LAND, LIBERTIES, AND LORDSHIP IN A LATE MEDIEVAL COUNTRYSIDE

University of Pennsylvania Press
Middle Ages Series
Edited by EDWARD PETERS
Henry Charles Lea Professor
of Medieval History
University of Pennsylvania

A complete listing of the books in this series
appears at the back of this volume

LAND, LIBERTIES, AND LORDSHIP IN A LATE MEDIEVAL COUNTRYSIDE

Agrarian Structures and Change in the Duchy of Wrocław

§§§§§§§§§§§§§§§§§§

RICHARD C. HOFFMANN

upp

Philadelphia
UNIVERSITY OF PENNSYLVANIA PRESS

This work has been supported by a grant from the National Endowment for the Humanities, an independent federal agency.

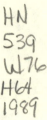
Library of Congress Cataloging-in-Publication Data

Hoffmann, Richard C. (Richard Charles), 1943–
    Land, liberties, and lordship in a late medieval countryside :
agrarian structures and change in the Duchy of Wrocław / Richard C.
Hoffmann.
        p.   cm.—(University of Pennsylvania Press Middle Ages
series)
    Bibliography: p.
    Includes index.
    ISBN 0-8122-8090-3
    1. Wrocław (Poland : Voivodeship)—Social Conditions.   2. Land
tenure—Poland—Wrocław (Voivodeship)—History.   3. Peasantry—
Poland—Wrocław (Voivodeship)—History.   4. Poland—History—To
1572.   I. Title.   II. Series.
HN539.W76H64   1989
306'.09438'5—dc20   89-14659
                                                                            CIP

Design by Adrianne Onderdonk Dudden

CONTENTS

PART TWO

ORGANIZING AGRICULTURAL RESOURCES

PART THREE

A SOCIAL SYSTEM IN ACTION

MAPS

TABLES

FIGURES

ABBREVIATIONS

All references in this book are given in a shortened form, usually the name of the author or editor and, where necessary, a short title. Abbreviations of certain much-used items and terms appear below. Complete citations are in the bibliography.

ACW   Alfred Sabisch, ed. *Acta capituli Wratislaviensis 1500–1562. Die Sitzungsprotokolle des Breslauer Domkapitels in der ersten Hälfte des 16. Jahrhunderts.* 2 vols. Cologne and Vienna, 1972–76.

AESC   *Annales: économies—sociétés—civilisations*

AHR   *American Historical Review*

APH   *Acta Poloniae Historica*

AsKg   *Archiv für schlesische Kirchengeschichte*

BUB   Georg Korn, ed. *Breslauer Urkundenbuch.* Breslau, 1870.

CdS   Codex diplomaticus Silesiae [the German series]

CdM   Antonin Boček et al., eds. *Codex diplomaticus et epistolaris Moraviae.* 15 vols. Olomouc, 1836–1903.

ChronBMV   Gustav A. H. Stenzel, ed. *Chronica abbatum Beatae Mariae virginis in Arenae*, pp. 156–286 in SrS, vol. 2. Breslau, 1839.

CPH   *Czasopismo Prawno-Historyczne*

DQ   Darstellungen und Quellen zur schlesischen Geschichte

DT   Helene Bindewald, ed. *Deutsche Texte aus schlesischen Kanzleien des 14. und 15. Jahrhunderts.* 2 vols. Berlin, 1935–36.

EcHR   *Economic History Review*

fl   florin or gulden (coin)

gr   groschen (coin)

HGZ   WAP, AMW, Q28. Heilige Geist: Zinsbuch 1430–37.

HPR   Colmar Grünhagen, ed. *Henricus Pauper. Rechnungen der Stadt Breslau von 1299–1358, nebst zwei Rationarien von 1386 und 1387, dem Liber Imperatoris vom Jahre 1377 und den ältesten Breslauer Statuten.* Breslau, 1860.

hl   heller or pfennig (coin)

j   jugerum (measure of land)

JEcH   *Journal of Economic History*

JEEcH   *Journal of European Economic History*

Jesuiter   WAP, Rep. 135, B72. Inhaltsverzeichniss der ausserurkundlichen Papiere des Jesuiter-Collegium zu Breslau, 1352–1788.

JSFWUB   *Jahrbuch der schlesischen Friedrich-Wilhelms-Universität zu Breslau*

JsKg	*Jahrbuch für schlesische Kirchengeschichte*
KdS	Karol Maleczyński, ed. *Kodeks diplomatyczny Śląska*. 3 vols. Wrocław, 1956–64.
KH	*Kwartalnik Historyczny*
KHKM	*Kwartalnik Historii Kultury Materialnej*
KLM	WAP, Rękopisy Klose, Kl 132 (Kl 128). [S. B. Klose's holograph copy of] Districtus Wratislaviensis liber de mansis comparatus sub anno 1443.
LB	Gustav A. H. Stenzel, ed. "Das Landbuch des Fürstenthums Breslau," in *Übersicht*, 1842, pp. 48–141.
LBU	Colmar Grünhagen and Hermann Markgraf, eds. *Lehns- und Besitzurkunden Schlesiens und seiner einzelnen Fürstenthümer im Mittelalter*. 2 vols. Leipzig, 1881–83.
LFE	Hermann Markgraf and J. W. Schulte, eds. *Liber fundationis episcopatus Wratislaviensis*. Breslau, 1889.
LN	WAA I, III a 31. Liber Niger.
m	mansus (measure of land)
mk	mark (money of account)
MPH	Monumenta Poloniae Historica
MSGV	*Mitteilungen der schlesischen Gesellschaft für Volkskunde*
NLChron	Leo Santifaller, ed. *Nikolaus Liebental und seine Chronik der Äbte des Breslauer St. Vincenzstifts*. Tongerloo, 1949.
NRB	Otto Meinardus, ed. *Das Neumarkter Rechtsbuch und andere Neumarkter Rechtsquellen*. Breslau, 1906.
PAN	Polska Akademia Nauk
PCC	Berthold Kronthal and Heinrich Wendt, eds. *Politische Correspondenz Breslaus im Zeitalter des Königs Matthias Corvinus*. 2 vols. Breslau, 1893–94.
PCP	Hermann Markgraf, ed. *Politische Correspondenz Breslaus im Zeitalter Georgs von Podiebrad*. 2 vols. Breslau, 1873–74.
PH	*Przegląd Historyczny*
"QBBB"	Wilhelm Schulte, ed., "Quellen zur Geschichte der Besitzverhältnisse des Bistums Breslau," pp. 171–279 in his *Studien zur schlesischen Kirchengeschichte*. Breslau, 1907.
QD	Quellen und Darstellungen zur schlesischen Geschichte
RB	WAP, AMW, C20. Registrum omnium bonorum sive villarum et allodiorum in districtibus Wratislaviensi, Noviforensi et Awrassensi super pecunia Burnegelt anno etc XXV.
RBM	Karel J. Erben et al., eds. *Regesta diplomatica nec non epistolaria Bohemiae et Moraviae*. 7 vols. Prague, 1855–92, 1928–29, and 1954–63.
Rep	Repertorium
RF	WAP, AMW, C24, 1–5. Repertorium Frobenianum. Repertorium Investiturarum in Praediis Ducatus Wratislaviensis, quae in Libris ejusdem Cancellarie continentur, 5 vols.
RH	*Roczniki Historyczne*
RI	Johann F. Böhmer et al., eds. *Regesta Imperii*. Vol. 8:1–2, *Die Regesten des Kaiserreichs unter Kaiser Karl IV. 1346–1378*, ed. Alfons Huber, 2 vols. (Innsbruck,

	1877–89); Vol. 11, *Die Urkunden Kaiser Sigmunds 1410–1437*, ed. Wilhelm Altmann, 2 vols. (Innsbruck, 1896–1900)
RS	Wacław Korta et al., eds. *Regesty śląskie*. 2 vols. Wrocław, 1975–83.
RSC, year(s)	[Registra succustodiae dextri chori ecclesie Wratislaviensis], 4 sequential manuscript account books as follows: WAA I, III d 28, Regestum succustodiae dextri chori ecclesie Wratislaviensis 1406–1459; WAP Rep. 15, 230, Registrum redditum succustodiae dextri chori ecclesie Wratislaviensis; WAP Rep. 15, 293, Registrum succustodiae dextri chori de anno 1471 usque 1488; WAA I, III d 49, Regestum Subcustodis 1507–1787. [The two WAP manuscripts are in fact dismembered parts of one original: 230 contains 1465, 1479–81, and part of 1484; 293 contains 1471–78, the end of the 1481 entry-1483, the middle of the 1484 entry, and 1485–88. WAA III d 49 actually begins with 1496.]
RUL	WAP, Rep. 135, C150e, Zg134/37. Regesten der Urkunden des Schlossarchivs Deutsch-Lissa 1404–1790.
RW	WAP, AMW, J 7. Der rechte Weg.
SLR	Ernst T. Gaupp, ed. *Das schlesische Landrecht oder eigentlich Landrecht des Fürstenthums Breslau vom J. 1356 an sich und in seiner Verhältnisse zum Sachsenspiegel dargestellt*. Leipzig, 1828; reprint Aalen, 1966.
SLU	Josef J. Menzel, *Die schlesischen Lokationsurkunden des 13. Jahrhunderts: Studien zum Urkundenwesen, zur Siedlungs-, Rechts-, und Wirtschaftsgeschichte einer ostdeutschen Landschaft im Mittelalter*. Würzburg, 1977. [Items in extensive documentary appendix are cited by number.]
Sobótka	*Śląski Kwartalnik Historyczny Sobótka*
SR	Colmar Grünhagen et al., eds. *Regesten zur schlesischen Geschichte*. 6 vols. in 8. Breslau, 1875–1925.
SrS	Scriptores rerum Silesiacarum
SSp	Eike von Repgow. *Sachsenspiegel*, ed. Karl A. Eckhardt, 2d ed. rev., 2 vols. Berlin, 1955–56.
SUB	Heinrich Appelt and Winfried Irgang, eds. *Schlesisches Urkundenbuch*. 2 vols. in 4. Vienna and Cologne, 1963–78.
SW	*Studia Wczesnośredniowieczne*
UBB	Gustav A. H. Stenzel, ed. *Urkunden zur Geschichte des Bisthums Breslau im Mittelalter*. Breslau, 1845.
Übersicht	*Übersicht der Arbeiten und Veränderungen der schlesischen Gesellschaft für vaterländischen Cultur*
UD	August Meitzen, ed. *Urkunden schlesischer Dörfer. Zur Geschichte der ländlichen Verhältnisse und der Flureinteilung insbesondere*. Breslau, 1863.
UFO	Wilhelm Haeusler, ed. *Urkundensammlung zur Geschichte des Fürstenthums Oels, bis zum Aussterben der Piastischen Herzogslinie*. Breslau, 1883.
VSWG	*Vierteljahrsschrift für Sozial- und Wirtschaftsgeschichte*

Tz-S	Gustav A. Tzschoppe and Gustav A. H. Stenzel, eds., *Ur-kundensammlung zur Geschichte des Ursprungs der Städte und der Einführung und Verbreitung Deutscher Kolonisten und Rechte im Schlesien und der Ober-Lausitz.* Hamburg, 1832.
WAA	Wrocław, Archiwum Archidiecezjalne
WAP	Wrocław, Archiwum Państwowe
WAP, AMW	Wrocław, Archiwum Państwowe, Archiwum miasta Wrocławia
WTN	Wrocławski Towarzystwo Nauk
ZVGS	*Zeitschrift des Vereins für Geschichte und Alterthum Schlesiens* [Alterthum dropped with vol. 40 (1906)]
ZO	*Zeitschrift für Ostforschung*
ZRG	*Zeitschrift des Savigny Stiftungs für Rechtsgeschichte*

PREFACE

It has taken twenty years to reconstruct, analyze, explain, and understand 350 years in the complex life of a past community. No medievalist should think that too long. The remnants from the past sought here have waited far longer and deserve commensurate patience.

This book grew from repeated engagement with the sources and will succeed to the extent it recaptures them and those who created them. To that end, I have purposely cast in it a reconstructive rather than an argumentative mode. In other words, the organization and presentation derive more from the concerns and texts of people past than from the disputes of later historians. As readers familiar with literature around my subject will recognize, the rich human reality in the medieval records has been too often neglected in cultivating a sterile national or ideological parti pris or constructing a rootless metahistory. Had I shaped this book around the historiography, I feared losing the documented past I sought and found.

Of course *Land, Liberties, and Lordship* was not conceived in an intellectual vacuum. Analytical frameworks of medieval economic history, of rural social history, and of East Central European history, are provided in Chapter 1. In addition, the broad substantive understanding of medieval agrarian history against which this sense of the Wrocław countryside evolved is available in my lengthy article "Tenure of Land, Western European," in *Dictionary of the Middle Ages*, Joseph Strayer et al., eds., vol. 11, pp. 671–686 (New York, 1988). The institutional perspective may be augmented by my "Tools, Agricultural, Western European" and "Villages: Community," pp. 72–82 and 439–441 in volume 12 of the *Dictionary* (New York, 1989).

In consequence I relegate most comparative issues and academic controversy to the notes. The form of citations required to save space, however, makes some notes less transparent than I would prefer. Cognoscenti may recognize the import of allusions to "Carsten," to "Buczek," or to "Grünhagen;" other readers are encouraged (implored) to trace references patiently from text to notes to bibliography. Then they will see both my large debts to and my occasionally sharp differences from two centuries of scholars in both Silesian history and medieval studies.

What follows is my sole responsibility, though I have necessarily drawn on uncounted friends, colleagues, teachers, and others. Much brief aid must go unremarked. But people who have made a particular and critical difference to the outcome of an effort deserve special thanks, if some, sadly, just to their memories.

Without the caretakers of manuscripts and books there can be no historical scholarship. Once at Wrocław I relied on the help, advice, and staffs of Miss Janina Pasławska, Director for Scholarly Research at the Archiwum Państwowe, and the late Most Reverend Wincenty Urban, then Auxiliary Bishop of Wrocław and Director of the archdiocesan library, archive, and museum. At York I depend on the great skills and good humor of the Interlibrary Loan section, especially through the years those of Mary Hudecki and Gary MacDonald.

Maps and figures were ably produced by the Cartographic Office, Department of Geography, Faculty of Arts, York University. Robert Ryan, Hania Guzewska, Carolyn Gondor, and Carol Randall helped my questions and answers achieve graphic form.

Financial support has been received from time to time from the [then] Canada Council, from the Faculty of Arts at York University, and from the International Research and Exchanges Board.

Intellectual mentors and helpful patrons at various stages of this project in Poland and North America have been Aleksander Gieysztor, the late Roman Heck, Harry Miskimin, Janos Bak, and Ambrose Raftis. Colleagues in the Department of History, York University, inevitably stimulate and inspire emulation. Dozens of fellow conferees, especially during the great annual medieval gatherings at Kalamazoo, have prodded hypotheses toward improvement. Paul Lovejoy and two then anonymous referees affirmed when needed that slowly assembled separate fragments did form a sensible whole.

The entirety is offered to the memories of three whose instruction and example taught the meaning of scholarship: Arnold E. Melzer, Robert L. Reynolds, Robert S. Lopez. May it hold a measure of their acuity and humanity.

Ellen and Kate had to hear so much so long. They kept it in perspective.

King City, Ontario
January, 1989

PART ONE

§§§§§§§

Contexts for a Rural History

§§ 1 §§
INTRODUCTION: APPROACHING AGRARIAN HISTORY IN MEDIEVAL EAST-CENTRAL EUROPE

An economic system is a set of dependent, interconnected economic relationships which, precisely because they are interconnected, arise more or less contemporaneously and disappear more or less contemporaneously, giving way to other relationships. The empirical dating of their emergence and dissolution enables us to fix the limits of a specific economic system in time. To construct the theory of a determinate economic system means to establish (always empirically) the fullest possible totality of dependent relationships present within the system, and to explain the connections between these relationships. . . . The task of economic history is to understand how men have carried out their economic activity in various social situations.

Witold Kula, *An Economic Theory of the Feudal System. Towards a Model of the Polish Economy 1500–1800*, pp. 179 and 182.

Of the many Middle Ages, some are now well known and some poorly known. This book explores a part of medieval Europe unfamiliar to most Anglophone and even most western medievalists to illuminate from a novel perspective issues central to historical inquiry—development and stability, prosperity and poverty, community and authority, freedom and loss of freedom. It examines structures and change in the rural life of a small east-central European region around the Silesian city of Wrocław between the late twelfth century and the early sixteenth.[1] The intent is to recreate, understand, and explain interconnected relationships among peasants and lords in this vanished society.

How are human experiences in the medieval Duchy of Wrocław to be reconstructed and meaningfully recapitulated? Three intersecting spheres of issues arise from the confrontation of modern scholarly minds with medieval economic, agrarian, and east-central European history. The object of study and the surviving sources shape the investigation and its results. This introductory chapter treats analytical and methodological considerations before sketching in brief the book's organization and argument.

Medieval economic historians have sought to describe and explain expansion, development, and contraction in the production, distribution, and consumption of goods and services. Generations of scholarship established the reality of change in medieval economic life and the inception by the turn of the first millennium of a long period of growth. This the demands of human numbers and ruling lords powered, the energies of peasants and artisans sustained, and the minds and travels of merchants coordinated into an emerging continental economic system.[2] Then scholars questioned whether continuous economic progress followed from medieval growth and showed that it was not uninterrupted.[3] Hence a long cycle of growth, depression, and renewed growth now seems visible across Europe from the High Middle Ages to the sixteenth century.

Causal questions remain. A search for answers forces attention to the distinctive experiences of those regional communities which collectively formed the mosaic of traditional Europe. Not just French knights, Italian traders, Flemish craftsmen, and English peasants peopled medieval Europe, making and enduring its history. Along the expanded continental frontiers of Latin Christendom in particular, the timing, form, and causes of economic change remain obscure. So, too, do ways these were manifest in the local and regional societies which framed the lives of most medieval Europeans.[4] One set of problems, then, concerns long-term economic change in a particular setting. How did people in the countryside around Wrocław participate in the secular evolution of the medieval European economy?

A second frame of analysis recognizes that a traditional agrarian society contains a peasant majority and an elite minority whose behaviors together form a structural whole with ramifications beyond the purely economic.

Conceptual models of "peasant society" identify for study potentially significant variables and contexts of social interaction. Traditional small cultivators constitute a subordinated part of a larger society, so the varying forms and incidence of elite dominance necessarily affect how peasants live. Yet equally significant are structures internal to peasant society: familial units of production, consumption, and residence; a primary orientation towards subsistence and self-sufficiency from the resources commanded by those units; participation of the units in local communities. Differential access to wealth, social behavior linking wealth and family, relative ease of movement and access to markets, and the authority, structure, and autonomy of the village can shape peasant lives as much as does the direct individual or collective confrontation between lord and peasant.[5] Peasants thus live in a complex reality webbed with connections among resources, technologies, lordship, kin groups, status groups, communities, and interlocking regional networks. Discoverable norms and acceptable variations pattern lives therein. Yet those lives are led by real individuals, not ideal types. Modern theory of peasant society offers only potential tools for the historian seeking from exiguous sources to reimagine human situations in a particular past setting.

Lords, too, were complete social beings, not just cardboard figures of power to be opposed to peasants. Recent scholars have learned how elite culture, kinship, and broader economic situations shape lords' handling and very notion of landed property.[6] To understand and explain medieval agrarian life, then, requires a view of landowners in their own social setting.

Third is the history of east-central Europe, too long warped by a one-sided western perspective on European civilization and too long vexed by modern ethnocentrisms and consequent medieval anachronisms.[7] Nineteenth-century nationalisms defined the territory as contested between German and Slav and imposed that conceptual framework upon its earlier history. Understandings of the medieval past thus long revolved around issues of ethno-cultural identity, contact, and conflict. To German allegations of a historic national mission on behalf of western civilization against the barbarous masses of the east, Poles, Czechs, and Magyars understandably opposed their own mirror images of autonomous members of the European cultural community defending themselves against naked aggression. Even syntheses of the medieval history of Silesia, a territory successively belonging to Polish, Bohemian, Habsburg, and (later) Prussian rulers and inhabited until 1945 by people of indubitably mixed origins, were made to revolve around axes of ethnic identity and national membership.[8]

Since the mid-twentieth century new perspectives on east-central European history have emerged. They focus on experiences (including conflicts) shared among people living between Elbe and Pripet as participants since the first millennium in the pluralistic culture of Latin Christendom. Oscar Halecki's propitious "borderlands of western civilization" suggested a broad understanding with rich comparative potential.[9] Walter Schlesinger broke in 1957 with at least a century of *Ostforschung* and *Siedlungsgeschichte* to declare that the old German east was no more and to call for reconsideration of its historical place as something other than "colonization."[10] František Graus offered the notion of a "melting pot" to frame issues of ethnic formation and, with special felicity for the medievalist, pointed out the need to recognize "there were more important problems than frontier disputes, linguistic quarrels and national prestige." By the mid-1980s even the historical doyen of the Polish state and nation, Henryk Łowmiański, could speak (in passing) of the medieval "formation of a particular Silesian nation" distinct from the Polish.[11]

The new conceptual environment encourages the medievalist to confront problems belonging to the Middle Ages and not to the nineteenth century. This necessarily includes giving to questions of ethnicity attention commensurate with their importance in relevant medieval texts and behavior. For much of the Middle Ages dominant processes of socio-cultural change drew east-central Europe ever closer to a common European evolution. At the end of the period came a fateful transition; while the region maintained full cultural membership in Europe, its social development diverged. The serfdom the West was rapidly leaving behind now appeared in the East where it had not been.[12] Issues of agrarian development and social change are thus central to that part of medieval European history which occurred in the East. These, too, help shape this effort to understand and explain the experiences of those medieval people who lived around Wrocław.

Conceptual assemblages labelled medieval, agrarian, and east-central European provide analytic environments for this book. They do not directly determine its method or its organization, for the intent of this history is not nomothetic. The objective here is less to test theories of medieval growth and recession, of peasant society, or of east-central European development than it is to use such ideas to help explore the life of a past society.[13] General interpretive questions must inform the historian's apprehension of an object of inquiry but specific people and communities made the object itself. Men and women living in a particular past left from their lives fragments which the present confronts.

The medieval Duchy of Wrocław (see Map 1.1) provides an object of study positioned on a continuum between the representative and the unique. To the western observer it lay tucked behind the eastern edges of the Bohemian massif on a tiny scrap (1500–1600 square kilometers or 600 square miles) of the north European plain in the center of the Odra river basin and the province of Silesia. Neither topography nor climate nor ethnicity nor even the influence of the city in its midst sharply separated this community from its neighbors; its discernable particularity resulted from the vagaries of now old and obscure politics. But those almost random borders delimited a dense web of interactions among the thirty to sixty thousand people living there at any one time between 1200 and 1530. Borders and behavior established a congruent map of medieval documents, shared and similar within, different and incommensurate without. A unity of sources reflects the unit of social organization then and permits a unit of analysis now.

The medieval duchy was surprisingly productive of materials for its historical reconstruction. Their survival in considerable volume, despite severe and irreplaceable losses to Wrocław archives in 1945,[14] has molded research strategies and tactics of presentation. Especially four key types of primary sources give form and content to this book.

Most medievalists are familiar with charters, formal written documents recording and providing proof of a juridical act, which often concerned the property or privilege of the recipient. Such texts, whether ducal, papal, episcopal, or by other authority, offer the first concrete evidence from around Wrocław and, numbering in the high hundreds by the early fourteenth century, almost all the early source material. Churchmen and a few townspeople with landed property then favored or kept charters; most transactions occurred orally in the presence of the local Piast duke and went unrecorded. But in 1336 a new absentee ruler, King John of Bohemia, established permanent official registers (*Libri terrae, Landbücher*) for all conveyances of properties held from him (as most were). The initial general series became in 1367 separate ones for permanent sales or inheritances (*Libri perpetuorum*), marriage settlements, and repurchaseable pledges or annuities. By the mid-sixteenth century they filled more than thirty hefty volumes. For easier reference to the then 10,000 chronological entries in the eight *Libri perpetuorum*, the secretary of the duchy compiled what came to be called the "Repertorium Frobenianum" [RF], an alphabetical listing of each rural settlement and the substance of every charter about it.[15] Until 1945 all the *Landbücher* were in the archive (if rarely used); since 1945 only RF survives. It provides, however, a nearly complete sequential record of secular properties and their holders in the late medieval duchy. Ecclesiastical cartularies complement it. The charters may be thought of as a large collection of snapshots taken from the point of view of landowners.

The Wrocław duchy is also comparatively rich in examples of a rarer source which can balance with broad panoramas the narrow focus of the charters. Large survey documents record information about many rural settlements at four different dates. Earliest and least comprehensive is a catalog of lands and rights compiled about 1300 by clerks of the bishop of Wrocław, the "Liber fundationis episcopatus Wratislaviensis" [LFE]. Sections covering the duchy contain quantitative details about fifty-nine places where the bishop was lord or took tithes. A half century later Emperor Charles IV had administrators of what was then his hereditary principality investigate all ducal resources there. The "Register of villages, demesnes, and ducal rights of the Duchy of Wrocław and the District of Namysłów" or, to the nineteenth-century editor, "Landbuch des Fürstenthums Breslau" [*LB*] was drafted by 1353 and partly revised over the next five years. Its topical and geographical sections record types and amounts of land, many owners, and other information from 284 identifiable settlements in the duchy. Two more surveys come from the first half of the fifteenth century; each was compiled to assess and collect a particular tax on land. The "Register of Burnegelt" [RB] from 1425 lists for each of 199 places the land subject to tax (lords' demesne farms and the lordships of some churches were exempt) and the payment made. Data from RB is augmented by contemporary surveys of estates belonging to two exempt owners, the Wrocław cathedral chapter and the Bishop of Lebus. The three texts together cover 211 places in the duchy just before the Hussite wars. The latest survey document was compiled in the midst of those wars. This "Liber de mansis" [KLM] from 1443 now survives only as a late eighteenth-century holograph copy by the Wrocław antiquary Samuel B. Klose, who also published selections in 1781. It lists 235 identifiable settlements. Each survey reports on land use and economic organization in a large but not complete sample of Wrocław duchy settlements. Handled with critical awareness in ways detailed in Appendix A, they yield quantitative profiles of the duchy's countryside at times significant to its economic history.

Surveys range broadly across the countryside of the duchy but rarely penetrate the life of its villages and farms. Only the occasional charter treats rural settlements as societies instead of just properties. But a third, mostly late kind of source, the land- or titheholder's own financial account, may go deeper, for these can record individual peasant holdings, obligations owed, paid, evaded, or forgiven, and even many years of this information. None date to the twelfth or thirteenth century and few to the fourteenth and early fifteenth, but they become more common in the late fifteenth and early sixteenth centuries. Nearly all that survive were kept by clerics, but their tithe accounts often cover lay-owned properties as well. Some late income accounts also have the quality of village court books.

Legal compilations are a fourth distinctive source of information about rural relationships in the late medieval duchy, for it produced two of these. The so-called "Silesian land law" [*SLR*] was codified in 1356 by knights and Wrocław citizens whom the king had instructed to reconcile indigenous Polish and immigrant German legal customs. They adjusted *Sachsenspiegel* to the special conditions of the duchy and established the basic law applied in its courts for the rest of the Middle Ages. Later experience created further precedents which a long-time court member compiled in 1490 as a private handbook, "Der Rechte Weg" [RW]. In succession the two texts give distinctive local views on normative behavior in the countryside.

Except for two Wrocław witnesses to mid-fifteenth-century wars, narrative writers had little interest in matters agrarian. The fiscal and administrative records, especially extensive by the mid-fourteenth century and unparalleled elsewhere in Silesia, make the Duchy of Wrocław peculiarly apt for systematic study. They allow intensive and near-complete investigation of relatively full and constant documentation from an entire area.

Extant materials also limit investigation. Most record sources reveal rural society down to but not below the social aggregate level of particular settlements. Except with landlord accounts and other late or unusual sources individual peasants or their farms can rarely be examined in depth. Villages can. All places recur in text after text. Documented statements can be made and compared. Hence this study approaches the duchy as a regional mosaic of discrete local communities with their own identities, their own topographic and social qualities, and their own histories. The 362 human settlements (some short-lived) in the medieval duchy all appear on Map 1.1. Most will reappear in maps, tables, and discussions throughout this book. The history of the region is, to a large but not exclusive degree, a composite of these local histories.

To maximize the breadth of detail and completeness in each local community history and the contribution all make to reconstructing the web of interrelationships which formed a regional history, all information on questions of potential relevance was assembled from available documentation. In isolation most recorded "facts" (like the presence of a mill in a particular place in 1342, the rate of rent demanded by the bishop elsewhere in 1277, or the quantity of "deserted" land in another place in 1443) have no significance. A family or village history lends context to some, but the narrative of one settlement still has only antiquarian interest. The atomic particulars of rural life gain interpretive meaning in mass. Hence quantified techniques and tabular, graphic, and cartographic representations will often summarize the collected data. These methods permit critical evaluation of general assertions and of the representative quality of any specific details.[16] Then case studies of communities, groups, or, where possible, individuals selected from the larger assemblages, restore a human and narrative dimension to the reconstruction. Points where probable inference from the available data reaches a limit are clearly indicated and speculative or hypothetical conclusions expressly offered as such. Neither quantification nor theoretical awareness replaces information not in the sources; they can only suggest where lacunae occur and how the fragments of the past which are recaptured may once have been aligned. This study is presented with the conviction that it is as important to declare what is not known as to indicate what is.

This introduction should also give practical help to readers disoriented by unfamiliar linguistic and other aspects of east-central European history. A guide to Polish pronunciation appears on p. 489. Personal and place names pose the greatest problem. These were originally recorded in the inconsistent orthography of medieval Latin and German, some subsequently underwent linguistic change and/or translation into another language, and many were then treated by scholars writing in modern German, Polish, or Czech. The aim here is to handle the material in English with consistency and a minimum of anachronism. Many readers will be satisfied to know the conventions here adopted:

GIVEN (Christian) NAMES use English cognates where available, modern Polish or German forms where they exist, or, for those without modern equivalents, orthographically-tidy versions of a medieval form.

SURNAMES are given in a standardized, preferably medieval and text-based form. Those of geographical origin have been translated into "of + toponym" unless they acquired an unambiguous family quality.

PLACE NAMES IN SILESIA are the modern Polish names where such exist. PLACES ELSEWHERE receive their common English name if they have one and their native name if not.

PLACES NO LONGER EXISTING or without their own modern name ("deserted villages") receive a standardized reconstruction (marked by asterisks, e. g. *Szczepin*) of the form used in medieval texts.

Where a MEDIEVAL NAME FORM is discussed or not otherwise identifiable, it appears in italics or quotation marks as appropriate.

A Gazetteer (pp. 531–551) locates and names in Polish and German places in the medieval duchy or relevant to its history. Readers needing greater justification of onomastic decisions should see Appendix C (pp. 405–408). Units of measurement and other specialized terms are defined in the Glossary (pp. 485–488) and additional information about medieval Silesian money is in Appendix B (pp. 400–404).

The interpretive and methodological approaches identified above run as threads through a narrative and structural analysis of a social and economic system set in a particular time and place, the late medieval Duchy of Wrocław. The system is the rural regime of "German law" (*ius Theutonicum*), the organization of the countryside around autonomous village communities of free peasant farming households with good tenurial rights. These institutional arrangements appeared around Wrocław in the early thirteenth century, were perhaps territorially dominant by its close, and continued to multiply for another hundred years. They meshed with characteristic relationships among lords and lords, lords and peasants, peasants and markets, technologies and resources, and peasants and peasants. People in these interconnections responded in certain ways to difficulties, conflicts, opportunities, and change. During the later fifteenth and beginning of the sixteenth century this web of behavior slowly gave way to the different connections of neoserfdom. This book would establish (always empirically) characteristic relationships within the regime of the German law, its emergence, and its dissolution in the countryside around Wrocław.

The investigative reconstruction is presented in four large segments. Part I builds necessary frames, here in Chapter 1 the analytical perspectives, in the next chapter the natural and human setting of the late medieval duchy, and in Chapter 3 the antecedent development of twelfth-century Poland and Silesia. The latter established the environment of economic growth and the relationships between the elite and landed resources needed for institutional innovation in the countryside. The following three segments look from different but intersecting perspectives at the subsequent rural order of the German law.

Part II considers the German law as an agricultural resource system, exploring how this regime was formed and functioned around Wrocław during the thirteenth through early fifteenth centuries. What the developmental initiatives of landowners and the collaborative energies of peasants created is the subject of Chapter 4. Chapter 5 examines landlord demesne farms, the empirically essential counterpart to German law tenant agriculture, during the same period. Chapter 6 treats relationships between lords, tenants, and their two kinds of productive enterprises, as these shifted through time and in a wider economic setting. The concern is for change in, but not of, the system, and the involvement of individuals and groups with such change.

Part III contemplates the same fourteenth- and early fifteenth-century rural order as a social system of lords and peasants. Chapter 7 is from an elite perspective, considering lordship rights to landed property, the persons who possessed these rights, and the social settings in which they handled them. Chapter 8 views from the village the activities of landowners, revealing the separation of the lord from village affairs and the inconstancy of connections between any particular lord and any specific lordship. This situation reinforced structural features of the German law regime, leaving the village community and its own society, as explored in Chapter 9, largely independent of regular or direct elite intervention. The German law village emerges as a multivariate and pluralistic social system with a strong head man, the *schulz*, as its center and its principal (but not sole) link to the surrounding society.

Part IV follows the German law regime to and beyond the limits of its adaptability during the fifteenth and early sixteenth century. In Chapter 10 exogenous pressures from the natural and socio-political environments of mid-fifteenth century east-central Europe are shown stressing all rural relationships in the duchy. Peasants struggled for survival, lords endured loss of incomes, and both grasped at opportunities within and without the old frame of possibilities. Two or three human generations experienced crisis. Chapter 11 traces their subsequent responses, some to rebuild what once had been and others to rethink earlier relationships. What had been learned of risks to lordly incomes in the German law regime combined with changing elite social contexts for landed property to end the traditional motility of lordship rights, strengthening the effective authority of lords and encouraging its exercise. In weakened communities without external sources of support, even peasants prospering from available lands and markets could not resist effectively. As Chapter 12 sets out, around 1500 people near Wrocław were in piecemeal fashion and incrementally replacing their German law regime with something else. Entry of a hereditary lord into the village and into the entire social space between the village and the larger society changed the system itself.

Map 1.1

THE LATE MEDIEVAL DUCHY OF WROCŁAW

— — — Wrocław Duchy boundary

- - - - - Boundary of later or
temporary additions

The following settlements belonged to the late
medieval Wrocław duchy only as indicated:

Domaniów	1347 to 1361
Janików	1342 to 1361
Jarosławice	from 1438
Ludów Śląski	from 1434
Szostakowice	from 1353
Wierzbno	1342 to 1361

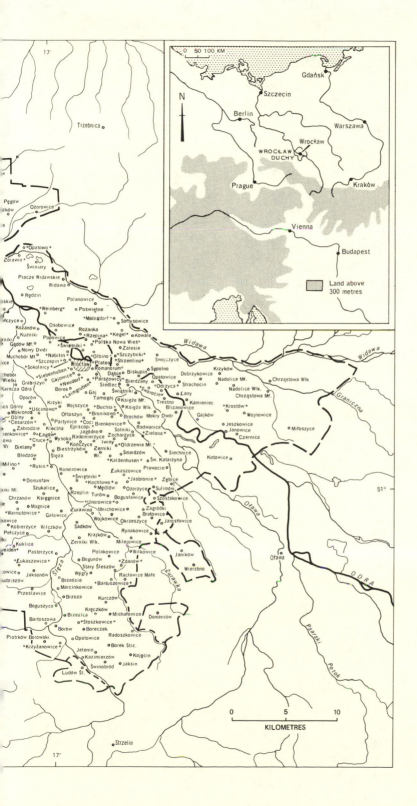

17°

Trzebnica ○

Inset map:

0 50 100 KM

N

Gdańsk

Szczecin

Berlin

Warszawa

Wrocław

WROCŁAW
DUCHY

Prague

Kraków

Vienna

Budapest

Land above
300 metres

Pęgów
zków
e
○ Ozorowice

Opatowo *

Żorawin *
Świniary

Pracze Widawskie
○
Widawa ○

Rędzin

Polanowice
Weinberg ○ Poświętne
*Molnsdorf ○
rfczyce ○ ○ Softysowice
Kożanów ○ Osobowice
Kuźniki ○ Popowice ○ Rożanka
rniki/ Gądów Mł. ○ *Rzepina* *Kegel* ○ Kowale
○ Nowy Dwór *Świetniki * *Polska Nowa Wieś*
Muchobór Mł. ○ *Nabitin * ○ Olbino ○ Zalesie
ice *Szczepin ○ *Sokolnicy * ○ Wrocław ○ Platea *Szczytniki*
chobór *Siebenhuben ○ Dąbie *Strzemlino* Swojczyce
Wielki Grabiszyn ○ Gajowice ○ Romanorum Biskupin ○ Sępolno Krzyków
Karncza Góra ○ *Neudorf* *Parszowice* ○ Opatowice Dobrzykowice ○ Nadolice Mł. ○ ○ Chrząstowa Wlk
Borek ○ Leimgruben* Bierdzany ○ Odrzyca * Strachocin Nadolice Wlk.
Oporów ○ Gaj Siedlec ○ Świątniki ○ Swarocin ○ Łany ○ Chrząstowa Mr.
Krzyki ○ Tamogai ○ *Księże Mł.* Trestno ○ Kamieniec
os Górny *Uściminowo* Wojszyce *Buchta * ○ Księże Wlk. Blizanowice *Krostów *
Mokronos Ołtaszyn ○ *Bronikowo* ○ Brochów Mokry Dwór Gajków ○ Wojnowice
Dolny *Cesarzów * Partynice ○ Klecina Episcopi *Bienkowice ○ Jeszkowice ○ Miłoszyce
*Zabrodzie ○ ○ Zagródki Solniki ○ Radwanice ○ Janowice
ienkowice* ○ *Łagów Jagódno ○ *Zielona * Czernica
owa *Cruce * Wysoka Radomierzyce Zacharzyce
Wr. Bielany Kończyce ○ Iwiny
○ Biestrzyków ○ *Oldrzewie Mł.* Siechnice ○
Bledzów ○ Zerniki Smardzów ○ Kotowice ○
Ślęza Wr. *Kaldenhusen * ○ Św. Katarzyna
Milino * *Rusin * ○ Komorowice Prawocin ○
○ *Świętniki * Łukaszowice
Domasław ○ *Kochlowo * ○ *Jasbromie * Zębice
niki Mł. Szukalice ○ Mędlów ○ Ozorzyce Sulimów ○
Chrzanów Księgnice ○ Rzeplin Turów ○ Bogusławice ○ Szostakowice
*Warmutowice * Magnice ○ *Unorowice * ○ Zagródki
○ Galowice Żurawina Mnichowice ○ Bratowice ○ Jarosławice
owice ○ Kobierzyce Wilczków Wojkowice Okrzeszyce ○
Pełczyce ○ Sadków ○ Rynakowice
ki Kuklice Pasterzyce ○ Krajków ○ Milejowice Janików ○
eiden* *Łukaszewice * ○ Zerniki Wlk. Polakowice ○ Wilkowice ○
owice ○ Bogunów *Zdanów * Wierzbno ○
○ Jaksonów Węgry ○ Stary Śleszów
udziszów Brzeście ○ Racławice Małe
Przesławice ○ Marcinkowice *Bartuszowice *
○ Brzoza Kurczów ○
Boguszyce ○ Kręcków ○
Bartoszowa Brzezica ○ Michałowice ○ Domaniów
Borów ○ Boreczek
Piotrków Borowski ○ Stoszkowice *
*Krzyżanowice * Opatowice ○ Radoszkowice
Jelenin ○ Borek Strz.
Kazimierzów ○ Kojęcin
Świnobród ○ Jaksin
Ludów Śl.

0   5   10
KILOMETRES

○ Strzelin

17°

51°

Widawa

Widawa

Graniczna

Oława

Oława

Oława

ODRA

Psarski

Potok

Ślęza

Żurawka

§§ 2 §§

ENVIRONMENTS:
THE DUCHY OF WROCŁAW
AS REGION AND POLITY

Poloniae diuiditur in sex ducatos, quorum duces sunt potentes quasi reges, sunt autem nomina ducatuum: Cracouiensis, Opuliensis, Bratislaviensis, Glogouiensis, Gnisnensis et magouiensis. . . . Terre est pascuosa, nemorosa, et late ualde. habundat in pane, sed caret vino: irrigatur Wandale iam dicto, Odera, nisa, bobera, et magara, piscibus habundat multum et carnibus; argentifodine et equi indomiti multi sunt.

Olgierd Górka, ed., *Anonymi descriptio Europae orientalis . . . anno MCCCVIII exarata*, pp. 55–57.

Natural and cultural environments give opportunities and limits to people living in them. An anonymous early fourteenth-century western writer had trouble with eastern European names, but captured important first impressions of the medieval Polish lands: broad plains, some wooded, some open; large river systems; several confusing political units. He saw best the nearer side of the country; three of the six duchies he knew were Silesian, and three of the five rivers, too. The broad and shallow basin of the Odra shapes Silesia as an extension of the great north European plain into the angle between the Sudetes and Carpathians. On the river in the heart of the province is the historic center Wrocław, and around it the duchy named for it.

Rolling mountain ridges are not distant—from the city's Świdnica gate their outlier, Mount Ślęza, looms barely thirty kilometers away—but this is a land of river and plain (see Map 2.1). Bisecting and further subdividing the region around Wrocław are bottomlands along the Odra and its tributaries, the Oława, Ślęza, Bystrzyca, and Średzka Woda on the left (southwestern) bank and the Widawa on the right. Bounded by ten-meter terraces, these low-lying areas were until the late eighteenth century easily flooded patchworks of meadow, pond, wood, and sand bar, creatures and victims of the meandering rivers.[1] Three quarters of the duchy lay above the terraces

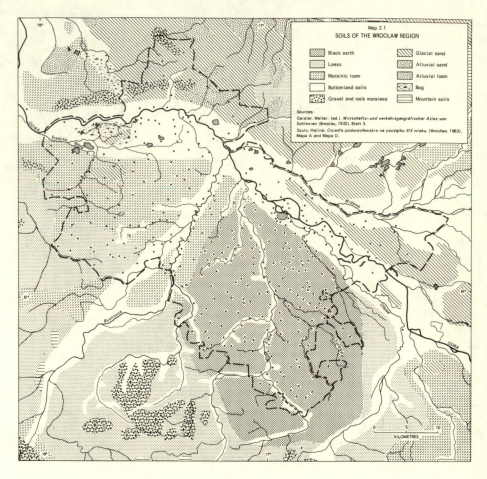

Map 2.1
SOILS OF THE WROCŁAW REGION

Black earth   Glacial sand
Loess   Alluvial sand
Morainic loam   Alluvial loam
Bottomland soils   Bog
Gravel and rock moraines   Mountain soils

Sources:
Geisler, Walter: (ed.), *Wirtschafts– und verkehrsgeografischer Atlas von Schlesien* (Breslau, 1932), Blatt 3.
Szulc, Halina: *Osiedla podwrocławskie na początku XIX wieku*, (Wrocław, 1963), Mapa A and Mapa D.

and the flood waters. South of Wrocław the gently undulating landscape is mantled by humus-rich black earth, a friable soil of post-glacial origin naturally devoid of heavy forest cover. Light and fertile, too, are the loess plains which roughly parallel the Sudetes range and penetrate the duchy along its southwestern edge. North of the loess and west of the black earth, naturally-wooded and less rich glacial soils, loams and sands for the most part, roll north to the Odra and rise across it into gravel terminal moraines. On the whole, however, the area contained in the later medieval duchy has barely a hundred meters difference in elevation, so that the principal topographic distinction is between bottomland and plain.

Like the surface features and soils, the climate of the duchy is but a local variant of that known across the great north European plain. Within the humid temperate belt stretching from northern France to the steppes, this area shares fairly cool, dry summers but no genuine dry season of the Mediterranean type. Wrocław is less cool and damp than the maritime west, but still more moderate than the truly continental climate of eastern Poland. Modern January temperatures average just below freezing and July around 18°C (64°F). Wheat grows better than elsewhere in Poland, but the hardier rye was long favored.

In the central Odra basin, distance and human densities, not physical barriers or different natural endowments, distinguish one regional unit from another. Since the High Middle Ages urban-centered districts have served social and administrative needs throughout Silesia and the rest of east-central Europe. The medieval district of Wrocław extended south from the Widawa and east from the Bystrzyca to irregular borders with districts centered on Oława and Strzelin. To its west, across the Bystrzyca and south of the Odra, was the Środa district, only half the size of the Wrocław district. It abutted the districts of Kąty on the south and of Legnica on the west. And to the north across the Odra, squeezed between lands of the often hostile duke of Głogów and Oleśnica, lay the very small district of Uraz, a castle and dwarf town on the bank of the river.[2] When in the early fourteenth century the districts of Wrocław, Środa, and Uraz came to define a realm ruled from Wrocław, it formed a rough rectangle of about thirty-five by forty-five kilometers with its longer dimension parallel to the southeast-northwest flow of the Odra.

The *ducatus Wratislaviensis* of the later Middle Ages—several hundred rural settlements, three administrative districts, a couple of little towns, and a major city with fifteen thousand inhabitants and commercial links far beyond the puny boundaries of this dwarf principality—had no geographic logic. Its very existence memorialized the breakup of an earlier political system into a zone of fracture between larger units, for this Duchy of Wrocław was the rump of a much larger Duchy of Silesia that during the High Middle Ages played a regionally significant role. The politics of the greater east-central European arena shaped the duchy and at times directly set conditions for life in field and hut and landlord's seat. Administrative practice created certain economic relationships, and the texts which record others. Understanding the rural society of the duchy in its historic setting thus requires some familiarity with the politics of Poland, Silesia, and the duchy from the formation of a Polish state until the first half of the sixteenth century. The goal of the overview in this chapter, however, is to report only enough about the evolution and organization of the polity to establish a context for the agrarian developments of the later Middle Ages.[3]

A surviving remnant

When the state-building activities and religious conversion of Mieszko I brought the Polish people to historical attention in the later tenth century, central Silesia was the homeland of the *Slenzani*, a Slavic people culturally Polish but then clearly in the Bohemian sphere of influence. The warlike and able Bolesław I "the Bold," second Christian ruler of Poland and heir to his father's expansionism, defeated the Bohemians and annexed Silesia to the Piast state in 999. The next year he sealed his victory by setting up a bishopric for the province at Wrocław, where fortified islands in the Odra and associated craft and trading settlements already bore economic characteristics of a town.

The vicissitudes of the early Polish state of which Silesia was an integral part have little direct bearing on later medieval developments. The breakup of that political organism begins the story of the Silesian duchies, Wrocław among them. Like Kievan *Rus*, early Piast Poland passed from an era of relatively strong centralized government to one in which regionalism gained the upper hand. Bolesław III "Wrymouth," last single ruler of Poland for nearly two centuries, institutionalized these tendencies by creating in his 1138 testament an appanage-seniorate system for his sons. Silesia fell to the eldest, Władysław II, who, as senior, also received Little Poland and Cracow, now gradually becoming the spiritual and political center of the Piast lands. Władysław tried to restore centralized rule, lost the ensuing fraternal war, and in 1146 fled with his immediate family to the Empire. After nearly twenty years of imperial military and diplomatic intervention for this potential client, in 1163 not Władysław, who died as "the Exile," but his sons, Bolesław "the Tall" and Mieszko, returned with German wives and knightly educations to divide Silesia between them.[4] To Bolesław fell the northern and central portions of the province, including the largest urban center, Wrocław. His descendants, who in some parts of the country survived until the eighteenth century, continued and ended the line of Piast dukes in lower Silesia.

Bolesław, his son, and his grandson ruled over a unified lower Silesia from 1163 to 1241 (see Table 2.1). Although Bolesław had a German wife and upbringing, owed his position in part to Imperial support, and welcomed knights and monks from Germany, he was no German prince. The search for national sentiment in the activities of a twelfth-century prince is an exercise in historical self-deception. Especially in the confused Polish situation, policies depended on personal loyalties and the need to create a firm local or regional basis for continued power, not on virtually non-existent national feeling. For it was in the Polish arena that Bolesław oper-

Table 2.1. Wrocław's rulers, 1163–1526

Sovereign Piast Dukes of Silesia at Wrocław	
1163–1201	Bolesław I "the Tall"
1201–1238	Henry I "the Bearded"
1238–1241	Henry II "the Pious"
1242–1248	Bolesław II "the Bald" (co-ruler 1243–48)
1243–1266	Henry III "the White" (co-ruler 1243–48)
1266–1270	Władysław, Archbishop of Salzburg (regent for Henry IV)
1266–1290	Henry IV "the Just" (minor 1266–70)
1290–1296	Henry V "the Fat"
1296–1301	Bolko I, Duke of Świdnica (regent for Bolesław III and Henry VI)
1296–1311	Bolesław III "the Wastrel" (minor 1296–1306; co-ruler 1306–11)
1296–1335	Henry VI (minor 1296–1306; co-ruler 1306–11; vassal of Bohemia, 1327–35)

Kings of Bohemia and Dukes of Wrocław		Appointed Captains of the Wrocław Duchy	
House of Luxemburg			
1327–1346	John (King from 1310; immediate duke from 1336)	1336–37	Conrad of Borsnicz
		1337–39	Henry of Hugowicz
		1339–41	Conrad of Falkenhain
		1341–43	Henry of Stercze
		1343–46	Conrad of Falkenhain
1346–1378	Charles IV (Charles I as king; Emperor from 1347)	1346–60	Conrad of Falkenhain
		1360–69	Wrocław city council
		1369–78	Těma of Koldice
1378–1419	Wenceslas (Wenceslas IV as king; Emperor, 1378–1400, then deposed)	1378–83	Těma of Koldice
		1383–89	Herman of Chusník
		1389–95	Henry Škopek of Dubá
		1395–97	Stefan of Opaczna
		1397–1400	John of Milheim
		1400–03	Beneš of Chusník
		1403–04	Wrocław city council
		1404–08	Beneš of Chusník
		1408–13	John of Chotievice
		1413–19	Henry of Lasan
1419–1437	Sigismund (King of Hungary since 1387; Emperor from 1410)	1419–20	Henry of Lasan
		1420–22	Albert of Koldice
		1422–23	Conrad, Duke of Oleśnica and Bishop of Wrocław
		1423–24	Albert of Koldice
		1424–37	Wrocław city council
House of Habsburg			
1437–1439	Albert of Austria (as Emperor, Albert II)	1437–39	Wrocław city council
		1439	Margrave Albert of Brandenburg
1439–1440	Elizabeth of Hungary (for Ladislas Posthumus)	1439–40	Wrocław city council
1440–1457	Ladislas Posthumus (minor to 1455)	1440–55	Wrocław city council
		1455–57	Henry of Rožmberk
		1457	John of Rožmberk

Table 2.1. (*continued*)

Elected Monarchs			
1458–1471	George Poděbrady (not recognized at Wrocław after 1469)	1458 1458–69	John of Rožmberk Wrocław city council
1469–1490	Mathias "Corvinus" Hunyadi (King of Hungary from 1458; not recognized in Bohemia)	1469–70 1470–90	Zdeněk of Šternberk Wrocław city council
Jagiellonian House			
1490–1516	Vladislav II "King O.K." (originally Władysław; recognized in Bohemia from 1471; King of Hungary from 1490 as Ladislas or Laszlo V)	1490–1516	Wrocław city council
1516–1526	Louis (in Hungary, Louis II)	1516–26	Wrocław city council

ated after the restoration. He acted as a Polish prince seeking to retain and improve his position in the oft anarchic seniorate system of his dynasty.

Henry I "the Bearded" (1202–38) successfully continued his father's main policies, basing a drive toward leadership of a reunited Poland on the relative economic advancement of his Silesian base. By the last decade of his life he had achieved hegemony from east of Cracow to the Pomeranian border. At home Henry and his wife, the German princess and future saint Hedwig, actively encouraged monastic foundations, old and new, and promoted economic expansion, both by natives, now underway for some generations, and by immigrant German peasants, miners, and traders.[5] Thus before 1223 he gave German municipal institutions to the older market settlement called Środa, midway on the route between the ducal castles at Wrocław and Legnica, and renamed it the "new market" (*novum forum*, then *Neumarkt*).[6] Henry I was followed by his one surviving son, Henry II "the Pious," whose pursuit of traditional family goals ended with him before a wing of the Mongol army which devastated east-central Europe in 1241.

Four youths were heirs to the Silesian duchy and other Polish lands left smoldering behind the withdrawing Mongols. Their age, rivalry, and custom of dividing an inheritance among all surviving males began several generations of fragmentation and impotence in the Silesian principalities. The slide toward a plethora of bickering dwarf states slowed only during the reign of Henry IV "the Just" (1266–90), and culminated in the passing of Silesia under the influence and suzerainty of the strong western neighbour, Bohemia. The process gave shape to the late medieval Duchy of Wrocław.

The eldest son of Henry II, Bolesław II, was declared of age in 1242, Henry III was named co-ruler in 1247, and the next year the Silesian duchy was partitioned among them and a younger brother, Conrad.[7] Henry III received the middle segment with Wrocław at the center, and held on to it through repeated fraternal conflicts and the loss of all the extra-Silesian lands of the dynasty.

During the succeeding minority and early rule of Henry IV, even the protection of the duke's uncle, King Přemysl Ottokar II of Bohemia, could not stop the extortion of the Środa district in 1277 by Bolesław of Legnica.[8] From a perspective of Slavic solidarity these years with Ottokar may have been a high point, but from that of power and prestige in the Silesian and Polish arena they were only a prelude to Henry's own assertion of dominance in Silesia and claims to leadership of Poland. For a time his efforts were hampered by struggles with Bishop Thomas II of Wrocław, who demanded full sovereign authority over two districts owned by his see; the conflict ended only in 1287 when the duke sacrificed the fruits of military victory by a grant of wide jurisdictional powers. The settlement, engineered by Jacob Świnka, primate of the Polish church and leader of the reunification movement, freed Henry to make good a claim to Cracow and Little Poland and to become by 1290 the preeminent Piast prince, ruler of the largest, wealthiest, and ideologically most critical portions of the Polish lands. Then, still young and with the kingdom not yet restored, this last duke of Wrocław capable of an independent political program suddenly died. Without heirs of his body, Henry IV left his Silesian lands to an old antagonist, Henry I of Głogów (perhaps to encourage greater unity), and abandoned the policies of a lifetime to grant to the bishop virtual sovereignty in all church lands.[9]

In 1290 Bishop Thomas held for Henry of Głogów the castle and cathedral islands at Wrocław but not the loyalties of wealthy German merchants in the city and German and Polish knights of the countryside. They instead offered the duchy to another Henry, Duke of Legnica and their late ruler's successful general, who accepted election as Henry V of Wrocław. His succession reunited the Środa district to Wrocław. But Henry V fell victim and captive to a coalition between his brother Bolko and Henry of Głogów. The cost of freedom in 1294 was surrender of all the mountain districts to Bolko, and to the Duke of Głogów those north and east of the Odra, including the Uraz castle and district.[10]

Henry V survived his humiliation barely more than a year, leaving the truncated Wrocław duchy to his minor sons and the regency to his aggressive brother, Bolko I of Świdnica. Bolko used his position to weaken Wrocław in favor of his own city and to oppose Bohemian designs on Silesia and Poland. After Bolko's death in 1301 the Bohemian regency favored by the city of Wrocław did occur, but the ensuing deaths of two successive Přemyslid kings of Bohemia and Poland, Wenceslas II in 1303 and Wenceslas III in 1306, extinguished that dynasty, permitted the restoration of a Piast Polish kingdom,[11] and delayed for nearly a generation the Bohemian hegemony over Silesia.

The Duchy of Wrocław left by Henry V was a third as large as his predecessor's, but male children would keep it together no longer than necessary. By 1311 Bolesław had taken the extremities around Legnica and Brzeg and Henry the middle, the Wrocław and Środa districts. When three years later this Henry VI of Wrocław bought back the Uraz castle and district, the Duchy of Wrocław had attained the shape it would keep for two and a half centuries.[12] By the early fourteenth century, hereditary divisions had split the Silesian lands left by Henry II in 1241 into nine separate principalities.

Political fission of Silesia during the late thirteenth and early fourteenth centuries was related to simultaneous changes in the economy, social structure, and local institutions. Developments visible since 1150 now accelerated the emergence of a social system combining Polish and German traditions, which would exhibit a tenacity capable of enduring later difficulties with a minimum of adjustment. Following chapters detail such changes in the rural economy in the Wrocław duchy, but those in the exercise of political power belong here. Part of the general economic expansion was the foundation of new villages with new German legal forms, and the conversion of older villages from indigenous to these imported customs. Concurrently, the Polish system of local administration by castellanies gave way to one of districts centered on walled towns. The judicial authority of the castellan over persons subject to Polish law devolved upon a new territorial court, the *czuda* or *Zaude* (known from around 1300), while the German law judge, no longer a special appointee for a few specific immunities, also became a territorial officer, the *advocatus provincialis* or *Landvogt*, who presided over a *iudicium provinciale* of assessors drawn from the urban upper classes and village heads.[13] Eventually in 1337 even the *czuda* was in the Duchy of Wrocław abolished at local request and the *iudicium provinciale* left as the one high court in each district.[14]

Grants of ducal prerogatives to Bishop Thomas II by Henry IV in the compromise of 1287 and his testament three years later are the first solid evidence for different shifts in the locus of governmental power. During the next two centuries and especially when the ruler's attention was otherwise engaged, local lords and landowners obtained by means legitimate or not originally sovereign rights over their properties and the people who inhabited them. Authority to tax and to judge the rural population would slowly drift from the Silesian dukes to the landlords, thus eroding the domestic power of the former and, by letting once-sovereign prerogatives support and augment seigneurial rights, strengthening that of the latter over the peasantry and in regional affairs. For some time after 1287, however, mainly churchmen would benefit from this trend.[15] Around Wrocław they had by then enjoyed a century of ducal and private donations which gave them close to a third of the rural lordships. The largest ecclesiastical estate, that of the bishop and chapter, governed independently of the ducal administration even the inhabitants of their scattered holdings. That practice would in the fourteenth century spark more than one dispute with secular authorities. Other ecclesiastical landlords were less autonomous.

The period of political fragmentation also coincided with foundation of urban municipalities on the western (i.e. German) model and the gain by some of these of wealth and political influence. After 1241 Wrocław received its first municipal charter, a set of privileges renewed and revised by Henry III in 1261. Long active in the commerce moving along the trade routes which skirted or crossed the Bohemian massif from the west to Cracow and points east, the Wrocław merchants engaged in politics to avoid tolls, preserve routes and markets, and retain or enlarge a territorial base commensurate with their commercial ambitions. Whether or not ethnic considerations influenced decisions like that to support Henry V in 1290, the political weight of the city could but grow in the dwindling confines of the duchy. By about 1320 Wrocław was an urban craft and mercantile center on a par with all but the greatest in western Europe and, since Peter's pence returns suggest a population of thirteen to fourteen thousand, probably the largest city east of Prague.[16]

The respite Přemyslid extinction had afforded Silesian Piasts trying to retain autonomy among their more powerful neighbours ceased by 1320. Their feelings of entrapment grew as the contest over the province intensified between the new Bohemian ruler, John of Luxemburg, and the revived Polish kingdom of Władysław IV Łokietek. After 1323 the Silesian princes, without abandoning many attributes of Polish culture, ceased identifying themselves with the *regnum Poloniae* and were drawn into the Bohemian orbit. Their change of allegiance is not easily explained. Though the later Polish Piasts never long relaxed their endeavor to regain the lost province, Polish foreign policy had other critical interests, the now-hostile Teutonic Order, the other lost province of Pomerania, and, from the 1340s, growing commitments in Ruthenia. The Bohemian effort gained from a long tradition of influence across the Sudetes and the active pursuit of objectives by the enterprising John.[17] The role of Wrocław is ambiguous, with some commercial considerations pulling the town magnates east balanced by fears for their urban independence and possible cultural preference for the "German" Luxemburgs. Closer to home, the city feared further division of its principality between neighboring dukes married to Henry VI's daughters.

The Bohemian thrust was not to be denied. In March 1327, but a month after most of the upper Silesian dukes had, in the face of a Bohemian army, accepted John's suzerainty, Henry VI of Wrocław travelled to Prague, the first lower Silesian ruler to follow suit. On 27 April the Bohemian king accepted Henry's fealty and conceded him lifetime possession of the duchy. John or his heir would, however, succeed directly to the ducal office upon Henry's death—which followed in late 1335.[18] By the end of John's reign (1346) the Bohemian crown included overlordship over all of Silesia except Świdnica-Jawor, which Charles finally acquired by marriage to its heiress in 1353. Polish opposition, diplomatic and at times military, continued until the 1348 Treaty of Namysłów produced what proved to be lasting peace.[19] That year Charles formally proclaimed Silesia an element of the impersonal Bohemian Crown and duchies like Wrocław, where the king was himself duke, especially incorporated into that entity.[20] For four centuries Silesian history, and especially that of the Wrocław duchy, was to be linked with Prague, not Cracow.

Absentee authority and its local exercise

Every sovereign over Wrocław after 1335 was at the same time holder of a foreign crown, suzerain over all Silesia, and hereditary duke of Wrocław. To reign in absentia over the Wrocław duchy required changes in local governmental institutions, a task soon taken in hand by the Luxemburgs, especially the pragmatic Charles, who, well before the death of his bellicose father, relieved him of mundane chores in the family domains. They needed and found machinery for governance and men to fill it.

An immediate need was for a resident officer to act for the king in the duchy. John followed the precedent established by his Přemyslid predecessors in their Polish and other outlying territories and appointed a "captain" (*capitaneus, Landeshauptmann, starosta*).[21] This official served at the royal pleasure and took overall responsibility for defence, internal security, finance, justice, and administration, that is, the full range of duties that had been the personal affairs of the resident prince. By John's 1327 confirmation of the duchy's privileges, only natives were to receive appointment.

The only full-time assistance for the captain, beyond personal household servants and perhaps a few troops, came from the chancellor and his clerks. Thus Dietmar Meckenbach, chancellor from 1351 to 1360, managed the survey of landholdings and taxable property that is now one of the finest

sources for any study of the duchy.[22] This official also recorded land transactions and judicial decisions involving landholding at the landlord level.
He charged for this service, but his records both determined tax assessments
and proved disputed ownership rights.[23] Although the chancery was, therefore, an office important to local landowners as well as the sovereign, little
is known of incumbents under the first three Luxemburgs. Most seem to
have been clerks in the king's service who held the job for some years and
then passed to other tasks.[24] Before 1421 only the chancellor in 1360–61,
Jacob of Kąty, came from a significant native family.

The Luxemburgs otherwise relied upon ad hoc committees and short
term panels of locally influential people to govern the duchy in their name.
This was notably true of the judicial system, another area where the new
dynasty made important changes. With abolition of the *czuda* in 1337, the
first courts above the village level became the district courts that met at
Wrocław and Środa.[25] These were courts of first instance for countrymen
not subject to a village court (i.e., exempt peasants, schulzen, and landowners) and for capital and other crimes reserved to the sovereign's high
justice, but they also heard appeals from village and seigneurial courts, in-
sofar as such were permitted. Under an appointed *Hofrichter* sat seven assessors, initially mostly schulzen. By the reign of Wenceslas IV the growing
rural activities of Wrocław citizens made the court of the Wrocław district a
townsmen's preserve, but in the Środa district village chiefs remained in the
company of townsmen and nobles.[26]

Under John and Charles two courts came to have competence over the
whole duchy. The more active of these, variously called the *iudicium curiae,*
Hofgericht, or *Mannrecht* during its long history, was a modification of the
old duke's personal justice to fit the situation of an absentee ruler. It heard
cases involving property directly subject to the sovereign and appeals from
the district courts. It was chaired (in the king's normal absence) by the captain or by the *Hofrichter* of the Wrocław district court. At first knightly
landowners in varying numbers found the judgements, but in 1343 King
John decreed a membership of twelve, half of them citizens of Wrocław with
eligible property in the duchy.[27] From 1361 the assessors were eight, but
still equally divided between townsmen and nobles selected annually by the
town council and the *terrigenae* (see below) respectively.

By the early fourteenth century, the Wrocław town council was also
serving as a court of last resort for appeals on points of law. This practice
slowly gave way to similar appeals to another body established by King
John in 1346 for a different purpose, the commission called the "Royal Six."
Originally these three knightly vassals and three town councillors were to
resolve legal ambiguities in the city's charters,[28] but their work eventually

produced the duchy's law code of 1356, and they then took on the role of final recourse when the law itself was at issue.

If justice was the main peacetime service provided by a late medieval government, taxes were possibly its greatest problem; especially for rulers with as many financial needs as the Luxemburgs, they were a major reason for its very existence. Two principal taxes had developed in thirteenth-century Silesia, the land tax (*petitio, exactio, Geschoss*) and the "mint money" (*pecunia monetalis, defectus monete,* or *Munzgeld*). The former began as a fluctuating and irregular assessment requested by the ruler in times of need, but by about 1300 it had stabilized as a fixed annual payment from rent-paying peasant and *gertner* holdings in the countryside and building lots in the towns. Landlords' direct exploitation demesnes and the holdings of schulzen were free from tax. By the fourteenth century the *Geschoss* had both money and grain components. Soon after this tax had become a regular obligation, the idea that the suzerain might get special help in emergencies reappeared as the *petitio specialis* or *Bede*. The second important general tax, mint money, like the *Geschoss* an annual impost on taxable land, originally indemnified the prince who refrained from exercising his profitable right to recall and remint coins circulating in his territory. Soon after its late thirteenth-century start, mint money in the Wrocław duchy was assessed and paid as part of the land tax. Added to these main taxes were tolls, customs, surviving obligations due to the prince under Polish customary law, and military services of village schulzen, mostly paid in cash by this time.[29]

With a fiscal system in place around Wrocław, the Luxemburgs needed do little more than learn and enforce it. For the sake of development on poor land John was even induced in 1341 to cut the tax rate in the Środa district from twelve groschen to six per rental mansus.[30] Thus the great survey done about 1353 for Charles IV exemplifies Luxemburg fiscal policy. The only surviving account from the duchy dates from 1377 and suggests the magnitude of the system at its height. Of total receipts worth not quite 1400 marks, the city of Wrocław paid 560 marks, the town of Środa was exempt, and rural areas added about 250 marks cash and grain worth almost 125. Tolls provided about 200 marks. Local expenses of more than 900 marks still left 400 for transfer to Prague or other royal business.[31]

The account from 1377 was kept for the Wrocław town council, which had administered the financial affairs of the duchy. Nearly a third of the disbursements went to Těma of Koldice, Czech courtier of Charles and Wenceslas and for fourteen years captain of the Wrocław duchy. Other monies went to imperial vassals and toward construction projects in the royal castle at Wrocław. Thus the account itself shows politics in the fourteenth-century duchy to have involved not just administrative machinery but an interplay of forces: the local nobility, the city of Wrocław, and, balancing or using the others from afar, the crown of Bohemia and its favorites. A "constitution" of several elements, often operated by domestic groups but repeatedly adjusted by royal intervention, structured political life under the Luxemburgs.

During the thirteenth century a more distinctive group of nobles had emerged from the complex social gradations of the early Piast state. Landed wealth, princely service, and a military calling sustained claims to privileged status, while the once absolute authority of the Polish sovereign was tempered by reciprocal forms of personal dependency and land grants that came to resemble the more structured western feudalism.[32] In Silesia, sovereign dukes multiplied and their principalities shrank, splitting family allegiances and blocking the spread of large family properties across the province. As a result, fourteenth-century Silesia sustained a relatively homogeneous subprincely secular elite without the sharp division between magnates and ordinary knights characteristic of the Kingdom of Poland. In this environment of dwarf states and well before the success of the Luxemburgs, a somewhat foggy notion of a noble corporate identity appeared within each district or principality. In the Wrocław duchy this germ of a noble "Estate" is visible in the "terrigenae" who in 1290 joined the city to accept Henry V as their ruler. By the mid-fourteenth century, a presumption of consent to taxation and major political action seems to have been accepted.[33] Again the Luxemburgs brought little change. John's confirmation of privileges in 1327 tacitly recognized the political importance of the *terrigenae*, especially in his guarantee to provide only native sons as his governors. Later, district nobles gathered to assist or to petition the monarch.[34]

Participation by individual nobles in governmental activity may best illustrate the political importance of this group during the fourteenth century. At the highest level, for a generation after 1327 the Luxemburgs kept their promise to reserve the captaincy for local men. The longest-serving among the early captains, Conrad of Falkenhain (1339–41 and 1343–60) had widespread rural interests in the duchy, some in association with Wrocław citizens.[35] Before 1360 individuals like him monopolized the chief office in the duchy. But urban interests came to oppose Falkenhain; in 1359 the city of Wrocław complained to Charles IV that his appointee failed to prevent disorder and to support townsmen against their enemies (without further specific charges).[36] For a year Charles sought compromise, allowing the town council to function as Falkenhain's deputy, but in 1360 the king appointed the city captain in its own right and ended leadership of the duchy by indigenous nobles. It did not, however, end their strong political influence. Half of the assessors on the duchy's *iudicium curiae* and "Royal Six" came from noble ranks. Membership lists from the former, available from 1361 on, demonstrate the regular representation of the major landholding families in the duchy: a Schellendorf and a Hugowicz, for example, each sat on half of the courts meeting between 1361 and 1420.[37]

Wrocław's acquisition of the captaincy in 1360 capped its growing wealth, prestige, and influence under the early Luxemburgs. The city bustled with craftsmen in textiles, leather, and metal whose products were shipped, together with a wide variety of goods in transit, across Europe by the mercantile elite who dominated municipal politics.[38] Their town council won toll-free trade, staple rights, and other commercial advantages. Magnates and other townsmen had by mid-century also invested heavily in rural land in the Wrocław district.

Urban influence in the politics of the duchy, already evident in the late thirteenth century, grew as well.[39] By the reign of Wenceslas, Wrocław citizens dominated their district court and shared the *iudicium curiae* with the nobility. Their membership on the latter was more widely distributed than that of their noble colleagues; only the Dompnig family held seats nearly as often as the great noble houses. It was rather as a corporation, embodied in their town council, that the citizens of Wrocław most actively engaged in the affairs of the duchy during this period. Helping to finance the anti-Polish campaigns of John and Charles during the 1340s brought the city control over royal incomes in the duchy, first as security for its loans and later as the council served as collection agent for the king's account.[40] Possession of the captaincy would merely regularize the town's influence. But before the Hussite wars Wrocław's domination of the government of the duchy remained incomplete, largely because the Luxemburgs repeatedly displayed a willingness to intervene, to maintain a royal presence when orderly government seemed at risk, and to use the resources of the duchy for their own purposes.

Disorder and disagreement between Conrad of Falkenhain and the city in the late 1350s had brought the captaincy to the town council, and new conflicts involving that office led to its removal in 1369. When the city became mired in jurisdictional disputes with its bishop, Charles reclaimed the captaincy and installed a neutral, the Bohemian nobleman Těma of Koldice. Whether Charles and his successors learned from the troubles of 1359 and 1369 or merely found in this office a useful reward for their followers, for the next fifty-five years the pledge of 1327 was ignored (see Table 2.1 above). The captaincy and the incomes attached to it went to one Luxemburg supporter after another, nearly all foreigners to the duchy. Of thirteen incumbencies between 1369 and 1424, only one can rightly be called native, the brief period during the captivity of Wenceslas in 1403 when the town council held the office in its own right, although some others acquired property or had *ex officio* interests in the duchy.[41] Then more typical, however, were men without roots there, like Henry Škopek of Dubá, scion of an old Czech baronial family, friend of Wenceslas, and simultaneously chief chamberlain of Bohemia; or John of Milheim, a Silesian émigré who rose via the royal court into the highest circles of Bohemian society.[42] Direct sovereign control of the office, as expressed in its occupancy by "foreigners," was often mitigated by the incumbents' absence on other royal business. Then the Wrocław town council acted as the deputy. Hence even after 1369 urban influences were surely more significant than during the 1340s and 1350s, but they rested on the insecure foundation of ad hoc arrangements and an inactive or otherwise occupied monarch. The direct and bloody intervention of Sigismund, who in 1420 personally dismantled a guild regime that had seized power in Wrocław two years earlier, demonstrates continued royal willingness and royal capacity to react directly to threats to internal security.[43]

External and internal security and a long-unequaled political stability were products of the Luxemburg regime in Silesia, and especially in the Duchy of Wrocław. After 1348 no major military danger faced the duchy from outside the province, while feuds among princes and nobles were held in check by the appeal of court life and high politics and the threat of royal intervention. Administrative mechanisms were adjusted to forms they would follow for two centuries and more. Even occasional disputes between king and bishop, city and cathedral chapter, or craftsmen and town council left the countryside undisturbed. The city and its commerce seem to have suffered little from the economic difficulties so prevalent elsewhere after mid-century, so by the turn of the century its population may have reached 19,000.[44] No longer the vulnerable dwarf state of the early fourteenth century, as part of the Bohemian Crown the Duchy of Wrocław belonged to one of larger and better-governed political structures in east central Europe. Despite the weaknesses of Charles's son, Wenceslas IV, the Luxemburg system in Silesia in 1400 had only begun to show hints of incipient disintegration.

An occasionally presumptuous pawn

A regional community in a larger state shares weal and woe. Only occasionally in the fifteenth and sixteenth centuries were conditions in the Wrocław duchy set by internal volition. Usually its inhabitants had to navigate in larger currents.

Around 1400 storm clouds did brew over the Luxemburg domains; the next two generations would see them sweep eastward from their Czech center more than once, adding to the impact of local disturbances in Silesia and the Wrocław duchy itself. Within a decade of Charles's death the absence of his firm hand became perceptible in the province as feuds among nobles, towns, and even dukes inspired local alliances to wage or combat them. Wrocław's once welcome role as financier to the crown now drew the duchy into a protracted feud with other creditors, the Dukes of Opole, who waged economic warfare by waylaying merchants and burning villages. Throughout the fifteenth century these most popular tactics blurred to imperceptibility (at least for the victims) boundaries between public warfare, private feud, and simple brigandage. Then in Wrocław itself a bloody guild revolt in 1418, the first serious uprising since 1333, was quelled only by the equally harsh hand of the new ruler, Sigismund.

In some ways the Wrocław revolt resembled the Hussite revolution which simultaneously gave social content to the Czech reformation and solidified the Czech people against the brother and heir of Wenceslas. Certainly the responses of Sigismund and the Wrocław leadership were identical. While some evidence indicates initial pro-Hussite sentiments among the lower social orders in Silesia, dominant political groups in the province leaned heavily toward the most rabid opposition.[45] Social reaction, religious orthodoxy, and ethnic antipathy may all have contributed to the initial ruling attitude. Silesian forces actively joined in Sigismund's efforts to invade Bohemia, crush the revolution, and claim his throne. Retaliation by the successful Czech defenders soon followed. From 1427 to 1434 the feared Hussite troops and their armored wagons, at times joined by local recruits or individual Polish allies, ranged throughout Silesia, burning churches and country estates, looting villages and monasteries, even taking and holding towns and castles. The Wrocław duchy, where the city government and cathedral chapter were the soul of the Silesian war effort, received special attention more than once. No part of the duchy was really spared; nowhere did the Silesians put effective opposition in the field. The sequel to the Czech raids was extensive rural depopulation.

When the Czechs and Sigismund were reconciled in summer, 1436, the fighting also ended in Silesia. But people had barely caught their breath before war (or virtual anarchy) broke out again after the Emperor's death in 1437. A contest between Austrian Habsburgs and Polish Jagiellonians for the vacant crowns of Bohemia and Hungary was in Silesia interwoven with provincial feuds, complemented by the collapse of order everywhere outside city walls or the burgeoning strongholds of local lords. Taking the sword and dying by it, men like Leonard Asenheimer, a Bavarian adventurer, set the tone of public life. He appeared in Silesia in 1442, brandishing a commission from Queen Elizabeth of Hungary to open up a second front against the Poles. A meteoric career began with military operations against Poland and the allied dukes of Oleśnica and easily survived expulsion from Namysłów for arbitrary and violent behavior as garrison commander. Having married into a prestigious Wrocław family, Asenheimer led town forces against a band of noble robbers to gain as reward the Środa castle. But then he started a private feud with a Moravian baron, who retaliated against Wrocław's commerce, and tried to make the Środa district his own independent principality. When Asenheimer laid violent hands on Środa's town court, officials there seized, tried, and executed him, thus precipitating three more years of feud with his henchman, the Duke of Cieszyn.[46]

Comparable conditions in contemporary Bohemia gave rise to the man who would focus the various currents of conflict in the crown lands and bring unity, if not to his state, at least to the history of the mid-fifteenth century, the Czech nobleman and Utraquist, George Poděbrady.[47] His rapid ascent to a key role in procuring Czech election of Ladislas Posthumus, son of Albert II, revived latent anti-Hussite sentiments in Wrocław. Fired by fanatical preachers, the city, and now especially its lower orders, became the center of an anti-Czech movement in the incorporated provinces. First the city refused to send emissaries to heretical Prague to swear allegiance to the young king; then, at the news of Ladislas's death and Poděbrady's own election in 1458, it turned to violent opposition. An able diplomat, the king soon stripped Wrocław of possible allies and, late in 1459, stood with his army before its walls. Only papal mediation procured a saving compromise. But three years later Wrocław's intransigence revived when Pius II broke with the king over the continuation of Utraquism in Bohemia. At Rome municipal delegations reviled moderation, in Bohemia jealous noble families rose in armed revolt, and on the southern border Poděbrady's onetime protégé, King Mathias "Corvinus" Hunyadi of Hungary, emerged as champion of the orthodox to accept partisan election as king of Bohemia in 1469. Again raiding warfare flamed along the Silesian borders, and did not end with the death of the "Hussite King" in 1471.

Poděbrady and his party had agreed to promote the succession to Bohemia of Władysław, son of Polish King Casimir IV.[48] His election by the loyalist Czech estates assured continued combat, pitting Bohemia and Poland against Hungary, Silesia, Moravia, and Lusatia, where Mathias had succeeded in establishing himself. From the standpoint of the Wrocław duchy, a satisfactory outcome was assured after Mathias repelled a joint Czech-Polish invasion and assault on the city in late 1474. The conflict ended, however, only with the Peace of Olomouc in 1478, whereby the

Jagiellonians recognized Corvinus as King of Bohemia ruling over all the incorporated provinces, and he in turn accepted Władysław (in Bohemia Vladislav II) as King of Bohemia ruling over Bohemia. With this division of the crown lands ended what is often called the "Second Hussite War" and, for the Duchy of Wrocław, more than a half-century of struggle, insecurity, and destruction.

Freed of immediate concern with defence and international politics between the 1480s and 1520s, many in the Wrocław duchy sought stable prosperity like that reputed to have prevailed in the days of Charles IV. But a shifted balance of political forces had brought with it other changes in life and thought that made for a fitful transition from medieval issues to those of the sixteenth century. At one level the vigorous new initiatives of Mathias contrast with the laissez faire weakness of his Jagiellonian successors, and on a more local plane the city of Wrocław, though adjusting to more painfully competitive commerce, moved steadily to tighten its grip on the duchy's governance.

In Hungary King Mathias ruled in the style of some western contemporaries, seeking to substitute a strong, centralized, hereditary monarchy for the aristocratic decentralization of his predecessors and fully willing to innovate for these ends.[49] His Silesian activities continued this thrust and met the same opposition from vested interests. The first sovereign in generations to treat the province as a unit, Mathias imposed his rule on the Silesian dukes, symbolically demoting them in the Olomouc treaty from the rank of princes to that of "barones Bohemie."[50] Over them he placed a provincial viceroy whose extensive powers in the king's absence were wielded first by Hungarians and later by Silesian dukes of proven loyalty. A Diet of Estates met in formal sessions, but only at the royal pleasure and for royal fiscal needs. Some of the monies thus wrung from the reluctant Silesians supported Corvinus's mercenary "Black Army," a terror to any locality, enemy or friend, in which it was billeted. The first standing army in this part of Europe freed the king from dependence on the forces of his nobility. Mathias's attempts to repair the mess in Silesia's currency, long disrupted by shortage and debasement, never succeeded.

In the Duchy of Wrocław Mathias especially tried to rein in subordinate authorities and assert royal rights. Even on the first visit to Wrocław, his warm supporter, the king surprised the town councillors by accepting their pro forma resignation of the captaincy into his hands and installing his own candidate, the Czech potentate Zdeněk of Šternberk. The need for more financial support against Poděbrady soon canceled this experiment, but the king later adopted the expedient of annually appointing to the post of senior councillor (*Ratsälteste*) his own man, who personally acted as captain. Nobles and rich townsmen alike opposed royal attempts to review and confiscate alienated royal rights and to treat as fiefs (with attendant obligations) what the holders could not prove were free and hereditary properties.[51] Since confiscated holdings often went as fiefs to royal partisans, Wrocław's senior councillor and captain in the late 1480s, Henry Dompnig, used his position and the king's absence from Silesia for personal gain. Dompnig's enemies said he connived with the viceroy to make himself pocket dictator of the duchy, browbeating the town council, seizing and destroying the charters of those whose lands he coveted, and forging his own titles and privileges. At news of Mathias's death in 1490 his Silesian program, like that in Hungary, collapsed; the head of Henry Dompnig rolled in front of the Wrocław city hall.[52]

Experience with a strong monarch in Mathias Hunyadi had alarmed powerful interests in Hungary as well as Silesia. His illegitimate son was passed over for the Estates' more suitable candidate, "King Dobře," Vladislav II of Bohemia, the old Jagiellonian rival of Mathias, whose career as an amiable weakling on the Czech throne had amply demonstrated his qualifications. Thus the Polish dynasty gained the crowns of Wenceslas and Stephen, but local strong men could control their own affairs. A year before his death, Vladislav compromised with his family's long-time rivals by entering into a marriage alliance with the Habsburgs. The youth of Vladislav's son and successor, the ill-fated Louis (1516–26), allowed him no greater freedom than his father from noble control. The growing Turkish threat to his southern frontier forced the king and his advisors to action, precipitating the catastrophe of Mohács where Louis and his army perished. The Habsburg, Ferdinand, recalling the treaty of 1515, had little difficulty in making good his claim to the Bohemian throne.[53]

Changes came to Silesia and Wrocław under but without the influence of the Jagiellonian monarchs. Only when Vladislav's brother, Sigismund, later king of Poland, spent two years as "Highest Captain of Upper and Lower Silesia" to reduce banditry and shore up an unstable coinage did the province attract governmental attention.[54] Otherwise local authorities dealt as best they could with routine administration and the innovations that trickled in from outside. Leagues of towns and princes tried to discourage feuds and violence and, in the so-called Kolovrat treaty of 1504, to limit the claims of the church against their subjects. Wrocław revived its obsolete claim to staple rights in the Polish trade, only to lose more from a retaliatory embargo on its commerce in Poland and Brandenburg. Clerics and teachers educated at Cracow or the German universities brought humanism to the city, inspiring local disciples and imitators among the literate classes.

In the wake of the new learning came the teaching of Lutheran reformers, who found a field fertilized by lay piety, clerical corruption, and traditions of dissension between the city and the ecclesiastical corporations who were its neighbors. By 1526 the Reformation had been installed in the town parishes and was percolating into the countryside. Whisperings of more radical reforms and muted repercussions of the peasant unrest which had swept Germany were likewise heard.[55]

Neither new ideas nor new dynasties nor even the new politics presaged by Corvinus, whatever their future effects on Silesian life, should obscure steadier internal trends of the late fifteenth and early sixteenth centuries. Despite, and at times because of, invasion, upheaval, and neglect, the city of Wrocław moved towards control over the duchy's government. During the Hussite wars the town council gained full legal possession of the captaincy—and then retained it into the seventeenth century. Even the six years between 1424 and 1526 with other captains were responses to external political needs of the sovereign, not to the earlier wish to dampen internal dissension.[56] Only Mathias Corvinus dared interfere, but even he did so only through the town government and without permanent effect. Wrocław also purchased the chancellorship of the duchy at this time.[57] Membership on the courts continued balanced between burghers and knights, but by the decades around 1500 the former had the greater wealth and continuity of membership. Wrocław's judicial dominance is suggested on the one hand by individual noblemen trying to evade jurisdiction when in legal difficulties with townsmen and on the other by the privileges the city acquired to call these cases directly to tribunals it controlled.[58] By 1522 the noble estate of the duchy was publicly whining to King Louis about not only Wrocław's economic privileges but its very political hegemony.[59] So long as the sovereign remained distant and uninvolved, the relative balance in the duchy between town and nobility reversed contemporary regional norms.

The city of Wrocław profited from the small size of its effective political unit, the absenteeism of rulers oblivious to Silesian affairs, and the disorders of the fifteenth century, to construct an incipient city-state in the duchy. But with the coming of the new dynasty these conditions so characteristic of late medieval Silesia were replaced by others more typical of its modern history. The Habsburg succession combined with simultaneous cultural and economic changes to mark a gradual but distinct break in the history of duchy and province.[60] In a long (1527–64) reign, Ferdinand slowly removed real power from autonomous lesser authorities, whose continued local functioning was now overseen by a centralizing administration staffed by loyal careerists. The domestic quiet which ensued let the king scrap the obsolete tax on rental land for one on the assessed wealth of the entire province and replace the 250-year-old groschen with a new monetary regime. In religion he even sacrificed confessional preference for tranquillity, allowing the numerous Protestant towns and dukes to retain and even propagate their beliefs so long as they neither aided embattled co-religionists in Germany nor imported violent confessional conflict into Silesia.

No single novelty brought to the Wrocław Duchy in the years after 1500 was unique or decisive. But just as an accumulation of innovations in the late twelfth and early thirteenth centuries broke with an earlier medieval past, so did those of the early sixteenth century end the socio-political system that had prevailed since then. Two centuries of Habsburg rule would be followed by another two centuries of Prussian rule before the cataclysm of 1945 would remove the seven century old German presence and restore Silesia to Poland.

The nature and development of the late medieval agrarian regime on the borderland between eastern and western Europe describes the intellectual frame of reference for this study. That conceptual focus now rests in its geographic and historic surroundings, the parameters of natural and political environment within which people made economic decisions, established the patterns of rural life, and reacted or adapted to change. The historical endeavor would reconstruct such choices, customs, and trends, proceeding from the recorded results and concomitants of human behavior toward the perceptions and motivations of those who experienced them. But the leap from behavioral precipitate, the "historical source," through actual event, the "fact of history," to the existential reality in the actor's mind is often barred by the isolated and cryptic qualities of the record. Cautious discrimination between generalization from particulars and inference of individual or even group motivations must be especially evident when one is using formulaic documents created for the non-agricultural purposes of the literate few. Except in sadly few instances, the chapters which follow must chiefly ascertain which events were general or frequent in the duchy while omitting through lack of knowledge all too many of the personal and individually human aspects intrinsic to any particular action. This constraint notably affects the task of reconstructing the rural economy of the late twelfth century and the subsequent spread of German law institutions across the countryside.

THE CHANGING POLISH
COUNTRYSIDE OF THE
HIGH MIDDLE AGES

Ecclesiam sancti Adalberti dedit Boguslaus frater comitis Petri cum villa Mochbor, cuius ascripti sunt: Zbilut cum filiis Dados, Zauis, Vilcan, Radon, qui cum deberet monetario marcam et dimidiam fere, Vlodimirus solum pro eo debitum tenet esset homo sancte Marie ecclesie.

A late twelfth century description of Muchobor Mały, a lordship of the Augustinian canons of St. Mary at Wrocław; *KdS* #68 = *SUB*, I, #58.

Indigenous dynamism and growth characterized Poland's economic and social history during the late twelfth and early thirteenth centuries as much as fragmentation and disunity did its politics. Since there is little written evidence for the country as a whole from this period, portrayal of so small an area as the future Wrocław duchy must draw heavily on wider studies of Polish or Silesian conditions, and often merely illustrate their local manifestations. This chapter, therefore, examines settlement patterns, lordship, and the peasantry to describe rural life in transition from relative stability toward accelerated change. In central Silesia as elsewhere, active expansion refutes once-traditional images of backward stagnation.[1]

Population and settlement

Polish scholars generally agree that with or before the twelfth century Poland's population followed that of western Europe into a phase of long-term expansion. Estimates for the kingdom suggest that densities rose by 80 percent between 1000 and 1340 with the first and greatest growth in the westernmost provinces.[2] If before 1200 an average of eight to nine persons per square kilometer lived in Silesia (including known woodland), by mid-century rural densities alone may have reached sixteen in the thickly settled central Odra basin. Around Trzebnica, on the lower slopes of Mt. Ślęza, and near Ścinawa the thickness of settlement may already have peaked.[3] Of course little direct demographic evidence supports such calculations. The one village in Great Poland where sixteen households in 1288 had descended from eight of the nine there in 1216 is, not surprisingly, a rare and fortuitous example[4]—and one not repeated near Wrocław.

Population growth in the late twelfth and early thirteenth centuries is commonly inferred from many signs of expanding human settlement and arable acreage. Southeast of the Wrocław duchy, where the upper Oława river carves fertile valleys into the Sudetes, Duke Henry established Cistercians at Henryków in 1228. A generation later the monks' need to defend their holdings against other claimants led them to record the histories of what they had acquired: "In the days when the old lord Duke Bolesław . . . distributed to his rustics land in various places, he gave that woods to a certain rustic of his own, Glambo by name. This same rustic Glambo first cleared that place which is now called Great Meadow."[5] Few such human accounts enliven the record of expanding settlement near Wrocław, but its reality is no less certain. On a fair-sized area of the black earth in the Wrocław district, from the Żurawka and the Ślęza rivers northeast almost to the Oława (see Map 3.1), formerly empty lands were cleared by twelfth century settlers.[6] But continued uneven human densities by the mid-thirteenth century call for review of the rural settlement pattern before a further look at agrarian institutions.

Map 3.1 reveals a concentration of human settlement near Wrocław along river terraces and other reasonably dry sites in and beside the bottomlands of the Odra and the Oława from Kozanów to Księże Wielkie and Blizanowice. (For rural place names omitted from a map for clarity's sake, the interested reader is referred to the Gazetteer and to Map 1.1.) North and east of the Odra the bottomlands seem much more sparsely inhabited. The black earth soils which spread southward from Wrocław beyond the later boundary of the duchy also contained fairly thick populations, especially in that recently cleared section already mentioned. Further south, a five to ten kilometer belt of unsettled lands separated villages near the junction of the Żurawka and Ślęza from another major concentration around the forks of the Ślęza, and along its branches beyond the southern limits of the black earth.

Westward from Wrocław, the black earth gives way to loams and bottomlands along the Bystrzyca and loess in the southern sections of the Środa district. Here early thirteenth-century settlement was scattered in a distinct band from the city to and beyond Kostomłoty. Most sites lay near the lower Ślęza, the Bystrzyca, and their tributaries. With few exceptions, the rest of what would become the Środa district then had but one focus of habitation

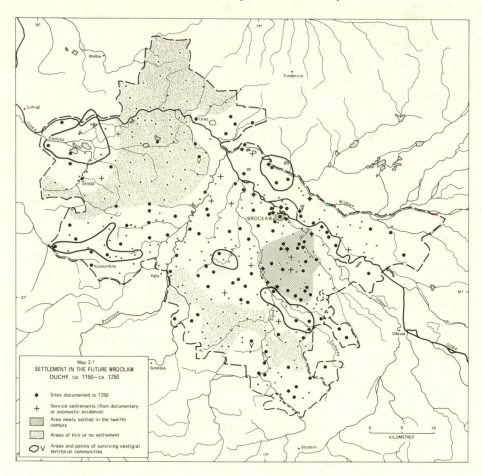

Map 3.1
SETTLEMENT IN THE FUTURE WROCŁAW
DUCHY, ca. 1150– ca. 1250

● Sites documented to 1250

+ Service settlements (from documentary
or onomastic evidence)

Area newly settled in the twelfth
century

Areas of thin or no settlement

○∨ Areas and points of surviving vestigial
territorial communities

in the area drained by the Średzka Woda. Near Rzeczyca a ford across the
Odra gave access to Lubiąż, Wołów, and points north. The last notable
concentration within the later Wrocław duchy was north of the city along
the Odra and its feeder streams between Uraz and Widawa. This, however,
was but a fringe of the densely populated area around Trzebnica.

Hence in general the rural population of the early thirteenth century
concentrated on the black earth and the loess, with some settlement on favored sites in the bottomlands but relatively little penetration of the extensive loams of the central Środa district and the sandy moraines north of
Uraz.[7] Locational attributes of settlement in the area around Wrocław thus
differed little from those elsewhere in contemporary Poland. The choice of
sites near water but located above flood level on dunes or terraces was typi-

cal from the earliest Middle Ages. By the twelfth century a growing population had spread to somewhat higher sites and opened up most good soils,
but still left relatively undisturbed the less fertile or poorly watered areas.[8]

Soils and water courses influence but only incompletely determine human settlement patterns. People's institutions also structure their distribution on the landscape. Under the earlier Polish agrarian regime, individual
farmsteads (*źreby, sortes*) were grouped into local economic complexes
(*campi*) which, in turn, formed a territorial community (*opole, vicinia*).[9]
Whether dispersed as isolated farms in woodland clearings or assembled
into hamlets, the economically autonomous and oft-times topographically
distinct *źreb* had long been the fundamental unit of settlement and production. Its name had the same ambiguity still present in English "lot," simultaneously signifying a parcel of ground and acquisition by chance, as in the
division of an inheritance. Each źreb was a relatively small economic unit,
the assemblage of cultivated lands which belonged to a single holder regard-
less of its compactness or his social condition. But most often it came to
connote a family holding with certain hereditary qualities. Land not used
for crops belonged not to households but to the *campus* association or *opole*
community for extensive use by all members. While *campi* could serve collective economic needs and *opoly* were foci of local social and governmental
affairs, both also joined scattered farms and hamlets into a spatial, if not
nucleated, settlement pattern. By the twelfth century, however, the fluidity
of dispersed territorial settlement and the ambiguity of landholding inherent
in this system were making it a thing of the past. With great landlords
anxious to delineate their properties, *opoly* and *campi* broke up into distinct
villages where źreby could be united and lands attached to specific holdings.

Around Wrocław, the transitional character of late twelfth and early
thirteenth century rural settlement structures made for variety and sometimes even confused contemporaries. Many attributes of the źreb can be
exemplified. Holders of these ranged in status from slaves through a duke's
miller and a small lord named Zlaucovo to the wealthy Count Mikora.[10]
Layers of rights over these holdings, indicative of their integration into relations of lordship and dependency, permitted the Wrocław cathedral warden and his brother to make a gift of six *sortes* belonging to Suyny, who
presumably worked or managed them.[11] Although by 1252 old notions of a
family-sized źreb must have weakened considerably for Suyny to have six
of them, large individual ones existed much earlier—witness Mikora's gift
at *Żórawin* in 1175 with fields, 25 horses, 6 oxen, and 3 cows.[12] But with
the źreb losing its normative role in rural organization, people found it hard
to relate to other rural institutions, especially the village. In several charters

during 1203–08 Henry I successively labeled *Opatowo* "villa," "villula," and "sors."[13] The autonomous farmstead still existed near Wrocław in the early 1200s but it was giving way to other settlement units.

Traces of the old territorial patterns survived as well, some even beyond the thirteenth century. Specific uses of the terms *campus* or *opole* are not numerous. In a charter of 1203 Henry I identified Jaksonów as being "in campo Zlesie" and incidental references to *viciniae* occur in texts as late as 1254.[14] More valuable affirmation of extensive "neighborhood" settlement complexes comes from the toponomastic history of localities in the Wrocław district and from slightly later patterns of inter-village cooperation in the Środa district.

In the bottomlands north of Wrocław, at least four places shared the name *Widawa* in the early and mid-thirteenth century. The modern site of that name belonged to St. Vincent's abbey and the Church of Wrocław had another three villages so labelled, gifts from their family inheritances by a dean, Crisanus, a cantor, John, and a canon, Vincent.[15] From these eventually emerged Krzyżanowice (north of the Widawa river and named from Crisanus), Polanowice, and Poświętne. South of the city another such community along the Żurawka river split during the twelfth and thirteenth centuries into six villages, each of which retained for at least a time the name *Żurawina*. Although most eventually received new patronymic place names, only one of the local magnates thus memorialized, the Cragek who gave Krajków to St. Vincent before 1149, otherwise attained documentary notice.[16]

West of the Bystrzyca, early territorial communities on the southern loess and in the northwestern lowlands are to be inferred from social networks among small Polish landlords revealed during two tithe controversies around 1300. An agreement between Stanisław, priest of Chomiąża, and the abbot of Lubiąż finds six individuals, lords of Jaśkowice, Szczepanów, "Zagadlovicz," Zakrzów, Zagórzyce (north of the Odra in the Wołów district), and an unidentifiable "villa Vincencii," jointly interested in the payment and disposition of tithes owed to the Chomiąża parish church. Their lordships covered most of the old-settled area north of Środa and, like the *Widawa* and *Żurawina* communities, both sides of the river.[17] At the other end of the district comparable relationships and probably kinship ties linked lords of Siemidrożyce, Rakoszyce, Jakubowice, *Czepankowicz*, Szymanowice, and perhaps Jarosław in a long struggle over tithes for the Kostomłoty church.[18] By these early fourteenth-century controversies, of course, *campi* and *viciniae* were moribund and all but forgotten, echoing at most in a few place names. Cooperation among neighboring lords in the two longest-inhabited sections of the Środa district was then the last trace of an older territorial unity which had preceded the village-based settlement pattern of the later Middle Ages.

Źreb and opole on the one hand, nucleated village on the other were, therefore, both components of rural settlement and concepts that differently structured institutions of landholding and agriculture. The gradual trend towards nucleation, a slow transition from one organizational principle to another, meant the long coexistence of two settlement forms, one featuring scattered farmsteads and small hamlets, the other good-sized villages. In the well-documented and advanced Trzebnica region Duke Henry donated villages of less than ten to almost twenty households, perhaps fifty to one hundred persons. Among the largest places known in the early thirteenth century, the fishing village of Kotowice had twenty-two families and (if the normal multiplier of 5.5 persons per household is reasonable) some 130 inhabitants. But elsewhere, notably in newly-pioneered areas like around Henryków, settlements more often held a mere handful of families, each on its źreb.[19] Archeological evidence indicates seven to ten households as a norm for Polish rural settlements.[20]

The countryside of 1200 was in flux. Expansion of cropland joined with transition from a dispersed toward a more nucleated settlement pattern long before Poland or Silesia felt the impact of German immigration and German customs. As źreby were amalgamated into villages and hamlets coalesced, numerous individual settlements disappeared, place names vanished, but both population and arable remained and grew.[21] For example, the abbey of St. Mary had in 1193 two "villae," Brochów and *Bronikowo*. A decade later *Bronikowo*, now said to be "beside *Buchta*," was further described as "sortes." The place name last received known mention in 1250, when Innocent IV confirmed the holdings of St. Mary. Meanwhile *Buchta*, too, came to the abbey by ducal gift in 1243 and promptly faded from the extant record. Neither *Buchta* nor *Bronikowo* were mentioned when Henry III confirmed St. Mary's holdings in 1256. By the fifteenth century all that remained was the tradition that, in the words of the abbey's chronicler, "once and at that time [1243] Brochów and *Buchta* were two little villages, but thereafter and up to now they are together one village within its boundaries, which is simply called Brochów."[22] *Bronikowo* was presumably absorbed, too.

Not far away Domaniów also grew by absorption of several neighbors. Sometime before 1224 Henry I gave to Peter, son of Woysław, the village called "Domavioua" which, after Peter's death, his heirs gave to Trzebnica. When Henry confirmed this gift he united to it the chapel there in "Domavioua" and villages of his castle guards and other men.[23] The two names, "Domanevo" and "Domanigeua Cirki," given this place in Pope Clement's

1267 confirmation charter for Trzebnica reflect the amalgamation.[24] Such reorganizations meant that, of 168 rural settlements documented in the Wrocław district before 1300, thirteen had appeared in the texts only to vanish again.[25] Like the "villam nomine Vstimouo que est iuxta Oporouo,"[26] most left but their names as mementos of a fast-disappearing old Polish rural society.

The development of seigneurial lordship

Demographic increase and arable expansion alone did not impel replacement of *sortes, campi*, and *viciniae* with nucleated villages and desertion of some settlement sites at the very time others were being created and expanded. Equally central to the evolution of Polish rural society were changes in the nature and exercise of lordship—the way those with power controlled and exploited rural populations, production, and resources. An increasingly autonomous group of landholders, lay and ecclesiastical, emerged in twelfth-century Poland.[27] In the early Piast state, noble wealth, status, and power had depended on a close personal relationship with the duke or king and active involvement in the administrative system of the castellanies. But for feebler twelfth-century rulers to keep their adherents required not merely maintaining them in castles but granting them lands and other direct sources of revenue. To these ducal losses were added extensive gifts to churches and monasteries.[28] Thus, although Silesian dukes probably still controlled nearly half of the land in the province in 1200, their relative position had been much reduced and would continue to diminish in the future.

Lay lords profited from the political disturbances of the twelfth century. High medieval Poland distinguished between the largest landholders, scions of families who had long possessed hereditary properties and gained more in ducal service (*nobiles*) and smaller lords, men who emerged more slowly through military service into the landed elite (*milites*). The noble status of the former was undisputed; that of the latter, the knights, dubious or, at best, plausibly ambiguous. By the thirteenth century the two groups shared, however, direct personal connections to the prince whom they served as cavalrymen and consequent customary privileges (*ius militare*), i.e., authority over those who lived on their lands and personal liberty from the judicial and fiscal powers of the duke's subordinates.[29]

Great lay landholders are much the better documented. Up to 1266 thirty-nine individuals can be found in the Silesian texts to have possessed three or more villages; of these, thirteen had holdings in the future Wrocław duchy.[30] Earliest and greatest of them was Count Peter Włast, a member of the Łabędziów clan whose ambitions unsettled the last years of the old Polish monarchy. His properties spread across the kingdom and included at least twenty Silesian sites. Close to Wrocław he gave Opatowice, *Olbino*, and Wierzbno to St. Vincent, Jelenin and Turów to the bishop, and Tyniec Mały to St. Mary, all together with other, more distant holdings.[31] Most of Włast's lands came from his rich family inheritance. This origin and the sheer size of his wealth make him a less typical figure than Count John of Wierzbno, an active politician at ducal courts during the 1240s–60s. Count John had hereditary properties and ducal gifts near Świdnica but, perhaps to get a seat or incomes closer to Wrocław, spent a hundred silver marks for Święta Katarzyna and Blizanowice in 1257.[32] When he later sold out, the purchasers, Eberhard and Simon *Gallici*, represented a new element that had been joining the Silesian ruling group since the late twelfth century, the immigrant knight and nobleman. The Walloon *Gallici* had arrived before 1200 and risen in the ducal service. By buying Święta Katarzyna and Blizanowice they added to their cluster of properties northwest of Oława.[33]

Some late twelfth-century knights were, like the first *Gallici*, immigrants to Silesia who took service with local princes. A few Germans accompanied Bolesław's return from exile and others followed. But before mid-century those who then settled in Silesia remained few beside the lesser native landowners.[34]

More typical of smaller lords were the Cragek who gave Krajków to St Vincent before 1149 or the Gosław who, well before 1250, bought a piece of Budziszów from Count Tvorimir.[35] Many such men were long connected to ducal service and benevolence. Leszek, a ducal chamberlain, held in Jarosław in 1218 and as late as 1257 Dukes Henry and Władysław gave Dobrzykowice to the former's knight Henry of Gurgowicz.[36] But others had also entered the ranks of lay landlords by mid-century: the lady Adelaide, widow of Gosław's son, sold Budziszów in 1251 and, more portentous of the future, in 1257 a "late citizen of Wrocław," Giselher, had already held Święta Katarzyna and Blizanowice.[37] So lay lords large and small were important elements of the rural scene, even if inadequate texts cannot support serious assessment of their relative control over men and land.

Lords whose massive establishment can be well traced to the twelfth and thirteenth centuries are ecclesiastical corporations. Although for more than a century after 1000 the bishopric of Wrocław was the sole organized body of the church in Silesia, by the 1250s at least twenty abbeys, convents, hospitals, and military orders had been founded and given often extensive lands. The eleven then holding in the Wrocław duchy already included over half of the ecclesiastical owners (and nearly all the large ones) to occur there during the Middle Ages.

Table 3.1. Ecclesiastical lordships in the Wrocław duchy (to the mid-thirteenth century)

		First list of properties			By mid-thirteenth century			
	Founded	Date	Total properties	In Wrocław Duchy	Total properties	Rank	In Wrocław Duchy	Rank
Church of Wrocław (bishop and chapter)	1000	1155	48	ca.18	ca.176	1	46	1
St. Vincent (at *Olbino*—Premonstratensian canons)	1130s & 1180s	1149	22	9	35+	5	14	2
St. Mary on the Sand Island (at Wrocław—Augustinian canons)	1149	1193	24	10	39	4	12	3
Trzebnica (Cistercian nuns)	1203	1203	18	3	51+	2	8	4
Lubiąż (Cistercian monks)	1163 & 1175	1175	15	4	43+	3	6	5.5
St. Clare (at Wrocław—Franciscan nuns)	1257	1257	7	6	7	11	6	5.5
St. Elizabeth (later St. Mathias) Hospital (at Wrocław—Knights of the Cross with a Red Star)	1253	1253	10	5 or 6	10	9	5 or 6	7
Holy Spirit Hospital	1214	1214	unknown		6	13	3	8
Leprosarium in Środa	1245	[no clear property lists]			2+	17	2	9
Knights Hospitallers	1150/1189	[no clear property lists]			12	8	1	10.5
Teutonic Order	[no actual center in Silesia]				6+	12	1	10.5

Note. Information summarized in Table 3.1 and Map 3.2 is chiefly from Korta, *Wielki własności*, pp. 58–93, although identification of locations in the future Wrocław duchy required re-examination of texts as follows: *KdS* #25, 35, 55, 71, 103, and 163; *SUB*, I, #19, 28, 45, 61, 83, 142; II, 100, 287, 364, 365, 397; *SR* #884, 935, 973, 1104 and 1331; *UFO* #60 and 77; *BUB* #17 and 48; *UD*, pp. 248–251. For the Środa leprosarium see Moepert, *Ortsnamen*, p. 28. The early Silesian history of the Hospitallers is in Szczesniak, pp. 16–22, and their ownership of Mnichowice demonstrated in Hoffmann, "Nazwy," pp. 2–9. Compare lists in Matzen-Stöckert, pp. 177–185.

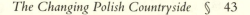

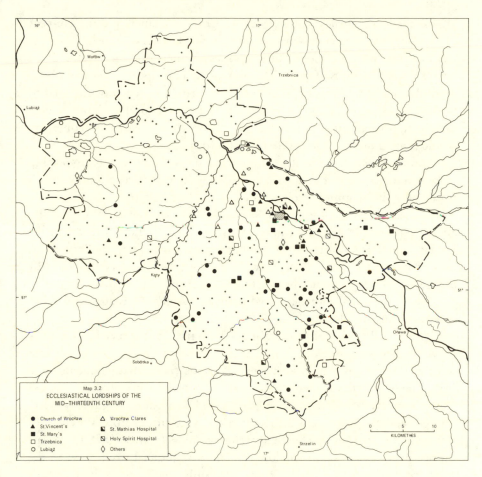

Map 3.2
ECCLESIASTICAL LORDSHIPS OF THE
MID–THIRTEENTH CENTURY

● Church of Wrocław △ Wrocław Clares
▲ St.Vincent's ◩ St. Mathias Hospital
■ St. Mary's ◪ Holy Spirit Hospital
□ Trzebnica ◇ Others
○ Lubiąż

The roster of church lordships (see Table 3.1) approximates with some variation in age and importance the more general picture for the entire province. After the bishopric, whose holdings in the Wrocław area lay scattered throughout most old-settled neighborhoods (see Map 3.2),[38] the largest estates were not, as for all Silesia, those of the Cistercian, but those of two older houses, St. Vincent and St. Mary, both established before 1200 in the immediate vicinity of the town.[39] Their concentrated holdings lay away from Wrocław, St. Vincent's around Kostomłoty and St. Mary's on the slopes of Mt. Ślęza, but both also had more dispersed lands nearer their suburban sites. The younger Cistercians abbeys, Lubiąż and Trzebnica, founded by Bolesław I and Henry I respectively, received their main estates elsewhere, and owned only scattered Wrocław duchy localities.[40] Later and lesser foundations, however, the Wrocław hospitals of the Holy Spirit and

St. Elizabeth (soon renamed St. Mathias from its chapel) and the convent of St. Clare, received endowments more confined to the diminishing duchy, and thus held local positions much in excess of their provincial rank. Even before the foundations of the 1250s, churches held property in nearly a hundred places around Wrocław, about three-fourths of those documented to that point and already about one-fourth of the total rural settlements ever known at any one time in the medieval duchy. The area had become and would remain one of much ecclesiastical lordship.

Lordship meant, especially for monastic houses, not merely ownership of land and power over tenants, but a concomitant reduction in the duke's fiscal and judicial authority over people. In Poland the immunity, too, was a twelfth-century innovation. In Silesia the first sign of a duke formally abdicating some of his governmental powers to a landlord appears in the Lubiąż foundation charter of 1175 where, after establishing the legal position of future German settlers (see Chapter 4), Bolesław continued, "If, however, Poles who do not belong to any other lordship become tenants of the abbot, they shall not be forced to pay anything or render any other services to anyone else."[41]

Through the mid-thirteenth century both fiscal and judicial immunities grew less rapidly under Wrocław's dukes than elsewhere, mostly being kept to partial grants on church lordships.[42] Various traditional payments were first to be removed, as when Bolesław II freed the bishop's holdings in 1248 from demands of ducal hunting parties and provision of guide service, cartage, and lodging.[43] Ducal jurisdictions were lifted more slowly still, although the customary thirteenth-century *Ius polonorum* gave much authority over peasants to their lords.[44] The first judicial exemption in the province, also to Lubiąż in 1202, included only low justice over Germans and Poles. By 1300 the abbey would be reduced to forging interpolations into this text in an effort to claim the high justice Henry I had kept.[45] The two older houses, St. Vincent and St. Mary, gained some judicial privileges elsewhere, but in the future Wrocław duchy by mid-century the former may have been trying to usurp such rights with claims that its Kostomłoty was the center of a *territorium*. St. Mary first obtained general exemption from the castellan's courts in 1258.[46] In the meantime the Holy Spirit hospital and the Clares had acquired some of the best privileges,[47] but this remained the only duchy in which the bishop had no immune jurisdictions.

Creation of lordships, great and small, lay and ecclesiastical, encouraged, almost presupposed, much land to change hands. By the mid-thirteenth century a genuine land market had certainly emerged. In the transfers that built monastic and episcopal estates, simple gifts from dukes and others predominated.[48] Similar grants, surely for services, probably moved many other properties from dukes to nobles.[49] But plainly "economic" transactions also occurred. To assemble and augment a compact estate for Trzebnica, Henry I used property exchanges extensively, giving to St. Mary *Milino* for Maślice and *Rogerowo* and to the brothers Wilk and Henry Górka Sobocka for Pęgów.[50] Although the churches may actually have purchased land only after a slowdown in lay giving around 1250,[51] laymen bought and sold much earlier. Individual twelfth-century examples, like Peter Włast's purchase of Tyniec Mały from two Jews or Razo's sale of Bartoszowa to the deacon Bartholomeus, can be matched with more later ones, some even stating the price paid.[52] Recipients had, however, to beware later challenges from descendants or collaterals of the donor or seller, who asserted that alienations of land required the consent of all kin. Lubiąż, for instance, long resisted and eventually had to pay off the families of donors of Bogunów and Bartoszowa.[53] Such risks lasted through the thirteenth century.

Disgruntled prospective heirs and occasional violent usurpations aside, the more careful landlords thus had various means to pursue coherent acquisition policies. No fully consolidated estates were thereby assembled, but many ecclesiastical owners worked to round out individual properties and to unite in their own hands all possible rights over them. The search for immunities was but part of this. For example, St. Mary got Tyniec Mały in its earliest endowment from Peter Włast, but then found its possession threatened under Bolesław I. Duke Henry restored its rights and, in exchange for other holdings, added the nearby *Milino* (which eventually merged with Tyniec). Then in 1204 the abbey acquired one ducal tax on Tyniec and in 1212 made another exchange to control its tithes as well.[54] Tithes on their own properties were a particular concern of church landlords.[55]

Twelfth- and thirteenth-century documents say more about which properties were held and disputed by members of the landholding elite than they do about how those same lords used and exploited their holdings. The mere fact of possession, however, tells little of how the rural economy worked. In choosing between working the land on his own account or through tenancies, a lord reacted to economic conditions and shaped the socio-economic situation of peasants. The issue will receive emphasis in later chapters and, as central to an understanding of agrarian development before and during the German law movement, needs careful attention here. Available early evidence confirms the presence of both demesnes and tenancies and allows some exemplification of demesne operations and peasant obligations, but it is inadequate to measure the relative importance of these two primary modes of estate management.[56]

Certainly large church landowners expected to exploit some properties directly. Papal protection charters for St. Vincent, St. Mary, Lubiąż, and Trzebnica specified full exemption from tithe on products from their demesnes.[57] And the expectations reflected reality. Trzebnica, for example, in 1203 received labor services from most tenants on its compact estate; in 1267 seven lordships there had granges. In the Wrocław duchy there was another at Domaniów.[58] Lubiąż received a well-stocked demesne at *Żórawin* in 1175, and in the thirteenth century operated its own farms at Bartoszowa and Wilkszyn.[59] Both St. Vincent and St. Mary received demesnes from Henry I in 1204 and possessed them during the next generations.[60] The bishop and the hospitals had *curiae* and their own plows, too.[61]

Large and small lay lordships also operated demesnes all this time. Until 1175 Count Mikora had arable and stock in *Żórawin* and more intensive operations in *Olbino*.[62] In the old-settled area around Kostomłoty and Siemidrożyce, the knight Albert, who had his own plow in 1228, differed little from Radak and Pansław of Rakoszyce, "knights who cultivate their own plowlands," in 1288. A Wrocław citizen named Hugo had a demesne farm at *Kochłowo* in the 1260s.[63]

From a few direct exploitations fortuitous reports indicate something of actual operations.[64] To judge from specific mention of fields on Count Mikora's farm at *Żórawin* in 1175 and seed "for sowing" at Szczytniki and a St. Mary property in 1204 and Polanowice in 1267, arable agriculture was not uncommon. Inventories of draft stock further substantiate this and, if, as at Trzebnica, a team of oxen may be equated with about one small mansus of arable, permit some estimate of scale.[65] The four demesnes so inventoried thus contained from two to six or seven mansi (i.e., 35 to 100+ hectares or 80 to almost 300 acres)[66]—no plantations, true, but equaling and well surpassing the larger peasant holdings. More extensive pastoralism is, on the other hand, suggested by the presence, in addition to draft animals, of twenty-five horses and three cows at *Żórawin* and two hundred sheep, four cows, twenty-two hogs, and much poultry at Polanowice (both in the Odra bottomlands where demesne stock farms were later common). More intensive husbandry of gardens and orchards took place on Mikora's other demesne in *Olbino*. Small labor services from local peasants in Rzeplin and Mnichowice helped operators of lords' farms there, but, as elsewhere in central Silesia, resident servants or hired hands must have done most of the work.[67] But the owner of a farm did not have to operate it and risk fluctuating returns. From before 1216 into the 1230s Abbot Conrad of Lubiąż leased *Żórawin* to a certain Raceno.[68]

Direct exploitation properties did play a noteworthy role in the rural economy of the period before the German law movement. Although central

Silesia of about 1200 was surely no land of a few latifundia, the peasant's family-sized rental holding did not have exclusive sway. But beyond eliminating these extremes, texts for this period cannot be pressed further to quantify the relative importance of direct exploitation and peasant tenancies in organizing rural settlements, in employing the agricultural population, in managing arable, or in contributing to landlord incomes (which need not be coterminous measures).

Inability to calculate the importance to landlords of tenants and their rent payments should not be taken as denying or minimizing the rental economy before the importation of German law institutions.[69] Leasing of demesnes was certainly a move in that direction, while charters for Trzebnica confirm significant incomes from peasant payments in cash and kind. Trzebnica and Lubiąż, Cistercian houses which might be expected to operate large granges and, like others in their order, even expel peasants to create them, ruled over many tenant villages, Bogunów among them.[70] Although Polish lords can receive little credit for technical innovations in agriculture,[71] they did introduce new ways to assess the obligations of their tenants. The value to high medieval Polish lords of their rental incomes is shown in the spread of the *aratrum* as a unit of agricultural management.

The źreb, which combined tenurial, familial, and settlement connotations, had into the twelfth century conceptualized an agricultural economic unit. Indeterminate size and value suited it poorly, however, for evaluating productive capacities and adjusting obligations to them. No assessments were, in fact, based on the źreb as a unit. Arable production in an area or estate depended less on the number of such farmsteads than on their command over land and the equipment to work it, notably the plow and its team (*aratrum, radło*). Within limits imposed by soil fertility and the prevailing techniques, possession of a given number of draft animals provided a roughly standard gauge of a peasant's productivity and the rents that could be squeezed from him. Draft stock was so used on the Trzebnica properties in 1204. Because animals and plows really reflected a unit of arable, from the eleventh century more and more Polish landlords used the term aratrum to designate not the machine itself but a unit of land, a consistent measure of productive resources upon which rents could be assessed. By the later twelfth century the aratrum had become the normal basis for assessing taxes and tithes as well.[72] Just as lords abandoned the indistinct źreb as a settlement unit in favor of the more sharply defined nucleated village, so they now filled its role as an economic unit with this more standard "plowland."

Twelfth-century use of aratrum in Silesia was confined to the Bohemian and Moravian borders, but its premier appearance in the heart of the province, Henry's foundation of Trzebnica in 1203, already found it assessing tithes at Ozorowice.[73] Later texts expressly refer to a measurement of land: three "plows" let out at Gajowice in 1245 and an "aratrum de terra" sold near Rzeplin in 1261.[74]

Introduction of the aratrum, a way to conceptualize agricultural resources by the capabilities of a machine rather than the needs of a human household, was one more sign of the growth of landlord power in the generations around 1200. Firmly anchored in their command over a rising share of the duchy's land and human resources, nobles and churchmen alike sought to eliminate rivals to their authority, be they ducal officials or competing lords. The emerging land market opened the possibility of using conveyances to "rationalize" the shape of lordships, while the new assessment unit offered a means of "normalizing" the incomes due from peasant tenants. Peasants were, of course, very much the objects of these developments, forced to accept transfer from Duke Henry to the Trzebnica nuns or to work on a demesne. Changes arising in the rural economy due to the growth of lordship impelled major transformations in peasants' positions. But Silesian cultivators themselves contributed other dynamic impulses toward a restructuring of their economic and social order.

Change in peasant society

A generically peasant status, a sense that rural agriculturalists were to be conceived as a single social order of *rustici*, emerged slowly in Silesia and Poland. Many defining criteria earlier split the Polish farming population into a multiplicity of status groups. Although texts from near Wrocław do not catalog in full the classes present and their legal, social, and economic attributes, the gradual move from variety towards uniformity is as visible here as anywhere else.[75]

One of the oldest classifications of the rural population, that by the specialized services they rendered the dukes and castles, was by the late twelfth century archaic and all but abandoned.[76] Its traces still dotted the landscape, however, for a good score of Wrocław duchy place names come from people like launderers (Pracze), shield makers (Szczytniki), swineherds (Świniary), or chamberlains (Komorniki).[77] A few ducal servants were still around, falconers in *Sokolnicy*, grooms in Kozanów, and chamberlains.[78] Older churches also had villages of special servants, *sanctuarii* with hereditary obligations to care for the building and its contents, and episcopal cooks.[79] For all of these their definitive obligations, sporadic or regular, were superimposed upon an ordinary peasant agricultural life.

Economic activities offered other descriptors of the rural populace. The "men vulgarly called . . . *lazaky, strozones, popraznici*" in a 1227 tithe agreement bore names from terms for clearing woodland by fire and farming the fertile ash for a few years.[80] Ducal plowmen (*aratores, rataj*) enjoyed full exemption from other obligations; their presence is evidenced in the place name Ratyń.[81] Gardeners appear in Kozanów, Piłczyce, and villages along the Widawa shortly after 1200, while specialized fishermen (*piscatores*) worked the waters of the Odra, notably around Kotowice. At the same time Dalemir in Zajączków was hereditary mason to Trzebnica—but negligence could reduce him to the status of *hospes*.[82]

A third common classification arranged peasants along a continuum between total servitude and full freedom. Over time, groups from both extremes tended to coalesce into half-free dependency with varying degrees of de facto inheritance and mobility rights. By about 1200 only remnants survived in central Silesia of free peasants whose hereditary holdings had been linked to military service with ducal forces.[83] Slaves, too, were in the main an early phenomenon. Peter Włast gave St. Mary two men who had been sold into slavery, Carnota and his nephew Bil, while other such *emptici* (*zakupi*) also belonged to the abbey in the mid-twelfth century. But Zonowid, whose father, the taverner Boleta, had been enslaved (for debts?) by Duke Bolesław, may have been among the last of this unhappy group.[84]

Persons of intermediate status, serfs in the usual sense of half-free peasants, became more common. On the Trzebnica estates in 1204 unfree *hospites* held many *źreby* of varying sizes. Strictly bound to their land, they thus had certain quasi-hereditary claims to it and were not prohibited from enlarging their holdings.[85] *Hospites* could, however, be transferred from (a tenure on?) one lordship to another. Henry I sent Rados and Bogumil from Uraz to be *hospites* in Trzebnica.[86] What seems to have been an overall shortage of labor, which made men more than land the critical resource on an estate, thus encouraged both negative measures restricting peasant mobility and positive ones of hereditary rights. Contemporary Polish customary law outlines procedures to reclaim an escaped serf,[87] but a new servile category with firm tenurial rights, the *ascripticii*, had also appeared. Zbilut and his sons from Muchobor Mały (see the beginning of this chapter) had more than a dozen peers at Janików, another lordship of St. Mary.[88] On the other hand, lords with empty lands to populate could try to win new settlers with the privileges of "free *hospites*," i.e., guaranteed tenure and the right to leave if all obligations were met and a replacement obtained.

With old specialized groupings all but gone, both independent peasants and slaves disappearing, and assessments based less on status than on resources (the aratrum), only nuances of inheritance and mobility rights continued to divide the mass of the Silesian rural population. By around 1200 general terms like *rustici* and *homines* had begun to reflect this broad similarity. *Rusticus* would label the peasant in the later Middle Ages.[89]

A peasant's social situation is not encompassed by status groups and lordship alone. Twelfth- and thirteenth-century Silesian peasants lived near others more or less like themselves who made up a rural community, formal or informal. The *opole* (*vicinia*), already introduced as a settlement structure, had social functions as well. Its members shared responsibility for local peace and order, including pursuit of thieves and homicides.[90] Wrocław duchy communities carried out work-a-day tasks, repairing roads and bridges and helping determine boundaries.[91] Leadership came from a *vlodar* or a *starosta*, whom the lord appointed to collect dues, perform minor judicial functions, and speak for the community. Community members might be called to advise a court but, unlike the later German practice, left the decision to the judge alone.[92] Other possible areas of community activity were less developed. Individual households took care of their own beasts without common herdsmen,[93] while parishioners played no role in selecting priests or maintaining the fabric.[94]

Just as social categories of peasants merged toward the normalized *rusticus*, so did their obligations shift from a motley assortment of specific services and payments in kind toward set amounts of grain and cash.[95] A national trend affected rents, tithes, and taxes alike, but Silesian evidence, especially about dues to the landlord, is pretty well confined to the Trzebnica area and Henry's grants to the convent. Here conditions about 1200 were mixed. Men like Rados and Bogumil from Uraz, landed *hospites*, paid their lord according to the number of their draft animals: if four or more oxen or two oxen and a horse, two measures each of wheat, rye, and oats plus a pot of honey; if two oxen, half. Those with their own land but borrowed stock owed a measure of rye, while if both stock and land came from another, the rent was but a measure of oats. All had also to reap grain from five parcels and mow three cartloads of hay. Radon, Kranch, and their nineteen fellow fishermen in Kotowice, all listed by name, each owed a bundle of fish called a *meth* every Wednesday and Friday, with two of them also obligated to another each Saturday, but each could replace the fish with two pots of honey and measures of wheat and rye. Some individuals owed money rents or had, like Radost the cooper, the option to pay in grain or cash, but everyone except the vine dressers had to work six weeks a year on the convent's fields.[96] These transitional rent types at Trzebnica in 1204 may suggest like mixtures of labor, in-kind payments, and a few money dues on other mid-Silesian estates, but comparable examples fail.

Grants of immunity report more fully the particular obligations of peasants to serve and pay the sovereign.[97] Most recorded for the Wrocław duchy were various aids to render to the duke and his men in the course of their official duties. Peasants had to stand watch (*custodes, strosa*), track thieves (*slad*), and provide guides (*conductum, prevod*) and lodging (*stan*). Closer to daily agricultural routines were services of carting (*plaustra, powoz*) and mowing (*preseka*). But payments, too, were taken, the hearth tax (*podwórowe*) and the plow tax (*poradlne*).[98] Immunities and other exemptions whittled away at the real meaning to peasants of many such obligations, while a progressive shift away from services may be seen in a text of the 1230s or –40s which listed guard duty among the "payments" (*solutiones*).[99]

The church in Poland traditionally demanded as tithe a full tenth of produce. *Ius polonorum* delayed legal removal of the harvest from the field until the tithe recipient had taken his tenth sheaf or at least received sufficient public notice. Difficulties arose from this practice and claims for exemptions and reductions on newly cleared lands caused differences between Henry I and Bishop Thomas, but papal judges delegate in 1227 reaffirmed the real tenth principle.[100] In the episcopal income register from around 1300 most Wrocław duchy places without German law paid the "decimis in campis" that custom prescribed. Still, barely a year after the decision of 1227, the lord of Jakubowice (no new settlement) paid tithe to St. Vincent at a half mark cash per plow.[101]

The move towards more systematic assessment of peasant obligations may have coincided with a rise of them. The national trend in rents did move upwards between the early twelfth century and early fourteenth, but it is hard to compare this absolute increase in amounts owed with the possible growth of agricultural productivity, or to determine if rents rose in Silesia before the German law movement.[102] Certainly Trzebnica peasants owed a lot. Six weeks labor and other services came to about 10 percent of their working time, while the tithe took another 10 percent of their output. The impact of rents in cash and in kind plus payments to the duke depends on estimates of total household production, but Maleczyński's assertion that gross compulsory outlays absorbed about half the incomes of the *hospites* sounds plausible.[103] And elsewhere farmers enjoyed fewer and later exemptions from ducal exactions.

By the 1240s Bishop Thomas was complaining that the demands of Duke Bolesław so oppressed the inhabitants of episcopal villages that they had refused their obligations to him, their lord.[104] Other peasants sought surcease in flight. The monks of St. Mary dragged from the vain asylum of the Wrocław cathedral Zonowid, son of the enslaved butcher Boleta, and other fugitives. Men in "Chinino," who owed rents to the knight Radak and tithes to the priest Clement, successfully disappeared.[105]

Causal connections among these phenomena are easier to assert than to test. One argument would have rising rents in older settlements driving peasants to flight. Under conditions of labor shortage and unused land, other lords would welcome fugitives, so those who feared loss of workers had to offer money rents as an incentive to remain.[106] Conversely, new money rents and fixed assessments have been alleged as the independent variable, the means for increased exploitation of the peasantry.[107] Evidence from the Wrocław duchy or Silesia can eliminate neither plausible alternative, especially since rent affected the peasant economy only relative to productivity—which also changed.

Polish agriculture, the peasants in their everyday activities, adopted in the twelfth and thirteenth centuries a bundle of new techniques associated with short-fallow cereal monoculture, the normative agricultural system of medieval Europe.[108] Slow diffusion of a more productive farming technology still left room for older, more extensive, forms appropriate to lower human densities. Silesian evidence confirms the survival of slash-and-burn agriculture in some well-wooded areas during the early thirteenth century, and pastoral economies long prevailed in the Odra bottomlands northwest of Wrocław. The bishop's men in Piłczyce ran swine there and cattle grazed woodlands and meadows around Głogi and Warzyn.[109] The twenty-one fishermen of Kotowice had their counterparts up and down the river. The small settlement of Rędzin, property of St. Clare, well illustrates the economic potential, even in the later thirteenth century, of a thinly-settled landscape. Several meadows supported herds of cattle, even some customarily brought from elsewhere. Fishers worked the rivers and ponds and others kept bees. Timber was a valuable asset, as was a vineyard leased out by the convent.[110]

The Rędzin vineyard is, however, a useful reminder that pockets of sophisticated labor-intensive agriculture also coexisted with other forms throughout the Middle Ages. Vintagers near Trzebnica, vineyards at Osobowice, and wine tithes from Wrocław's outskirts attest to early and continuing attempts at viticulture.[111] Technical advances in horticulture gave hops growers at Małkowice the peculiar distinction of being the first documented Polish users of intentionally hauled and spread animal manure.[112] But both extensive and intensive specialities remained incidentals against the general orientation towards regular cereal production.

In the central activities of Polish agriculture innovative crops, tools, rotations, and field systems appeared and spread from the twelfth century. Common millet, once frequent in archaeological sites, gave way to rye, wheat, oats, and barley. Although wheat, the preferred cereal, occurs often in lists of obligations, in actual quantity produced it probably took a distant back seat to the better-adapted others.[113] Even if the traditional ard (*radło*) broke but did not turn the soil, it remained the basic tool for tillage until around 1200. The heavy plow (*pług*) had been adopted in a few Polish sites by 1225 and spread rapidly in the rest of the century. Better harrows and sickles came in as well.[114] Although the new plows were still drawn almost exclusively by oxen until around 1300, an improved horse harness was learned, possibly from the east, some two hundred years earlier. Horses pulled carts and, where their speed was a real asset, harrows. The abbot of St. Vincent in 1204 may have thought horses were "harrowers,"[115] but the equation of two oxen with one horse to assess the dues of Trzebnica *hospites* suggests that peasants' beasts were less able to specialize.

In the West, increased regular cereal production with a more powerful but ungainly plow and greater use of horse power accompanied diffusion of a three course rotation and often changes in the layout of parcels to make the classic three field system. Polish agriculture took a similar course. Triennial rotations of winter grains, spring grains, and fallow appeared here and there during the eleventh century but full development of even an irregular three course rotation occurred only after 1100. Inventories from a farm of St. Mary in 1204 and Polanowice in 1267 distinguish between summer and winter seed. Arable land could be reorganized during merger of independent *źreby* into new nucleated villages, but in all probability regulated rotations and fixed field systems came in only with the German law.[116] Except for this last, however, the Polish agrarian economy around 1200 plainly knew and was itself adopting the technical features of western production.

A final sign of rising grain production and of the technical adaptability of country people before the entry of German peasants and customs is the spread of the vertical-wheeled water mill into rural Poland around 1200.[117] Indubitably authentic Silesian texts of the twelfth century mention no such machines,[118] but several do soon thereafter. Near Wrocław a miller with his own *źreb* ran a mill at Piłczyce on the Ślęza, and Trzebnica owned another on the Widawa near Mikora's bridge, both by 1225.[119] The eight mills recorded by 1260 stood in most of the more densely settled sections of the Wrocław district.

Changing agricultural practices, obligations, and status of Silesian peasants in the century before the coming of the German law can no more be explained apart from their interactive relationship with landlords than can their evolving settlement patterns. If extortion of higher rents forced intensification of production, so, too, did the simple consumption needs of a growing peasant population, especially close to Wrocław where land well-suited for major expansion of cropland was scarce by 1200. Lords and peasants together proved willing to accept innovations in technical equipment and in how they handled their productive resources. Improved rotations systematized grain farming in much the way the aratrum regularized rent assessments and newly nucleated villages shaped settlement patterns. But not all change could come piecemeal, and not all forces promoting rural change sprang from the countryside of lords, peasants, demesnes, villages, and fields of rye. To complete this assessment of rural life around Wrocław in the late twelfth and early thirteenth centuries, two important phenomena remain, premeditated efforts towards rural development and the increased seepage of a market economy from the towns into the countryside, both of which transcended simple changes in settlement patterns, lordship, or the peasantry.

Transforming forces

In 1208 Henry I added to the Piłczyce holdings of the church of Wrocław the village of his grooms called Kozanów, the fields of his gardeners (bounded by a pear tree and a willow on the bank of the Ślęza opposite the pear, both marked with signs), the źreb of his miller with the mill on the Ślęza, some fields beyond the tavern there, and a swamp called "Lang" (between the Odra and a pond behind the bishop's grange). He also gave the bishop and his men from Piłczyce the use of the oak woods for pannage, dead wood, and other purposes harmless to the oaks, and he "personally made a circuit of the above-mentioned."[120] Sixteen years later, at Domaniów, where Trzebnica had received both private and ducal gifts, Henry again "made in his own person a single circuit out of these."[121] The practice called *ujazd* (*circuitio* or *circumequitatio*), whereby the duke personally rode around an area to establish its boundaries, came into Silesia from Bohemia or Moravia around 1100. An 1177 circuit of Bogunów is the first known near Wrocław.[122] The duke's act defined a space or *circuitus*, and sometimes resulted in a new place name.

Performance of *ujazd* could serve several reorganizing and developmental purposes.[123] Most simply and directly it separated from surrounding territory a spatial entity and established the latter as one lordship. Henry's gift of Kotowice "with the men and with all that I have there circled" is typical. When he goes on to report that Bishop Cyprian had added the tithes from that circuit, the practice becomes the prelude to further consolidation of rights within the set bounds.[124] Internally, *ujazd* melded individual źreby and hamlets into larger nucleated settlements as just described at Domaniów and Piłczyce.[125] Finally, many ducal circuits delineated sections of woodland then opened by the lord for clearance, either to extend present fields or to start a new village. The *circuitus* of Wilkszyn contained in 1218 "a certain portion called birchwood (*Brezni*)," later the site of Pisarzowice, while that of Zalesie in 1254 joined to the older settlement an oak woods called *Guy*.[126]

Ujazd regulated relationships among members of the ruling group to affirm a particular lord's authority over specific lands and peasants, but it did not determine how the lord chose to use them. Other mechanisms promoted growth, attracted settlers, or "modernized" lord-peasant relations within a lordship. Places called *lgota* (from Czech *hlota* = "lightening") mark attempts by landowners to gain or retain tenants through rent reductions and other freedoms, a practice which also spread from Czech into Polish regions. Of the seventy-odd Silesian examples only one, Ligotka (just south of Środa), is in the Wrocław duchy, and it enters the documentation in 1289 only as the owner converted it to German law.[127] However, developmental efforts were not restricted to these sites or methods. If Lubiąż in 1175 anticipated Poles moving from other lordships and Bolesław I encouraged clearances around Henryków, other lords, too, had programs of expansion well before they turned to the German law.[128] Even in the 1260s Henry III and Bishop Thomas could anticipate setting out villages at Polanowice and Czernica with either Polish or German law.[129] At Krępice in 1295 Zdzisław gained liberty from services and special payments, free alienation and inheritance rights, and pasture for his sheep in return for one mark a year, even though the village and his tenancy stayed under Polish customary law.[130] A good score of settlements created and/or reformed with Polish customs are evident near Wrocław to and beyond 1300.[131] Indigenous arrangements offered flexibility enough for a wide range of initiatives, including the hereditary money-rent tenancy normally associated with the imported German law.

Money rents of any sort and development of a market in lordships presumed regular circulation of money in the countryside. Thus both attest to penetration of a market and exchange economy into rural areas and rural relationships. The diffusion of monetary considerations eventually affected lords and peasants alike, but its initial and continuing focus was urban. A chief accomplishment of post-war Polish historians has been to demonstrate the presence, prosperity, and dynamism of early medieval Polish urban centers, numbering some dozen around 1000 and perhaps fifty by 1200. Wrocław was a specific manifestation of a pattern.[132] Many medieval towns were chiefly characterized by their function as nodes of long-distance trade. Those in Poland about 1200 participated actively in such commercial exchanges. Major routes linked Wrocław to Italy via Prague, to the Low Countries via Magdeburg, and to Poznań, Gniezno, and the Baltic. Wrocław merchants journeyed eastwards through Cracow to Lublin, Ruthenia, and Kievan Rus. Annual fairs drew traders from afar.[133]

But while a purely mercantile town can be isolated from its immediate surroundings, Wrocław, like other contemporary Polish towns, was integrated with the countryside as a center for consumption, manufactures, and local exchange. Important consuming groups, ducal officials, monks, canons, and cathedral clergy, made up much of its population. Nobles from the region still spent considerable time there. Simply to feed and house town dwellers drew heavily on nearby resources.[134] Iron and gold smiths, potters, glass, leather, and other craft workers plied their trades in early medieval Wrocław.[135] On the left bank of the Odra, where the area of the later walled city was probably fully occupied by 1200, a marketplace, taverns, and butcheries served retail needs. A few minutes' walk to the west, beside the old church of St. Nicholas in *Nabitin* stood another tavern.[136] On the other side of the main branch of the Odra, reached via bridges to the Sand and Cathedral islands, *Olbino* was then a chief commercial district. Lubiąż received three hundred denarii a week from its butcheries there; St. Vincent owned a tavern, more butcheries, and a slaughter house, and ran a week-long fair until the 1230s.[137] So just as its fairs and long-range connections made Wrocław the highest level central place in Silesia, the marketplace, taverns, butcheries, and the like manifested its (expectable) role in more local exchanges.

Wrocław did not monopolize local exchange in Silesia or the duchy. Elsewhere in the province lesser towns connected their areas via Wrocław to long-distance trade flows, but the confined space of the future duchy limited lower level facilities to local markets and, at the most rural, taverns.[138] Some two hundred weekly markets in late twelfth-century Poland provided the means critical for penetration and deepening of monetary exchanges in the countryside.[139] Of some twenty-five to thirty such Silesian points for the sale of foodstuffs and craft products, at least two, Kostomłoty and Środa, joined Wrocław in its duchy.[140] The former, a "forum" belonging to St. Vincent by the mid-twelfth century, contained as well a tavern and some butcheries.[141]

Taverns provided full-time services. They not only lodged travellers and sold beer, but also retailed food, salt, and handicrafts. Tolls and taxes were taken there.[142] Of the nine sites of taverns recorded up to 1250 in Polish settings of the future duchy, three are the expected towns and markets, but at the others monetary exchanges entered more rural places.[143] Some idea of their cash turnover is suggested by the weekly dues of twenty denarii paid to Trzebnica from each in Uraz. The competition felt from such local sale points was shown when Wrocław bought in 1266 a ducal ban on new tavern construction in the nearby countryside.[144]

Thus several structures eased monetary circulation and exchange among country people. When in 1237 Henry I let Trzebnica have silver incomes from the Wrocław mint coined for necessary purchases of fish, eggs, and cheese, and when the 1267 inventory of the Polanowice demesne listed cash values for sheep, oxen, cows, draft cattle, and swine, these firm local instances of the effective penetration of monetary exchange confirm the general evidence of peasants at markets and in taverns to be found in the *Ius polonorum.*[145] Not just an accounting convention or an affair of urban merchants, the monetary economy had entered rural life.

In the generations around 1200 Polish lords and peasants around Wrocław ably and willingly used markets and adapted agrarian institutions to what was becoming, at least in part, an economy of monetary exchange. Expanding use of money was but one of the changing conditions, some exogenous, some deeply indigenous to the rural world, but all fundamentally autogenous to Polish society, which induced adjustment and rewarded flexibility and innovation. Polity, town, and countryside moved on their own terms in the direction of structural characteristics like those of the "modern" contemporary west: nucleated settlements of dependent peasant agriculturalists; strong "feudal" lordship; and an exchange sector centered in urban communities. Dominant groups in mid-Silesian society favored these converging tendencies and accepted arrangements like *ujazd, lgota,* fixed assessments, and markets which promoted desirable changes and were malleable enough to fit an economy with major local and regional disparities. In this context encouragement of immigration and importation of western patterns for rural organization in a convenient and proven German form were a logical next step.

PART TWO

§§§§§§§

Organizing Agricultural Resources

LOCARE IURE THEUTONICO: INSTRUMENT AND STRUCTURE FOR A NEW INSTITUTIONAL ORDER

Dedimus et concessimus domino Lamberto de Tinez et suis heredibus curiam nostram in Zabloto et quicquid ad eam de terra pertinet, ad locandum ibidem Theutonicos in iure et libertate Theuthonicali, prout sibi videbitur expedire.

Abbot Albert of St. Vincent contracts to establish German law at Zabłoto, 1240; *SUB*, II, #193.

Abbess Gertrude of Trzebnica followed up her house's successful consolidation of holdings in Domaniów by issuing a charter in 1234 to "locate" Germans on the former grange there. Under their "iure Teutonico" they owed the abbey eight scot cash rent per "mansus" beginning on Martinmas, 1235, and full grain tithes at harvest time. The two and a half mansi assigned to the parish church were exempt from such obligations, as were two more "mansos feodales" of the "scultetus," who also received a tavern in the village and, if the convent agreed, a stall for the sale of meat. With the permission of her father the duke, the abbess further freed the inhabitants from all obligations of Polish law, so they enjoyed pure German law. Thus capital offenses came to judgment in the village where the ducal schulz of Oława and the village schulz together presided, while disputes they could not judge went directly to the duke or a castellan acceptable to both parties. Military service and taxes were the same as those of the convent's other Germans and subjects.[1]

More than a century later, nearly half the settlements in the Wrocław duchy had institutions like those installed by Gertrude. Still, King John gave Nicholas Sittin permission for "iure et titulo emphithetico seu theutonicali exponendi et locandi" Bielany Wrocławskie, and his son Charles encouraged all "nobles and inhabitants of the districts as well as citizens of our cities of Wrocław and Środa" to undertake such "locations, constructions, and plantations."[2] The grant of German law and the village which it created are central to the late medieval countryside. In this chapter terms and concepts are presented briefly and then the introduction of these institutions to the duchy is examined from several perspectives.

Cultural interaction along the Germano-Slavic frontier during the thirteenth and fourteenth centuries was so pervasive that the term "German law" can have several denotations. For urban centers, grants of German law provided newly formalized municipal constitutions modeled on those of western cities.[3] Silesian dukes chartered most towns by around 1300. The old market at Środa had become the German law *Novum Forum* by the early 1220s.[4] Successful tests on lesser centers encouraged like privileges for Wrocław after the destructive Mongol raid of 1241. Twenty years later Henry III and Władysław substituted the better-known urban code of Magdeburg.[5]

A second meaning of German law in the Polish setting referred to material provisions of private, criminal, and procedural justice borrowed from *Sachsenspiegel* and Magdeburg practice and grafted on to that of indigenous courts.[6] In the Wrocław duchy this conversion from Polish to German legal norms chiefly affected the landholding group; it resulted in abolition of the Polish law *czuda* court in 1337.[7] But the grants of German law to Domaniów and other villages concerned different relationships.

The liberties a rural community in east-central Europe obtained as German law originated in the earliest medieval promises of freedom to people who would settle unfarmed land. Practices from the Low Countries and from Franconia joined into characteristic customs and terms as German settlers crossed the middle Elbe during the twelfth century. Their way of setting up a village acquired the name "German" law (liberty, custom, etc.) as it was brought into Bohemia, Silesia, and further regions of Poland around 1200.[8]

A rural community received German law by a process called *locatio*. Connotations of the term derived from both German *besetzen*, to "settle" or "establish," and the older Latin *locare*, "to put out at lease." The owner of the land obtained the consent of the sovereign, some of whose rights might be touched, and then usually found a contractor to set up the village. After agreeing on the incomes the lord would expect, this *locator* divided the land among prospective tenants, retaining for himself a fief-like, rent-free holding larger than that of ordinary peasants. Personally free and with the right to leave whenever clear of debts to the lord, the German law peasant received firm hereditary rights in return for payment of fixed obligations owed through the *locator* to the lord.[9] The nexus of the lord-peasant relationship became exchange of secure tenure for fixed rents, usually cash and grain. A labor component was almost never included. Unlike arrangements in Domaniów, tithes were normally assessed in set amounts of grain or money. German law peasants did none of the services Polish custom gave the state, for these, too, were stabilized in coin or grain. And new tenants were often exempt from all obligations for some start-up years.

But *locatio* set up more than a relationship between the landlord and each peasant. Village churches received a landed endowment to support the rector. New villages were often larger than older ones of the vicinity. In villages with German law judicial administration and income were split; the duke reserved capital cases and made low justice the prerogative of the land-lord. He in turn kept only an appellate and superior jurisdiction at three special court sessions each year (*Dreidingen*) and entrusted everyday matters to the *locator*, now become the schulz, a hereditary village headman and judge. The schulz presided over a panel of jurors chosen from the village community. Thus a German law village replicated the commune of a German law town, having its own customs, certain collective responsibilities for police and defense, perhaps some common lands, and, usually, jurisdiction over the common-field arable, for agriculture in these villages followed a regulated three course rotation.[10]

For communal rotations to work, surveys saw to it that each tenant's land was distributed evenly across the fields. The unit used by surveyors to measure arable acreage, the *mansus*, was the basis for all assessments. By the mid-twelfth century in the area of German eastward expansion, the term *mansus* had lost its reference to a varying quantity of land for one household and become a reasonably fixed measure of area. More westerly and mountainous regions employed *mansi* of different size, but the plains from Brandenburg east to Prussia and south through Silesia into Little Poland used the so-called "Flemish *mansus*" (unknown in Flanders). Contemporaries calculated this at thirty *jugera* of three hundred square rods each, or nine thousand square rods. Later survivals confirm that *jugera* used in central Silesia measured about 56 ares and the mansus some 16.8 hectares (about 42 acres).[11] But while the whole of the village arable could be measured in contiguous mansi, each peasant had only a collection of scattered strip parcels, the *Gewende*, in the open fields. No necessary relationship prevailed between number of mansi and number or size of tenancies. Land remaining after the survey and subdivision was called "leftovers" (*remanencia, super-fluitas, excrescentia, Überschar*), and was outside the regular rotation.

To list such attributes of villages with German law may obscure their *diagnostic* features, for in the cryptic isolation of extant texts not all can surely distinguish a place with from a place without German law. Certainly explicit reference to *ius Theutonicum* in a privilege for *locatio*, a lord-*locator* agreement, or some fortuitous record is the safest ground for inference. Lacking this evidence, schulzen and general freedom from the fiscal burdens of Polish law (not the specific exemptions of an immunity) seem, in Silesia at least, confined to German law villages.[12] This is not so for free years, clearances, churches with landed endowments, or single-village parishes. Mansi also soon measured all sorts of arable. Fixed tithes and signs of a survey can be more tricky; generally confined to German law places, they occur just often enough elsewhere to be inadequate indicators on their own.[13] In this study they are taken only to date the presence of German law earlier in a place with later firm evidence.

Many different meanings have been attributed to the spread of villages with German law into Silesia and other Polish provinces.[14] For some authors ethno-cultural questions are of chief importance. Did ethnic Germans thus gain predominance in the Silesian population? Did natives abandon one national identity for another? Was it a "colonization" movement? Other authors have various socio-economic concerns. Was German law a way to import "rural feudalism?" To shift from a natural to a money economy? Did it tip the balance of lord-peasant relations or result from an earlier tilt? Were its instigators after lower rents, higher incomes, new land to work, improvement of old arable, or clearance of woodlands? Did they consciously imitate western patterns, carefully bring along their traditional techniques, or simply do what happened to work for their needs? Some interpretations focus on motives, others on long-term effects. Some are mutually tenable, others not. Not all start from good knowledge of the Polish economy, and not all contribute equally to understanding a medieval society. Even chronology is disputed.

This treatment of German law in villages of the Wrocław duchy proceeds with caution, eschewing or at least postponing assertion of meaning for collation of texts, mapping of sites, comparison of privileges, and distinguishing motives from effects. It seeks to learn from the evidence of this region the participants in, circumstances for, and application of *locatio* there. Concerns of medieval villagers, of their lords, and of modern retrospect are considered, but all depend first on when and to what extent these institutions appeared and spread in the duchy's countryside.

Chronology

German peasants probably entered Silesia at the end of the twelfth century. Plans for their arrival in the Lubiąż foundation charter of 1175 came to fruition somewhere on the abbey's holdings by 1202. Four years later Germans who had a formal agreement with their lord, Duke Henry, lived near

Wrocław at Psie Pole (outside the later duchy).[15] During the next decade records are of localities in the mountains, but by 1218 Germans lived in a few villages around Oława and, perhaps by 1223, others around Środa. Authentic *locatio* charters for specific villages, however, date only from 1221, when Henry I both conceded to St. Mary's abbey "ius Theutonicale" for its *hospites* at sites near Legnica and Wołów and himself contracted for the putting out of fifty mansi near Ząbkowice.[16] Nevertheless, diffusion in the next generation does not seem rapid, with only some forty sites of *locatio* identifiable by 1241. Then started what is recognized as the wholesale spread of German law across Silesia.[17] But whereas Karol Maleczyński would have the process end around 1300, his German counterpart, Hermann Aubin, argued for its continuity until the mid-fourteenth century Black Death cut off the supply of potential settlers.[18] This issue deserves special attention in the evidence from what was becoming the Wrocław duchy.

The earliest cases of German law in the future duchy involve several suspicious documents. When these are removed or recognized as the products of not yet standardized chancellery practice,[19] no firm evidence predates the 1220s, but by the end of that decade Duke Henry had certainly established German law in some unidentifiable villages near Środa and Abbot Witosław of St. Mary (1219–28) had probably carried out the *locatio* of Tyniec Mały.[20] This leaves, however, Gertrude's 1234 *locatio* for Domaniów as the earliest undisputed grant in the future duchy. Thereafter St. Vincent obtained permission to put out Wierzbno (1235) and Zabłoto (1240) and used the latter right away.[21] A 1244 ducal privilege for Janików plus the probable setting out of Kostomłoty brought to six the number of Wrocław duchy rural sites identifiably recorded with German law by 1250.[22]

Table 4.1 summarizes the increase after 1250 of places with evidence for German law institutions. For the duchy as a whole the greatest rate of change came during the second half of the thirteenth century, when the number of sites grew more than ten-fold and their share of known rural settlements more than six-fold. But the arrangements are first noted for even more places during 1300–53. From the mid-thirteenth to the mid-fourteenth century, moreover, settlements with German law increase so much faster than do all places documented as to guarantee that the change is not merely a result of more complete sources. After 1353, with records for all places then existing, the growth of evidence slows; only a handful of new sites appear after 1425.

Districts in the duchy follow the general pattern of rapid then decelerating diffusion with certain divergent features. The Środa and Uraz districts were affected most strongly in the thirteenth century and exhibit little or no percentage change after 1300 and 1353 respectively. In the Wrocław district

Table 4.1. The spread of German law institutions, 1250–1530

	1250	1300	1353	1425	1480	1530
Entire Wrocław Duchy						
Settlements[a]	128	234	354	362	345	340
Number with						
German law (%)	6 (5)	73 (31)	176 (50)	219 (60)	225 (65)	232 (67)
Wrocław district						
Settlements[a]	98	168	231	236	218	215
Number with						
German law (%)	3 (3)	40 (24)	104 (45)	144 (61)	148 (68)	154 (72)
Środa district						
Settlements[a]	25	53	103	106	107	105
Number with						
German law (%)	3 (12)	24 (45)	57 (55)	60 (57)	62 (58)	63 (60)
Uraz district						
Settlements[a]	5	13	20	20	20	20
Number with						
German law (%)	0 (0)	9 (69)	15 (75)	15 (75)	15 (75)	15 (75)

[a] For 1250 and 1300, settlements then documented.

Note. German law is here diagnosed from ducal grants of permission, *locatio* contracts, schulzen, general freedom from Polish law burdens, and, if followed by one of the above, fixed tithes and "leftovers." Dates for profiles were chosen on both substantive and methodological grounds. All coincide with significant points in the duchy's rural development in 1300, 1353, and 1425 with major documents whose survey of large numbers of villages bring up to date earlier changes and permit construction of comparative statistics. See Appendix A.

Totals exceed the 67 by 1341 which might be adduced from Maleczyński's tabulation (*Historia Śląska*, I: 1, 398–426) because he: (1) used very narrow criteria; (2) wrongly identified some places; and (3) missed for some sites early evidence of a sort he accepted elsewhere. Compare with his listing the following texts: *KdS* #310; *SUB*, I, #270; *SR* #792, 807, 1641, 1953 (rightly Jaksin), 2107, 2107b, and 2226 (rightly Świojczyce); *LFE* B150. Totals fall below the 291 places that Matzen-Stöckert, pp. 219–227 and 290–298, eventually lists under several formal headings in alphabetical order by modern German name as meeting by 1342 her criteria for German law. No temporal variables are considered. The large number is because Matzen-Stöckert (1) uses the larger modern rather than medieval district (*Kreis*) boundaries and (2) accepts in practice any reference to mansi as "Merkmale deutschen Rechts und deutscher Besiedlung" (pp. 290–298), even though she earlier (p. 217) queried this criterion. This results in listing as sites of German law by 1342 places like, among others, Kębłowice, Kończyce, and Strachowice, where actual *later* grants are known (see note to Table 4.2), and places like *Milino* and *Łagów* that demonstrably were always pure demesne farms, though surveyed in mansi.

the spread began more slowly, hit a peak after 1300, and continued beyond 1353, when the proportion of such villages there passed the mean. The long-term tabulation indicates that less than a third of the places in the duchy certainly had German law institutions by 1300, and perhaps two-thirds had them by the early fifteenth century. The temporal scale of Table 4.1 is, however, too crude for refined consideration of the diffusion process involved.

Figure 4.1 breaks down by decades the evidence tabulated from the

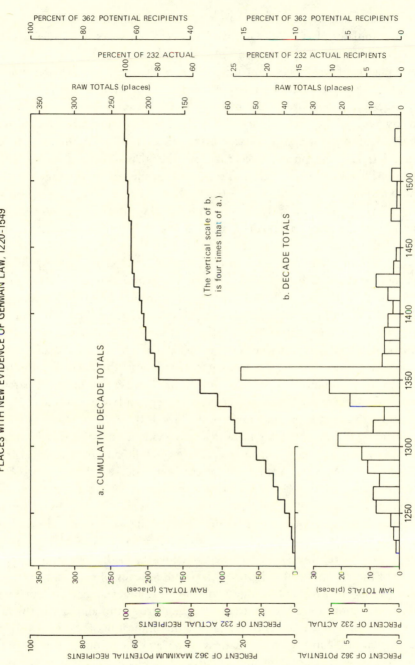

Figure 4.1
PLACES WITH NEW EVIDENCE OF GERMAN LAW, 1220-1549

a. CUMULATIVE DECADE TOTALS

b. DECADE TOTALS

(The vertical scale of b.
is four times that of a.)

duchy and displays it as both a frequency distribution and a logistic curve that cumulates places with German law every ten years. Consider first the shape of the curves. In accord with normal diffusion theory, cumulative acceptance of the innovation follows an S-shaped path, starting slowly, climbing steeply in the middle portions, and then tailing off. The largest decade totals, too, are in the middle.[23] Closer examination reveals previously undetected irregularities in the diffusion process. Settlements with new symptoms of German law crop up in ever-larger numbers until the first decade of the fourteenth century, but then drop off sharply in the 1310s and 1320s before a resurgence in the 1330s pushes the per decade totals to new maxima in the 1340s and 1350s. With 80 percent of such arrangements in place by 1359, their spread fell to a low level for the next two generations before a final peak in the 1420s pushed the total to 95 percent. The rest trickled in over the next century.

The tabulation suggests a movement with two major waves, the first gathering strength before 1250 to reach a maximum around 1300 and the second rising higher and faster in the years around 1350. The second and third decades of the fourteenth century form a noticeable trough. But Figure 4.1 also demonstrates disadvantages in using this evidence to ascertain chronology. Because most such references document the *presence* of German law institutions in a village, not their installation, the data used for both Table 4.1 and Figure 4.1 can only summarize relative conditions at particular times and record *termini ante quibus* for German law in particular places. Because the three most noticeable peaks, 1300–09, 1350–59, and 1420–29, coincide with unusual texts bringing new evidence of villages which may quietly have acquired German law before, the ebb and flow inferred from Figure 4.1 may be the creation of documentary survival.[24]

Actual grants of German law to rural settlements better measure the rhythm (though not the extent) of the movement in the duchy. They are datable for seventy-four villages, fifty-two in the form of ducal privileges for landowners and thirty-three as owner's *locatio* contracts (eleven contain elements of both types).[25] A marked irregularity in the temporal distribution of these is apparent in Figure 4.2. The frequency of surviving contracts and grants shown there changes with notable independence of surviving documentation overall. Despite accelerating growth in all records through the thirteenth and fourteenth centuries, this indicator of the intent to put particular lordships out to German law replicates the bi-modal feature of the retrospective evidence tabulated in Figure 4.1. One wave of *locationes* in the thirteenth century was separated from another in the 1340s and 1350s by a good forty years of almost no interest.

The German law movement in the Wrocław duchy occurred as an ir-

Figure 4.2

PLACES WITH DATABLE GRANTS (PERMISSIONS AND CONTRACTS) OF GERMAN LAW, 1220-1549

a. CUMULATIVE DECADE TOTALS

(The vertical scale of b. is four times that of a.,
but neither matches those of Figure 4.1)

b. DECADE TOTALS

Note. For sources see Notes to Maps and Figures.

regular diffusion process. The first introductions of the 1220s found slow imitation until the 1250s and 1260s. A dip in datable grants in the 1270s may reflect passage of this first crest beyond the duchy into Upper Silesia, where activity was then intense. More grants around Wrocław in the 1290s pushed those extant to a new peak and argue for understanding the second half of the century as a single period of intense conversion to German law. Of course not all plans succeeded. Although Bishop Thomas II turned Piłczyce over to brothers named Werner and Lodoycus for *locatio* in 1291,[26] no German law village resulted. Perhaps the failure of the 1291 attempt presaged the sudden abandonment of German law grants after 1300. In any case, the hiatus of the first third of the fourteenth century is plain. The Piłczyce *locatio* was renewed only in 1353,[27] when Bishop Przesław and a new *locator*, John Sechsbecher, joined in what had become a new and major upsurge of interest in grants of German law.[28]

Comparable data from Great Poland indicate that this temporal irregularity went beyond the Wrocław duchy. Although a bare 20 percent of the villages in that much larger region are found with German law by 1370, it too had a late thirteenth-century wave with two distinct crests (1250s and 1280–99) and an early fourteenth-century reduction of activity. The upswing there began about 1350 and was still going at the end of research so far carried out.[29] The evidence from this neighboring region thus adds plausibility to the chronology here adduced for the Wrocław duchy and encourages viewing the spread of German law in a changing regional economic context.

Ethno-cultural dimensions

Use of quantitative techniques to measure the spread of German law in the duchy ought not obscure this movement's human character. Real individuals and groups introduced these institutions. *Locatores*, peasants, and landlords played distinct and equally critical roles. But first a different human dimension needs attention. The institutions were, after all, called "ius Theutonicum," *German* law, but early thirteenth-century Silesia was a Polish society, differing only subtly from landscapes to the east. To what degree, then, were ethnic variables central? How much was the German law movement a physical movement of Germans who, by replacing the indigenous population, began Germanizing Silesia or, rather, the Wrocław duchy?

Postwar research has reduced the number of immigrants into the Polish lands, once thought to be very substantial.[30] There is no evidence for mass migrations. Instead Walter Kuhn argued for the relatively small scale movement of at most 200,000 Germans to all of their settlement areas in the twelfth century and as many again in the thirteenth. Silesia received only some of the latter and the Duchy of Wrocław a part of those. But Kuhn further maintained that the empty lands to which the migrants came offered such favorable conditions that high reproduction rates soon meant large ethnic German components in local populations.[31]

In all Silesia less than a score of texts specify German peasant settlers before the mid-thirteenth century, with the earliest in the general vicinity of Wrocław those already mentioned on the lands of Lubiąż in 1202 and at Psie Pole in 1206.[32] The privilege for St. Mary of 1221 first calls people at Tyniec and elsewhere "hospites," but later assigns to them military duties "like other Germans."[33] Up to mid-century only the grants for Domaniów and Zabłoto specify *locatio* of Germans. Thereafter that for Pisarzowice suggests them as one alternative, and three ducal contracts of the early 1260s imply a distinction between *hospites* coming in and Poles already there.[34] Other grants of German law in the duchy are silent on this issue.

Later texts give little more help, for Germans are noticeable around Wrocław only about mid-century, when they complained to the papal legate about having to observe the more stringent Polish Lenten fast.[35] By 1283 Henry IV considered German names customary for places with German inhabitants, so little surprise is occasioned by his successor's referring in a 1293 charter to Kojęcin as "allodium Koianzin siue vulgariter Baumgarthe."[36]

Even if German had become a common tongue around Wrocław by the end of the thirteenth century, neither a massive influx of German peasants nor an overwhelming explosion of their children can be supported for this area. This was no virgin wilderness inhabited by a handful of primitives and invaded by an advanced society. Individuals and small groups of German peasants were attracted by the leaders of another organized European society. They soon assimilated to the country they had entered. The *Life* of St. Hedwig written in the late 1200s calls "German" only visitors from that country, not Silesian-born descendants of immigrants. Persons of German ethnic origin, perhaps 20 percent of Silesia's inhabitants by 1300, but surely less near Wrocław than in the western mountains, must be viewed against the growing indigenous population and other in-comers.[37]

German law did not require Germans. At the future Pisarzowice in 1251 Lubiąż contemplated establishing "Germans or men of any other language."[38] Immigrants who antedated both significant German settlement and the use of German law institutions were *Romanos*, Walloons from around Liége and Namur, who first settled in the eastern suburb of Wrocław (*Platea Romanorum*) under the auspices of Bishop Walter (1148–69), a fellow countryman.[39] Their descendants received German law from Bishop Thomas in 1260.[40] By then other *Romanos* had acquired similar freedoms in Wierzbno and Janików, where they kept their identity into the fourteenth century, and had been instrumental in the *locationes* of Tyniec Mały and Zabłoto.[41] Thus non-German immigrants participated in perhaps four of the six German law grants that survive from Wrocław duchy villages before 1250, one more than those specifying German peasant participation.

Of course the indigenous Polish population retained far greater numerical importance. Polish place names remained overwhelmingly dominant in the Wrocław district right up to modern times, and even the German historian of those in the Środa district admitted to Slavic roots for nearly two-thirds. In Wrocław itself, priests at the St. Christopher and St. Clement churches preached in Polish around 1500 while Polish-speaking peasants drank and sang in suburban taverns.[42] Far from abandoning the vicinity of Wrocław in the face of German immigration and the German law, the Polish peasant population was soon swept up in the movement. Poles in some old villages below Mount Ślęza had German law before 1250, while Henry III included indigenous farmers in *locationes* at Łowęcice, Warzyn, and Gosławice in the 1260s.[43] The *locatores* whom Henry chose, Cunczco at Warzyn, Dresco at Łowęcice, the brothers Beneda, Walter, and Gosław at Gosławice, point as well to native involvement in even this "expert" role.[44] The German law movement in the duchy, then, can scarcely be seen as ethnically exclusive.

The names of the brothers Beneda, Walter, and Gosław should give warning that questions of ethnic or "national" identity put to medieval texts and behavior soon impose preconceptions of modern east-central Europe. When two brothers were Henricus and Jascocel and two others Starostca and Gregor, who was a "German" and who a "Pole?"[45] Which was the common tongue in 1339, when the bishop of Lebus referred to a Wrocław duchy settlement as "allodii Gelenyn siue Aptowicz wlgariter nuncupati"?[46] Study of Silesian German dialects has long shown and that of early immigrant knights more recently confirmed that Silesians of German extraction came chiefly from Meissen and Lusatia, which were in the thirteenth century themselves bilingual territories.[47] Not surprisingly, then, Silesian dialects of both languages borrowed heavily from one another for long after 1300.[48] Throughout the later Middle Ages many individuals bore names like Cunczco, Hanko, or Friczko, where a Slavic diminutive modified a Germanic root. These ostensible indicators of ethno-cultural identity, vernacular languages, were moreover until the middle to late fourteenth century in texts from the duchy overlain by the mark of another consciously acquired culture, Christian latinity. The system of personal names that replaced vernacular Slavic among the late thirteenth-century Silesian elite was as much western Christian as German.[49] Is a scribe's "Joannes," then, a German *Johann* or *Hans*, or a Polish *Jan* or *Janko*?[50]

National identity and consciousness were in the Middle Ages phenomena of social strata well above the peasants.[51] For most of the High Middle Ages Polish rulers, like Bolesław and the Henrys in Wrocław, welcomed migrants whom their country could use and absorb. Then, for reasons having nothing to do with agrarian life, just about 1300 the Polish elite entered a new and especially critical phase in its development of nationality, and especially equated this with language.[52] Silesia did not fully share in this phase, and thus, by not changing, became less "Polish" than the Poland that did. It did not, however, become German. Elite consciousness in that province remained through the later Middle Ages more complex and not characteristically defined by language. Immigration and intersettlement had created a multicultural mix that was itself definitive.[53] The shift in Silesia from a relatively uniform Polish culture to a pluralistic one was a necessary but certainly an insufficient precondition for a subsequent process of becoming "German." Germanization was not thirteenth century or even medieval, though it began then. It lasted and remained incomplete into the twentieth century.

German immigrants contributed greatly to the important changes which did occur in thirteenth-century Silesia. They were not ethno-cultural but socio-economic. In the countryside an old Polish agrarian regime became something else, the regime of German law. This institutional complex Germans first brought and continued to use, but it quickly lost ethnic exclusiveness. As the innovation diffused more rapidly around Wrocław after mid-century the people bearing it no longer bore ethno-cultural labels. Those tags no longer described what was happening. German law was spread and operated in the countryside around Wrocław by persons in particular socio-economic roles: *locator*/schulz, peasant tenant, and landlord. Providers of entrepreneurial expertise, productive manpower, and motivating drive, these were the participants in *locatio*. The first two belonged to the village.

Villagers with German law

Locatores played a role critical to the success of each venture, both as short-term *locatio* and as enduring village. At Zabłoto in 1240 Lambert of Tyniec undertook the responsibility for "locating Germans there in German law and liberty."[54] More than a century later Hanco Dremelik's initial task in Siechnice, though described more verbosely, had changed little: "full power of putting out, inheriting, locating, and selling the said mansi of fields to rustics, inhabitants, and cultivators with hereditary right."[55] How the job was carried out remains a mystery. Were criers sent out to recruit peasants as was done to repopulate deserted lands in the late fifteenth century? The special agreements which peasants and *locatores* must have made were, of course, oral. It is not hard, however, to imagine Lambert, Hanco, or one of their peers organizing surveys, distributing parcels of arable, arranging for initial seed supplies, and settling disputes. Each also had to make sure that the tenants understood and accepted the obligations on their holdings.

For Lambert and his heirs at Zabłoto, the task of *locatio* probably merged almost imperceptibly into a lifetime of local leadership, for he received the "ius sculteti" of the new village.[56] Successive roles of settlement agent and village head had been combined around Meissen and Magdeburg in the 1150s, and the pattern once established became the rule in most regions where Germans settled.[57] The position is well described in grants from around Wrocław.

The schulz was responsible to landlord and sovereign for maintaining their rights over the village and for overseeing the village community. Chief of his duties was judicial. In the words of Abbess Euphrosina in the Kotowice *locatio* of 1294, "The above-mentioned schulz shall judge the judgment of all cases in the court," forwarding to her two-thirds of the incomes from justice and keeping one-third himself.[58] Like schulz Conrad of Kostomłoty in 1278, also subject to the standard two-to-one split of incomes, most schulzen found their competence limited to minor but frequent breaches of village custom and other lesser crimes. For more important matters Abbot William of St. Vincent or his representative chaired the "supremis iudiciis, que vulgariter fogtding appelantur, ter in anno . . . ," but Conrad had to pay the expenses thereby incurred. Since the abbey lacked high justice rights, however, "maiores causas . . . capitis vel manus sentenciam" were judged by the duke's judge at Środa, the district town. Conrad's help in transmitting these cases still brought him a ninth of the monetary returns.[59] All such provisions were common to the duchy's German law village schulzen. When there was more than one *locator*, as with Arnold and Tilo at Muchobór Wielkie after 1291, they chaired the court in rotation.[60]

The job of the schulz was not, however, simply judicial. After handing out tenures to the peasants, he undertook to supervise conveyance of these holdings and to ensure payment of the rents specified in his (not their) agreement with the lord.[61] Although thirteenth-century *locatio* agreements pay more attention to declaring that grain dues moved at peasant expense to the lord's collection point, later ones articulate strongly the responsibility of the schulz for what his villagers owed.[62] To the sovereign, finally, schulzen owed not only collection of taxes from the peasants but also, unless waived for cash, military service with their lords' contingents.[63] The Wrocław duchy's *locatores*-schulzen crystallized in their successive roles the central features of the German law, rental tenancy, separation of the lord from everyday interaction with the peasantry, and creation of a formal village community under the schulz's leadership. Much depended on their abilities, honesty, and expertise.

Judging from those who appear in extant German law grants, many Wrocław duchy *locatores* possessed the requisite local knowledge and experience. The first named, Lambert at Zabłoto, came from one of the very few older German law villages in the area, Tyniec Mały, where he would have learned the customs of St. Mary's villages he was to apply.[64] *Locationes* during the next generation were handled by minor officials, former judges, and even experienced schulzen from elsewhere.[65] In the 1280s and 1290s, however, a different group provided most of the known *locatores*, the citizens of Wrocław. Of nine individuals then identified as more than names, six came from the city. Among the latter were leading merchants and councillors like Arnold the Notary and Gunther the Small, as well as Henry Molheim, the only person to undertake two *locationes*.[66] The sadly rare references to *locatores* in grants from the mid-fourteenth century include three more townsmen, all wealthy city politicians who had earlier leased or exercised sublordship over the ecclesiastical properties they were to put out to peasants.[67] They probably did not themselves see to the work, since the tendency then was rather to draw *locatores* from lower social strata, like the former schulz and peasant from Siedlakowice who shared the role at Pustków Żurowski in 1352.[68] Transformation of the locatorial function from a task worthy of various reasonably prestigious non-peasant individuals to one increasingly entrusted to peasants themselves suggests a declining status for it and the generalization of requisite knowledge among the rural populace. But those rich townsmen draw attention to the profits therein.

The successful *locator* had two sources of gain. In the short term he probably charged the peasants for granting holdings, but, since this practice belonged to oral and customary arrangements between these two parties, no positive Silesian evidence survives.[69] His more permanent returns, however, are well documented. Besides judicial incomes, the office of schulz was endowed with valuable properties and privileges. The two rent- and tithe-free mansi, tavern, and butchery of the Domaniów schulz were entirely typical, but others also acquired milling rights, bakeries, fisheries, extra meadows, and free pasturage for one to four hundred sheep on the village lands.[70] The *locatio* charters show no discernible pattern in the range of these privileges nor in the fraction of the arable assigned to the free *scholtisei*. In eighteen measurable cases from the thirteenth century and another three from the middle to late fourteenth century, the average *scholtisei* at *locatio* comprised just more than one-tenth of the village lands.[71] Since, however, villages receiving German law in the thirteenth century were usually larger than those later, the three or four mansi received by rather normal early schulzen like Lambert at Zabłoto in 1240 or Tilo and Arnold at Muchobór in 1292, were twice the amount obtained by *locatores* at Siechnice, Borek, or Bliż a century later.[72] The good-sized rural estates acquired by *locatores*, especially when added to their other privileges and emoluments, endowed dynasties of wealthy countrymen with resources to match their responsibilities as intermediaries between lords and peasants. The grants, however, do not tell whether the recipients of these lands intended to operate them directly or settle tenants of their own.

The whole bundle of a schulz's properties and privileges was hereditary, alienable, and divisible, in legal terms, a *feudum improprium* (or *degeneratium*).[73] Although most contracts merely refer in passing to the rights of the *locator* and his heirs, that for Siechnice expressly extended the succession to Nicholas, brother of schulz Hanco Dremelik and himself schulz in Kuchary near Oława, if Hanco died without issue.[74] More usually, however, only a surviving spouse, sons, or daughters could inherit. Thus at Wierzbno within fifteen years of the 1253 *locatio* the three mansi received by *locator* John had been divided among his sons and at least one share sold, with the lord's consent as required, to an entirely different individual, Jesko of Rybicz.[75]

One last sign of the value of the *locator's* role (and perhaps of changing markets for their services) is their growing need to pay cash for the position. First evident in the duchy with the knight Dirseco's sale of locatorial rights over Pietrzykowice to Dietmar in 1264,[76] this practice appears in four of the five surviving agreements from the 1290s, when city entrepreneurs were paying ten and more marks per mansus for the right to settle peasants and become a schulz.[77] A century later the *scholtisei* with one free mansus in Bliż set Peter Furman back seventy marks.[78] Intervening changes in the coinage (see Appendix B) would make the silver value of Furman's free mansus about four times greater than in the 1290s. Both the fees and their probable increase suggest that the supply of prospective *locatores* had so outstripped demand for their services that lords could profit from shifting their properties to German law as well as from rents thereafter.

Locatorial profits and landlord incomes alike came only from the hidden foundation of the German law movement, peasant farmers and their families. The interests of the German law texts conceal the producers behind a rarely-parted veil of implicit assumption. Peasants are more frequently named individuals in the handful of pre-1250 writings that reflect Polish conditions than in the massive documentation from the age of German law between 1250 and the 1420s. Ironically the very gains in peasant wealth and

status achieved by assessment according to arable acreage and insertion of
the schulz between lord and peasant made superfluous consideration by
those who wrote of those who farmed. Become lords of land, the literate
could leave the men to the schulz. The quality of the evidence thus forces
discussion of the *rustici* into an impersonal normative mode.

Having seen something of village institutions from the schulz's perspective makes familiar the view of the peasants.[79] In a move with portents for
a distant future, the duke withdrew his officers from regular involvement
in rural affairs, granting to lords what was seen as "low justice" (itself an
imported concept) and retaining only capital and appellate jurisdiction plus
a part of the incomes therefrom.[80] But lords, too, became distant figures
who exercised personal justice only in *Dreidingen*[81] and entrusted to schulzen everyday management of village life. A schulz, then, capped the local
hierarchy of a German law village. The peasants owed allegiance to him.[82]
Although his hereditary tenure and formal subordination to the landlord
deprived them of influence over his appointment, peasant assessors, usually
seven in number, found the judgments in his court. Whether chosen by
their peers or named by the lord or schulz, the assessors brought the weight
of recognized custom and respectable village opinion to bear on minor
criminal matters, disputes over village property, and the recurring decisions
required to manage the common fields.[83] Other responsible householders
represented their community in its parochial guise, caring as vestrymen for
their church, its furnishings, and grounds.[84]

With the German law the peasant achieved personal freedom and a
firmly hereditary tenure to land. Names denoting personal servitude are
absent from the grants, first replaced by *hospites* and then by words describ-
ing residence and employment: *rustici, villani, agricoli, incolas villae, rurico-
larii*, and *Gebuern*, all used interchangeably.[85] The great mass of the rural
population had become one; exceptions were limited on the one hand to the
all but landless *gertner* and on the other to schulzen, taverners, and like possessors of free "fiefs" descended from the *locator*'s endowment. Tenure
structured the social hierarchy.

In the vocabulary of the grants, peasants held *mansi censuales* (*Zinshufen*)
as *hereditates rusticorum* (*Bauernerbn*).[86] All blood relatives could inherit by
taking possession in the schulz's court, but the peasant was free to sell,
pledge, or exchange his holdings in whole or in part without, in most cases,
the consent of the lord. Like Sventoys of Jenkowice in 1297, the schulz
controlled conveyancing of *hereditates*.[87] With such mobility of property
coupled to the peasant's personal liberty, assessments had to lie on a different
base, the mansus, a term introduced to Silesia and to the duchy strictly in
the context of German law. Every German law contract or grant that treats

of obligations imposes them on mansi. By 1305, for instance, disputes over the tithes of Juszczyn revolved only around the number of mansi actually in the village, the *rustici* maintaining thirty-two against episcopal administrators who asserted thirty-five and a half.[88] That the mansus, however, bore no necessary relationship to holding sizes, even at *locatio*, is confirmed by a provision at Muchobór Wielkie in 1291 which limited individual tenants to two or at most three mansi.[89] The sizes of peasant holdings in villages established under German law are otherwise no concern of the *locatio* charters, for the scale of farms related less to community institutions or peasant status than to the economics of peasant farming.

Accentuated cereal production with a regulated three course rotation on common field arable was the chief technical feature of agriculture in a German law village. Bishop Lawrence referred in 1223 to the "division of mansi into lots according to the German custom," and a generation later his successor's contract with Albert for German law at Święte required the first rents from fields already cleared "when first they gather the summer with the winter crops."[90] In all, thirteen of the twenty-four Wrocław duchy grants of years free from obligations are divisible by three (and another four cases with four years simply allowed completion of a full rotational cycle before demanding rents).

Less direct evidence shows more broadly the cereal-growing emphasis of German law villages near Wrocław, for these arrangements spread least where concentrated grain production was least feasible, in the bottomlands. Of the thirty-three sites ever documented on the flood plain of the Odra from Uraz west to the mouth of the Średzka Woda only twelve (36 percent) acquired German law, a proportion well below the ratio for the duchy as a whole (60 percent). That peasants in one poor village there, Chomiąża, had to have Abbess Euphrosina in 1285 halve rents and grant more free years,[91] helps explain why only four places there got it before 1300. In the duchy as a whole, villages with German law fail to replicate the approximately equal numbers of settlements with bottomland and with upland sites. Of the seventy-three places receiving *ius Theutonicum* before 1300, barely one in four had a bottomland site, while of the 232 which ever had it, the proportion does not reach two in five.[92] Heavy soils and the danger of flooding, then, posed a barrier to the reasoned adoption of these arrangements.

The amount of innovation and increased productivity represented by the cereal-growing emphasis and regulated three course managerial practices of the German law is, however, unsure. Certainly both grain production and the rotational technique were earlier known in Poland and the Wrocław area, but to label the latter "more Theutonico" suggests a role in their diffusion among peasant farmers. Some authors further connect the spread of these techniques to a rise in productivity from seed-yield ratios of about two to one in the twelfth century to three or four to one by the mid-fourteenth.[93] This plausible assertion gains no support from Wrocław duchy texts, German law or other. But to the extent that German law made normal in peasant agriculture improvements formerly restricted to a few well-run estates or holdings and impelled each farmer to convert to near-monoculture of cereals and a three course rotation, production of grain per unit farmed would rise.

New techniques imposed conversion costs, and villages newly founded with German law had to work hard before the land could produce at all. In either instance, peasants creating a German law village needed some start-up capital. Although nothing is really known about who supported villagers who could not farm yet uncleared lands, lords could help by initially foregoing rents. Costs for peasants were cut in this way in twenty-four of the villages which received grants up to 1312, but not in later contracts.[94] Settlers on new land received from two to twelve free years but those on older arable also could get from one to six years off some of their obligations. One of the longer grants went to peasants at Mrozów in 1277, where those who had to clear the woodland got twelve years, but those whose land was already open only four. Other than this general adjustment of incentives to the difficulty of the task, little consistent variation emerges from the grants.[95]

After their free years expired, German law tenants assumed the burdens established in the *locatio* contract. In its overwhelming reliance on fixed obligations assessed according to arable area alone, the German law furthered the earlier Polish trend towards standardization. Tenants of St. Mary and St. Vincent owed the state *annona ducalis*, one measure each of wheat and oats from each mansus, a payment which remained well into the 1300s.[96] Others merely found the *poradlne* converted to a assessment on mansi and then giving way by the fourteenth century to a fixed land tax of a quarter mark per mansus.[97] Of obligatory services under Polish law, however, only assistance in building fortifications and defensive militia duty remained. All others were explicitly abolished for German law villagers.[98]

Labor services and in-kind payments to the lord all but vanished. In the handful of German law grants that mention labor, only the first contract for Szukalice in 1253 suggested work at the lord's pleasure might replace the money rent; this clause disappeared from the revised contract of 1254. Elsewhere services atrophied to a mere two days' sowing owed by the Mnichowice tenants on the demesne at Turów, three days' plowing at Przesławice, and a few mentions of carrying duties, chiefly of peasants' own grain payments to a monastic or ducal recipient.[99] Unlike the case in Great

Poland, German law labor services in the Wrocław duchy seem not to have risen in the fourteenth century; they are essentially absent from grants after 1300.[100] Minor payments are few and varied: a continuation of Polish honey dues at Gosławice, hay at Muchobór, candle wax from the old cathedral demesne of *Cruce*.[101] In most German law villages such customary gifts were confined to symbolic recognitions of the landlord's superiority, the "honors" (*honores, Ehrungen*) of a couple of chickens at Christmas and fifteen eggs at Easter, for instance.[102]

The bulk of the obligations set for peasants in contracts of German law around Wrocław was yearly fixed grain and money payments for rent and tithe. In the absence of real tenths as tithe, most of the thirty extant contracts which state the obligations of rental mansi followed a pattern set by Abbot Albert of St. Vincent for Zabłoto in 1240, where he established each payment but did not distinguish tithe and rent.[103] This ambiguity, especially if seen from the peasant's perspective as equally external demands on his harvest, seems almost the norm in Polish texts of this period.[104] Thus a focus on the physical rather than the legal aspect of major peasant obligations accords with contemporary literate as well as peasant attitudes. Tenants owed *maldratas annone* and *fertones, Maltern* and *Virdungen*, the grain at Martinmas (November 11) and the money at Walpurgis (May 1) and Michaelmas (September 29).[105]

Normal grain dues per mansus were twelve measures (of perhaps 128 liters) "triplicis grani," i.e., four each of wheat, rye, and oats. That made one *maldratum* of cereals and gave rise to the common phrase *decimum maldratum* (*Malterzehnt*).[106] A higher payment of fifteen measures claimed from peasants at Rzeplin in 1253 was quickly revised the next year to conform with the twelve measure norm.[107] The standard mix of grains was occasionally altered in villages on loams and in the Środa district to delete or reduce the wheat component for more rye and oats.[108] Payment of grain as a real tenth of the harvest, on the other hand, came in German law grants only from a few ecclesiastical properties on old-settled black earths in the Wrocław district.[109]

Money payments, if labeled, usually "rent," were, like other transactions, measured in the thirteenth century by a weighed mark "usual silver," but later by the mark of 48 Bohemian groschen that became the standard circulating medium in Silesia.

Levels of fixed dues set in *locatio* contracts changed somewhat over the hundred and sixty year span during which they were established.[110] Inhabitants of most places that acquired German law during the mid-thirteenth century paid like those in Wierzbno, an annual twelve measures and a quarter mark the mansus, while exceptions differed more in the structure of obligations than in the total owed. But by the 1280s and 1290s, rents had crept upward. The traditional twelve measures and a quarter mark remained the norm in the contracts, but others ran uniformly higher—to an extreme of one and a quarter marks plus the grain at Szczepankowice in 1286. This upward drift continued into the few *locatio* agreements which survive from the mid-fourteenth century. Cash components rose without compensatory reduction in the grain. By the end of the thirteenth century the mean cash payment had drifted upward from about 34.4 grams of fine silver towards 50 grams. With the coins available during 1347–78, the four contracts then endorsed called for money rents between 57.6 and 172.8 grams, but subsequent debasement let later nominally higher rents contain no more specie.[111]

Peasants produced grain, however. The economic position of a German law peasant can be apprehended only in terms of his obligations relative to the productive capacity of his farm. A peasant at Zabłoto working one mansus of common-field arable under the quite standard arrangements made in 1240 had to pay two measures of grain to the duke and twelve measures plus a quarter mark cash to the abbey.[112] With a three course rotation this farmer would plant about 11.2 of his 16.8 hectares, half in rye with some wheat, half in spring oats and barley. Assuming that he seeded about 228 liters to the hectare and that his yield was 4 to 1, his total would be 9216 liters or 86.4 measures.[113] He had to store 21.6 measures of seed for the following year, 25 percent of the harvest. Then fiscal and fixed grain obligations absorbed 14 measures and, at the thirteenth century grain price of about .05 marks per measure, he had to sell another five measures to get the cash for his money rent. So the Zabłoto peasant paid out 19 measures (22 percent of his harvest)[114] and was left with 45.8 measures (53 percent). At 107 liters to the measure, this man's grain provided an annual caloric minimum for fourteen adults or, in a diet with other foods, a basic cereal component for nineteen adults.[115]

These levels seem very high, probably because the 4 to 1 yield ratio they assume was a rare maximum for medieval central European peasant farmers. Such an individual probably thought a 3-to-1 yield a successful year.[116] At this lower ratio his harvest of 64.8 measures was reduced by a total of 19 (29 percent) for fixed obligations and 21.6 (33 percent) for seed reserve to leave him 24.2 measures (38 percent), enough to feed a still respectable seven to ten adults.[117] By comparison with his counterpart on the Trzebnica estates a generation earlier, whose obligations gobbled up a good half of his production and whose productivity as measured by the seed-yield ratio was probably still lower,[118] the Zabłoto peasant did all right indeed. If he could work more than a mansus, his net receipts increased proportionately, but his share of the product remained constant. His real advantage came from the fixed rents themselves, for any productivity gains beyond a bare minimum to cover his obligations were his alone. So were those from higher prices.

To the Wrocław duchy peasant, then, considerable advantage accrued from participation in the German law movement. He gained personal freedom with some possibility of upward mobility. His reorganized community and newly secured tenure offered some added independence even without a move. A native who received German law in his home village may have found in reorganization of arable an opportunity to increase productivity, while newly fixed rents permitted him to retain much of any gain. For new settlers, Germans or Poles, security, autonomy, and fixed obligations were coupled to an opportunity to acquire land, bring it into production, and make a new home on it. Despite the benefits, however, German law in the Wrocław duchy was no peasant movement. No evidence suggests villagers learning about the innovation from their neighbors and then pressing for like privileges of their own.[119] Peasants joined, made it work, and gained, but the leaders and movers were not peasants, not even *locatores*, but lords, the people who collectively received twenty to thirty percent of the Zabłoto peasant's harvest.

In the lord's interest

Because innovations by landlords had already contributed much dynamism to the late twelfth- and early thirteenth-century Polish economy, their active involvement with German law causes no surprise. Who were they and in what settings did they turn to these innovations? The best answers come from examining those owners who aimed in the surviving grants and contracts to establish German law institutions in settlements of the duchy. Table 4.2 summarizes for discussion the groups so recorded.

The preeminence of churches in the extant evidence of the German law movement around Wrocław stems in part from their penchant for written records and in part from the many ecclesiastical holdings there.[120] Churchmen were demonstrably instrumental in early stages of the movement here, sponsoring on their lands all fifteen of the *locationes* known before 1260 and almost four-fifths of those carried out by 1279. Although their share dropped in the last two decades of the century, later in the diffusion process they were again among its leaders.

Within the ecclesiastical group, individual corporate participants ranked close to their relative position as lords (Table 4.3). Thus the largest single holder, the Church of Wrocław, also far surpassed the others among grantors of German law, and of the leading clerical proprietors only the Wrocław

Table 4.2. Landlords appearing in grants of German law, 1221–1399

	Dukes	Churches	Nobles	Wrocław citizens	City of Wrocław	Total
to 1249		6				6
1250–1279	4	13	1	1		19
1280–1299	3	5	7			15
1300–1339		2	1			3
1340–1359		11	2	10	1	24
1360–1399		6		1		7
Total	7	43	11	11	1	74

Note. For sources see note to Figure 4.2 in *Notes to Maps and Figures.*

Table 4.3. Ecclesiastical landlords in more than one *locatio*

	Church of Wrocław	Saint Mary	Saint Vincent	Trzebnica	Saint Mathias	Lubiąż	Holy Spirit
to 1249		2	3	1			
1250–1279	9		1			1	1
1280–1299	3			1			
1300–1339		1				1	
1340–1359	3	1		1	3		
1360–1399	4	1					1
Total	19	5	4	3	3	2	2
Rank among church landlords by mid-13th century	1	3	2	4	7	5	8

Note. For sources see Figure 4.2 and Table 3.1.

Clares did not participate to the extent their estate would suggest. But the concentration of recorded activity by certain corporations into relatively constrained periods and their common possession also of land elsewhere, advises a closer look at the particular policies followed by at least an exemplary ecclesiastical lord.

St. Vincent's Premonstratensians slowly developed a program of German law conversion on holdings in and outside the later Wrocław duchy during the mid to late 1200s. Despite having ruled German peasants at Psie Pole since 1206, the monks let their Augustinian neighbors at St. Mary first experiment with the new institutions, and in 1228 they borrowed words and substance from earlier St. Mary charters to arrange their own first privilege to establish *hospites* at a place they had long owned west of Świdnica.[121] Seven years later Henry I conceded German law for the *Romanos* in Wierzbno, but exercise of the privilege in an actual contract was much delayed.[122] Experiment and imitation continued. In contracting in 1240 for the Zabłoto grange, St. Vincent anticipated for the first time in the Wrocław area settlement of Germans and expansion of existing arable through new clearances. Local customs, the specific rent, and the *locator*, however, still came from older German law villages of St. Mary.[123]

After the accession of Abbot Vitus in 1248 the Premonstratensians embarked on a confident German law program, using the up-to-date customary law of Środa and, increasingly, a normal rent rate of a quarter mark plus twelve measures in three grains. Now the new arrangements were installed at the heart of the abbey's chief property complex, the ancient market village at Kostomłoty and Ujów nearby.[124] By 1254, though no genuine town, Kostomłoty was being called a *civitas* by Henry III. Środa law on the Kostomłoty plan went to two more villages here, Gorzec in 1252 and Kilianów in 1259.[125] Meanwhile success around Kostomłoty also presaged *locatio* for other older villages, Wierzbno among them, during the 1250s.[126]

After a short wait, in the early 1270s *locatio* of Czeczy brought to four the Wrocław duchy properties put under German law and another near Strzelin increased those in a cluster west of Oława, both still following the Kostomłoty model.[127] Legal reforms in 1278 even saw that place as the center of a "territorium Cozzenbloth," a reasonably contiguous complex of nine abbey villages organized into a semi-autonomous regional estate under the administrative supervision of the abbot's *Vogt* and his court.[128] But thereafter the flow of grants from St. Vincent slowed down and went towards more distant villages, some near Oława and Trzebnica, others in Upper Silesia.[129] That to Czeczy was its last known grant in the duchy or the area of Kostomłoty.

Of the thirty-five Silesian properties owned by St. Vincent in the mid-thirteenth century, the abbey installed German law on thirteen, making it a leader in this phase of the movement.[130] On fourteen lordships held in the future Wrocław duchy between 1250 and 1300, the Premonstratensians granted four *locationes*, three near Kostomłoty and the other on the opposite side at Wierzbno. But three much closer properties, Księże Wielkie, Grabiszyn, and *Olbino* (where the abbey itself was), received German law only after 1350 and seven more places owned by the abbey between 1250 and 1300 never obtained it from them.[131] The policy of St. Vincent, then, concentrated in the mid-thirteenth century on conversion of older and distant villages in reasonably compact groups. Scattered outlying holdings were good for first experiments but then only late or sporadic attention, while the numerous sites closest to the abbey itself remained untouched until the late fourteenth century, when a half-hearted resurgence of interest reformed some of these demesnes.

Patterns like that of St. Vincent may be seen for the Church of Wrocław, Lubiąż, St. Mary, and other major ecclesiastical lords.[132] Churches' grants in the duchy rarely articulate the topoi of economic improvement familiar elsewhere,[133] but this motive to reform what were mostly older settlements and properties is most likely. Ecclesiastics withdrew first from active supervision of their tenants and in the fourteenth century from much of the demesne farming they had done until then.

Ducal participation in German law *locatio* had different correlates. Bolesław I and Henry I promoted Polish law development, German immigrants, and new institutions,[134] but their effect on rural areas of the future Wrocław duchy is obscure. Though Henry made at Środa a German law town, the plausible references to associated villages are late and imprecise. Hence surviving ducal charters come only from the period 1261–93 when several different sovereigns sought some defensive presence and financial return by filling in settlement along their (momentary) borders. In the early 1260s Henry III of Wrocław, faced with continued threats to the thinly settled central Środa district and to areas northwest of Uraz, used German law and his own followers to expand or found villages at Warzyn, Łowęcice, and Gosławice.[135] Having extorted Środa from Henry IV in 1277, dukes of Legnica at Mrozów in that year and Mokra in 1289 continued like promotions along what had now become their frontier against an irredentist Wrocław.[136] By 1289, however, Henry of Legnica was the ally and friend of Henry IV and using Wrocław citizens as *locatores*. Then, having become with the city's support duke of Wrocław as well, this same Henry (V) sponsored more citizen entrepreneurs installing German law at Nadolice Wielkie and Kozanów.[137] Finally, having in 1294 stripped the Uraz district from the Wrocław duke, Henry of Głogów anchored his defenses there by founding in the woodlands no less than eight new villages.[138]

Noble landholders trailed dukes and churches in adopting German law for their properties; even if their activity was severely underdocumented, it could not have equaled their share in rural lordships.[139] The earliest private lay contract for a village with German law on a lordship in the duchy came from Dirseco, lord of Pietrzykowice in 1264. He accepted the then normal rent of a quarter mark and twelve measures and the law of Środa for the inhabitants, but kept a full five mansi as a direct exploitation demesne.[140] His peers in the 1280s and 1290s then turned so eagerly to German law as to replace the ecclesiastics as the leading group. But their activities lacked other distinction and diminished in the next century.

Some citizens of Wrocław acquired rural lordships soon after 1250, but for some time members of this group dealt with German law for villages chiefly as *locatores*. Even the marked early fourteenth-century growth in their holdings resulted only with the 1340s in their promotion of those institutions there. Then came two intensely active decades.[141] Nicholas Sittin, owner of demesnes and rental land at a good dozen sites south of Wrocław plus several well-secured annuities and farms of royal incomes, is a suitable example.[142] Having acquired the large demesne at Bielany by 1336 and then bought a few other nearby bits, he obtained from King John in 1341 general freedom from fiscal exactions of all kinds and permission to put out to German law it and ten more mansi he intended to buy.[143] Some of the neighboring land was not for sale, notably the cathedral chapter demesne at *Cruce*, so Nicholas took it on perpetual lease in 1344 with the explicit proviso that he could put it, too, out to German law.[144] In 1353 Bielany, no longer a demesne, had forty-three rental mansi and a schulz with four more. Nicholas Sittin was followed in its lordship by his heirs.[145] Like him, citizen owners put out old demesnes to German law tenants, abandoning direct exploitation for rentier incomes. King John voiced the motives of all townsmen in a 1341 privilege to put tenants on the former Blizanowice demesne: he hoped that the expected larger revenues might make them the more eager in his service.[146]

Especially after pioneering dukes and churchmen had demonstrated the value of German law institutions, landowners installed them, certainly, for their economic advantage. In changing circumstances around thirteenth- and fourteenth-century Wrocław, however, this one underlying purpose applied *locatio* to German law there in three distinct settings: to reform traditional villages; to expand settlement; and to convert demesnes to tenant villages. Changing balances among them gave different effect to this practice during the almost two centuries of its use.

German law grants reformed institutional structures of older villages throughout the thirteenth and probably well into the fourteenth century. Consider again Domaniów. Here the nuns of Trzebnica acquired in the 1220s several small settlements and had them merged into one lordship by the duke's personal *circuitus*. Here dwelt one-time ducal *homines*, peasant soldiers called *pogrodschi*, and probably some other peasants, but by 1234 the convent also ran a grange. Abbess Gertrude's grant in that year thus grew out of and carried further these developments. The physical and proprietary amalgamation of the *circuitus* paved the way for juridical union under a schulz. Obligations were now fixed on a standardized *mansus*; a revision by Abbess Euphrosina in 1286 found only the minor increase from eight to nine scot. The initial grant mentioned German settlers, but nothing later indicates more than one kind of peasant status or tenure here; if any survived 1234 the new survey of 1286 surely removed them. With local affairs entrusted to the schulz and community and with a regular income from rents, the convent could close the inconveniently distant grange. From a motley mix of lordships, inhabitants, and probably also obligations—from an institutional arrangement where an efficient lord pressed directly on the peasants and only an efficient and knowledgeable lord could obtain her rights—Domaniów became a self-regulating annual source of 250 to 300 measures of grain and 13 to 15 marks cash.[147] Similar transformations and gains for lords and probably peasants are also well-recorded elsewhere.[148] In an area as densely settled by 1200 as the Wrocław duchy, *locatio iure Theutonico* may have affected the most people as such a tool for the institutional reform of existing properties and lord-peasant relations. Among the seventy-three settlements on Map 4.1 where by 1300 lords had planned and, mostly, installed German law, thirty-nine are older communities transformed by this means.

Another nineteen of the seventy-three places with German law by 1300 occur in or at the edge of areas of scanty human habitation. Use of this institutional tool to organize pioneers to expand settlement and arable in the duchy is chiefly evident on the high loams of the central Środa district and the morainic hills north of Uraz.

In an extended triangle from south of Środa widening eastwards to a line from about Leśnica to Wilkszyn it is hard to find a significant population before 1250.[149] Since the German villages around Środa attributed to Henry I cannot be identified (Proszków, Bielany, Jugowiec, Juszczyn, and Żródła seem likely candidates), visible efforts of expansion began at the edges. In the early 1250s the leaders were churchmen—the Holy Spirit Hospital at the older but peripheral Karczyce, Lubiąż at a site called "Birchwood" ("Brezina"), the later Pisarzowice, and Bishop Thomas at Święte—all using German law to promote settlement.[150] In the only extant contract of these the bishop allowed extra free years for settlers clearing new land. Use by Lubiąż of "Germans or others" established the mixed ethnic participation that seems to characterize this movement. *Locatores* hereabouts in the next generation bore names like Dresco, Gosław, and Witosław as well as Wilherus and John.

Leadership now passed from clerics to sovereigns, as different dukes sponsored *locationes* which spread from the edges, at Łowęcice and Gosławice, into the heart of the once empty section, at Mrozów and at a place called "Swampy" (Mokra).[151] At the latter everybody got ten free years, a plain sign that hard work would be required. By about 1305, however, barely fifteen years after the contract, new settlers at Mokra had brought

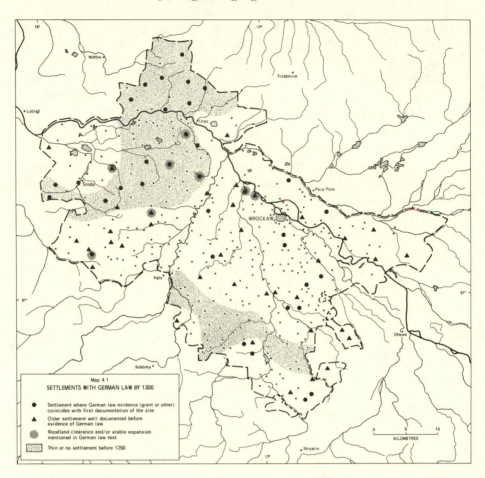

Map 4.1
SETTLEMENTS WITH GERMAN LAW BY 1300

● Settlement where German law evidence (grant or other)
coincides with first documentation of the site

▲ Older settlement well documented before
evidence of German law

◉ Woodland clearance and/or arable expansion
mentioned in German law text

▒ Thin or no settlement before 1250

0   5   10
KILOMETRES

into production more than twenty-four mansi; episcopal authorities claimed that the tithe payment of three marks (*locatio* set ⅛ mark per mansus as the tithe rate) ought to be more.[152]

Meanwhile the late thirteenth century also reveals for the first time several places with names suggestive of recent settlement but whose German law came without benefit of extant contracts or grants. By 1278 "Springs" was inhabited, and then soon "Lampert's village," "Moorland," and "Hugo's village."[153] Ligotka, whose name recalls that Polish customs also could promote new settlement, received from a knight's widow in 1289 German law with three free years.[154] On the once empty loam only Krępice, a village of free Polish peasants directly under the duke, enters the written record during the second half of the thirteenth century without any sign of the German law.[155]

North of the Odra swamps near Uraz, German law settlers moved into the morainic woodlands much like their counterparts to the south. Up to 1250 only the easternmost corner held a detectable population, developing under Polish customs with support from Duke Henry and the Trzebnica convent.[156] Ducal promotion of settlement in the infertile frontier hills above Uraz began with the *locatio* of Warzyn by Henry III and Conrad, Vogt of Lesnica, in 1261. The inhabitants received the law of Środa and Poles specific exemption from customary services.[157] Warzyn and Uraz together provided bases for further expansion from either flank of the still wooded uplands. Henry III may have anticipated another push from the east only two years later, for the contract usually identified with Gosławice a ways to the south included *Gurse* on the Środa side of the Odra and a "villa Woycechonis" that is highly suggestive of Wojciechów, first unambiguously documented just after 1300.[158] Those references, however, pretty well rule out the success of that duke's possible effort, for contemporaries there credit another Henry III, the aggressive Duke of Głogów, who held Uraz from 1294 until his death in 1309, with erection of new villages at this and several other sites: Górowo, Bukowiec, Borów, Rościsławice, Jajków, Radecz, Wały.[159] They lay with Godzięcin and Bagno, themselves first called "Tyrgarten" and "Heinrichsdorf" by Henry of Głogów himself in 1301, around the remnant woodland which he preserved and where only a tiny demesne, "Tannynwalde" (Jodłowice), appeared from 1313.[160] Meanwhile, and arguing as well for at least some immigration under auspices other than ducal, the formerly unknown Golędzinów and the older Pęgów and Ozorowice had also acquired German names, "Chunzendorf," "Henningesdorf," and "Sponsbrük," and Abbess Euphrosina had transfered Kotowice to German law.[161]

With the area now suffused with good-sized villages of a regular plan, the virtual completion of settlement gained recognition in 1312 when the heirs of Duke Henry divided his realm. They disposed of Uraz castle "with [for the first time] its district."[162] Here again German law had worked to attract settlers who filled and made remunerative for the promoters what had been uninhabited territory. Shortly after 1300 no major empty spots remained in what had just become the Wrocław duchy.

After a quiet human generation the movement to install German law institutions revived strongly around the middle of the fourteenth century. Attempts at *locatio* were now chiefly directed to a third application, conversion into tenant holdings of the remaining direct exploitation demesnes. As is clear on Map 4.2, activity concentrated on the old-settled black earths of the Wrocław district. Map 4.2 displays only those places which, because they received *grants* of German law after 1300, could not have acquired it

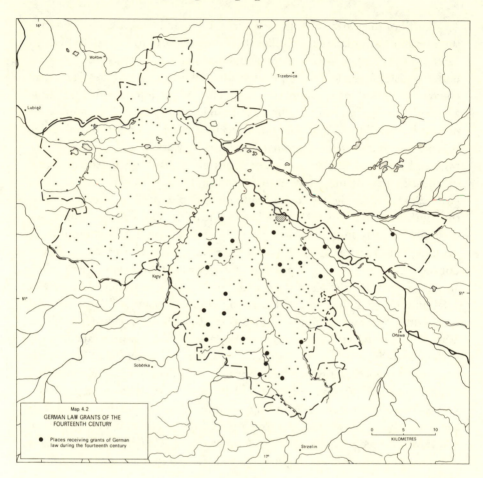

Map 4.2
GERMAN LAW GRANTS OF THE
FOURTEENTH CENTURY

● Places receiving grants of German
law during the fourteenth century

earlier in silence. These were small holdings, not the great villages of the thirteenth-century *locationes*.[163] Landlords (and knights, churches, and citizens all participated) now became more outgoing about their motives. Jesco of Smolec wanted in 1339 to put out his village and demesne there to peasants for an annual rent "in order to increase its usefulness,"[164] and the like attitudes of townsmen have already been mentioned. Lords wanted to get out of agriculture and make money in the process, to, in the words of Charles IV's general privilege from 1354, "locate your demesne properties with all sorts of persons as tenants and on those your said demesne properties to have constructed and established new villages for the augmentation of the land and the usefulness of the common good."[165]

Gądów Mały well illustrates the circumstances and meaning of *locatio* at this time. Lordship over this demesne was divided, with about eight mansi under Trzebnica and four under the Church of Wrocław, but successive lay subholders long managed and operated a single farm.[166] Then in 1345 Nicholas Brunonis, a Wrocław citizen, obtained royal permission to put out to "farmers and countrymen for an annual rent his demesne called Gądów" of twelve and one-third mansi under the joint lordship just described.[167] When the 1353 tax survey was compiled, nine mansi were rented out and a schulz had the other three.[168] Peasant tenants, gertner, and schulzen are thereafter regular in their appearance at Gądów Mały, but of the demesne no more is heard. The move away from direct exploitation in the fourteenth century was larger than the German law grants, for lords needed no privilege, locatorial assistance, or new institutions to parcel out demesnes in existing villages. The broader topic is taken up in later chapters. Pertinent here is the recognition that the German law grant offered sufficient flexibility and familiarity for lords to resuscitate it for a new and profitable role.

The economic impact of institutional change

Around Wrocław to locate to German law was a landlord's tool for innovation. It continued and accelerated the twelfth- and early thirteenth-century trends toward arable expansion, standardized assessments, fixed liquid incomes, and withdrawal from direct agricultural management, first over peasant tenants, then over demesne production. Lords transformed their incomes from a heterogeneous mix of labor services and real payments to consistent amounts of money and grain. They enlarged their incomes by expanding the land tilled under their auspices, to that end often settling empty frontier areas with defensible peasant communities. Lords stabilized their incomes at the new levels by abandoning their own farms and shifting the costs of production to the peasants. The institutional forms of German law thus standardized in the duchy of Wrocław trends common to most of high medieval trans-Alpine Europe and evident in Poland since at least the late twelfth century. It follows from the development of the Polish economy in the period before the German law that the forms themselves, the German law per se, were not necessary to the process but simply those procedures used to accomplish it. For this they were well chosen.

The norms of German custom came to Silesia for the sake of landlord and ducal incomes, but the effects of this innovation exceeded those intentions. The German law reforms created structures basic to the later medieval countryside around Wrocław. Rural settlement was by about 1300 all but complete because German law privileges had attracted settlers to formerly ill-favored areas. Villagers lived in semi-autonomous communities and

farmed reasonably secure tenures as free men because German law privileges did dissuade indigenes from flight. And the new rural "division of
labor" between peasant agricultural producers and rentier lords characteristic of the German law village had forced both into a closer and more regular involvement with the market. Lords over German law villages needed
to convert their receipts of cash and grain into consumables, even some
foodstuffs. To pay the money rent peasant tenants had to sell some five to
ten percent of their harvest; with higher productivity and fixed rents, they
could sell more and then satisfy on the market wants they had once foregone
or met at home.

Thus a further change wrought by the German law was still deeper
penetration of the market economy into the countryside. Country people
interacted more and more with the duchy's urban centers, chiefly Wrocław,
where they exchanged their produce for city goods. By the early fourteenth
century the city numbered thirty-two stalls for the sale of bread and more
for meat.[169] The municipal government had an inventory of about two hundred malter (2400 measures) each of rye and malt valued at some four hundred marks—not the product of city gardens.[170] The ready buyers drew so
many peasants with their grain carts to town on market days that not all
could find room and special regulations had to cover those who sold outside.[171] The city, moreover, not content or confident with its ability to attract local exchange, acquired and enforced in the later thirteenth century a
monopoly over that in the neighborhood, the so-called *Meilenrecht*.[172] The
very fear of competition verifies the extent to which market-oriented specialists found ready buyers in the countryside, while Wrocław's commercial
growth confirms the emergence of a complex regional economy where
town and country had constructed a real, if unequal, symbiosis.

By the end of the thirteenth century, therefore, the form of relations
among landlords, peasants, land, and markets around Wrocław was increasingly a product of the German law movement. The institutional order created with German law established the strengths and weaknesses of this rural
economy, opening certain options and closing others. In its parameters the
secular ebb and flow of economic activity, and the more constant cycles of
agrarian life were henceforth played out.

§§ 5 §§

DEMESNE FARMING IN THE AGE OF GERMAN LAW

ISTA SUNT ALLODIA ET NUMERUS MANSORUM IN DISTRICTU WRATISLAUIENSI.
Lemgruben prope Wratislauiam habet 16 mansos: cruciferorum corporis Christi
Gay allodium Ernkonis 6½ mansorum.
Gay allodium puerorum de Lubow 5 mansorum.

Part of the fiscal survey of 1353; *LB* #221–223.

Creation of a German law village did not always take the landowner out of agriculture. Like canon John at Rzeplin or the knight Dirseco at Pietrzykowice in the 1260s,[1] many lords reserved for their own use some of the resources described in the *locatio*. Older settlements still unreformed were also commonly *allodia*, demesne lands "under the lord's own plow," in contrast to the *mansi censuales* of tenants in a *villa*.[2] Kozanów, a settlement of ducal servants that came to the Church of Wrocław in 1208, was in the first half of the fourteenth century a well-stocked *allodium* of ten mansi entrusted by the cathedral chapter to one of its members.[3] Nearly half of the duchy's settlements were then such independent direct exploitation properties. To the tenant farming of the German law village must be opposed the landlord farming of demesnes, a competitive mode for the organization of agriculture and the exploitation of landed property.

While the thin record up to the mid-thirteenth century could at best affirm the presence of landlord farms in the central Silesian countryside, more numerous and explicit documents of the late 1200s through early 1400s sustain deeper study of their situation and operation. This chapter examines in succession the quantitative importance, size, location, production, labor supply, management, and values of direct exploitation properties. Though shrinking in numbers, they were significant structures in the rural economy of the duchy, producing with hired workers goods intended for the owner's consumption and market sale.[4]

Demesne farms

Land and fiscal records from the duchy's medieval settlements establish the continuous quantitative importance of demesne operations, both in terms of their presence in most places and their control over an appreciable share of arable resources.[5] Taking the principality as a whole, the episcopal income register of 1300/05 (*LFE*) and other reasonably contemporary texts confirm the existence then of 234 rural settlements (maybe a hundred more, though present, had yet to enter the documentary record). All but fifty-one (22 percent) of these had land in demesne. In eighty (34 percent) this was beside peasant farms, but 103 (44 percent) were run entirely on the landholder's account. A half century later, when Charles IV's fiscal survey (*LB*) covered 284 places in the duchy and 70 more from other texts make the total of 354 a probable enumeration of all then settled, the frequency of demesnes had changed little. The 274 localities with landlord farms still came to more than three-fourths of the total, 161 (45 percent) as independent demesne settlements and 113 (32 percent) dividing local resources with tenants. Even in 1425, interpretation in the context of other records of the *burnegelt* tax return (RB) argues for approximately equal division of the 362 places then inhabited among those without demesne (116 or 32 percent), those with tenants and demesne (125 or 35 percent) and those entirely in demesne (121 or 33 percent).

The most probable estimates of the distribution of arable land in the duchy suggest around 35 percent in demesne during the first half of the fourteenth century and 20 to 25 percent by the eve of the Hussite wars. The perceptible drop is a sign of a secular retreat from landlord farming which shall require careful study, but the evidence still confirms the lasting place of this mode for the exploitation of agricultural resources. The significance of demesne enterprises to the rural life of the duchy will emerge from a closer look at their operation.

Demesne lands in most settlements were several times larger than even a good-sized peasant holding. In the eleven places where land in demesne can be measured from the episcopal income register of about 1300, it averaged 8.6 mansi, while the much larger such sample available in 1353 (146 places) works out to an even ten mansi. By 1425 this may have shrunk some; the thirty-four adequately informative entries provide a mean size of 7.6 demesne mansi per settlement. Such calculations can deceive, however, for places differed greatly and many held more than one demesne farm. On founding the collegiate church of Holy Cross in 1288, Henry IV established farms of four mansi to meet the personal needs of each canon,[6] but this uniformity may have more to do with the living standard of such prelates than the economic efficiency of sixty-five hectares. Certainly many land-

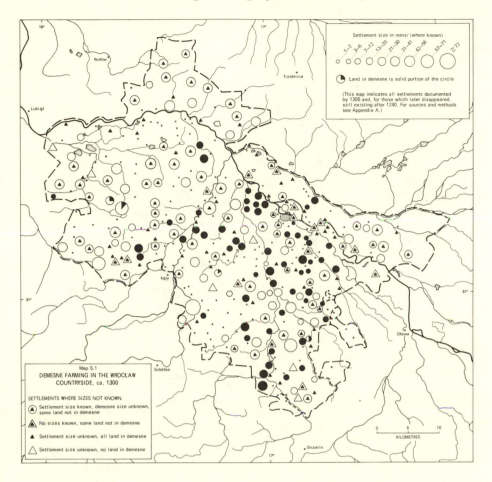

Map 5.1
DEMESNE FARMING IN THE WROCŁAW
COUNTRYSIDE, ca. 1300

owners, from Dirseco with his five mansi at Pietrzykowice in 1264 to the
Holy Spirit hospital with two mansi in Lisowice about 1430, did work this
or less. But the rest of Lisowice then reveals the much larger scale at which
other demesne farmers operated all through the period, for Conrad Campen
ran a full twelve mansi.[7] Over a century earlier Jenczko of Zgorzelec and
Henry Molheim, both townsmen, were working demesnes owned by the
bishop at Komorowice with fifteen mansi and at Ozorzyce with eighteen,
while St. Mary farmed another fifteen at Muchobor Mały before 1311.[8]

The separate farms for which sizes are given in the 1353 fiscal survey
have a simple arithmetic mean just over seven mansi.[9] Where that large record can be checked against conveyances to assure complete listing of local
lords and their holdings, most demesnes seem to fall in the range of four to
eleven mansi. At Piersno, for instance, the four farms of five knights from
the Walch, Runge, and Bramir families were between 3.5 and 6 mansi each,

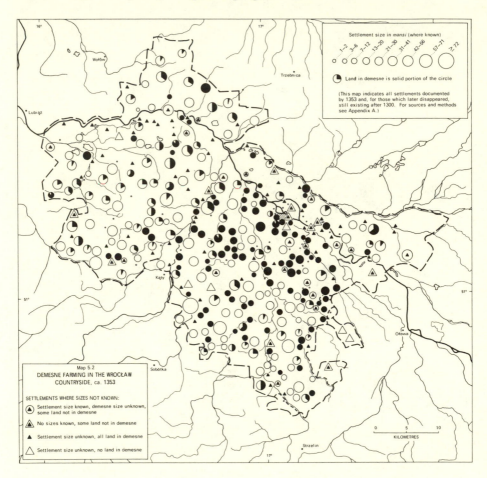

Map 5.2
DEMESNE FARMING IN THE WROCŁAW
COUNTRYSIDE, ca. 1353

SETTLEMENTS WHERE SIZES NOT KNOWN:

Settlement size known, demesne size unknown, some land not in demesne

No sizes known, some land not in demesne

Settlement size unknown, all land in demesne

Settlement size unknown, no land in demesne

Settlement size in *mansi* (where known)

Land in demesne is solid portion of the circle

(This map indicates all settlements documented by 1353 and, for those which later disappeared, still existing after 1300. For sources and methods see Appendix A.)

and at Grabiszyn St. Vincent had 10.5 mansi, two townsmen 10 and 9, and an unidentifiable layman 7.5.[10] The normal demesne farm, then, controlled something in the order of a hundred hectares (250 acres). Even the largest did not rival the huge grain farms of the sixteenth and seventeenth centuries, but only the smallest failed well to surpass the biggest peasant and even most schulz holdings. In land alone, demesne operations represented a significant allocation of productive resources.

Direct exploitations were always found throughout the duchy, but their situation and production developed differently in certain areas. Maps 5.1, 5.2, and 5.3 show demesnes and their share of settlements in a real rural landscape evolving over time. Significant regional patterns emerge. Around 1300 demesne farms were everywhere numerous, thickest on the oldest-settled black earth and loess but fully a part of newer establishments on the

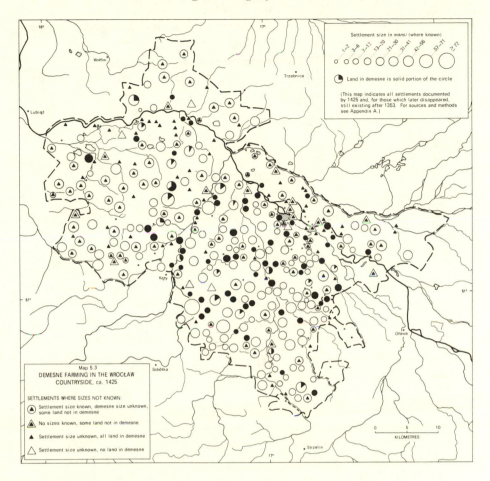

Map 5.3
DEMESNE FARMING IN THE WROCŁAW
COUNTRYSIDE, ca. 1425

Środa loam and the uplands north of Uraz. Although this broad distribution
had changed little by mid-century, the then complete record allows clearer
perception of some evolving distinctions. While demesnes in 1353 seem less
frequent on the black earth south of a line running roughly from Oława to
Kąty, they remained widespread. Especially great concentrations, areas of
much demesne and few tenancies, dominated the black earths of the middle
Wrocław district and the bottomlands along the Odra.

An association of demesne farming with well-watered lowlands, especially on properties operated without peasant tenants, becomes still more
plain on Map 5.3,[11] where the demesne-tenancy combination emerges as the
typical arrangement on the uplands of the Środa and Uraz districts. By
1425, however, the solid block on the black earth had gone; with a few
exceptions most of the higher Wrocław district was a land of tenant farm-

ing. Over the century and a quarter thus depicted, and especially from 1353 to 1425, the landlord's farm became less a general element of the duchy's countryside and more a particular feature of two landscapes, the independent demesne in the damp and wooded river bottoms and that co-existing with peasant tenants on the mediocre but dry loams and moraines. These configurations match regional differences in the products of these properties.

Demesne production

Wise property managers produce whatever their resources best offer to effective demand. Woodland in Brodno brought the Trzebnica nuns ten marks a year and fisheries not seized by a local knight another five.[12] Elsewhere more intensive activities were pursued. The Wrocław Clares had a vineyard at Rędzin by 1287 and in 1370 bought another in *Szczepin* from the abbot of Henryków, while nobles and a citizen of Środa bought and sold one at Chwalimierz about the same time.[13] Just south of Wrocław the Corpus Christi Commandery had intensively-managed vegetable gardens in *Neudorf*.[14] Productive capital investments on demesne holdings included numerous water and a few wind mills, taverns, malt kilns, a woad mill, and near the city, a fulling mill and tile works.[15] Variety and ingenuity never ceased, but the overwhelming mass of demesne farms concentrated on the staples of cereal and animal husbandry.

Grain farming might, of course, be the a priori assumption for agricultural enterprises in this historical and ecological setting. What else were arable mansi for? Cereal production can, moreover, be verified for demesne farms in fifty-one settlements from reasonably explicit references dating between 1250 and the early 1430s. Livestock, perhaps less easily presumed, were demonstrably raised in forty-nine places. In all, such references identify demesne production in eighty different places (20 have evidence of both grains and stock), a quarter to a third of those known to have had direct exploitation properties during this period. The sample thus provided spreads well across the duchy and represents a full variety of landlords and a realistic division of managerial arrangements.[16] When localized as on Map 5.4 and viewed as an aggregate in Table 5.1, it demonstrates distinct fourteenth-century farming regions, reasonably consistent areas where a certain mix of product seems closely linked to particular resources and forms of management.

Available data confirm grain cultivation on demesne farms throughout the duchy, but more emphasis on it in some areas than others. These crops are verified in the great majority of places with recorded production on the

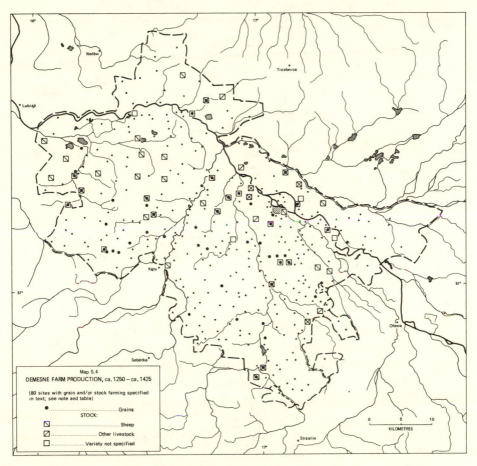

Map 5.4
DEMESNE FARM PRODUCTION, ca. 1250 – ca. 1425

(80 sites with grain and/or stock farming specified
in text; see note and table)

● .... Grains

STOCK:

◨ .... Sheep

◪ .... Other livestock

▢ .... Variety not specified

Note. For sources see *Notes to Maps and Figures.*

black earth (82 percent) and the loess (100 percent) but this frequency drops off slightly on the loam (62 percent) and markedly in the bottomlands (39 percent). Farms on the black earth but with significant bottomland resources (like Gądów Mały, Kozanów, or Borów) follow the latter rather than the former pattern. Those on the black earth were, as expected, chiefly independent demesnes, but those on the loam mostly lay in larger villages with peasant tenants.

Animal husbandry is better treated according to the kinds of beasts reared, but in general is recorded very often on bottomland demesnes (89 percent), at a more moderate level on the loam (65 percent), and less commonly on the black earth (36 percent). Sheep farming was the more widespread, but concentrated on the loam, where more than half of the farms were engaged in rearing more than half of the sheep anywhere documented.

Table 5.1. Sites of recorded production on demesne farms, ca. 1250–ca. 1425

| Soil types of sites | Grains | Livestock | | | | Total sites on soil type |
| | | all | Specific varieties mentioned | | Variety not specified | |
			sheep	other[a]		
Black earth	18	8	4	3	2	22
Black earth with bottomland	2	5	5	3		5
Bottomland	7	16	8	8	4	18
Loam or moraine	18	19	18	3		29
Loess	6	1		1		6
Total	51	49	35	18	6	80

Note. For sources see Map 5.4. Table 5.1 is not a contingency table because several sites have more than one product recorded.

[a] Cattle, horses, goats, or swine.

The others lived mostly in the bottomlands, while only a handful of black earth farms raised them. Again, most demesne sheep farming on the loam and moraine occurred in properties adjoining tenant neighbors—unlike the independent demesnes which prevailed in the lowlands. Cattle, horses, goats, and swine were uncommon on upland sites irrespective of soil. Some of the records which do exist are surely of draft animals alone.[17] In the bottomlands, however, almost half of the farms kept good-sized herds; almost two-thirds of the known such beasts appeared on the bare quarter of sites with lowland resources. There, too, were most of the sites where extra pastures, stock barns, or stored feed confirm animal husbandry but not the varieties kept.

In the fourteenth century, then, landlord agriculture showed aspects of regional specialization. On the fertile and well-drained black earth uplands surviving evidence argues for cereal monoculture on independent demesne farms, while the equally dry but less fertile loams and morainic soils held more mixed farming enterprises which raised sheep and grains beside a community of tenants. Direct exploitation in the bottomlands, usually on properties without peasant neighbors, de-emphasized cereal production to rear livestock, sheep and/or the cattle, horses, and hogs distinctive of this area alone. This general pattern, already very like that current here in the early nineteenth century,[18] provides a context for the particulars given by unusually rich records from certain properties.

Grain farms on the independent demesnes of the Wrocław district black earths had, at least to start, the advantage of efficiently consolidated arable. When William Zenicz, a Wrocław citizen, bought *Łukaszewice* in 1306 its ten and a quarter mansi were all "in one piece around the farmstead."[19] Although the notary Mathias combined two previous holdings in three parcels to establish his farm at Smardzów in 1281, he easily operated the ten or so mansi as one unit until after 1314.[20] In contrast, at Sulimów in 1361, where tenants had also farmed since at least 1357, the demesne land disputed between Helwig Molnsdorf and John Flamming seems from description in the arbitrater's award to have been divided into open field strips like that of the peasants.[21]

Explicit reference in the Sulimów award to equal parcels in "winter getreydis . . . , sommer getreydis . . . , vnd broche" verifies the three-course rotation suggested by the general situation and by the harvests actually recorded from these farms. Rye and barley predominate among incidental references to payments made from black earth demesnes,[22] but the much fuller financial accounts from the royal demesne at Borów in 1377–78 and the hospital property at Wysoka in the 1430s give few grounds for generalization. At Borów rye and barley did comprise most of the grain accounted by the administrator, John Nossen, to his superiors, the Wrocław city council, but unspecified amounts of oats were consumed on the farm itself.[23] The Wysoka records also seem less to treat as an enterprise the nine mansi farm than its account with the hospital business manager. Annual returns for all cereals, for spring and winter grains, and for specific varieties fluctuate too wildly to draw technical conclusions.[24] In any case, these demesnes on the best grain land in the duchy do seem less reliant on rye than were Polish royal demesnes and most peasant holdings.[25]

Demesne grain farms on the black earth possessed a full complement of the equipment required for effective operation. Hans Flamming's barn at Sulimów is described as a sturdy structure,[26] while the responsibilities accepted in 1410 by Canon Matzeo de Lamberto de Neapoli along with lifetime use of the chapter's demesne in Biestrzyków included upkeep and improvement of the walled tower and other buildings. Matzeo further received draft animals valued at ten marks, two carts, plows, and small tools worth another mark.[27] Draft animals were certainly among the more expensive items. Three horses bought for Wysoka in 1434/35 came to over five marks.[28] Although the main capital outlay on the Borów property in 1377 was for new and improved buildings, money had also to be found for plow parts and sickles.[29]

The fields of Borów were up on the black earth, but it also had extensive valley lands at the forks of the Ślęza. Sale of livestock products accounted for more than half of the cash incomes received in 1377. Most lucrative were the sheep, which brought 12mk for wool and 1mk 10gr for skins. Sale of horses yielded more than 10mk, while cattle products (calves, cows, hides and cheeses) and pigs returned a bit more than 4mk each.[30]

Stock raising which equaled or surpassed grain farming in importance characterized the bottomlands, although the relative emphasis on particular animals differed. On the city's holdings in Szczytniki the annual fees for pasturage in 1387 brought 9mk 18gr from cattle, 1mk 6gr from swine, and 1mk from goats, compared to a little more than 3mk for arable and more than 12mk for hay meadows.[31] In the 1430s the hospital property at Trestno produced butter, cheeses, veal, and pork plus some cereals, chiefly oats. Haying and raking were major expenses.[32] Herd sizes, ignored in the income accounts, are specified in eight demesne inventories dating from the 1260s through the 1360s. That from Gądów Mały, a farm belonging to the widow of a Wrocław magnate, is not atypical; her 1336 will disposed of two hundred sheep, twenty cows, four draft animals, and thirty hogs.[33] Sheep are most common and most numerous throughout; cattle and swine about equal in number but never totaling more than the sheep herd; and horses, despite the Borów accounts, rather rare and few. But pastoralism still left room for grain. The chapter's property at Polanowice in 1267 had a good supply of seed grain, while at Gajków almost a century later millet was grown.[34]

Lowland stock raisers took advantage of rough pasture and natural meadows to support their large herds. Lubiąż ran animals in woods near Rędzin, while in the later fourteenth century the nuns of Trzebnica thought worthwhile the forged attribution to Henry I of their claim to pasture cattle and horses on the forested alluvial sands around Golędzinów. They also thought too low the ten marks they got for waste pasture at Brodno.[35] Meadows could be even more valuable. A parcel of only seven jugera near Siechnice was in 1409 disputed between St. Mathias and three peasants from Św. Katarzyna. Claiming that the hospital had illegally detained this property for twenty-four years, the plaintiffs demanded damages of sixty-three marks for, "in the opinion of the community" each jugera yearly yielded three cartloads of hay or could be leased for eighteen groschen.[36]

Farmers whose drier sites lacked these lowland resources had either to acquire such lands elsewhere—like the sons of Peter Stengil who added to their arable in Łukaszowice a meadow over between the Oława and the Odra[37]—or to buy the needed feed—like the manager of Wysoka who in 1435 spent five marks for hay from Księże and Gajowice.[38] In winter, however, stall feeding on stored fodder, some of it even cultivated, was not uncommon. The Głogi farm in the late thirteenth century had cattle and hay barns, and fodder was stored at Uraz in 1403. The Borów horse herds ate locally grown oats, but those few used for draft purposes at Wysoka (not a bottomland farm) lived on oats shipped from Trestno.[39] Less suited for intensive grain cultivation than the upland sites, bottomland demesne farms had better access to resources for productive and technically advancing pastoralism.[40]

Because accounts and inventories do not survive from fourteenth-century demesne farms in the sheep-grain areas on the loam and moraine, their operation is not well documented. Reports of tithe taking procedures and disputes arising from them confirm cultivation practices like those on the black earth, and the many sales of annuities payable in rye argue for the preeminence of that grain over wheat.[41] Herds when numbered, compared in size with those in the bottomlands, but most references are only to a *pascus ovium* or *schafferey* appurtenant to the demesne.[42] But the resources that fed sheep on the loam differed from those in the lowlands, for they grazed less on natural waste or meadows (rare in this upland area) than on the fallow and stubble of the entire village. Thus a demesne of three mansi at Stabłowice sold by John of Neuss to Reinhard of Stabłowice in 1337 included free sheep pasturage rights on twenty-two mansi, while Peter Dammerow at Strachowice in 1370 ran the herd from his four mansi on another twelve as well.[43] Without enough land specially suited for pastoralism, lords in the good-sized villages of the loam captured some of the benefits of stock raising by exploiting in addition to their own arable that of their peasant tenants. When Henry V leased the old castle lands in Bielany outside Środa he promised that peasants were not to impede the demesne flocks.[44]

Large herds and extensive grain fields may suggest some major contributions by demesne farms to markets in agricultural produce, but only a handful of especially full accounts even hint at the disposition of production.[45] From Borów in 1377–78, besides livestock 120 measures of barley were sold each year, but wheat sales fell from 84 to 36 measures while rye climbed from nothing to 228. Only oats and some foodstuffs were consumed on the property.[46] From the hospital farms of Wysoka and Trestno during the 1430s, however, little was marketed. Of the 404.75 measures of grain accounted at Wysoka in 1434/35 (one of the best years), only 39.25 measures of wheat were sold. Most of the rest was kept for the hospital's use as grain or malt.[47] The difference probably derives from the dissimilar needs of an absentee royal government and a charitable corporation with mouths to feed. The more normal situation of an individual lay owner, knight or citizen, likely fell between these extremes, with some household consumption covered directly from these properties but other by sale of surplus production. Certainly the woad mill at Jakubowice in 1391 makes sense only if it processed more dyestuffs than those required by Jacob of Jacobsdorf or the purchaser, Katherine Karschow and her son, John.[48]

Labor

Who worked these good-sized enterprises? In the age of German law forced labor from ordinary peasant tenants was not available for serious production on the lord's account. Few thirteenth-century contracts for German law mentioned labor service and those only a couple of days a year for sowing or plowing. Later references are even more rare, three days plowing on the Clares' demesne at Pietrzykowice in 1329 and two on that at Jarosławice sold by John Brunonis the younger to St. Mary in 1336.[49] By 1405 the bishop of Lebus claimed no labor from his five properties in the duchy or from eight of the other ten he had in Silesia.[50] Nor could forced labor by small holders (*gertner*) take up the slack. Only from *Olbino* and Poświętne do fourteenth century Wrocław duchy records verify such obligations—for three and two days haying each year.[51] Hired labor thus predominated on demesne farms.

A permanent work force of servants (*famuli, gesinde*) probably carried out most routine tasks on most direct exploitation properties. Such people plowed and seeded the Wysoka demesne in 1433/34.[52] Otherwise their pay and status receive more mention than the work they did. *Famuli* at Borów earned at least nineteen groschen including drinks in 1377, while those at Trestno got bread made from a mixture of wheat and rye in 1434 and those at Wysoka a total of seven and a half marks in the following year.[53] These incidental references can only hint at the importance of hired hands, in part because the Holy Spirit Hospital maintained a separate *registrum famulorum* for servants on all its properties—itself clear evidence of their vital role.[54]

Gesinde worked for individual farm operators rather than being in any way tied to a property. Those of the Henry who took possession of a five mansi demesne at Sośnica in 1375 came under his jurisdiction, not the village lord's.[55] And in 1425 at least four *famuli* were entrusted with the responsible task of making the tax payments due from their employers' landholdings. Peter Kemmer, the only such servant there named, paid almost a mark for Ulrich Pak, and an anonymous *famulus* of George Seidlicz, castellan of Uraz, still more.[56] Trusted employees crucial to the ongoing operation of a demesne farm, full-time servants could be costly but still proved inadequate both for skilled tasks and for major seasonal labor needs, especially in grain production.

Employment of daily wage workers was therefore a marked and costly feature of demesne operations. Carpenters who made capital improvements at Borów received more than six marks and others at Wysoka more than seven. The Borów manager also hired a smith. Less skilled incidental tasks included hauling wood and earth and, at Trestno, ditching worth thirty-one marks in 1433/34 and more than six marks plus a food wage three years later. Nevertheless harvesting imposed the largest regular labor cost on the demesne farmer. Reaping at 1mk 17gr came to almost half the payments made at Borów for workers other than specialized craftsmen.[57] By the 1430s all costs had risen, but that for harvest labor remained relatively large, in 1434/35 totaling 26.5mk of the 48mk wage bill and 86 mark gross expenditures at Wysoka and 18.5 of an incomplete 21.5mk total at Trestno. The hospital's administrator paid 4gr per man day for reapers of rye and per jugera for those cutting oats,[58] but an appreciable portion of all wage bills went for food. About a dozen small holders from *Olbino*, who cut hay for three days in the royal meadows, received three and half marks cash, sixty small loaves, and a quantity of cheeses.[59] Added to the cash outlay for harvest at Trestno in 1436 were seventeen large loaves, six measures of flour, two sides of mutton, and six joints of beef.[60]

Some wage workers were employed but casually. Martin and his "socio," Rakche's son, Bartus, Mattheus, and Maczko put in about seventeen days between them on the Trestno property in 1436/37, earning as "laboratores" twenty heller a day.[61] Migrant laborers came from Poland in the late fourteenth century as well as in the better documented sixteenth.[62] Most important contributors to the labor supply of demesnes were, however, the *gertner*, small holders who supplemented their meager landed resources with regular wage work.

Gertner (*ortulani*) were common inhabitants of the duchy's countryside throughout the time here discussed. Thirty-five of the places entered in the 1425 tax account contained them, but that listing is certainly incomplete.[63] Nor is it wise to infer from their presence in *Olbino* alone among the many settlements cataloged by royal officials in 1353 that the group developed rapidly during the later fourteenth century. *Ortulani* lived at Piłczyce and Kozanów as early as 1208 and, like Wilczko, Peter, and Peter Wlossin at Siemidrożyce or Poscho at Strachowice, are known from a good dozen places by the mid-fourteenth century.[64] It looks, then, like gertner were a significant presence during the entire later Middle Ages.

Traditional interpretations of the gertners' economic position tie them closely to work on landlord farms. Sixteenth- through eighteenth-century distinctions between "free gertner," whose small hereditary holdings owed only money and a little service, and "threshing gertner," whose less secure tenures required harvest labor for a fixed customary share of the crop, are read back into the thirteenth and fourteenth centuries when neither the specific terms nor the sharp conceptual differences can be found. Free gertner then allegedly reflect German law norms at the small holder's scale, and threshing gertner persons and arrangements descended from earlier Polish direct exploitation properties.[65] Taken on their own terms, however, Wrocław duchy records of the fourteenth century support no such rigid classifications, but a broader grouping of small holdings, some but not all of which belonged to people who worked wherever needed as agricultural laborers.

The mere presence of an *ortus* or *garten* says nothing of the occupation of its holder, only that the parcel lay outside the main fields and their regulated routine.[66] Wrocław citizens and ecclesiastics had gardens before the city's walls, as did people from Środa around their little town.[67] Respected peasants like Paul, a vestryman from Miękinia, owned them, too.[68] Gertner in several villages just south of Wrocław where they comprised nearly the whole population by the later fourteenth century (*Leimgruben*, *Neudorf*, and Gajowice for certain, perhaps others), had already found the full time employment as intensive market gardeners that would later characterize them as *Kräuter*.[69] Others lived in more ordinary villages but where no demesne meant no jobs on it. Seventeen of the thirty-five settlements with gertner recorded in the 1425 tax return had then no demesne; ten of them had had none for fifty years or more.[70] Small holders had in the Wrocław duchy, then, no necessary connection with the labor needs of landlord farming.

So to clarify the structural position of fourteenth-century gertner (by pruning it of early modern anachronisms) is not to deny their extensive employment on demesne farms but to argue that, in view of the other opportunities open to small holders, demesne managers had no oligopsony on their labor. Nevertheless gertner did live and work on direct exploitations throughout this period. Six from Siemidrożyce, Jakubowice, and Sikorzyce who testified in 1329 at hearings on a tithe dispute ranged in age from about twenty-five to over sixty. Rogala, who remembered the 1268 canonization of St. Hedwig, had lived in his village from birth. Peter Propst, the youngest, told of working for the local priest at tithe collection time, while another Peter once drove his lord to Wrocław in a wagon.[71] Later reports lack both the human touch and the details of what tasks gertner actually performed, but repeatedly confirm their connection to demesne farms. Around mid-century eleven gertner pertained to the demesne of Witco of Schonfeld at Cesarzowice in the Środa district, and others to those of John Tute in Rościsławice and Jachinus in Sadowice.[72] In 1436/37 the Holy Spirit Hospital spent over four marks repairing two houses of gertner at Trestno. No doubt the residents received at least some of the twenty-one marks plus foodstuffs paid out in that same year for haying, reaping, cutting straw, and ditching.[73]

Administration

Thus far demesne farms, their production and labor supply have been treated without much regard for the locus of operational and strategic decisions and the account to which incomes were credited or losses assessed. This approach suited the lack of demonstrable differences in agricultural practice among landowning groups, but from each lord's perspective the choice between direct exploitation and leasing a property to a different operator had considerable import. Was he to bear the risks and costs of farming for the sake of unsteady returns in kind or on the market or to avoid them and settle for fixed incomes? Variations on each response fit the differing needs and changing economic environment of Wrocław duchy landlords.

All sorts of landowners continually exploited their demesne lands themselves. The three mansi reserved by Canon John at Rzeplin in 1253–54 were by 1262 managed directly by the chapter's procurator; later on individual canons took particular properties under their personal supervision.[74] The old knight Paschco ran his own holdings in Siemidrożyce in the 1320s, while Nicholas Rempel's supervision of workmen at Ratyń in 1423 indicates that even the greatest of urban magnates occasionally did so too.[75] The account books from Borów in 1377 and Wysoka and Trestno in the 1430s were also those of landlord farmers, the city council as vice-captain for the king and the Holy Spirit Hospital.

Of course few landowners could devote their full attention to running a farm, so they entrusted day to day operation to a *colonus* (*hofeman*) and, if the scale of their properties so warranted, more general supervision to an *advocatus* (*vogt*) or other estate manager. Paschco of Siemidrożyce had *coloni* named Michael and Clement and an *advocatus*, Jan Duczman.[76] Bartus Flach, *colonus* at Trestno, regularly appears in the accounts, handling some operating expenses from the farm's resources and paying to the hospital the produce it needed.[77] At least at Borów, these were salaried employees, the *advocatus* getting 8mk 32gr, the *colonus* almost as much cash plus two cattle worth 38gr; all these payments moreover, were handled by John Nossen, the town councilor made responsible for this property.[78] A lord who ran a demesne on his own account could further choose to manage for market sales or household consumption.

Leasing was an equally common strategy for acquiring income from demesne holdings, one which in varying degrees sacrificed some returns and flexibility for reduced risk and expenses. Relatively short limited-term leases preserved many of direct exploitation's advantages while avoiding labor and other operational costs, so many used them. The three mansi, "leftovers," farmstead, and stock in Lubnów owned by John, son of John Cnuso, went in 1336 at seventeen marks for three years to Nicholas of Radecz, while some twenty years later the Lübeck family's property at Borek brought thirty-nine marks on lease to Conrad and Nicholas Rorich.[79] Terms ranged from the landowner's pleasure or annual up to ten years and the lessee accepted responsibility for production and upkeep. Few lessees are identifiable. To judge from the rare informative instances, a landlord's return on arable put out at short-term lease approximated that from normal peasant tenancies—around a mark per mansus per year in the mid-fourteenth century.[80] Of course use of the owner's equipment, buildings, and stock gave him an effectively lower return on capital value, but then again possible adjustments for each new lease were an advantage ruled out when peasant tenants had hereditary rights.

Life leases played a limited role, less designed for "economic" exploitation of demesne holdings than were the short term arrangements. Ecclesiastical lords, notably the bishop and cathedral chapter, used lifetime tenures to assign corporate resources to the support and/or management of individual members or employees. Arrangements for Kozanów in 1321 are a useful case in point. An episcopal property, the demesne here had recently been recovered from hereditary lay lessees and the full sublordship given to the chapter. Under the terms of the gift the chapter was to entrust Kozanów for life to a selected canon, who would operate the farm and use the surplus incomes to support poor clerks. He was further to maintain the inventory and equipment of the demesne and (another sign of the special value of bottomland resources) sell off no timber, using it only for upkeep of the property.[81]

Life leases also rewarded useful contacts and loyal employees while retaining title to the farm so granted. Peter, protonotary of Wrocław, received from the Clares in 1287 demesne lands between Osobowice and Rędzin to hold for life "iure locationis" in return for an annual rent of three marks silver and two large measures of wine. He, too, had to maintain the inventory, which would all revert to the convent at his death. In the early 1420s Wolff, *advocatus* of the episcopal household in Wrocław, had like rights over three mansi of the bishop at Biskupice Podgórne.[82]

Hereditary "leases," also sometimes called "sales" (by sellers who retained rights) or "fiefs" (which paid rents), much outnumber in the extant record other leasehold arrangements. The owner of the demesne all but alienated his property in return for a large sum of money, retaining only a low rent, investiture, first refusal, and repurchase rights, but permitting the newly created sublord full powers to alienate, divide, sublet, and pass on the property to his heirs. Because his church was in financial difficulties in 1291, Bishop Thomas II "sold" his demesne farm at Piłczyce to Werner and Lodoycus Pannewicz in this way for ten marks a mansus. The purchasers owed each year rent of a quarter mark per mansus, whether cultivated or not, and tithes to the church of All Saints, which provisions remained in force whether they chose to put the property out to German law peasants or to retain it as a single farm.[83] The latter choice prevailed. Still an *allodium*, Piłczyce passed by inheritance and sales through at least three successive lay families before the last sold it, now partly out to tenants, in 1360 to the Corpus Christi Commandery. After the Hospitallers agreed to accept the arrangements of 1291 and be episcopal "vassals," Bishop Przesław confirmed their possession as the perpetual "fief" it had long been and reaffirmed his right to buy them out for their cost plus the value of any improvements. Such arrangements continued into the sixteenth century.[84] Other ecclesiastical and especially episcopal demesnes were during the late thirteenth and early fourteenth centuries handled in much the same way. When the cathedral chapter bought up Gądów Mały in 1370–71 and Nowa Wieś Wrocławska between 1391 and 1393, it extinguished generations-old lay sublordships that had begun well before either property had been converted from a demesne farm to German law tenancies.[85]

During the late 1200s and early 1300s lords who established hereditary leaseholders on their demesnes clearly sacrificed long- for short-term returns. Initial prices were reasonably high. St. Vincent got about eleven marks the mansus for Księże Wielkie in 1274, the Kamieniec Cistercians around thirteen and a quarter for Mokry Dwor in 1286, and St. Mary a whopping thirty-five and a third for Muchobór Mały in 1311, all values quite comparable with those contemporaries were paying for demesne land bought outright.[86] Having thus paid well for their holdings, the lessees offered little indeed in annual rents to their overlords. The eighth mark, fifth mark, and quarter mark per mansus from Księże, Zagródki, and Muchobór fell at or below the returns other owners were then getting from arable out to peasant tenants.[87] Even worse from the owner's point of view, hereditary leases froze revenues from demesne properties at what became by the mid-fourteenth century laughably low levels. The annual one-ninth mark per mansus received by Kamieniec from Mokry Dwór in 1286 was then fairly small; it was ludicrous when confirmed a hundred years later.[88] Such worthless incomes could easily be neglected and the demesne farm, like that of St.

Mary at *Neudorf*, pass imperceptibly into the unencumbered possession of the lessee.[89]

The lessees, most of them Wrocław citizens, benefited greatly; the owners, most of them churches, lost. Why then did abbots and bishops put out their holdings in this way? Echoing Bishop Thomas, abbot William of St. Vincent and abbot Philip of St. Mary each justified his "sale" to a townsman of Księże and of Muchobór by specific reference to the financial need of his corporation.[90] The hereditary lease functioned, then, to conceal or at least to legitimize the effective alienation of mortmain property by hard-pressed ecclesiastics.

From the mid-fourteenth century, however, owners of demesne farms began to treat hereditary leases as long-term economic strategies for property management. Examples are few, but rent levels now seem more closely aligned with those demanded of other sorts of tenants, while grain components also helped the landlord maintain the value of his incomes in an age of debasement. To hold the seven mansi demesne of *Cruce* from the cathedral chapter "in emphiteosim perpetuam" in 1344 Nicholas Sittin was to pay each year ten marks cash, nine "stones" of wax, and, like some earlier lessees, the tenth sheaf from the field.[91] St. Mary, itself the hereditary lessee of Zagródki from the bishop under terms dating back to 1295, leased it out in 1376 for two marks and a chicken from each of the six mansi there,[92] a rate four times that the abbey owed to the bishop and, like others then, well in accord with those received from German law tenants. Relic leases established in an earlier generation may still have prevented realistic returns from some properties, but the hereditary lease appears after the 1340s to have been a legitimate option to escape entirely the costs of demesne farming without going so far as to break up a good-sized holding among peasant tenants. Since it did, however, remove all flexibility in administration and severely hinder regular adjustment to changing coin and commodity values, the hereditary lease still represented for the landowner the largest withdrawal from demesne agriculture short of abandonment itself. The lessee, whether holding under this or some other arrangement, was nevertheless a demesne farmer, who indicated by his or her very action the continuing value imputed to good-sized direct exploitations.

The value of demesne properties

Properties in demesne were considerable assets for landowners, whether viewed as sources of revenue or potential objects for sale. Returns on leases provide one measure of their relative worth. With the exception of those hereditary leases from the 1270s to 1330s which really concealed alienations, annual rates were usually about like those from the owners' ultimate alternative, peasant tenancies.

Most to be desired, of course, is information on the actual value of demesne production in a settlement or on a lord's estate where it may be compared with incomes from tenancies.[93] Even the best evidence from the Duchy of Wrocław fails in this regard. For Borów, the fullest account, no size is ever recorded. Receipts were certainly considerable, 54mk 38gr specified in 1377, almost 63mk in the summary totals for 1378.[94] But 1377 was a year of major capital improvement on this farm and total expenditures of 64mk 37gr 2hl meant a loss on annual account of 10mk 10hl (about 15 percent of costs). When monies listed as spent on improvements are removed, however, "normal" expenditures come to some 38mk and incomes exceed expenses by around 17mk (about 45 percent). This figure approximates the contemporary return on 170mk invested in annuities or the rentals from ten peasant mansi at the then average level of about 1.5mk (in cash and grain).[95]

Because production from Trestno and Wysoka was used in the 1430s for direct consumption at a time of rural anarchy and unstable prices, the Holy Spirit Hospital never valued it in monetary terms. Quantities of produce could be large but varied greatly and, even with what look like incomplete expenditure accounts, cost an appreciable amount. The nine mansi at Wysoka yielded from 64 to 737 measures of grain in different years. Trestno's four and a half mansi gave in 1434 meat, dairy products, and 186 measures of grain for about 42 marks expenditure (including some improvements), but only 84 measures and the other items when more than 22 marks were spent just on harvesting the very next year.[96] The significant quantity of demesne produce is plain, its profitability relative both to production costs and to the opportunity cost of tenancies foregone, more ambiguous.

The land market, already active by the mid-thirteenth century, supplied perhaps the best measure of the continuing, though changing, value placed by Wrocław duchy landlords on demesne farms. Per mansus prices from eighty-eight sales of demesne arable in forty-four different places between 1260 and 1431 are summarized in both nominal and silver terms on Figure 5.1.[97]

Leaving for the next chapter the matter of value relative to rental lands, variations over time in that of demesne land are fully evident. Whereas demesne mansi went for around twenty marks in the decades before 1300 (and may have been drifting higher, too), the first third of the fourteenth century, especially the 1310s, showed a major surge. Henry Doring paid fifty marks royal groschen per mansus for Samotwór in 1313,[98] a value (nominal or silver) twice that known for any sale before the turn of the century and

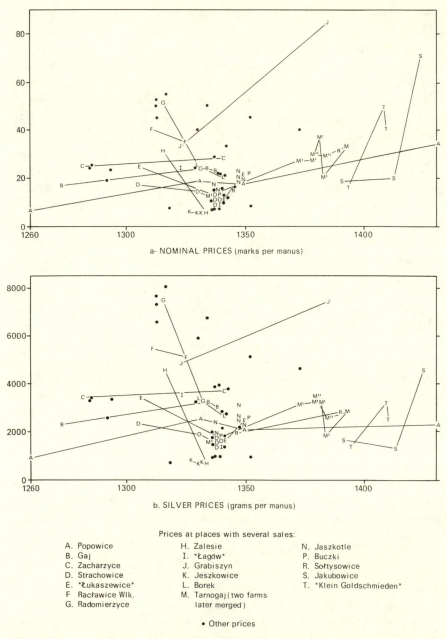

Figure 5.1
DEMESNE LAND PRICES, 1260-1431
(88 sales in 44 places)

a- NOMINAL PRICES (marks per manus)

b. SILVER PRICES (grams per manus)

Prices at places with several sales:

A. Popowice	H. Zalesie	N. Jaszkotle
B. Gaj	I. *Łagów*	P. Buczki
C. Zacharzyce	J. Grabiszyn	R. Sołtysowice
D. Strachowice	K. Jeszkowice	S. Jakubowice
E. *Łukaszewice*	L. Borek	T. *Klein Goldschmieden*
F Racławice Wlk.	M. Tarnogaj (two farms	
G. Radomierzyce	later merged)	

• Other prices

Note. For sources see *Notes to Maps and Figures.*

exceeded by only two prices known after 1320, but itself not unusual in the decade when it was tendered. The subsequent retreat from these levels, fully depicted on the figure, is exemplified in six successive sales at Strachowice. Although 3.5 mansi had gone for 17.2mk each in 1305, 7 more brought only 14.3mk in 1330 and four sales in 1338–39 which covered a total of 4 mansi (2, 1.25, and two sales of the same 0.75 mansus) ran between 10 and 12 marks and averaged 11.[99] The drop well exceeded changes in the circulating coinage and returned the price of demesne land to levels not far from those of a generation or more earlier.

Records of prices for demesne land become dangerously sparse after mid-century, but repeated instances from the same properties do seem to suggest a nominal increase that stayed barely but perceptibly in advance of the decaying currency. One farm at Tarnogaj that had gone for 12.3 marks (1659 grams silver) per mansus in 1336 doubled its value to 27.2 marks (3135 grams) by 1373. Debasements in the following generation, however, held its silver value to the same or even lower levels despite nominal prices that went over 30 marks a mansus in 1382 and 1393. Another farm here followed a like pattern, but larger nominal increases at Jakubowice or Popowice, for instance, did allow for real price growth.

Demesne land prices soared to a peak between 1310 and 1320 from which the next two decades saw an accelerating fall to a new low by the 1340s. Thereafter they rose slowly in approximate counterpoint to the debasement of the groschen. These fluctuations, notably the distinctive character of the first third of the fourteenth century, should recall like peculiarities in the rhythm of the German law movement. They begin to become more understandable if, the nature and continuing importance of demesne farming in the duchy having been established, the focus now shifts to the interaction between demesne and tenancy in the full context of agricultural conditions from the late thirteenth century to the Hussite wars.

§§ 6 §§

DEMESNE, TENANCY, AND AGRICULTURAL CONDITIONS IN A LONG FOURTEENTH CENTURY, CA. 1300 – CA. 1425

> Bresa habet 45 mansos, quorum plebanus habet 3, ad allodium pertinent 18, scultetus 5, censuales 19.
>> Brzezina in the 1353 survey for Charles IV; *LB* #205.
>
> Bresa 30 mansi censuales. Item 4 mansi in allodio ibidem. Landisloth presentavit 17 grossos.
>> Brzezina in the 1425 tax return; RB, fol. 11r.

After the canons of St. Mary consolidated their lordship over the old Polish settlement at Tyniec Mały by acquiring the tithes and a part of the adjoining *Milino*, in the 1220s they "modernized" it with the first grant of German law still surviving from the later Wrocław duchy. For a century Tyniec remained a German law village of St. Mary and the rest of *Milino* a complex of small demesne farms owned and operated by knights and Wrocław citizens.[1] Then in the 1330s Abbot Conrad (1329–63) bought out these holders and merged *Milino* as a demesne farm to Tyniec. What had in 1337 been his "allodium Tynczia penes prope parvam Tyncziam" was in the 1353 fiscal survey assessed at fourteen of the forty-eight mansi in the village.[2]

Shortly after the survey Abbot Conrad gave the abbey's demesne at Tyniec on a life lease to his uncle, Nicholas Falkenberg. But Falkenberg failed to meet the terms of his tenure, so a later abbot, John of Prague (1375–81), redeemed the holding for the abbey and invested in new construction there. As late as 1414, when the abbot's enemies in a feud destroyed the property and kidnaped the *advocatus*, St. Mary still farmed the demesne.[3]

Those damages may have convinced the next abbot, Mathias Hering (1416–29), of the risks of farming in an increasingly unsettled age, or perhaps he calculated the relative value of demesne products against tenant rents, but his decision to withdraw from direct exploitation at Tyniec was ascribed in the later tradition of the canons to Polonophilia and financial irresponsibility. As their chronicle put it, "this lord abbot Mathias also put out the demesne in Tyniec Mały as peasant holdings for certain Polish rustics at a fixed yearly rent in cash and grain. These built a little hamlet there, which the brothers ironically called Matczkendorf, and paid neither the inheritance money nor the annual rents. Even after an agreement was made about this, they observed it very little."[4] But defaulting on rents was around 1430 in no way confined to the Polish peasants of Tyniec, so this and Abbot Jodocus's subsequent restoration of the demesne belong to a later story, not to the long fourteenth century.

Management of holdings at Tyniec Mały by successive abbots of St. Mary illustrates in its general course and several specifics long- and short-term tendencies in the agrarian development of the duchy from the late thirteenth century to the eve of the Hussite wars. Note in particular the extension (or maybe even creation) of a large demesne farm in the 1330s, the shifting choice between direct and leasehold operation, and the final attempt by the lord fully to leave farming. This well-recorded property and village thus draws attention to some dominant themes of a long fourteenth century—a retreat from demesne cultivation and the competitive value of tenant farming—and to briefer phases in their impact. The phenomena are set out in the first half of this chapter. They acquire historical significance in their economic context of demographic and market conditions, treated in the third section of this chapter. Putting all together results in reconstructive explanation of the changing conditions of agriculture. Although growth and development continually evident in the thirteenth century gave way to certain difficulties soon after 1300, in the Wrocław duchy expansiveness returned before 1350 and tailed off but gradually after the first local experience of epidemics in the 1360s. By the early 1400s the countryside still showed none of the symptoms of crisis or depression which then so typified much of the West and some other regions of east-central Europe, like Brandenburg.[5]

The retreat from demesne

Data used in Chapter 5 to demonstrate the continuing quantitative importance of demesne farms in the duchy's fourteenth century settlements also showed a decline in their relative and absolute frequency. Of the 234 places known in 1300 more than three-fourths (193 = 78 percent) contained demesne and little more than half (131 = 57 percent) tenancies. The more full list of mid-century showed rather little change. But by 1425 demesnes were

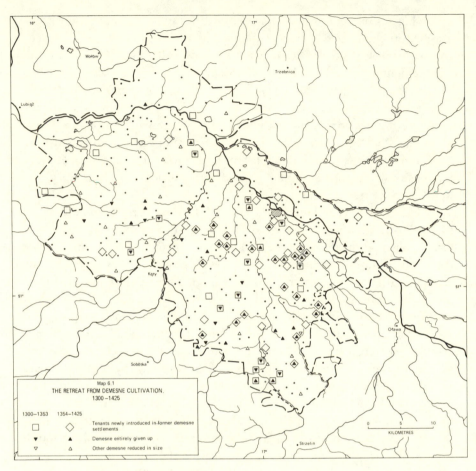

Map 6.1
THE RETREAT FROM DEMESNE CULTIVATION.
1300 – 1425

1300–1353	1354–1425	
□	◇	Tenants newly introduced in former demesne settlements
▼	▲	Demesne entirely given up
▽	△	Other demesne reduced in size

Note. For sources see *Notes to Maps and Figures*.

to be found in only two-thirds of the duchy's settlements, just about as many as had peasant tenants.[6] The amount of land in demesne also dropped, probably from one mansus in three of the duchy's arable in the first half of the fourteenth century to one in four or five by the first quarter of the fifteenth.

Chapter 5 concerned surviving demesnes; this section looks at the others, those reduced in size or wholly transferred to tenant farmers between 1300 and 1425. One or both verifiably occurred in the 122 places shown on Map 6.1. The appearance of this evidence in time is more precisely presented in Figure 6.1. Lords thus demonstrably withdrew in whole or part from direct exploitation in about one-third of the duchy's rural settlements. This shrank or eliminated by 1425 some 40 percent of the demesne farms which had existed a century or so before.[7] But this general retreat from

Figure 6.1
THE RETREAT FROM DEMESNE CULTIVATION, 1300-1425

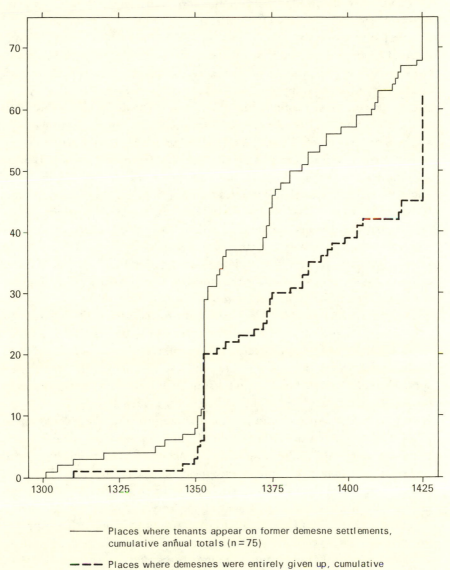

———— Places where tenants appear on former demesne settlements,
cumulative annual totals (n = 75)

— — — Places where demesnes were entirely given up, cumulative
annual totals (n = 62)

demesne was accentuated by and characteristic of particular periods, regions, productive specialities, and landlord groups.

Demesne cultivation was abandoned most fully where it had once been most common, on the old-settled black earths of the Wrocław district, and most rapidly during the middle and later years of the fourteenth century. Around 1300 the demesne farms present across the duchy were especially thick on the good soils south of Wrocław. During the next half century (to 1353) peasant tenants appeared on twenty-nine former demesnes, while twenty of these passed entirely into their hands. This happened, moreover, to the same temporal rhythm already seen in the German law movement and in the behavior of demesne land prices, which set off the first third or so of the century from earlier and later periods (Figure 6.1). On only four sites did tenants replace demesne holdings before the mid-1330s and only one demesne farm entirely disappeared during this time. Between 1337 and compilation of the 1353 fiscal survey, however, seven sites gained previously unknown tenants and five lost their former demesnes. The years 1350–52 alone bring twice as many new tenant communities as any decade since 1300. Then the survey itself introduces another eighteen sets of *mansi censuales* and eliminates *allodia* from another fourteen sites. On Map 6.1 changes up to 1353 are especially common around the forks of the Ślęza and on the more recently settled black earth just to the north. Elsewhere they occur in approximate proportion to the density of settlement.

The survey of 1353, however, caught a rural economy in unusual flux. By the end of the decade seven places which were demesnes in the original survey had newly added tenants, while one such landlord farm was entirely broken up. In all and even without the survey evidence, more new tenant communities (11) appeared and more demesnes (5) were surrendered in the 1350s than in any but one other decade from 1300 to 1419. The exception is equally remarkable. After a notable decline in such activities during the 1360s (no new tenant communities appear between 1360 and 1372), the 1370s brought a resurgence that matched the 1350s in both indicators and ushered in continued conversion of demesne lands and farms which tapered off only a little by the 1420s. Finally the tax roll of 1425 and other supporting evidence add seven more previously unknown tenant groups, eliminate seventeen previously documented demesne sites, and, by comparison with entries for 1353, reveal a reduction in size of another twenty-three surviving demesnes. In all, tenants were introduced on forty-six sites and demesnes entirely given up on forty-two sites between the survey of 1353 and the mid-1420s.

Spatial distribution of these events after 1353 approximated that of demesne farms then, but that meant especial concentration in the Wrocław district black earths. Within a bare two kilometer radius of Iwiny, for instance, tenants appeared on no less than seven of the ten sites then inhabited. Whereas only Smardzów had been converted (shortly) before 1353, by 1425 old demesnes in Bienkowice, Solniki, Zacharzyce, Iwiny, and Radomierzyce were totally in tenant hands, those in Żerniki Wrocławskie and Jagodno had been cut back, and only *Kaldenhusen* and *Oldrzewie Małe* remained untouched. In contrast, of the twenty sites in the Uraz district, fourteen had demesne lands in 1353 and by 1425 only in Kręsko were they gone, only in Pęgów visibly reduced.

To summarize the evidence from Figure 6.1 and Map 6.1, during the long fourteenth century landlords withdrew from demesne farming most rapidly between 1340 and 1360 and again after 1370, but much less before the 1330s and during the 1360s. They did this the most on the Wrocław district black earths, first in the south, then further north. The least change seems to have been on the Środa loams and northward through the Odra bottomlands into the moraines north of Uraz.

The regional features of places where lords got out of direct exploitation recall those established in Chapter 5 for demesne production. (Cereal monoculture in independent demesne farms characterized the black earth, mixed grain and sheep raising demesnes in larger villages the loam and moraine, and pastoralism the independent demesnes of the bottomlands.) The inference that demesnes which had concentrated on grain farming were those most given up is supported by a further look at the same eighty properties which gave the production information. Table 6.1 summarizes the fate of those farms.

Cross tabulation in Table 6.1 of production types and the histories of the properties does show disproportionately high association between grain growing and the abandonment of demesne. Although the sites of cereal monoculture made up but 39 percent of the sample ($31/80$), they were 58 percent ($11/19$) of the places where demesne cultivation ceased entirely. Conversely, sites where pastoralism alone is known, only 36 percent ($29/80$) of the sample, were 45 percent ($19/42$) of those demesnes which survived unchanged to 1425. As might be expected, mixed farming took an intermediate position; more than either of the more specialized forms, these places were scaled down in size but not abandoned. Viewed another way, of the almost half (47.5 percent) of these properties where demesne production was reduced (in part or entirely), more raised grain ($28/38 = 75$ percent) than animals ($22/38 = 59$ percent), while on the three quarters (76 percent) where at least some demesne lasted through 1425 (even if less than formerly), stock raisers ($41/61 = 67$ percent) outnumbered cereal farmers ($36/61 = 59$ percent) by a similar margin. Withdrawal in whole or in part from demesne culti-

Table 6.1. Production and the retreat from demesne:
80 sites with recorded demesne production

	Grain only	Mixed farming	Stock only	Total
No demonstrable change in demesne	15	8	19	42
Demesne reduced but not abandoned	5	8	6	19
Demesne cultivation abandoned	11	4	4	19
Totals	31	20	29	80

Note. The 80 sites are those shown on Map 5.4 and discussed pp. 98–100. Those where demesne was cut back between 1300 and 1425 appear on Map 6.1. Two more are here added to the category of abandoned demesnes: Rzeplin, where the demesne farm of the 1250s and 1260s disappeared later in the thirteenth century (*LB* #142); *Cesarzów*, merged with Zabrodzie a century later (RF, IV, 3038 and 3077–3083).

As a contingency table that cross tabulates the production and history of the 80 sites, Table 6.1 can be tested to assess the statistical likelihood that the two variables are mutually independent. It yields a chi-square of 7.790 as compared to a critical value of 7.77944 at 4 degrees of freedom and an alpha of 0.1. The probability is, therefore, better than 90% that production and the later history of a demesne are related variables.

vation was, therefore, significantly but not exclusively from grain production, especially that practiced as monoculture on the independent demesne farms of the Wrocław district black earth plains.

Of course location, resources, and production speciality were no more than conditions for a managerial decision to discontinue direct exploitation. Landlords themselves had to make it. Some groups participated more than others in this progressive withdrawal from agricultural production. Table 6.2 classifies the holders of lordships in the 98 sites where a change of settlement type most precisely dates the movement out of demesne. Ecclesiastics and Wrocław citizens were responsible for most introductions of tenants and most terminations of demesne farms. Often, as at Gądów Mały in 1353 where Nicholas of Nysa held under the bishop and Trzebnica, they collaborated in such endeavors.[8] The large role of churchmen, however, may reflect more their numbers among the local landowning elite than any special interest and opportunity to stop demesne farming. What they did was not incommensurate with how much land they then had. But townspeople, who at this time were just carving out their lordships, did take properties out of demesne more than their share of land might predict. Whereas in the early 1300s almost nine of their holdings in ten contained some demesne lands and only one in five lands out to tenants, by the eve of the Hussite wars they took rents from tenants on about four-fifths of their properties and operated on their own account on little more than half.[9] The nobility, in contrast, showed rather less inclination to give up their own farms and

Table 6.2. Landlord groups and the retreat from demesne

	Ecclesiastical corporations	Knights	Wrocław citizens	Others and unclassified
Tenants introduced under: (75 places)	26 (35%)	14 (19%)	30 (40%)	11 (15%)
Demesne cultivation stopped under: (62 places)	27 (44%)	12 (19%)	26 (42%)	7 (11%)
For comparison: percent of settlements where the group owned land in:				
1300	42	17	12	11
1353	35	37	25	15
1425	34	22	28	11
average of years shown	37	25	22	12

Note. The table includes only the places where tenants appeared or demesne disappeared between 1300 and 1425 (Map 6.1) because information about those where demesnes were reduced in size between two surveys is too imprecise to attribute it to a particular lord. Sublords are, however, included. Comparative statistics on lordship are from Appendix A, Table A.1, rows 7, 10, 13, and 16.

live from rents alone. Although they participated in about a fifth of the conversions away from demesne, they owned on average a good quarter of the lordships in the duchy. Citizens, then, participated most enthusiastically in the long-term shift away from demesne cultivation, the churchmen about in accord with their share in lordships overall, and the knightly families trailed.

Few other detectable consistencies mark landowners who moved out of demesne cultivation. The Church of Wrocław, largest lord in the duchy, cut back its operations on the most sites (13, all during or after the 1350s), but other important corporations behaved differently. Those demesnes of a St. Mary or St. Vincent, for example, which had survived the thirteenth-century enthusiasm for German law reforms remained in operation through the next century and a quarter or, in rare instances like Księże Wielkie, became villages only in the early fifteenth century. Of the major ecclesiastical landholders, only Lubiąż cut back demesnes on more than two sites. Its shutdown of granges at Bartoszowa, Pisarzowice, and Wilkszyn, all but complete by 1353, pertained, however, less to precocious participation in a fourteenth century move away from direct exploitation than to the end of the old Cistercian economy on distant and isolated properties.[10] Relatively more active were the lesser and more locally-oriented younger houses. In the 1350s two successive masters of St. Mathias hospital installed tenants at Siechnice, Boguszyce, and Mokronos Górny and closed down demesne farms at the latter two and Dobrzykowice.[11] Citizens also terminated their own farms most actively in the 1350s, 1370s, and 1410s; none verifiably did so before 1353. These represented a good cross-section of the urban oligarchy, including already-wealthy merchants like the Stengel, the upwardly mobile Dompnig, who in two generations rose from simple furriers to recipients of a noble patent from Charles IV, and the taverner, Peter Roster called Mühlschreiber, sole bearer of that name ever on the city council.[12]

Noble landlords had not only less interest in leaving demesne farming, those who did so were out of step. Most tenants introduced under such owners had appeared by 1353. Otherwise they, too, seem fairly representative of their class. Names like Schellendorf, Hugowicz, Siedlicz, Borsnicz, and Radak were those of major landowners and politicians, but the Nebilschütz, Jesir, and Dirsdorf families had little wealth and influence. With landowners, then, as with location and productive speciality, certain quantitative characteristics of the movement out of direct exploitation coexisted with variety reflective of the general situation in the duchy.

Statistical association between a decline in demesne farming and black earth sites, grain monoculture, and citizen ownership provides no adequate explanation of this long term shift in agricultural organization. For one thing, the three variables thus suggested as independent were themselves closely linked; cereal production centered on the fertile black earth and townsmen first and most extensively acquired properties there, close to the city. Then, too, exceptions to the general patterns affirm that no single set of conditions determined change in property management.[13] Individual landowners had to weigh their demesne operation against their own economic (and social) goals, its efficiency in meeting these, and its performance relative to what might be predicted from those alternatives they could conceive. Was rural property to yield goods for domestic use or a monetary income? Were liquid incomes better assured by sale of demesne produce, sale of rents in kind, or money dues? How did the foreseeable yield from a demesne farm compare to the costs of production (however operationally defined)? Did this profit margin differ from that predictable from tenants? Were prospective tenants available? Sadly but not at all surprisingly, these central parameters of landlord decision making remain entirely concealed. They are an unknowable center of values and motives which can be but inferred from the known externals of presumably relevant preconditions and eventual results. That many demesnes proved marginal in the fourteenth century, especially in the 1350s and after 1370, has been demonstrated. That these were lands of marginal fertility is unlikely: the black earth was the best soil in the duchy; it remained densely inhabited; and the poor and last-settled Uraz uplands were least affected by withdrawal from demesne. Hence further understanding requires a shift of focus from the demesne to the more successful competitor, tenant farming. What values and returns did that have for lords and what conditions did these imply for peasants?

The value of tenancies

Sale prices were one indicator of the value lords put on demesne property. The same information for land out to tenants is slightly less common, but offers suggestive points of comparison with the serial data already seen. In the same format as used for prices of demesne land, Figure 6.2 displays nominal and silver values paid between landlords in 51 sales of tenant-held rental mansi located in 32 different villages between the mid-thirteenth century and the coming of the Hussites.

Consider first the temporal pattern suggested by this evidence. Up to about 1300 a mansus with tenants seems normally to have brought ten to fifteen marks; silver prices averaged about 1800 grams. The trend was at most slowly upward or at least stable. But the first two decades or so of the new century show a perceptible slip. Rental mansi then often brought ten or fewer marks and only 1500 or less grams of the monetary metal so that the 1310s mark a distinct nadir in the long-term movement of these prices. Then an upward advance resumed, especially in nominal values. By the 1340s and 1350s prices in the fifteen to twenty mark range were not uncommon and a generation or so later the normal level may have pushed over twenty marks. Debasement much moderated the silver so conveyed. Although the many sales of the 1320s and 1330s averaged about 1600 grams and those around mid-century about 1700, the greater numbers of coins given later held no more specie. In real price terms, then, the value of rental mansi seems to have peaked by about 1300, dropped through the first quarter of the century, risen to almost its old maximum through the 1350s, and leveled off over the next several decades.

Compare these rental land prices with those for demesne land (Figure 5.1). A perfunctory glance at the two graphs spots the higher and more volatile prices of demesne land. Whereas less than a third ($26/87$ = 30 percent) of the demesne sales brought less than 2000 grams of silver per mansus, a bare quarter ($13/51$ = 26 percent) of the sales of tenant mansi ever topped this level. At their lowest in the 1310s and 1320s tenant lands still brought a good 80 percent of their peak values; demesne prices of the 1330s and 1340s, however, averaged less than half what they had in the previous two decades. Lordship over tenants meant control over less expensive but more stable resources.

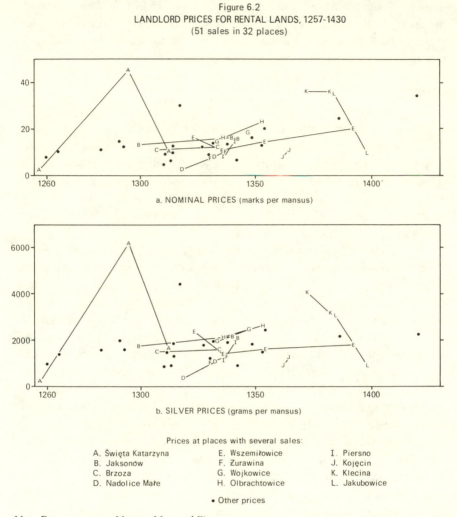

Figure 6.2
LANDLORD PRICES FOR RENTAL LANDS, 1257-1430
(51 sales in 32 places)

a. NOMINAL PRICES (marks per mansus)

b. SILVER PRICES (grams per mansus)

Prices at places with several sales:

A. Święta Katarzyna	E. Wszemiłowice	I. Piersno
B. Jaksonów	F. Żurawina	J. Kojęcin
C. Brzoza	G. Wojkowice	K. Klecina
D. Nadolice Małe	H. Olbrachtowice	L. Jakubowice

• Other prices

Note. For sources see *Notes to Maps and Figures.*

But closer examination reveals differences in the behavior over time of the two price series. Especially during the first half of the fourteenth century, when the data are most complete and the fluctuations most pronounced, they vary inversely with one another. In the first couple of decades after 1300 demesne land prices moved to an all-time peak while rental lands sank to the lowest levels known. Then in the 1330s they reversed directions. By mid-century a new relationship had tenant-held lands steadily increasing in value and demesne holdings at or near the lowest point of their curve. The data are inadequate to confirm a precise relative chronology, but it does look as if the upturn of rental land prices predated 1330 and thus began slightly before the collapse of the others. After the 1350s a different rhythm seems to take over. Both series (now approaching a limit of insufficient evidence) moved more slowly, adjusted in approximate unison to the decaying currency, and maintained a barely upward if not stable trend.

The graphs of both price series resemble those for the retreat from demesne (Figure 6.1) and for the German law (Figures 4.1 and 4.2). For almost a century the shared rhythms are plain. When demesne prices were relatively low and rental land prices relatively high, both conversion of demesne to tenancies and creation of new German law villages were common, reaching peaks in their own curves. These were the conditions of the late thirteenth century and in the decades around 1350. The intervening period, especially the second decade of the fourteenth century, differed: notably high demesne prices then coincided with low rental land prices and a slowdown in both grants of German law and moves by lords out of farming. After the 1360s movements are less distinct. Demesne land prices leveled off rather low and rental land prices flattened out rather high. Following last major surges in the 1370s, first the German law grants, then the withdrawal from demesne gradually slowed.

Prices are in one sense certainly connected to supply and demand. When the desireability of land in demesne was reflected by the high values of the 1310s, few owners converted their farms to relatively less desirable tenancies; as price trends reversed by mid–century, owners broke up demesnes to increase the supply of rental land. But supply and demand are not the ultimate creators of land prices, for land acquires value as a resource for production and, eventually, incomes (however expressed). Demesne farms were worth having because lords could get from them agricultural products for consumption or exchange. The competitive use, tenancies, yielded to the landowner his rents. The price of tenant–held land, then, should reflect, at least in part, an evaluation of the revenue lords could expect to receive from the peasants who rented it. The incomes of lords were the obligations of peasants.

The German law made the chief obligations of tenants on Silesian rental mansi fixed amounts of grain and money.[14] Previous investigators of these agree on their form but not their height during the mid–thirteenth to the early fifteenth century. Peasant dues were then progressively monetized as ever more places had grain payments reduced or eliminated in favor of cash. Little even suggests significant labor rents (see p. 104 above). The level of obligations, however, has been debated. August Meitzen examined closely a half dozen villages to conclude that there was no significant change in real rent values.[15] Later writers opposed this, arguing from broader but less thorough inquiry that money rents did rise during the late thirteenth and the fourteenth century.[16] But they did not pursue the effect of coincident changes in the coins with which the rents were paid. The likelihood of some movement was here foreshadowed in looking at German law grants, where rents for new tenants rose slowly during the thirteenth century and reached by the mid-fourteenth levels twice those of a hundred years before. Examination of all records of rent from the duchy will extend and modify that impression.

Relevant information occurs in two situations. For a very few villages obligations are reported at more than one date, thus revealing, in an extremely small sample, change over time in the same places. They are almost all church properties but include sites across the duchy. More common are citations of the rents in a particular place at a single date. To use these by themselves risks perceiving as changes over time what were really variations among villages. Hence the tactic here adopted is to display the data in full (Figure 6.3a). The result shows that both sets of references give the same general pattern, with fluctuations in the larger set of single views corroborated by those in villages seen more than once. The information is, of course, too sparse to create a smooth curve of changing rent levels, but it is possible to calculate average obligations for sets of villages with evidence from limited periods of time (Table 6.3).

The mixed character of rents set in both cash and grain further complicates their study. At least notionally, peasants produced only a quantity of cereals, so the dues as paid already represented a partial conversion of wealth in grain to wealth in money. Eventual consumption by a lord or other recipient might well follow further and complete transformation into a sum of cash. Thus changing grain prices varied the relative value of each component and of the total payment. In addition, changes in the silver content of the circulating coinage changed that of the nominal "mark" and hence the quantity of monetary metal actually transferred in any payment. Full understanding of variations in the level and components of rent demands analysis first of nominal obligations and then of their values as both silver and grain equivalents (Figure 6.3b and Table 6.3), but should not press the numbers beyond the level of visual inspection.

Consider first the separate forms in which rent was paid. A progressive shift towards money and away from grain assessments dominates the entire period. The average nominal payment in money more than doubled from the mid to the late thirteenth century and doubled again between 1300 and the years around 1350.[17] Then the rise slowed. The median cash obligation in 1386–1430 was somewhat more than that for 1326–75, but the mean insignificantly less.

Silver values conveyed in those coins display the dampened rise to be

Table 6.3. Major tenant obligations, 1234–1430
(average annual per mansus)

	1234–1278 (20 cases)	1280–1300/05 (20 cases)	1326–1375 (17 cases)	1386–1430 (19 cases)
Money dues				
cases	20	18	17	18
nominal value (marks)	.22 median .25 mode .25	.54 median .33 mode .25	1.0 median .75 mode .50	.98 median .98 mode 1.0
as silver (grams)	30.9	74.4	122	74.0
grain equivalent (measures)	5.6	13.5	12.3	12.1
Grain dues				
cases	18	18	14	18
grain (measures)	12.8 median 12 mode 12	11.1 median 12 mode 12	8.8 median 12 mode 12	7.5 median 4.5 mode 0
silver equivalent (grams)	70.5	61.0	87.5	47.5
Total dues				
cases	18	16	14	17
silver equivalent (grams)	105 median 101 mode 101	132 median 101 mode 101	186 median 191 no mode	125 median 118 no mode
grain equivalent (measures)	18.5 median 18 mode 18	23.8 median 18 mode 18	18.8 median 18 mode 18	19.9 median 21 no mode

Note. Data, sources, and methods are as Figure 6.3. Rows that treat separately the money or grain component use all information on that component (including zero values when these are known), but the section on total dues uses only cases for which both components are known. These totals are like those from addition of the separate component values except in the period 1326–1375. Lack of information about the grain payments (if any) at two places with rather high money dues, Wilczków in 1352 and Szczytniki in 1360, causes their entries to drop out of the total computation. Thus, for 1326–1375 only, the sums of the two separate components are greater than those given as totals: 209.5 grams as compared to 186 and 21.1 measures to 18.8.

expected as debasement became an increasingly important fact of economic life. In the thirteenth century, when coins still circulated by weight and fineness, the nominal increase was also real. Thereafter the early fourteenth century climb was cut to some 80 percent in specie and later major devaluations pulled silver payments back down to the level of a century before.

Fluctuating grain prices also pulled down the ostensibly rising quantity of goods which peasants had to transfer in the form of money rents. The

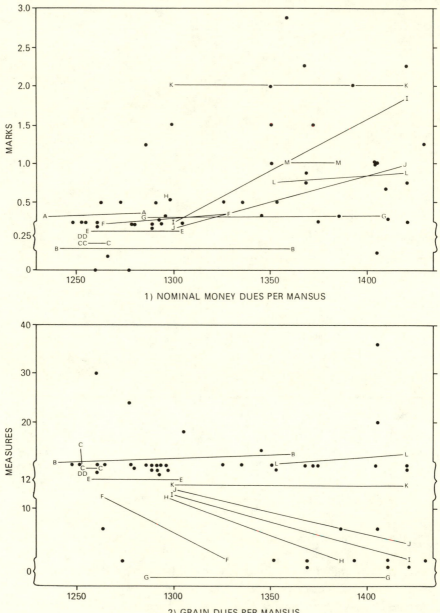

Figure 6.3a
MAJOR TENANT OBLIGATIONS, 1234-1430

1) NOMINAL MONEY DUES PER MANSUS

2) GRAIN DUES PER MANSUS

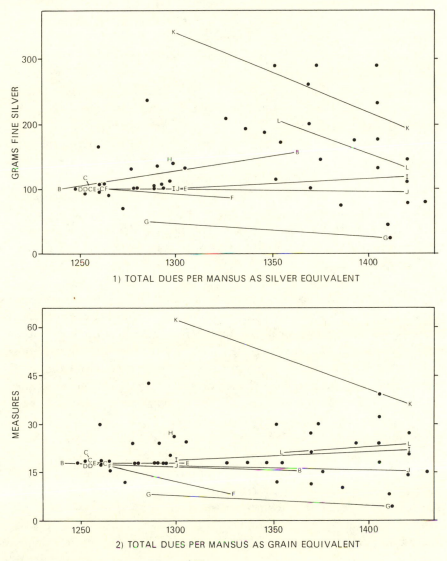

Figure 6.3b
MAJOR TENANT OBLIGATIONS, 1234-1430

1) TOTAL DUES PER MANSUS AS SILVER EQUIVALENT

2) TOTAL DUES PER MANSUS AS GRAIN EQUIVALENT

Note. For sources see *Notes to Maps and Figures.*

grain value represented by these payments peaked before 1300 and then slowly declined through the next century and a quarter. Nevertheless, whether considered as a silver or a grain equivalent, the share of the total obligation paid in the form of money increased from less than a third in the mid-thirteenth century to over half by around 1300 and about 60 percent by the middle and late fourteenth century.

Dues in grain fell. While the average rental mansus owed twelve or more measures of mixed grains around 1250, a half century later this figure had dropped below the twelve measure mark, chiefly because fewer places seem to have owed very large quantities of grain. Another century and villages with no cereal dues at all had become common.[18] The mean grain obligation was below eight measures by around 1400 and the median (perhaps a better estimator for such wide-ranging values), a mere 4.5 measures. The combined changes in price and currency made the smaller mid-fourteenth century average payment of grain worth more silver than that a century before, but thereafter the value in specie of these dues dropped as well. Grain payments had made a good two-thirds of the value owed in the mid-thirteenth century. They fell to half or less by about 1300 and slowly declined to perhaps a third over the next century.

Hence the difference between the obligations of late thirteenth century peasants in Radoszkowice and those of their early fifteenth-century heirs was reasonably representative of the whole duchy. The earlier payment of a quarter mark cash and about twelve measures of grain had become by the early 1420s one of 47gr 4hl (.985 mk) and three measures. Their lord the bishop, who had around 1300 received in rent and tithes from the nine rental mansi 2.25 marks plus 108 measures, later took in from the same holdings 8.875 marks plus 27 measures.[19] But what combined values had these changing mixes?

Figure 6.3b and the lowest rows of Table 6.3 consider the cases where obligations in both components are known (including zero in either) and, using half-century average grain prices from Table 6.4 below and the silver content of the contemporary coinage, estimate both silver and grain equivalents for these totals. The former measures the specie value of lords' receipts and peasants' payments and the latter how much product a peasant had to turn over to a lord's control. Because several variables affected them, the equivalents do not always move in the same way. Between the middle and the late thirteenth century the silver value of the mean rent assessment (though not the median or mode) rose by about a fourth of the initial figure. An even greater rise took place within the next fifty years, for the average of the mid-fourteenth century comes to at least half again that of its beginning. By the eve of the Hussite wars, however, the specie value conveyed had come down from the mid–century peak and averaged at or below the amount known from the years around 1300.

Grain equivalents peaked earlier and were less volatile throughout. Tightly grouped at about eighteen measures in the mid–thirteenth century cases, the mean value by the turn of the century had climbed by almost a third, chiefly because of several instances with notably high obligations. In the first half of the fourteenth century, however, higher grain prices pulled down the cereal value of money rents at the same time as cereal rents were being phased out. The result was a drop between 1300 and 1350 by a fifth in the grain equivalent paid and then most likely little major change in the following seventy-five years.[20]

The movement of rent, then, differs with the perspective from which it is examined. Changes in grain equivalents, which might be called the producers' and consumers' point of view, did not coincide with those in silver equivalents, the criterion appropriate for people who would convert incomes into other than food. During the second half of the thirteenth century, a period of frequent German law *locationes*, total rent values, however calculated, rose by some 25–30 percent while being transformed from payments mostly in grain to approximately equal values of grain and cash. Recognizing that, though technical improvements likely then spread among peasant farms, too little is known of productivity to assess the share of output transferred in rents, Wrocław duchy peasants were paying more and landlords receiving more at the close of the thirteenth century than in its middle. But the years around 1300 were a peak in the grain it took to meet the peasants' obligations. Although the silver value of rents increased by about half to a new maximum over the next couple of generations, higher prices meant less cereal covered those costs, especially since the trend toward a larger money component continued. The peasant surely gained thereby and the landlord lost to the extent that he had once sold or himself consumed his grain. But at the same time the lord did get larger liquid revenues, thus reducing the need to enter the market as a seller (itself not without costs) to convert receipts to cash. The intense mid–century efforts of landowners to make of demesne farms fixed rent tenancies and the long-term shift toward money rents suggest that lower grain equivalents were a price lords willingly paid for more silver.

Trends in the late fourteenth and early fifteenth century were less well-defined. Total values of rent probably declined but, in an age of frequent debasement, more steeply in silver than in grain. Perhaps this also explains a slowdown, if not halt, in the movement away from rents in kind. All else being equal, peasants continued to need less of their harvest to meet landlords' demands and now paid their money dues in poorer coins as well. On the long term, then, the two centuries from the coming of the German law until that of the Hussites did witness rent increases in the order of 10–20 percent, depending on whether grain or silver equivalents are used. On a shorter scale, however, what lords took of the peasants' product, grain, rose mostly in the thirteenth century, and that considered as specie, before the mid-fourteenth. Stable or falling rental values thereafter paralleled slowly diminishing interest in both grants of German law and subdivision of demesne farms.[21]

The two measures of the value rental lands had for owners, sale prices and revenues from rent, show reasonable consistency during the long fourteenth century. Both were relatively high when German law grants and withdrawal from demesne farming were common; both were lower when direct exploitations were being retained and institutional reforms rare. Clearly, then, a certain "pull" sometimes exercised by the rising worth of tenancies encouraged landowners to convert their own enterprises into rentier lordships operated by peasant households. Demand for and profits from land out to tenants induced a response to increase its supply. Owners desiring to give up farm operation, wishing for more secure incomes from rising rents, and willing to pay higher prices for rental lands, could not, however, themselves create the occupied tenancies they wanted. Tenant farming requires persons willing to take up land under the conditions offered and rising rents need people to pay them. Demography thus unavoidably affected the economic framework which shaped interaction between demesne and tenancy. At the same time, the impact of the market on rural relationships is again seen in the divergent values of rents calculated in silver and in grain. A full context for rural developments between the late thirteenth and the early fifteenth centuries includes population and prices, as fragmentary as information about them may be.

Population and market conditions

Postwar decades saw lively interest in Poland's demographic history. In general, research on periods before the partitions concentrated on those provinces which belonged throughout to the Polish state, Great Poland, Little Poland, and Mazovia, but, where the sources permit, Silesian conditions have been noted or at least hypothesized from comparative evidence. Knowledge of late medieval Polish population supplies a framework for the Wrocław duchy. Students of this field have tried to establish long term trends from estimates of aggregate population at certain key (and well-documented) dates, each of which epitomizes demographic conditions over a longer span of time. Especially relevant here are totals and intervening trends for 1000, 1340, and 1578, the origins of the Polish state, its reunification, and the waning days of its renaissance prosperity.

Few agree on the precise levels reached at any particular pre-modern date. Serious questions remain about proper use as demographic evidence of mid-fourteenth century records of Peter's Pence, a head tax paid from Polish dioceses to Rome.[22] But consensus has been reached on the secular trend. For the kingdom as a whole the steady increase of the high Middle Ages (80 percent from 1000 to 1340), accelerated thereafter. The rate of annual growth, 0.18 percent before 1340, climbed to a mean for the period 1340 to 1578 of 0.30 percent so that by the latter year Poland's population was two and a half times that of the mid-fourteenth century.[23] Long-term rates so high leave little margin for periods of major depopulation followed by still faster increase; no demographic decline is believed to have marked the Polish later Middle Ages. On the contrary, regions once thinly inhabited were then settled most rapidly so that by the mid-fourteenth century the kingdom as a whole knew a density of some eight to nine per square kilometer, equal to that of Silesia a century and a half before. Later growth continued to mitigate, but did not eliminate, regional disparities.[24]

Silesia's aggregate population development has been less well served by sources and scholars than that of the reconstituted Polish kingdom. Considerable growth surely characterized the thirteenth century but the known intensity of local opposition to the Peter's Pence makes of the mere regional (archdeaconry) totals (which are the only form in which the source there survived) unsatisfactory demographic evidence.[25] Tadeusz Ładogórski manipulated these numbers to achieve an aggregate 407,000 people in the mid-fourteenth century bishopric of Wrocław, and thought this corroborated from another calculation of a thousand parishes each with four hundred souls.[26]

A total in the range of 400,000 to 500,000 for the province in the mid-fourteenth century fits poorly the accepted and more soundly based late sixteenth century level of about 1,250,000.[27] Implausibly high rates of increase are required for Silesians to have multiplied two and a half or three times in two centuries. Unlike in Great Poland and Mazovia, in Silesia human settlement stopped expanding in the late 1300s and began again only around 1500. Severe local population losses and retreat of settlement were in the interim not uncommon.[28] Further research by Władysław Dziewulski on the district of Nysa, where Ładogórski had thought assuming 3.66 persons per mansus would corroborate estimates from Peter's Pence, argues for distinctly larger families, smaller holdings, and thus higher densities and total numbers.[29] In consequence, Ładogórski himself conceded that markedly greater evasion of the Peter's Pence in Silesia than in the kingdom made his original estimates for the province too low.[30] A rough approximation of 600,000 to 800,000 would put the average population density in the mid-century province at around fifteen per square kilometer (not quite twice that of 1200) and bring the growth needed to attain late sixteenth century totals down to a more palatable doubling over two hundred plus years. It looks, however, like Silesia failed to replicate the kingdom's continued expansion beyond the late fourteenth century, maintained a stable or declining population for the next hundred years or so, and only then put on a new spurt of growth.

In the center of the province were the highest densities of the mid-fourteenth century, almost 20 or 12–15 per square kilometer according to the Peter's Pence calculations of Ładogórski and Walter Kuhn respectively.[31] These suggest a rural population in the Duchy of Wrocław between 30,000 and 20,000. Estimates from the number of known settlements or the total of occupied mansi depend critically on assumptions about average sizes of villages, farms, and households. Dziewulski's upward-leaning factors, 140 per village and 5.5 per mansus, give totals at or above 30,000; Kuhn's minimal three per mansus only 21,000.[32] Data on family or household size are, for this time and place, effectively inaccessible; all authors assume six. In the few villages with records at this time, peasant farms averaged about 1.4 mansi. This would suggest just over four persons per mansus and a rural population of 28,000–30,000 (18–19 per square kilometer).[33] With an allowance for the lesser towns, the duchy's population outside Wrocław itself probably just passed 30,000. The city, by comparison, is best estimated at 14,000 to 17,000 by the late 1300s[34]—a plain sign that its economic region and role went far beyond the principality.

Evidence of population trends is perhaps more relevant and surely more confidence-inspiring than the pseudo-precision of estimated aggregates, especially since surviving signs of short-term events and movements suggest in matters demographic, too, a now-familiar periodicity. Vigorous expansion of rural settlement during the late thirteenth century so filled the once-empty Środa and Uraz districts that by 1350 all modern sites of human habitation are recorded in contemporary texts. Also symptomatic of favorable demographic conditions in rural Silesia during the late 1200s is the general silence of contemporary annalists on the subject of famines. Some immigrants even arrived after flight to escape food shortages in their homelands. The early fourteenth century "Elder Wrocław Annals" mention a famine so affecting Germany in 1264 "that many persons, leaving their fields, fled to Poland."[35] Indirect evidence thus makes most probable continuation of population growth up to about 1300.

Did demographic expansion in the duchy falter in the early fourteenth century? Much suggests it. After the first decade numbers of settlements continue to enter the documentary record but explicit signs that any are "new" villages cease for at least a generation. In contrast, lands gone deserted, formerly known only in conjunction with short-lived military or meteorological disasters, seem to become more common. As early as 1305 episcopal surveyors found Jugowiec a "villa deserta" which yielded no rents,[36] but most such records are somewhat later. Kalinowice, a property of the knightly Colmas brothers, lay empty in 1337.[37] One Wrocław citizen, John Schel, so feared depopulation that he then wrote into a contract for an annuity on rental mansi at Wróblowice a guarantee of payment even if the village "were deserted to the last mansus."[38] As late as 1353 the royal fiscal survey lists deserted arable in 20 of the 284 places (7 percent) for which it gives quantitative information.[39] Nor are plausible grounds for a flattening or downturn of the demographic curve absent from the early fourteenth century. The famine of 1315–17 spared the duchy no more than other parts of trans-Alpine Europe.[40] Another major food shortage, accompanied by epidemic disease, swept the continent's midsection in 1338.[41]

If signs of problems but no acute crisis make the Wrocław duchy resemble some parts of early fourteenth-century western Europe,[42] its escape along with a larger Polish area from the premier demographic event of the later Middle Ages, the Black Death of 1347–50, signifies the more peculiar course of the ensuing several generations.[43] Direct evidence of population change fails for the decades of mid-century, but the overall scarcity of deserted holdings, the progress of German law, the occurrence of places like Wierzbica, "nova locatio" in 1353,[44] and the continuing rise in silver rents are hardly signs of stagnation or decline in human numbers. The plague did come after harvest failures in 1362 when it caused many deaths, and again in 1372, when its mortality seems less serious.[45]

The evidence of later trends is ambiguous, supporting neither continued all-out expansion nor major depopulation before the 1420s. Fewer places had empty holdings in the 1425 tax return than in 1353, and the number of deserted mansi dropped by half.[46] Still, *Zielona* lay uncultivated in 1362 and in the 1390s Lubiatów, Wróblowice, and Nowa Wieś had holdings "die da wüste lagen."[47] Landless gertner lived in many villages but wholly new settlements had become a thing of the past. Landlords still found tenants for demesne lands they would no more farm themselves. Rural population growth may have stopped after the bad years of the 1360s and early 1370s, but the countryside of around 1400 cannot coherently be understood as one stalked by the specter of demographic collapse.

Table 6.4. Silesian cereal prices estimated by Friedensburg, 1250–1550 (fifty-year per measure averages)

	"Grain"	Wheat	Rye	Barley	Oats
1250–1300 nominal	.04mk				
silver	5.5g				
1300–1350 nominal	3.75gr				
silver	9.0–14.5g				
1350–1400 nominal		4.5–5gr	3.5–4gr	2.5gr	1.3–1.5gr
silver		8.2–12g	6.4–9.6g	4.6–6g	2.4–3.6g
1400–1450 nominal		[n o e s t i m a t e s a t t e m p t e d]			
silver					
1450–1500 nominal		9–10gr	6–7gr	4–5gr	3–4gr
silver		10.4–16.7g	7.0–11.7g	4.6–8.4g	3.5–6.7g
1500–1550 nominal		18–20gr	14–16gr	12gr	8–9gr
silver		15.1–25.6g	11.8–20.4g	10.1–15.4g	6.7–11.5g

Note. From Friedensburg, "Getreidepreise," pp. 42–45, with silver values added in accord with Appendix B. Ranges of silver values are the extremes, the lower price at the lowest silver content during the fifty-year period, the higher price at the highest value. Generally, however, the best coins circulated at the beginning of each period.

Like human population, commodity prices interact in complicated ways with other variables in an economic system. High prices, whether from excess demand or failure of supply, induce other changes as people respond to these consumers' difficulties and producers' opportunities. To the extent that the market infiltrates a traditional rural economy, the price behavior of agricultural goods becomes a useful indicator of its conditions. The countryside around Wrocław was thoroughly penetrated, if not dominated, by commercial relationships. Some demesne farmers produced for the market. Hereditary tenants sold grain to pay more of their rents in cash. Price changes affected the value of those rents. City dwellers, in turn, had to—and at the busy grain market of the 1321 municipal ordinances did[48]—buy food, whether from peasants, demesne lords, or recipients of rents in kind. Even skimpy price data, then, offer suggestive signposts toward an understanding of the fourteenth century rural economy.

Price citations are themselves a scarce commodity in medieval Silesia. For non-agricultural goods they are unknown, for livestock, all but absent,[49] and for cereals, rare enough to have attracted only a now-aged study by Friedrich Friedensburg.[50] Having examined all Silesian evidence then in print, Friedensburg pointed out that, as well as prices from sales of actual grain (more rare curiosities than elements for a series), those from sales of grain annuities comprise a reasonably consistent sequence relating cereals to money. Chroniclers, who normally noted only peculiarly high or low prices, still thus preserve contemporary attitudes towards the value of this commodity and indicate the frequency of major famines or grain price inflations. Friedensburg used all three types of sources together to estimate average cereal prices in fifty-year periods, up to 1350 for what the texts simply call "grain" (but was most often probably rye), and thereafter for wheat, rye, barley, and oats. Table 6.4 reproduces his estimates in the contemporary coinage and appends to them a conversion to the range of silver values which then prevailed.[51]

Because Friedensburg began with what is now considered an incorrect value for the Polish mark[52] and thought older prices always less volatile than newer ones, he claimed the nominal prices of the thirteenth and fourteenth centuries were stable. His own estimates, however, deny it, for a shift from one skot per measure ($\frac{1}{24}$ = .04mk) in the late 1200s to 3.75 groschen (.078mk) in the early 1300s doubled the nominal price. Replacement of poor Silesian coins by the better Bohemian groschen meant that silver prices doubled as well. If, however, the "grain" of the years before 1350 is to be equated with rye thereafter, nominal prices did change little between the first and the second half of the fourteenth century. But in that case, debasement of the groschen meant silver prices fell by some 30 percent. Although

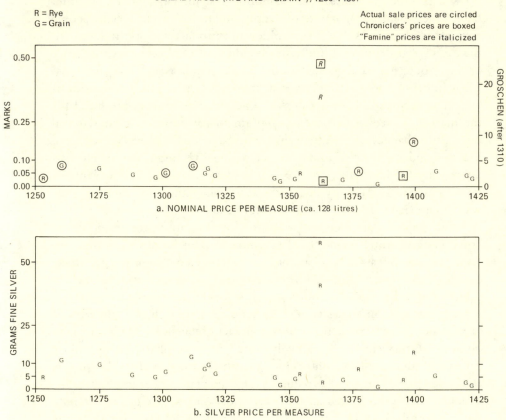

Figure 6.4
CEREAL PRICES (RYE AND "GRAIN"), 1250-1430.

R = Rye
G = Grain

Actual sale prices are circled
Chroniclers' prices are boxed
"Famine" prices are italicized

a. NOMINAL PRICE PER MEASURE (ca. 128 litres)

b. SILVER PRICE PER MEASURE

Note. For sources see *Notes to Maps and Figures.*

unwilling to suggest a normal price for 1400–50, Friedensburg dated to this time a significant nominal increase. Prices in the second half of the fifteenth century were about twice those of a century earlier, which offset intervening decay of the currency and pushed silver prices upwards by a third or so (not quite to the level of the late thirteenth century). Finally the pioneering author detected sharp inflation in the first third of the sixteenth century, a doubling of nominal (and silver) values. The temporal sequence thus suggested would have rising silver prices into the first half of the fourteenth century, a fall from then to around 1400, higher levels by the end of the fifteenth century than at its beginning, and acceleration of the upward movement after 1500. But Friedensburg drew his citations from all over Silesia and then acknowledged Wrocław prices as often much different than elsewhere in the province.[53] It therefore becomes necessary to examine what can be learned about cereal prices in the duchy itself, here at least up to the 1420s.

Paucity of source materials forces two conditions on the study of fourteenth century grain prices. As Friedensburg discovered, most surviving information is about "grain" or rye, not other crops, so these two prices must receive primary attention. Secondly, most references are to sales not of actual grain but of annuities and rents paid in grain. Friedensburg's assumption that such rents went for ten times their expected annual value seems justified and is here provisionally adopted.[54] The few sales of real cereals then serve to corroborate impressions gained from this evidence.

Figure 6.4 gives nominal and silver values for "grain" and rye in the Wrocław duchy and indicates the sort of record which supplied the citation. Again the familiar scatter diagrams allow at least some apprehension of general trends. An overall sluggishness differs sharply from what will be seen in the next century (Chapter 10). Over the entire period here portrayed, nominal money prices for a measure of "grain"-rye look relatively stable, mostly running in the range of two to three groschen (.04–.06mk). This implies a slow decline in the quantity of silver so exchanged and a failure of prices in the duchy fully to adjust to changes in the circulating medium.

Shorter movements also faintly mark the data. It looks as if prices moved slowly upward in the late thirteenth century and peaked in the second decade of the fourteenth. Narrative sources describe shortages then but cite no prices.[55] By mid-century, however, normal levels were back around two groschen or below five grams of silver. Nominal stability and silver deflation seem, therefore, chiefly characteristic of the second half of the fourteenth and the early fifteenth century, although interrupted by famine prices in 1362 and, even if no price citations survive, presumably in 1372.

Two real transactions from this period also support this finding. Wheat from the demesne at Borów went for 4.7gr the measure in 1377, barley for 2.5gr, and oats for 1.5gr, while purchases by the Wrocław citizen Michael Bank in 1426 averaged 5.15gr for wheat, 3.23gr for barley, and 2.2gr for oats.[56] The slight nominal rise for each grain did not compensate for less silver in the groschen. Whereas the three cereals brought 11.3, 6.0, and 3.6 grams the measure respectively in 1377, in 1426 Bank paid out but 6.9, 4.3, and 2.9 grams.

Evidence from the duchy thus confirms and specifies what is discernible in the wider Silesian estimates of Friedensburg. Stable or slowly rising grain prices of the later thirteenth century climbed higher in the early fourteenth, but from 1350 onwards the silver value of cereals, already well below its earlier peak, slid slowly downwards from not adjusting to a poorer coinage. The chronology ought to sound familiar; the direction of trends recalls the price of demesne lands. Several pieces of the fourteenth-century puzzle are, at least in hazy outline, now available for concurrent consideration.

The changing conditions of agriculture

Concurrent variations in grants of German law, the retreat from demesne farming, grain and land prices, and the movement of rent, when considered in the structural context of the fourteenth-century duchy, imply the character and causes of successive phases in the region's rural economic history. The long expansion of the twelfth and thirteenth centuries was checked soon after 1300, when production failures induced a generation of stagnation, but resumed in the decades around 1350. From the late thirteenth through the mid-fourteenth century, then, the duchy's rural inhabitants experienced a cyclic succession of growth, recession, and renewed growth, powered, it seems, by the interaction of population and production. The epidemics and famines of the 1360s and early 1370s closed the stepwise ascent. Bereft of the driving force of demographic pressure but, after 1372, evidently free for fifty years from serious food shortages, the region slid towards a stable equilibrium. Only the enduring wish of lords to withdraw from direct exploitation and then the weakening of the imported circulating medium, the Bohemian groschen, continued to modify rural economic relationships. By 1400 growth had perhaps ceased, but the absence of change by 1425 in settlement patterns, rent levels, or prices denies the onset of crisis or depression before the Hussite wars. This chronology, itself an interpretive summary of thematic investigations in this and previous chapters, is now to be explained in more detail.

From the late thirteenth century through the 1350s the variables open to serial assessment move in two concurrent but inverse waves. Despite difficulties of measurement, when the rates of German law grants and withdrawal from demesne were high, so too, were silver or grain equivalent rents and the silver price of tenant–held land, but grain and demesne land prices were low. When the latter two rose, the former four declined. Knowing the structural significance of these, the nature of their movement can be inferred.

In the last third of the thirteenth century locals and immigrants continued the century-old process of gnawing away at regional frontiers of settlement. Especially in the Środa and Uraz districts the German law grants which were then so common provided an institutional form for it. That the expansion occurred as, at least in part, a response to population pressure and demand for land, is shown by the course of rent. The low obligations of mid-century, useful incentives to attract settlers or to encourage institutional change, had by its end risen significantly, whether valued in grain or in silver. Peasants paid the higher rates despite (or even on) the nearby frontier of cultivation and their rights of mobility under German law.

Price movements reflect both the rationale for and the success of this expansion. Among landlords the silver values paid for lands out to fixed-rent tenants rose from the 1270s to the first decade of the next century, then reaching an all-time peak. Those for demesne holdings simultaneously fell. Firm demand for rental properties made sense because the rising value of fixed rents held for the owner considerable advantages over producing on his own account grain that went for low and, until perhaps the very end of the century, unchanging prices. The unprofitability of cereal production for the market is, however equally indicative of the success with which producers met a necessarily expanding demand for food. Urban consumers, the most significant regular purchasers of grain, were adequately supplied, while the peasantry met its own larger needs without driving up the price by entry into the market as buyers.

The efforts of rulers and landowners to promote economic growth by institutional reorganization and incentives for new settlers had, therefore, succeeded. Expansion drove rents upward, with or without improved productivity, but the pressures thereby exerted against productive resources were not until 1300 enough to inflate grain prices as well. An enlarged economic "pie" offered bigger incomes to at least those landlords who had taken advantage of their opportunities. The class of cultivators was collectively larger and wealthier and probably better off individually, too. The duchy had passed from its half- and spottily-developed state of the twelfth century to a more uniformly advanced condition.

In the first third of the fourteenth century, buoyant expansion was sharply reversed. Production failures, notably but not exclusively that of 1315–17, forced grain prices abruptly upward. The price of demesne land followed. That of rental land tumbled. If grain was profitable, so, too, was direct exploitation. To follow the reasoning by which low cereal prices explain the retreat from demesne, this period of high ones ought to find lords less attracted to such institutional and managerial transformations. This was then the case. For four decades German law grants in the duchy almost stopped. Very few demesne farms were parceled out to tenants. The dominant institutional trends of the thirteenth century thus ceased.

Some evidence even hints at a return of the pendulum, an early fourteenth century revival of demesne farming. Even before the famine years, the dean of the Wrocław chapter was refurbishing and restocking his farm at Wilkowice, while Conrad Molheim, a city man, contemplated enlarging his twelve mansi demesne at Swojczyce by purchasing more land from local peasants.[57] Another citizen, Arnold Rulandi, moved in the midst of crisis. In 1315 he bought from Hoger Preticz four mansi in Muchobór Wielki and by obtaining exemption from peasant dues converted them into a demesne. Within another year he had also obtained from local peasants (had they to sell land to get food?) two more mansi there. By 1319 he had combined all into one good-sized farm.[58] The abbot of St. Mary expanded his demesne in Tyniec by purchase of *Milino* in the early 1330s. High grain prices made it wise to control land with cereal crops, whether for household consumption or market sale.[59]

Reinforcing the incentives prices gave early fourteenth-century lords to keep demesne farms were the ultimate consequences of production failure: famine, mortality, and a plateau or dip in the previously rising demographic curve. Whether judged from German law grants or from other evidence of newly-founded villages, the expansion of settlement ceased shortly after 1300. By the 1330s at least some properties were abandoned and, as peasant demand for land fell short of supply, lords were again offering reduced obligations to attract replacement tenants. Agnes of Neuss held out two years with full exemption to any who might restore her four mansi in Stabłowice.[60] She was outdone by King John himself, who in 1341 "in view of the sterility and poor quality of land in our Środa district," halved his taxes on rental mansi there.[61]

The generosity of John and Agnes was not necessarily all voluntary, for peasants on the duchy's less fertile lands could on their own reduce obligations by simply refusing to pay. At Błonie the community's debt of eleven marks to the Wrocław citizen, Jacob of Opole, went as far as the *iudicium curiae* in 1336, while a few years later at Leśnica parish dues were defaulted. Licit and illicit reductions suggest that people in the countryside (and especially on the loams whence most examples come) could no longer sustain the rising obligations of the thirteenth century.[62] Demesnes may have been retained as much from shortage of prospective tenants as from changed preferences of landowners. As elsewhere, then, the production failures, which struck hardest in the second decade of the century but continued at a lower level for another twenty years, distinctly marked the duchy's agrarian development.[63] Their effects, transmitted by changes in price levels and demographic relationships, reversed tendencies that had long been dominant, making direct exploitation of agricultural properties more advantageous and reducing the prospect of durable gains from fixed rent tenancies.

Particular local factors reinforced the trends. The Bohemian groschen which then conquered the circulating coinage of Silesia was not in its first decades a very stable standard of value. Debased five times from its introduction in 1300 to the early 1340s, the coin lost some 30 percent of its silver content in a bare generation.[64] An astute landlord who anticipated from this past a future of instability might well dislike the prospect of fixed cash rents. Such reasoning is, of course, unrecorded, but in the 1330s people with financial claims in villages around Wrocław showed just the doubts about their money it would presuppose.[65] The political disarray which brought Bohemian coins into the province in the wake of Bohemian power damaged the duchy's productive capacity as well. When Henry VI and his brother, Bolesław III of Legnica-Brzeg, contested their inheritance, the impotence of the Wrocław duke not only forced his appeal to King John, it also let Bolesław's troops lay waste his countryside.[66] And so long as the Bohemian hegemony was actively disputed by a resurgent Polish kingdom, the change in rulers did not bring peace and security. In the autumn of 1338, already a year of food shortages, a Polish force looted and burned villages around Oława, Wiązów and Strzelin, and along the Widawa north of Wrocław.[67] Both political and more fundamental economic reasons, then, brought hard times to the early fourteenth century duchy, its peasants, and its landlords. Only one who produced a marketable surplus in those years of poor harvests could take any advantage of the general misfortune.

After the distinctive behavior of measurable index variables during the first third of the century, its middle years resemble those before 1300. By 1350, perhaps by 1340, the price of tenant held land was again on the upswing and those of demesne land and grain falling. Rents moved, in nominal and silver terms, well above those of a half-century before, but so long as grain prices remained relatively higher, this lowered the equivalent of obligations increasingly assessed in cash. Even so, the apparent increases did not go undisputed. Rent claimed by John Reste from Wilczków in 1352, at two marks the mansus among the highest known, had to be imposed on recalcitrant peasants by formal sentence of the *iudicium curiae*. At Święta Katarzyna in 1361, when the lord, Helwig Molnsdorf, seized a legacy for overdue rents, the disgruntled heirs declared feud and mounted a campaign of arson until the city council mediated an agreement.[68] Despite such incidents, the revived interest of landowners and peasants in tenant farming is confirmed by a spurt of new German law *locationes* in the 1340s and 1350s and, in the latter decade, conversion of many demesnes.

Evidence for the demographic trend around 1350 is not wholly satisfactory. Real new settlements are unrecorded, but some where new tenants had free years during the 1350s suggest extension of arable into uncultivated tracts.[69] More questionable, because so little is known of the density of settlement on demesne farms, are the demographic effects of conversion to tenant holdings. When John Kuschberg parcelled his demesne of nine mansi in Chrzanów to five *rustici* there, did the new farms of Nicholas Hubner, Katherine Hubner, Twerco, Nicholas Kleindienst, and Michael Curonis represent additions to the local population or merely the endowment of one-time demesne servants or the enrichment of Kuschberg's peasant neighbors?[70] Indirect indications, however, argue for population growth. Rents went up and landlords subdivided their properties with the firm expectation that willing tenants would provide a steady income from them. In 1354 Charles's general privilege for *locatio* seems to assume rising profits for all.[71] Serious population shortages are most implausible, mere stability unlikely, and some genuine growth looks like the most probable feature of mid-century, enough, in fact, to promote and support the return of relative prosperity.

The upswing of mid-century, for such is the most likely interpretation of the available data, seems linked most closely to a return of the buoyant population trends and production success of the late thirteenth century, to, in other words, a rebound from the induced difficulties of the intervening generation. Renewed granting of German law in the duchy preceded by only a decade or so a like resurgence in Great Poland, while landlords in Brandenburg also responded to lower grain prices by dividing demesne farms among peasant tenants.[72]

More local and ephemeral factors had less impact. The duchy's rural economy was growing well before peace finally returned to central Silesia. The Wrocław city council reported widespread destruction, injury, taking of hostages, and seizure of booty when Polish forces raided the Uraz district and threatened the city itself during the early summer of 1348.[73] Even in 1355 and as close to town as Muchobór, brigands harassed nearby peasants.[74] Nor could stable currency really be anticipated before the 1350s at the earliest. After John's last debasement in 1340, Charles opened his own reign with another in 1347. Contemporaries could not know or with reason expect that this would be the last tampering with the coinage for thirty-one years. And finally, escape from the plague might account for central Silesia's differences from other regions in the 1350s, but not its economic resurgence a decade or so before.

But the plague eventually did come, and with it and the famines of the 1360s a transforming shock to the duchy's rural development. Some immediate consequences are striking. Menczelinus, former schulz of Pęgów, bought a five mansi demesne at Stabłowice in 1362 itself. His privileges tell that he meant to emulate what others had done for the past twenty years and divide it among hereditary tenants. Not a year later, however, Menczelinus, his plans abandoned, sold the property, still a demesne farm, to Jesco of Smolec. This particular holding was never parceled out.[75] Had Menczelinus suddenly found tenants hard to find? More general evidence suggests it. German law grants fell from ten in the 1350s to two in the 1360s, lowest decade total since the 1330s. Evidence of new tenant communities on former demesnes went from eleven to zero—only to bounce back to eleven in the 1370s. On the longer term, however, the 1360s mark a more interesting change, the end of smooth cyclic movements and neat coincidence among measurable indices.

In the half-century that separated the second epidemic of 1372 from the coming of the Hussites, a more stable equilibrium replaced the cycles that had long dominated the duchy's rural economy. It is as if the mortalities had set for the region's population a ceiling that remained even after the plague reverted to an endemic state and production returned to an adequate normalcy. Following the famine of 1372 grain prices regained the nominal stability characteristic of earlier generations and hence, with debasement of the groschen, moved downward in terms of silver. Other indicators of demographic trends support no major movement up or down. The absence of new settlements and the low level of German law grants (which stopped after 1400), make significant growth dubious. On the other hand, deserted holdings recorded in the tax return of 1425 and other contemporary listings were more rare, small, and scattered than at mid-century. Landless gertner in more than thirty-five places in the duchy in 1425 also seem too common for a society where population decline was opening up slots among the well-endowed. Such evidence, so much in contrast with that of desertion and depopulation on poor soil areas of Brandenburg and Upper Silesia,[76] confirms the absence of a significant demographic crisis in the duchy before the Hussite wars.

   With population and production levels reasonably stabilized, the chief independent variables affecting the course of the rural economy in the late fourteenth and early fifteenth century became the continued preference of landlords for fixed rent over revenues from direct exploitation, and the return of monetary debasement. After raising the silver content of the groschen in the first two years of his reign, Wenceslas IV dropped it in 1380 below his father's level. There it stayed for twenty-six years. But two successive reductions in 1406 and 1408 pushed the coin to only 72 percent of the earlier value (55 percent of that in 1347–78) before minting ceased entirely in the early 1420s. Against this background established price relationships continued. Those for rental land adjusted well enough to maintain high silver levels to the end of the fourteenth century, while those for demesne land and grain, both still low compared to earlier in the century, lagged somewhat and thus dropped still more after 1400.

   But now rents failed to keep up with the price of tenant-held land. Although the average grain equivalents due around 1400 had changed little from those of mid-century, poorer coins meant a decisive drop in the quantities of silver peasants had to pay out. That this reflects less a major weakening of peasant demand for land than stability and debasement is supported by the only evidence extant of prices peasants paid for land. The inhabitants of Krępice, though operating small farms entirely analogous to those in neighboring villages, still preserved a status as peasant fief-holders that had once derived from their connection to the duke's *curia* at Leśnica. As free holders of land directly subject to the ruler their conveyances took place before the *iudicium curiae* rather than the court of a schulz and were registered like those of landlords' properties. Between 1366 and 1427 twenty-five of these sale charters (perhaps 15 percent of the total) so specify prices and sizes as to permit calculation of a per mansus price.[77] Fourteen sales from before 1396 averaged 12.9 marks or 1180 grams of silver; eleven sales between 1401 and 1427 averaged 18.4 marks, enough higher to raise the silver value to 1475 grams.

   Several reasons might be advanced for Wrocław duchy landlords continuing to convert demesne into tenant land against what looks like a drop in the value of their rental incomes. Low cereal prices offered little incentive to continue grain farming. They surely help explain both why arable demesnes had a higher casualty rate than stock farms and why citizen landowners most sought to get out of grain production. Peasant demand for tenancies had softened, but at a constant nominal rent rate tenants could still be found and thus the costs of production still be shifted to them. And debasement was by the 1370s no longer the operative assumption. Charles had kept the money stable since his accession. Wenceslas's single initial manipulation would not alone replace an expectation of stability with one of monetary decay. Tradition, then, in the absence of different motives and of logical alternatives, could long justify continued replacement of grain growing direct exploitations with fixed rent tenancies. Especially in so far as labor and managerial costs on demesnes failed to fall in tandem with grain prices and rents, tenancies may well have been the least painful alternative.

The rationale for certain group responses to economic change is less certain than the changes themselves or than their probable causes. Economic expansion, powered by population growth and the production success that supported it and channeled by creation of new villages and conversion of demesnes with fixed rent tenancies under German law, extended in the Wrocław duchy well into the fourteenth century, though temporarily interrupted in its second and third decades. Finally halted by the plagues and famines of the 1360s and early 1370s, the long period of growth still did not give way immediately to crisis, depression, or a distinctive new economic direction.[78] In the years around 1400 a rural population that was probably as large as it had ever been lived in equilibrium, perhaps delicate, with its productive resources and supported, albeit involuntarily, the demands of landlords and the consumption needs of townspeople.

PART THREE

§§§§§§§

A Social System in Action

THE LANDED ELITE:
LANDLORD RIGHTS IN
SOCIAL CONTEXTS

Otthocarus de Glubos cum uxore sua Elizabeth et filio Ottokaro resig-
nat Matthia de Mulhaim Militi villam suam Kobirwicz cum sculteto et
ejus servitio supremo et infimo judicio liberam sine omni servitio in
feudum. Conrad de Falkenhain: Capitaneus: in Crastino Michaelis ao
1350.

Conveyance of Kobierzyce; RF I, 462.

Part II examined the economics of agriculture during the thirteenth
through the early fifteenth centuries. To that end, conceptual aggregates of
"lords" and "peasants" participated in the organization and distribution of
production. Part III breaks up those aggregates for a different approach to
many of the same sources. The aim in the next three chapters is to examine
agrarian society during the same period. Chapters 7 and 8 treat seigneurial
lordship as an object shaped by elite social behavior. What was lordship?
Who possessed it? What did they do with it, why, and with what effects on
the countryside? Chapter 9 then looks within the village at groupings and
relationships among peasants and between them and their surroundings.
Although tentative in some details Part III argues strongly for a view of
rural conditions in which lord–peasant relations per se were only a part, and
at times a dependent one, of a larger socio-economic whole. As Chapter 3
treated several aspects of transformation in an earlier Polish situation, Parts
II and III in combination reconstruct multiple facets of agrarian life under
the regime of German law—and Part IV will follow the subsequent deterio-
ration of those social and economic structures.

In Part II the plans and decisions of lords visibly prompted change, but
the grounds for those decisions were not wholly clear. What mattered for
the record lords had compiled was not agricultural activities; these the texts
usually ignore. They chiefly preserve actions and dealings among individ-

uals in the landholding group. That the operative interests of people who were lords around Wrocław thus derived less from their position vis à vis peasants and more from their relationships with other members of the elite is made plain in the record of every lordship. To know the problem this and the following chapter must resolve, consider, for instance, the dossier of Kobierzyce.

In 1333 a knight called Otto of Glubos received Kobierzyce as a fief from Duke Henry VI. Place and man are not earlier recorded, but neither seems a newcomer, since the village had a Polish name and the knight was privileged for past services. With thirty mansi out to peasants and their schulz, Kobierzyce likely was Otto's largest holding, for he had only small parcels elsewhere.[1] After the duke's death, Otto had King John formally confirm his hereditary and "royal" rights over the village.[2] He died himself before April 1344, leaving at least two sons, both knights. Ottocar inherited Kobierzyce and his brother, a junior Otto, an endowment of incomes that Ottocar agreed to pay from the village.[3] That same year, Ottocar used Kobierzyce to secure a debt of 29 marks he owed to Christian of Kąty from Wrocław. Five years later, he again used half the village to dower his wife Elizabeth. On 30 September 1350, Ottocar, Elizabeth, and their son, also Ottocar, sold Kobierzyce, described as a service-free fief with the schulz and high and low justice, to Mathias of Molheim, a knight and a citizen of Wrocław.

The Molheims had been knights like the Gluboses, but moved to the city where Mathias was from 1309 to 1367 a municipal politician and purchaser of real estate. The documents are silent about his tenure at Kobierzyce, which passed to his sons Mathias, Conrad, John, Haske, and Buske.[4] The lordship was thus divided, if not immediately in 1367 when the younger Mathias alone sold an annuity to his uncle Conrad, then surely by 1375 when he sold his fifth portion outright to another wealthy and influential city man, Peter Schwarz. The other four brothers Molheim retained their four-fifths share as a fief until 1383, when they sold it to John Bayer. Bayer, who also had acquired Schwarz's part, disliked constraints in his feudal title to Kobierzyce. In late 1394 or early 1395 he induced King Wenceslas to transfer the entire village from fief to property status, in particular so that it could be inherited by women as well as men.[5]

Soon the Bayer heirs were applying the new privilege to carry out a hereditary succession more complex than that of the Molheims a generation before. One (unnamed) son received half Kobierzyce in the early 1410s and sold it to another Wroclaw citizen, Nicholas von der Heyde, while retaining a right of repurchase. Another son, Caspar, died childless soon after his father. Caspar's half of Kobierzyce passed to his mother, Dorothea, who had in the meantime married yet another town magnate, Wenceslas Reichel. In 1417 she sold her half to von der Heyde with full hereditary title.

The property was thus reassembled, but the parade of new owners not long halted. Within five years von der Heyde had perished and Kobierzyce passed to his children. On 12 November 1423 the heirs sold the entire property, half with hereditary, half with repurchaseable title, to another townsman, Peter Ungerathen. Peter's son Conrad paid the burnegelt tax of 1425 on Kobierzyce, which had changed in no known way since the 1353 fiscal survey,[6] but later that same year Peter arranged the disposition of his estate in a way that allotted other properties to Conrad. Kobierzyce Peter again divided, this time between his daughters Martha and Agatha, married respectively to John Voyt the Elder and John Voyt the Younger of Złotoryja. When Agatha's John died she married Balthasar Schawerke (sometimes called Zaucken) and in 1434 sold her share to her sister's husband. John the Elder had received Wrocław citizenship in 1428 and already controlled the half held in his wife's name. Just over a year after reuniting the property he, too, sold it all—to Franz Krig, citizen of Wrocław, for 300 marks.[7] The Krig family retained possession of Kobierzyce until 1455.

Through the long fourteenth century the texts say little about what went on at Kobierzyce, but much about its owners and what they did with the lordship. Many people, men and women, knights and citizens, possessed it. They bought and sold it, passed it by inheritance, borrowed against it, and changed the terms of their title. Clearly lords were neither stereotypes nor stable, but has the detail they recorded any meaning now? The story of this lordship is one of several hundred. How can the blur of events be ordered and connected to agrarian history?

This chapter takes its strategy from the texts themselves. Lordship is here treated from the point of view of the actor, the landowner, rather than that of the object, the rural settlement. First, how were property rights in the duchy defined? Second, who had them? The status groups possessing lordship are profiled and the distribution of properties among them tabulated. Then the estates of churches and of laity require different approaches. Of the former histories can be sketched, but lay estates are better grasped through the processes whereby individuals obtained and disposed of landed property. The question is thus transmuted from the static listing of owners to the dynamic of lords handling property in market and family settings. For good social reasons, most landed estates and the families who held them were transitory features of the duchy's rural landscape.

Knowledge gained in this chapter about the duchy's ephemeral lords will in the next be applied to a study of how and to what effect these lords exercised their rights over individual rural settlements. A major argument of the two chapters on lordship taken together will be that for most lords a primary attribute of landed property was its instrumental character. Its value could be increased or converted to other values through market or status mechanisms. The ease with which a member of the fourteenth-century landed elite could deal with his peers to have his holdings satisfy his needs reinforced the autonomy and freedom of peasants. Rapid circulation of lordship rights deprived those who held them of incentive or ability to interfere in the lives of tenant farmers and village communities. An analytical path which starts from the apparently meaningless parade of lords at Kobierzyce will thus make understandable the behavior as individuals and groups of men and women at the top of the duchy's social order. By an indirect route, it will elucidate anew the special structural backdrop for lord-peasant relations during the late thirteenth through early fifteenth centuries.

Titles to land

A tenurial space between peasants on the one hand and superior territorial authority on the other first approximates the lord's position. Where German law arrangements shaped agrarian society, a lord held over land cultivated by peasant tenants a higher right which justified their payment of rents to him. Older institutional patterns that survived in the demesne also depended on the lord's legitimate right of possession and use but left him a greater managerial role. Lords did not themselves farm, but lived from those—their tenants, employees, or servants—who did. Fourteenth-century Wrocław duchy landlords thus exercised rights that were legitimized in the law and custom of their territorial polity. Ducal authority, first personal and then through the *iudicium curiae*, offered procedures to register, convey, and defend the title and content of estates in land.

A lord could hold rights over land by a bewildering array of titles. When citizen magnate Nicholas Sittin divided his estate among his heirs in 1357 he specified that Bielany and half Domasław were his by "iure proprietatis," Pasterzyce and Pełczyce were "bona feudalia," and the rest of Domasław a fief specially privileged for females to inherit.[8] A distinction between fief (*feudum, Lehen*) and property (*proprietas, Erb und Eigen*) might appear most significant, the one implying a conditional grant for military service, the other unrestricted possession and use, but the fourteenth century blurred this neat dichotomy.

Many lords during the fourteenth century held ducal fiefs, a western idea accepted in Poland and Silesia a hundred years before. Some tenures by *ius feodale* conformed to the classic model. A feudal obligation to serve with a war horse lay upon Henry Wende for Proszków in the 1340s; his heirs still owed it under Wenceslas.[9] Other fiefholders enjoyed privileged exemption from this burden. For their loyalty to Henry VI, the knights Sidilmann and Tammo, first known local members of the large Schellendorf family, were freed in 1324 from service for their fiefs at Ratyń and Lutynia.[10] Similar liberties accumulated in successive generations; by 1425 few feudal tenures actually imposed on the possessor a special personal obligation to fight for his lord.

Rights of inheritance and sale also normally benefited those with fiefs. As important a fief as the castle at Uraz, with its strategic position and control over nearby villages, was in 1337 sold for 1200 marks groschen to Conrad of Borsnicz by Henry of Hugowicz.[11] Wojnowice, repeatedly specified as a fief in the conveyances, passed by a succession of sales and inheritances between 1376 and 1408 through the hands of a foreigner, two knights, a citizen, and three young children.[12]

A woman's acquisition of a fief was theoretically improper, however. The customary code drawn up by the Royal Six in 1356 specified that daughters were to receive only annuities from the feudal possessions of a deceased. Many lords seem to have disliked this restraint on the rights of their girls and sought special exemptions. Thus Richard Gubin and John Gotke, two Wrocław citizens, obtained from Charles IV in 1363 a privilege allowing women to succeed in default of male heirs to their fiefs at Sadków.[13] In practice, and even in places where no special permission is known, women inherited and bought admittedly feudal tenures in the late fourteenth century duchy. At Bukowiec in 1374 one Katherine sold to Nicholas of Pathendorf the single mansus of fief which she had from her husband Henry. Margaret Reste bought the lordship at Wojnowice from John of Vestinburg in 1368 and held it by hereditary feudal right.[14]

By the end of the century, those lords who held by feudal title found their economic freedom peculiarly inhibited by only one major extra-familial constraint—the duke's right of escheat in default of appropriate heirs. Thus, when Witzke Stroppen died without heirs in 1413, his half of Golędzinów was taken for the king by the captain John of Chotievice and granted to Peter Schellendorf.[15] The danger of loss was magnified if unscrupulous officials used the threat of illegal escheat to extort payments from legitimate heirs. John Polanowicz accused the fallen city politician, Nicholas Rempel, in 1423 of having extorted thirty marks and three loads of beer from him to avoid interference with his inheritance in Pasterzyce.[16] The remedy was obvious: have the crown convert title from fief to property and thus surrender its right as overlord. Most examples seem to date from the reign of Wenceslas. Thus, in 1395 the king allowed Peter Bayer to end the feudal status of his holdings at Jaksin and in 1413 did the same for another townsman, John Sachse, at Sośnica.[17] Even though lords of fiefs could treat their holdings with nearly complete liberty, they still found it useful at times to obtain a different title.

The hereditary and proprietary title, which then coexisted with feudal title, evolved from the old Polish *ius militare* and northern German customary law, especially *Sachsenspiegel*. By the thirteenth century, customary rights of Polish knights included hereditary claims (*ius hereditarium*) over lands possessed by kinsfolk, irrespective of whether these lands came from an independent patrimony or a ducal gift. Thus the entire kin group, male and female alike, had recognized rights to landed property and could exercise powers of preemption and repurchase over individual possessions which threatened to pass out of the lineage. On such lands daughters normally claimed a share in an inheritance. Military obligations were limited to a "public" duty to defend the homeland itself.[18] In practice, therefore, a family's holdings were often well (but not equally) dispersed among its members and numerous individuals had to participate in any transfer outside the kin group.[19] Since a potential hereditary claimant could appear to challenge a sale long after it seemed complete, the citizens of Wrocław obtained from Duke Henry in 1327 the privilege of refusing to respond to cases brought against them "in jure, ligwa et zeuda Polonicali."[20] Ten years later King John abolished the czuda and, with it, the authority of Polish law in the duchy.

German legal custom, however, had provisions like and easily influenced by Polish practice. *Sachsenspiegel* restricted preemption and repurchase to a smaller circle of direct relatives and to property in land and subject people; moveable goods were freely alienable. Daughters inherited landed property only in the absence of sons. The codification prepared in 1356 for the duchy, though based on the Saxon code, modified these provisions. In accord with the custom of Magdeburg (used in Wrocław's city court) and with the indigenous precedents outlined above, daughters in the duchy possessed rights to hereditary landed property equal to those of their brothers. Respecting lineage rights the local custom was still more liberal, requiring consent from legitimate children only, and then only for land which the possessor had himself inherited (*irstorben gut*).[21] Thus, just as rights of the lord over fiefs had attenuated during the fourteenth century, so too did those of the lineage over hereditary property. Other features remained unchanged, notably partibility. The citizen magnate Lutko von der Nysa anticipated in 1389 equal division of his landed estate (exclusive of fiefs) among his five living children (two sons, three daughters) and any future offspring.[22] Some obligation to public service continued, too, at least without special privilege. The brothers Grzebkowicz sold three mansi of demesne at Miękinia in 1401 with the proviso that purchasers of this hereditary property would share proportionately in the lordship's military obligations.[23] Thus although fief and hereditary property began as two distinct forms of title to land, the differences had become minimal. Landlords had complete practical authority to use and to dispose of their holdings.

Some private owners exercised on their rural properties authority not innately their own. Neither feudal or proprietary title nor lordship over a fully-privileged German law village itself conveyed to the possessor jurisdiction over capital offenses (high justice) or rights to take taxes. During the fourteenth century these public powers became private and associated with lordship (by a process to be studied in Chapter 8), but were not a necessary component of it. The right of patronage over a local church also could and often did belong to the local landowner. Nevertheless, in the period before the Hussite wars, however much possession of certain governmental or ecclesiastical rights may have described many Wrocław duchy lords, these were not the rights which then defined them as a group or by which they are now to be identified from the extant texts.

In a few instances an individual's status as lord in a settlement is ambiguous, particularly where more than one layer of private rights intervened between peasants and duke. Possessors of perpetual leases or rear fiefs at the bishop's Piłczyce, for instance, commonly exercised rights of use, inheritance, and alienation like those who held directly under the duke.[24] Another kind of right was inserted between the nominal landlord and his peasant tenants if the lord alienated incomes from the property. This could be permanent, as when Canon Nicholas Gleiwitz gave to the abbey of St. Mary fifty marks perpetual annuity from Siedlakowice,[25] or it could be limited through a set term or right of redemption. Often specific incomes and properties secured a repurchaseable annuity or other financial obligations. When a landholder so alienated his revenues to a creditor or a sublord in effective possession he much attenuated his authority over the property concerned. Who ought then to be considered the lord has no a priori and in rare cases no satisfactory answer. Within the limits of the evidence, the discussion that follows treats as members of the duchy's landed elite those who possessed direct and legitimate private authority to live from the payments and products of agriculturalists in a particular settlement.

Possessors of title

Who, then, during the long fourteenth century held rights of lordship or ownership over land in the countryside around Wrocław? What kinds of persons were they and what quantities of wealth did they control? Evidence to answer these questions dramatically improves from the late thirteenth century on. By collating information from especially charters of conveyance and fiscal records it is possible to identify in sequence by name and status most lords in most places most of the time. (For more on sources and methodology see Appendix A.) Consider first the status groups so identified.

One kind of landowner needs little collective introduction. About 1300 ecclesiastical corporations in the duchy were almost as privileged as their counterparts elsewhere. Although only the bishop's church claimed full sovereign authority over its lands, and that only after the death of Henry IV in 1290, most foundations had some immunity from secular authorities and all shared in an institutional durability very different from other landowners. Most church estates matched in permanence the corporations to which they belonged.

Among the laity, in contrast, only a couple of lords so endured. One was the sovereign himself, the ducal office with lands under its direct control which passed from one incumbent to another, from the last Piasts to the Luxemburgs. Another was the municipal corporation of Wrocław, holder through its council of some extramural property since the city's German law foundation and later a purchaser of more land.

Most lords in the duchy were private lay persons, whose standing and variety had clarified and modulated since the mid-thirteenth century. The great majority came from two privileged status groups, the knights and the citizens.

By around 1300 Silesia lacked large non-Piast landholders like the magnates of contemporary and later Poland, if only because the small scale of its sovereign duchies no longer left room for large barons. The "knighthood" (*militia, Ritterschaft, rycerstwo*), now unambiguously acknowledged as noble, was left as the highest social rank beneath the prince. Terms and concepts denoting particular of its social features interchangeably labeled membership therein. "Knight" (*miles, Ritter, ryterz*) often denoted men of this group, but some records reserved that term for the personal status of a dubbed or belted knight and used instead "squire" (*armiger, Knecht, giermek, panosza*) as the generic marker for elite males. In other contexts the same individuals might be titled "lord" (*dominus, Herr, pan*), ranked as "nobles" (*nobiles, Adeln, Edelgeborne*), or take a place among their prince's personal "vassals" (*fideles, vassi, Mannen*) who made up extra-urban political society (*terrigenae, Landschaft*).[26]

Knightly noble status had grown from the privileged and landed military order whose direct relationship to the prince was encompassed in the thirteenth-century Polish *ius militare*, but the people who claimed this rank in fourteenth-century Silesia were of mixed origin.[27] Unlike the late medieval Polish kingdom, the province continued to acknowledge the power of the prince to ennoble commoners; a few so entered its elite. More late medieval knights descended from German warriors who had immigrated to Silesia from Lusatia, Meissen, and neighboring areas in the thirteenth and early fourteenth century. Many of these were of ministerial origin, but in the Polish principalities, where this status was rare, they were called "knights" (*milites*) and thus assimilated to the privileged ranks of comparable native fighters. Descendants of the latter, moreover, contributed a major share to an elite which by 1350 freely intermarried.

By around 1300 the customary *ius militare* treated privileged possession of land as including authority over dependent cultivators and personal exemption from public officials but also a reciprocal direct dependence on the prince with an obligation to serve him as a cavalryman. Thus the Polish knighthood and its Silesian offshoot knew none of the gradations of rank derived further west from a hierarchy of vassal obligations. Increasingly, moreover, the *ius militare* came to be identified with land, and an individual's position among the knights with possession of land. Since land of feudal or proprietary title passed by inheritance in the lineage, so did knightly status. In law in the revived kingdom and in practice in Silesia, too, therefore, status and kinship were immediately joined: knightly rank derived from membership in a lineage of knights, not association with any particular land.[28] As a group in the Wrocław duchy, knightly families held themselves subject only to the prince, his captain, and the courts to which they provided the panel of assessors, the *iudicia provincialia* and the *iudicium curiae*.

The status of townspeople, and particularly those of Wrocław, originated in a formal grant of specific rights to members of a recognized collectivity. A "citizen" (*civis, Burgher*) shared in the privileges and expenses of the urban corporation. For some decades after Wrocław received its German law charter, the status derived from family residence and home ownership within the corporate limits, but a hundred years later those who leased their dwelling could gain citizenship by providing the cost of service in the local militia. Finally, an ordinance of 1374 simply required residence, payment of taxes, and performance of duties in the town watch. Wrocław's citizenship was not, therefore, confined to a wealthy, hereditary, mercantile, or previously landed elite among the city's inhabitants; most lay households were those of citizen heads.[29]

A leading stratum within the town did exist in those families with a tradition of membership on the city council, then sometimes called the *gentes* or *Geschlechtern* and by historians the "patriciate," but this group lacked formal definition. Wealth and, for craftsmen, abandoning artisanal for mercantile activity could bring the ambitious into it. Without the qualities of a true hereditary caste, therefore, these rich holders of political authority in the city turned over with generational regularity.[30]

All citizens enjoyed personal freedom and the privileges of their status, especially to work at crafts and trades under their own town laws and to be judged in their own courts as guaranteed by the duke. In the local hierarchy of honor, such armed and privileged freemen equated their rank with that of the knights. Especially before the mid-fourteenth century, intermarriage and individual mobility in either direction was familiar. Men could, with no special dispensation, assert both titles simultaneously, as "miles dominus Joannes Plessil, civis Wratislaviensis" did in 1339.[31] Even King John's reform of the *iudicium curiae* in 1343, while differentiating between the two status groups, pointedly equated their representatives. Perhaps influenced by the growing distinction of noble rank in Poland and Bohemia and reacting to a purportedly more "middle class" Wrocław citizenry, late fourteenth century knights less willingly accepted ordinary townspeople as their peers. Even the urban elite then found movement into the other order advisable, whether by intergenerational mobility or by royal letter patent.[32] Still, in a region where the city possessed such wealth and exercised such power, *civis Wratislaviensis* or *Burger zu Breslau* remained a proud and meaningful title.

Townspeople in medieval Silesia were never barred as such from possessing lordships, but at first citizen status had only negative effect. It proved the personal freedom and direct dependence on the sovereign needed to hold land from him. Thus wealthy townsmen soon acquired lordships and held them, like any other laymen, in what began as individual and became familial relationships to the duke. A Środa citizen named Godco or Goczko, for instance, long owned three mansi at Jastrzębce under terms exactly like those of the *ius militare*.[33]

Eventually citizens of Wrocław used their town's political weight to extract from the Luxemburgs collective privileges for their lands in the duchy. Early in 1327, as Henry VI took his stand with the Bohemian ruler, first he, then King John, freed these townsmen from all fees owed to convey rural properties and permitted the city's own legal custom to govern their possession of all but fiefs. Ten years later John ordered judicial disputes over citizen lands in the Wrocław district to be heard in the Wrocław district court even if the other party lived elsewhere. Wenceslas IV in 1396 extended the jurisdiction of the Wrocław district court (on whose panel of assessors citizens predominated) to cover citizen lordships anywhere.[34] Besides such official privileges, Wrocław citizens could benefit collectively and individually in their rural affairs all across the duchy whenever their city council functioned as captain. Economic and political advantages gained by citizen landlords over potential knightly competitors emphasized their separate status and compensated for any weakening of social parity between the groups.

A few lay landowners can be placed in neither of the two status groups. Some of these were distinctly free but non-noble countrymen, owner-operators of small farms held directly from the duke without knightly privileges or obligations. Others were village schulzen or prosperous tenants who had obtained lordly rights without giving up their place in village society. They are counted here among the holders of lordship but receive special attention in Chapter 9 for their peculiar position between lords and more ordinary peasants. There is also in the extant records a residue of lords whose status or family remains unknown. Their quantitative importance is by all measures surprisingly small, but they, too, were treated separately in preparing the data discussed below.

The nature of the evidence from the Duchy of Wrocław means that most lords are first identified as such individually on a village by village basis, just as in the case of Kobierzyce. So isolated, each name or sequence of names, even if labeled according to status, tells nothing of general patterns. Features and trends emerge only when all such information is combined into a list of all landowners documented in the duchy at a given date. Early in the century the coverage is still fairly sparse, but by mid-century, lords are consistently known in 80–90 percent of the rural settlements then inhabited. After separate entries are linked, in recognition that the same individual owned property in more than one place, and status or other attributes recorded for each owner, the result is a composite summary of the distribution of lordship rights in the year studied. Profiles for 1300, 1353, and 1425 are displayed in Table 7.1, where the share of each status group is approximated by the relative number of places where its members held land, of separate holdings they possessed, and of individual landowners in the group. What can be inferred from this information?

Ecclesiastical landowners are the best-documented group but still illustrate problems of coverage which must frame any discussion of long-term trends. An important concentration of church lands had developed during the twelfth and thirteenth centuries in what later became the Wrocław duchy. This continued during the subsequent period, when the more than a hundred places with clerical lands (line 5) represented 62, 39, and 43 percent of the settlements with known lordship in 1300, 1353, and 1425, respectively (line 6). But in 1300 the extant record was still heavily biased in favor of identifying ecclesiastical owners. Churchmen had long paid peculiar attention to written proof of their rights, while the laity were just starting to show such interest. The large contemporary survey text that justifies

Table 7.1. Groups in possession of lordships: 1300–1353–1425

	1300	1353	1425
a. The samples			
1. Settlements in the duchy[a]	234	354	362
2. Settlements with known lordship	163	317	291
Known lordship samples as %[b] of:			
3. Settlements documented to 1540 (row 2/384 × 100)	41%	83%	76%
4. Settlements in the sample year (row 2/row 1 × 100)	70%	89%	80%
b. Settlements with lordships of:[c]			
5. Ecclesiastical corporations	101	123	124
6. Settlements with ecclesiastical lordships as % of those with known lordship (row 5/row 2 × 100)	62%	39%	43%
7. Settlements with ecclesiastical lordships as % of settlements then in the duchy (row 5/row 1 × 100)	42%	35%	34%
8. Knightly nobles	39	131	80
9. Settlements with knightly lordships as % of those with known lordship (row 8/row 2 × 100)	24%	41%	27%
10. Settlements with knightly lordships as % of settlements then in the duchy (row 8/row 1 × 100)	17%	37%	22%
11. Citizens of Wrocław	27	88	101
12. Settlements with citizen lordships as % of those with known lordship (row 11/row 2 × 100)	16%	28%	35%
13. Settlements with citizen lordships as % of settlements then in the duchy (row 11/row 1 × 100)	12%	25%	28%
14. Other landowners[d]	25	54	38
15. Settlements with other lordships as % of those with known lordship (row 14/row 2 × 100)	15%	17%	13%
16. Settlements with other lordships as % of settlements then in the duchy (row 14/row 1 × 100)	11%	15%	11%
c. Individual holdings[e]			
17. Holdings with known lordship	207	579	415
Holdings of:			
18. Ecclesiastical corporations	104	125	124
19. Ecclesiastical holdings as % of those with known lordship (row 18/row 17 × 100)	51%	21%	30%
20. Knightly nobles	48	226	118
21. Knightly holdings as % of those with known lordship (row 20/row 17 × 100)	23%	39%	28%

Table 7.1. (*continued*)

	1300	1353	1425
22. Citizens of Wrocław	28	147	118
23. Citizen holdings as % of those with known lordship (row 22/ row 17 × 100)	14%	25%	28%
24. Others	27	81	55
25. Other holdings as % of those with known lordship (row 24/row 17 × 100)	13%	14%	13%
d. Lords			
26. Total landlords known	85	351	213
27. Ecclesiastical corporations	16	17	18
28. EC landlords as % of known (row 27/row 26 × 100)	19%	5%	8%
29. Knights	35	167	84
30. Knightly landlords as % of known (row 29/row 26 × 100)	41%	47%	39%
31. *Knightly landowning families*[f]	*23*	*79*	*39*
32. Citizens of Wrocław	25	97	65
33. Citizen landlords as % of known (row 32/row 26 × 100)	29%	28%	30%
34. *Citizen landowning families*[f]	*21*	*60*	*39*
35. Other lords	9	70	46
36. Other landlords as % of known (row 36/row 26 × 100)	10%	20%	22%

Notes.

[a] For 1300 only, settlements then documented.

[b] All percentages are given to the nearest whole number.

[c] In section b, rows 5–16, each settlement can count once for each status group. Thus a place where two knights had property contributes only one to the entry in row 8, but one where both a knight and a citizen had property counts for each group. Thus raw counts need not total the same as in row 2 and percentages need not add to 100.

[d] "Others" here include dukes, municipal corporations, citizens of Środa, schulzen and other free but non-noble countrymen, and persons of unidentifiable status.

[e] In section c, rows 17–25, each individual's property in each settlement where he holds counts once for his group. Thus in contrast to section b, rows 5–16, two noble landlords in one place contribute two holdings to the noble count. Raw counts total to those in row 17 and, except for rounding errors, the percentages to 100.

[f] As identified by common surnames.

Sources: See Table A.1 and discussion in Appendix A.

empirically an early fourteenth century profile of lordship is not secular but episcopal. The *Liber fundationis episcopatus Wratislaviensis* mentions many lay lords for their tithe obligations but covers church lands more thoroughly.[35] And because churches rarely alienated land and did not die, their lands are more easily detected even with relatively few texts. Thus, especially because the count of church lordships grew little in the fuller records of later years, the proportion for 1300 must be considerably deflated to approximate the share of all lands then held by this group. An estimate that ecclesiastical landowners possessed something like a third of the duchy's lordships in the early fourteenth century would accord well with the evidence that most individual ecclesiastical estates grew little or not at all in the next hundred years (see below). As before, most church lands were in the Wrocław district.

It follows that lay persons and institutions controlled about two-thirds of the fourteenth-century duchy's rural lordships, most of which belonged to clearly identifiable townsmen and knights. Their joint share likely grew in the decades before mid-century and stabilized for some generations thereafter. But the particular histories of the two groups differed dramatically: from owning several times the property of the few citizen lords around 1300, the Wrocław duchy nobility saw its position challenged by 1353 and, increasingly at its own expense, equaled or even surpassed by citizens by 1425.[36]

Wrocław citizens barely lagged behind churchmen in their use of written instruments, especially for the acquisition of property. This nearly complete early record makes the best starting point for assessment of their landed position. In 1300, twenty-five Wrocław citizens together possessed twenty-eight parcels in twenty-seven places, or, at most, 10 to 15 percent of the duchy's rural lordships (Table 7.1).[37] Only Werner Schertilzan's land at Bogdaszowice was then outside the Wrocław district (Map 7.1).[38]

The main growth of citizen landholdings came in the first half of the fourteenth century and continued at a much reduced rate into the early fifteenth.[39] By 1353, when all the evidence identifying landowners is at its best, nearly a hundred townsmen had property in eighty-eight places (Table 7.1). Their share of lordships had probably more than doubled to include a quarter of the settlements in the duchy. They remained overwhelmingly within the friendly confines of their own district: only one citizen property was in the Uraz district and seven along the eastern fringes of the Środa district (Map 7.1). But the inalienable church lands so common across the Wrocław district hampered further expansion of citizen interests there. After 1353 net additions to citizen-owned settlements slowed markedly, to a rate below even that of the late thirteenth century. In 1425 sixty-five citizen lords with land in 101 places had not quite a third of the duchy's lordships. In the Wrocław district itself, they owned marginally fewer places than in 1353. Men of Wrocław who sought new rural acquisitions turned after the mid-fourteenth century to the Środa district, which contained by 1425, especially in its southern reaches and northeast corner, nearly a quarter of the settlements they then possessed.[40] The composite data thus shows Wrocław

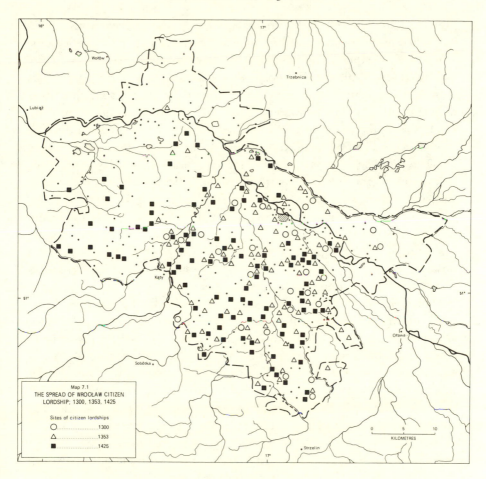

Map 7.1
THE SPREAD OF WROCŁAW CITIZEN
LORDSHIP; 1300, 1353, 1425

Sites of citizen lordships

○ 1300
△ 1353
■ 1425

citizens becoming lords of rural land in a wave which gathered slowly in their own district before 1300, rose rapidly to a crest there during the first half of the fourteenth century, and then washed significantly into the Środa district as it lost momentum in the generations before 1425.

Knights and their families are less fully documented than other important landowners. Slowest to care for written evidence of their possessory rights, many noble owners are first recorded not acquiring but already holding the property in question. How and when they came to be there is unknown. Later on, extant texts can pass silently over a generation or more of what is probably but not verifiably a noble family's continuous tenure. Nevertheless, the historical pattern of knightly lordships is demonstrably the inverse of that described for Wrocław citizens. Statistics for 1353 provide the most secure starting point because coverage is then most complete

(Table 7.1, rows 3 and 4). 167 members of knightly families then had 226 individual holdings in 131 places, which are 41 percent of the settlements where lords are then identifiable and 37 percent of those places then in any way recorded (Table 7.1) Balancing the possibility that nobles' properties then still more often went unrecorded against the fact that knights often owned only a part of the land at a given site would cause these figures to imply that in the mid-fourteenth century the knights controlled a third or more but not a half of the duchy's countryside.[41]

The problem is to ascertain the trend of noble ownership during the half century before 1353. Texts from around 1300 identify knights in only 24 percent of the sites where lords are then known, which is only 17 percent of sites then documented in any way and probably closer to 12 percent of those actually inhabited. And since it is not hard to find knights receiving grants of previously ducal land from Henry VI,[42] something like a doubling of their aggregate landholdings between 1300 and 1353 might seem plausible. Three reasons make this most unlikely. First, since the well-documented church estates alienated no appreciable land at this time, there is no evident source for simultaneous large-scale net growth in both citizen and noble lands. Second, at most places where knights held property in 1353, the first identifiable owner is a knight already in (not taking) possession when recorded after 1300.[43] Third, many places owned by non-nobles in 1353 had also first entered the documentary record in noble possession since 1300 and in the interim visibly passed to others.[44] The probable conclusion must be that knightly nobles did not in fact increase their total holdings after 1300 but then held as much as and most likely more than at mid-century (in excess of 40 percent), and that the net trend of their wealth drifted downwards during the first half of the century.

After mid-century noble lordships around Wrocław diminished more quickly. Between 1353 and 1425 the number of places with recorded lands of knights dropped by fifty-one (39 percent) while those with any identifiable lord declined by only twenty-six (8 percent). In 1425, nobles owned land in eighty settlements, 27 percent of those where lords are identifiable and 22 percent of those in the duchy.

The best approximation, therefore, of the trends in knightly wealth around fourteenth-century Wrocław is a slow but accelerating decrease from about two-fifths of the local lordships at the beginning of the century to one fourth just before the Hussite wars. Their decline had geographic attributes, too, for noble landowners effectively abandoned the Wrocław district and made the Środa and Uraz districts their redoubts.[45]

All persons other than churchmen, knights, and Wrocław citizens never had as many lordships as any one of the three main groups. Miscellaneous and unclassifiable landowners held, in the three years profiled, between 10 and 15 percent of places and of individual holdings (Table 7.1, rows 14–16 and 24–25). The relative importance of distinguishable groups among them reflects changes in the Silesian socio-political order. Weakening of the sovereign's direct power and access to landed wealth was manifest in a rapid loss of ducal lands: eighteen or more places managed on the dukes' (Wrocław and Głogów) accounts about 1300 were reduced to three by 1353 and none by the early fifteenth century.[46] Newer sorts of owners filled the gap. The municipality of Wrocław had from its foundation extramural pastures and meadows, and during the early 1300s added land in Szczytniki, Kowale, *Leimgruben*, and *Rzepina*.[47] Countrymen who were not knights but who nevertheless held land with full ownership rights had some quantitative importance, too. By 1353 they comprised more than 5 percent of known owners and in 1425 almost 10 percent, but their holdings were small and most lived in a few villages. Finally there were lords for whom surviving documents allow no designation of status. They too, are more numerous in the relatively full records for 1353 and 1425 than in 1300. At their peak in 1353 they included a little more than 10 percent of all named lords, but a smaller share of known holdings.[48]

Thus, to summarize the knowledge gained from tabulating all available evidence for the possession of lordships, three groups—the church, the knightly nobility, and the citizens of Wrocław—together dominated the class of lords in the fourteenth-century duchy. While the clergy changed little their total share of around a third of the duchy's lordships, the knights most likely retreated steadily from possession of somewhat more than the church in the generation around 1300 to about a quarter of the total by around 1425. Townsmen, however, rose during the same period from being owners of approximately one property in eight to a share equal to that of the nobility.[49] Citizens and clerics divided the Wrocław district between them; knights were preeminent in the Środa and especially the Uraz district.

What size were lords' estates around fourteenth-century Wrocław? Information on the total area or value of properties is not available. Only counts of lordships possessed by each lord and a frequency distribution of those counts are possible (see Table 7.2). Profiles at the familiar three dates suggest a division between large, mainly ecclesiastical, estates and small, mainly lay, estates, with more land in the latter by mid-century.

Again the data for 1300 present the greatest interpretive problem. Nearly half (47 percent) of the lordships identifiable in the documentary record for that year belonged to churches with property at three or more sites in the duchy (classified as large estates). Subsequent additions to ecclesiastical property lists were so few and generally so well-recorded that the

Table 7.2. The scale of lordship: 1300–1353–1425

	Total sample[a]	Small estates (1–2 holdings)					Large estates (3–15 holdings)					The very large estate of the Church of Wroclaw
		Church estates	Noble estates	Wroclaw citizen estates	Other[c] estates	All small estates	Church estates	Noble estates	Wroclaw citizen estates	Other[c] estates	All large estates	
1300 landowners	85	7	32	23	7	69	8	3	2	2	15	1
as % of total[b]	*100*	*8*	*38*	*27*	*8*	*81*	*9*	*4*	*2*	*2*	*18*	*1*
holdings	207	8	39	21	9	77	49	9	7	18	83	47
as % of total	*100*	*4*	*19*	*10*	*4*	*36*	*24*	*4*	*3*	*9*	*40*	*23*
1353 landowners	351	6	155	87	67	315	10	12	10	3	35	1
as % of total	*100*	*2*	*44*	*25*	*19*	*90*	*3*	*3*	*3*	*1*	*10*	*0.3*
holdings	579	8	184	100	69	361	69	42	47	12	170	48
as % of total	*100*	*1*	*32*	*17*	*12*	*62*	*12*	*7*	*8*	*2*	*29*	*8*
1425 landowners	213	5	79	54	44	182	12	5	11	2	30	1
as % of total	*100*	*2*	*37*	*25*	*21*	*85*	*6*	*2*	*5*	*1*	*14*	*0.5*
holdings	415	6	94	62	45	207	76	24	56	10	166	42
as % of total	*100*	*1*	*23*	*15*	*11*	*50*	*18*	*6*	*13*	*2*	*40*	*10*

Notes.

[a] The "total sample" of landowners and holdings replicates those in Table 7.1 (originally Table A.1), rows 25 and 17.

[b] All percentages in each row are of the entry in the column labelled "total sample," which is the same in both parts of the table. Percentages greater than one are rounded to the nearest whole percent.

[c] "Other estates," include those of dukes, municipal corporations, citizens of Środa, schulzen and other free but non-noble countrymen, and persons without identifiable status.

Sources: See Table A.2 and discussion in Appendix A.

raw figure of 96 holdings in 94 places is likely almost complete coverage for this group and their relative importance in 1300 thus much exaggerated in the written record of lordship. A better assessment recognizes in these 94 sites about 40 percent of sites recorded by 1300 and 25 percent of sites ever inhabited in the Middle Ages. Hence the nine large church estates controlled about a third of the properties in the early fourteenth-century duchy.

How then was the lay-owned two-thirds of the duchy apportioned in the early fourteenth century between large and small estates? If the ratio for the 103 lay-held properties in 91 places for which ownership is documented can stand for all lay-owned land, small lay lords had about 40 percent and large about 20, with the latter equally divided between the duke and good-sized private holders. In sum, the best approximation of the scale of lord-ships around 1300 would place a half or more of the duchy's land under the control of relatively large holders and a half or a little less under that of small ones. Few large lords and even fewer of the lordships in large estates were secular and private; the duchy was already a place of small lay and large ecclesiastical lords.

Ownership records for 1353 and 1425 cover 80 to 90 percent of the places then in the duchy. They confirm the picture dimly seen in 1300 and suggest more subtle trends. In both the mid-fourteenth and the early fif-teenth century small lords overwhelmingly dominated the group of land-owners and possessed half or more of the properties for which the lords are known. If it is not an artifact of the extraordinarily rich mid-century record, the evidence suggests the years around 1353 as a maximum in this broad distribution of lordship rights. At the same time, large ecclesiastical estates remained important and good-sized lay estates began to develop. Already by mid-century townsmen with more than two rural holdings had in-creased five-fold their numbers and the lands they controlled; by 1425 they outnumbered all other large lay lords and controlled more property too. Nevertheless lordships in small citizen estates remained a majority of the townsman-owned properties and lay lords of this scale—citizens, knights, and others—continued to hold more than any other group (ecclesiastical or large lay).[50]

The section should end on a note of caution. Tabulating properties and those from various status groups who owned them is not an ideal quanti-tative technique. Counts are made only of transformed data, the recorded presence of lords in places for which the history of lordship is recoverable from extant texts. But to count simply the conveyances themselves would omit property long held by a family or a corporation and to rely on survey texts alone would replicate their systematic lacunae (see the discussion in appendix A). The objects here tabulated may also uncomfortably resemble the "manors" whose counting once raised the spleen of specialists on Tudor-Stuart England.[51] Of course a lord's "holding" or "property" in a given place could vary greatly in size and value. The method used was not chosen freely from a set of alternatives, but is simply the only one available to estimate, however crudely, the distribution of lordships in the four-teenth-century duchy. That evidence is not strained by the following sum-mary conclusions:

1. After the disappearance of direct ducal lordships early in the century, churches, knights, and citizens of Wrocław owned the great majority of the land.
2. Corporate church estates, mostly quite large, covered a relatively stable one-third of the duchy's lordships, mostly in the Wrocław district.
3. Citizens of Wrocław increased their possessions, chiefly in the Wrocław district, from about one property in ten around 1300 to almost one in three by 1425, with more of the expansion coming before mid-century than after it.
4. Knights may have controlled more land than churchmen in the early part of the century but, by 1425, held about a quarter of that in the duchy, primarily in the Środa and Uraz districts.
5. Private lay landowners of whatever status were rarely very wealthy in land.

No contradictory hypotheses plausibly interpret the available evidence, while more precise assertions can be only spurious and speculative. These collective approximations suffice to give rough shape to a socio-economic structure of the landed elite and to provide a context for investigation of individual lords, their estates, and their behavior towards landed property. Now the special features of ecclesiastical and of lay landowners require their separate treatment.

Church estates in the fourteenth century: motion without movement

Estates of ecclesiastical foundations are the best documented in the duchy. Only here are reasonably full narratives possible, although, ironically, losses in 1945 of almost all the unpublished administrative records of monastic houses have left large gaps in a field scholars elsewhere have worked inten-sively. For the older foundations especially, most with much land outside as well as within the Duchy of Wrocław, political disarray around 1300 threatened violent expropriation and offered donations from penitent or competitive regional rulers. In a subsequent more stable environment these estates experienced less change, and that more from causes particular to each. Donations stopped and other forms of property acquisition never took up the slack. For generations before 1425 the large, old church estates had become stable structures.[52] After illustrating this evolution with a look at the bishopric and some monastic houses, the following discussion contrasts the greater and later dynamism of other, smaller, foundations with more local interests and functions.

As earlier, the largest landed estate in the fourteenth-century duchy and entire province belonged to the Church of Wrocław. The bishop governed with full princely rights whole districts around his usual residence at Nysa, and he, his canons, and other cathedral clergy added in the Wrocław duchy more than forty villages and independent demesne farms.[53]

The bishop's peaceful exploitation of his estate depended on good relations with secular authority. If this were too ambitious, it abraded the jurisdictional claims of *ecclesia*; if too weak, it left the church's riches open to plunder. Bishop Thomas II (1267–92) suffered military defeat and economic hardship before his penitent victor, Duke Henry IV, conceded juridical sovereignty over the episcopal principality of Nysa and endowed a new college of canons at Holy Cross just down the street from the cathedral.[54] Bishop Henry I (1301–19) found Duke Henry VI unable to protect episcopal lands and subjects from attack, pillage, and seizure by private lords at feud with him. Clerics in the 1330s were still redeeming those losses—and then suffered again when Bishop Nanker (1326–41) and King John dueled over tax payments and possession of a strategic castle.[55] Less portentous local issues which later exacerbated relations between the governing town council of Wrocław and the cathedral chapter resident across the river channel, sooner or later involved the estate of the church. First city and canons, then king and bishop, wrangled in 1367 about the authority of secular courts over a church subject from Strzeganowice.[56] In 1381 Wrocław defended its monopoly over the sale of much-favored Świdnica beer by seizing at the city gate kegs sent for canon Henry's Christmas from his brother, the Duke of Legnica. Excommunications, interdicts, and intrusion on church lordships fast followed.[57]

Normal economic and administrative procedures also affected the lands of the Church of Wrocław. After the chapter leased *Cruce* in perpetuity to a Wrocław citizen in 1344, he merged it to adjoining lands in Bielany Wrocławskie and its separate name, identity, and ecclesiastical lordship slipped from the minds of men.[58] The dead hand usually held, however, so the unity of the estate of the Church of Wrocław mainly fell victim to its own administrative subdivision into many autonomous prebends and corporations. Only a fraction, for instance, of known church properties were carefully surveyed for Bishop Conrad in 1421/25, for only these belonged directly to the bishop and were administered as a unit through his own officers.[59] Separately endowed and managed were the estates of the prior, dean, archdeacon, scholasticus and school, chancellor, chapter corporately, canons individually, and vicars.[60]

Less a single economic enterprise and less unperturbed by worldly considerations than its long roll of renewed and reconfirmed privileges might suggest, the estate of the Church of Wrocław in the duchy was nevertheless large and amazingly stable from the mid-thirteenth century to the eve of the Hussite wars. How stable? Of the forty-five lordships expressly confirmed by King Wenceslas in 1382 to end the "beer war" and celebrate accession of a new bishop, also Wenceslas, forty-four had been in the possession of the Church in 1353, forty in 1300, and thirty-three can be traced back to the papal bull of protection given the bishopric in 1245.[61]

Some monastic estates approached that of the episcopal church in age, size, and stability, but their greater managerial unity makes for more coherent stories of alternating prosperity and difficulty. The Premonstratensians of St. Vincent, whose estate scattered south of Wrocław and clustered around Kostomłoty was second in size only to that of the bishopric, experienced typically muted vicissitudes of fortune. They lost some holdings during the late 1200s, partly by the reshaping of rural settlement patterns, but also from sales and lay usurpations. Abbots sold Popowice and Opatowice, but at Kowale, Krajków, and Szczytniki lay lords simply appear in the abbey's place.[62]

A hint of better times for St. Vincent might be the repurchase of Opatowice in 1325,[63] but real efforts to increase its estate came only under Abbot Nicholas in the 1340s. He bought—for donations to St. Vincent had become entirely passé—lands, jurisdictions, and annual *census*, wherever, it seems, he could find them.[64] His successors concentrated their acquisitive impulses on extending rights or enlarging holdings at places where the abbey already had interests. The economic well-being of the abbey may have been threatened briefly when it was outlawed by Charles IV in 1377 and longer when it endured a costly thirteen-year dispute over the 1409 election of abbot Andreas Rugeler,[65] but in 1425 its estate was as large and long-established as ever. All six of St. Vincent's village lordships listed in that year's tax account could be traced back to the thirteenth century and of the seven demesne farms and other holdings not then taxed, none wholly post-dated the 1340s.[66]

The Augustinians of St. Mary on the Sand Islet owned in the Duchy of Wrocław a little less than their traditional rivals of St. Vincent because their largest property complex lay around Sobótka just south of its boundary, but otherwise the histories of the two houses were similar. Not one of St.

Mary's nine properties in 1425 had been acquired any later than 1353 and most long predated the fourteenth century. This house, too, suffered late thirteenth-century losses—blamed by its own chronicler on then abbot Nicholas Quas (1283–91)—which leaders in following generations laboriously restored.[67] After the reputedly prosperous tenure of Abbot Conrad of Włocławek (1329–63), some lands were put out at long lease but none fully alienated.[68] Comparably undramatic, if in some cases slowly dwindling, were the estates of other old (and distant) churches and foundations.[69]

In contrast to the stability and marginal losses which came during the fourteenth century to characterize the estates of most older houses with extensive lands elsewhere, corporations with real local interests and involvement around Wrocław experienced at least periods of prosperity and expansion. The city's convents and hospitals attracted landed donations well past 1300 and later often used their incomes to buy more lordships nearby.

Enclosed nuns of St. Clare at Wrocław, for example, recipients of a significant estate at their 1257 foundation, kept the patronage of the ducal house until its extinction. Duke Władysław, archbishop-elect of Salzburg, gave Księginice in 1268 and the regent, Duke Bolko, added Maślice upon the entry of his wards, the daughters of Henry V, in 1301. Henry VI offered Chrząstowa Wielka in 1327 to atone for damages caused by his officials.[70] Already in 1317 and 1324, however, St. Clare had also attracted the piety of a rich city family: John Markgraf and his wife, who would as a widow live with the nuns, donated their property in Pietrzykowice.[71] More often, however, the considerable gifts of townspeople, whether testamentary or upon entry of a kinswoman into the convent, came as cash or annuities on income-producing property. Though commonly hedged about with conditions so the incomes supported for life the donor's kin, all eventually came into the convent's free disposal.[72] This financed purchase of more land: seven mansi at Jeszkowice in 1333 and probably Iwiny and *Weinberg*, which the nuns had confirmed by King John in 1344/45.[73] After these steady additions, the mid-fourteenth-century estate of St. Clare had thirteen lordships and matched that of St. Vincent as second-largest in the duchy.[74] Then a tide plainly turned. No further new holdings are recorded and some late acquisitions were surrendered. By 1425 the convent's rural estate had shrunk to a size more moderate by ecclesiastical standards, eight well-documented and long-held properties in the river bottoms and black earth near the city.[75]

Surely in financial trouble by 1425 after a century of steady property accumulation was the hospital of St. Mathias, one of several charitable foundations which, like the convents, had prospered for much of the 1300s. The Knights of the Cross with the Red Star who operated St. Mathias did not change their original endowment in the duchy during the later thirteenth century, but in 1305 they bought from the knight Przesław of Maniów his holdings at Dobrzykowice.[76] Some economic tension may have affected the corporation during the 1330s, for, although forty marks were available to buy Strachocin in 1332, more was donated by the seller, John Stille, and Mokronos Dolny was sold to some laymen about the same time. As late as 1341 Master Conrad Glesil had to give special pledges for payment of overdue annuities.[77]

Mid-century administrators restored the hospital's finances, but left to their successors the surest assertion of prosperous confidence, new acquisitions of property. John Siebenwirt (1370–91) purchased Kamieniec Wrocławski in 1375 and repurchased Mokronos Dolny in 1386, while Peter Neuniz (1391–1402) similarly acquired Gajków in 1393.[78] But when, even before Neuniz's death, Pope Boniface IX could in 1399 allow appropriation of the Gajków parish church because the hospital's total incomes came to less than two hundred marks a year, perhaps the recent purchases had strained its resources.

Clearly the next couple of decades were difficult. Despite sale in 1405 of Boguszyce, debts mounted, two successive masters resigned under pressure, and in 1424 King Sigismund ordered the Wrocław city council to assume trusteeship of the hospital's finances. Mokronos Górny was sold within the year and then a meadow at Siechnice. Although the nine properties still listed for St. Mathias in 1425 put it near the top of the corporate lords, indebtedness would remain heavy and more sales would follow.[79] After considerable growth during most of the fourteenth century, therefore, the St. Mathias hospital was one of the few corporate landlords to display real economic distress even before the Hussite wars.

More or less ancient and as varied in sacramental, ascetic, or charitable purpose as the broad responsibilities claimed by the medieval church, the duchy's ecclesiastical landlords formed a distinct group among those who jostled for position atop rural society. But the churchmen did not, on the whole, jostle all that much during the long fourteenth century. Their share of properties shifted little and few houses seriously changed the relative size or location of their holdings. A map depicting ecclesiastical properties in 1353 or 1425 would contain more items but otherwise differ in no fundamentals from the situation portrayed for the mid-thirteenth century in Map 3.2. Eighty-five percent or more of church properties and all of most church estates in the duchy were in the Wrocław district.

The sheer total volume of church holdings in the duchy made them significant, though they could little represent any lords but themselves. These few perpetual corporations possessed an institutional continuity which encouraged long-term consistencies in their behavior and even conscious restorations of long-lost properties. Units of ownership among ecclesiastics were mostly larger than the norm, for they accumulated over centuries and escaped the biological cycles which inevitably dominate the history of lay estates. Ecclesiastical lordships were stable, but not static. The different particulars of each corporation's institutional function and relations with secular authorities, the managerial skills of administrators, and the slowly changing fashions of piety among the wealthy made distinct the experiences of a St. Vincent, a St. Clare, and a St. Mathias. Nevertheless, simple institutional continuity of owner and estate set ecclesiastics apart from secular individuals who shared the same elite position and role. Lay lords, numerous and mortally ephemeral, lived with other considerations and require different treatment.

Lay lords, families, and transitory estates

Transient lay-owned estates and impermanent families are characteristic of the Wrocław duchy's fourteenth-century landed elite. Of the 195 secular landowners known in 1425, only the city of Wrocław was also so listed in 1353 or 1300. Each early-fifteenth-century church estate plainly derived from a late-thirteenth-century predecessor. No knight or townsman of 1425 had the same estate as an ancestor in 1300; almost none had a single property from so distant a kinsman; few could even claim as their predecessors earlier landowners of the same name. This volatility of lay property stemmed from the social situation of lay lords. The lordships—many or few, however obtained, and with whatever degree of economic coherence—held by most lay lords were normally accumulated by the current holder and after his or her death soon again scattered by normal family obligations and the ever-available market. Concurrently, leading and lesser names among the possessors of land changed with generational regularity.

Conditions of flux are poorly grasped through that accumulation of separate narratives suitable for the church estates. Incomplete (if very plentiful) data and the unsynchronized and irregular occurrence of contingently critical events (sales, births, deaths, children's gender, etc.) preclude genuinely statistical methods as well. Instead, this section shifts attention from particular units undergoing idiosyncratic change to the processes which systematically brought people and property together and moved them apart. How did lords get land and develop estates? How did families later give up or keep an individual's holdings? In what follows the techniques used among the laity to build and transmit estates are established by composite generalization from law and practice, and their application illustrated with a few exemplary individuals. Collectively these social processes created, shaped, and shattered ephemeral connections between lords and landed properties to make lay estates evanescent.

How, then, was landed property acquired by those building estates around Wrocław? Already under the last Piasts private lay people used all means known to their successors: grant, purchase, and inheritance. The ruler rewarded with land the past or anticipated services of individuals of various ranks. Henry IV gave Krajków to Master Wiland the stonemason (*lapicida*) and his like-named son, a ducal servitor, as a service-free hereditary fief.[80] In 1292 a man of greater political weight, Nicholas, Count Palatine of Poznań, similarily received Janików, Swojczyce, and Kamieniec Wrocławskie.[81] Townsmen like the judges of Środa, Apeczco and Henry, acquired their four mansi at suburban Bielany and rural knights like Albert and Arnold Pak their village of Kulin, all from their loyal followership of Henry VI.[82]

Yet several of the same individuals in the same properties, and others like them elsewhere, also gained rights by other means. The younger Wiland took Krajków by inheritance, as did Albert of Gostyn, son of Count Nicholas, at Swojczyce, and Albert and Ulrich Pak, sons of the elder Albert, at Kulin.[83] So did the lady Florcha and her sons Jeszko and Przesław, widow and offspring of Dobrogost, who held part of Dobrzykowice in 1301. They then sold the property to Florcha's brother, the knight Przesław of Maniów, who three years earlier had bought other land there from another knight, Conrad of Sulz.[84] If citizens did have more consistent access to liquid wealth, they may have bought land for cash more than did other lords. In twelve months following May, 1324, John Stille, a Wrocław merchant, spent 57.5 marks in three separate deals with the heirs of Conrad of Strachocin to acquire their inheritance. John had, moreover, during the four years preceding the first full purchase, already loaned 29 marks to the owners of Strachocin for which he held a lien on the property.[85] But convoluted financial dealings were never the preserve of townsmen alone. In 1311 a knight, Frederick of Waldow, initiated private possession of Gniechowice. For a pledge of all ownership and sovereign rights the duke exercised there, he loaned to Henry VI an agreed sum of 2000 marks, of which only 1450 were paid in cash, 50 credited to the duke's existing debts, and 500 remitted for Frederick's loyal services. But if the full 2000 were not repaid in two years, Frederick and his heirs had perpetual feudal tenure in Gniechowice.[86]

Under the later Piasts and their Luxemburg successors landed property was available from several sources and could be acquired through various means. Recourse to these by contemporary builders of private estates cannot be quantified, but normal ranges of behavior are visible from a few illustrative careers.[87]

Property dealings of Otto of Glubos, whose tenure at Kobierzyce helped introduce the issues of this chapter, neatly bridge the transition from the last Piast, a man accessible to his more important subjects and generous with what began as a still appreciable sovereign estate, to King John, no less desirous of supporters but with less to give and less easily familiarized with a minor Silesian knight.[88] Otto did not lose from these changes in the availability of largess, but he did not gain either. From Henry VI in 1333 Otto had received his good-sized fief of Kobierzyce, freed for his loyalty from any obligations to service. When John took over, Otto saw to the confirmation of the earlier gift, but received no more from his sovereign.[89] To increase his estate Otto turned instead to the land market and to collaboration with wealthy men of the city. He and Nicholas Sittin bought from Sophia, wife of another townsman, Nicholas Reichenbach, demesne farms at Bielany Wrocławskie and Bledzów.[90] Otto kept the latter and his partner, the larger but more distant Bielany. This knight, first of his kin to own land in the duchy, thus followed the old way for a new man to gain landed wealth, the grant for service, with the new, purchase. Otto's two properties were conveniently in the middle of the Wrocław district.[91]

Despite the modest success of nobles like Otto of Glubos, the aggregate evidence proves the achievers on the mid-century rural land market were city men with liquid, if not often great wealth. Hennig Winter, though a merchant related to the well-to-do Głogów family, married the daughter of an artisan and gained only brief membership on the Rat. His one known lordship, a demesne farm at *Stoszkowice*, he bought in 1345 from Bishop Przesław, to whom it had been a gift from Margrave Charles.[92] Although the general stability of church estates removed from the market most land clergy acquired, special circumstances often made some available to interested laity. This one, Winter, represents nevertheless the small end of the range of citizen lords.

Peter Schwarz ("Niger"), who died in 1383, was a great Wrocław magnate, active continuously from 1342 to 1380 on either the city council or court and heavily involved in rural land and lordships. His approach to landed property is an instructive blend of familial connections and the power of the purse, both in service to a cool business head and the prestige value of a well-privileged estate. Peter's father Thilo, a merchant and councilman, had married him well to Hedwig Sittin but left him no land. Peter added to the profits of long-distance trading a still more lucrative activity as financier, which yielded not only income from loans but contacts and privileges, too.[93]

Through his career Peter dealt in landlord rights over a total of sixteen places in the duchy, actually owned land in thirteen, and retained to leave as a legacy four properties, Żerniki Wielkie, Solna, Jaksonów and Węgry, which about the time he acquired them came to 117 rental mansi.[94] Peter bought everything he owned, mostly from fellow citizens, some from nobles, one sublordship from the Church of Wrocław, but his chests of coin were not his only resource. Kinship and other connections helped. Of the four holdings he retained, three (Żerniki, Solna, and Jaksonów) came from his Sittin in-laws, and of his other landed interests, three more also found the Sittin involved as vendors or co-purchasers, and two were obtained from his regular business associate, Nicholas of Cracow.[95]

Caution and a concern to reduce risk also characterized Schwarz's dealings in rural property. His first three ventures, purchase of Gniechowice in 1338, taking ducal rights over Żerniki as a pledge in 1343, and buying eighteen rental mansi at Jaksin in 1344, were all partnerships. Other joint acquisitions followed. Peter took further care by delaying outright purchase of land and lordship until he had learned of it through prior tenure of annual rents on it, a practice he followed at Żerniki, Węgry, and Solna.[96] Overall, of the thirteen places where he actually obtained land, he did so in seven only after demonstrably prior experience with the place and/or the seller thereof.[97]

A like rationality controlled Schwarz's subsequent handling of his estate. Like some contemporaries, he acted as if he distinguished within the whole of his landed interests a core of holdings which would and did remain permanent possessions. By 1349 he had a decade's experience with country property and, though owning land in several places, had only annual rents on Węgry and Solna and nothing in Żerniki or Jaksonów. In that year, however, he began to purchase Solna and Żerniki from the Sittins. The former took two transactions, the latter four, but by 1356 they were his alone. Meanwhile the lands of the Colner family at Wegry had also come on the market and Schwarz was interested. First he obtained from Charles IV fief rights hereditary in both sexes for all he might acquire there. Then he achieved his expectations in three transactions with the Colner between 1352 and 1355. Finally in 1357 he bought the Sittin holdings at Jaksonów, a place equidistant from the other three villages. In an active career on the real estate market which covered more than thirty-five years, Schwarz completed the purchase of these properties in only eight. Then, although he controlled several other lordships at the time, Schwarz went back to Charles IV in 1359 to request and receive for these four alone special confirmation of his title and its conversion from "feodalia" to possession "in iura hereditaria."[98] With its components tidily grouped within eight kilometers of one another in the south of the Wrocław district, the estate of Peter Schwarz was complete. After 1359 he made for sixteen years no new acquisitions and concerned himself with property and titles only to defend against claims raised by Henry Sittin his rights in Żerniki.[99]

Lordships other than the select four had different objective features and received different treatment. They were broadly scattered across the Wrocław district and in most cases served more speculative ends. Rights and incomes at Gniechowice and Jaksin were back in the hands of the original sellers within a decade of Schwarz's purchase; the transactions may have covered what were really loans to the Reichenbachs and Falkenhains. Wierzbno and Janików Schwarz bought from Nicholas of Cracow in 1351 and sold to Hermann Borsnicz in 1357. A woods and fortified dwelling at Lesnica passed in a single charter of 1348 through his hands from the Sittin to a knight, Henry Schwarzenhorn.[100] For this wealthy townsman, then, rural lordships could be treated as mere commodities, a use of temporarily surplus liquid capital, but they could also serve for the construction of a landed estate to complement his rise to the pinnacle of power in his city. The means and sources of property acquisition Schwarz employed, however, cash and family connections, also typify the behavior of a successful entrant into what had become a self-perpetuating urban élite in mid-century Wrocław.

The rise to landed wealth and control over much of the duchy's countryside by rich citizens like Peter Schwarz and more numerous lesser ones like Hennig Winter ought not obscure the noble contingent among late fourteenth-century lords. The career of Krig Hugowicz aptly illustrates how a knight and descendant of knights could still build a considerable estate. Krig's lineage, once ministerials from near Meissen, had been established in the hills west of Uraz since his grandfather had served Duke Henry of Głogów, and in Krig's childhood had given King John loyal vassals and a captain of the duchy.[101] When he took a wife (of unrecorded parentage) in 1356, the couple received as her dower his father Poppo's share in the old family property at Warzyn. At Poppo's death in 1367, Krig, probably the eldest of three surviving sons, inherited two lordships, Bagno and Wały, which his father had purchased.[102] Krig increased his holdings thereabouts by dealing with his relatives. From his brothers, John and "Popchin" ("little Poppo"), he bought in 1367, the same year he served on the duchy's court, part of their paternal legacy at Kręsko. In 1389 a distant kinsman, Merboth Hugowicz, sold him the Żerkówek demesne. These lands and two farms of uncertain location called "Schossiz" and "Kaldenhus" went at Krig's passing in 1395 to his sons.[103] The legacy was as large and as internally well-situated as that left by Peter Schwarz a decade before.

Taken collectively the efforts at estate-building of Otto of Glubos, Hennig Winter, Peter Schwarz, and Krig Hugowicz illustrate some continuing features of property acquisition in the fourteenth-century duchy. Land normally changed hands in units of a single village or less. Very rarely could an individual other than an heir obtain in a single conveyance of any kind property in more than one place. Whole estates of any appreciable size moved only by inheritance (and even that was unusual if there were more than one descendant; see below). This meant that each estate builder, even one who inherited some land, had gradually to accumulate his holdings. Only slowly and with unsure success could an individual seek to construct a consolidated estate, one with a monopoly on lordship rights in a single place or a group of nearby places. And finally, though wealth in money, however made available, was probably necessary and at times perhaps sufficient to create a landed estate, those men who proved most successful augmented that wealth with prior or concurrent ties of personal influence with and especially kinship to those who had lordships at their disposal.

Counterposed to the recurring process of estate building were alienations of land. Every buyer needed a seller, every recipient a donor. In the fourteenth century duchy both market and kinship-based mechanisms broke up existing estates as they helped create new ones. What rules governed and practices shaped an individual lay owner's handling of landed possessions while he lived and his heirs' behavior with them after he died? A survey of legal and practical alternatives for alienation and familial transmission of land precedes illustration of how these combined to dismember some exemplary lay estates and leave expatriate, impoverished, or extinct the descendants of him who had once collected the properties.

The capacity and willingness of all sorts of lay lords to sell all sorts of property needs no further illustration.[104] As earlier remarked, the law did recognize one prior condition for alienation of some real property, consent of the vendor's kin, though after mid-century this meant only legitimate children and only for the sale of inherited real property.

In practice, however, prospective sellers may not have been so free, for the liberal rules were not fully accepted by some who saw themselves as potential heirs to an alienated property or even by some defenders of a completed transaction. Because so many conveyances today survive only as summaries which may omit mention of formal consent, it is the more significant that in certain cases visible pains were taken to meet or exceed legal requirements. Far beyond the obligations imposed by law went the citizen Henry Doring in 1341 (after the abolition of Polish law in the duchy). To give a demesne at Baranowice to his three daughters, he mustered the public acquiescence of three sons, a son-in-law, three grandsons, and a granddaughter.[105] Even under the unambiguous post-1356 law, people asserted and sometimes even acceded to claims without legal basis. Dirsco Roraw, son of Simon in an old knightly family, finally had to admit in court in 1386 that he had challenged "czu unrechte" his forebear's gift to St. Mathias of a mill and meadow at Siechnice. John of Żybiszów sold to John Bank's children in 1376 land at Żybiszów, part inherited, part purchased from co-heirs some years before. Fifteen years later one of the buyers, John Bank the younger, had to compromise with the seller's two brothers, his wife, and his three sons because, said they, he had not acknowledged their "hereditary lordship."[106] No clear documents ever prove that a kinsman's refusal of permission prevented a sale, but such cases are not to be expected among records of successful conveyances. Similar reasons explain the lack of unambiguous preemptions or legally privileged repurchases by relatives.[107] Nevertheless, the behavior of Wrocław duchy lords did display a tacit assumption that over (especially inherited) land extended a residual right of family members, notably of those who had once belonged to the same nuclear unit, to constrain the current holder from acting against their interests.

Family connections also gave positive direction to the transmission of property. Law and social custom alike required certain endowments of kin by a living owner and directed the descent of land to his heirs after his death. But these obligations had unequal impact on a landed estate.

Formation of a new marriage drew differently on the resources of the bride's family and those of the new husband. From the former, Polish and German customary law expected that the daughter take with her to her spouse endowment in movables (*dos, bestatunge, sponsalia*) of a value set by her father, brothers, or guardian and equivalent to her share in the paternal estate.[108] This dowry should have had little direct effect on real property rights and, correspondingly, rarely appears in the land records of the duchy.[109] Against the movables in her husband's estate a widow had two legitimate claims: the *Gerade* comprised items such as women's clothing and furnishings used by the wife of a household; the *Morgengabe* was normally items of value like stock or household goods which the husband had specified as a free gift after consummation of the marriage. Although neither was thus defined or described as charges against landed property, either could exceptionally be so expressed and paid.[110] More commonly, however, a man's landed wealth went to his wife's dower.

With the dower (*dotalicium, lypgedinge*), an arrangement common to German and Polish social custom in the later Middle Ages, the husband reciprocated the dowry. As negotiated by the families before the betrothal, this meant that value from the husband's property approximately equal to that of the dowry was combined with the dowry and secured on his property to the wife for life as her widow's portion, contractually immunized by formal registration from any interference. In the words of the duchy's mid-century law, "No one can break the woman's dower."[111] In practice, the dower could be a charge against the husband's lands,[112] but more often in the extant records the wife obtained a right to the land itself. Thus in 1336 Hedwig Plessil received Siedlakowice as "vera dothalicio quod vulgo lipgedinge dicitur" from her knightly husband John and in a later generation Elizabeth Reichenbach had more than thirty mansi at Gniechowice but Agnes of Lubnów only two at Lubnów.[113]

These ladies had not gained ownership rights to the real estate, or even possession during the lives of their husbands, but an interest which legally required their public consent for any diminution or alienation. Thus Elizabeth, who received in 1344 from her husband, Gregory of Chomiąża, a dower including four mansi at Łowęcice, appeared before the court in 1352 to agree to his sale of annuities on that land, and Agnes, wife of Lawrence of Cracow, citizen of Wrocław, assented "for her dower" to her man's 1376 sale of Swojczyce.[114]

But in turn law and the actions of charters and courts agreed that a wife's or widow's rights over such lands were themselves limited to a lifetime usufruct after the husband's death. His heirs retained true proprietary rights. A woman who alienated her dower or tried to pass it to her own heirs risked forfeiture of all her rights.[115] Nevertheless some did so. Elizabeth, widow of Conrad of Wierzbice, specified that she held Gajków as property by right of her dower when she sold it in 1344. In the next decade Mechtild Swenkenfeld first three times in five years publicly consented to her husband's sale of annuities on his land in Stary Śleszów and then, nine months after the last of these and as his widow, sold the four mansi there.[116] Hence, despite law and custom, some dowers did remove property from the husband's estate.

The normal limits on dower rights may alternatively have motivated some husbands to transfer genuine ownership rights to a wife. John Stille contracted with his wife Lusha in 1336 to provide in lieu of both her dower and her *gerade* thirty marks annual income from half his city and country property, twenty for life and ten for her free disposition. So long as she did not remarry, she would also control all the property he had left and be guardian of their children. Lusha's actual widowhood in 1340 brought her all that and ten marks more.[117] This endowment still resembled a dower, but other women gained actual conveyance of land during the husband's lifetime. John "Schinkall" (or "Krikhall," the manuscript is not clear) gave his wife Margaret as a dower all he had in Juszczyn in 1355 but in 1383 transferred instead his ownership of half the village.[118] Of course again not every such gift is specified as replacing a dower nor need all have done so. Many reasons could explain a transfer of property to the name of a spouse. Nevertheless, such conveyances can be seen as the logical (and empirical) extreme of the effect of marriage on landholding. Husbands met the socially recognized obligation to provide for wives' widowhood (to say nothing of any personal affections which may have existed), normally by dower, which temporarily withdrew a part of the landed estate for a woman's exclusive use, and occasionally by permanent severance of some of their land.

Other familial responsibilities also drew land or landed incomes from a living possessor of lordships. Principal recipients were unmarried female kin, a daughter like the Gertrude to whom Henry of Blesov's widow gave lands in Nowy Dwór and Małkowice; a maiden sister like Sophia Borsnicz, provided with life use of Marszowice by her brothers Conrad and John; or a widowed aunt like Margaret Lederhosynke to whom Nicholas and Jacob Bock ceded their inheritance at Okrzeszyce.[119] Often the lady entered a convent and the donation served expressly to cover her living expenses.[120] Doubtless such arrangements saved heads of households much of the expense of a dowry. On occasion, though, a father either anticipated the hereditary descent of his properties or arranged it in advance. After Peter Dirschkowicz had spent years gaining all of Piotrowice, in 1408 he turned it over to his children, giving the lordship jointly to his six sons and four hundred marks thereon to his unmarried daughter.[121]

Intra-familial conveyances which anticipated while the parent was alive a subsequent hereditary descent propel the discussion toward inheritance practices, for heirs who accepted their portion in advance were barred from later participation in the division of the inheritance unless they first returned their endowment to the common fund. On this principle the duchy's law was clear and in agreement with *Sachsenspiegel*.[122] Records of lordship do not confirm or deny restorations by the previously endowed, but do show exclusion of such heirs. Anna von der Nysa received from her father her endowed support in the St. Katherine convent only with the proviso that she therewith resigned all hereditary claims to his estate. Peter Walch took over from his father, Simon, a small demesne at Rościsławice on a Monday and on the Wednesday turned over to him all expectations to any paternal or maternal inheritance there.[123] Endowment and exclusion without restoration can favor one potential heir over others, but in the instances found they did not so function among lay lords near Wrocław in the later Middle Ages. Like other intra-familial transfers by living owners, these practices detached portions of an estate well before its normal passage to the heirs.

Hereditary devolution certainly outstripped other family-based transfers as the principal influence of personal status on the movement of lordship rights. Particular effects of inheritance in the duchy came from distinctive emphasis on the rights of females and on equal division among heirs of equal degree.

Thirteenth-century Polish and indigenous Silesian practices influenced the duchy's law to balance the rights of female heirs with those of males more evenly than did *Sachsenspiegel*.[124] A wholly new article (359) of the

1356 code articulated the principle: for fiefs ("lehngut") sons were to receive the land and unendowed daughters an annuity on it; all other property ("erbe vnd eigin vnd farnde habe") was divided among heirs of both sexes. Elsewhere the same principle modified clauses from *Sachsenspiegel* concerning representation and the rights of collaterals or ascendants.[125] The law did not, however, here discriminate between inherited and acquired lands or require that land pass to daughters in the presence of sons. Within its constraints certain options were open to landed families.

To what extent in practice did women receive land and rights over it in satisfaction of their hereditary claims against an estate? They obtained fiefs more and proprietary land less than legal prescription might suggest. Most fiefs did normally pass through a succession of males, while their daughters and sisters held only life monetary interests.[126] The law, after all, had teeth to bite those who flouted it: when Andreas Pieserer, who "had no feudal heirs (*lehnserben*), only daughters," tried in 1423 to pass his fief at Stabłowice through his daughter to her husband, Paul Wiener, it escheated to the crown.[127] As earlier mentioned, most men in Pieserer's position obtained (surely not for free) a royal privilege permitting female succession in a fief.[128] Since people were thus prepared to pay for female succession to fiefs, it is not surprising to find women actually inheriting property for which there was no legal bar. Mechtildis, wife of Vladimir of Świdnica, had half Ślęza from the estate of her father, Peter Ruthenus, before 1338, and Margaret, wife of John Thiele, most of Smolec Wielkie from her father and brothers "of Smolec" before 1436.[129]

Even where not required by law, women commonly received claims against land which actually passed to men of the same degree. Some of the ladies had their rights described explicitly, like Margaret, daughter of Mathias Smedichen and wife of Nicholas Sachse, who in 1409 inherited twelve and a half marks annual rent on the schulz and several named peasants in Domasław.[130] Probably more of them simply converted to cash a share in inherited land by selling it to a brother or other co-heir. One daughter of Jarosław at Smolec Mały, Ilske, thus gave up her hereditary share to her brothers Peter and John in 1390, and her sister Margaret did it three years later.[131]

Women among the duchy's landed elite did acquire land by hereditary right, but the reluctant acquiescence of their families likely has to do with the predictable results of female tenure, removal of the holding from association with the rest of the estate and the loss of family control. Women rarely long retained personal possession of landed property. If it were not quickly returned to the main body of a family estate by sale to male co-heirs, a married woman normally turned it over to her husband. Katherine

Engilgeri inherited part of Gajowice in 1314 and ceded it to her spouse, John Schertilzan. One daughter of Mathias Smedichen, late lord in Domasław in the early fifteenth century, gave her property there to her husband with tenure for her life and inheritance thereafter; her sister sold her share to her husband outright.[132] Married or not, women could themselves sell their inheritance out of the family. Two female heirs, a widow and a daughter both named Margaret, so concluded in the mid-1420s the tenure of Andreas of Smolec's family at Smolec Mały and Smolec Wielki.[133] Female succession may have been preferable to an estate falling back to the crown or, as shown below, to collaterals, but it necessarily carried all or part of the property out of the family with little prospect of return. To the extent that lay lords valued continuity of a family estate, therefore, they had reason to provide daughters and sisters with movables for their inheritance and to reserve the land, even if thus encumbered with annuities, for male heirs.

Landed heirs around Wrocław frequently took up and long retained inheritances as joint tenures, a custom also well-known among contemporary Polish landowners and in the German customary laws.[134] Tilo Scriptor, a citizen of Wrocław, left his demesne at Radomierzyce to his children Franz and Anna jointly in 1354; a generation later at Smolec Mały the sons of Jarosław held their paternal inheritance in common for at least three years, while at Smolec Wielki those of Andreas did so for seven.[135] Such joint possession meant mutual rights of inheritance among brothers and, if it continued through the appearance of a second generation, among collaterals as well.[136] The citizen John Reste acknowledged in 1318, when he arranged for his brother Gisco to succeed in default of his own children to his fief at Wilczków, that brothers, cousins, and uncles with hereditary rights could help keep land within the family.[137]

But owners and authorities in the Wrocław duchy refused to permit collateral claims arising from joint inheritance and tenure to override or supersede without compensation those of direct legitimate heirs, even if these were women. An interesting mix-up among the prolific Schellendorfs, whose principal holdings at Ratyń and Lutynia were long shared among several sets of brothers and their descendants, clearly establishes the priorities. In 1336 John "the notary" Schellendorf and his brothers asked King John for the right to inherit land then held as a paternal inheritance by their kinsmen, the brothers John and Conrad Schellendorf, who, the petitioners asserted, had not sons, or daughters, or the ability to produce them. On the assurance the incumbents lacked children, the king assented. Soon he was disabused. John and Conrad appeared to declare that they had a sister, wives, and daughters and to demand the fraudulent privilege be quashed. The (blushing?) king voided his previous charter and publicly verified the rights of the ladies as superior to those of the collaterals.[138] As with preemption, authorities in the duchy favored nuclear family ties over more distant ones.

At some point, finally, the duchy's landowning families did partition estates equally among surviving heirs and/or descendants of deceased heirs. In accord with the law most testaments and special privileges foresaw this practice.[139] The heirs collectively established portions of equivalent value, sometimes using a panel of disinterested arbitrators—as for a farm of less than a mansus at Sulimów where each field was divided equally between two hereditary claimants in 1361—and sometimes balancing family members' rights in a series of agreements. Nicholas Zweibrodt had many children and several properties at his death about 1390, although two endowed daughters had resigned further rights. In 1396 the seven eligible heirs agreed that John the Elder, Henry, Conrad, and Agnes would take the lands in the Środa district (a farm at *Niebelschütz* and one called "Igelsjagd"), while John the Younger, another Henry, and Nicholas shared those in the Wrocław district at Zabrodzie and *Cesarzów*.[140] The result among the Zweibrodt family would be fractional holdings more complicated but no less typical than those held almost a century earlier by the children of Conrad Strachow at Strachocin, where Magdalena, Stanisława, Paulina, and Henry each inherited, possessed, and ultimately sold one fourth of the lordship.[141]

Equality of portions among heirs of equal degree was the custom in the fourteenth century duchy, so it is important to acknowledge that it was not universal, even among male heirs. At least some families knew ways to avoid the fragmentation of an estate which partition normally entailed. During the first third of the century Herman Reichenbach, a knight, had a handsome estate at Gniechowice, Damianowice, and Sośnica in the southwest of the Wrocław district. By 1337 Herman and his (eldest?) son Conrad were dead, survived by sons Henry and Stephan (who still had to prove his majority), a daughter Katherine, and the several sons and daughter of Conrad. The latter collectively ceded all their rights to their uncle Stephan. Henry and Katherine never claimed more than incomes or rights of approval as potential heirs. By the late 1340s Stephan was confirmed as legitimate lord over all three villages, which he thirty years later passed to his own two sons.[142] Despite the presence of other heirs, familial agreement enabled this one son to preserve for a generation and more his father's undivided estate. Lutko von der Nysa in 1372, however, just received half of Domasław from his father Otto in preference to other children.[143]

Ways to prefer a single line of descendants belong with joint tenure and a hesitance to give land to women among the few elements counter-

vailing a pattern of handling property which, through quite free alienations, the giving of wives' and daughters' portions, and the prevalence of
equal partition, ought quickly to have dispersed an individual's landed estate. This combined effect of accepted social processes may now be illustrated from some individual estates.

The typical small citizen estate of the fourteenth century is briefly observed because only briefly existent. Berthold of Racibórz, a lawyer, left at
his death around 1350 four mansi of demesne he had bought at Rożanka and
two more at Partynice. His three children handled their inheritance in con-
ventionally egalitarian style. Stanisław and Berthold the Younger, a cleric,
together took Rożanka and their sister Gertrude, Partynice. The brothers
kept Rożanka in common and purchased more land there. But the priest
had all after Stanisław died and sold it out of the family in 1361. When in
turn Gertrude sold Partynice in 1373, she ended her family's role as local
lords.[144]

Of the same generation as the younger Racibórzes, Sidelinus Scheitler
bought feudal tenure of Jaksin with eighteen rental mansi and six in demesne in 1363. His sons Nicholas and Ambrose took joint possession in
1369, kept it until late 1393, and sold to another townsman. Nicholas had
just then himself obtained the much smaller Żybiszów, but this was the
family's last land in the duchy. When Nicholas left no descendants, Ambrose inherited and then sold in 1418 his brother's acquisition.[145]

The Racibórz and Scheitler families consistently followed norms of
equal and joint inheritance. Brothers especially received and held land in
common but were undeterred from alienating their inheritances. Although
the second generation of Racibórz lords briefly enlarged their legacy, neither
small estate endured. No land stayed in either family for more than one
hereditary step away from the person who first acquired it.

The estate founded by the now-familiar Otto of Glubos fell victim to
the same practices as those of his citizen contemporaries. When Otto died
in early 1344, the family had the fief at Kobierzyce and the smaller property
at Bledzów. The former went to Ottocar, the latter to Otto. But the brothers' shares were equilibrated by "a certain sum" in cash for the younger
Otto charged against his brother's Kobierzyce. This effort to conform to the
principle of equal division yet keep intact the larger of the family holdings
failed. Before the year was out Ottocar needed extra guarantees for yet another debt to his creditor Christian of Kąty. Had he trouble covering his
brother's claim? The texts fail at a critical point. They make plain, however,
the rapid collapse of the Gluboses' landed position. Otto, a knight like his
father, vanished from the duchy after selling Bledzów in 1346 to his father's
associate, Nicholas Sittin. Ottocar gave his wife, Elizabeth, half Kobierzyce

as dower in 1349, but this only ensured that she and their son joined him to sell the whole village the very next year.[146] In less than a decade the elder Otto's estate had evaporated. So had his descendants, at least from the lands around Wrocław.

Like the small estates of knights or townspeople, those of large lay lords were crushed to bits by accepted social mechanisms. Despite landowners' efforts to mitigate the effects of recognized social obligations, large property complexes were normally still more ephemeral than small, although the sheer bulk of a well-off family's landed position took longer to erode away. Greater numbers of lordships and kin also make for longer and more complex illustrative examples. Grasping the fate of the estate of Nicholas Sittin, a rich mid-century town councillor and sometime business acquaintance of the Gluboses, requires some detail; only special highlights in that of the locally outstanding noble, Conrad of Borsnicz, will then need attention.

Nicholas Sittin's estate anticipated in size that of his younger fellow councillor, Peter Schwarz. His own handling and the eventual disposition of his properties resemble in the prominence of equal portions and ensuing transience as a unit those of the lesser landowners. Here, moreover, the effects of biological accident and female inheritance were magnified, for the death without issue of Nicholas's elder (though illegitimate) son, Franz, spoiled the father's first provisions for his heirs.[147]

Early on Nicholas had dispersed the small landed legacy of his merchant father and before first recording plans for his own in 1351 he had also relinquished in transactions with or obligations to his kin three of his own acquisitions.[148] What then remained still testified to more than a decade's wise accumulation: the "feudum honorabile" of Bielany to which Nicholas had merged a mansus from *Łagów* and his leased demesne of *Cruce* and put out to German law tenants; the large village of Domasław nearby as a service-free fief; hereditary proprietorship over Wojszyce and over half of Pasterzyce, where his sons Franz and John already had the rest.[149] No knight and scarcely a citizen then held more.

During the 1350s Nicholas added little to his estate, but arranged its descent so his sons should receive equal shares in almost all the land and his daughters little land but sizeable portions in cash and annuities. For his wife he reserved in May 1351 life use of Domasław as dower. At the same time Franz and John were declared joint heirs to Bielany and Pasterzyce.[150] Six years later Nicholas's testament confirmed his earlier dispositions and accounted for all his properties and family responsibilities. By this will of 1357 Nicholas alloted to Franz and John together Bielany, Pasterzyce, and also half of Domasław plus new lands at Pełczyce. To his daughters he left three hundred marks in a common legacy and individual bequests. Anne and

Katherine would get joint tenure of the other half of Domasław (a fief with privileges for female succession) and dowries of one hundred thirty and one hundred marks respectively. Elizabeth and Margaret would each obtain 33.5 marks in annual rents (a capital value of 335 marks) secured on Wojszyce. All else (Wojszyce, city real estate, and movables not committed to pious cash bequests) was for equal division among all the heirs.[151]

Further proof that Nicholas meant to leave nearly all his land equally to his sons came in the next few years as father and children clarified ambiguities left in 1357. In 1359 they specified that lordship over Wojszyce was to go jointly to Franz and John. This removed the girls' shares there and left only a half of Domasław as land for females. Five months later Nicholas reiterated his sons' joint tenure and mutual inheritance if one were to die without issue.[152] Was all this necessary for Nicholas to ensure in particular the descent of full rights to the illegitimate Franz? Extant texts do not say. Franz died within a year or so of June, 1360, perhaps in the epidemic of plague.

Neither surviving summaries nor original texts in the duchy's property records speak of human motives, much less of feelings. None are stated here. Still it seems as if Nicholas Sittin had a special favor for Franz and maybe a dislike for John. The death of Franz without surviving issue should have left the whole landed estate to John, but Nicholas did not accept this. He completely changed his carefully-arranged succession, abandoning his effort to transmit intact to males nearly all his lands. In a new will of 1362 an equal division among the five surviving heirs would be achieved by partition of lands to the daughters. John should now receive the father's city shop and all of Bielany, while the girls together shared six hundred marks, Domasław, Wojszyce, and another three hundred marks "to restore" the two properties. All jointly would get Pasterzyce. John was in no way favored here and received less than he would have under the 1357–60 agreements. In 1362 only Anne gained a special bequest, of two hundred marks to buy a house.[153] For the entire fief at Domasław to sustain two more female portions required a new royal charter. This, in his last documented act as a landowner, Nicholas obtained in late June, 1363.[154] He died by the next summer's end.

The townspeople who gathered in November, 1364, to formalize partition of the estate of Nicholas Sittin manifested in their own personal connections the incipient separation of its four lordships. John Sittin was there, as was Margaret. Katherine came with her husband, Hartlieb. Anne and Elizabeth had, like their father, died in the past seventeen months, so their hereditary claims were represented by their children, Elizabeth's from her marriage with Otto von der Nysa and Anne's from hers with Arnold Fusil.

The widowers appeared for their offspring. About all that Nicholas's arrangements left was to share out what he had designated to several heirs in common, so the family agreed that Anne's children (the young Fusils) and Margaret should assume joint tenure of Wojszyce as their complete shares.[155] By 1371 this lordship belonged in part to a Margaret, wife of Peter Beyer, who might be but is not verifiable as the Sittin daughter, and to John Herdain, no Sittin kin at all. Wojszyce would not again be associated with descendants or other lands of Nicholas. To the von der Nysas, heirs of Elizabeth, their grandfather's will directed half of Domasław and at least a third of Pasterzyce. Their father, Otto, had by 1371 all of the latter, which he sold. The half of Domasław passed to his son Lutko, Nicholas Sittin's grandson, who eventually sold it in 1399. The other half, the portion of Katherine Sittin, she had sold ten years before.

Thus only at Bielany Wrocławskie did Nicholas Sittin's rural property descend to one who could continue the lineage. John Sittin sold ten mansi to a maternal relative, but otherwise kept possession and passed it to several daughters and a son. When the son, Nicholas, named for his grandfather who had acquired Bielany, sold his one-fourth share there in 1414, he was just following the previous lead of his own sisters and ending the Sittin family's last connection to any of the lands which had once comprised his namesake's impressive estate.[156] That estate, however, had vanished long before. In accord with its creator's wishes after the death of Franz and with the pattern accepted among landed families, the Sittin estate had been torn apart to endow individuals of the following generations.

Like the minor knight and the townsman, the great noble lord did not establish equivalent position and durable wealth for his descendants. Conrad of Borsnicz, knight, royal vassal, and captain of the duchy in 1336, fathered at least five sons and two daughters (see Table 7.3). His estate matched his status and progeny, for at his death between 1339 and 1348 he left Marszowice from his own inheritance, Ozorowice from a joint purchase with his brothers, and his personal acquisitions of the Uraz castle and ducal rights over church lordships at Turów, Muchobór, and Wilkszyn. Marszowice, however, he and his brothers had charged for the lifetime support of their sister, Sophia, and Ozorowice secured the rich dower of his wife Agnes, valued at forty marks annual income—whence the widow later sold off ten mansi and a four mark annuity.[157] Only the sons received the land—and quickly disposed of the tendentious rights over the bishop's distant villages.[158]

For a time fraternal joint tenure and the favoring of one brother looked to have anchored the family position. Only Herman[2] had succeeded at Uraz and he had been married well—his father-in-law was Palatine at Polish

Kalisz. But Herman could or would not sustain his position. Uraz he sold piecemeal out of the family by the 1360s and his claims on other lands he dribbled away to his brothers. Herman and Dsirshe had to the knowledge of the Wrocław land records no living children, so after cession in 1371 of his last known rights, Herman left no further trace there.[159] But meanwhile a second Conrad was emerging as preeminent among the brothers, first leading in their joint ventures, then patiently gathering into his own hands all the rights and properties of his lineage.[160] Within a decade of Herman's disappearance from the duchy's elite, Conrad had used the opportunities offered by joint tenure among all male heirs to recreate something very like the estate of their father. It lacked the old centerpiece, Uraz, but retained from the father's own family holdings Ozorowice and Marszowice and replaced his scattered jurisdictional claims with closer lordships at Gosławice and Pęgów.[161] This large, almost self-contained, estate in the bottomlands and hills up the Odra from Uraz all went to his own eight sons. Conrad was, in fact, alone among his brothers in detectably fathering a further generation of Wrocław duchy landowners. In property and progeny he filled the role for which Herman may have been intended.

The younger Conrad's landed estate descended to his male heirs in a manner like that of his father but with more normal results. By agreement in 1398 the acknowledged eldest, Friedman[2], separated the peripheral lordship at Marszowice, where his descendants eked out a barely landed position for another century.[162] The younger seven brothers had jointly the more compact estate at Ozorowice, Pęgów, and Gosławice. None of them asserted their father's role; they broke and dissipated the family estate. Three never after 1398 even tried to use their inheritance and four brothers probably shared out the land. Conrad[3] and Herman[3] themselves let Pęgów and Gosławice pass to strangers. Czenko and Henry split Ozorowice and their sons, the third generation from the captain, both sold out as soon as they took possession.[163] One after another the unraveled ends of the Borsnicz line and the scattered fragments of the Borsnicz estate fell into undocumented oblivion. The second Conrad had but postponed for a generation the impoverishment and disintegration of yet another good-sized lay estate.

The descent of five estates through the families of the men who created them has illustrated typical inheritance patterns and their effects. Preference for male heirs but admission of females to land was one theme; more pervasive was equality among all heirs. Females, as Nicholas Sittin likely knew, guaranteed the rapid dispersal of property into other families. Confining land to males might help, but partition eventually followed. A family could try to mitigate the effects of equality among heirs by favoring one or by confining to its own members its transfers of property. The sons of the elder

Table 7.3. The family of Conrad of Borsnicz

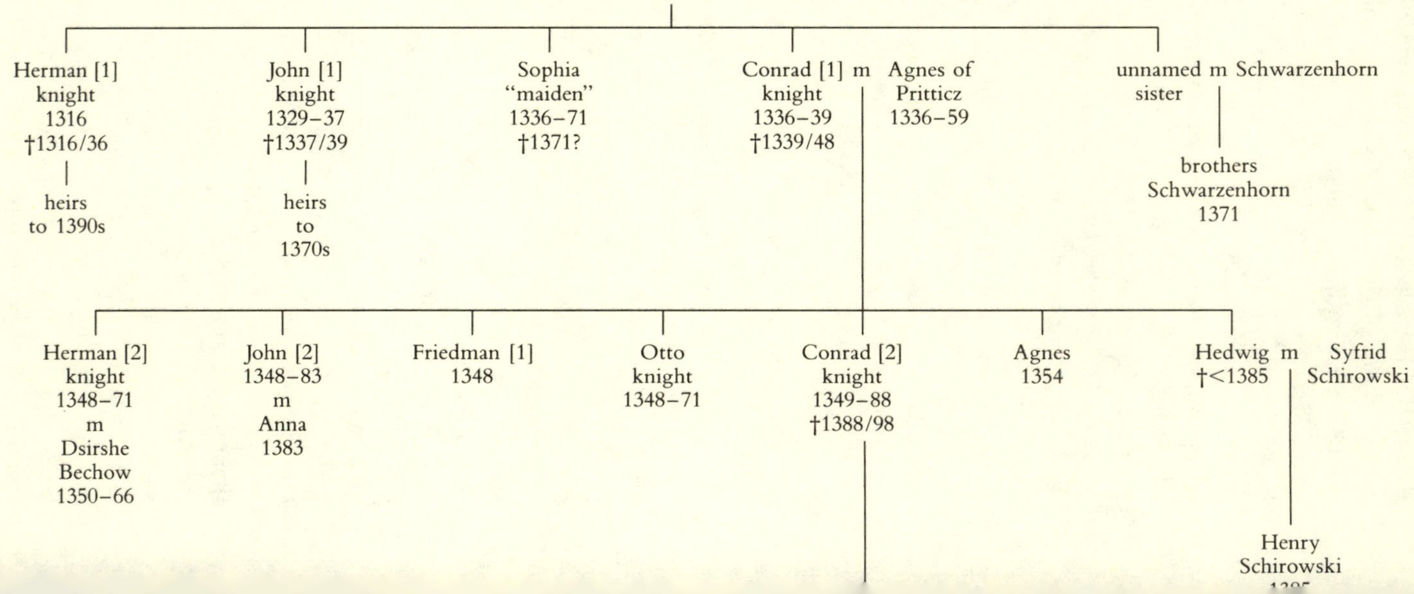

Herman [1]
knight
1316
†1316/36
—
heirs
to 1390s

John [1]
knight
1329–37
†1337/39
—
heirs
to
1370s

Sophia
"maiden"
1336–71
†1371?

Conrad [1] m Agnes of
knight   Pritticz
1336–39   1336–59
†1339/48

unnamed m Schwarzenhorn
sister

brothers
Schwarzenhorn
1371

Herman [2]
knight
1348–71
m
Dsirshe
Bechow
1350–66

John [2]
1348–83
m
Anna
1383

Friedman [1]
1348

Otto
knight
1348–71

Conrad [2]
knight
1349–88
†1388/98

Agnes
1354

Hedwig m Syfrid
†<1385   Schirowski

Henry
Schirowski
1385

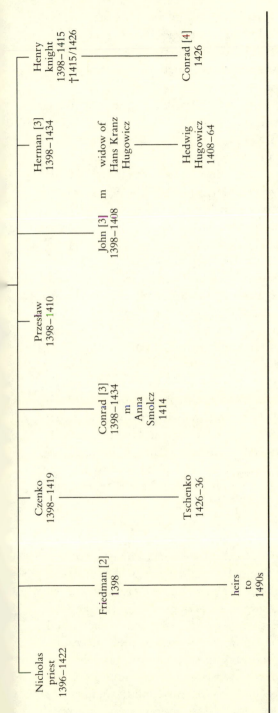

Nicholas
priest
1396–1422

Czenko
1398–1419

Conrad [3]
1398–1434
m
Anna
Smolcz
1414

Przesław
1398–1410

John [3]   m
1398–1408

Herman [3]
1398–1434

Henry
knight
1398–1415
†1415/1426

Friedman [2]
1398

Tschenko
1426–36

widow of
Hans Kranz
Hugowicz

Conrad [4]
1426

heirs
to
1490s

Hedwig
Hugowicz
1408–64

Note. Dates are those of documented actions (for collaterals only in a Borsnicz context). † indicates death between the dates shown. For sources, see notes to the discussion in text.

of Conrad Borsnicz did so to the benefit of Conrad the younger, whose sons did not—and showed that a plethora of male heirs could erode a family's lands as thoroughly as could a surplus of daughters.

Hence lay lordship in the fourteenth century duchy was suffused with instability. Estates were ephemeral. In the families described only the younger Conrad of Borsnicz passed to his heirs a set of lordships resembling that of his father. Family properties were transient. Of the twenty-one places which one member of these families ever once passed to another, only three stayed in the same family to a third generation. Family position was evanescent. Of the five families only the Sittin and Borsnicz lasted as lords into a third generation—and those grandchildren had but one property each where their grandsires, Nicholas Sittin or either Conrad of Borsnicz, had ranked at the top among contemporary landowners. Family rights to property had reality, but they were normally expressed as a congeries of individual claims upon a predecessor's wealth, not as a collective dynastic interest transcending the temporal limits of a one-time nuclear group. Each turn of the life cycle destroyed the creation of the dying generation. Members of a new generation started afresh with, perhaps, a chunk of inherited property, but no effective sense that they shared a corporate and enduring family estate. This set the duchy's fourteenth-century secular elite, knight and citizen alike, apart from many in pre-industrial Europe[164]—including its own eventual successors.

This chapter has looked long at those who held lordship rights between the late thirteenth and the early fifteenth century. It is time to recapitulate its argument. A position between the public sovereign and the peasant cultivator of private authority or "ownership" over land had more than one legal origin, but during the time here examined distinctions in law blurred. For most practical purposes lords had a recognizably free, alienable, and divisible title.

Most possessors of lordly title in the fourteenth-century duchy are identifiable most of the time. As a group they had several measurable features. About one-third of the duchy's lordships were in a few ecclesiastical estates, mostly of quite large size. The oldest and largest of these had become externally stable structures and added almost no new properties. Each was, however, for various reasons, subject to periods of managerial difficulty causing loss of rights that had later to be reclaimed. Smaller and younger corporations with clear local purposes remained more dynamic, experiencing periods of increasing wealth and of economic problems on their estates. Lordship rights on ecclesiastical estates were more fluid than the extreme stability of total numbers and property lists might suggest.

Two settlements in three had lay lords. Most lay estates were private and quite small, containing land in only one or two places. The once very large and in 1290 still appreciable ducal estate had gone by the 1350s. Of this development knights were at first the chief beneficiaries, although by the early 1300s likely no longer making net additions to the 40 percent of settlements they then held. Noble lordships peaked and then declined in number, dropping to the 25–30 percent range before the Hussite wars. A steady aggregate increase in lordships possessed by citizens of Wrocław reciprocated the fall of first ducal, then noble, properties. Townspeople had about one property in ten around 1300 and better than one in four around 1425.

In operational terms the chief feature of lay landowners and their estates was their transience. Individual knights and citizens built their own landed estates and passed them to their families. But by and large neither estates nor families long outlived the estate-builders. That transience was rooted in the social environment of knights and citizens, notably in their understanding of obligations to kin. Law and accepted social custom directed the use of a landed estate to satisfy those obligations. Landowning families normally recognized full rights to sell land, commonly practiced equal partible inheritance, and often accepted the rights of women to receive land and take it with them to another family. Rather than using their relatives to perpetuate their estates, they used their estates to enrich their close relatives. From a lay lord's perspective, property (lordship rights) had a strongly instrumental quality. It served social objectives. A consequence of this socially reasonable behavior was ephemeral contact among families and lordships.

Now the next chapter can explore the effects and implications of these characteristic fourteenth-century lords in villages around Wrocław.

THE LORD AND THE LORDSHIP: WHAT DID A LANDLORD DO?

Breytenaw hat XVIII Huffen Czynsshaftig, do gebit itzliche XVI Scot, halp vf Walpurgis vnd halp vf Martini, vnd eyn wasser, das do heyst Tyffenzee, mit wezen vnd welden, die zu Kumeyse synt geschreben, die gehorn alhyer, dorzu ist ein zee, der heyst Glogowiz, vnd eyn andir wasser, das heyst Weline, die synt vf dis Jar vormyt vor V marg an I Firtung. Item eyn wald, der heyst Swynsaw, do ist der Bowden gantz des Closters vnd das Holtz halp doruff. Item do ist eyn Huffe, die heyst die wilde Huffe, mit eym possche, gestrauche vnd eyn wezen, vnd ist gesundert vom gebawr erbe, vnd gehört zum Closter, Sundir eyn Mönch hat sie vorsetzt vor X marg, dem Schultisse zu Breytenaw. Item das Closter sol auch haben die Fyscherey an eynem Vber der Oder, das do trit kegen Breytenaw, doryn hat sich Gregor Wende geleget, Item vf der Schultisse hat das Closter den Rossdienst.

   Summa des Geldes vf Walpurgis VI marg.

   Summa vf Martini VI marg.

Item vom Wasser V marg adir wie man es kan vermitten.

Brodno is described in the *Urbarium* of the Trzebnica convent, 1410; *UD*, p. 263, #4.

The problem now is to knit together the agrarian history of Chapters 4 through 6 and the social elite discussed in Chapter 7. The solution goes back to the individual lord and property, a person in a specific social situation making use of a particular landed possession. How was this done? How did the way it was done affect the place of lordship as an institution in the fourteenth century duchy? First the characteristic distance of landowners from everyday farming and social activities of the rural population is established. To an important degree the ruling elite neither managed nor led the peasant majority but confined its role to the taking of incomes. Lordship was a claim to revenues, which gave it value to the lord.

    This chapter goes on to show that a lord who would not live from a nominally fixed annual return but wanted to put his claims to other uses, had normally to break a lordship into legal and/or physical fragments and by status and market mechanisms disperse these into the hands of others. Use subdivided lordship, but its parts remained to be gathered by seekers of easily maintained landed incomes. In some circumstances lords with certain interests and strengths gained at the expense of others and throughout the long fourteenth century all exploited their sovereign's financial and political needs to acquire his lucrative authority over peasants. But none among the landed then held decisive superiority over their peers and the circulation of property rights continued. The effect, viewed with the perspective of historical distance, was a cycle of different landowners simultaneously and successively fragmenting and consolidating lordship over settlements throughout the duchy. To conclude from the side of lordship's putative object, the village community, the cyclic structure resulting from rational behavior among the elite significantly inhibited interference by social superiors in the affairs of peasant families.

Distance

Fourteenth-century landowners around Wrocław maintained a physical and mental separation from the agricultural production and peasant communities present on their properties. Three bodies of evidence and reasoning jointly indicate this distance from agrarian life and suggest that lordship itself was then primarily equated with the right to draw regular revenue from the activities taking place on one's property. Some elements of this argument are new; others have previously been raised under different rubrics and here need only be recalled. What can be learned of the lords' way of life, what has been shown of agrarian organization, and what is implied by the sorts of records landowners did and did not have kept, offer no reason to believe that lords took the time to intervene, had the opportunity to intervene, or even thought of intervention as a plausible option.

Fourteenth-century texts mention only incidentally how lords lived— and indicate they had things to do other than run their landholdings. For one thing, only nobles were normally resident on (one of) their rural properties at all.[1] Citizens had town houses not then recorded for knights and rarely lived in the countryside.[2] Extramural burghers were not a phenomenon of late medieval central Silesia nor, in the duchy at least, were rural houses of religious.

Rural residence may have made nobles more familiar with country life, but it did not make them gentlemen farmers. Their social order traced its origins to a military profession as well as landed wealth and even a century's peace in Silesia did not efface this orientation. The royal tax survey of 1353 lists in a special section military service due from sixty-three properties and at least fifty-three named individuals. Only two of the latter are recognizably citizens; twenty-one belong to well-known knightly families. Nor is the record a mere formality. Entries specify equipment and the length of time a particular individual or group was to serve from a named tenure: "From Piotrków service is done with a charger through the year but there Paul of Harta and Henry of Cracow serve 10½ weeks and after that the Dirsdorfs for the rest of the year."[3]

If in that mid-century generation of knights only Herman of Borsnicz, castellan at Uraz during the Polish raid of 1348, visibly himself took arms in anticipation of combat, such was not the case for a later cohort. In July, 1410, a large Silesian mercenary contingent served the Teutonic Order, struggling to hold Marienburg after the Polish victory at Grunwald (Tannenberg). Of the 126 family names the pay books list, at least 23 were well known around Wrocław.[4] Among the 73 men who bore those names were 10 Luckow, 9 Schellendorf, 12 Siedlicz and Zedlicz (often ambiguous without specific kinsmen and properties), 6 Borsnicz, and 5 Hugowicz, to mention only some of the more numerous. Their amateur status is to be doubted.[5]

Even more than rural knights, town-dwelling citizens and clergy had interests other than rural lordship. The wealthiest townsmen pursued commerce, finance, and city politics; their lesser fellows lived from retail trade and crafts. About the only mention of a citizen participating in the everyday life of his rural estate is, in fact, a proverbially rule-proving exception: Nicholas Rempel took refuge at Ratyń in 1423 after failing to force his own election as chief of the city council. He ignored the summons of city officers, who found him supervising woodworkers and watching his schulz conduct a village court.[6] Ordinarily, landowners had other things to do and, as Rempel's schulz manifests, had lordships organized to minimize occasions for their direct participation.

A feature of the fourteenth-century agrarian regime was shown in Chapters 4 and 6 to have been the retreat of lords from direct involvement in the economic and social life of their properties. The German law movement provided owners with a way to raise returns from their acreage through technical improvement, arable expansion, and a shift to the peasantry of the costs and risks of production. In return lords offered secure tenancies, fixed rents, and village autonomy, a promise, that is, to leave the peasants more or less alone. To fill the leading role thus vacated by landowners, the *ocatores* who organized the reform for them became schulzen, intermediaries between tenants and lords. Acts of *locatio* outlined the intent; the performance of fourteenth century schulzen is described in the next chapter. But German law reforms were, especially in the fourteenth century, just one aspect of a process whereby landowners parcelled out demesne lands to tenants, abandoning in their own interests the fluctuating yields and rising costs of direct agricultural exploitation. Landowning groups joined at different rates in these developments, but all shared the general trend. By the eve of the Hussite wars lords had for two centuries been reducing their direct role in rural life.

One crude measure of the opportunity agrarian organization left for intervention by lords is the relative proportion of properties with rental, demesne, or both types of land. Tabulations for 1300, 1353, and 1425 (Table 8.1) confirm the generality in major landholding groups of the trend to rentier lordship. Knights, clergy, and citizens differed in degree, not kind. By 1425 each group had increased the share of its holdings entirely out to tenants and reduced those with demesne. The sharpest contrast was between the two older, reputedly more traditional orders: churchmen steadily favored tenant farmers and shifted land out of demesne; knights always had the most pure demesnes and the most holdings with demesne and tenant farms side by side. Against these two consistent patterns, citizen properties changed: in 1300 more than three-fourths were in demesne but by 1425 only one-fifth. Noble behavior and residential pattern thus corresponded; this group with the greatest need to supervise lived closest to their properties. Citizens, however, neither sought nor retained the access to resources required for the innovative capitalist management sometimes attributed to them.[7] Instead they eagerly emulated the clergy's transfer of arable from direct to indirect exploitation and thus conceded efficiency and profit in favor of regular fixed receipts of cash and grain.

Lords who employed estate administrators—and numbers did—were further removed from life on their lordships. Where a surrogate managed demesne, installed new tenants, collected dues, and exercised jurisdiction over the whole estate,[8] the lord could forget he owned working farms and peasant communities. The managers common on church estates by 1400 are likely older than the texts can prove.[9] On lands of lay lords unusual documents fortuitously reveal in 1329 John Duczman, "advocatus" for lord Pascho of Siemidrożyce and expert in tithe collection procedures, and in 1425 the "famulus" who handled taxes for George Seidlicz, castellan of Uraz.[10] Even more than the normal German law village already made him, such a lord was but the recipient of incomes.

Dominant trends and common institutions in the agrarian regime of the fourteenth century thus reinforced a passive role for landowners. Lords certainly created the regime and it served their interests, but it did so by minimizing rather than requiring or encouraging their activity in farming or

Table 8.1. Landlord groups and managerial arrangements: 1300–1353–1425

	1300	1353	1425
Holdings of known lordship	207	579	415
Ecclesiastical corporations			
Holdings	104	125	124
Rental land only	28%	36%	48%
Rental and demesne land	19%	17%	25%
Demesne land only	53%	47%	27%
Nobles			
Holdings	48	226	118
Rental land only	18%	18%	20%
Rental and demesne land	41%	44%	39%
Demesne land only	41%	38%	41%
Citizens of Wrocław			
Holdings	28	147	118
Rental land only	11%	30%	43%
Rental and demesne land	11%	19%	36%
Demesne land only	78%	51%	21%

Note. For sources and methods see Appendix A and Table A.4.

peasant affairs. Others, notably peasant farmers, managed and bore the risks of agricultural production. Others, notably village schulzen, dominated the life of the village community. Those who claimed lordship over rural property and its inhabitants could and increasingly in the fourteenth century did spend their time on other things and, from afar, take the revenues to which their superior rights entitled them. Landed property was thus to its owner not so much, so often, or so regularly an object, natural and human, to be manipulated for production of a valued good as one which itself yielded the object of value, an annual income. At this mental (and often real) distance, what mattered to the landowner was not the qualitative mix of resources possessed but the specific rights which defined revenues. A lord did not operate an enterprise, but exploited property and defended against his peers his claim to do so. He cared about what he owned not for what he could do with it but for what he got from it—incomes which were clearly established as his.

The characteristic documents created for fourteenth-century lords manifest the mental equation of lordship with a certain revenue. Both estate surveys and conveyances record expectations and entitlements as if rights alone fixed the relevant reality.

Estate surveys are not really numerous from about 1300 to 1425, but more do come from this period than from times earlier and later combined. In the bishop's *liber fundationis* of 1295–1305, the city's rental book of 1354, and the early fifteenth-century *urbaria* from Trzebnica, Lebus, and the *mensa episcopalis*,[11] every lordship is described in the same way. What mattered to the bishop's clerks about 1300 was that "in Strzeganowice, an episcopal village, are 30 mansi each paying 14 measures, 4 of wheat, 4 of rye, 4 of oats, and two of barley, all other services, and 8 scot." Their successors noted the later subtenure of Gisco Reste and transfer of the property to the cathedral chapter.[12] Administrators at the Trzebnica convent a century later needed—see the epigraph of this chapter—more but no other kinds of facts to state what concerned them about Brodno. Dozens of fourteenth-century entries so prescribe or assert the fixed ideal, "they pay," "they owe," "it returns." Left unconsidered are the possibilities that they might not always pay or that the woodland might be exploited differently. Only an illegal challenge by some other lord like Gregor Wende or a legal transfer of rights to one like Gisco Reste might change the situation. And if that occurred even a half-century later—the chapter got Strzeganowice from Bishop Przesław in 1352—just a note kept the record adequately up to date. Thus for the purposes of those who compiled and used the surveys, lordship was adequately described by asserting the title and equating land with expected incomes.

Next to the few survey texts, numerous to the point of overwhelming were the charters of conveyance and confirmation, made out in individual copies, preserved by recipients, and transcribed into official registers and private and corporate chartularies. Whether extant whole or in summary form, these have been a prime resource for much of the reconstruction and analysis now done here. But their purpose then was very like that of the surveys because they recorded in authoritative form as precisely as needed (but no more) what property, rights, and objects a particular person legitimately exploited. Rarely quantitative and detailing the incomes only when these were themselves at issue, a charter proved entitlement to take from the described property. The right and who held it were all that mattered. Even every surviving inventory of demesne equipment and stock from before the 1430s was written down not as a managerial record but to clarify who had what rights.[13]

If title were ambiguous, disputes and legal challenges of particular incomes arose. Of these there were plenty, but almost always over who had a certain right and not over its reality. To resolve a dispute demanded only enough inquiry or negotiation to establish the limits of each competing lord's legitimate claim. An exemplary case came up in 1345 over the boundary between Albert Shrolle's property at Kamieniec and that at Gajków of the widow of Conrad of Wierzbice. Lacking adequate charter evidence, the *iudicium curiae* sent the Hofrichter and two others to ask the eldest inhabitants ("altsesin") and neighbors ("nackebewr"). The delegation rode along the land to hear the witnesses first agree on one boundary Shrolle had denied and then deny one he asserted. Later Schrolle took them to a meadow and the neighbors swore it had been used by Conrad forty years earlier, then to another where Shrolle's haymaking on both sides of a bush was declared a false novelty. Finally, after local elders denied Shrolle's claim to a millet field, he stomped off in disgust. The judges' report simply specified the particular landholdings in more detail than before (thus recording minutiae normally passed over in silence) and ended the controversy.[14]

In contrast to the many records which treat property as an object of rights with known yields, all but absent from the fourteenth century are precisely those texts used to manage resources in situations where a recalcitrant reality refuses to conform to the model set by law, title, and recorded obligation. A working manager copes with change and difficulty by keeping account books to tell at least what needs doing and what has been done. Registers of real annual expectations, returns, and the lack thereof are common in and after the mid-fifteenth century (see Chapters 10–12 below). Earlier, however, not only are survivors rare, no others leave traces in contemporary records, in pre-war studies, or in the catalogues of archives now partly destroyed. If fourteenth-century lords kept running or summary accounts comparable to those of their successors, these have been obliterated with incredible thoroughness. For instance, only five texts from before 1430 give the names and holdings of several or all tenants in a village. None of these lists payments actually made or covers more than a single year. The 1430s alone provide more (see Table 9.1 below).[15]

The rule that fourteenth-century landlords did not record the real workings of their properties is proven by one exception, the municipal corporation of Wrocław. In the city's account book for 1318–57, its clerks thought worth separate entry only sums spent on property rights at *Szczytniki* and Kowale. Occasionally they referred to other expenditures and to receipts from these lands, but every time grouped them with substantively unrelated items.[16] The same habits shaped the councillors' account for 1386.[17] Finally in 1387 a full income account specified for each remunerative right or piece at Szczytniki exactly who paid, when, and how much.[18] It is the one fourteenth-century instance of a landowner plainly treating a property as yielding incomes only when supervised for compliance with obligations. Only here is the equation of lordship and revenues not automatic and assumed. But the equation remains, for all the account mentions are the receipts.[19] Nothing else mattered enough to be recorded.

To say that a significant distance separated fourteenth-century landowners from economic production and social life in the countryside thus summarizes well-documented behavior: lords were otherwise occupied; other persons took charge of the agrarian economy and its social organization; lords claimed fixed incomes; lords had recorded ideal entitlements to objects and revenues, not actual fluctuations in production and receipts. To infer a mentality or a framework within which landowners perceived lordship necessarily goes beyond the documents. Still, landlord behavior gains coherence if behind it is postulated a congruent mental distance from everyday realities of agricultural society. Lords acted in the fourteenth century as if they had little concern for what went on on their lands or for manipulating (making use of) the objects they owned. They and others behaved as if lordship were little more than receipt of certain revenues. The incomes and not the natural and human resources which produced them had significance and made lordship valuable to one who possessed it.

Revenues, their uses, and the subdivision of lordship

Fourteenth-century landlords stood so far back from rural economic activity that lordship was essentially a definable claim to certain revenues. Because possession of land was good for annual incomes, it was good for other things as well. This section first evaluates revenues from land. Then it shows how income-yielding property enabled owners to provide security for kin, acquire clients, and obtain liquid capital from the market. But so to use his rights over a settlement caused a lord to disperse them among potential and actual competitors.

To consider annual incomes from landed property in the duchy is to assess from the side of landowners the payments of peasant tenants and the yields of demesne farms treated in Chapters 4–6.[20] To review in brief, the owner of a village was entitled to receive rent for the land, small dues symbolic of his lordship over those who lived on it, and a third of the proceeds from justice administered in the court of the schulz. Rents and dues were nominally fixed at so much per mansus, collected by the schulz, and transferred to the landowner. In actual receipts cash supplanted real produce through the century, so that by about 1400 some villages paid entirely in money except for the odd chicken or dozen eggs. Thus, despite their nominal stability, incomes from rental land did change on rare occasions, in individual villages and by those gradual increments also as a duchy-wide aggregate, in composition, nominal quantity, and value received by the landowner. Grain equivalents from the normal rental mansus probably rose about 30 percent during the second half of the thirteenth century, but a nearly compensating decline during the first half of the fourteenth approached stability after the 1360s or -70s. In the silver equivalents more important to rent recipients,[21] however, rising returns continued past 1300. Rents in the century's middle third held half again as much monetary metal as those paid when it began. Thereafter (more precisely between the 1370s/80s and the 1420s/30s) the amount of silver conveyed in normal rentals dropped by about a third, mainly from debasement of coinage.

Returns from demesne land are almost inestimable. It is only to be doubted that they regularily comprised an order of magnitude much different from those derived from mansi out to tenants. Incomes from direct exploitation were, however, more often in kind, considerably more variable from one year to the next, and always representative of a greater investment by the lord himself in operating and fixed capital. Landowners did not in the late fourteenth and early fifteenth centuries treat demesne farming as a desireable remedy for their slowly diminishing receipts in silver from land out to tenants.

Average rents per mansus indicate returns to landownership overall, but not what the lord of a given property might receive. Only a very few places described in surveys of ecclesiastical estates offer such information. Because of their owners' status and because they are almost all tenant villages, such examples cannot be treated as wholly representative. They still provide the only immediate and realistic impressions of the size, range, and composition of landed incomes.

Piłczyce and Radoszkowice both belonged to the bishop of Wrocław, were surveyed in both 1300 and 1421/25, and, with about twelve mansi each, can stand for a unit of arable and settlement common in much of the Wrocław district. At the start of the fourteenth century Piłczyce was leased as a demesne farm for payment of six marks in lieu of field tithes. A century and a quarter later the bishop may have regained direct control of the demesne but his clerks recorded no further details on what that yielded. Four mansi were now out to peasant tenants. These paid 3½ marks cash and 4½ malder of grain or (at about 3 groschen the measure, see Figure 6.4) not quite seven marks total value. But the bishop also got 2 marks 27 groschen yearly from eight gardens and six marks from the fishery—more from the non-arable resources than from the land itself.[22]

At Radoszkowice peasant tenants held all the land. In 1300 their nine customary rental mansi yielded 2¼ marks "racione census et iudicia et omnia servicia," and another 1 mark 9 scot in lieu of tithes on livestock and the dinner owed to the lord when he came to judge. Grain tithes were taken as a real tenth sheaf from the fields. One peasant simply gave a mark for his two mansi and the schulz nine scot for his obligation to service. The bishop's incomes from his direct lordship thus came to 5 marks plus the grain tithes. But at Radoszkowice the bishop also claimed ducal fiscal rights then worth each year 5 marks 15 scot in coin and 6 malder of grain.[23] More than a century later his returns from Radoszkowice had changed rather little, although all entitlements had been amalgamated into fixed yearly revenues totaling 11 marks plus 2 malder 3 measures of grain.[24] Thus from these rather small Wrocław district peasant communities the landowner's rights over regular arable farmers consistently brought around a mark per mansus but as much or more could also come from claims on other village resources or from adding the sovereign's to the owner's rights.

Some larger village lordships confirm both the order of magnitude and the variability owners could expect in landed incomes. Siedlakowice brought the bishop normal or better returns without any mention of extraordinary resources or legal claims. Early in the fourteenth century the 20½ rental mansi there paid 5⅛ marks plus grain worth at contemporary price levels about twenty more. By 1421/25 money for all rents, meals, and services totaled 48 marks 42 groschen from the village of 25 mansi.[25] At the other extreme, Lipnica gave little to the Trzebnica convent in 1410: the twenty-five mansi paid cash at a rate which yielded to the lord a mere 8 marks 16 groschen and the cavalry service of the schulz.[26] Between that one-third mark per mansus and the two marks from Siedlakowice a decade later is as large a difference as known in the fourteenth-century duchy.

The welfare equivalent of a certain amount of property or annual income is not easily established, even though it should be a major factor in evaluating lordship rights. Never do extant texts record total holdings, revenues, and expenses of a single lord—or anything concrete of incomes or expenditures for any lay owner at all.[27] But incidental data from the first half of the period here discussed suggest roughly what was needed to support a member of the elite at some minimal scale appropriate to his or her rank. One endowed altar priest in the cathedral was to live on ten marks and another from lordship over 6⅔ tenant-held mansi.[28] Girls destined for the convent life cost less, three to eight marks or barely three mansi of demesne.[29] But widows were a little better off, with endowments in the range of six to ten marks a year or four to twelve mansi common among the ordinary run of knightly families during the years around 1340–50. On the high side, John Ohme's daughter Elizabeth received from her father's neighbor and her new husband, Henry de Calow, four mansi in demesne, seven out to tenants, that of the schulz at Pracze, half a mill, and an annuity of one and a half marks.[30] Of course, a bride had the advantage that her dower resulted from negotiation between her husband's family and her own. Undesired daughters and unbeneficed priests had best like what those responsible for them thought sufficient.

It looks therefore as if men of the early fourteenth century agreed that three or four mansi could support with their annual returns to lordship a barely sufficient living for a person with some pretense to elite and economically non-productive status. If so, then the owners of normal-sized demesne farms, small villages, or portions of larger ones, the kinds of minor lords who so dominated in their numbers the duchy's elite, could likely live appropriately from their landed incomes at least into the third quarter of the fourteenth century. Smaller owners, those with but a mansus or two or three, probably even then needed other sources of revenue, either by themselves operating the farm (see Chapter 9) or by engaging in non-agricultural occupations (i.e., townspeople). By 1400, however, the shrinking value of peasant payments had probably pushed upward this margin of economic hazard for small landowners.[31]

Considerations other than quantity probably also influenced lords' evaluation of their income-yielding properties. Of one obvious possibility, enhanced personal status from receipt of landed and physically unearned incomes rather than equal amounts from personal labor in a trade or craft, the fourteenth-century sources say nothing. On the other hand, administrative costs to the lord of rental or indirectly-exploited demesne land were almost nil. He spent no working capital or time to get his revenue. And nominally fixed rents offered to the fourteenth-century landowner real short-term advantage in the reasonable expectation of the same returns year after year. The rate on investment for a Wrocław citizen may have been higher in a successful commercial venture, but so, too, were chances of failure and loss of capital. Landed incomes had low risk.

The yield of annual revenues made a lordship good for other things. Expectation of future returns made rights over land a good way for an owner to provide economic security for family members and to reward followers. Confidently anticipated incomes gave access to a capital market. They could be exchanged for credit now or the ownership rights themselves sold for whatever a willing buyer might offer. But unlike living from current revenue, a lord's use of land for social, political, or capitalized ends promoted partition of a lordship's separable and remunerative rights into many other hands. That lords were little reluctant thus to destroy the integrity of a lordship confirms their income-oriented mind set and helps explain their limited hegemony over the fourteenth-century countryside.

The previous chapter amply illustrated lords transferring property to their relatives and the importance of partibility in such conveyances. Needed here is only confirmation of the regularity with which this broke up the lordship over individual settlements.[32] Clearest proof that partition resulted from choice, not necessity, comes from landowners rich enough to have had alternatives if the prospect of partition were repugnant. Stephen Reichenbach had in 1348 lordship over Damianowice, Sośnica, and Gniechowice and still determined, in the event of his death without issue, equal division of the latter village between his brother Henry and his married sister Katherine.[33] Intentions became outcomes. Citizen lords repeatedly divided Skałka: into at least four pieces among the heirs of John Schertilzan around 1350; into at least three among those of Nicholas von der Nysa less than a decade later; into at least two after the gift to his children by Lutko von der Nysa in 1413.[34] Knightly families did the same.[35] Sometimes portions were split into further portions like Peter Megerlin's half of Małkowice, which was quartered for two daughters, one son, and an unidentified claimant.[36] Nor were testaments and hereditary partitions the only ways landowners carved up their lordships in the interests of kin. Five small owners at Gaj between 1344 and 1372 sliced from their properties a mansus or less for a wife. In at least four of these, the woman's property subsequently passed to another owner.[37]

Gifts and inheritances of land sliced vertically through a lordship to define territorial portions, each legally autonomous and directly dependent upon public authority. A lease or subinfeudation of land, on the other hand, cut a lordship into horizontal layers of rights, each defined legally and superimposed one upon another over the same territory. Although the importance of short-term financial motives for churches leasing their demesne farms has already been remarked,[38] lords also established subordinate tenures to acquire or reward followers and gain the elevation of status provided by public recognition of superior position. Again the best evidence comes from the bishop himself. Around 1300 he had on church lands near Kryniczno several "fideles" exempt from regular rents. One, Conrad, even bore the title "dominus." They owed to the bishop what was customary for episcopal servitors, a regular tour of duty at his court and military service on horseback.[39] The mediocre size of lay estates left little room for subordinate elite tenures. Just the odd reference hints at higher prestige for those with authority over landed subordinates who were not peasants. Franczco Radak claimed by virtue of his hereditary lordship over Kokorzyce "respectum cum Homagio" from "domina Gerdruda de Kokirdorf" and her son.[40]

Whether capital or clients motivated a landowner to establish long leases or fiefs, they meant two or more lords divided the lordship in classic "feudal" form. About 1400 the sublord at Sośnica judged his own dependents and kept those incomes.[41] Within the terms of their tenure subordinate lords used their lands in their own interests, passing them by inheritance, alienating them to third parties, dividing them into separate pieces, even subletting or encumbering the land with annual rents. At Rynakowice the two mansi subinfeudated to Nicholas of Jenkowice in 1321 were by the 1350s split through sales and inheritances into three separate pieces. Despite the bishop's nominal overlordship, every transaction since 1321 had occurred before secular authorities. To reassert his rights as owner after the rich citizen Peter Bayer reconsolidated the two mansi in 1365, Bishop Przesław had to give him land at Wilków in exchange.[42] Thus little differentiated a subordinate lord's use of his lands from that made by men who held directly under the duke.

The latent competition between landowner and possessor by lease or rear fief sometimes surfaced. After leasing *Burkhardsmül* from St. Clare for some years, Andreas Radak, lord of adjoining Gałów, refused in 1316 to surrender it unless he received twenty marks for improvements he claimed to have made. The convent in turn claimed sixteen marks in overdue rents. A compromise solution saw Andreas keep the mill and the sixteen marks in return for his forgetting the twenty marks worth of improvements and giving the nuns a competing mill on his Gałów land and access across Gałów to *Burkhardsmül*.[43] More than a half century later the canons of St. Mary lamented loss of authority over and revenues from the part of Gajowice which the Commandery of Corpus Christi held. This the Hospitallers had merged to *Neudorf* so the abbey had lost "by negligence" its lordship and nearly two marks in annual rents.[44] To restore a unified and effective lordship by any means other than capitulating to a sublord in effective possession, the landowner had to emulate the bishop at Rynakowice in 1365 and buy the subordinate out of his tenure. Otherwise the one who had once meant welcome cash or a worthy follower continued to contest the lordship.

Land gave incomes and land stored wealth. Besides passing that wealth to kin or dependents a lord could use it and the incomes to obtain liquid capital. Short of actual sale, two generic methods were familiar: the sale of rent (*census, Zins*) and the pledge (*pignus, Pfand*). Although legally distinct, both were ways to convert rights over land into cash or credit values for any of an owner's purposes.[45] Sometimes the impetus came from the "normal" explanation for credit and debt in a relatively stable agrarian society, financial need and the costs of living beyond regular incomes.[46] More social obligations, not necessarily or purely financial, gave another reason. Rents often endowed brides, widows, and churches.[47] Financial and personal motives mixed when a debtor pledged his property to cover losses not of the creditor but of a third party standing personal surety for payment.[48] Finally, some borrowing against landed property and incomes aimed at future gains. Their commerce on credit in cloth from Ypres induced Vogt Bruno of Leśnica and Mathias of Molheim in 1336 to pledge their properties,[49] while George Salusch and his family sold *census* totalling 8½ marks against Zabór Mały before they bought Zabór Wielki in 1422.[50] Neither sort of borrowing alone need signify the impoverishment of a lay landowner. Both met any need for liquid capital.

An annual rent was a fixed payment from a specified income-bearing property, hereditary and alienable for the purchaser and redeemable by the seller for the initial sum paid. The most complete sale agreements named dates for payments, ranked the priority of this claim on the yield of the property, and designated other of the owner's possessions to make up any shortfall. Reinczke of Swenkenfeld promised in 1357 that the three marks *census* his wife sold on the demesne at Bogdaszowice to Else of Czindal was due half at Walpurgis and half at Michaelmas. In case of default Else was to seek satisfaction against the demesne or other Swenkenfeld land there.[51] Thus the property on which the rent rested itself secured its payment. Normally fourteenth-century landowners sold annual rents in cash; those in grain are rare.[52] Lords could alienate any sum up to the annual yield of the property. No known landowner sold less than a mark a year and some much more, in a single or several successive transactions. On Sadków men from the Lobil family made six sales between 1350 and 1357 of rents totaling forty-one marks, more than there were mansi in the village. Nicholas Lompniz sold two marks rent on 2½ mansi at Małkowice in 1356 and seven on 1¾ mansus there the next year.[53]

The capital a landowner received for encumbering property with an annual rent rose in stages through this period. Most records of *census* omit the price, but those assembled in Figure 8.1 seem to indicate a pattern. Between the 1330s and 1350s few rents on rural property brought the seller as much as ten times what he was to pay each year. Most lords got between eight and nine—and thus borrowed at annual interest between 11 and 12.5 percent. Supporting the impression from the incidentally informative cases is Charles IV's statement in 1353 that eight times annual returns was the "common custom of the land of Wrocław." But then rates ascended to a new level for a generation and more. Between 1360 and 1420 forty-one of the forty-seven sales with known prices went at ten to one (i.e., 10 percent interest). In 1395 the king even legislated this for repurchase of any *census* without other proven price. The period of stability ceased, however, by the 1420s. A 20-mark rent got 240 marks in 1422, and equal or higher prices common in the next decade marked a slide in interest rates to and below 8.5 percent. Near the extremes, a landowner of the 1430s could get almost twice what his predecessor a century before had accepted.[54]

Such quantitative evaluation is not feasible for capital acquired by pledging land. Partly this is because the secured sum, which is often stated, was in this procedure related to the value of the pledged property, which is not stated; nor is reported the annual income foregone by the debtor who turned over the pledge. Then, too, men transacting a loan against a pledge likely conspired to record only the obligation itself and avoid accusations of

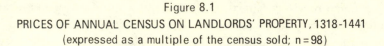

Figure 8.1

PRICES OF ANNUAL CENSUS ON LANDLORDS' PROPERTY, 1318-1441

(expressed as a multiple of the census sold; n = 98)

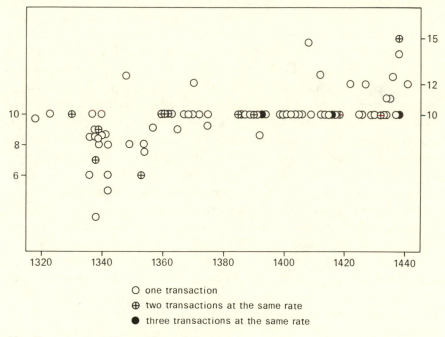

○ one transaction

⊕ two transactions at the same rate

● three transactions at the same rate

Note. For sources see *Notes to Maps and Figures.*

usury. Pledging landed property offered the owner a more flexible way to borrow than did the straightforward sale of rent. Some loans against a pledge (and the clear examples all seem to predate the 1350s) were like the modern hypothec, a lien against property without transfer of possession or title to the creditor unless the obligation is not met.[55] More common were pledges congruent with the classical Roman *pignus*, a transfer of possession and use (but not genuine title) until the obligation was met. Among the more explicit agreements of this sort was one made in 1341 between Henry of Gerstinberg and John Schellendorf to secure the former's debt of 29.5 marks. Until payment was made, John had the use of all Henry's holdings at Jarnołtów except the woodland.[56] Incomes accruing from the property given in pledge did not reduce the debt itself.

Loans secured against land by pledge or by sale of rent could presage genuine transfers of ownership. The debtor might forfeit for non-payment or agree after an additional and final payment to convert the creditor's right to full lordship. The latter possibility was taken into account when Cybeley pledged eleven and a half mansi at Nadolice Małe to Conrad Schertilzan for ten marks due at Michaelmas, 1318; if Cybeley did not pay, Conrad or his legitimate successor in the pledge could buy the property for another twenty marks.[57] Other lords simply let their creditors foreclose on the pledged land. Margaret of Ząbkowice lost property at Gaj to Emeric the physician for a 4¼ mark debt in 1336 and Hans and Paul Steube all of Solna to Franz Schellendorf in the early 1420s.[58] And there were owners who simply followed mounting debts with a sale, whether to the former creditor or to one previously uninvolved.[59] That expedient suggests again that for many landowners borrowing against their lands had begun in a style of life too costly to maintain from annual revenues alone.

Yet even where alienation did not follow borrowing against land and whatever the precise legal mechanism through which a lord borrowed, it inevitably fragmented authority over the lordship. That some of the lord's rights now belonged to another was fully known to the peasants who made the rights remunerative. When John Plessil sold four marks on Solna to a Wrocław citizen, the schulz and four men swore for the community that the payment would be made. Reinczke of Swenkenfeld declared his wife's sale of rent on the demesne at Bogdaszowice in the village court itself.[60] Then the fully alienable *census* could drift by further sale to persons whose only link to the land or its owner was this legitimate claim to certain incomes. Twenty-one marks of the *census* sold on Jaksin in the mid-1340s by lord Conrad of Falkenhain passed in 1350 to at least the third successive possessor, Gertrude of Doyn. who had to be reminded that Conrad had a right of repurchase.[61] The landowner's sole recourse was to exercise that right and, in effect, pay off a lien which may have begun with a different owner long before.[62]

Not surprisingly, disputes erupted between owners and other claimants to peasant payments. Henry of Schirow challenged the claim by Conrad Borsnicz to thirty-two marks on Schirow's demesne at Sadowice arising from the will of his mother, Borsnicz's sister. The lord of Jastrzębce and the Środa priory-hospital squabbled publicly over less than a mark in annual rents from a scrap of field at Lipnica.[63]

Peasants were in the middle of these confrontations, liable to be threatened with court action or worse by whichever side they failed to pay. Tenants attracted to newly-rented land at Sulimów in 1392 even had the owner and his family swear to represent them if they should ever be pledged on the lord's account.[64] But being between two or more claimants to landlord rights did not always harm a peasant community. Villagers at Wilczków who refused rents claimed by John Reste in the early 1350s exploited his loss by fire of an older charter and played off an annual rent due to an altar in a church in Wrocław.[65] The credit and liquid capital a lord got for landed property thus cost more than the incomes ostensibly sacrificed.

A lord's final option was to realize on the sale market, always active in the fourteenth century, the value it placed on his land. The title had to be clear of claims by kin or creditors or those outstanding made known to a buyer who accepted them. Then the vendor could have his money, whether he had held with full rights like Peter Zeuissil who got thirty-five marks for Sikorzyce in 1339 or as a sublord like John Smedichen who got four hundred for Piłczyce under the bishop in 1435.[66] They dealt on a market with distinct structural features.

Table 8.2 summarizes what has already been learned of land prices for consideration now from the perspective of owners wishing to liquidate the capital tied up in a property. Those with demesnes possessed assets of greater and more volatile unit value than those with land rented out to tenants. Probably this difference reflected gross returns to direct exploitation equal to or greater than yields from rents plus the presence on working landlord farms of assets other than land. But unless *net* annual incomes from demesne land much exceeded those from rental land (and differences in operating costs make this unlikely), the higher prices probably meant lower rates of return to the wealth tied up in a demesne farm. At their closest, in the middle third of the fourteenth century, prices for demesne land still exceeded those for rental land by 17 percent. From the seller's point of view, therefore, sale of demesne rather than tenant-held property usually generated more capital at less sacrifice of current revenue. On the other hand, a direct exploitation provided consumables and possibly contained the owner's dwelling. Temporal variation in demesne land prices was, as previously shown, directly related to the movement of prices for grain. Shortfalls in food production made especially the second and third decades of the fourteenth century a seller's market for demesne farms. Would that those prices could be compared with revenues.

In Table 8.2, prices received for rental land are set against revenues from major peasant obligations. Normal silver prices seemingly ran about thirteen times customary annual returns in the late 1200s and around 1400 but only about about ten times at mid-century. Seen another way, the wealth tied up in land out to tenants was returning 7 or 8 percent a year before 1300 and around 1400 but about 10 percent around 1350. Most of the time, therefore, an owner who needed capital could sell his whole lordship over rental land for significantly more than he could get by sale of the rent as *census*. It makes sense that the whole lordship would be worth more than part of it, but poor evidence for the formation of land values can prove none of the plausible reasons for this. Among these belong non-rental incomes (espe-

**Table 8.2. Sale prices for demesne and rental land,
late 1200s–early 1400s: nominal (marks per mansus),
silver (grams per mansus), and comparative values**

		ca.1280–1300	ca.1300–1335	ca.1335–1360	ca.1360–1425
demesne land prices[a]	nominal	22.5mk	32.5mk	17.5mk	35.0mk
	silver	3000g	4500g	2250g	3000g
rental land prices[b]	nominal	12.5mk	10.0mk	15.0mk	22.5mk
	silver	1700g	1500g	1800g	1700g
For comparison:					
average rent per mansus[c]	silver	132g	n.a.	186g	125g
census price (as multiple of annual payment)[d]		n.a.	n.a.	8–9	10

Notes.
   [a]Data summarized from Figure 5.1 approximate mid-ranges of normal values during the periods indicated.
   [b]Data summarized from Figure 6.2 approximate mid-ranges of normal values during the periods indicated.
   [c]Data from Table 6.3.
   [d]Data summarized from Figure 8.1 approximate mid-ranges of normal values during the periods indicated.

cially fiscal and judicial), minimal operating costs, low risk, and the enhanced status of a *dominus hereditarius* (*Erbherr*).

   Prices for rental land peaked (in silver) during the mid-fourteenth century, but were still a bargain for prospective purchasers because high real
rents maximized the rate of return. Why did mid-century sellers not then
get still more? On the supply side, some seem so pressed for ready cash they
depressed the market. The heirs of Conrad Reichenbach in 1337 included
his debts and their own financial need as grounds for selling half Gniechowice for only five hundred marks—it had in 1311 been pledged for two
thousand.[67] On the other side prospective buyers, and that then meant citizens of Wrocław, could put their money instead into relatively low-priced
demesne land (and gain all the profits from *locatio* at high rents) or into the
commercial prospects promised by the new Luxemburg connection.

   Was the market unusually affected by distinctive behavior on the part
of landowners from the city? Some activity looks like short-term speculation in an environment of quick turnover.[68] For example, on 3 November
1417 Peter Raster bought from Beda, a close relative by marriage, *Piotrowice Małe*, two-thirds of Chrzanów, a fourth of Stary Śleszów, and a
share in half of Pracze Widawskie. Over the next few months he added

Barbara Monsterberg's rights to Chrzanów and the part of the same half of Pracze which Dorothea Schonhals had owned. Then on 5 May 1418 he sold everything he had in the four places back to Beda.[69] Did Raster exploit his kinsman and fellow-councillor or were the two matrons rooked? Or do the bald summaries of conveyances conceal some quite different motivations? No prices are known.

Close examination of fully-documented cases reveals the behavior of citizens on the land market to have been more complex than simply buying cheap and selling dear. In what one student thought "ein Spekulationsgeschäft," the citizen brothers John and Henry Gürtler bought the demesne *Klein Goldschmieden* from the heirs of Michael Runge for 70 marks in 1394. In 1409 Henry sold it to their fellow citizen Nicholas Steinkeller for 220.[70] Even allowing for a 26 percent debasement of the groschen in the interim, Gürtler had in fifteen years nearly tripled his money. But he had also improved the title by obtaining in 1397 the claims of John Tschore, another citizen. Gürtler seems here to have been the astute speculator, but where does that leave Tschore or Steinkeller? The latter, in fact, took a beating on the property in the very next year, selling it to Mathias Wisgott for a mere 180 marks.

Earlier Tarnogaj was manipulated by other townsmen. In 1383–84 Franz Schreiber bought and combined two demesne farms which had for the past generation made up that place, paying 20.2 marks the mansus for one and 29.1 for the other. His total investment came to 272.5 marks. Within two years Schreiber's intentions were clear: he obtained royal permission to sell this fief to ecclesiastics. And in 1393 his plans came to lucrative fruition when he received for the entire settlement 360 marks from the mansionarii of Holy Cross. In less than a decade he had made 10 percent on one purchase and 30 on the other. But Schreiber had not merely bought low and waited for a price rise. He had assembled one larger farm from two and had gone to the effort to have waived in his favor the prohibition against sales to the church. And just before Schreiber other townsmen had done rather poorly in their own brief ventures at Tarnogaj. Peter Strasberg from Poznań and John Grolok, citizen of Wrocław, bought one farm in 1379 for 150 marks and sold it in 1382 for 200—but the intervening 25 percent debasement of the groschen gobbled up their gains. They sold to a Wrocław notary named Erasmus, who lost a whopping 87.5 marks when he sold out to Schreiber one year later.[71] The high-speed dealers did nowhere near as well as the slower improvers of rights at *Klein Goldschmieden* and Tarnogaj, even though all were citizens.

Reasons other than speculative intent explain rapid turnover of some citizen landowners. Between the 1380s and the 1430s eight town families in succession owned Damianowice, which thus looks like a prime object of speculative enterprise—except five of the transfers occurred after females inherited the property.[72] The mass of the evidence thus does not argue for land speculation as more than an occasional activity of citizen lords.

Rapid sequences of sales did distinguish the fourteenth-century market in land,[73] but all sorts of lay lords fully participated. Krajków, for instance, belonged to several independent owner-operators: of twenty-nine sales of land there between 1350 and 1399, only two involved citizens in any way.[74] The demesne at Żar passed by sale among the Schellendorf and other knights seven times between 1366 and 1390, and their peers transferred four times between 1363 and 1367 an eleven-mansi piece of Źródła.[75] Any member of the elite could see that an active market made land a secure, remunerative, and easily liquidated way to store capital for which a preferred use was lacking. The effect of rapid turnover was thus more uniform than its causes. Landowners seeking alternatively to embody and to free their capital contributed little to the strength of lordship in places like Źródła, Damianowice, or Tarnogaj.

The same corrosive effect derived from a further characteristic of the market in land: lords wishing to sell could break up a lordship by alienating fragments piecemeal to different buyers. The parts so separated were like those created through inheritance and other family transfers, territorial segments of more or less arbitrary size and definition. Like rapid turnover, fragmentation by sale had no detectable association with any particular generation, status group, or form of title to land. No kind of lord flinched from carving a chunk from his property to consummate a desired sale. Squires Pasco and Andreas Grzebkowicz sliced off the demesne at Karczyce and sold it to Tammo Schirowski in 1343 but kept the village lands for another five years before ceding them to Henry Koltsch, a citizen of Środa. The same person would not again own demesne and village at Karczyce until the 1430s.[76] In 1355 a citizen, Barthel Schertilzan, simply chopped his demesne farm at Swojczyce in two, selling 3½ mansi to the Holy Trinity Hospital and keeping the other two.[77]

What may be the ultimate instance of fourteenth-century lords arbitrarily splitting a village lordship took place at Nowa Wieś Wrocławska in 1391. Nicholas Plener and Nicholas Oberer bought sublordship under the Bishop of Wrocław and agreed to divide the property. Since one side of the village had 9⅝ mansi and the other 9⅞, they decided one lord should take the schulz's 3¾ rental mansi and ⅞ free mansus and count these as being on the opposite side of the village street. But since that side also had two empty mansi and the other only a quarter, they compromised on equal bearing of those losses. Each would thus, they said, have 10¾ rental mansi, half the gertner (whose precise division is not, thank goodness, detailed), and an equal share in the undivided remainder, which ostensibly included the "herschaft."[78] No doubt the possessions of each Nicholas were then clearer to them than they now appear, but the entire episode again confirms the overwhelming importance to lords of property as a source of revenue. Division in the process of sale was as normal as division in the course of any other use to which land might be put in the lord's interest.

What values had a lordship to a fourteenth-century possessor of it? The collective answer is revenues, security, clients, credit, and liquid cash. Each had its own complexities and patterns and each satisfied different needs of a landowner. To separate them is partly a tool to analyze the behavior of lords who turned their properties to their needs as these arose. The effects on each lordship came out of the fortuitous combination of individual circumstance. But to exploit a lordship in any way other than living from its annual yield or selling it whole for its capital value commonly resulted in its division into separate rights and/or physical portions. Providing for one's kin from one's land created hereditary or other fractional shares. Granting it to a vassal or a lessee or borrowing against it multiplied layers of rights over the same property. And selling for liquid capital often meant physical fission, too. However generated, the segments gained immediately their own institutional life and moved independently to new possessors via channels set by status relationships or the market. "Lordship" in use thus tended to become a mere list or collection of potentially or actually discrete claims to take an income from a certain property, not a unified possession or a unique social role. Though ostensibly derived from the economic and geographic realities of a particular place, lordship rights floated free from these through the hands of the élite, their direction and accumulation more determined by social and market forces among the group of landowners than by the shape of the rural world itself. Use atomized lordship in the fourteenth century Wrocław duchy and, not coincidentally, opened to a wide spectrum of individuals entry into the landlord group.

Consolidation, simple and extended

Of Franz Schreiber's dealings at Tarnogaj in 1383–84 a near-contemporary remarked, "it seems that out of two demesne farms each of five and a half mansi, purchased from two persons and united, the aforesaid Franz made a village."[79] This anonymous compiler of a chartulary for the mansionarii of Holy Cross thus uniquely displayed his perception of a countercurrent to subdivision of lordships. The pattern of behavior may be called consolidation and provisionally defined as an individual landowner gathering dispersed owners' rights over and portions in a single place.[80] No other writer so directly revealed a consciousness of the phenomenon, but consolidation was common to every sort of landowner and is central to any understanding of lordship in the fourteenth century. This section treats the simple collection of scattered ownership rights and then extends the concept to include creation of new lordships by amalgamation of old ones. A further stage created new lordship rights by acquisition of authority formerly lodged elsewhere in society. A continuum joined the assembly of dispersed old incomes and the gain of new ones by those with private title to land.

Throughout the period and all across the duchy patient men accumulated by market and status-based means the scattered claims which, when assembled, made a unitary lordship over the lands and inhabitants of a rural settlement. Actions of the wealthy townsman Franz Schreiber at Tarnogaj mirrored those of dozens of his peers over generations. Back in 1313 Nicholas of Pasterzyce, also a citizen, bought four mansi at Sadków from William of Zenicz and his wife and another four from the sons of Gerhard of Molheim to gain that entire property.[81]

Knights from new and old families consolidated lordships as well as did any townsman. Peter Dirschkowicz came to Piotrowice in 1401 to buy from John Seidlicz of Samotwór all of his holdings there: eighteen rental mansi, two gardens, two shares in the tavern, and royal taxes worth two marks. The next year he obtained from Henry Rimbabe a third of the demesne, appurtenant woods and meadows, five rental gardens, nineteen rental mansi, another share in the tavern, a third of the patronage, the schulz's service, and various minor rights. In 1405 Peter got nine and a half mansi from Franz von der Stroze, in 1406 the shares in the demesne, rental land, mill, tavern, and patronage of John and Margaret Rimbabe, and in 1408 the other mill previously owned by Franz Borsnicz. The last outstanding fragment of Piotrowice became his five years later, when Knecht Hugowicz turned over two mansi once associated with the latter mill.[82] Much earlier, Poppo Hugowicz established the position of his family by three purchases at Bagno in 1337–38 and then waited patiently until 1365 for the final piece.[83]

Only clerical landowners look rarely to have pieced together a lordship from its parts, but appearances can deceive. Church estates grew little during the fourteenth century and corporations had never to partition their lands among heirs. Like the mansionarii of Holy Cross, who bought all Tarnogaj from Franz Schreiber, clerics willingly paid to benefit from other's work at consolidation. But they preferred when able to liquidate sublordships or leaseholds in their own villages, merging claims rather than territorial parcels. That strange division of sublordship rights over Nowa Wieś between Nicholas Plener and Nicholas Oberer in 1391, for instance, was ended by the cathedral chapter buying out both within two years.[84] Whether a landowner sought by purchase to eliminate competing layers of rights or parcels held by another, therefore, these efforts simplified and at the extreme reunited the lordship over a rural settlement.

These simple consolidations of traditional owner's rights counteracted the subdivisions previously seen. When one individual accumulated others' claims against a settlement he improved his own position as lord over it, diminished the unit cost of collecting revenues, and reduced conflict among landowners. The sole lord over a rural community had perhaps greater prestige than one with a limited claim against it. Land and incomes grew without the transactions costs which equivalent acquisitions in a new place might add. A concerted program to buy up the rights of others in a place where one already had claims was, therefore, well-advised for an individual who felt his lands too small and had the liquid wealth to acquire more.

Beyond individual advantage, however, simple consolidation of ordinary landowner's rights did not go. Increasing the scale of one's holdings raised revenues but only in proportion to the new acquisitions themselves; sheer size brought no additional advantage. Nor did such consolidations otherwise directly raise the rate of return to lordship. The nature, value, and totality of landowners' claims against the village or demesne changed not at all. What two, three, or more had taken now simply went to one. Simple consolidations of owner's rights by individuals were, therefore, but part of the continual reshuffling of incomes within the landowning group. The consolidator paid for more revenues and received them, but these personal gains could only mitigate the late fourteenth-century malaise of traditional landed incomes and those dependent on them.

Simple consolidation of dispersed but traditional rights of ownership merely redistributed landed incomes from less fortunate lords to ones with the capital to accumulate more claims. But the idea of consolidation could be extended to new opportunities as well. At this time around Wrocław lords did not demand more from peasants or press more closely the productive capacity of their lands, for they could easier augment customary revenues by dealing with others in the elite. The consolidation process draws the investigator beyond mere reunion of existing owner's rights to other important ways fourteenth-century lords made their titles more remunerative. One was by creating new lordship units from previously separate farms and hamlets.

Territorial manipulations by lords for improvement's sake have been earlier encountered. Those in the fourteenth century and especially its middle and later decades built up new lordships as a regular extension of the incremental methods used to consolidate single existing ones. The twenty-year effort of the well-to-do citizen Richard of Gubin to reunite Chrzanów, for instance, also increased by half the lordship's size. It had sixteen mansi in 1353, the year before Richard made his first purchase there, and after nine transactions ending in 1376 he owned them all. Since 1366, moreover, Richard had also been buying land at *Warmutowice*, which the fiscal register had rated at eight mansi. Three purchases of nominally 7½ mansi he completed by 1372—the last time *Warmutowice* is recorded. By 1396 Richard's heirs had only Chrzanów, which in 1425, though assessed at its old sixteen mansi, paid tax for twenty-two. Assessment and payment coincided in 1443.[85] Plainly Richard had during the 1360s and -70s pieced together two adjacent lordships and merged them into one. His activities were in many ways typical. Most such efforts to create a larger lordship by combining small ones took place in the Wrocław district, where properties and settlements did run smaller than elsewhere.[86] Many initiators came from the citizen owners then so numerous there.[87]

But the lord's restructuring of territorial units was no more peculiar to citizens than was any other approach to landed property. St. Vincent's abbey bought ten mansi at or around Sołtysowice in 1346–47. In the same vicinity were then another ten mansi sometimes called *Molnsdorf* and a third place called *Kegel*. Between mid-century and 1391 two generations of the Dumlose family from Wrocław gathered these. Meanwhile another member of that family, Franz Dumlose, had become abbot of St. Vincent and in 1390, a year before his death, bought out four mansi the Rothe family had held since mid-century. Finally under the successor of Franz St. Vincent completed the territorial consolidation of lordship in this bottomland area, acquiring from the last of the Dumlose the lands "zu dem Kegel zu Schulteisewicz und zu Molnsdorf als diezelben guter zuenander geslagen und eyn gut wurden sein." Last to come in were eleven marks of *census* on the former Dumlose lands which the abbey redeemed in 1419.[88]

A most complex and wholly innovative amalgamation of what had been separate properties was carried out by a family with no known elite status apart from their ownership of land. Beginning with a mere perpetual lease of 1½ mansi at Bielany in 1351, men and women named Zweibrodt created in their own name the village now called Zabrodzie.[89] After vague but visible incremental additions, there in a 1398 sale charter materialized their previously unknown "gutt und dorff Zwaybrodt, als es von den fuhrwergken Zeseraw, Bengkwitz, Logaw, und andern zusammen geschlagen ist. . . ."[90] Later records confirm that from three or more separate little demesne farms on the black earth between Bielany and Cesarzowice the Zweibrodts had formed a new rental unit of some twenty mansi.

The effects and thus the significance of fourteenth-century landowners' constructing new territorial lordships go just a step beyond the simpler consolidations of broken old ones.[91] Lords did modify first the nominal and institutional and eventually the settlement geography of the area. From an immediate economic perspective, however, this chiefly raised the size of but not the rate of return from their holdings. Like earlier improving landowners, however, some creators of new lordships, the Zweibrodts and Richard of Gubin among them, followed their amalgamations with settlement of tenants, suggesting some opinion that a certain minimum size would help make the new village viable. Other small demesnes, however, were converted to rental land without territorial changes, while St. Vincent kept Sołtysowice as three demesne farms into the sixteenth century.[92] Again, the prestige of owning a larger lordship rather than just a couple of farms, (which certainly should have accrued to the Zweibrodts) and some reductions in administrative costs seem the most probable general results from the point of view of the owners.

The privatization of higher authority

A compelling reason for lords to consolidate as well ducal rights over land and dependents is as obvious now as in the fourteenth century: *iura ducalia* had clear financial worth. In 1343 John of Głogów from Wrocław valued those over Janików and Wierzbno at a total of eighty-four marks cash each year and from each rental mansus four measures of grain. At St. Mary's Tyniec Mały in the 1430s the land tax and high justice annually came to eighteen and a half marks and thirteen and a half malder of grain.[93]

Transfer from the public authority of the sovereign to the private possession of the landowner of rights to tax and to judge the rural population is a commonplace of late medieval and early modern east-central Europe, one signpost marking divergence of the region from the route taken by the west. With due regard for particulars and timing, Silesia and the Duchy of Wrocław participated fully in this historic shift of authority.[94] Here it occurred locally and individually, affecting specific rural communities and benefitting certain landowners and groups in advance of others. It arose in the fourteenth century from a conjunction of the sovereign's political and the landowners' economic needs. Less oddly than it may seem, peasants were then little affected.

Since the early growth of seigneurial lordship in twelfth-century Silesia, sovereign dukes had retained a right to tax rental land and to judge capital cases and appeals from village courts. For practical purposes by the fourteenth century this meant their officers took the land tax and administered what was then thought of as "high justice," with a third of the revenue generated by village courts. Yet rulers in Silesia generally and of Wrocław in particular had by the same time nearly exhausted their resources suitable to win and hold loyal followers while their political needs for them had, if anything, grown.

Thus the dukes, whether local and native Piast or absentee Luxemburg, slowly and grudgingly gave out the so-called *iura ducalia* to men they would favor or reward. Some such rights went for services rendered or expected, as when Henry VI granted the Pak brothers, Albert and Arnold, his high justice over Kulin in 1326 and Jaksonów in 1330.[95] Elsewhere the same kinds of claims secured loans. King John's rights over Wierzbice covered 71¼ marks from Conrad of Borsnicz in 1339 and 200 marks from Henry Schwarzenhorn in 1345.[96] And, like other remunerative rights in the fourteenth-century duchy, some *iura ducalia* rulers simply sold or exchanged outright—like the geschoss and jurisdiction at Brzezica conveyed by Wenceslas to Zdenko Dompnig for a hundred marks in 1405.[97] By all legitimate means fourteenth-century rulers of Wrocław divested themselves piecemeal of their direct authority over the countryside.

Fiscal and judicial components in *iura ducalia* could go together or separately. In many villages private possession of the right to tax well predated that to judge; in some only the taxes are ever recorded as alienated by the duke.[98] Jarosław is a case in point. Otto of Borsnicz proved before the *iudicium curiae* in 1344 his complete lordship and possession of all taxes there, but admitted that the king's district judge handled capital offenses. Through more than sixty years and successive landowning families the conveyances reiterate these provisions. Then in 1432 Sigismund Sachse had confirmed a gift of the village with high justice rights.[99] This should not be attributed simply to poor documentation. Some ducal charters giving or confirming sovereign rights to private lords explicitly reserve the high justice. These occur at many times, but are most common among those Henry VI issued after his submission to John of Bohemia.[100] Taken together they indicate, first, a preference by Henry to retain jurisdictional authority and, second, since lords show no sign of complaint, a principal concern on their part with cash returns rather than control over tenants.

Quite in keeping with the income orientation towards property prevalent among landowners, even when they possessed both kinds of ducal rights, the value was expressed in terms of the yield from taxes alone. What Nicholas Stewitz called his high justice at Żurawina in 1428, he described as an annual quantity of cash and grain.[101]

Possession of ducal rights by private persons in general is not possession by the local lord in particular. Although the Wrocław duchy developed no lasting or major private overlordships apart from the ownership of land,[102] up to mid-century numbers of grants went to others than the lords of the settlements affected. Lipnica belonged to Trzebnica, but Henry VI enfeoffed his vassal Rosco with his rights there in 1316, and he later gave those over Bartoszowa and Szukalice, properties of Lubiąż and the Church of Wrocław respectively, to the knightly brothers Conrad and Mulich of Rideburg.[103] Nor were churches the only landowners so affected. King John pledged to to Henry of Kuschberg royal incomes from the Schellendorfs' lordship at Lutynia and Charles's emissaries exchanged to John and Peter Colmas the king's claims on the Molheim lands at Polakowice.[104] Like other private possessions, ducal rights moved freely through market and hereditary channels. Those over Tyniec Mały Charles gave in 1371 to Tĕma of Koldice and they passed in 1390 to John Seidlicz. By the 1430s they were split between a citizen and a monk at St. Vincent, son of the knight Peter Melin.[105] The village pertained, of course, to St. Mary.

Naturally there was friction between separate land and judicial lords. Henry VI anticipated it in July, 1321, when he pledged his rights at Jelenin and Radoszkowice to the brothers Adlungsbach, for he promised to represent them if the bishop and chapter, owners of the villages, raised complaints, lawsuits, or threats of excommunication.[106] He should have had in mind the contemporary squabble over Zabłoto between the landlord, St. Vincent, and Mathias of Molheim. In October of that very year a papal order forced Molheim to admit the abbey's lordship rights, but he clung to the *iura ducalia* and passed them in 1332 to his son-in-law, Conrad of Falkenhain. Even after a generation, when Conrad's sons had sold their claims to the abbey, the recollected tension caused St. Vincent to demand of them a special oath repudiating any further intervention at Zabłoto.[107]

The abbey's main practical response at Zabłoto was that of most landowners who found another private individual exercising sovereign jurisdiction over their property. Whether conflict had erupted or not, owners simply sought to consolidate to their lordship rights the *iura ducalia* as well.

A systematic effort was initiated in the mid-1340s by Bishop Przesław, who found knights with ducal authority on many lands of his church.[108] Its lordships around Wrocław had remained under secular jurisdiction and offered rulers like Henry VI tempting means to reward supporters. For the Luxemburgs, however, the bishop had political value worth the effort to assuage this irritant. First Margrave Charles confirmed and his father endorsed the general exemption of church property from royal taxes. Then in August, 1345, the king explicitly reconfirmed all privileges, this time naming nine lordships in the duchy where a private individual then held ducal rights.[109] The next winter he appointed a special commission to resolve disagreements over *iura ducalia* between the bishop and Mulich of Rideburg, Mathias of Molheim, Petzko of Adlungsbach, Poppo of Hugowicz, Hermann of Borsnicz, and Hartung and Ramvold of Nymands. The panel had to be renewed by Charles in 1348 and further noble parties added, but at the end of that year agreement was reached. For sums paid partly by the bishop and partly by the commission, each knight ceded to Przesław and his church the "jura ducalia" and "jus supremo" he had held. Charles himself closed the episode when, on next confirming the privileges of the bishopric, he specified freedom from secular jurisdiction in those and more villages.[110]

Lay landowners had no less concern than the clergy. In exchange for the Colmas brothers' ducal rights at the bishop's Rzeplin the king's commissioners had given them those at Polakowice. The local lord, Agnes, widow of Henry of Molheim, bought them out within the year. At Piotrków Borowski Tilo and John Rothe consolidated the lordship between 1363 and 1384 and then in 1404 took over the high justice and geschoss which the Rausendorf brothers and Bernhard of Dobroszyce had from the king.[111]

When did lords in the duchy get ducal rights on their properties? The surest criterion of this increment to lordly authority is a positive textual statement that the owner of a settlement held capital jurisdiction. Since separate transfers of fiscal rights and/or possession by non-owning private parties occurred earlier if, indeed, at all, this is also the most conservative measure of landlord powers. That the lord had *iura ducalia* so defined is recorded before 1550 at 139 places in the duchy, sometimes as actual acquisitions but a little more often as one specified element of lordship rights. Figure 8.2 tabulates these references as 5-year steps in a cumulative total. All the available evidence so portrayed over time indicates that lords in most places had ducal jurisdiction by the second quarter of the fifteenth century: surviving texts record it in 110 settlements (79 percent of the 139) before 1425 and the total reaches 124 (89 percent) by 1440. As a documentable phenomenon in the Wrocław duchy, therefore, landowners obtained *iura ducalia* mainly during the long fourteenth century, perhaps somewhat earlier than elsewhere in Silesia.[112] Their actions must be understood in that situation, not later ones.

Figure 8.2 also highlights phases in the acquisition by landowners of ducal authority. These suggest its dynamic. Steep rises on the graph and many actual grants correspond with rulers in need of support and/or money from the landed elite. Henry VI's tenuous security is reflected in nearly one new site of lordly high justice for each year of his reign; both reached a climax in 1326–27 when his perhaps frantic search turned to Bohemian suzerainty and lords of eight settlements gained ducal rights of jurisdiction. Four knights won reward for their service and the others were two fashion-

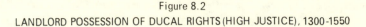

Figure 8.2

LANDLORD POSSESSION OF DUCAL RIGHTS (HIGH JUSTICE), 1300-1550

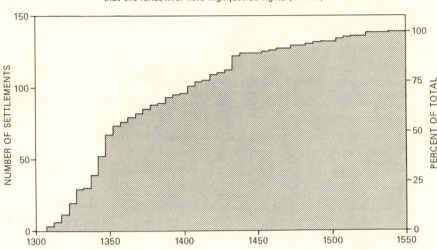

5-year cumulative totals of places with new evidence
that the landowner held high justice rights (n=139)

able religious foundations, St. Mathias and St. Clare.[113] King John's succession and worry over a restless province beside unreconciled Poland then meant flurries of benefits to landowners in 1337 and 1345. In the latter year, for example, John gave to two knights and a townsman his rights over Ogrodnica, Strachowice, and Gądów Mały and sold to Paschco Grzebkowicz those at Jarząbkowice and Karczyce.[114] Then the longest annual list of new lordships with ducal rights in owners' hands came three years later from Charles's collaboration with the bishop's consolidation drive. Finally, five new records of ducal rights in 1404–05 include two cash transactions whereby Wenceslas, still shaken from his captivity by disgruntled Czech barons, transferred to two Dompnigs his rights over their Święta Katarzyna and Brzezica.[115]

In and after the 1350s the curve in Figure 8.2 levels out as Charles IV displayed the contrasting behavior of a relatively secure and solvent ruler. Most new evidence then is of previously unrecorded ducal rights being written into conveyances. Wise owners took precautions when Charles and his servants were verifying royal prerogatives. They gave ducal incomes and jurisdictions special treatment in the survey of 1353.[116] The title of Nicholas Seidlicz to tax at Małkowice there noted as illegal was in 1358 declared void. And on Walpurgis, 1361, Małkowice paid the king five marks as *exactio*.[117] Thus the passage of judicial and other rights over rural property and people from public to private landowner's possession took its basic tempo from the needs and prospects of the ruler. Lords held out their hands but could not determine when they would be filled.

Different sorts of landowners consolidated ducal rights at different rates. Knights had considerable initial advantages and wealthy old church corporations a not unrelated handicap. Citizen landowners started slowly but had by about 1425 a share commensurate with their expanded acreage.

The knights' precocity stemmed from their close personal ties and political importance to Henry VI and the early Luxemburgs. To name men who received from their ruler before mid-century *iura ducalia* on their own properties is to call a roll of the duchy's knightly lineages, large and small: Pasco Grzebkowicz, Conrad of Borsnicz, Arnold and Albert Pak, Andreas Radak, Conrad of Falkenhain, Henry of Hugowicz, Pasco Rimbabe, Stephen Reichenbach, Otto of Glubos, Henry Wende, Siffrid of Schirow, Peter of Pritticz, Peczco and Zacharias of Gugelow.[118] Even in 1371 Těma of Koldice could still benefit like his earlier peers from royal gift of prerogatives over Tyniec, Sadków, and Jerzmanowo. By then the great surge of noble acquisitions had tapered off but this group likely possessed in the early fifteenth century a higher share of ducal rights over their lordships than did any other.[119]

Men of Wrocław exploited the needs of their early fourteenth-century dukes more to their collective than to their individual advantage. Though citizen landholding grew, townspeople showed in ducal rights only an erratic interest less than proportional to their place in the landholding group. Individual citizen lords were inconsistent. The Dompnig-Bayer-Budissin consortium worked in 1343 to keep their Wojnowice exempt from the district court but placidly accepted for nearly a half century this same jurisdiction over Żurawina.[120] Opportunities were not refused but likely not aggressively pursued, either.

Citizen landowners later lost their diffidence toward *iura ducalia* and by the turn of the century happily exchanged credit or cash for them. Zdenko Dompnig had King Wenceslas confirm in 1395 his claims in Jaksonów and ten years later spent a hundred marks for the taxes and high justice at Brzezica.[121] More recently landed citizen families treated ducal rights like any other in consolidating their new lordships. The fast-rising Nicholas Rempel went from buying up the claims of the Schellendorfs at Ratyń in three deals during 1404–06 to getting from the king full fiscal and judicial authority there.[122] Where the rights were already privatized, the process simply enveloped them with the land. Mathias Jenkwicz added the geschoss and high justice at Sadków from Erasmus Peseler in 1408 to the two shares in the lordship he had the previous year from the heirs John and Leonhard Reichard. And as citizens bought up noble properties where such rights were already the owner's, their share in ducal jurisdiction over the countryside continued to grow.[123] Much is associated with the increase in good-sized citizen estates. Unlike the knighthood, citizen holders of *iura ducalia* were more often relatively large than small property-owners. Many small men had, of course, only fractions of settlements in their control. But whether the connection is directly causal or not, as more citizen lords built up bigger estates around 1400 this group also accumulated ducal rights in similar proportion.

When knights and citizens wanted *iura ducalia* they had little problem getting them. Not so the clerics. The struggles of the relatively laggard corporate ecclesiastical landlords to obtain ducal authority on their estates perhaps better indicate the importance lords allotted to such rights than do the many easy acquisitions by the laity. The corporations were victims of their own precocious literacy and later political impotence.

Institutional lords who had relied on written records of their property and privilege in the thirteenth century, when the concept of *iura ducalia* was just evolving, found in the fourteenth that their treasured proofs of ownership did not specify exactly what now troubled them. One response was to interpolate into the texts of authentic older charters phrases appropriate to update a title and legitimate the rights one claimed. This the Cistercians of Lubiąż did in the early fourteenth century, modeling on their authentic grants from Duke Bolesław and his son a whole family of charters. High justice over the abbey's lands and subjects was the principal issue, causing the artificers to put into the mouth of the duke statements of gift with a richly anachronistic legal vocabulary.[124] In the Wrocław duchy this gained little, for Lubiąż eventually had to use other means, mainly cash, to get ducal rights on its lordships.[125]

Undeterred by the experience of Lubiąż, its sister foundation at Trzebnica undertook an elaborate parallel program under Abbess Katherine (1372–1404). At least thirteen charters, eleven of which dealt exclusively with ducal rights on the convent's properties, were composed in imitation of Henry I's authentic early thirteenth century grants. One claimed for the nuns' lordships at Brodno, Chomiąża, and Lipnica full tax exemption and high and low justice rights; another did so for Kotowice.[126] This time, moreover, the ruse worked. That for Kotowice the *iudicium curiae* accepted in 1398 as limiting jurisdiction there to the convent's own court, and in 1404 Wenceslas himself confirmed notarized copies of both texts at the request of the abbess. The king had then to order his captain, and the captain, the castellan of Uraz, to observe the convent's rights.[127]

The reluctance of the castellan to defer to Trzebnica (he did not surrender his claims on Kotowice until 1408) reveals a more immediate cause of the churches' slow acquisition of these rights: they were already in the hands of the duke's noble followers. Clerics in the fourteenth century faced competitors more favorably positioned than they, both to obtain and to retain these rights. The situation caused conflicts and engendered programs of consolidation already discussed. Some houses, the Clares and St. Mathias, for example, won with little difficulty directly from Henry VI jurisdiction over their properties.[128] The bishop had influence worth Charles's cultivation. But the older monastic foundations especially, bereft of pious favor and political weight, found the going slow indeed.

The experience of St. Vincent with its centerpiece lordship of Kostomłoty can stand for several older houses' tardy success at what was plainly a process of consolidation. Neither the Premonstratensians' twelfth-century title nor their thirteenth-century German law grant excluded the duke's authority. In 1329 Henry VI gave his right to take incomes from Kostomłoty to the noble brothers Stercze. This they sold in 1361 to Conrad, John, and Otto Borsnicz, although the abbey had since 1345 royal permission to buy it itself. The annual three marks from the schulz in lieu of cavalry service Conrad turned over to the abbot for thirty marks in 1369. The *geschoss* and mint money of thirty-six marks a year he kept until 1388 and then got 387 marks for it. The abbey's chronicler may have called this the "jus supremum et omne ducale judicium in villa Cossenplotcz," but such was not the case.[129] Capital and appellate jurisdiction long remained a royal prerogative, so complaints of the abbey about the actions of the Środa district court rose in shrill crescendo with the king's every visit to Wrocław. Definitive quiet came only after 1439, when King Albert conceded without limitation that none from Kostomłoty could be called to any but the abbey's court.[130] More than a century had passed since the Stercze had first intruded an unwelcome competing presence on the abbey's lordship and more than a half century since public justice itself became the issue.

Despite the eagerness with which some foundations pursued ducal rights over their lordships, seeking by ingenuity and persistence to compensate for their lack of benefactors, political clout, and willingness to spend, they were among the last to eliminate such competing authority.

What significance ought to be attributed to the mainly fourteenth-century transfer of ducal fiscal and judicial authority to private ownership in the Duchy of Wrocław? At the time it goes far to explain the economic survival and relative well-being of landowners through an age of decaying incomes from land and traditional lordship itself. In the crudest terms the landowning class thus obtained a markedly larger share of the surplus extracted from the peasants by their superiors. This occurred whether the private holder had ducal rights on his own or on another's property. When a lord obtained the *iura ducalia* on his own land, moreover, he increased his annual income per mansus owned, his power over his property, and even his status, both absolutely and relative to potential and real rivals. Neither the aggregate nor the individual gains to landowners came at the expense of peasants, the sum of whose obligatory outlays and deference to the elite remained unchanged. The immediate loser was the public authority, the duke or king, whose incomes and whose capacity to influence rural affairs passed to the landlords. On a longer perspective, of course, for lords to achieve public authority over the peasantry, as they almost had around Wrocław by the Hussite wars, established what became a key component in a later more authoritarian and exploitative agrarian regime.[131] Under other circumstances lords could use this institutional mechanism to gain wealth, power, and status at direct peasant expense. In its fourteenth-century setting, however, private acquisition of ducal authority was a less portentous affair. After the needs of rulers provided the opportunity, lords extended a pattern of behavior here labeled consolidation to redistribute elite incomes in their own favor.

The church also laid autonomous claim to authority over a lord's property and to revenues from its inhabitants and product. By around 1300 *ecclesia* had firmly established its largest demand against rural production, the tithes. The old assertion by Polish knights that the *ius militare* allowed them freely to allocate their tithes was crushed by synodal legislation and obliterated in disputes like that over the tithes of Siemidrozyce, definitively won in 1330 by the priest of Kostomłoty for his territorial parish.[132] Only a guerilla resistance, like that of a Środa citizen who claimed in 1388 that his little lordship in Bielany owed no tithes, sporadically continued.[133] Otherwise only clerics might take the tenth from their own lands—and bicker among themselves over it.[134]

So all grudgingly paid tithe, but in rural society the parish church and clergy more immediately manifested the socio-political as well as economic claims of *ecclesia*. These, however, could be subjected to a landowner's influence through the right of patronage, the *ius patronatus ecclesie* or *Kirchlehn*. Notably including authority to present a candidate for the vacant benefice, patronage had in early Poland been royal, but by the time patronage over specific rural churches around Wrocław enters the surviving record (mainly during the fourteenth century), it was most often appurtenant to private lordship.[135] A church at Bogdaszowice is first recorded in 1319, when half the patronage belonged with half the scholtisei and thirteen mansi to Jacob and John Schertilzan.[136]

Where lordship and patronage did not coincide, owners tried to create that alignment. St. Vincent, by 1300 lord for a century and a half over Wierzbno, then induced the knight Stephen to donate to it patronage over the church there.[137] The lord of Pracze, Henry Cal, set up in 1348 a new church for that village, Polanowice, and Rędzin, carving a parish by agreement from that of the All Saints church in the Wrocław suburbs.[138]

Still the pairing between landowner and patron was never everywhere perfect. As at Leśnica, where in 1326 Henry VI gave his patronage right to the canons of Holy Cross, who were not lords there, church corporations possessed rights over a fair number of parishes on lay property.[139] And especially in the Wrocław district many parishes covered several contiguous lordships, only one of which had the patronage. St. Mathias's demesne at Siechnice was in the parish of Święta Katarzyna, where the patronage belonged to laymen. In 1347 the hospital had to enter a special agreement with the then rector, Henry of Głogów, paying him twelve groschen a year to provide services in its lordship.[140] Such difficulties likely accentuated the value to lords of the more normal assimilation of patronage to lordship.

For lords who had it patronage was like any other right appurtenant to ownership of land. Conrad of Borsnicz used it with the rest of Ozorowice to dower his wife Agnes and at Skałka it was first inherited by one daughter of Lutko von der Nysa and then sold by her to another.[141] Naturally these practices meant patronage rights could themselves be divided and reconsolidated along with the rest of the lordship. Peter Dirschkowicz bought one third at Piotrowice in 1402 with the holding of John and Margaret Rimbabe.[142] All instances confirm, however, that patronage once joined to land ownership was not thereafter parted from it. In the words of a 1352 conveyance of fifteen mansi at Żurawina, with the land went the "ius patronatus ecclesiae in dictis mansis."[143] Though like ducal authority in having a purpose and legitimacy ostensibly quite separate from the land, patronage, too, became but a part of the lord's unified prerogatives.

Patronage augmented a landlord's influence in his lordship but remained bound by canon law. The patron had to present a genuine cleric and once installed the priest possessed his own rights. Lay lords were stymied. Ecclesiastical landowners alone could go beyond patronage to appropriation of their parish churches, incorporating the benefice and duties of the local rector to the resources and identity of the lordly foundation itself. After long experience with patronage over rectors at Kostomłoty St. Vincent obtained in 1386 the right to appropriate the rectory and all its incomes, thereafter providing the care of souls by appointment of a member of the abbey itself. St. Mathias did the same with its church at Gajków in 1399. That both these actions belong to the larger process of consolidation is shown by their immediate context. Appropriation by the landowner at Kostomłoty preceded by two years elimination of competing lay claims to tax the village and that at Gajków followed by six years the hospital's purchase from John Schlantz of lordship there.[144]

Fourteenth-century lords consolidated traditional rights of ownership over their rural properties and added by similar means rights not previously theirs. They bought up separate portions and bought out overlapping claims. They built new lordships from loose collections of neighboring properties and improved their authority with rights to judge and tax peasants and to nominate a priest. Yet no such gains resulted from collective action by landowners as a group, for as a group they took none and lacked corporate identity. Lords came from certain status groups but acted as individuals or corporations with specific social or institutional obligations. Each separately and in competition with others pulled together power over properties that comprised rural settlements and resources. In the process landowners not only improved their personal wealth, they gained as a class at the expense of persons and institutions whose claims upon peasants did not rest on title to the land itself. Lords at this time achieved substantial monopoly control over the elite's demands against the peasantry of their villages and of the Wrocław duchy. They had by the early fifteenth century authority over their villages. Yet rents did not rise. The quality of lord-peasant relations did not change. The distance of lords from their properties did not diminish. Why not?

The cyclic structure of fourteenth-century lordships

Consolidation and fragmentation were not in sum patterns of behavior by different lords, on different properties, or at different times. Taking the long fourteenth century in the duchy as a whole the practices treated in this chapter belonged simultaneously to the same set of people and the same set of lordships. A fully consolidated lordship augmented with an absorbed hamlet, ducal rights, and patronage, remained for its owner valuable for the same social purposes as any other bundle of remunerative rights. Neither narrow nor extended consolidation immunized a lordship from subsequent subdivision. Rights still passed among participants in an open and competitive market, whether by status or purely economic mechanisms. Thus the trend to bring into the hands of those who owned the land still other claims on the people who inhabited it merely added to an existing circulation.

Lordship over a settlement in the fourteenth-century duchy was not a permanent relationship or one which moved in one discernible direction, but a characteristically cyclic structure which oscillated unsteadily but repeatedly between what were from each successive lord's perspective phases of acquisition and dispersal and from the viewpoint of the village and its inhabitants, phases of consolidation and subdivision. Figure 8.3 schematizes this circular movement to integrate conceptually the behavioral reality already documented at length: one landowner's use of a property created the fragments which another would consolidate.

To explicate and demonstrate the figure, consider again the history of Kobierzyce, which posed the problems about the record, characteristics, motivations, and results of landowner behavior which have been examined since the start of Chapter 7. That history may now be seen as a typical variation of the cycle. The single private lordship created by Henry's grant to Otto of Glubos in 1333, with the ducal rights added by John, lasted through the sale to Mathias of Molheim and ended with hereditary partition among his sons. Ensuing subdivision continued up to the new consolidation (at least two purchases) by John Bayer around 1383. But Bayer's unified lordship over Kobierzyce endured only until his death before 1410, when shares passed to his sons and their mother. Nicholas von der Nysa consolidated those again in 1417 to complete a second cycle. The third began in less than a decade when the successor to Nysa's heirs, Peter Ungerathen, divided the property between his two daughters. Thus in the ninety-seven years of Kobierzyce's documented history before 1430 lordship there had passed through five different kin groups and nearly three full alternations between unity and subdivision.

In the histories of village lordships which resulted from the behavior of successive landowners the cycle itself emerges as the structural constant. The polarities or phases of unity and disunity or subdivision and consolidation have no consistency or pattern across the time of the fourteenth century, the space of the duchy, or the socio-cultural divisions within the landowning class. Village lordships are always to be found at all phases of the cycle. Division of Chrzanów in the 1350s was contemporary with a Kobierzyce still one under Mathias of Molheim and a Raszków being reunited by Henry Clonicz. These three each had one lord in the 1390s, but by 1425 only Chrzanów remained united.[145] At Węgry in the 1350s some owners were partitioning an inheritance and and others buying up the fragments with a view to reuniting them; those at Jenkowice then simply let a division go on. By the mid-1420s, however, entirely different landowners had united Jenkowice and divided Węgry.[146] Of course by some random chance some lordships may never have been divided, but by the same token

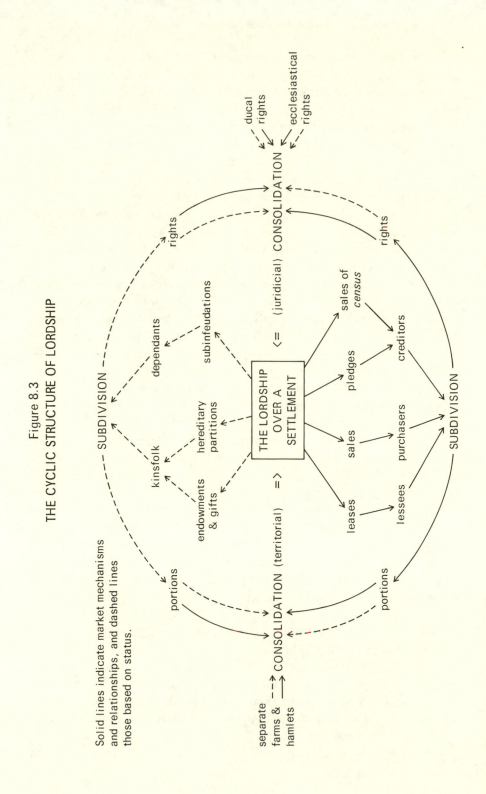

Figure 8.3
THE CYCLIC STRUCTURE OF LORDSHIP

Solid lines indicate market mechanisms and relationships, and dashed lines those based on status.

others were never united. Moreover even the incomplete records of leases, pledges, subinfeudations, and sales of rents leave no lordship unencumbered.

That all status groups among landowners actively consolidated and dispersed rights and portions of lordships has been assiduously detailed. Forms of movement varied for each, with hereditary partition important on lay properties but leases or the like more common for corporate lords. Lay mortality naturally made their lordships the most vulnerable and thus the most volatile, while rules against full alienation and the durable memory of corporations reduced motion on ecclesiastical properties. But the cycle worked there too. St. Mathias consolidated in 1277 pieces of Mokronos not fully included in its foundation gift and defended these in 1314. It beat off demands for payments from this property which the rector of Jaszkotle raised in the early 1330s. But if the hospital had ever controlled the whole area called Mokronos, it then did so no longer. Lay lords of knightly and of citizen extraction owned a part from before 1336 until 1386, pledging it for debts, creating dowers, buying and selling in whole and in pieces. St. Mathias "restored" its lordship over what had become Mokronos Dolny by purchase in 1386. But soon thereafter the hospital's early fifteenth-century financial troubles began a whole new round of subdivisions and separate claims which lasted into the 1480s.[147] Rights over ecclesiastical lordships circulated more slowly, more reluctantly, and less automatically, but the pattern remained.

Practically free movement of rights over property among lords in the duchy allowed the cyclic structure. Its reality in the fourteenth century meant, however, that the terms "lordship" or "village lord" had but ephemeral or artificial meaning. The lordship was then but a village community or a demesne settlement which defined territorially a bundle of rights. A village lord was then but a congeries of separate claimants to the payments which those rights legitimized. The claimants themselves and the composition of each one's claims changed erratically for reasons unrelated to the particular qualities, geographic, economic, or social, of the object on which the claims rested. The village community, however, remained. Thus a landowner could most easily obtain more incomes by dealing with other claimants to the territory already owned in part (i.e. attempt consolidation) or with like persons with similar claims elsewhere. For the villagers the same reality meant that today's lords would probably soon change and could if necessary now be played off against one another. Rarely did the fourteenth-century peasant community face a single overwhelming and predictably continuous aggressive authority. The community was stable and enduring, and the lord, a shifting manifestation of a different, though dominant, society.

A long and complex treatment of the place and role of landlords and lordship in the fourteenth-century duchy has identified a part of a socio-economic order in large-scale equilibrium. The landowning group is defined by its feudal and proprietary tenure, its non-agricultural way of life, and its effective, even growing, monopoly on access to status and power. But entry into that group was for most of the period relatively open, dependant primarily upon wealth and thus clearly competitive. Competition for landed incomes reinforced divisions among the landholding group which derived from the external attributes of status and the internal ones of kinship and relative wealth. These divisions then motivated individual behavior with property. Arching over the perpetual movement of landowning families and of property among them which so dominates the bulk of the documentation is but one major trend, the growth of landowners' rights manifest in their acquisition of *iura ducalia*. These contained the potential for direct domination of the peasantry. But in the century before the Hussite wars such domination remained inhibited by enduring features of the rural social order: the fragmentation, broad distribution, small scale, and instability of much landownership; the social context and income-oriented purposes of most landowners; the institutional arrangements of the German law village. No one-way causal relationships among these variables are to be detected or imputed on other than a priori grounds. The rural order of the fourteenth century, lords and villagers together, represented no mechanical device but an organic structural unity, probably imperfect and certainly exploitative on any absolute scale, but well-enough integrated and mutually reinforcing to survive and react to many changes through minor equilibrating adjustments. It has been seen from developmental and resource-oriented economic perspectives and now from the socio-economic perspective of its rulers. Chapter 9 looks inside the village itself.

VILLAGERS IN AND BEYOND
THEIR COMMUNITIES

Stabilwicz xlij mansi censuales et thaberna, quattuor ortulani et molendinum cum tribus rotis. Jacobus scultetus presentavit xviij grossos de xxx mansis, iiijor ortulanis et tribus rotis. Hartungus Kewle habet iiijor mansos. Petrus de Samphar habet v mansos et ipse scultetus iii mansos, non dederunt.

Stabłowice in the tax return of 1425; RB, fol. 5r, or Korta, "Księga," #77.

Medieval lords commanded the resources of literacy; medieval peasants did not. Hence some activities of landowners were intentionally preserved in writings that still survive and others of their doings left traces enough to see, but the life of the peasant majority is illuminated only by happenstance in records made for the purposes of others. The distance separating lords from their lordships around fourteenth-century Wrocław left villagers to their own devices, and left their lives out of the texts. And in their rare appearances tenants are only accidentally other than anonymous owers of dues. But country people cannot just be stereotyped in their role as tenants. The tenant-rent-landlord nexus omits other stratifications in medieval rural society and other connections in and among its villages.[1] Too much is left empty of humanity.

This chapter cannot fill the void. It gleans from textual byways sown to no crop. The chief goal is to celebrate with vignettes, mimes (for the words of peasants are then almost never heard), and occasional set pieces the variety, autonomy, interactions, and relative material well-being of fourteenth- and early fifteenth-century villagers around Wrocław. It first presents rural residents who occupied a social place between the normal landowner and peasant tenant, people on a margin that was also a strategic conjunction for the whole social system. Then it displays sides not seen so far of more ordinary villagers, the range of their wealth, their freedoms, and their access to special economic opportunities. Last comes a partial retracing of spatial and financial connections which helped bind into a regional society men and women in different places and groups. For some topics—schulzen, peasant wealth, and rural credit, for instance—benchmarks are established to treat later changes in Part IV. For now, however, Chapter 9 completes discussion of the structural foundations for a relatively autonomous, confident, and prosperous regional rural community in the generations before the Hussite wars.

Between lord and peasant

The commonplace ordering of pre-modern society into lords and peasants distorts the complex rural stratification of the fourteenth- and early fifteenth-century duchy. Differences among lords have been shown; those among peasants shall be. But for some persons economic activities at variance with their tenurial status and for others performance of a peculiar role sustained intermediate social positions which the dichotomy ignores. Surviving evidence reveals three such groups—small holders of full property rights, village schulzen, and parish priests—for separate treatment below. The first were the oldest but had become an archaic anomaly; the last were in but hardly of the village; the second held a central position in the rural order created with the German law.

Property records for several places settled before or without German law contain not one lord or lordship cycle but many small owners. Best known is Krępice, for which August Meitzen long ago published the texts, but for much of the fourteenth century Pełczyce, Krajków, Chrzanów, Okrzeszyce, and perhaps others were similar.[2] No full survey survives from these, but most landholders were plainly very small. At Krępice in 1384 a good quarter of the village was covered by Bartko and Hannos Adam with 1½ mansi, Mignow Strige with 1, Peter, son of Henry, with 1½, Stephen Curzonak with 2½, and Simon Gumba with ½.[3] At Pełczyce before 1387 and at Krajków between 1336 and 1438 not one of the many conveyances handled more than two mansi.[4]

Yet these small holders had the same tenurial rights as great lords, for they held hereditary fiefs from the duke and conveyed them before the captain and the *iudicium curiae*.[5] When Matzke of Krajków died without issue in the late 1390s, his two mansi escheated to the crown, only to be regranted to Henry and John Kochern and their "Lehnserben" in the very terms by which Wiland the stonemason had received that land from Henry IV in the 1280s.[6] Those at Krajków were free of service, but others owed military duties or a cash commutation.[7]

In socio-economic situation these landholders were less like their tenurial peers than like well-off peasant tenants or schulzen. At Krajków around mid-century certainly three and probably five fiefholders with less than two mansi cultivated their own farms; those with like tenures at Chrzanów were even called *rustici*.[8] The purely local importance of these people confirms their mediocrity. Most surnames came from the village itself. Thus the line of "Bogus de Polsicz" ("Bogusław of Pełczyce"), who took over 1.8 mansi of hereditary fief at Pelczyce in 1322, can be traced there alone for at least three generations, while their neighbors and peers included Rupert "of Pełczyce," his sons, and the heirs of Michael "of Pełczyce."[9] Plainly, these holders of small fiefs were not larger lords elsewhere. An earlier age might have thought them peasant warriors or even *milites*, but they were no longer so designated in the fourteenth-century records.[10] Most bore names of Polish origin (and Bogusław of Pełczyce sat on the czuda in 1323[11]). Only their conditions of tenure distinguished them from operators of tenant farms.

The fourteenth century was a rather well-documented but otherwise unremarkable phase in the slow disappearance of the peasant proprietors. Some villages were quickly transformed. For example, at Okrzeszyce between 1375 and 1387 men called "von Okerschitz" sold one after another seven hereditary fiefs totaling only eight or nine mansi to citizens Nicholas and John Bock. Thereafter the lordship remained in the hands of citizens and other larger owners.[12] At Zakrzyce during 1427–29 the noble Hans Radak bought out five predecessors.[13] Peasant proprietors survived into the 1430s at Krajków, but had vanished by the time the conveyances resume in 1484. Those at Krępice lasted into the 1520s to pose to their rulers an impossible paradox—how could people rightly serfs hold fiefs? But that anticipates (see p. 357 below) an age different from the fourteenth century, when people who held like lords but worked like peasants were just fading relics from an older social organization.

Village schulzen were between lord and peasant, too, but not as social anachronisms. They mediated the principal junction in the rural order established by the German law. A privileged hereditary village headship had been brought to Silesia to reward the *locator* and to both separate and connect lord and tenants. Schulzen were made responsible for running the village court and collecting peasant dues and invested with a substantial *feudum improprium* owing military service.[14] Now fourteenth- and early fifteenth-century schulzen are visible in the structurally intermediate position implicit in their antecedents. The economic resources of schulzen sustained their actual exercise of leadership in and representation of their communities.

The personal background of many schulzen remains obscure. Too common are mere names like the John of "Muschow" and John Koscitzko of Lubnów who in 1365 together bought the office at Rościsławice. Up to the mid–fifteenth century individuals from outside the peasantry did accept and serve in this position. Clerics bought it at Popowice near Środa in 1388 and again in 1403,[15] and schulzen who identified themselves as town citizens are even more numerous. Around Środa its burghers appear as such in several villages, while even proud Wrocław magnates like the wealthy tailor and ducal confidant, Dietrich Haso, purchased these offices and passed them on to their heirs.[16]

But along with the slow disappearance in the fourteenth century of *locatores* from upper social strata and in keeping with the special juridical position of the office, schulz came to denote a status of its own. Most of the economic and social doings of schulzen discussed below catch the eye because they and others refer to them as such. This assertion of a particular identity is supported by the relative frequency with which schulzen themselves obtained the same office elsewhere and dealt with others of their own sort. Thus Peter Furman, "once schulz in Solna," became in 1393 the new schulz of Bliż and in the following year "Mathias, once schulz in Brzoza," purchased the office in Świnobrod.[17] More complex situations arose as well. In 1420 the duchy's court confirmed a village court decision about the scholtisei at Domasław. Interested parties included Jacob, schulz of Wojszyce, with his wife Margaret, and the "Erblinge des Gutes . . . Andres der Schultis von Dombslau" and his wife.[18]

Unlike peasant proprietors, fourteenth century schulzen reinforced by their economic resources and activities their intermediate social rank. The lands and privileges of their endowments could support independence and enterprise. To take an unusually detailed but still typical mid-fourteenth century instance, when Hanco Dremelik, a peasant from Kuchary, handled the *locatio* of Siechnice, he received for a forty mark cash outlay free hereditary possession of the schulz's office plus two mansi of arable, the local fishery, a tavern, a butchery, a plot of reeds for thatch, and free pasturage for 150 sheep.[19] The components of Dremelik's scholtisei were common to many of his peers, but his two mansi, though good-sized by ordinary peasant standards, fell below the norm for schulzen in the duchy. The fiscal survey of 1353 specifies holding size for 128 of the 137 schulzen mentioned; the mean endowment was 2.7 mansi.[20] An average in the order of 2½ mansi is further confirmed by the tax returns of 1425 and 1443.[21] Though less than half the size of the average demesne farm in the same texts, such a tenure ranked somewhat above that of the average parish priest and was matched by only about one peasant tenant in twenty (see below). Seen as a farmer alone the schulz stood well above most of his fellow villagers.

But Hanco Dremelik and his peers usually controlled more than just arable in the open fields. Special economic privileges made that land more valuable and provided opportunities not always open to mere tenants. In particular, many schulzen enjoyed rights like those of Gerhard from St. Vincent's lordship at Zabłoto, whose reissued privilege of 1363 let him run up to 300 sheep on village land.[22] To judge from the surviving evidence only schulzen and demesne farmers could raise sheep on a large scale, asserting the right to graze their herds on the village pasture and stubble without interference from the peasants. Although a few had a general privilege, most extant references specify a substantial stint, 150 at least and up to 400.[23] Commercial prerogatives and monopolies, initially rights of the lord, also often passed to the schulz. Almost every scholtisei adequately described in the documents included the local tavern, mill, or both. When more elaborate marketing facilities were present, like the stalls for bakers, butchers, and cobblers at Janików that appear in a 1351 charter, these, too, often belonged to the schulz.[24]

Hereditary village schulzen did not limit their economic activity to exploitation of their landed and legal endowments. They showed much enterprise in profitable and prestigious aspects of the rural economy. Some took up parcels of land on lease or even regular rental mansi.[25] Others, though still operating on a relatively small scale within their home village, acquired land in demesne and with it the rights and duties of a lord. Nicholas, schulz of Jerzmanowo, bought three mansi there in 1337 to be held with hereditary fief rights, while his successor, John Strolicz, gave a similarly described holding to kinsmen in 1363. The schulz of Buczki in 1340, Tisczco, even had a miniature castle with a drawbridge on his service-free demesne of four mansi.[26]

Certain schulzen went beyond the mere addition of a few more mansi and utilized their position and resources to establish their own lordship over major portions of their village. From before 1310 to 1369 almost a quarter of Małkowice belonged to its schulzen. On the five mansi which had been added to the original endowment, *rustici* were tenants and subjects of the schulz himself.[27] In the early fifteenth century Matzke, schulz of Bukowiec, also owned 10¾ mansi, some demesne, some rental, of the forty-odd in that village.[28]

Schulzen with ambitions and the wealth to pursue them also found opportunity outside their home villages. Almost forty cases are extant from the 1340s to 1420s of individual schulzen who obtained in other villages demesne and rental lands measuring from less than a mansus to more than ten. Just as patient as any lordly investor was the schulz of Wojkowice, Stephen, in his consolidation of hereditary fief rights over Pasterzyce. Beginning in 1396 he bought out first one heir, Katherine Wolnigk, then another, Nicholas Wolnigk (who had himself merged the portions of three others), and finally, nineteen years later, the last competitor, Katherine Domerow, to accumulate 12½ mansi, the local mill, and all rights over the river there.[29] Pasterzyce is about six kilometers from Stephen's base at Wojkowice, but other schulzen ranged farther afield. Paul Werber, schulz of Żurawina, went more than fifteen kilometers in 1388 to buy the demesne at Kazimierzów, which his family then kept for three generations.[30] Such acquisitions demonstrate the wealth of certain schulzen and make them the only distinct group to join the knights, citizens, and clerics as lords of rural settlements in the duchy. At least some schulzen thus crossed the boundary from the village to the dominant strata of society.

Land purchases, big farms, large herds, and control over market and service facilities hint that schulzen could mobilize considerable capital. But positive evidence for mercantile or financial interests is uncommon. Werner, schulz of Węgry and largest buyer in 1377 of draft horses from the demesne at Borów, took six on credit for 4¼ marks and paid in two installments.[31] His predecessor, Bartholomeus, put even more cash into annual rents. When *census* sold for just below ten times the annual return, he bought a total of thirteen marks on the holdings of Henry Swenkenfeld, hereditary lord of Stary Śleszów, and then dealt as an equal with a consortium of Wrocław merchants to simplify the complex network of rights over that village.[32] And a few other schulzen loaned on landed security, both to small men like Seiffrid of Lemberg, whose single mansus at Pełczyce was pledged to schulz Peter of Wilczków in 1340, and to figures as impressive as Conrad of Falkenhain, once captain of the duchy, who with his brother borrowed from the schulz of Jaksin, John the Red, 30½ marks against all their rights in the village.[33]

Signs of prosperous and enterprising fourteenth- and early fifteenth-century schulzen are strong; those of economic difficulty are rare and ambiguous. Certainly schulzen borrowing money by the sale of annual rents are more common than those lending it. That fits all expectations of what records were made and survived, but is no firm evidence of financial trouble.[34] The right of alienation did put the office and its holdings on the market. When these passed as a unit, as happened at least seven times at Bielany beside Środa in 1357–94, the economic resources remained intact, although such turnover might weaken the ability of successive incumbents to exercise real leadership in the village.[35] More deleterious, surely, was the fragmentation that arose from partial sales or hereditary partition. As early as 1339 the scholtisei of Galowice had been broken into at least three parts and that at Michałowice in 1417 was in five. Sales of single schulz mansi are fairly common.[36]

Sales of the office early gave lords an opportunity to replace hereditary schulzen with their own temporary appointees. This they did not do around Wrocław before the 1430s. Instead the pattern was that followed at Ogrodnica in 1319, where the landowners resold with full freedoms three mansi that had fallen to them from the *scholtisei*.[37] Overall, then, the individual misfortune which surely struck some schulzen in the duchy during the century or so before the Hussite wars little affected the collective well-being and independence of these people.

Prosperity provided the resources and prestigious office the opportunity for schulzen to assert genuine and recognized leadership in their villages and neighborhoods. They converted intermediate status and wealth as village notables into a critical function as mediators between the peasant community and its superiors in society at large.[38]

The judicial and collecting roles assigned schulzen in *locatio* charters were no mere formality. Fourteenth century texts confirm that they presided in person over village courts then normally conceived as "Schultis und Scheppen," schulz and assessors.[39] Although by rights limited to matters of low justice, they found themselves responsible as well for more serious violations of order. Schulz and assessors from Zabłoto were hailed into the district court at Środa for failing to investigate a murder in their village,[40] while part of the schulz's task at the customary *Dreiding* was to chair the entire village community sitting as an investigative jury of presentment to reveal crimes not otherwise charged.[41] That schulzen normally did collect rents is corroborated by some village records and by one of the few passages where the duchy's mid-fourteenth century legal code diverged from *Sachsenspiegel*. Where the prototype referred to persons in general who asserted that rents had been paid, the revision specified "a schulz who claims that he has paid his rents to his lord."[42] That the schulz's own holding was free of rent makes the change more telling. Surviving account books of some ecclesiastical officials verify schulzen handling tithes.[43] And they often took charge of tax collections. The schulz paid to fiscal authorities the entire sum due from nearly a fifth of the villages in the tax return of 1425.[44]

To tasks intrinsic to the office fourteenth century schulzen added others indicative of their high standing in rural society. Before about 1350 they monopolized the seats on district courts. Replaced thereafter in the Wrocław district by townsmen, schulzen kept into the fifteenth century three of the seven positions on the Środa district court.[45] There in 1428 the schulz of Czeczy, Peter, joined those of Lipnica and Jastrzębce and four local landowners. Peter also served on the private "landing" of his lord, St. Vincent, with six others, most of them schulzen, too, under the chairmanship of the abbey's *Vogt*.[46] Before such courts other schulzen appeared, registering cases from their own courts or, as those of Milejowice and Mnichowice in a dispute over boundaries and water rights, acting for their village communities.[47] Their status made them valued guarantors for the fulfillment of agreements: that the lords of Solna and of Bogdaszowice would turn over alienated rents; that a convicted highwayman would not retaliate against his accusers; that a respondent would come to court.[48] In the latter case the schulz of Stary Śleszów appeared at the court of Żurawina on behalf of a native of that village, one of several signs that schulzen were known and respected outside their own settlements.[49] Even when the hard times of the early fourteenth century caused a few village communities to refuse obligations, schulzen remained at their head—as in a 1336 rent strike at Błonie.[50]

In situations abnormal or routine, in terms of status or wealth, in structural position or social role, the fourteenth century schulz held to his place between lord and peasant. Unlike the lord he belonged to the village. He gave the community leadership and handled its relations with external authority.

Because rural parish clergy gain status on other than tenurial grounds and because they bring a higher power and authority to a community, they sometimes provide leadership like that here attributed to schulzen. Not so around Wrocław in the fourteenth and early fifteenth centuries. Village priests, though a discernible group and not to be equated with mere peasant tenants, rarely functioned as men of high local standing.[51]

Control over appointment of rural clergy rested with a landlord patron or someone even farther away from the village.[52] As a result, typically identifiable priests shared few interests with peasant parishioners. They came from elite families and often looked toward higher ecclesiatical career prospects. Luther Schellendorf from one knightly lineage received his post in Chmiełów from another, the Seidlicz, patrons there in the 1350s.[53] The rector at Święta Katarzyna was then Peter Hirschberg, a descendant of the citizen Gunther "the Small" whose heirs had in 1312 obtained the lordship and patronage.[54] Priests of elite origin but without family holdings in the duchy were less common. Pasco of Biechów came to Janików from Great Poland in 1348 by papal provision. He was already a canon at Gniezno and at Poznań and now also received a prebend in the Wrocław chapter.[55] But canons were joined in the possession of rural parishes by men with experience at lower levels of the hierarchy. A mid-century cathedral altarist, then also priest of a parish near Oława, testified that he had begun as a clerical "servant" to the head of the priory-hospital in Środa and later served for a year under the prior's patronage as rector at Głogi.[56] If not a mere niche for a younger son or source of added income for a prelate, the rural church could be a stepping-stone quickly abandoned by an ambitious seeker of higher office.

Like schulzen, village priests controlled an endowment of land and re-munerative rights. The rector at Borek Strzeliński in 1405 had 4 mansi of arable, tithes in kind and money worth 30½ marks, and 19 malter of rye as "mass grain." "A good offering" was worth another 8 marks.[57] St. Law-rence at Borek was, however, an unusually large and well-endowed bene-fice. That set up at Pracze Widawskie in 1348 got 1½ mansi, mass grain, and other incomes for which the priest of All Saints at *Olbino*, who con-sented to division of his parish, took only 36 groschen a year in compensa-tion.[58] A glebe (*Widmut*) of around two mansi was norm and average in all survey texts.[59] That this standard was even intentional is suggested by smaller endowments being raised to it.[60] On his land the priest had a farm-stead (*Pfarrhof*) and himself ran or leased out a rent- and tax-free farm.[61]

Compared to the relative consistency of rural priests' landholdings, their rights to payments from the local population varied considerably. Episcopal and ducal gifts of tithes to ecclesiastical corporations and the com-mon conversion of real tenths to fixed assessments in grain or cash had created several different situations. Some rectors themselves paid tithes from their lands to a corporate tithe lord,[62] some were exempt,[63] and some took tithes from their parishioners and—as around Domaniów in 1316–17 and in the Kostomłoty-Siemidrożyce area in the 1320s—fought fiercely among themselves over them.[64] The impression remains, however, that as many rural clerics may have paid tithes as received them. Most probably did neither.

The personal interest of most village priests was limited to those parish dues which they did collect. For the care of local souls the rector was enti-tled to the "mass grain" (*annona missales, Messkorn*), normally a measure of rye and of oats from each cultivated mansus, rental or demesne. Then there were the *colenda* or *fructus*, a more voluntary payment in cash or grain, and various fees for special services or sacraments, all of which could, as at Siechnice in 1347, be commuted into an annual cash payment.[65] Some rural clergy also received pious gifts, like the 9¼ marks willed to the priest of Bukowiec in 1414.[66]

Evidence for economic activity by rural clergy does not compete with that about schulzen. Priests vigorously defended their perquisites, collected their dues, and looked after their farms, but otherwise dealt mostly in a familial setting. In all the transactions made by Conrad of Windmoel, priest of Kryniczno (one of the few who bought significantly as well as sold), he accompanied his uncles or siblings.[67] As a whole, though the resources available to village clergy may have approached those of a schulz and could contribute to a good estate for a man inclined to pluralism, they seem less well off and far less enterprising than the village headmen. Coupled with revenues from family properties, a rural rectory might provide a suitable living for a lord's cadet, but further gains for those who wished them came via preferment in the church, not local entrepreneurship.

It thus causes no surprise that the rural clergy of the fourteenth century duchy lacked the leadership and prestige of contemporary schulzen. Of course some involved themselves in their parish work by repairing and improving churches, like Jacob of Jelin, rector at *Szczepin*, who in 1347 rebuilt his filial church at Muchobór, and others achieved sufficient respect to receive gifts and added endowments from the villagers.[68] But in contrast were those reluctant pastors like Henry, Wrocław canon and priest of Jaszkotle, who in 1334 had to be forced by threat of excommunication to serve his parishioners resident at Mokronos,[69] or the canons of St. Vincent against whom abbots around 1400 wielded papal bulls to compel proper attention to their churches.[70]

Priests did willingly and regularly interact with the laity for the sake of their tithes and other incomes, seizing all ecclesiastical weapons to extract payment from reluctant debtors. Gregory of Gorka, priest at Domaniów, went repeatedly for four years (1387–90) to the church courts at Wrocław in what, when the records break off, remained a vigorous yet vain attempt to get tithes out of his parishioners, the brothers Kursantkowicz.[71] Jost of Domasław even tried secular justice and appealed to the Wrocław district court to get the villagers of Chrzanów to recognize his pastoral rights.[72]

Contentiousness over matters financial marked as well the rural clergy's dealings within the church. The decades-long duel between rectors of Kostomłoty and Siemidrożyce over tithe rights was but a well-recorded instance among the many which pitted one priest against his neighbor and colleague or another against a tithe-claiming corporation or patron.[73] Threats to their parish incomes from the competing services of friars (who by mid-century were penetrating country districts) provoked the duchy's rural clergy to near-unanimous outrage.[74]

Against the picture of legalism and avarice little suggests that outside their formal capacity rural priests regularly acted as members of a respected village elite. Their appearance away from their villages as witnesses or agents of courts was, so far as is known, confined to ecclesiastical hearings and assemblies.[75] With this record, no wonder the only heretic clearly linked to the Wrocław duchy in the fourteenth century, a "totus rusticanus" named Stephen who was burned in the city in 1398, denied that bad priests had authority over laymen.[76]

In the fourteenth and early fifteenth centuries the elite of the Wrocław duchy, nobles, prelates, and urban magnates, did not, even in their capacities as landowners, lords, and governors, often confront the mass of peasant tenants whom they exploited and ruled. Between the dominant and the subordinate orders were the groups just discussed, proprietary peasants, schulzen, and parish priests. The first, hard to detect except as they vanished by selling off their little hereditary fiefs, then had little significance greater than reminding historians of the slow and incomplete character of even a transformation so great as that brought to central Silesia by the rise of seigneurial lordship and the adoption of German law. The perhaps one hundred priests who served at any one time in the duchy's rural churches were recognizably representatives of a universal institution—but at the same time men whose normal relationship with their charges and whose familial or career interests outside the village deprived them of any real standing beyond their office. It was rather the schulzen, the two hundred or so autonomous village headmen, who occupied the juncture critical to the social order of the German law village and thus to the duchy's countryside. Independent, aggressive, and prosperous, the hereditary schulzen of the late fourteenth century provided to their neighbors the leadership and to their lords the responsible local intermediary that made the system work.

Fragments from peasant lives

A peculiar status or role set the people so far considered apart from the great mass of their fellow villagers, the *rustici*. Wrocław duchy peasants, the largest part of a larger, dynamic, and inegalitarian whole, shared those characteristics. They prove neither equal, nor uniform, nor static, nor entirely local in their interests and activities. To move from a stereotype toward appreciation of the pluralism possible within the regime of German law pushes beyond earlier treatments of rent rates and the techniques of grain production to several other aspects of peasant situations. This section discusses some uncommon shreds of evidence about differences in material resources and well-being, about legal freedoms and their exercise, and about economic niches other than subsistence farming on open-field arable.

　　To get acquainted with people and farms on the rental land that was the foundation of the rural economy, consider the twenty-one tenants who in 1431 owed to the Holy Spirit Hospital a quarter mark tithe from each of the 26¼ such mansi in Łowęcice.[77] Eight of them, Lorke Boam, Michel Bwrsen, Chunad, Mathis Merkel, Borsicke, Michel Czin, Jocup Kreczimer, and the priest from nearby Radakowice, possessed but a half mansus each. Jocup Kreczimer's kinsman, Jan, however, had three times as much land, a mansus and a half, as did four other tenants, Hans Scholcz, Michel Kopew, Chinko, and Lorenz Malkewicz. Miczno Rosannke, Jozef, and the unnamed schulz each had one mansus, and Lorke Boczno one and a quarter. Bigger farms were also common: Steffan Boczno, the schulz in Radakowice, possessed two rental mansi in Łowęcice; Andres Malkewicz and Nored worked two and a half each, and the largest tenant, Jocup Czepan, three and a half.

Besides the bicultural flavor of this village on the Środa loam 175 years after its *locatio* to German law, what does this catalog convey? All farmers in this snapshot of Łowęcice were not the same. The many poorest among them, those at a half mansus, together controlled only 15 percent of local arable. The biggest tenants, the five at or above two mansi, had 40 percent. The middle range in this village farmed at or near the average of 1.25 mansi. They made up the largest group (43 percent) and controlled the most land (45 percent), but not a majority of either the villagers or their resources. Thus Mathis Merkel, Lorke Boczno, and Andres Malkewicz, for example, each represented a different size of agricultural enterprise and peasant household economy, all noteworthy for their share in the population and/or production of early fifteenth-century Łowęcice.

Because variety more than common patterns marked the distribution of land in peasant villages around Wrocław, the profile just seen in Łowęcice was neither normal nor deviant. This conclusion follows from the fourteen known records of several if not all tenants and farms in a village from the period under consideration. As totaled at the end of Table 9.1 and portrayed in Figure 9.1, the aggregate of these 173 farms verifies significant inequality within the peasant group itself: the poorest 10 percent of tenants possessed 3 percent of the land and the wealthiest 10 percent controlled 22 percent. A standardized "index of inequality" measures the departure from an even distribution. An overall rating of .294 is high (unequal) for a sample from which non-peasant landholders have been removed.

The degree of inequality differed from one village to the next (Table 9.1). Relatively equal in their possession of land were peasants at Kębłowice in 1374 and at Mnichowice in 1381, where the majority held at or about the local mean and the index was .182 or .210. Inhabitants of Zębice or Bogdaszowice in 1433 knew another situation: widely ranging sizes of farms, much land in the hands of the locally well-off, and indices of inequality at .332 and .331 respectively. And quite apart from the shape of the distributions, the average and the most common holding sizes varied. At Kebłowice all tenants had either a half or one mansus, while in Mnichowice the majority possessed two but others ranged from three-fourths to three. Still different were conditions at Łowęcice, where, as described above, the highest number fell at the lowest local holding size but others farmed up to seven times more. From village to village, from farmstead to farmstead, then, late fourteenth-century peasants faced their economic needs with widely variant land resources.

The data summarized in Table 9.1 support no plausible explanations for differences in the distributions of land among tenants. Even in the small sample from this period, distinctive soil types, majority culture (Polish or German personal names), dates of German law grant, and social status of landowners associate with both large and small farms and greater or lesser degrees of equality.[78] Simple determinisms are thus ruled out. Stochastic mechanisms are not—but the small sample and the absence of cases from the Uraz and much of the Środa district (where farms in the *late* fifteenth-century were notably large) make testing for probabilistic relationships vain.

The data do hint at growing inequality and shrinking of the mean holding. No index number from before the 1430s approaches the aggregate total, but four of the nine from 1431–33 exceed it. The average tenant in the earlier data had 1.45 mansi, and in the later 1.29. In the one place allowing longitudinal comparison, Bogdaszowice, the mean holding in the whole village of 1433 differed little from that of the three peasants known in 1364, but the standard deviation (a measure of dispersion about the mean) and the index of inequality rose. The few facts are inconclusive, but smaller farms and greater difference between rich and poor peasants correspond with signs that rural populations and access to markets grew in the duchy up to the time of the Hussite wars.

But the difficulty in trying to grasp peasants' economic situations is to assess the welfare equivalents of different farms. At Łowęcice in 1431, how much better off than Mathis Merkel and his household on his half mansus was Andres Boczno on his 1¼? How about Andres Malkewicz on his 2½? Now go from the Środa loam to the Wrocław district black earth, and back two generations to Mnichowice in 1381—were the brothers Wernherus and Miczko, who held two mansi jointly, their brother-in-law, Jekelinus, who had two mansi himself, and the other three tenants of such a holding there[79] about as well off as Andres Malkewicz fifty years later? There are the limits of the fourteenth-century evidence about land in peasant farms. It tells rather much, all things considered, of differential access to land, it eliminates several possibly related factors, but ultimately it *explains* little of this central reality in everyday peasant life. There are, moreover, other ways to check on the economic well-being of Wrocław duchy peasants.

Debt and material indigence, quite apart from landlessness, were certainly never absent from this peasant society. Wernherus, Miczko, Jekelinus, and the other tenants at Mnichowice in 1381 entered the documentary record because for some reason they needed ready cash and to get it sold to the Corpus Christi Commandery repurchaseable annuities ranging from one-half to two marks. At Kębłowice in 1374 the villagers incurred a *census* of five marks to cover forty-five loaned by their schulz, the townsman Nicholas Borg.[80] Loans for annuities could be but a stop-gap, for unless the capital

Table 9.1. Tenant holdings in fourteen villages, 1351–1433

Place, date, and area covered	Number of tenants	Holdings at size (mansi) of:														Mean	Std. dev.	Index of inequality
		0	.25	.5	.75	1	1.25	1.5	2	2.25	2.5	3	3.25	3.5	3.75			
Chrzanów 1351 on 9 of 16 mansi	5					2			2			1				1.80	.75	.228
Bogdaszowice 1364 on 3 of 20 rental mansi	3			1		1		1								1.00	.41	.188
Kębłowice 1374 on 6.5 of 16 mansi	9			5		4										.72	.24	.182
Mnichowice 1381 on 16 of 18 rental mansi	9				1	1	1		5			1				1.78	.67	.210
Św. Katarzyna 1409 on 6.25 of 32 rental mansi	3							2					1			2.08	.87	.210
Jarząbkowice 1431 on 16 of 18 rental mansi	12					9			2			1				1.33	.62	.210
Łowęcice 1431 on 26.25 of 26.25 rental mansi	21			8		3		5	1		2			1		1.25	.70	.331
Wróblowice 1431 on 19.25 of 19.25 rental mansi	12					5		3	3						1	1.60	.70	.226
Żebice 1431																		

	n													
rental mansi	29	4	6	4	7	4						1.08	.73	.331
Budziszów Śr. 1433 on 12 of 12 occupied rental mansi	10	3	4	1	1		1					1.20	.95	.330
Ilnica 1433 on 15.5 of 15.5 rental mansi	10	1	4	2	1	1	1					1.55	.80	.274
Karczyce 1433 on 27.5 of 28 rental mansi	23	5	11	3	2	1	1					1.20	.64	.260
Radakowice 1433 on 24.5 of 24.5 rental mansi	15	1	4	5	2	1	2					1.63	.69	.257
TOTAL: on 226.5 m.	173	30	56	29	26	1	5	7	1	2	1	1.32	.74	.294
% of tenants	100	17	32	17	15	1	3	4	1	1	1			
Cumulative %		21	55	75	90	91	94	98	98	99	100			
Land in holdings (m.)	0	15	56	43.5	52	2.25	12.5	21	3.25	7	3.75			
% of land	0	7	25	19	23	1	5	9	2	3	2			
Cumulative %		8	33	55	78	79	85	94	95	98	100			

Note. Sources (in order as above): RF, II, 675–699 (the 9 mansi turned over to *rustici* in 1351 were probably the only ones in Chrzanów not then in demesne); RF, I, 29r–34r; LN, 46r–47r (these 6.5 mansi are the first rental land in Kębłowice; later medieval texts fail to detail the land type distribution here; Sommerfeldt, pp. 82–83; UD, pp. 148–151; HGZ, fols. 16r–16v; 12r–12v; 15v; 14v–15r; 22r; 20v; 21r, 19v; 21v. Free and demesne holdings, where present, are here omitted. To reduce rounding errors, cumulative percentages were taken from cumulative raw totals rather than addition of the separate percentages.

Figure 9.1
AGGREGATE DISTRIBUTION OF TENANT HOLDINGS
IN FOURTEEN VILLAGES, 1351-1433

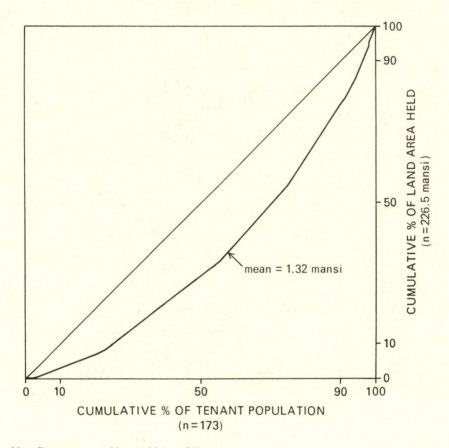

Note. For sources see *Notes to Maps and Figures.*

sum were repaid the annual payment became a permanent charge against the peasant's holding. Even loss of all his possessions just made the debtor liable in his person.[81] Also indicative of the normally minute scale of liquid wealth among peasants was the customary maximum fine in village courts, one heller.[82]

Money may often look rare in villages, but some peasants thought and dealt in values far above the petty sums just mentioned. Three "rustici ville Sancte Katherine" (Święta Katarzyna) sued the St. Mathias hospital for sixty-three marks worth of hay taken from disputed meadow lands.[83] In 1352 John Ratht of Siedlakowice, a property of the Church of Wrocław, joined with the schulz of Solna to undertake *locatio* of the chapter's demesne at Pustków Żurówski. The partners paid a hundred marks, fifty in cash in three installments over nine months and fifty as an annual payment of fifteen marks (three time the normal rate).[84] In economic terms at least, these prosperous peasants resemble schulzen and minor landowners more closely than they do the poorer tenants. An inheritance case heard by the village court of Żurawina in 1384 involved (and it sounds very like a wife's share only) thirteen marks in cash, twenty sheep, four horses, three cattle, five hogs, eleven geese, women's clothing (a coat, fancy clothes, a dress), and bed linen.[85] Nor was actual passage from the peasantry to the propertied orders unknown. Henry Scholtz and Thomas Krocker, "gebauern von Wilxen" in 1377, purchased half the lordship over Piskorzowice. Six years later, when Scholtz's heirs sold out to Krocker, this former peasant sported the title of Wrocław citizen.[86]

Upward social mobility became almost necessary for a well-off peasant tenant. Recognized custom limited his possession of rental land to what he could work with his household and paid laborers, forbidding him to sublet it or otherwise contract it out.[87] Only by shifting his economic role from agricultural producer to rentier and manager and his status from tenant to landowner could the wealthy peasant move beyond the limits imposed by a household unit into the scale that, under the prevailing technology and institutions, only rule over tenant farmers sustained. But then he lost as well some of the advantages of a peasant's household economy and entered the economic circumstances of those lords discussed in earlier chapters. No doubt those few who, like Thomas Krocker, faced this choice paid the price willingly.

In most respects legal custom of the fourteenth century duchy left to peasants great economic security and freedom vis-a-vis both landowners and their own kin. The codification of 1356 took over from *Sachsenspiegel* the guarantee that the tenant possessed by hereditary right his "erbe czins gut vnd recht an dem gute," and limited his obligations to payment of the annual rent: "No tenant shall be obligated to his lord for more than his rent, which he shall give each [required] day annually."[88] Tenant rights were improved over *Sachsenspiegel* in clauses covering late payment of rents (a penalty but no doubling) and disputes over actual payment (two witnesses, not three).[89] Even a tenant without hereditary rights could be expelled by a landlord only after a full season's advance warning.[90] As *gewonheit* such practices were enforced by Wrocław courts and, in special appeals for consultation, the Magdeburg assessors.[91]

The law of property and inheritance fostered formation of nuclear household economic units and protected them against the claims of collaterals. One of the few outright legal innovations by the Royal Six replaced, for the peasantry, the Saxon custom of a wife's entailed portion with the Franconian one of common property in marriage. Thus, whether a marriage proved fertile or not, half the couple's property remained with the survivor, and legitimate offspring supplanted all claims from ascendants of a deceased spouse.[92] The source of property brought to the marriage no longer mattered. In 1415 Bishop Wenceslas set similar rules for immune ecclesiastical properties not certainly subject to the duchy's code, and these were evidently soon enforced.[93]

But the solidity of particular tenurial units was not permitted to override the wish of peasants, like lords, to help each heir start a viable new household. Unlike later peasant custom in central Silesia, the duchy's code of 1356, the contemporary systematic city compilation of Magdeburg and other precedents, and the later ordinances of Bishop Wenceslas assume and confirm full partibility among men and women.[94] This practice seems to represent both an indigenous Polish peasant custom and that of city folk, as opposed to immigrant German peasants. It also reaffirms that lords had in the fourteenth century no strong ground to compel the unity of peasant farms.

The firm legal position of Wrocław duchy tenants was reinforced by their right to move. In the fourteenth century lands held for hereditary rents were freely conveyed before the court of the schulz. Payments for and the requirement of the landlord's consent to such transactions, standard at the end of the fifteenth century, seem to have been rare or absent before the Hussite wars.[95] The code of 1356 instead permitted renters freely to depart from the village after giving notice of their intentions.[96] This exceeded the liberty allowed under the statutes King Casimir gave contemporary Great Poland and under the Roman law and other precedents which later applied in the duchy itself.[97] It derived from the same provision of *Sachsenspiegel* that a Brandenburg court in 1383 interpreted as permitting departure from a properly maintained holding even without provision of a new tenant and in defiance of the landlord.[98] The reality of these legal rights is evidenced by their effects, pervasive indicators of mobility among fourteenth century peasants.

Most internal migrants are recorded as such only at their destination, so their socio-economic antecedents are almost always obscure. Nevertheless, much affirms that reasonably permanent moves were not uncommon among peasant households. A sixty-year-old peasant, Hermann Berner (another text reads "Corner"), told ecclesiastical judges in 1329 how he had once held lands in Szymanowice but now was tenant of three and a half mansi in Kostomłoty.[99] More systematic assessment of rural migration depends on conveyances or lists of tenants mentioning that an individual came from elsewhere or containing surnames derived from place names.[100] Thus at least five nearby villages contributed landholders to Krępice between 1385 and 1409. The most distant of these, "Niclas Heinrich Messners Sone von Radagsdorff" (Radakowice), who bought a half mansus in 1405, had, however, only come about six kilometers.[101] Two (15 percent) of the fourteen tenants at Mnichowice in 1381 had names from elsewhere: Bartko "of Turów" came from the very next village, but Henry "Petirkow" had come a good fifteen kilometers if from Piotrków Borowski (and more if from a synonymous place outside the duchy).[102] A like proportion of identifiable migrants, 21 of 140, were in the early 1430s among those in eight villages in the east of the Sroda district who paid tithe to the Holy Spirit Hospital.[103]

Migration of other country people, most of whom must have been peasants, helped sustain the duchy's urban populations. Thomas Krocker, peasant of Wilkszyn in 1377 and citizen of Wrocław six years later (see above), followed an already well-trod path. The brothers Hermann, John, and Nicholas "from Pasterzyce" acquired Wrocław citizenship before 1330 as, presumably, did the "Heinke Muchebor" who later shared tenure of one of the city's shambles.[104] Środa attracted the inhabitants of its district. No less than five of the town's eleven old and new councillors in 1359 had names recalling those of nearby villages: "Thilo de Pfaffendorff" (Popowice), "Niczco Golow" (Gałów), "Michael de Wrowelwicz" (Wróblowice), "Gutmannus de Steffansdorff" (Szczepanów), and "Johannes de Hugoldisdorf" (Jugowiec).[105] Far wider and, in a tax account recording all heads of household in 1403, better documented, was the pull exerted by Wrocław itself.[106] One taxpayer in five had a surname derived from a place of origin; 205 (9 percent) were based on the names of at least 95 Wrocław duchy villages and towns.[107] Most of those in the duchy lay quite close to the city—a quarter within eight kilometers and half within sixteen—but other migrants had come rather far. The journeys of Petir "von Kossinplocz" from Kostomłoty and John "Schoneiche" from Proszków had been thirty or more kilometers.[108] Except as affected by distance, however, no parts of the duchy or kinds of rural arrangements or lordships contributed on the available evidence notably large or small numbers of migrants.

Permanent and at times distant migrations by individuals in the peaceful fourteenth century emerged from more numerous regular and irregular everyday movements and contacts by men and women all across the duchy. Towns held many attractions—trade, the courts, piety, and administration—to bring country people inside their walls for a few hours or days. Five men of Krępice traded horses at Wrocław in 1401.[109] Casual encounters among outsiders and townsmen reached the written record when violence or tragedy drew official attention: Albert and Nicholas from Rożanka were punished for wounding Nicholas Neudorf in the street before the suburban *Olbino* tavern;[110] Paschco Affencrey of Szczepanów died in an accident while visiting Środa.[111] To the public courts in Wrocław came folk like John Schuwert of Tyniec Mały and Anne, taverner of Domasław, to settle a disputed debt, and Hannos Kusicske of Rościsławice, Jocusch of Wszemiłowice, Hannos of Bukowiec, and Hannos Woynewicz (Wojnowice) to guarantee a friend's obligations.[112] To their lord's court at the St. Vincent abbey went a couple from Grabiszyn, John of Leimgruben and his wife Nethe, clutching a flask of wine and a capon in hopes of a favorable hearing on their assault charge.[113]

The countryside also knew these work-a-day interactions. The squabble between city council and cathedral chapter that cost Wrocław the captaincy in 1369 began when the lord of Gądów seized and brought before secular courts a peasant from the chapter's exempt lordship of Strzeganowice.[114] A woman named Else, disgruntled former maid to Alexius Wyner at Sulimów, pursued her case against her ex-employer with the help of a legal guardian Stephan, son of Henry, from Klecina;[115] half the width of the Wrocław district separated her one-time work place from the residence of a man she should have known and trusted.

The best impression of how normal movement was comes from records of uncommon events. Official inquiries to decide local disputes by reference to custom and practice heard reputedly knowledgeable witnesses from a wide neighborhood. Judges delegate in the tithe dispute between priests of Siemidrożyce and Kostomłoty listened not only to locals and landowners but also to people from Ilnica, Sikorzyce, Wilków, Jakubowice, Zabłoto, and two places outside the duchy about the past controversy and ways tithes had been and were collected.[116] The practice continued. Plausibly informed testimony on highly specific factual issues indicates a substantial range of peasant movement. Witnesses in 1456 as to the traditional location of a stone in a ditch on the disputed boundary between Wojkowice and Mnichowice were more than twenty-five countrymen from fourteen other places up to fifteen kilometers away (almost a day's easy travel).[117] Peasant life, though rooted by its very nature in the soil of arable mansi, reached out to personal interactions beyond the fields of the village that, whether regularly or incidentally, temporarily or permanently, joined villagers to the larger society and helped knit a regional community in the fourteenth-century duchy.

But full-time arable farming in the classic three course common field pattern did not occupy all people then usefully described as rustics. More specialized economic activities both in agriculture and out provided other opportunities for individuals and families and further variety to the rural scene.

In a suburban zone south of Wrocław distinctive communities of market gardeners (later called *Kräuter*) developed during the fourteenth century.[118] Small tenancies measured in jugera, not mansi, and paying unusually high rents for their size were present on municipal and ecclesiastical property outside the Świdnica and Oława gates by a little after 1300,[119] but whole villages on this pattern were established during the expansive mid-century years. Using the proven *locatio* format in 1345, Abbot Conrad of St. Mary entrusted to a man named Hermann 54.5 jugera (i.e., less than two mansi) from the demesne at Gajowice. Gertner on them would receive hereditary tenures and pasture rights for annual rents of 24 groschen per jugerum from existing and 18 groschen from new gardens. Tithe of another half groschen the jugerum went to the local rector. The lower rent came to about 11.5 marks per mansus or, in the coins struck during 1347–70, about 1325 grams of silver, four times the highest known for regular tenant arable in that century.[120] With revenue prospects like that, no wonder the city and corporate landowners put out several hundred more jugera in *Leimgruben*, *Neudorf*, Gajowice, and Borek over the next generation.[121] By 1425 the tax collectors (and their record is incomplete) counted fifty *ortulani* at *Leimgruben*, another twelve near the gallows outside the Świdnica gate, and receipts that indicate sixty-eight more at *Szczepin*.[122] Even the lowest rent known on these lands, an eighth mark for each of the city's sixteen jugera near the gallows, matched or exceeded all regular tenant obligations from between 1350 and 1430.[123]

These gertner could afford high rents because the nearby city offered a rich market for the produce of intensively-worked small holdings. Of the twenty-three tenants on the city's thirty-three jugera near the Świdnica gate in the late 1350s, only one, John of Chmielów, farmed as much as four jugera; thirteen held only one.[124] But John and his neighbors cultivated not scattered open field strips but unitary fenced parcels that stretched back from their roadside houses. The compilers of the 1443 tax account said Gajowice "had no mansi," which precisely describes early modern maps of fields in this area.[125] On small enclosures individual management entirely replaced communal regulation to allow the intensity of labor which alone gave the farms their economic viability. This meant, in particular, heavy and regular manuring of the already-rich black earth with cartloads of urban night soil.[126] Organic recycling, institutional peculiarities, and the unusual proximity of a large market for perishables fostered an island of uniquely commercialized agriculture in this small corner of the duchy.

Places just north of Wrocław had gertner, too, but past *Olbino* low rents on small holdings suggest no economic peculiarities.[127] More specific to all the lands among the river channels were fishermen. Four of their huts comprised the whole of Zakrzów throughout the Middle Ages, the inhabitants of Szczytniki counted several *piscatores* among their number, and, at the other extreme from Zakrzów of the Odra's course through the duchy four more lived under the bishop at Kotowice.[128] Mostly they were part-time specialists, fisher-peasants whose living came as much from their fields as from their nets, spears, hooks, and boats. Those at the other Kotowice, who received seven of the thirty-three mansi in the *locatio* of 1294, paid during harvest time no fishes to the nuns of Trzebnica.[129]

Like their more purely agricultural fellows, fishermen, even those for whom no landholdings are recorded, found monetary obligations superseding dues in kind. At the end of the thirteenth century those of the bishop and of Trzebnica owed quantities of fish every few days, although the latter could substitute a cash payment.[130] By mid-century, however the weekly heaps of fishes had become, at least on the city's lordships at *Szczytniki* and *Platea Romanorum*, a symbolic large salmon for the ceremonial table of the *Rat* and, respectively, annual dues of six and ten marks.[131] The bishop, too, now took a thirty groschen "fischerczins" from the disputed fishery between Kotowice and the St. Mathias properties at Siechnice and Gajków.[132] Though surely as involved with the urban market as any *Kräuter*, the Odra fishermen occupied another of the niches open to common folk in the duchy.

Mercantile and craft occupations also supported country families. The *locatio* for *Łukaszewice* in 1350 contemplated for a rather ordinary village a tavern and establishments of a smith, baker, butcher, and cobbler, while a later privilege claimed by lords of Małkowice added tailors and weavers.[133] Elsewhere worked millers, carpenters, tilers, and, at Wierzbno in 1318, a cloth shearer, Eberhard "Rasor."[134]

Tenurial situations of rural craftsmen could differ. A few whose speciality demanded skill and fixed capital investment had proprietary rights,[135] but some dependency was more common. Taverners especially often held their inns as hereditary free fiefs like those of schulzen because these establishments had once been part of the schulz's endowment and prerogatives.[136] Most tradesmen, however, were regular hereditary tenants of a free fief-holder or the landowner. Wynrich, son-in-law of Peter of Karszów, so accepted the traditionally hereditary rights, holdings, and obligations of the tavern in Domaniów from the local priest in 1309.[137] The brothers Muldner, Tile and Peter, successively held their inn at Rościsławice in the early fifteenth century from the lords of the village.[138] Normal customary tenants, too, were millers at Widawa in 1298 and Jurczyce in 1399 and village blacksmiths at Ilnica and Radakowice in the 1430s.[139] Generally, therefore, rural craftsmen, especially those whose job depended on fixed capital installations like mills or taverns, had hereditary and fully alienable rights like those of their neighbors who farmed.[140]

Common tenurial subordination caused the rents and dues of most craftsmen to resemble those of their neighbors. Innkeepers and millers often paid out considerable sums to their landlords and and had also to maintain their establishments.[141] As a rule taverners owed cash, at least a mark a year, more often two or three, and, at Borów in 1377, as much as five. Added payments in kind, whether the few hens and eggs of the brothers Muldner at Rościsławice or the two *maldrata* of the innkeeper at Piotrowice, were uncommon.[142] Millers, in contrast, more normally expected to pay in goods or services. Until bought off by the incumbent in 1352, the tenant of the Winkelmill on the Bystrzyca between Stabłowice and Leśnica owed six *maldrata* of rye and a mark cash. At Jurczyce free milling of the demesne's grain was provided.[143] The value of this miller's labor cannot be estimated, but the other rents assessed against inns and mills fall at or above the highest paid in the fourteenth century from a peasant mansus. Known craftsmen of other sorts paid rather small money rents, mostly deriving from tenure of a house or small holding rather than the trade itself.[144] Fees to practice were, however, probably more common than the surviving evidence, for these made profitable the initial locatorial monopoly over village crafts. The *Vogt* of Leśnica licenced cobblers for six groschen a year.[145]

It is not often feasible, however, to distinguish special craftsmen's obligations from those which derived from agricultural land. Like Hildebrand, a seventy-year-old cobbler from Kostomłoty who in 1329 "lived from his craft and his fields,"[146] many did (or could) not earn a living from their special skills alone. Taverners and some craftsmen worked fairly normal-sized peasant farms, whether appurtenant to their shops or separately held. Jesco Mabiken's inn at Wierzbno in the 1320s came with two mansi and that of John Walpurg at Stabłowice in the 1350s with one. Mathias Kowal arrived at Ilnica in 1436 to work a half mansus as well as' his smithy, but two years later had tripled his land.[147]

Incomes from rural craft work are almost without record. Millers in Silesia customarily worked for a share of the grain. If the units of volume in a 1336 ordinance by King John had their later values, this was 3 to 4 percent around Wrocław.[148] Otherwise there are only the substantial cash payments to uncounted smiths and carpenters on the Borów demesne in 1377.[149]

Rural specialists, as at least part-time representatives of an economic order more dependent on exchange of goods and services, handled money more often than did ordinary peasant householders.[150] Their access to liquid capital made them creditors of less fortunate countrymen like John Schuwert of Tyniec Mały, who owed 26 groschen to Anna, taverner in Domasław, in 1402, or Lawrence, schulz of Jarząbkowice, who borrowed five marks from a miller in 1419.[151] Some made good-sized (if traditional) investments, buying off hereditary rents on their holdings or expanding their arable acreage. One taverner, Stephan of Mrozów, purchased from an impecunious noble lordship over more than five and a half mansi, part arable, part pasture, in the demesne at Lenartowice.[152] Such signs of wealth, when coupled with the high rents paid by many craftsmen, argue for appreciable profits from rural trading. But the behavior of the Unverworns, taverners at Jarząbkowice in the 1430s, suggests that even well-off retailer-peasants perceived advantages in full-time agriculture. The father, Nicholas "tabernator dictus Unverworn," tenant of one rental mansus, died in 1434 and was followed in inn and land by his son, Stenczil. But by 1436 Stenczil and his brothers, Andres and Paul, had used the bad times and resulting difficulties of their neighbors to take over three more mansi. With the tithe account from 1437 Stenczil and Andres (no more is heard of Paul) dropped all mention of tavern-keeping and with two mansi each enjoyed some of the larger farms in their village.[153]

Men like Nicholas Unverworn, innkeeper of Jarząbkowice, or Hildebrand, the Kostomłoty cobbler, practiced their crafts to the envy and spite of influential urban interests. Wrocław and Środa alike would curb rural competitors and enforce division of labor between an agricultural countryside and a commercial and industrial urbanism. Wrocław's thirteenth-century *Meilenrecht* over rural taverns and craftsmen (see Chapter 4) remained a pillar of city policy.[154] Środa asserted the same in its district.[155] But at the same time the towns needed country produce—grain, meat, hops, fish—in consistent quantities and at low prices. So engrossing and forestalling brought heavy fines and, from the 1320s onwards, the rulers and the *Rat* collaborated in establishing weekly free markets, first in bread, later in meat, to encourage country folk to carry their crops to town themselves.[156] Even established rural markets outside the *Bannmeilen* faced urban opposition and pressures. St. Vincent needed royal help in 1367 after the Wrocław city council, then captain, denied its ancient right to hold a market in Kostomłoty.[157]

Attempts to suppress rural commerce and draw exchange entirely into the purview of the cities, were, however, but a jostling for position within a complex hierarchical structure of regional economic relationships. Country people required certain non-agricultural goods and services, many available in the towns but others better dispersed into more numerous smaller centers. Networks of marketing, processing, religious, and financial arrangements cut across the socio-economic strata so far discussed, tied persons of varying status into communities, channeled their movements, and helped link the duchy into a regional whole. As by work, wealth, and status, rural life was patterned by neighborhood contacts and financial contracts.

Networks: spatial, social, and economic

By the late fourteenth century Silesia and the Wrocław duchy held a discernible place in the network of commercial routes which webbed Europe's interior. At Wrocław the important road from Flanders via upper Saxony to Cracow and Hungary intersected two heavily traveled north-south arteries. Men and goods from southern Germany, Italy, or the Balkans could approach through Prague, Vienna, or the Moravian passes and go on to either Poznań or the lower Vistula and Gdańsk. Along the major routes lay other Silesian centers while lesser but still regionally significant tracks drew to the city traffic from more isolated provincial towns. Środa marked the midpoint on the main road between Wrocław and Legnica where a lesser one forked off to the northwest.[158] But in the duchy the two cities, one large, one small, simply capped a hierarchy of places which, by offering goods and services rural people needed, drew them from their villages.

Below the level of the chartered cities five places possessed the semi-urban character indicated by names like *forum, oppidum, Märktel*, or *Stetil*. Where the highway to the west crossed the Bystrzyca, twelve kilometers from Wrocław and twenty from Środa, the one-time ducal residence of Leśnica had an *advocatus* by 1261 and in the early fourteenth century even claimed the title of *civitas*.[159] But its inhabitants never bought out the hereditary *Vogt* to achieve self-government and official texts in and after the 1320s normally designate it "Lezna oppidum," or "Markte und Stetel zur Lessen."[160] Uraz had its own tiny district but otherwise resembled Leśnica. On the Odra terraces where a secondary route from Wrocław turned towards Wołow, the "civitas et castrum" so-called in 1312 was later usually labeled "castrum et oppidum," though its inhabitants asserted citizen status.[161] On the old-settled loess Kostomłoty had been a Polish law *forum* and the administrative centre for the several properties of the St. Vincent monastery there, but it struggled to maintain its economic role against the town the dukes established at Kąty and then against regulatory pressures from Środa and Wrocław.[162] In another area of dense settlement, the southern corner of the Wrocław district, a ducal possession, Borów, did not succeed. It had a *Vogt* and was called an *oppidum* between 1294 and 1337, but then all signs of urban or commercial life evaporate.[163] The role of local center passed to the nearby Borek Strzeliński, where in 1386 King Wenceslas confirmed what may have been an older right to hold a weekly market.[164]

On the land (and Map 9.1) these rural markets fill in the interstices among the chartered cities in the duchy and its environs. None is within ten kilometers of a city; the successive pair of Borów and Borek Strzeliński are the only two that close to one another. Thus the greater proportion of the duchy was served by a city or a market within an easy day's journey (10 km

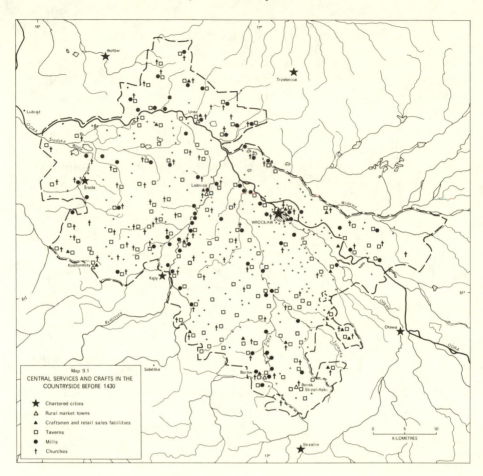

Map 9.1
CENTRAL SERVICES AND CRAFTS IN THE
COUNTRYSIDE BEFORE 1430

★ Chartered cities
△ Rural market towns
▲ Craftsmen and retail sales facilities
□ Taverns
● Mills
† Churches

one way). One significant exception tests this rule. Well beyond ten kilometers from any market were villages on the old-settled black earth and
lowlands of the Wrocław district from around Tyniec Mały east to Mnichowice and then northeast to the Nadolices and Chrząstowas. The anomaly attests neatly to the attraction of Wrocław and to the history of
settlement in the Wrocław district. The unserviced strip was until at least
the mid-thirteenth century the outer limit of the densely inhabited zone
around Wrocław. Woodlands beyond turned men's attentions back to the
city until the very decades when the markets were established.[165]

Besides any special products which a visiting peddler might offer on the
weekly market day and besides the ubiquitous taverns discussed below, rural markets offered only very basic local retailing, processing, and services.
Where particular trades or shops are mentioned, those of butchers, bakers,

and cobblers all but exhaust the list. By the early 1400s Leśnica and Uraz had about a dozen of each, and bath-houses, too.[166]

The same consumption goods and services also characterized crafts practiced in villages without market rights. The cobbler's stall, shambles, and stand for the sale of bread conveyed in a charter of the *scholtisei* at Blizanowice in 1380 well represent most recorded village trading facilities.[167] Much rarer were smiths or members of the textile crafts, weavers or tailors.[168] Only the extramural suburbs of Wrocław contained noteworthy industry: a slaughter house and retailers' shops, a fulling mill, tile works, and establishments of malters.[169] In general, then, operators of rural retail and manufacturing establishments served a market pretty well confined to their own peers and neighbors. The needs they satisfied arose not from long-distance commerce but from daily life in the villages.

The most basic and numerous facilities for exchange in the countryside were not specialized retail shops but taverns. Like their early medieval predecessors, fourteenth-century innkeepers lodged travelers, brewed and poured ale, and traded in small amounts of several commodities.[170] That *taberna* or *Kretscham* (the Silesian German word from Polish *karczma*) meant more than a mere right to sell beverages is confirmed by detailed provisions for upkeep of buildings and other facilities in rental agreements like one the owner and taverner at Domaniów made in 1309–10.[171]

In contrast to the handful of market towns and other craft or sale facilities on Map 9.1, taverns at 140 rural sites in the fourteenth century duchy numbered one for about every eleven square kilometers or every 200–225 rural inhabitants. But the distribution was not uniform. In the Środa and Uraz districts, where villages of thirteenth-century origin were characteristically large, most had their own tavern, while in the sections of the Wrocław district where small villages marked earlier dense occupation, most did not. But because distance between villages varied inversely with size, actual density of taverns was less uneven. Greater irregularity occurred close to the cities. Only seventeen taverns, many of them very old, lay within ten kilometers of Wrocław and only ten that distance from Środa. Such densities of but one tavern per eighteen and thirty-one square kilometers respectively plainly indicate the economic and political strength of the towns. Żerniki Wrocławskie, a good-sized place on the black earth only eight kilometers southeast of Wrocław, was the one village in the duchy more than four kilometers from a tavern. Just to the south, however, in the very area poorly served by markets, taverns were unusually thick.

Taverns provided the most basic goods regularly obtained on the market by the rural population and mills the most important economic service. After two centuries' spread, the water mill was fully dominant.[172] In all, seventy-seven rural sites in the duchy contained a mill by 1430 (Map 9.1) Even omitting second mills at some sites (and both mills and people in the cities), this meant at least one mill for every four hundred country folk or twenty square kilometers.[173]

Availability of water power controlled the siting of mills. Notable concentrations developed along the fast-flowing mountain-fed Bystrzyca system and on the upper Ślęza, where most mills had at least two wheels and some up to four.[174] In contrast, the often inadequate flows of the bottomland rivers, the Odra, Oława, and Widawa, supported fewer and generally smaller mills.[175] Still the impression is of intense exploitation of even the least water-courses. Neither the rivulets in the hills above Uraz nor the meager and slow-moving Średzka Woda avoided working their way to the Odra. The number of mills on even quite tiny streams was presumably a response to the high cost of moving heavy grain, meal, and flour overland, but the uneven distribution of water power resources meant that this necessity could be at best reduced. That movement of cereal products to and from mills must have been significant is attested by repeated reference in mill privileges to access rights and the upkeep of roadways. Even at Rościsławice, where the water could not have supported a major commercial enterprise, charters of 1365 and 1435 specified free entry for cartloads of grain on their way to the mill.[176]

The church provided to inhabitants of the duchy's countryside a third central service which, like the more crudely economic ones, helped shape social interactions.[177] The rural parish system was completed in the fourteenth century. A new parish at Pracze Widawskie in 1348, for example, spared people there, in Rędzin, and in Polanowice the seasonally troublesome journey across the bottomlands to their former church at *Olbino*.[178] Nevertheless different structures continued to distinguish parishes on the old-settled black earth and loess from younger ones on the loam and moraines (Map 9.1). In the Wrocław and the south of the Sroda district most places had no local church and belonged to a parish covering several nucleations. St. Lawrence at Borek Strzeliński, for instance, also served Jelenin, Boreczek, Kręczków, Michałowice, Kojęcin, Jaksin, and Świnobrod.[179] Travel from homes to churches was less needful in areas of the Środa and Uraz districts where German law settlement in the thirteenth century had established churches in most villages. In the area reaching from Wilkszyn and Brzezina northward past Golędzinów, all served until the 1280s by the church at Uraz, appeared by the 1350s at least four, perhaps five, new parishes.[180]

Parish communities were active but certainly not well documented. The lord and villagers of Pracze together agreed with the priest of All Saints over their new local church, while other disputes regularly ended with groups of parishioners accepting the decision.[181] Lay people contributed to the physical fabric and services of rural churches and helped administer parish temporalities.[182] Contemporary witnesses swore that voluntarily-allocated tithes from nobles and peasants over a wide area of the Środa district built the church at Mrozów around 1300.[183] At Wierzbno in 1318 schulz and peasants together added to the landed endowment of their church a second mansus to support another altar priest and bell-ringer.[184]

Each of the central facilities which dotted the countryside, crafts, taverns, mills, and parish churches, exerted a certain but different attraction on inhabitants of the surrounding area. Villages with several of these, even though they had no market rights, clearly drew greater social attention. Map 9.1 contains thirty places which, thanks to three or more central facilities, might be called central villages. These places were larger than the average rural settlement,[185] and had distinct locations. They were common in the Uraz district and in a band paralleling the Bystrzyca about midway between Wrocław and Środa and not unusual in the south of the Wrocław district, but rare closer to the cities. It looks again as if the economic strength, attractions, and political power of the cities suppressed autonomous nuclei in their immediate vicinity, while the weaker markets were less able to eliminate rival concentrations in the countryside.

Traces thus emerge from the records of the late fourteenth-century duchy of a regionally structured economic and social network which derived from the distribution of population and natural resources as these had developed historically. Instead of a purely agricultural countryside opposed directly to commercial and administrative cities, the interaction was mediated by a hierarchy of facilities in the land itself. The retail trades in particular formed a system of taverns and marketplaces which drew their customers from what look like spatially coherent localities and neighborhoods.[186] Like coherence in terms of population and historical evolution of settlement made the religious system fully compatible with that for exchange. But these neat arrangements were cross-cut, thanks to the irregular availability of water power, by the distribution of milling services. Thus a peasant from Zabłoto, for example, could patronize his local tavern and seek religious comfort or market dealings at Kostomłoty a couple of kilometers south, but had to carry his grain at least twice as far to mills at Buczki on the Średzka Woda to the north or Piotrowice on the Strzegomka to the southeast. Across the duchy, then, overlapping and interlocking neighborhood and regional networks served the particular needs of small groups of people and fed upwards to the urban centres, Środa and, eventually, Wrocław itself. At the peripheries, especially the far north and south, political boundaries may have distorted relationships, but overall the duchy probably encompassed the normal social interactions of its inhabitants of whatever degree.

Nodes in the network of central places can be documented with considerable accuracy and with great probability it can be inferred that country people and their lords used these to meet their needs. But because the activities there focused and the contacts there made generated little in the way of written records, not to be seen are the particular interpersonal relationships created and sustained while men and women marketed, milled, drank, or worshiped. How the contacts must have occurred is plain; that any certain ones did is not.

The reverse is true of the financial relationships preserved in records of rural credit and debt. Where, as often happens, a borrower and lender lack visible acquaintance through neighborhood, lordship, or kinship, the paths by which they came together are now lost. That they did so, however, is itself prima facie proof of connections between villagers and others outside their communities. Country people participated fully, if not always equally and at their own initiative, in a web of financial contracts, obligations, and exchanges which spread across the fourteenth-century duchy. Their evident involvement is the more striking because, unlike their lords, most peasants dealt before village courts where written records were not normally kept and from which almost none now survive. Nevertheless villagers may be detected as debtors and as creditors and, to a degree, their financial dealings may be placed in a meaningful context.

Some villagers incurred personal or communal obligations at their lord's behest. A landowner with a financial liability could formally transfer it to the peasants who owed dues to him. Thus in 1341 the Stille lords of Olbrachtowice covered the forty marks they owed the Wrocław Jew Jacob by having the village community pledge to pay him within a year. Likewise in 1416 Peter and Woytko, tenants of four mansi at Żerniki Małe, saw the mark a year they owed to canon Nicholas Seidlicz shifted as an annual rent to their lord's colleague John Sweidenicz, who had paid ten marks for it. The peasants stood before the bishop's official to hear the conveyance and a threat of excommunication for default.[187] By such means might ordinary countrymen encounter townsmen, clerics, Jews, and others who had no place in their rural communities. Contacts of this sort arose, however, from socio-economic knowledge and relationships of lords in their own stratum of society.

Villages and villagers also entered into financial dealings on their own, thus demonstrating their independent acquaintance with sources of credit. Many such arrangements followed existing connections with the landowner, the schulz, or neighbors. Stanko, schulz of Oporów, sold for eleven marks to his lord, the cathedral chapter, a mark annual rent on his scholtisei in 1364 and a St. Vincent tenant at *Olbino* in 1413, Peter Melczer, sold to the abbey a half mark on his holding for five.[188] George, schulz of Gajowice, advanced five marks to Anna Hellebrandynne, a tenant there, for a mark and a half in *census*.[189] Ordinary villagers, whether owner-operators or tenants, might be sources of funds, too. At Krępice in 1337 the one-time ducal cook Nicholas had pledged his two mansi to Wenceslava, widow of Beburco, for a ten mark debt. Almost a century later at Zębice Andreas and Martin Smolin arranged to pay to their fellow tenant Climke Belak debts totaling sixty groschen.[190] These relationships are not surprising.

Less predictable lines joined villagers and other potential lenders. Churches and those in them were happy to take *census* from country people with their own property or with tenancies under other lords. For instance, the schulz of Wojkowice in 1331, whose lord was John Colner, borrowed fifteen marks from the cathedral vicars. In 1418 George, schulz of Gajowice under St. Mary, sold a rent to a nun at St. Dorothea while his own lord loaned a larger sum to the schulz of *Szczepin*, a village which belonged to the Clares.[191] Other peasants turned to urban capital. In the 1330s the entire commune of Błonie contracted debts to the citizen Jacob of Opole and some two or more generations later that of the bishop's lordship at Kryniczno sold a *census* to Peter Molner and his sister Clara, both of Wrocław.[192] Individuals, like Peczco, son of Peter of Ołtaszyn, who in 1338 sold to Andreas Fusil a half mark on his two mansi at Łukaszowice, did the same. At Krępice the proprietary peasants used city lenders extensively: of the seven *census* contracts known there between 1368 and 1380 six were made with Wrocław citizens.[193] But since all these creditors lacked obvious prior connection with those to whom they loaned, these dealings confirm peasant involvement in a socio-economic world beyond their village and lordship.

The skimpy data further suggest something of the place of credit and debt in fourteenth-century villages. Of course the reasons and context for assuming a financial obligation are rarely detectable, but, like landowners, peasants with debts were not always poor and destitute—at least before the 1430s (see Chapter 10). That some farmers did so reveal financial difficulties is no surprise. Nicholas, son of Martin of Krępice, sold annuities on his little property in 1368 and 1370, and in 1387 fell so far behind in his payments that he forfeited the land.[194]

Other cases seem more ambiguous. A proprietor like the men of Krępice, Nicholas of Stary Dwór had a small farm he worked himself at *Łukaszewice*. There he sold 1¼ marks annual rent to the citizen John Wenczlaw in 1383 and again in 1386. In 1388 he admitted owing 1 mark 18 groschen to a fellow named John Leen, but ten years later himself enforced a malder of rye owed by Michael Gomolka. Nicholas's heirs then sold still more rents. As equivocal are the cases of two schulzen who sold annuities in 1418: Peter Weinhold thus obtained sixty marks from St. Mary, but he possessed a free demesne farm in Buczki as well as his scholtisei, tavern, and three mansi at *Szczepin*; George of Gajowice then got ten marks for one on his scholtisei, but himself lent money seven years later.[195]

And some rural debts had clear investment quality. Philip the schulz of Solna and his kinsman John Ratht of Siedlakowice sold large annuities and made deferred payments to finance buying the demesne at Pustków Żurowski from the cathedral chapter.[196] Three men from Węgry effectively used short term credit in 1377, buying horses from the royal demesne at Borów with payments deferred from Martinmas to Christmas and February.[197]

Especially given the character of the surviving documentation, short term credit with a fixed date for payment like that used by the Węgry horse buyers is surprisingly well recorded. It must have been a common expedient. Having paid 2 marks 6 groschen in late December, the son of the Węgry schulz saw no difficulty in rounding up the same sum in another six weeks. The operator of a tile works in Kowale expected to pay off an eight mark debt within four months in 1340 and Janusch, son of Adam of Krępice, two marks in three weeks.[198] Individual villagers thus as a matter of course took a few months to pay off relatively modest sums, a sign of both the difficulty and the possibility of peasants' laying their hands on cash. The recorded incidence of fixed terms at a year or more further substantiates this conclusion, for most of these obligations rested on whole village communities and often represented but the transfer at the lord's request of regular seigneurial dues to the lord's creditor. The villagers of Olbrachtowice had a year to pay the forty marks their lords owed Jacob the Jew.[199] Individuals with a debt in the same order of magnitude might need even longer. At Krępice in 1387 Elizabeth, wife of John Willusch, and her son Nicholas Steynchen undertook to cover a debt of sixteen marks by installments to be paid on Michaelmas over the next three years.[200] Even then, they were able to pay as much in one year as Martin Smolin at Zębice thought in 1436 he might be lucky to cover in two.[201] But that comparison simply marks the contrast between the late fourteenth century and the period after 1425. Earlier, country people did seem to expect they could handle a moderate additional cash outlay within a relatively short period of time.

Ordinary rural debt and credit did not apparently extend beyond about a three year term. This was the domain of the *census*, hereditary, repurchaseable, and normally incurred for sums of five marks or more. As among the

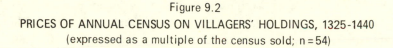

Figure 9.2

PRICES OF ANNUAL CENSUS ON VILLAGERS' HOLDINGS, 1325-1440

(expressed as a multiple of the census sold; n = 54)

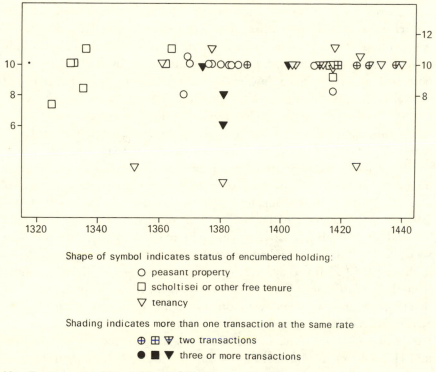

Shape of symbol indicates status of encumbered holding:

     O peasant property

     ☐ scholtisei or other free tenure

     ▽ tenancy

Shading indicates more than one transaction at the same rate

     ⊕ ⊞ ▼ two transactions

     ● ■ ▼ three or more transactions

Note. For sources see *Notes to Maps and Figures.*

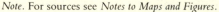

landed elite, this most popular way to borrow was used continually (and surely far more than the texts now record). Instances enough have already been seen of country people selling annual rents to a variety of lenders. The tabulation in Figure 9.2 of the prices villagers received indicates a normal rate in the later fourteenth and early fifteenth centuries of ten times the annual obligation. But, unlike their social superiors, these borrowers got no rates much below that 10 percent interest. Indeed some tenants had to take far worse. The repurchaseable annuities owed from tenures in Mnichowice in 1381 mostly ran at eight to one (12.5 percent), but Hanco Longus paid a mark a year for six (16.7 percent) and Andirko Sweczik four for nine (44.5 percent!).[202] Why? Even a poor gertner's widow at Gajowice in 1413 managed to get five marks at ten percent from her village lord, St. Mary.[203] It is a salutary reminder that villagers in the fourteenth-century duchy did live as the lower echelon of a thoroughly stratified society. Their position was not so extreme, however, as to make their dealings in annual rents or other forms of credit different in kind from those of other social groups. Though at some disadvantage, they made credit, too, a normal aspect of village and country life.

The full involvement of village people in the duchy's network of financial relationships is further affirmed by a few who gave credit and loans. A couple of dozen extant cases dating between the 1330s and the 1430s include creditors from all landed village groups: schulz Peter of Wilczków and his peer at Domaniów, Jesco; owner-operators Wenceslava at Krępice and Nicholas of Stary Dwór; Anna the taverner in Domasław; Climke Belak, tenant at Zębice.[204] Village lenders used all normal forms of credit: short-term loans, the pledge, and the loan against an annual rent. Especially remarkable in the activities of even the handful who are known is the spatial and social scope. Those from Krępice kept their recorded deals within their own community, as did the men of Zębice, but others exploited broader contacts. The schulz of Domaniów knew the need of the schulz of Barto-szowa and the taverner of Domasław, that of a man from Tyniec Mały. These dealt with their relative equals and extended credit on a horizontal social vector, but others did so vertically. Bartholomeus, schulz of Węgry in the late 1350s, left perhaps the most extensive record. In 1356 he bought from the lord of Stary Śleszów, Henry Swenkenfeld, a five mark *census* on that property and two years later another of eight. Then on 10 October 1358 Bartolomeus came to an agreement with Swenkenfeld's other creditors, the citizen consortium of Peter Bayer, John Budessin, and the brothers Domp-nig. He sold to them the eight mark rent on Śleszów and they to him six marks on the Rulandi family's lordship in Blizanowice.[205]

In a couple of remarkable instances villagers even became creditors to their own lords. In April 1336 John the Red, schulz of Jaksin, gave to his landlords Albert and Conrad of Falkenhain 30.5 marks against the pledge of their entire lordship and rental incomes in that very village.[206] A generation later the village communities of Wierzbno and Domaniów engaged more obscurely in the financial manipulations of their lord, the Duke of Brzeg. After complex dealings among Duke Louis, the city of Brzeg, and the duke's favorite, Bishop Mathias of Trebigne, the two villages ended up holding twenty marks on the duke's tolls so long as they had to pay for him an obligation to the bishop.[207] At least on occasion country people were able and willing to deal as equals on the credit market with even the highest of their superiors.

Beyond impressions the meager evidence on village lenders will not go. And like imprecision must be conceded to the whole network of village financial dealings. It cannot much be analyzed because the sources are simply not there. But its very existence affirms once again the multistranded quality of the Wrocław duchy's rural regime in the fourteenth century.

Financial contracts simultaneously manifested prior and established new bonds between individuals and among groups. Within village society loans and debts reiterated ties of neighborhood and local prestige, but also marked their extension into surrounding communities. Beyond village society credit provided another connection to members of the elite, one which paralleled but also augmented lordship. The community of Siedlakowice, for instance, dealt with St. Mathias in 1339 and with the citizen Tilco Rothe the next year because its knightly lord had alienated to them his incomes from there.[208] That case grew from lordship but others arose independently, if rarely in the full light of good documentation. Nicholas of Stary Dwór owned his land at *Łukaszewice* but for his own reasons sold rents on it to the Wenczlaws from Wrocław, who, since they owned no lordships, thus acquired a link to the countryside.[209] Thomas Sybisch of Zagródki counterbalanced his tenurial dependence on St. Mary with rents he sold to the altarist at St. Elizabeth in Wrocław, and Michael Stossche of Domasław his on the landowner Nicholas Skopp with one to the citizen Henry Gramschicz.[210] Why these particular relationships arose, none can now say; the point is that they did arise, and by their very occurrence show that credit and debt were an autonomous mechanism for linking people across social boundaries. Despite the vestigial quality of the evidence, financial dealings affirmed and articulated the juncture of elites and villagers into a regional socio-economic community.

The accessibility to fourteenth-century peasants around Wrocław of economic opportunities and financial resources outside their village community and their landowner's authority go together with other documented features of their surroundings to explain at least structurally the relative autonomy and prosperity they then enjoyed. Lordship was central and inequality and exploitation pervasive, let there be no doubt, but by comparison with what had gone before and with what would come, a pluralism much mitigated these realities of traditional rural life.

To reiterate, the norms of the German law village provided security of tenure, autonomy in local affairs, and fixed obligations assessed on arable acreage. The joint movement of prices and of the coinage made these dues a slowly diminishing proportion of each peasant's output. Landowners operated within the norms partly from a lack of occasion to intervene directly in agrarian affairs and partly from an inclination to treat landed revenues as a means to achieve social utility in dealings with their own peers. The lords' use of their ownership rights kept these so widely and so often (re-)distributed as to inhibit the concerted intent required to change lord-peasant relationships, especially since alternative actions at their own social level promised more sure increments to individual or family wealth. The ability of the lord to rule his lordship was hampered, too, by assignment of rural leadership to a well-entrenched member of village society, the schulz, who by office and local prestige mediated the juncture between the community and superior or external authority. And then the peasant tenants themselves could and did freely pursue their own economic interests by trading goods on the market, by dealing in their farmland, by turning to small-scale crafts and services, and by moving from one settlement and situation to another. Within the village and beyond its limits no single human authority or nexus inevitably shaped or constrained the life chances of a fourteenth-century peasant. So long as livings were to be made with available tools from the resources of the plains, river bottoms, and hills, rural people could at least maintain a relatively favorable position.

PART FOUR

§§§§§§§

The Erosion of a Socio-Economic Order

§§ 10 §§

THE STORM, CA. 1425 – CA. 1480

Destructa, depopulata et incinerata est fere tota Slesia. . . .

A contemporary abbot of St. Mary recalls the Hussite wars;
ChronBMV, p. 219.

From the late 1100s until the early 1400s the Wrocław duchy experienced agrarian development. Population grew. Land under the plow increased. German law spread. Landlord farms were parceled among peasant tenants. At the same time local elites made private lordship their principal access to wealth, eased direct ducal jurisdiction off the land, and opened their ranks to the ambitions of urban capital. Bohemian hegemony curbed dynastic and private violence. The counterpart to the steady trends were effectively stable structures: peasant autonomy and prosperity in the German law village; the lordship cycle and distance of landowners from everyday rural affairs; the integrative role of market, regional, and other relationships. Men and women in the fourteenth-century duchy surely knew change, mobility, and latent or acute conflict, but long experience made acceptable a certain range of behavior and understandable certain patterns of individual and group action. Their world was a predictable one.

After 1425 all this changed. Forces outside the control of Wrocław's peasants or lords lashed the duchy with furious blows, ripping its socio-economic fabric and laying bare or exacerbating its weaknesses and conflicts. This chapter describes how physical insecurity, meteorological instability, and monetary disarray disrupted all rural relationships. After the perils it treats their results among villagers and lords. Whether the rural order of the fourteenth century contained within itself the germ of its own destruction or no, it came to founder in a much larger mid-fifteenth-century maelstrom. This was a time of crisis.[1]

Forces of disruption

Quietly continuing patterns of rural life and development were in the mid-fifteenth century shattered by the peculiar conjunction in central Silesia of three greater chains of events from beyond the regional horizons of villagers and landowners. A complex crisis of medieval Czech civilization set off the Hussite revolution, which burst bloodily into the crown lands, there to reverberate through two generations of endemic violence and to destroy rural production and resources. Natural disasters from newly erratic and hazardous weather patterns had similar effects. And because Wrocław's chief coins were Bohemian groschen, monetary chaos across the Sudetes intensified the general European silver shortage to rend further the web of exchanges joining country people to the urban economy and elite society. The incidence and initial impact of each hazard is of first concern here.

The literate elite of fifteenth-century Silesia told in self-righteous sorrow how physical insecurity became normal in their countryside. The rhetoric is verified by records of devastated communities and individual casualties. Of course war, banditry, and feud were rarely unfamiliar to medieval Europeans, and a peasant economy where relatively low investment in capital goods made land and labor more critical factors of production was better placed than a modern one for rapid recovery from destruction. Still, the particulars of war, local violence, and their immediate consequences in the duchy from around 1425 to about 1480 explain many of the rural changes hereafter treated.

Public order in Silesia had begun to deteriorate well before banners bearing the chalice crossed the Sudetes, for in the 1390s the weakening position of Wenceslas loosened the grip of his servants and friends.[2] For loyal Wrocław the king's financial need now meant struggle with other royal creditors. To press one claim against the city, the dukes of Opole declared feud late in 1399. Their troops entered the duchy to loot, burn, and seize merchants for ransom. Twice more they returned, once grabbing 130 horses and another time goods valued at more than three thousand marks. Wrocław alleged damages totaling 13,244 marks, but the only named site of rural losses was Święta Katarzyna, where the king compensated Jeschko Dompnig with a higher fiscal privilege.[3] A decade's alternation of force and diplomacy climaxed in the city's seizure of the traveling Bishop John of Kujavia, brother of the reigning dukes. He gained quick release but not the demanded apologies and penance. So in early 1413 his brother Bernard again invaded the duchy, plundering and burning Bogunów, Węgry, Wilczków, Jaksonów, Magnice, Pasterzyce, Gałowice, and Żerniki Wielkie, and driving his booty, livestock and peasants alike, off to his mountain strongholds.

A few months later Duke Bolesław burned more villages, Gniechowice among them.[4]

Other landowners and peasants suffered from more private appeals to force. Abbot Andreas of St. Vincent reported to Rome in 1412 the devastation of Kostomłoty by a marauding band. On nearby abbey lordships tenants nightly feared attack, men and cattle were seized, and all faced ruin. Two years later Abbot Peter Czartewicz of St. Mary foolishly called Duke Henry of Oława a "Schuesterchen." The latter salved his honor by sacking the abbey's properties around Sobótka and its demesne farms at Tyniec Mały and Brochów. The manager at Tyniec lay hurt in Oława's dungeon and damages purportedly came to ten thousand florins.[5]

Such incidents were but an ominous prelude. The tax roll of 1425 still had few defaults and the least deserted land of any large survey. The Hussite wars really began what proved to be a long period of unrelieved rural destruction. From 1428 to 1434 Czech forces, stung to retaliation by Silesian atrocities during anti-Hussite crusades, ranged freely about the province. Three separate invasions of the Wrocław duchy can be documented and specific points of damage identified. Of course the surviving texts (and Map 10.1) can only confirm where losses did occur. Nothing warrants that the listings are comprehensive; probably they are not. Tactics then normal increased the harm of these conflicts. Major pitched battles between organized units were exceptional. Only the assaults on Wrocław in 1459 and 1474 involved them. More normally, raiding parties fanned out from strongholds or bivouacs to scorch the enemy earth. Villages burned; peasants fled, fell prisoner, or died; their goods filled the bellies and wagons of their persecutors or further fed the flames.

In late March, 1428, Hussite forces entered the duchy from the west after cutting a swath of destruction past Świdnica, Legnica, and Głogów. Capturing Środa and Kąty en route, they passed south to meet reinforcements near Niemcza. An official of the Teutonic Order reported from Wrocław in early April that the invaders numbered some 24,000 and gained strength from the Silesian peasantry. Their commander, Prokop the Great, then hoped to win over local people. Contemporary witnesses, the knight Martin Ehrenburg and the Wrocław canon Sigismund Rosicz, agreed there were many fatalities and fires, but the former reports selective destruction of churches, rectories, taverns, and demesne farms, including that at Gniechowice.[6]

After circling east and across the Odra, the same Hussite column returned in early May, now less discriminate and less welcome. They passed right around Wrocław, fired the church of St. Nicholas in the shadow of the walls, and camped just beyond the southeastern suburbs. "Retiring from

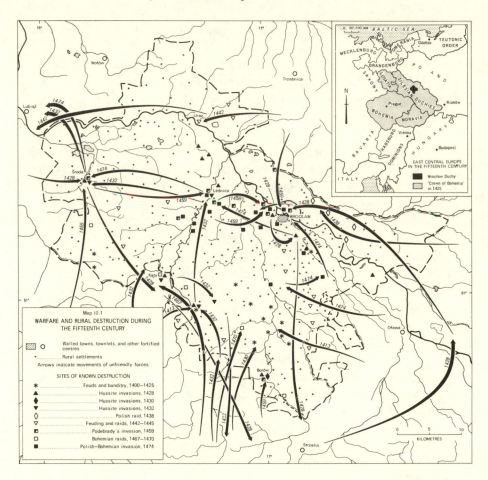

Map 10.1
WARFARE AND RURAL DESTRUCTION DURING
THE FIFTEENTH CENTURY

Walled towns, townlets, and other fortified centres

Rural settlements

Arrows indicate movements of unfriendly forces

SITES OF KNOWN DESTRUCTION

* .... Feuds and banditry, 1400–1425
▲ .... Hussite invasions, 1428
◆ .... Hussite invasions, 1430
▼ .... Hussite invasions, 1432
◇ .... Polish raid, 1438
▽ .... Feuding and raids, 1442–1445
◪ .... Podebrady's invasion, 1459
□ .... Bohemian raids, 1467–1470
■ .... Polish–Bohemian invasion, 1474

there, they burned many villages around Wrocław and Strzelin, taking with them innumerable beasts and spoils."[7] This was the route only of the main body. Damages recorded at Wilkszyn, Pisarzowice, and Miłoszyn were more than fifteen kilometers from the nearest reported point of advance. And losses at Bartoszowa, Stabłowice, Brochów, and Kotowice must also be attributed to this foray.[8]

Actions in 1430 spread less widely. Late in April heretical troops moved from upper Silesia to again capture Niemcza. From there they regularly foraged for cattle in the southern reaches of the duchy and caused the inhabitants to abandon Borów.[9]

In 1432 Hussites carried sword and flame through areas earlier spared. A party from what had become a permanent base at Niemcza moved north to take Kąty and loot a herd of horses from Wierzbica. In skirmishes on

16 June this vanguard routed Wrocław troops from positions near Strzelin. Two days later the main body bivouacked on the border of the duchy. They advanced to take Gniechowice, burn Wierzbica, and traverse the Wrocław district to Leśnica. After paying their customary warm attention to that small town, they followed the main road to Środa and moved on to demolish the monastery at Lubiąż.[10] It was the last major officially heretical visitation.

Yet the peace finally reached between Sigismund and the Hussites in 1436 only briefly spared the battered duchy. The king's death in 1437 unleashed dynastic struggles in east-central Europe and factional feuds around Wrocław. Polish claims to the crown of Bohemia were advanced against those of Albert II von Habsburg through raids along the Silesian border. A contingent from Great Poland sliced through the Oleśnica and Brzeg duchies in the fall of 1438 to reach within a "mile" of Wrocław and, from a camp at Kamieniec, "loot and burn Swojczyce, Dobrzykowice, Kowale, and many other villages."[11] By the early 1440s the melée swirled with regional and local combatants: the city of Wrocław; Bishop Conrad the Elder, hereditary duke of Oleśnica; his reigning brother and antagonist, also Conrad; the Poles, normally aligned with the latter; Leonhard Asenheimer, acting in his own interests and in the name of Queen Elizabeth of Hungary; and the knightly von Czirne family, local landowners, both one-time military leaders for Wrocław and erstwhile allies of the Hussites, and now possessors of the Uraz castle.

From June, 1442, to September, 1443, raid and counter-raid flared along the boundary between the Uraz and Trzebnica districts and at times deep into the Wrocław district. The Czirne waged simultaneous private war against bishop and chapter by burning church-owned villages. At Uraz, Świdnica Polska, Siedlakowice, Racławice Małe, Pęgów, Mnichowice, Milejowice, Lutynia, Kryniczno, Golędzinów, and Bogusławice country people suffered in their possessions and their persons.[12] Those at Ołtaszyn, Biestrzyków, and "many other villages of the Wrocław church and chapter near Wrocław" again fell victims in 1445 to a different feud of their episcopal lord with Duke Bolko of Opole.[13]

After this turmoil the duchy enjoyed more than a decade's official calm. But men of all sorts had learned too well the lessons of the sword and the firebrand. Public and organized violence suggested its use for other purposes. Private appeals to force fill the documentary record as never before 1425.

Prominent among the visibly violent were the landed lay elite. From noble ranks, for instance, Czasław Sommerfeld, hereditary lord of Jastrzębce, demanded in the 1440s payments from tenants in Lipnica of the

Środa priory-hospital. He dragged the peasants into his own court and later assaulted the indignant prior in the very sacristy of his church.[14] A generation later Junker Debitsch, lord of Lubnów, pursued a dispute with Andreas Mico, steward of the demesne farm at Zabór Mały, by abducting his sick wife and keeping her in the stocks until she miscarried. In Mico's complaint this followed Debitsch's seizure of the former's property and his charters of title to it.[15]

Town families did not defer in this respect to the knights. At Cieszyce in 1440, for example, Dominic Dietrich, recognized bastard of a Dompnig girl, attacked Thomas Leuen, breaking into his house, seizing his money and movables, and dragging him behind two horses until he nearly died.[16] Henry Hoppe, a landed but not rich city juror, cloaked in legality his 1483 persecution of a Kuklice peasant. With apparent authority but not the Rat's permission he broke the poor man's thumbs with the "maiden" and had him nearly drowned. It cost Henry a fifty florin fine.[17]

Villagers also used force to pursue their interests against neighbors and lords. In April, 1439, the town council of Środa indicted Nickel Cluge from Głoska for having led an assault on men from Uraz, who were robbed and some killed on a woodland road. Two months later the council required the schulz and nine others from Nickel's home village to stand surety for his good behavior. He had, it seems, threatened further violence against the town and against his own lord, Peter Falkenhain.[18] Some village violence plainly belonged to on-going feuds. At Bogunów in 1447, for instance, one faction beat another, the dependents of Hans Bank, in a pitched battle. A fragmentary court record lists casualties and claims of theft on both sides.[19]

Arson or its threat was a popular way to press against lord and community an unacceptably neglected claim. Village courts and landowners, among them Franz Krig from Magnice and Nicholas Skopp from Domasław, publicly proclaimed their safe-conducts for the unknown persons who "gebrant und schaden geton hat" if these would appear in public to negotiate their grievances.[20]

To violence against familiar rivals was added its less discriminate use by genuine brigands, not all of them anonymous or foreign. George Czirne, lord of Uraz in 1438, and Melchior Ungerathen, city councillor and lord of Gniechowice in 1460, were alleged horse thieves.[21] In late 1476 Wrocław reported to King Mathias that the then lord of Uraz, Melchior von Laban, preyed on Polish merchants, and that Czech bandits had kidnapped the councilor Wenceslas Bank from his own farm at Kazimierzów. Seven months later the *Rat* complained further of a gang from Świdnica who had taken stock from Kulin and Wojtkowice and escaped across the duchy's border.[22] Less lucky or well-connected highwaymen and robbers of churches who fell into the city's hands went quickly to the gallows or the stake.[23]

It is probable, if not demonstrable, that the general breakdown of local law and order, the endemic quality of feuding and banditry, destabilized rural life in the duchy as much as the wars which, though more dramatic and generally dangerous, were less prolonged.[24] Perhaps not surprisingly, this alternative explanation was neglected in April, 1459, when Wrocław and other Silesian rulers blamed on the Hussite invasions of three decades past their still desolate countryside.[25]

That Silesian letter to Pope Pius II was an early ranging shot of renewed general conflict, for the interlude of formal peace had crumbled with the rise of George Poděbrady to power in Bohemia and the move of Wrocław to intransigent opposition. A second Hussite war began with the king's invasion and siege of the city in the autumn of 1459. Two eyewitnesses, the canon Rosicz and the city secretary, Peter Eschenloer, tell much about military operations in the vicinity.[26] The king and his Silesian allies advanced from Świdnica to Środa in the first week of September. When that town capitulated without delay they moved up on Gałów and Leśnica to storm the castles and burn the houses. After beating off a Wrocław counterattack, royal troops destroyed Żerniki and Złotniki. On 29 September an assault by Oleśnica forces massed on the northern approaches to the city, penetrated to the Odra at *Olbino* before being repelled. The swath of burned-out villages extended as far as Widawa. Meanwhile Borów again fell victim to skirmishes along the southern edge of the duchy. A last assault before papal emissaries gained a truce reached and destroyed Popowice and suburban *Szczepin*.

The armistice just let alignments form for general conflict in the crown lands by the mid-1460s and entry of Mathias Corvinus in 1469. Most fighting was in the mountains, but even before the second offensive of 1474 some Czech incursions into the duchy can be traced. Eschenloer tells of pillaging around Kąty in August, 1467, and says that by 1470 this had become common. Lay and clerical landowners blamed the city for their suffering and paid Czech commanders protection money to escape further harm. One raid the secretary specified as taking livestock from Kuklice.[27] The following spring (4 April 1471) that same village community received a written notice from one of their tormentors: failure to make the promised payment within four days would, he threatened, make things "ten times worse for you."[28] Peasants learned well that little separated war from brigandage. No popular support for the invaders is recorded.

When the folk of Kuklice faced raw extortion George Poděbrady lay two weeks in his grave. They could rejoice little, however, as new diplomatic machinations far away pitted Jagiellonian Poland and Bohemia against Corvinus's Hungary, Moravia, Silesia, and Lusatia. And they and their fellows paid the price for Wrocław's improved readiness when a combined

Czech-Polish army again threatened in autumn, 1474. In September, as the enemy assembled, King Mathias ordered a scorched-earth defense. On pain of confiscation all cattle, fodder, grain, and other movables were brought to the towns. He stockpiled great stores for his troops. At Wrocław families of "armen Gebaurs Volk" camped with their livestock along the walls, in the fields of uncut grain near the Oleśnica gate, and in suburban *Szczepin* and *Platea Romanorum*. By month's end an epidemic carried them off by the hundreds. Also quartered in the suburbs were the king's Black Army, who lived up to their evil reputation by stealing everything portable and tearing down houses for firewood. Eschenloer thought them worse than the enemy.[29]

As military reporter the town secretary is joined by Benedict Johnsdorf, then abbot of St. Mary.[30] The Czech and Polish contingents linked up near Oława in mid-October and advanced to establish a base at Święta Katarzyna. From there they moved up to assault the suburbs for two weeks. During this time Johnsdorf reports that "they set so many fires in the Wrocław district from morning to noon that the sky and the sun were obscured by the fumes and thick smoke." Having exhausted the forage southeast of the city, the invaders moved westward through Brochów, Gajowice, Muchobór Mały, and Grabiszyn to Gałów, Leśnica, Złotniki, Jerzmanowo, and Samotwór. Now the chronicler declares that more than three hundred fires of burning villages could be seen from the city's towers. But Mathias's tactics had worked. The Polish army, weakened by short supplies and the coming winter, accepted a truce and retired. The Black Army returned to its preferred occupation, pillage. The land about Wrocław lay desolate.[31]

All the violence, death, and destruction just narrated took place in the close confines of the Wrocław duchy in barely over fifty years, two or three human generations. Between 1428 and 1474 alone Map 10.1 displays sixty-four places where attacks are documented. None now can say how many more went unrecorded. Danger had become a normal part of fifteenth-century rural life.

Occasionally contemporaries openly blamed specific troubles on the harm they had suffered. Monks of Lubiąż, for instance, lost in 1428 at Bartoszowa, "quasi medietas per hussitas conbusta et in rebus et in pecoribus spoliata," two-thirds of their revenues in cash and all in grain.[32] Years later other farms and communities had not yet recovered. In 1441 the "hoff, dorff vnd guth Kottewicz an der Oder . . . von den ketzern vorbrant vnd vorwust ist" and two years thereafter the peasants of Komorniki still had their taxes fully dismissed "propter exustione et Rapcone Equorum et aliarum rerum spoliatone."[33] Even the victory of 1474 had its clearly perceived costs in the villagers who by the next spring, wrote Johnsdorf, "omnibus rebus suis spoliati penuria et fame mortui sunt."[34] Thus concretely did witnesses draw the causal connection between war and the reduced incomes, depopulation, desertion, and impoverishment which this chapter shall soon argue were general in the mid-century duchy. But not only human violence directly caused distress; nature, too, destroyed lives and livelihoods.

Like the political, environmental conditions worsened in the mid-fifteenth century as temperate Europe's climate drifted toward the "Little Ice Age." In east-central parts of the continent the onset of cooler and wetter long-term weather patterns was accompanied by great short-term instability, with severe alternations between dry years and wet, warm years and cold.[35]

A change in dominant weather conditions is not, of course, documented from systematic observations taken in the central Odra basin, but is firmly indicated by the available local evidence. Rarely in the fourteenth century did meteorological events draw the notice of Silesian annalists or otherwise enter the documentary record. The odd storm aroused brief excitement, but only a flood in August, 1387, which destroyed mills and demesne buildings in the bottomlands, drew broad attention.[36] In the fifteenth century, however, references multiply to years of drought or excessive precipitation, remarkable heat, or severe cold. Both Rosicz and Eschenloer noted sometimes brutally variable weather and consequent human difficulties. Their reports, often corroborated by other records, mark as especially unstable the 1450s and 1460s, with twelve remarkably cold and snowy winters, four summers with major flooding, and four others of drought.[37]

Behind the annual variability which the chroniclers saw was a larger phenomenon which they likely did not, a generation-long wave of frequent and heavy summer rains and floods. Curt Weikinn's compilation of hydrographic references from central Europe has data to calculate the frequency of the Odra's flooding during June, July, and August. After 1387 no such events are recorded until 1405 and not again until 1444. There followed nine years of flood in thirty-one: 1444, 1445, 1454, 1456, 1462, 1464, 1468, 1470, and 1475—and then a twenty-year respite before another wave between 1495 and 1525.[38] Nineteenth- and twentieth-century observers of similar occurrences noted that eastward-moving storms then stalled as they crossed the Sudetes and soaked the whole basin between Głogów and Opole.[39]

Like the harm from war and violence, that from the weather was plain to fifteenth-century writers. Hard winters and summer droughts rarely much affected rural life and agriculture. Only because many country folk had not yet rebuilt from the 1474 invasion, says Eschenloer, did they suffer greatly and some die from the severe cold of 1475–76.[40] Some notably dry summers (1459, 1469, 1472, 1473) gave good harvests and others (1437,

1471) dangerously poor ones.[41] But summer rain and floods put at risk capital equipment, livestock, and the grain harvest. In 1470 regular heavy rains after mid-June stunted all crops, rotted the grain in the fields, and prevented harvest. The Odra and all its tributaries rose to drown meadows and halt nearly all farm work around Wrocław well into October. Six years earlier mid-August floods swept away bridges, mills, animals, and people all along the rivers.[42] In pre-industrial temperate Europe, excess moisture posed the greatest environmental danger to human food supplies and property.[43] And too much water was what country people often faced around mid-century Wrocław.

In summer, 1470, Peter Eschenloer saw three threats to the well-being of his city: the heretical enemy, the incessant rains, and the king's new monetary policy, which brought "perdicione maxima terrarum et hominum de pauperacione."[44] The last complaint echoed a theme by then a half-century old, the dangerous disarray of the coinage. The problems mid-fifteenth-century Silesia had with its currency were regional manifestations of a general European silver shortage, compounded by the collapse of Bohemian royal authority and by the uncoordinated, self-seeking, and futile responses of local powers.

The Prague groschen Silesians used for most major transactions lost in the last decade of Wenceslas's reign more than a fourth of the silver it had held for the twenty years after his accession. Small mintings of the late 1420s showed no improvement and ended with a thirty-year halt to the work of the Czech moneyers. Then Poděbrady briefly (1460–71) restored the coin to almost 90 percent of its turn-of-the-century value, but his successors soon cut it to levels below that of Wenceslas's final years. Meanwhile, under the auspices of Mathias between 1466 and 1482, Wrocław struck still weaker versions.

The city's own small coins could not fill the gap. Already in 1422 the city reduced the specie in its mintings of heller by a fifth from the standard maintained for the past forty years. In 1429, to wring from its financial resources every drop for the anti-Hussite effort, it coined them with no silver at all. Scorned by contemporaries for hurting the urban poor and other trading towns, these were quietly abandoned in 1438. Then for more than two decades the market had to rely on old coins and issues from other Silesian or foreign mints. New Wrocław heller finally made in 1460 were 22 percent below the 1422 issue and reduced further in 1470 and 1474.[45] No wonder counterfeits and poor foreign issues circulated freely and Silesian politicians vainly sought an agreement on coinage. Yet the distressed voices are, like that of Eschenloer, urban.

Country people innocently observed the monetary crisis. They bore for it no responsibility and were little threatened in their everyday routines. Rural folk used coins, to be sure, but they were not really the peasants' affair. Peasant use of money signified their partial envelopment in an urban-based exchange economy, whether for the sake of their own needs or (most often) those of their lords. Neither agricultural production nor the direct consumption of it by farm families depended on coins as on peace and an equable climatic regime.

But monetary disorder put into question the structured relationships between agriculturalists and others, rural laborers and craftsmen, lords, creditors, and urban consumers or suppliers of city-made goods. Recipients of nominally fixed or customary sums of money were now especially at risk. Those with power used it to guard the value of their incomes. Very quickly parties to transactions found a measure of security by specifying the coins acceptable to fulfill obligations. In late summer, 1429, for instance, the Postel family of Uraz sold a two mark *census* on their holdings. The buyer, Anna Bendlerynne from Wrocław, paid twenty marks in groschen and had specified in the charter that the annuity was due in the same coin, not heller.[46] Debasements might still cut the specie received as dues or in redemption, but creditors did in this way avoid being stuck with other coins of less or unknown value.

A further step of self-defense was to gold, as in Mathias Jenkwicz's 1470 sale to the vicars of Holy Cross of a four mark *census* on his lordship at Sadków. Jenkwicz owed a mark heller each quarter but he received payment and was permitted to repurchase in neither heller nor groschen but florins, eighty-nine by count. Use of the stable gold coin spread into the countryside by at least the 1460s; more, it seems, for relatively large, though not uncommon, payments than for everyday peasant transactions.[47] But then people with such obligations had to get ever-greater numbers of silver coins to exchange for gold; the gulden (florin, ducat) worth about twenty-three groschen around 1420 cost thirty-one about 1450 and more than fifty in the 1470s.[48] Direct evidence thus confirms awareness in the countryside of monetary confusion but few immediate effects on peasants themselves. The danger was that lords or creditors, financially crippled by this or other disruptions of the mid-century economy, might think to recoup their losses at peasant expense.

Merely to detail physical insecurity, meteorological disaster, and monetary chaos in the mid-century duchy is to start to catalogue the blows these struck against the rural economy and the people who lived in or from it. A sparse supply of non-standard or worthless coins distorted habitual relationships on the market or between lords and peasants. Floods ravaged lowland fields and structures; rain rotted and drought parched the standing grain.

Political or private violence imperiled the livelihoods and lives of peasants. As never in the generations before, these multiple shocks reverberated through the agrarian order to mark the mid-fifteenth century as a time of prolonged general crisis. Nearly all groups numbered among the victims; only a few gained beyond survival.

Victims and survivors: the shape of crisis in the village

Evidence is voluminous for fifteenth-century changes in natural and human conditions for rural life. Evidence directly relating rural life to its setting is less common, though firm. Much more just depicts crisis in the mid-century countryside. The exogenous shocks and their certain effects were set forth first to serve as a backdrop for examining mutually corroborative signs of problems and of responses to them. Now this section considers the situation of villagers. Whatever in particular damaged their production and equipment, they suffered famine, disease, and death. Land went derelict, obligations went unpaid, and people fell into poverty. Only a few, it seems, seized with success the opportunities thereby opened. Here, too, belong issues of social conflict and unrest. A following section will then treat the less vital but better recorded difficulties of the landed elite: falling incomes and property values; loss of managerial initiative and even, among some groups, of enthusiasm for landed possessions. From top to bottom the structure shook.

Sure indicators of stress in an agrarian economy are rising prices and acute shortages of food. Uncommon around Wrocław for the previous half-century, both became disturbingly frequent after 1425. They hurt urban grain purchasers and rural grain producers alike. Rosicz, Eschenloer, and other witnesses habitually comment on good and bad harvests and communicate their sense of normal and abnormal market conditions. Extant statements of grain prices appear in Figure 10.1. Within what seems a mid-century swell in nominal non-famine levels, the remarkably expensive years still stand out. Then prices often doubled, tripled, or soared even to sixteen times normal.[49]

That the problem around mid-century Wrocław was failure of production, not distribution, is plain from pathetic reports of country people flocking to the city in search of food. The first major famine occurred in 1431, when Rosicz saw "multi venientes de villis pre fame, inedia ac tristitia mortui sunt. . . ."[50] Following four years of war and the previous summer's desultory raids, this began nearly a decade of recurring shortages. After the Hussite offensive just before harvest in 1432, supplies were again tight in 1433 and 1434. "The poor gathered in Wrocław from many small towns

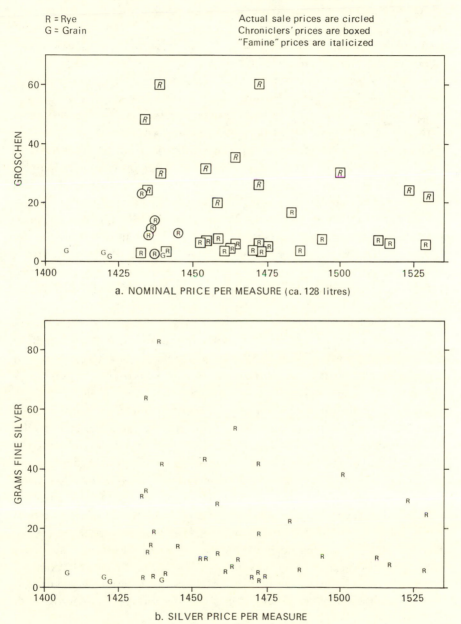

Figure 10.1
CEREAL PRICES (RYE AND "GRAIN") 1400 -1530

R = Rye
G = Grain

Actual sale prices are circled
Chroniclers' prices are boxed
"Famine" prices are italicized

a. NOMINAL PRICE PER MEASURE (ca. 128 litres)

b. SILVER PRICE PER MEASURE

Note. For sources see *Notes to Maps and Figures.*

and villages in a very great multitude, having their lodgings in the squares and cemeteries; they perished from famine and cold."[51] These conditions came again in 1437 after a drought and again in 1439 after renewed conflict before the 1440s brought respite.[52] A second wave of inflations and famines hit in 1458, 1464, 1470, and 1472 (all followed difficult growing seasons and the latter two also military danger and manipulation of the coinage).[53]

Peter Eschenloer's narrative of 1472 well describes the subsistence crises. After 1471's dry summer caused a premature harvest, the "Teurung" began during February in Silesia and nearby regions. By early March in Wrocław rye sold for 18 groschen the measure, wheat for 24, and oats or barley for 10. The city council proposed selling rye from the reserves at 12 groschen, but the communal assembly refused. Then on Easter (29 March), as rye hit 22 groschen, it demanded such sales. In the next six weeks prices soared—rye brought 60 groschen and wheat went only for gold. Wrocław sold rye even to non-residents for 20 groschen. "There one saw the poor people come in crowds from Silesia and all the lands around; the peasants gladly bought a measure of bran for ten groschen." But the relief measures curbed mortality and with the new harvest rye fell to a more normal 6 groschen by late July.[54] Governing urban authorities had learned to handle the emergency needs of their community and the crowds of rural refugees. But that they had to rescue the latter at all reveals the inability under stress of at least some countrymen to feed themselves and to push the shortfall off on market consumers. When harvest failed for whatever cause, peasants in the mid-century duchy had to enter the market as prospective purchasers and drive prices still higher.[55]

Epidemic disease joined famine to ravage the duchy's inhabitants. No texts offer clear symptoms for diagnosis, but recurring plague seems likely. Most outbreaks began in late summer and early fall and kept going into the winter. Wrocław was free of great sickness from 1372 until "maxima pestis in Silesia" struck in 1412 and 1413. The Hussite wars were followed by another outbreak during 1437–39.[56] The next delayed until 1451–52 and for a time the frequency picked up. An epidemic in 1460 was followed by especially heavy mortalities from August, 1464, to late February, 1465.[57] Then for two years Eschenloer notes plague raging unabated through the province, "and also in the Duchy of Wrocław, but not in the city of Wrocław, except occasionally by contagion from villagers."[58] So peasants died in their villages in times of peace as they did huddled about the walls of Wrocław in time of war in 1474.

Famine, plague, and war together depopulated the mid-century countryside. Extant narratives dramatized the lethal effects especially during the 1430s, 60s, and 70s. A more sober record source, the 1430–38 income reg-

Table 10.1. The decline of tenant numbers in villages with obligations to the Holy Spirit Hospital, 1431–1438

| | Number of tenants in earliest and latest years with full data | | | | |
	1431	1433	1436	1438	Percent change
Bogdaszowice		29	22		−24
Budziszów, pow. Śr.		10	10		0
Ilnica		10		10	0
Jarząbkowice	15			12	−20
Karczyce		23		17	−26
Łowęcice	20	17			−15
Radakowice		16		12	−25
Wróbłowice	12			8	−33
Zębice	12			6	−50

Source: HGZ, *passim*.

ister of the Holy Spirit hospital, confirms the losses suffered by people in one group of villages during the first phase of generally acute danger. For nine settlements it regularly (though not each year in full) lists by name the peasant tenants, their tenures, and the dues they paid. Eight were lay-owned sites in the east-central part of the Środa district; the other, Zębice, was a hospital property southeast of Wrocław.[59] This text, already exploited in Chapter 9 for what the earliest entries say of pre-war peasant society, richly details the changing situation of the 1430s.

Tenant numbers in each village at the earliest and latest date for which the income register identifies all land appear in Table 10.1. In only two did the number of households remain unchanged; nowhere did it increase. Gaps and incommensurabilities in the information from this text prevent calculation of a total decline, but the experience of these nine communities may be generalized from the mean annual drop of 4.5 percent for the maximum durations indicated. If that rate held for the full seven years of the register, net losses came to almost one household in three. Might it be thought a near-maximum? The 1430s were especially hard times and all these places lay close to known Hussite depredations.

The one other contemporary running list of tenants covers those at Radomierzyce who in 1449–57 owed tithe to the assistant warden (*succustos*) of the cathedral. The seven farms there to begin that more benign period were also present at its end, albeit mostly with new possessors.[60] Nothing so close to genuine population data is available for later years of crisis.

Records of deserted arable are in this situation plausible surrogates

**Table 10.2. Deserted land in villages with obligations
to the Holy Spirit Hospital, 1433–1438**

	Years with full account	Tenant mansi	Mean percent deserted
Bogdaszowice	3	30	6
Budziszów, pow. Śr.	2	12.5	2
Ilnica	5	18.5	25
Jarząbkowice	5	18	14
Karczyce	3	28	18
Łowęcice	2	26	14
Radakowice	5	24	11
Wróblowice	4	25	12
Zębice	6	12	4

Source: HGZ, *passim*.

for the absent rural population estimates as well as autonomous indicators of economic crisis. Early fifteenth-century evidence, it will be recalled, showed a society exploiting its known resources nearly to the full. In 1425 one settlement in fifteen (6.5 percent) had any unused farmland and that was just one percent of the land assessed. The eight villages in the Środa district with obligations to Holy Spirit then held more than 190 mansi, but only three at Radakowice lay idle.[61] Table 10.2 makes clear the abrupt change after 1425. Not one of these peasant communities worked all of its land in the mid-1430s. In the average year with a full account, one mansus in eight had no cultivator. This corresponds with the incidental reports of abandoned farmland elsewhere in the late 1420s and 1430s.

Might the rural depopulation and abandoned arable of the 1430s have been short-term phenomena, with peasant refugees returning when acute danger had passed? The duchy's tax account from 1443 decisively demonstrates the reverse.[62] Five years after the last entries in the Holy Spirit accounts and more than ten since the last Hussite incursion, deserted farmland which paid no tax was common in the duchy's countryside (Map 10.2). The board of landowners responsible for the collection found it in 112 of the 235 identifiable settlements they recorded, 47.5 percent.[63] For 165 places they set down enough data to calculate that 20.9 percent of land (829 of 3962 mansi) then lay idle.[64] It is the highest rate of desertion known from any medieval survey in the duchy. In villages with obligations to the Holy Spirit hospital conditions had worsened since the mid-1430s. In 1443 six of the nine had more abandoned land and in total almost one mansus in five and a half was not being worked.[65]

Map 10.2 confirms the importance of the Hussites in causing what was

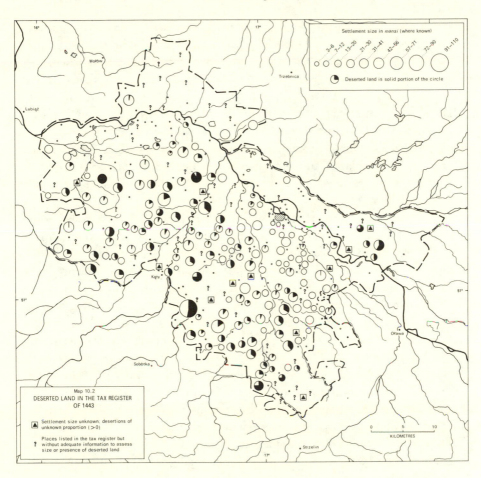

Map 10.2
DESERTED LAND IN THE TAX REGISTER
OF 1443

by 1443 a decade and a half of rural distress. Where the tax return gives good coverage (too much is missing from most of the bottomlands and the Uraz district), deserted land is more common in the southern parts of the Wrocław district and along the routes which cross the Środa district but less near Wrocław itself. A check on known Hussite activities (Map 10.1) finds a like pattern, especially when it is recalled that peasants close to Wrocław took refuge in the inviolate city but that Środa, Leśnica, and other minor centers fell victim the same as open villages. But how much did the original inhabitants remain or other survivors seek out safer sites?

Rural depopulation cannot be measured in and through the warfare, bad weather, food shortages, and disease of the 1460s and 1470s. The tax register of 1443 is the last known survey from the medieval duchy, so only incidental references can suggest the continued or repeated emptiness of much land. The *ex parte* plaint of Silesian authorities in 1459, "hodie multe [sc. villas et possessiones] casse et vacue sunt et manent sine cultore," has some ring of truth.[66] Thereafter conditions deteriorated to Eschenloer's mournful countryside "empty of men and beasts" in 1475. In that year and the three following there were new desertions at Iwiny.[67] And eventually late fifteenth-century landowners confirmed abandoned fields and farms by their efforts to repopulate them (see Chapter 11). So the countryside was significantly and long emptied by the dangers of mid-century. Peasants died and were not replaced; they left their threatened farms and did not return. Known resources lay idle for generations as they had not for more than a century before.[68]

Mid-century villagers defaulted on their traditional obligations to the elite even more than they deserted their land. High rates of non-payment were recognizeably (even by some disappointed recipients) related to the peasants' economic difficulties. Quantitative and anecdotal evidence indicates massive default during and after the Hussite war and again in the 1470s, but also its considerable persistence through the intervening period. Paradigmatic are the tithe accounts for Radomierzyce, where the warden claimed two marks from twelve mansi. This he got each year for twenty up to 1426 and for nearly fifty after 1486, but not in the interim. No receipts were entered during 1427–36 and, after full payment for 1437, further arrears accumulated through 1440. The following seventeen years (1441–57) produced the full amount only three times and nothing at all in 1447, so the total fell short by 15 percent. Fragmentary returns from the 1460s and early 1470s show no defaults, but then nothing came in during 1474–80 and barely half in 1481–85.[69] Each part of the paradigm is replicated in discontinuous evidence from other places.

During the 1430s people failed 53 percent of the time to pay their full obligations to the Holy Spirit Hospital (Table 10.3). Anecdotal traces of like behavior elsewhere are then almost common, often pointing to problems which began late in the previous decade. For instance, the Polish peasants settled by Abbot Mathias Hering (1416–29) on St. Mary's old demesne in Tyniec Mały were, said the unsympathetic later chronicler, delinquent in annual rents and other dues. An agreement made in 1430 had no effect, so in 1434 Abbot Jodocus bought them out.[70] But they were not unusual. Oswald, schulz of Muchobór Wielkie, stood accused and guilty before the *officialis* in 1431 of neglecting the mark *census* he owed the cathedral vicars, as the next year did his colleague of Wierzbice, then several payments behind on his annual six marks to the Clares.[71] Even whole villages, Rynakowice and Jelenin among them, were excommunicated by papal order for defaulting on customary rents which their lord, the bishop and chapter, had pledged to two townsmen.[72]

**Table 10.3. Default on obligations owed to the
Holy Spirit Hospital, 1433–1438**

	Years with full account	Mean number of tenancies	Mean percent defaulting
Bogdaszowice	3	25	58
Budziszów, pow. Śr.	2	10	15
Ilnica	5	10	63
Jarząbkowice	5	11	56
Karczyce	3	17	82
Łowęcice	2	18	40
Radakowice	5	15	51
Wróblowice	4	11	46
Zębice	6	8	51

Source: HGZ, *passim.*

Such references largely peter out during the 1440s, 50s, and 60s, but in at least one place, Komorniki, occasions for non-payment of one obligation or another arose continually even then. The village paid no tax in 1443, when the ruling Wrocław council exempted it for having been looted and burned. Three years later comes to light a long intermittent conflict with the priest of Środa over defaults of parish grain dues. An incident involving one peasant in 1446 was followed in 1450–52 by the entire community refusing to recognize or pay the vicar. Most of the ten householders capitulated after excommunication by the *officialis*, but the schulz, John Grundt, held out against a mobile interdict for another five years. When Grundt did give in, moreover, he got to settle his arrears for well below one year's assessment from his seven mansus holding. New refusals scarcely a decade later marked the advent of yet another vicar. Arbitrators for the bishop and Rat together in 1475 verified customary distinctions between those holdings subject to the disputed dues and those exempt. At their request, the vicar forgave two years of full arrears and half of two more. Despite the concessions, at least two peasants held out against renewed excommunication until 1481, when they were punished by the secular authorities.[73]

By the time the men of Komorniki were again paying as they were required many other villagers had also failed to meet claims against them. The warden then also had tithes at Iwiny, where he received full payment up to 1474 and after 1479, but less than half during 1475–78.[74] Soon thereafter St. Vincent was pursuing in two separate cases delinquents from Siemidrożyce, *Czepankowicz*, Jenkowice, Sobkowice, and Jakubowice and from Janików and Jarosławice.[75] So the 1470s were not just at Radomierzyce a second crest in the mid-century wave of non-payment.

The social incidence of default on obligations varied with its intensity.

When non-payment was high, it was general as well. For example, 82 percent of expected payments from Karczyce failed in the 1430s to come to the Holy Spirit hospital (Table 10.3). In 1433 nine of the twenty-three farms were partly or wholly unworked; none of these paid. Of the remaining fourteen tenants, only three clearly met their obligations—but none of those three paid in 1434 and 1435. By 1438 Karczyce was home to seventeen tenants, nine of them survivors from 1433 and eight more recent arrivals or successors. Only six paid in full on time, three from the older set and three from the newer. But none show signs of continuous or apparently concerted default, either. The well- and the poorly-endowed paid or not with bewildering inconsistency.[76] The same happened at the hospital's own lordship of Zębice. The only tenant there to pay each year was Michael Gos, whose three-quarter mansus farm of 1433 had grown to two mansi by 1437–38. Every other, large or small, old or new, had at least one year of insufficient payment, even though only two of the ten original farms ever went deserted. Payments were incomplete, late, and often in kind or labor. But only the wholly deserted tenures failed year after year to give something.[77]

Lower rates of non-payment commonly meant a few persistent delinquents. For instance at Budziszów in the 1430s, where as little as 15 percent of payments were missed, only two men defaulted more than once. Andreas Pulis or Bartek Rusticus and usually both (each had two mansi), came up short or entirely delinquent in every year of the account.[78] Likewise in 1449–57 at Radomierzyce 70 percent of arrears and 63 percent of ultimate non-payments rested on the two mansus farm of Hans Maitraiter.[79] The consistent offenders were not characteristically among the smaller of the peasant landholders.

The responses of lords to peasants who defaulted on their obligations corresponded in part to the distinction between situations of high general delinquency and low with a few repeated culprits. This suggests an interpretive understanding. Certainly efforts to enforce lords' rights and punish offenders dominate the extant anecdotes. To judge from surviving documents St. Vincent, for instance, did nothing else.[80] But the sources for nearly all the incidental references—acts of judicial coercion by authorities which the successful plaintiff then retained—can record little else.

Yet even some coercive texts contain traces of accommodation with defaulters. The heirs to the scholtisei at Siechnice, for example, had to turn over their holding to their landowner and creditor, St. Mathias, for their hundred marks of overdue rents. This was no simple foreclosure, however, but a sale with right of repurchase for the same sum plus the value of any future improvements. Later testimony confirms that the schulz's tavern at least was then burnt down and unrestored.[81] Were the destruction and the retained rights connected? Likewise at Tyniec Mały in 1434 Abbot Jodocus did not just expel but, as the chronicle twice makes explicit, "bought out" the long-delinquent tenants.[82] Even at Komorniki, where texts from the dispute with the Środa vicars clearly imply the community's concerted refusal to pay, the victors tempered their legally enforceable claims, once releasing the schulz from the ban for far less than his full arrears and later remitting all back and some future dues. How much had this to do with the desolation of that village recorded tó explain its tax exemption in 1443?

Coercion argues for a perceived ability but unwillingness to pay. If applied with any rationality, it is to raise the cost of refusal beyond that of acquiescence. Accommodation may suggest, however, some perception by the claimant that payment was abnormally difficult and that squeezing still harder would be counterproductive. This reasoning was certainly applied by the Wrocław Rat to Komorniki in 1443. Both of its objective ingredients—economic misfortune and an alleviated response to default—were clearly present at Siechnice in 1438 and cannot be ruled out at Tyniec or later at Komorniki either. These isolated cases can only pose the hypothesis that lords accommodated default by mid-century peasants because, to some degree, they perceived non-payment as resulting from rural economic distress. It is confirmed from the responses documented in the income registers for a full range of situations for default.

In the high default conditions of the mid-1430s at the villages with obligations to the Holy Spirit Hospital signs of coercion are rare. Only a dozen of the hundreds of payments involved special oaths, pledges, guarantors, warnings, and even excommunications.[83] The hospital's accounts more often record arrangements to ease the burden its claims posed on the peasants. It accepted payment in forms other than those required, dismissed individual's arrears, and at times generally reduced the rate of an obligation for an entire village. At its own Zębice, a tenant or two each year and in 1433 and 1435 half or more of them replaced the assessed 1.25 marks per mansus with grain, livestock, and/or labor. Martin Smolin, for instance, who then had two mansi, gave in 1433 some coin and some oats and in 1434 a milk cow and six others; in 1435 he mowed to work off his rent.[84]

At the tithe villages the hospital more commonly just forgave the arrears of men like Nickel Kopaczke at Bogdaszowice in 1437, who owed sixteen groschen but "Pauper est valde. . . . Datur 6 gr . . . media dismissa est."[85] In most vills during 1434–36, between a third and a half of the peasant holders so benefited, and in other years smaller though measurable numbers. Collective privileges were also well justified. The account for Łowęcice from 1434 simply follows the heading that each mansus owes twelve groschen for tithe with "Note this year dismissed for 8 groschen because of damage from Hussites." It was the second year of general reduction there, and was paralleled elsewhere.[86] Such consistent behavior implies a conscious policy to accommodate individuals and communities in serious economic trouble.

Evidence for accommodation less commonly overbalanced that for coercion in instances where a few chronic delinquents stood out against general compliance. The one excommunicant at Ilnica was the long-recalcitrant Michael Radak, and at Budziszów, where the low overall rate may well be related to the tithe reduction given in 1434, only the two regular offenders, Bartek Rusticus and Andreas Pulis, were formally warned.[87]

Thus, even in the eyes of lords harmed by the defaults of mid-fifteenth-century peasants, much was to be attributed not to their culpability but to their economic distress. How much of the delinquency known only from lords' coercive opposition had the same origins cannot, of course, be estimated. Taken as a whole and admitting possible exceptions, however, the wave of defaults must be understood primarily to indicate peasant economic difficulty. People could no longer meet the demands their superiors had long placed upon them. The rural impoverishment so inferred in the mid-century duchy is further corroborated by direct signs of indigence, by a changing role of credit and debt in the village, and by decline in the price of peasant land.

Mentioned above was "pauper" Nickel Kopaczke at Bogdaszowice, whose arrears the hospital forgave in 1437. In all, the account book at least once so designated twelve individuals,[88]—without once making plain the intent of this expression of poverty. Taken collectively these people otherwise differed little from their neighbors. Farms of a half to two mansi covered the normal range in their villages. No "poor" paid full obligations and most were freely dismissed, but that also happened to others, and even to the same people in some years when they were not so labeled. Half came from Bogdaszowice and more than half were "pauper" in 1434, when the accounts reflect great economic distress. Nevertheless the compiler of these records saw reason to remark upon the poverty he thus detected in the countryside, and he did so for peasants both well and meagerly endowed.

Related direct signs of impoverishment occur more generally among mid-fifteenth century schulzen, villagers earlier noted for economic and tenurial independence and occasional ascent to lordship. Now the odd scraps of evidence begin to drift the other way. A telling such incident closed in 1434 the known history of the Werber-Kindelswirth lineage, schulzen at Żurawina, whose acquisition of the independent demesne at Kazimierzów in 1388 had so epitomized their rise. Caspar Kindelswirth, from the third generation to combine possession of the office and the property, sold Kazimierzów to his own village lord, Peter Stronichen.[89] Retrenchment by once well-to-do schulzen families was not balanced by rising new ones, so by 1480 village headmen had left the landowning group. Some schulzen found themselves in trouble in their own villages, too. Default on rents by the family at Siechnice in the 1430s was, given the outcome, a fair indicator that they lacked funds, but they were not the only ones to surrender lands and office to their lord. Within ten years of the Siechnice deal, schulzen were selling out to the local landowner in Damianowice, Stabłowice, Świniary, and Tyniec Mały.[90] The loss of well-being had reached the top of village society.

The place of credit and debt in village social relations shifted in ways suggesting ominous mid-century conditions and auguring ill for the future of community autonomy. Especially in a broad range of records involving repurchaseable *census* during and after the 1430s, older pluralistic and investment qualities perceptibly yielded to a landlord connection and emergency purposes. In thirteen of fourteen known *census* newly contracted between 1431 and 1441, villagers borrowed from the local landowner or persons linked to him. For instance, gertner at *Olbino* and the peasant landholder Martin Hoffman at *Polska Nowa Wieś* sold annuities to St. Vincent.[91] Miczko Crik, tenant of two mansi at *Łukaszewice* under the citizen Dietrich Wenzel in 1431, got twenty marks for his two mark *census* not from the lord himself but from the lord's own guild of taverners in Wrocław. Schulzen at the cathedral chapter vills of Oporów and Polanowice in 1458 borrowed from the cathedral vicars.[92] Conversely, the few rents then sold by villagers to persons not clearly associated with their lord were to members of the elite.[93] To judge from surviving cases, in the mid-fifteenth-century village lenders ceased to provide this form of credit and lords themselves much curbed the independent lending activity of outsiders.

Slightly later legal opinion and privilege speak in the same vein of a growing, though not yet complete, identification between lordship and the handling of peasant debt. Among precedents followed by duchy and city courts was an appellate decision from 1472 which authorized Dominic Dompnig as "erbherr" of an unnamed village to fine, sequester property, and exact corporal punishment in enforcing the sworn debt of two named tenants.[94] Three years later King Mathias gave the city of Wrocław far-reaching liberties to offset purported excesses of landlord power. According to the Rat "inhabitants of the villages, namely the peasants resident in the Wrocław, Środa, and Namysłów districts," had debts to people from Wrocław, which local lords and district courts did not help enforce. Mathias therefore permitted people of Wrocław to sue delinquent peasants in courts the city influenced (municipal, Wrocław district, and *iudicium curiae*), forbade interference by lords of debtors, and ordered other district courts to recognize the attorneys of the citizens.[95] Urban lending to peasant tenants thus did continue despite the dearth of specific documentation, but local lords did not always take kindly to these autonomous claims against their dependents. Such risks gave townsmen good reason to divert investments from rural *census* or other credits to safer places.

Beside the traces of an emerging landlord monopoly over provision of credit to villagers are signs that sales of *census* now served emergency needs for resources and thus at least bordered upon genuine subsistence loans. In 1438 five tenants at Domasław of Nicholas Skopp agreed to pay a half or whole mark annual *census* for debts already of five or ten marks, which could be redeemed for the amount owed. These villagers thus used annuities to service but not to reduce what they already could not pay. The taverner Peter Mynke secured his loan in 1438 with two mansi as well as his inn. By 1440 his debt of ten marks had grown to twenty, requiring another two mark *census*, and his landholding had shrunk to one and a half mansi. Despite the credits Peter sank deeper towards insolvency.[96] Exceptionally, Martin Hoffman of *Polska Nowa Wieś* proved able in 1459 to repurchase half of the *census* he had sold to his lord, St. Vincent, in 1441.[97] Most necessities were not so soon overcome. For instance, the one mark sold in 1466 by John Kretschmer, tenant at Rożanka under Katherine Schwenkfeld, was redeemed in 1654.[98]

Small-scale credits among villagers did remain part of everyday life. At Krępice in 1451 Peter Closse faced a threat from Martin Jesche to foreclose on his landholding for the sixteen marks it secured. At Zębice in 1435 one way such debts could arise is made clear. Wenczko Welag bought from Paweł Lutek a half mansus and agreed to pay the fourteen mark price in semi-annual installments of one mark each.[99] But fixed-term credits could be emergency expedients, too: thirteen men of Chrzanów pledged their lands in 1433 for payment in three installments of the 11.25 marks they owed their parish priest for back tithes.[100]

A final indicator of rural impoverishment are the falling amounts peasants paid one another for land. Again the only serial data come from that unusual village of peasant proprietors, Krępice, where a buoyant peasant economy was earlier seen (p. 146) pushing steadily upward the coins and the silver given for arable mansi. That postwar generations could not sustain these levels is clear from Figure 10.2. Where the eleven sales with recorded prices from 1401–27 had averaged 18.4 marks or 1475 grams of silver per mansus, the eight extant from 1431–62 came to only 13.65 marks or 637 grams. While nominal prices dropped almost a third, silver values crumbled to less than half their previous level. Properties for which more

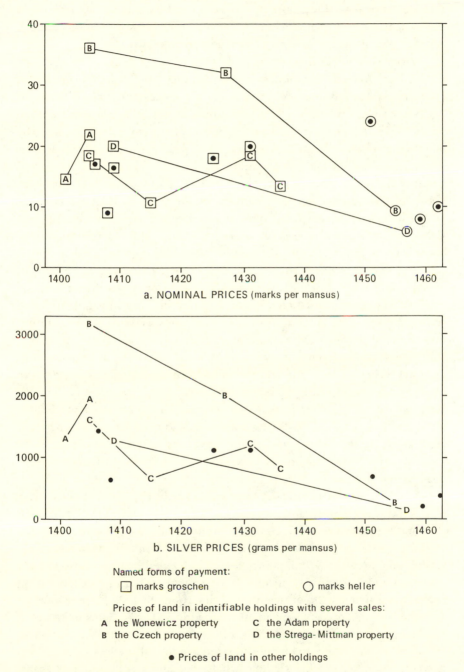

Figure 10.2
PEASANT LAND PRICES AT KRĘPICE, 1401-1462 (n = 19)

a. NOMINAL PRICES (marks per mansus)

b. SILVER PRICES (grams per mansus)

Named forms of payment:
☐ marks groschen   ○ marks heller

Prices of land in identifiable holdings with several sales:
A the Wonewicz property   C the Adam property
B the Czech property   D the Strega-Mittman property

● Prices of land in other holdings

Source: *UD*, pp. 197–299.

than one sale price is known control for different land quality and confirm the decline. For instance, the brothers Strega bought a holding of locally average value in 1409 for more than twenty marks a mansus; after their last descendant died without issue in 1457 it sold for only six.[101] In this village, at least, effective peasant demand for land had collapsed.

Lower land prices may be traced in part to fewer peasants and surplus arable, but monetary conditions were also a factor. Up to 1430 all sales at Krępice were priced in marks groschen. One transaction in 1431 was paid "halb groschen und halb heller," and then four of the last five recorded prices (1451–62) were quoted in the poor small coin which, even if the better new Wrocław heller of 1460 were used, held per mark only 58 percent of the silver of the weak contemporary groschen.[102] Thus in both form and quantity the liquid capital handled by men of Krępice had sadly diminished. If the village were in this representative of the duchy, such collective impoverishment may help explain why, as remarked above, Wenczko Welag at Zębice in 1435 spread over seven years payment of the fourteen marks for his new farm. He and thousands like him lacked the cash to do otherwise.[103]

Yet the case of Wenczko Welag and the broader evidence of land prices at Krępice contain an ambiguity that draws attention to another side of the mid-century peasant situation. One aspect suggests economic difficulty and retrogression; another reveals opportunities for survivors in an economy now short of productive labor, seeking food, and suddenly rich in unused land. Some countrymen and -women suffered; others might hope to gain. For each seller of land who realized less than once expected, there was also a buyer who gained productive resources more cheaply than before. Wenczko himself, bearer of a name not previously recorded in Zębice, got a small farm for only fourteen marks and did not even have to pay that right away. By the following May, moreover, he sat with the village assessors, a man of standing in his new community.[104] And other survivors achieved more.

Arable that former cultivators had left could be exploited by those who stayed and wanted more land. Records of the late 1430s from the Holy Spirit Hospital mention veteran villagers enlarging and immigrants establishing new farms from this resource. At Jarząbkowice Mathias Newgebawir succeeded John Newgebawir in possession of one rental mansus between 1431 and 1433 and, though paying only a part of his tithes in 1435, hung on through the worst years of default and desertion. In 1436 he took over as well the mansus Pleskotynne had abandoned in 1433–34. Thus in 1436–37 Mathias worked two mansi and in 1438, three, raising his family's farm from one of the smaller to one of the largest in the village.[105] At Ilnica three newcomers began in 1436 seeding a half, one and a half, and two mansi previously deserted, and two years later paid tithes on their new farms.[106]

Such enterprise had visible effect on the distribution of land among peasants. Even the first few decades of rural disruption shaped a pattern unlike those detected before 1430. This is shown in the later entries from the Holy Spirit hospital accounts and in similar records of Krępice in 1443 and Radomierzyce in 1449–57, all summarized in Table 10.4a and displayed in the aggregate in Figure 10.3. Comparison with earlier data (see Table 9.1 and Figure 9.1) identifies two significant shifts both in the aggregates and in the three villages (Jarząbkowice, Wróblowice, and Zębice) with records from the early and the late 1430s. Peasant holdings increased markedly in size: the modal property doubled from one mansus to two in the aggregate and in most individual places; the mean holding rose from below to well above a mansus and a half. At the same time, peasant landed endowments became more equal: the index of inequality dropped from .294 to .226 for the whole groups surveyed and comparably in two of the three villages. Fewer people had more land more evenly distributed among them in the late 1430s through 1450s than had their early fifteenth century predecessors.

Less certain is the persistence beyond the 1450s of survivors' better and more equal access to land resources. Table 10.4b and the corresponding line in Figure 10.3 summarize land distributions among peasants in six villages for which tithe obligations to the church at Środa were recorded in 1494, a decade and more after some political security had returned to the Wrocław duchy. These cultivators had the large farms familiar from the mid-century data, but also internal inequality like that common a hundred years before. But interpretation of this evidence (which is all that is extant from the later fifteenth century) poses insoluble problems. The neighborhood is not represented in other known data on peasant land distribution and is distinguished by its very early, poorly documented, German law settlement in association with the town (see p. 87 above). Without controls from another date, the possibility that the 1494 distributions here reflect influences other than those of the fifteenth century situation cannot be rejected.[107]

Information from 1494 does not, however, refute the general assertion that recorded peasant holdings were in the fifteenth century larger than before. Thus, to the extent that peasant well-being derived from access to arable resources, the average mid-century peasant had the potential to be better off than his fourteenth-century counterpart and, if the threshold of a reasonable economic subsistence in normal times approximated the one-mansus farm, the segment of the rural population operating below this margin had been much reduced. Less than ten percent of tenures fell below a mansus in the post-1438 record as compared to nearly twenty-five percent in the pre-1433 one. At Zębice, where the extant evidence is most complete and immediately comparable, eight of twelve farms contained a mansus or less in 1431, but only two of seven did in 1438.

Table 10.4. Distributions of peasant land in the mid and late fifteenth century

a. Peasant holdings in five villages, 1438–1449/57.

Place, date, and area covered	Number of tenants	Holdings at size (mansi) of:												Mean	Std. dev.	Index of inequality
		.5	.75	1	1.5	1.75	2	2.25	2.5	3	3.5	4	6.5			
Jarząbkowice 1438 on 18.5 of 18.5 rental mansi	10			3	1		4			2				1.85	.55	.223
Wróblowice 1438 on 13 of 13 rental mansi	8			2	2		4							1.62	.37	.131
Zębice 1438 on 11.75 of 11.75 rental mansi	7	1	1			1	2	1	1					1.68	.71	.234
Krępice 1433 on 14.5 of 19 occupied mansi	9	1		3	2		2					1		1.61	.96	.300
Radomierzyce 1449/57 on 12 of 12 rental mansi	7			1	2		4							1.72	.41	.097
TOTAL: on 69.75 m	41	2	1	9	7	1	16	1	1	2		1		1.70	.67	.226
% of tenants	100	4	2	22	17	2	39	2	2	4		2				
Cumulative %		4	7	29	46	49	88	90	93	98		100				
Land in holdings (m)		1	.75	9	10.25	1.75	32	2.25	2.5	6		4				
% of land		1	1	13	15	3	46	3	4	9		6				

Holdings at size (mansi) of:

Place, and area covered	Number of tenants	.5	.75	1	1.5	1.75	2	2.25	2.5	3	3.5	4	6.5	Mean	Std. dev.	Index of inequality
Popowice (pow. Śr.) on 11 of 11 rental mansi	6			1	2		2			1				1.83	.59	.192
Bielany (pow. Śr.) on 11 of 11 rental mansi	6			3			2					1		1.83	.90	.296
Chwalimierz on 13.5 of 14 rental mansi	7			1	1		4			1				1.93	.56	.132
Jugowiec on 26 of 26 rental mansi	9			2	1		1			1	2	1	1	2.89	1.24	.290
Komorniki on 39.5 of 40 rental mansi	18			4	2		7			1	1	3		2.19	1.03	.262
Ogrodnica on 22 of 22 occupied rental mansi	12	2		3	1		2			3	1			1.83	1.03	.310
TOTAL: on 123 m	58	2		14	7		18			7	4	5	1	2.12	1.14	.298
% of tenants	100	3		24	12		31			12	7	9	2			
Cumulative %		3		26	40		71			83	90	98	100			
Land in holdings (m)		1		14	10.5		36			21	14	20	6.5			
% of land		1		11	9		29			17	11	16	5			
Cumulative %		1		12	21		50			67	78	95	100			

Note. Data for Table 10.4a from HGZ, fols. 122v–23v, 124v, and 118v–119r; KLM, fol. 32; RSC 1449–57. As in Table 9.1, free and demesne land, even leased to peasant farmers, are excluded. Inhabitants of Krępice differed only in tenurial status from the other peasants here tabulated (see Chapter 9). The distribution of land among farms at Radomierzyce did not change in the nine annual listings between 1449 and 1457. Data for Table 10.4b are in Heyne, *Neumarkt*, pp. 386–91. Cumulative percentages are calculated from cumulative raw totals rather than by simple addition of the percentages themselves.

Figure 10.3
AGGREGATE DISTRIBUTIONS OF TENANT HOLDINGS IN THE MID- AND LATER FIFTEENTH CENTURY

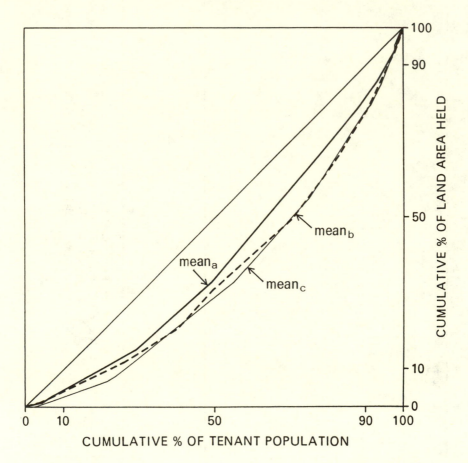

a ——— 41 tenants on 69.75 mansi in five villages, 1438–1449/57. (data from Table 10.4a)

b − − − 58 tenants on 123 mansi in six villages near Sroda, 1494. (data from Table 10.4b)

c ——— For comparison, 173 tenants on 226.5 mansi in fourteen villages, 1351–1433. (from Figure 9.1)

Note. Figure displays cumulative percentages constructed in Table 10.4 a, b. For properties of the Lorenz curve and index of inequality, see note to Figure 9.1.

Nor did the better-endowed peasants of the mid-fifteenth century lose to their lords what they could gain from the larger production of their lands. Nominal stability in per mansus rent rates during the middle decades of the century is indicated by the surprisingly sparse contemporary evidence and confirmed by the richer record around 1500. Throughout the 1430s inhabitants of the Holy Spirit hospital's lordship at Zębice owed their usual mark and a quarter plus "honors." (At times they found it hard enough to meet that claim.) In the next half century the only comparable statement of rent rates (as opposed to tithes) comes from the city of Wrocław's lands at Kowale in 1468—where one mark the mansus was precisely that demanded since before the 1360s.[108] Yet such durability of old dues was likely far more common than is explicit mid-fifteenth-century evidence for it. As is shown in the next chapter, four of the five villages where rent levels in 1500–30 can be juxtaposed with rates from 1350–1430 experienced no nominal change.

Unchanging obligations allowed peasant tenants to reap benefits from debasement. Even if a cultivator at Kowale in 1468 refrained from passing to his municipal lord counterfeit coins or bad heller and paid his rent in the city's own current minting of groschen, he thus disbursed less than half the silver so spent by his predecessor of the 1420s. Where the more common mixed payment in grain and cash was owed, peasants had less advantage.

But whether a tenant paid dues wholly or just in large part in cash, a chief opportunity during the fifteenth century came from the market for his grain. When cereal prices crept upwards in normal years and soared in the recurring shortages, those with grain to sell won the higher profits. Certainly tenant farmers controlled the largest share of the cereals produced in the duchy. Lords' demand for money payments forced such peasant producers to put on the market some portion of the crop. Rising prices then let this share be reduced and more consumed at home or else gave extraordinary returns from a fixed amount marketed.

Did peasants around Wrocław respond to the price trend favoring mid-century grain producers? The testimony of a city magnate and rural landlord in 1485, when prices may have receded from their earlier peak (see Figure 10.1 above), argues that some had. A tenant at Żerniki Wrocławskie, Paul Merot, wanted to give up his farm to the lord, Franz Bottner, pleading an inability to obtain servants. Bottner replied with a different and explicitly price-dependent explanation: "When times were good so the grain was worth much, he worked the holding. Now, however, the grain is worth little and he wants . . . to leave the holding."[109] Quite simply, those peasant tenants who survived had not only a freer supply of farmland, they also profited from an enhanced price for their product. Bigger farms left more grain to be sold and higher prices for it meant less grain went to meet the landowners' fixed claim for cash.[110]

More available land and consequently larger farms, a drop in the real value of obligatory cash expenditures, and a rise in the market price for grain have been here presented as peasant opportunities in the conjuncture of the mid-fifteenth century because they offered ways to improve economic well-being. But to treat them as such requires an assumption that people could work the land, harvest the crop, market that surplus to farm and family needs, and pay the rents. Then the peasant was well, even better, off. But the economist's assumption of *ceteris paribus* failed around mid-century Wrocław. Many peasants did not work their land; they abandoned it. Many peasants did not harvest their crops; they watched raiders take or destroy them. Many peasants did not supply to markets their surplus; they desperately demanded food. Many peasants did not pay their rents; they defaulted, pleaded poverty, and often enough had their pleas accepted. Making the potentials into reality was likely about as common as were the successive years then free from political or natural disturbance. Given some time without danger, the changed man-land ratio and the fossilized rates of expropriation could let a family which escaped the normal hazards of human biology and farm operation do well. But let the barn, house, and seed store be burned and the draft stock fill the bellies of soldiers, and then the emaciated survivors who returned from urban refuge could do little with their greater acres, and gloat little that the obligations they could not pay had in fact lost value. Opportunity was for *lucky* survivors.

What have so far been called opportunities for mid-century villagers not only required individual good fortune, they derived from the prior misfortune of other peasants who fled their lands, sought food, and died. Hence these chances for gain should be recognized as contingent upon disorder's having made necessary some remunerative efforts at reconstruction. But the disruption of rural routines itself might plausibly be thought an opportunity for peasants to pass on to the exploiters the risks of agricultural production and to use in peasant interests the exogenous weakening of authority. So to construe the fifteenth-century situation would see in it an enhanced potential for peasant resistance, whether ad hoc against randomly weakened claimants or with more systematic intentions.[111] By such reckoning, at least some of the defaulted obligations and violence in the countryside would signify not poverty and danger to peasant producers but a perceived chance to better their position.

In the Wrocław duchy, individual peasant acts of "self-help" may lie behind threats like that by an anonymous would-be arsonist against the lord of a demesne at Biskupice in 1431.[112] Vincent Schulcz defended his leasehold tenure at Prawocin in 1433 against the new purchaser of lordship there, the knight Tristran von Redern, by having the courts confirm his written title, but at Domasław in the 1440s the peasant Wawirske had to be constrained by three guarantors to take to the courts whatever claim he was pursuing against the lord, Nicholas Skopp. Wawirske had in protest refused to work his land. So, too, at Budziszów in 1452 two brothers named Schulcz pursued a feud with the abbot of St. Mary's until for peace he accepted arbitration.[113] But none of these shows so plain an intention as the peasant brothers on other lands of St. Mary near Legnica, who so effectively avenged maltreatment of their father that they won compensation, memorial masses, and immunity from retaliatory prosecution.[114]

When Wrocław duchy peasants resisted what look like traditional demands of lords, the church, or public authority, they normally did so as corporate communities led by their schulz and assessors. Whole villages, not individuals, were accused of non-payment by episcopal creditors and by the cathedral vicars during the 1430s and by officials of the Holy Cross Chapter and of St. Mary a generation later.[115] Those disputes involved rents, but village-wide refusals of tithes and other church dues are more fully documented. That at Komorniki has already been seen but deserves added mention not only for lasting well longer (1446–59 and 1470–81) than what might be thought the economic problems of even a thoroughly devastated village, but also for including community rejection of the sacrament offered by the disputant rector and lengthy defiance of episcopal excommunications.[116] Clearly something more than poverty motivated those men. Around Siemidrożyce, too, the struggle during the 1470s between the tithe claimant, St. Vincent, and schulzen and peasants from a half-dozen villages[117] gains significance from recollection that those same tithes had been intermittently disputed for almost two hundred years. In a time of troubles people tried again. St. Vincent's own tenants at Zabłoto and Kostomłoty meanwhile unleashed collective violence against toll-collecting facilities in Środa, while the community of Świniary was fined in 1468 for refusing military obligations.[118]

Of course the prime opportunity for peasant resistance to the central Silesian agrarian regime had come earlier, in the 1420s and 1430s, when Hussite ideas, examples, and military might swept northeastwards across the Sudetes. By the first Hussite offensive into the Wrocław duchy in 1428 the Silesian ruling elite had established its anti-Hussite stance and its military impotence. Was this the favorable revolutionary moment for which waiting rural masses could be aroused? Not demonstrably around Wrocław. This is not to deny the existence of individual Polish and Silesian Hussites, but the significance of them in the duchy's countryside. Unless an implausible quantity of one-sided evidence has vanished, the governing authorities from the city had by 1428 hunted local heretics for years with notably slim success.[119] Nor had they simply overlooked the reservoir of pro-Hussite enthusiasm for which the invaders hoped. The bishop's peasant levies did flee the battlefield at Nysa (like most crusaders who faced Prokop's veterans), and in an atmosphere of Hussite restraint which initially spared peasant farms enough people joined them to worry the Teutonic Order's representative in Wrocław, but that was all. The conciliatory deportment and the reports of mass peasant collaboration quickly ceased—and this despite the on-going fearful vigilance of the authorities.[120] No references to peasant support occur in narratives of later campaigns in the Wrocław area, only descriptions of indiscriminate damage and flight. King Sigismund feared in 1431 that "many people" helped supply the heretics, but the Wrocław judicial records for 1430–35 contain only ten relevant cases—including a knight and a man jailed for merely saying he would like to join the Hussites.[121] If country people around Wrocław did sympathize with the Hussite cause, they did not actively seize upon Hussite presence and military success as an opportunity to dismantle the system in which they lived.

The episode of the Hussite wars thus confirms in its ambiguity the limits to peasant resistance in the mid-fifteenth century. Conspicuously absent was mass enthusiasm for the heretics and their ideas, but so was unprovoked hostility to them in defense of the existing regime. Instead, after a period of caution in 1428, Hussite behavior provoked fear, rejection, flight, and occasional defense of the peasants' own resources against these new competitors. Subsequent disorder let individuals and communities pursue their separate interests against older predators, too. Thus from the peasant point of view (which, remember, is always only to be inferred from lords' accounts of peasant behavior), the whole mid-century storm did enhance chances for resistance, even if these were not always taken and resistance chiefly meant retention by peasants of resources otherwise transferred perforce to the lordly elite. More importantly, however, the storm just destroyed peasant resources, and they could at best seek to pass on the lords' share of the losses. From the lords' point of view, though, resistance and destruction had identical effect, a severe blow to landed incomes.

Landed interests at risk

Compared to mid-century peasants the landed elite suffered less often in their persons but no less sharply in their interests. Indeed the goods and bodies of lords could fall victim to the same hazards as those of their tenants. Thus the chronicler of St. Mary lamented the Hussites' demolition of the Brochów demesne in 1428 and the Poles' burning of Chrząstowa Mała ten years later. The knight Nicholas Stewitz got royal compensation in 1429 for harm the heretics had done him, but Lorenz Jenkwicz, lord of Galów in 1465, got nothing when Wrocław destroyed his defenses lest they serve an enemy. In 1476 the important citizen landowner Wenceslas Bank was taken hostage by Czech raiders.[122]

The impact of immediate material damage was multiplied by peasant responses to their misfortunes. Deserted land and unpaid dues shifted heavy losses to landowners. Much peasant distress is in fact known only because lords recorded and explained their own. This section argues that disruption of rural life and production caused for landowners monetary losses which, with concomitant higher expenditures, stressed the finances of the landed elite. Unremitting rural difficulties reduced the value of landed assets and influenced the management of property.

How were landed wealth and incomes affected? On occasion some lords assessed the costs. The Cistercians counted the Hussite raids of 1428 as costing Lubiąż more than five thousand marks and some four hundred malter of grain.[123] In the 1430s the provisors of the school fund at Holy Cross complained of non-payment of a twenty mark *census* from Gałów and their successors in 1478/79 received barely half the rents expected from four Wrocław duchy properties.[124] At that time the chronicler of St. Mary was lamenting the falling revenues of all Silesian lordships, secular and spiritual.[125] As Canon John Steinkeller pointed out in 1475, repair of damaged property cost a lot, too.[126]

The fifteenth-century financial ruin of once-prosperous Silesian church corporations is a commonplace of secondary studies and contemporary narrative. The Church of Wrocław, deeply enmeshed in regional politics, suffered on a scale far transcending the Wrocław duchy alone. Bishop Conrad (1417–47) was driven to bankruptcy and talk of resignation; his successor, Peter Nowak (1447–56), spent most of his tenure frantically pledging properties and incomes for the tens of thousands of florins needed to pay his mercenaries and redeem his castles.[127] Of course the disaster engulfed the cathedral chapter and its lordships around Wrocław, compelling distasteful expedients like the 1434 sale to two townsmen of a 130 mark *census* on nine chapter villages to raise 1300 marks and ransom the bishop from the brothers Czirne. Even in the quieter 1460s, when Bishop Jodocus gave to the chapter his rights over Kryniczno, the canons had to sell a 16 mark *census* and reappropriate another to raise the 665 florins needed to buy out the lay holder, Peter von Falkenhain.[128] But the troubles of landownership in the duchy are more visible on the estates of churches with more limited interests.

The hospital of St. Mathias had required trusteeship by the Wrocław city council as early as 1424 (see p. 174 above), but through mid-century the troubles of this middling corporate lord deepened. To the alienated lands of Mokronos Górny were added by 1431 those of Mokronos Dólny, while a dispute with the Jenkwicz family at Gajków first cost the hospital excommunication over a fifty mark debt and then 12.5 marks in annual incomes to cover another 225 marks it owed. When it still could not pay in 1433 it had to pledge its lands at Kamieniec, Dobrzykowice, and Bierdzany, and its mill in the city. The tax clerks in 1443 deleted Dobrzykowice and both Mokronoses from the list for St. Mathias and placed them among the lay villages. Still more land had to be sold in the 1450s and Bierdzany, briefly redeemed, again in 1471 went (with right of repurchase) to townsmen.[129]

Unlike shaky St. Mathias, the Corpus Christi Commandery had around 1400 been actively expanding its estates. But times changed for the Knights of St. John, too. By the early 1430s much of the commandery's lands lay deserted. Borów, reputedly waste for eight years, was sold in 1439 and Radomierzyce soon thereafter. Some financial help came in 1443 when the city scribe Peter Heger donated Blizanowice, though there, too, 3.75 of the 16 mansi lay empty. But continued problems caused the city to request a visitation of the house in 1448 and the Grand Master of the Order to assume direct control over it.[130]

On the much larger estate of the Augustinians, severe economic strain had set in by the 1440s and not yet abated when their chronicler wrote in the 1470s. Some financial weakness he traced to the excessive generosity of Abbot Mathias Hering (1416–29) but more dire conditions he attributed to the Hussite assaults which lasted into the abbacy of Jodocus (1429–47). Even so, when that abbot began with internal managerial reforms, the outlook for St. Mary was promising. Soon Jodocus was buying up the claims of others against abbey properties and still flush enough to sink some 161 marks or 276 florins into two silver statues of the Virgin. His ambitions misread the resources of his house. In 1440 he had to sell one new and one older image worth together more than four hundred florins, "because of the poverty of the monastery arising from the destruction of its properties by the abominable heretics and others, for paying debts contracted as a result, and especially for paying for the highest rights then purchased over Jarosławice."[131] All this, the chronicler continued, so ate up the savings made in the reforms that the wealth of the monastery had, even as he wrote in 1476, never been restored.

Abbots of St. Mary after Jodocus had problems more immediate than his old liabilities.[132] Their chronicler's litany of feuds, floods, debts, managerial failure, and forced sales is echoed by his counterpart from the rival

St. Vincent, Nicholas Liebental, and sustained in the record sources.[133] The condition of not just St. Vincent or monastic houses, but the whole church around Wrocław was caught in 1480 by the incoming abbot, John Löbschütz, who told a judge that:

> he found the monastery as if desolate and widowed without honor throughout, both in matters spiritual and in matters temporal, for scarcely ten brethren in all were to be counted and also all the demesne farms lay deserted, unfenced and uncultivated, or else alienated from the monastery.[134]

Evidence from large and small ecclesiastical estates thus concurs in depicting difficulties and crises for landed wealth.

But what of all those lay lords? Their individual economic conditions are just as obscure in the fifteenth century as the fourteenth. Neither financial statements nor estate surveys survive. What is now understood of the many grounds for property transactions is sufficient warning that personal estate histories reconstructed from conveyances imply no more about short-term yields and profits to landowners than is already known from reports of abandoned land and unpaid rents.

One fortuitously well-recorded case is, however, telling. Back in 1422 the noble Salusch family had sold *census* on their hereditary holdings in Zabór Mały to finance purchase of Zabór Wielkie. This investment made, they sold no more incomes during that decade. Nearby properties certainly suffered from Hussite raids in 1428, but nothing is said of conditions at Zabór. Then in 1430 the Salusches suddenly and heavily re-entered the credit market to borrow during the next four years through five sales of rent on Zabór Mały more than sixty marks. The sequel was not that of a decade before. By 1435 George Salusch confessed to arrears totaling 210 marks and surrendered to his chief creditor, Henry Strelin, most of the family's land in the village.[135] Thus began a generation-long slide to oblivion. In following years other landowners appear at Zabór Mały and the Salusches sold off the demesne farm itself in 1456. At Zabór Wielkie they alienated lordship over tenants in 1476, more revenues in 1492, and the last morsel of demesne in 1497. They finally disappeared after divesting relict rights at Zabór Mały in 1501.[136] Clearly, however, the early 1430s and the abrupt change then in this family's context for debt marked a shift in their economic fortunes; their critical losses of property followed before 1480.

Financial weakness like that of the mid-century Salusches and the church corporations was more general than extant account books and narratives can show. This is evident from the quantitative indicators used in previous chapters to elucidate the usefulness of landed property to those who possessed it. Trends in the price of land, in its allocation between tenants and demesne, and in grants of German law diverged from those of the previous century. A different aggregate pattern marks a mid-fifteenth-century collapse in the value of lordship.

Prices for land in transactions among fourteenth-century lords were handled in Figures 5.1 and 6.1. Demesne land then had a value higher but more volatile than rental land. After mid-century both climbed just faster than the groschen was debased. Around 1400 demesne land normally sold for something less than thirty marks the mansus (2000 or more grams of silver) and rental land went in the range of twenty-five marks (2000 grams or less). Figure 10.4 now continues presentation of the available data.

Useable records of land prices are few from the fifteenth century but give unequivocal answers to a limited set of relevant questions. Nominal and silver prices for both kinds of land crested in the first quarter or third of the century and then fell. By the 1480s silver equivalents running near 1000 grams per mansus were half the earlier peak. Two forces seem to have been at work. With respect to supply and demand, lower returns and higher risks from the possession of landed property surely made it less desirable. On the monetary side confusion of coinage and a shortage of specie had effect. For the first time in the known documentation, rural land went for gold florins rather than silver groschen in a sale of demesne at *Skaszyce* in 1472 and then in all three recorded sales of rental land during and after the 1480s. The 1472 transaction occurred just after the Wrocław and Prague mints had twice coined groschen with different silver content and the groschen-florin ratio twice fluctuated by more than a hundred percent.[137] Nevertheless, conversions at contemporary ratios consistently place the silver values of prices quoted in gold in the same ranges as those quoted in silver. At the lower prices of the later fifteenth century the historic margin of demesne over rental land vanished—probably because lords involuntarily held much land their tenants had abandoned.

Congruent with reversal of fourteenth century price relationships was a halt to the still older movement of land from demesne to rental tenancies. Instead with the 1430s some land passed from peasants to lords. An abrupt and telling such shift took place at Tyniec Mały where in 1434 Abbot Jodocus of St. Mary replaced tenants installed barely more than a decade before with a demesne worked by abbey servants. Two years later St. Mary's direct possessions there grew by another four mansi when the schulz surrendered his office and endowment.[138] For what the lord at Tyniec achieved intentionally others had less enthusiasm. At Zębice the procurator for the Holy Spirit Hospital, Martin Faulseite, tried repeatedly in the late 1430s to find someone to take over 2.5 mansi abandoned to the hospital for non-

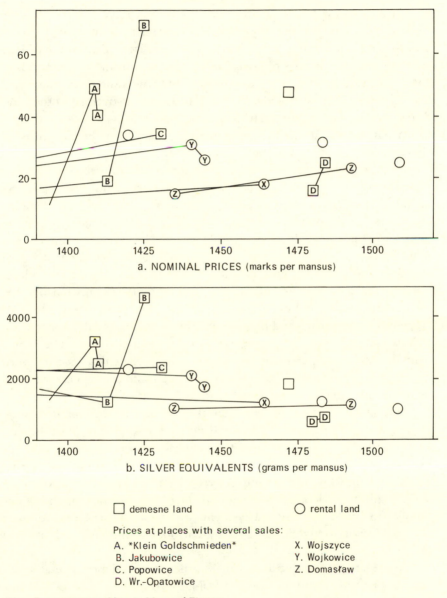

Figure 10.4
LANDLORD PRICES FOR DEMESNE AND RENTAL LANDS, 1409-1509
(16 sales in 12 places)

a. NOMINAL PRICES (marks per mansus)

b. SILVER EQUIVALENTS (grams per mansus)

□ demesne land   ○ rental land

Prices at places with several sales:
A. *Klein Goldschmieden*   X. Wojszyce
B. Jakubowice   Y. Wojkowice
C. Popowice   Z. Domasław
D. Wr.-Opatowice

Note. For sources see *Notes to Maps and Figures.*

payment of hereditary rents.[139] Such occurences would explain tax return entries like those for Brzezina, where the demesne grew from four mansi in 1425 to nine in 1443.[140] Such a reversal was unknown since before the 1350s. But can it be generalized?

Quantitative indicators of the mid-fifteenth-century balance between landlord and peasant farms suggest less a movement counter to the four-teenth-century trend than a firm halt to it. The relative distribution of land after the first two decades of crisis can be estimated from the tax return of 1443. This text distinguishes less consistently between demesne and rental lands than between cultivated and abandoned, and its coverage of the Uraz district is thin. So when a stratified profile from the 1443 record estimates 68 percent rental land and 21 percent demesne, that should be recognized as approximating the 66 percent and 27 percent from 1425.[141]

Quantitative comparison can be extended to 1480 only for the recorded presence of tenants, demesne, or both in each settlement. The 362 places inhabited in 1425 were almost evenly split among those without demesne (32 percent), with both tenants and demesne (35 percent), and entirely in demesne (33 percent). Hence two-thirds contained some rental land and the same proportion some demesne land. By 1480 some small sites had been abandoned or combined with neighbors to reduce the documented places of human habitation to 345. Of these 112 (32 percent) had only tenants, 131 (38 percent) tenants and demesne, and 102 (30 percent) demesne alone. At 70 percent with tenants and 68 percent with demesne, the difference from 1425 is minimal.[142] So the change was of trend, not structure. The retreat from demesne so important in the fourteenth-century countryside stopped during the mid-fifteenth. In the aggregate, at least, landowners were no longer dismantling their direct exploitation farms.[143]

Fifteenth-century lords ceased another activity of their predecessors, the granting of German law. Chapter 4 detailed how 95 percent of the sites ever recorded with these institutions surely had them before 1425. Not one known grant was made between 1395 and 1502.[144] This causes no surprise in view of the close connection between later phases of this movement and the shift from demesne to tenant farming. But evidence for and grants of German law are mostly independent of the conveyances used to tabu-late managerial arrangements, so they corroborate the new stability just inferred.

Aggregate quantitative data, which earlier measured incremental devel-opment in a consistent institutional setting, portray in the mid-1400s a dif-ferent situation. Familiar changes and movements cease. Lords do no longer what they had been doing, but do not undo what they had done. They seem paralyzed. And yet, partial disaggregation of data on land management sug-gests no mere petrification of conditions since 1425.

Surviving evidence identifies owners in 1480 of 328 holdings in 266 of the 345 rural settlements then in the duchy.[145] A tabulation of managerial arrangements on estates of churches and nobles shows little change from patterns earlier established there. As in 1425 about half of the properties of clerics were entirely out to tenants, something more than a quarter contained rental and demesne land, and just above a fifth were only demesne. Knightly owners simply accentuated their old emphasis on mixed or bipartite holdings: from about two-fifths in 1425 the tenancy-demesne combination rose to more than half in 1480, while those of a single type declined proportionately.

Such continuity of traditional managerial approaches did not extend to those citizen landowners whose collective participation in the shift from demesne to tenant farming so marked the countryside of the long fourteenth century.[146] By 1425 only a fifth of the rural holdings of Wrocław citizens had lacked rental tenants; more than two-fifths contained only such lands and a third were mixed. Arrangements on the 87 known citizen properties in 1480 differed. The share entirely in the hands of the owner remained the same, but that without any demesne fell to a fourth and that with both managerial forms rose above half. Looking only at the presence or absence of each kind of land on the properties of townsmen, the frequency of tenant land had not changed (79 percent in 1425 and 78 in 1480), but that of demesne land increased by more than half to 75 percent. The very group which had in the fourteenth century most actively sustained the then-dominant trend toward tenant farming reversed its practice in the mid-fifteenth. Because the quantitative data are only a counting of commonly recorded manifestations of behavior, they cannot communicate the intentions and constraints behind the acts. But understanding of lords in the mid-century crisis can grow from examination of the status and wealth groups among them.

Documented holders of lordship rights in 1480 are reconstructed in Appendix A, where the methodological difficulties and necessary qualifications are generally spelled out.[147] Landownership at the end of the crisis period is the worst covered since the early fourteenth century: the 266 places for which extant records then identify at least one owner are but 77 percent of those inhabited. The profile of lords in 1480 is, moreover, the first constructed solely from transaction charters and similar records specific to each place without the support of a major contemporary survey. The principal drawback is a bias favoring detection of ecclesiastical landowners, whose continued possession of rights needs less frequent documentation than does identification of often-changing secular lords.

With this caveat in mind (or, controlling for a smaller sample weighted towards church properties), the overall shape of the landowning group in

1480 is familiar. Ecclesiastical corporations held land in 42 percent of the settlements with known lords, nobles in 28 percent, citizens of Wrocław in 29 percent, and members of other status groups in 11 percent. Counting holdings of individual lords as in Table 10.5 gives 35 percent belonging to churches, 26 percent to nobles, 27 percent to citizens, and 12 percent to others. The complete available record thus offers no grounds to infer significant change between 1425 and 1480 in the distribution of property among status groups. The best estimate of magnitudes would place about a third of lordships in the hands of churchmen, something more than a quarter each in those of townsmen and knights, and around an eighth in other hands. This stability itself, however, departs from the fourteenth century trend, for the steady accumulation of lordships by citizens of Wrocław has been wholly checked.[148] Equally familiar are the tabulations of properties by size of estate. Fifty-two percent of holdings in small and 48 percent in large estates is no real change from the equal division of 1425.[149]

More ought not be made of such consistencies among landowners around mid-century Wrocław. They do not imply the end of a market in land or creation of permanent estate complexes with stable ownership. Ceaseless movement of rights and properties through status and market mechanisms still preserved that genuine constant of fourteenth century lordship, its cyclic structure. At Rakoszyce, for instance, Peter Stronichen assembled fragments from several holders in the early 1430s and sold the entire lordship to Peter Krig in 1436 but by the 1450s and early -60s the Krig heirs had again divided it.[150] At the same time Ulrich Luckow was working hard to pull together the legal bits into which Chwalimierz had been sliced after Agnes Vogt of Środa gave it to three daughters and a grandson in 1425.[151] As earlier, constant motion within the gross structural stability of the whole landowning elite helped shape distinctive experiences for some of its constituent groups, families, and individuals.

The preponderance of large church estates in Table 10.5 is now familiar, and their apparently greater share in 1480 a result of skewed information from that date. But the gross stability of properties with ecclesiastical claims should not conceal how financially strapped houses lost rights and revenues when they put land out on long leases or sold with right of repurchase. In the 1430s and the 1460s, for example, the Piłczyce demesne farm was worth more than 400 marks to sublords, while the bishop and Church of Wrocław retained only the woodland.[152] St. Mathias pledged Bierdzany to Henry Jenkwicz in 1432. Before the hospital foundation regained it sixty years later at a cost of more than 400 marks, no less than six conveyances among lay lords intervened and all took place before the duchy's secular courts.[153] St. Mathias had rights at Bierdzany through mid-century, to be sure, but these had lost most short-term significance.

Table 10.5. Distributions of holdings by status of lord and scale of estate, 1425 and 1480 (percentages)

	Ecclesiastical corporations	Nobles	Citizens of Wrocław	Other lords	Total
a. 1425 (n=415 holdings)					
Large estates (>2 holdings)	28	6	13	2	50
Small estates (1–2 holdings)	1	23	15	11	50
Total	29	29	28	13	100
b. 1480 (n=328 holdings)					
Large estates (>2 holdings)	33	5	8	2	48
Small estates (1–2 holdings)	2	21	19	10	52
Total	35	26	27	12	100

Note. Data on holdings of size and status groups in 1425 and 1480 from appropriate rows of Table A.2 are transformed into percentages for display as contingency tables summing to 100.

Estates of noble families seem from Table 10.5 to have changed little in share or size characteristics. But the table cannot show important and novel shifts in the location of noble properties. The disappearance at this time of relict knightly claims in small settlements south of Wrocław was more than compensated by a significant revival of noble landed fortunes along the Bystrzyca, in the Środa district, and, though they had been less challenged there, the Uraz district. In more than a dozen places where townsmen had wholly replaced knightly families around 1400, others of the latter returned by 1480. As early as 1433 the citizen Beda sold all of *Piotrowice Małe* to Wenzel Seidlicz of Samotwór; it stayed in noble hands thereafter. Another Beda lordship, Kadłup, still belonged to that man's heirs in 1443 but after 1457 to the Rimbabes and a relatively new knightly family, the Kreiselwitzes.[154] At Sośnica, where several city names appeared among early fifteenth-century landowners, Katherina, widow of John Seidlicz, took over in 1446, to be followed by her sons John and Conrad until they sold to a new townsman, Mathias Jenkwicz, in 1475.[155] Instances like this last, where thirty years of knightly lordship fall between the profiles of Table 10.5, suggest that the mid-century resurgence of noble landholding exceeded what can be measured here. Not all came at the expense of citizens: the prior of Corpus Christi sold Borów to Sigmund Parchwicz in 1439.[156]

Did the renascence of noble lordship in outlying sections of the duchy partly derive from a superior capacity of the nobles to defend their local interests? In mid-century conditions personal presence and a willingness to use extralegal coercion could help a landowner. The problem of usurped property rights around Wrocław exercised spiritual and secular authorities, from the Council of Basel in 1437 to King Mathias in 1475.[157] Particular cases justified their fears. Complaints to the duchy's court in 1454 included that Krig and Hans Runge had long seized *census* due from Piersno and *Opalin*. At least twice in the 1440s and 50s Czasław Sommerfeld at Jastrzębce successfully used strong-arm tactics, first against the Środa priory to squeeze rents from peasants at Lipnica and then against the town itself to sell beer from his illegal tavern. In both cases he eventually gained official cover for his acts.[158] But others than nobles could also play such games and victimize knightly families. For fifteen years the Luckows lost their hereditary rights over Chwalimierz to maneuvers of the soon infamous Henry Dompnig.[159]

But Henry Dompnig is for his behavior an acknowledged exception among fifteenth-century lords from Wrocław. Table 10.5 suggests his big new estate was an exception, too, for the most certain indication there contrasts the growing share of small citizen landowners and the shrinking share of large ones. While in 1425 one rural property in eight (13 percent) belonged to a townsman with more than two holdings, in 1480 these numbered but one in twelve (8 percent). Properties in small citizen estates, on the other hand, rose from 15 to 19 percent of those known.

Why the differential? Answers probably lie in the way townspeople saw in landed property a secure, remunerative, and relatively liquifiable store for surplus capital.[160] For one thing, wealth for investment in rural estate may have been less available in mid-century Wrocław than before. Eschenloer suggested profits from trade and crafts were hurt by the political conflicts[161] and surely losses in capital facilities and in returns from existing rural holdings constrained the funds available to acquire more. The city borrowed heavily and even exacted forced loans from rich citizens.[162] Wealth in the municipal debt was diverted from investment in land.

Next to the plausible shrinking of urban wealth available to buy land should be ranked its lessened allure. Endemic warfare, non-payment of rents, and the collapse of land prices threatened what had once drawn merchant capital into the countryside. Even successful city families might now decline a chance to possess rural land. The Popplaus gained their first success in trade at Legnica and in the early 1430s moved to Wrocław to achieve wealth and in 1446 a seat on the Rat. But they bought no rural land before the 1480s. In fact, when Caspar and Nicholas Popplau got Łowęcice in 1458 through a kinsman's legacy, they sold it within five years.[163] With less to invest and land less favored as an investment townsmen scaled down their estates. But buyers still had to be found and land near the city or potentially profitable without relying on peasant rent-payers still had its uses, so the shift was a marginal one, less a flight from the countryside than a collective unwillingness to hold more than a limited amount of land. This context lends meaning to both the fall of land prices and some citizens' new appreciation for demesne land.

The hazards and the opportunities of landownership in the mid-century duchy arose from the ways exogenous destructive forces diminished rural wealth and production. Those with demesnes lost capital equipment and revenue but could find their land enlarged. But to restore production in the forms to which they were accustomed required the very capital that seems to have been short. Lords with tenancies lost incomes when occupants died, deserted their farms, or failed to pay their rents; recuperation depended on peasant labor, also in short supply. It is not unlikely, however, that the rental economy suffered more and thus that the greater losers among lords were those clerics and citizens who had traditionally maintained the greatest distance from agricultural activity. For the latter land had been a surplus investment more than a source of livelihood or status. When risks rose, city people less willingly gambled for the sake of their returns, and rather cut down the size of their estates. Churchmen sustained equal but corporate financial losses. Their lands provided, however, much of their income and their own rules forbade most alienations. When forced to disinvest they retained residual rights to their estates.

The mid-century storm shook and rocked the Duchy of Wrocław by obliterating the constancy and predictability which had earlier sustained gradual, patterned, and consonant rural development. Insecurity and instability now endangered all. How did people in this society react? From lord to peasant they tried to cope, to get by, to survive. More than any major structural changes the time of troubles shifted the dynamic from one of development to one of survival.

Some people the changes of mid-century forced back from now exposed socio-economic positions. Lords from Wrocław cut back the size and scatter of their estates, giving up holdings their forebears had acquired in the Środa district and relying less on income from tenants. Churchmen surrendered annual revenues for needed capital values. Peasant farmers sacrificed production for safety when they had to (and could) and then shifted those losses to their lords by not paying dues. Vulnerable elements in the rural population were destroyed by war, disease, and famine.

Losses suffered by peasants and landowners made opportunities for those who survived or were less affected. Even by the late 1430s the duchy had vacant niches and unused resources. But conditions to invest wealth or labor in the countryside were poor. High and unpredictable risks discouraged traditional initiatives. The spread of these, in fact, halted: no more grants of German law to develop empty land or redevelop demesne farms; no further growth of landownership by townspeople. Even the involuntarily enlarged demesnes, new concentrations of resources with potential for innovative management, were not so handled. Nor did peasants seize the chance to challenge a regime that exploited them. So one important casualty was the incentive for the kinds of developmental responses available in the existing structures. The storm rather left survivors catatonic.

A paralysis of human initiative—or simply a clinging to whatever in the wreckage seemed still to work—left the rural socio-economic system to run on its own inertia for some two or three human generations. Surviving peasants took up what vacant land their households could operate and thus built larger farms more equal in size. Lords coerced defaulters whom they thought recalcitrant and collaborated with those they deemed blamelessly incapacitated. Rural institutional arrangements held their traditional courses. The balance between tenant and landlord farming stood as it had been set before the troubles began. The cyclic structure of lordship remained largely undisturbed and the gross pattern of ownership rights much the same.

In a way, then, what changed in the mid-fifteenth century was that so much did not change at all. Trends of a century or more were broken. Ordinary operations of rural institutions had repeatedly been interrupted and humans made to pay a painful price. And yet so much of the structures remained. As the winds abated people could still see, recall, or find recorded what had been. They had survived severe testing and into different circumstances. Would they rebuild along the old lines? Not all would happily exchange their new position for the old. Not all could. Not all the old foundations and old assumptions still held. As the tumult stilled men struggled to shape their own desires, some resuscitated, some new. But had there been a subtle mental shift? Much in the countryside of 1480 looks no different but the response to it of important actors was.

AFTERMATH: AMBIGUOUS RECONSTRUCTION

Illic aethero surgentes culmine montes
Mirantur segetum velut Idae Gargara spicas,
Lustrat dum Phoebus Nemeae prope sidera pestis,
Atque gregi frutices; sed opimaque pabula pastor
Invenit, optata minans in rupe capellas
Quique pecus fluidas felix comitatur ad undas.
Hinc ubi tardus adest crescentibus Hesperus umbris,
Ipse pedo saturum fumantes pellit ad aedes.
Pingue solum scindis curvo telluris aratro,
Rustice; consurgite tibi plurima semine radix.
Plena gerit stabulis pulcherimma filia mulctra;
Hinc tibi non modico candescit lacte catinus.

Silesian humanist Pancratius Vulturinus recalls his native countryside,
1506; *Panegyricus Slesiacus*, lines 71–82.

The rural order of the German law survived the mid-century storm. Peace and security after 1480 promised repair of its tattered fabric as peasants and lords joined again the threads of old relationships. They could not know what the historian's retrospect must: their generations would close what those after 1200 had opened. Not in the insecure welter of the mid-fifteenth century, but in the quiet of the years around 1500, authority and power transformed the rural duchy. While some restored what had been, others responded to contingencies of recent experience and new situations. Both belong to a Janus-faced age.

These closing chapters will not strive to capture all accessible features of rural life between the 1480s and the 1520s. The issue is the end of that German law past which has been the focus throughout. The intent here is limited to showing how, in the historic situation around 1500, beside genuine and restored continuity fundamental change took shape. The paradoxes of the process are no less integral than its decisiveness. Hence this chapter begins with the return and immediate effects of a secure rural environment and goes on to examine how lords and peasants took that occasion to repair what had been broken. The same stability let people deal with hazards and opportunities revealed by the recent past. This chapter therefore ends by considering how landowning groups modified relationships among their members and their properties in ways which ended an old structural constant, the lordship cycle. The next and final inquiry follows those lords into their lordships where, in their innovative reshaping of fundamental links with peasants and resources, they supplanted the regime of German law with that of neoserfdom.

Calm

After 1480 the surroundings of agrarian life in central Silesia slowly regained relative stability. In consequence a slow recovery of rural populations and production fostered conditions much like those before the storm.

Formal war involving the Duchy of Wrocław ended with the Peace of Olomouc in 1478 and the Jagiellonian succession of 1490; it came not again for more than a century. Memories of invasion faded. Curbing disorder was a slower task in which setbacks could mean local emergencies no less acute than before. The closing years of Mathias's reign endured the depredations of his army,[1] while the Jagiellonians mostly left the problem to regional initiative. Wrocław and other territorial authorities reiterated agreements to mediate disputes, pursue felons, prosecute crimes committed in other jurisdictions, and detain persons "die nicht herren haben,"[2] but feuds and brigandage tapered off rather than stopping abruptly.

The less frequent failures of public security drew more attention than did undramatic successes. There was "Black Christopher" von Reisewitz, who in a notorious career of *Reiterei*—large scale highway robbery, theft, and extortion—ranged with impunity across central Silesia for a dozen years. A thin line separated such a robber knight from another waging quasi-legitimate private war. Duke Bartholomeus of Ziębice, Christopher's titular lord, burned four Wrocław duchy villages in 1512 in a vain effort to save his man from the city's gallows. Sometimes even the forces of order came to mutual blows, as in the 1508–09 exchange of retaliatory raids between Wrocław and the duke of Legnica, sparked by pursuit of a brigand across the border.[3] As late as 1519, rural property holders could appreciate why the master of St. Mathias would rebuild his Siechnice mill not on the exposed old site outside the village but inside, where "if the village is guarded, so too is the mill."[4] Villages were guarded even if less threatened than a generation before.

People around Wrocław in the late fifteenth and early sixteen centuries remained alert to the natural and the monetary scourges of their predecessors. Like the political, the natural environment had stabilized. Meteorological conditions of sixteenth- through eighteenth-century Europe are reputed more constant than those of the fifteenth, though sharply cooler than during the high Middle Ages.[5] Not overall climate but frequent and violent variability of weather helped cut agricultural production in the mid-fifteenth century, and this certainly moderated. Contemporaries thought noteworthy only brief summer floods in 1501 and 1515 and a drought in 1532.[6] Food shortage and pestilence diminished, too. Wrocław's chroniclers report during 1480–1530 just three famines and those much mitigated by effective use of municipal grain reserves as in 1472.[7] The fifty-year period suffered only six episodes of plague, which witnesses make out to be less long and virulent than earlier ones.[8]

Much less good may be said of Silesian mints and their products. The dreary tale of many different bad coins and repeated vain reforms dragged on into the 1540s (see Appendix B). With no dependable circulating medium and silver supplies at least somewhat short into the early 1500s, the economically active in Silesia grasped all sorts of stratagems. The Popplaus, major Wrocław merchants at the turn of the century, kept their books in Hungarian florins, with which they traded in Poland, Bohemia, and Hungary, but to the west they dealt in Rhenish florins worth 25 percent more and at Wrocław itself in marks valued at a hundred to 171 Hungarian florins.[9] The noble Reynbabe brothers sold to the vicars of Holy Cross in 1514 an annual *census* of six "heavy Hungarian florins or as much other coin as makes up a florin" and set the repurchase price at sixty "sufficiently heavy" florins.[10]

To lesser folk groschen and heller mattered. A contemporary remarked in 1511 how Wrocław's commoners suffered from confusion among several heller valued at anywhere between eight and twelve to one kind of groschen or another. In 1514 the cathedral chapter and the people of Jagodno had to ask a mediator whether 48 or 32 "white groschen" constituted a "legal mark."[11] Most inventories and accounts from this period specify coins and exchanges, but now as then, uncertainty stalks efforts to work out silver values and compare payments over time.

Retreat of war and reduction of tempest, famine, and plague, if not ordering of monetary chaos, restored to the agrarian economy aspects of normalcy missing for more than two generations. With a rebound of rural populations, trends in food supply, prices, and rents, levels of default on obligations, and relations between demesne and rental lands returned to patterns resembling more those of the late fourteenth century than of the mid-fifteenth.

Silesia surely shared sixteenth-century Europe's population growth, but no precise chronology of the new upswing is demonstrable for the country-side around Wrocław.[12] Without even plausible surrogates for aggregate rural numbers, the trend must be inferred from general indicators of labor supply and reduced, but not yet absent, signs of empty farmland. This evidence suggests a slow process of repopulation that had by 1530 not yet regained levels of a century before. Certainly complaints of labor shortage did not end with Paul Merot's plea that farm servants were unobtainable around Żerniki Wrocławskie in 1485. Fifteen episcopal villages near Wrocław where thirty-one gertner lived in 1421/25 had only fourteen in 1530.[13] Rural employers wanting cheap labor set maximum wages, forced able-bodied vagrants to work or leave, and hired migrant harvesters from Poland.[14]

The slow growth so hinted at can be confirmed only by haphazard records of settlement and desertion at specific sites, for this time offers no extensive surveys. In the six villages of the duchy near Środa where the town's rector claimed tithes in 1494, he marked as deserted only eight of 148 mansi, but several tenants had recently taken over abandoned holdings. Twenty years later the then incumbent, John Ruster, who could not have assumed his post before 1497, reported that at some unspecified earlier time he had for the duration of his tenure converted to cash the full grain tithes of Komorniki "nam eadem villa erat deserta et quasi in nichilum redacta."[15] Sale charters and other texts refer in passing to desertions at particular places, many of them demesne farms. A half century after Abbot John Löbschütz complained about St. Vincent's "allodia deserta," Buczki, Janowice, *Niebelschütz*, Zurawiniec, Strachocin, Chrząstowa Mała, *Łażany*, and *Krostów* were still not all worked.[16] No wonder the Kolovrat agreement between the Silesian Estates and the Church of Wrocław in 1504 devoted a long article to restoration of lands left empty by their former cultivators.[17]

Set beside signs of unused arable resources the richness in food for which early humanist panegyricists lauded Wrocław,[18] and there is good reason for the decline of grain and land prices from their mid-century levels. Figure 10.1 showed a slide from the 1470s into the 1520s of both nominal and silver prices for cereals, though it may be more noticeable in fewer mentions of famines and grain price inflations than in lower "normal" levels. This impression gains support from Franz Bottner's 1485 allegation that grain had cheapened.[19] Perhaps the best generalization now presentable is that during the years around 1500 cereal prices were subject to less violent fluctuation than a half century before, and that their levels lay below those both of that earlier and of a later time.[20] The implication is an improved supply from fields and farmers less subject to human or natural harassment.

That land, too, remained on a buyers' market around 1500, the meager evidence of prices indicates (review Figure 10.4). The peasant series from Krępice stops after 1462, and only five landlord prices are to be found between 1480 and 1509. Yet these have some interest. Three of the five were for florins, not groschen, reflecting the drift away from the latter coin in large-scale transactions. And all prices are distinctly low in comparison with those of the fourteenth century and the 1440s. Even assuming (as for Figure 10.4) that groschen prices were paid in Bohemian rather than Mathias's weaker coins, both demesne and rental lands were going for half or less the amounts of silver given during the lowest fourteenth-century periods for each.

Think for a moment of grain and land as elements in an agricultural production system, and their prices as derived from market supply and demand. In terms of silver both price levels around 1500 were lower than in the mid-fifteenth-century, while that for grain was higher and that for land lower than in the fourteenth. These relationships may be hypothesized to reflect a situation in which (1) the landed population was still as a result of mid-fifteenth century losses below late fourteenth-century levels, so land remained surplus; but (2) market demand for the product of the land, grain, moved, with a growing population, towards that of around 1400, though in a situation of continuing tight silver supplies. Conditions around 1500 thus more closely resembled those of a century before than they did those which had intervened, and the differences between 1500 and 1400 were a continuing result of the intervening events.

Earlier chapters showed that lords' prices for land did not simply and directly reflect peasant demand. Traditionally, at least, landowners in the Wrocław duchy viewed land as a source of revenues, much of which came from rent rather than market sales. Good information on rent levels was a great gap in the data available from the mid-fifteenth century, even though difficulties in the making of other kinds of payments then were well confirmed. Now, however, rich records of peasant obligations and their payment show long-term nominal stability, real decline, and much less default. Here, too, the countryside of about 1500 looks more like that of 1400 than that of 1450.

Table 11.1 summarizes nineteen statements of major tenant obligations extant from 1481 to 1532. Six of these are from three villages where dues and their payment can be tracked year after year; in eight more a late record can be juxtaposed with an earlier one from the same place. Consider first such well documented villages. Rents traceable within the period now studied were taken in cash alone without change of nominal rates. Peasants at Tarnogaj owed the same 1.75 marks per mansus in 1532 as their forerunners in 1481, while the two marks of their contemporaries at Małuszów went

Table 11.1. Major tenant obligations, 1481–1532 (rates per mansus)

| | | Late fifteenth- early sixteenth-century rate | | | | | | Compare last known earlier rate (if any) | | | | |
| | | Money dues | | Grain dues | | Total obligation | | | Nominal | | Total obligation | |
	Date	Nominal marks	Grams silver	Measures	Grams silver equivalent	Grams silver equivalent	Measures grain equivalent	Date	Money (marks)	Grain (measures)	Grams silver equivalent	Measures grain equivalent
Tarnogaj	1481	1.75	109.2	0	0	109.2	10.4					
Popowice [Śr.]	1494	.62	37.4	12	122.9	160.3	15.7					
Wierzbica	1496	1.17	71.6	12	122.9	194.6	18.9					
Siechnice	1500	.5	30.7	12	122.9	153.6	14.9	1354	.5	12	173.8	18
Matuszów	1502	2.0	122.8	0	0	122.8	11.8					
Kulin	1509	1.5	92.1	0	0	92.1	8.8					
Domasław	1514	2.0	122.8	12	122.9	245.7	23.8					
Mędłów	1518	2.5	149.0	0	0	149.0	14.7					
Brodno	1523	.67	39.7	0	0	39.7	3.9	1410	.67	0	42.9	8
Chomiąża	1523	.5	29.8	0	0	29.8	2.9	1410	.33	0	21.4	4
Lipnica	1523	.33	19.8	0	0	19.8	1.9	1410	.33	0	21.4	4
Kotowice [Trz]	1523	1.0	59.6	0	0	59.6	6.0	1294	.375	12	100.4	18.3
Zębice	1529	1.25	66.0	0	0	66.0	7.3	1430	1.25	0	80.4	15
Biestrzyków	1529	1.0	52.8	0	0	52.8	6.0					
Mędłów	1531	2.5	132.0	0	0	132.0	14.7	1518	2.5	0	149.0	14.7
Czernica	1532	1.85	97.9	0	0	97.9	10.9	1273	.5	0	68.8	12.5
Muchobór Wlk.	1532	3.3	160.0	0	0	160.0	19.4	1291	.5	12	134.8	24.5
Małuszów	1532	2.0	105.6	0	0	105.6	11.8	1502	2.0	0	122.8	11.8
Tarnogaj	1532	1.75	92.4	0	0	92.4	10.4	1481	1.75	0	109.2	10.4
MEAN (n = 19 cases)		1.48	83.7	2.5	25.9	109.6	11.3					
median		1.5				105.6	10.4					
mode		2.0		0		100+/−10	11+/−1					

Note. Sources: WAA I, IV a 41–43, *sub annis notis*; Heyne, *Neumarkt*, pp. 386–388; Pfeiffer, *Patriziat*, p. 218; *UD*, pp. 69–70 and 164; WAA I, III d 34; WAA I, III d 13–16, *sub annis* 1518 and 1531; Wutke, "Oybin," pp. 40–41; Domański and Sille, pp. 209–213; WAP, AMW, Q29, 1, fols. 2 and 4r; WAP Rep 15, 228, pp. 44–52. The supplemental entries for comparison are from Figure 6.3.

The shorter span of time permits a presentation of data different than for the long fourteenth century in Figure 6.3 and Table 6.3, but the procedures are the same as there described. Marks are marks groschen, converted when necessary. Grain obligations in the main part of the table are converted to silver equivalents at 8 groschen (.17 mk) the measure using the 1487–1516 groschen of 1.28 grams silver.

back at least thirty years and the 2.5 marks of those at Mędłów at least thirteen. Nominal stability extended from the early fifteenth or even the mid-fourteenth century at another four of five known early sixteenth-century villages. Only at Chomiąża was a pre-war rate plainly raised, though not enough to compensate for less silver in the groschen. All the more did those unchanged lose silver value.

This picture of nominal stability and real decline in rent rates requires adjustment when all evidence from around 1500 is taken into account. The villages in Table 11.1 averaged a hereditary obligation of 1.48 marks plus 2.5 measures the mansus, or, with conversions appropriate for this period, the equivalent of 109.6 grams of silver or 11.3 measures of grain. Similar information a century older was summarized in Table 6.3: nineteen village rent rates from 1386 to 1430 averaged .98 marks cash plus 7.4 measures of grain, which then worked out to total values of 125 grams silver or 19.9 measures. Between the years around 1400 and those around 1500, then, average money dues rose by about half and average grain dues dropped by two-thirds, so the shift from grain to money had continued. In total value, however, hereditary dues had not kept up with movements of price and currency. The equivalent from a mansus of rental land around 1500 was more than 10 percent lower when measured in silver and more than 40 percent lower in grain than it had been a century before. If rental incomes set sale values for land, no wonder lords were paying and accepting less. For tenants, however, the slow rate of economic recovery meant some of the good aspects of the mid-fifteenth century lingered even as the insecurity which had caused them faded away.[21]

If early sixteenth-century peasant farmers benefited from the common survival of hundred-year-old rent rates, they (and their lords) also enjoyed a renewed ability to pay what they were assessed. Rates of default at well-recorded villages after the 1480s were sharply lower than before. From Tarnogaj the mansionarii of the Holy Cross church recorded payments of hereditary rent in almost every year from 1464 to 1512/13. In the twenty-two full annual accounts kept from 1481/82 to 1512/13 the village paid in full in twenty years. In the other two years defaults totalled 2.5 percent of the annual assessment, so that for the whole twenty-two years 99.8 percent of rents were paid and only 0.2 percent defaulted.[22] At Małuszów, lordship rights belonged to the mansionarii of the chapel of the Virgin in the cathedral; their rent roll is complete for twenty-one years between 1502 and 1532. Defaults are there recorded for most years, seventeen, and on average about one peasant in seven failed to pay in full each year. The shortfall in rent totalled, however, only 7.6 percent of the amount required.[23] A third extant account was kept less tidily by the cathedral vicars for Mędłów in 1518–24 (and again after 1531). Here three tenants paid consistent amounts each year the record is complete, though in each case the collector always accepted without comment a little less than what the assessed rate should have required. Since the fourth tenant gave the assessed amount each year, Mędłów provides no evidence of recognized defaults at this time.[24]

Obligations other than rents on hereditary tenancies show the same pattern. The tenant of a Rożanka garden belonging to the Holy Spirit Hospital paid his half mark without fail from 1498 to 1515 and those who owed from land in suburban *Platea Romanorum* a mark to an altar in a Wrocław parish church paid annually from 1512 to 1540.[25] Two long-running tithe accounts kept by the assistant warden at the cathedral are similar—and thus differ from their own earlier parts. From Iwiny entries survive from 1471–88 and 1497–1525. The two mark tithe came in every year without fail between 1480 and 1524; defaults were noted in 1475, 1477–78, and 1524/25. For Radomierzyce the continuous record from 1480 to 1526 shows no or partial payment only before 1485 and in 1524/25. The one year after 1490 in which the canon failed to receive his due from these two villages he even knew to blame "the Lutherans."[26] Short of heretical intervention, the world had returned to normal; obligatory payments were made and accepted.

One more "normal" or traditional aspect of the late fifteenth and early sixteenth century around Wrocław was continuity in basic managerial structure, the organization of rural land into demesne farms and peasant tenancies. As for 1480, distributions of land cannot be measured, but continuing runs of conveyances and other texts still permit tabulation of settlement types. Reference to the comparative static profiles constructed in Appendix A (Table A.3) indicates, again as for 1480, little change since 1425 in the nature and organization of the settlements that made up the countryside of the duchy. A few more places had disappeared or been absorbed by neighbors and a few more previously known only as demesne farms give evidence of some tenants. Nevertheless, up to 1530 this indicator shows no sign of major change in the kinds and distributions of important rural institutions. Not quite two fifths of the duchy's settlements contained both demesne and tenants, a third held only tenant cultivators, and just under a third were landlord farms alone.

The improvement of rural security after 1480 brought with it conditions more like a century than a half century before. To reiterate: populations regained their numbers, land came back into cultivation, grain prices came back down from a mid-century peak, nominal rents held or advanced slightly beyond earlier rates just as they had around 1400, peasants again paid those rents, and basic organizing structures remained unchanged. That intervening depopulation and debasement had for some such features modified meaning (land prices) or value (prices and rents expressed in silver equivalents) does not confute the continuity thus reestablished across the chasm of mid-century. The similarities comprehend most of the indicators which earlier framed discussion of the economy of the long fourteenth century.[27]

Yet the countryside of 1500 was not that of 1400 *redivivus*. Human actions were contingent upon intervening experiences, especially since few people active in the last two decades of the fifteenth century could have known the first two. While some grasped again old institutional tools and followed old ways, others took up new weapons to defend and improve pregnantly novel positions. Hence what follows looks next at traditional responses to the return of stability—incentives for arable expansion; peasant prosperity on larger holdings with good market access; estate-building by church- and townsmen—but then at behavior attuned to different socio-economic imperatives—new roles for citizen lords and their properties; the shifting character of municipal and noble estates; a consequent change to the cyclic structure of lordship. No age of transition is simple.

Picking up the pieces

The relative quiet of the late fifteenth and early sixteenth centuries let people in the countryside around Wrocław take up strategies and goals that troubled times had pushed aside or thwarted. Written records or other traces attested to the way things had been, and suggested how they might again be.[28] Folk in central Silesia knew how to gain from bringing together willing peasant workers and empty land, no matter that in 1480 not climax forest but two or three human generations of second growth covered the soil. They were familiar with customary patterns for organizing rural communities, operating peasant farms, and trading on the market. Churchmen found in their chartularies privileges just as useful to a fifteenth- as to a fourteenth-century abbot or prior. Merchants and master craftsmen in a city loyal to a Jagiellonian could see from their peaceful walls the same places to invest surplus funds as had those subject to a Luxemburg. To take up where others had left off, to restore what once had been, to build further in familiar directions, such human efforts adjusted new and restored conditions to an existing socio-cultural heritage. Time-tested modes of behavior were again appropriate.

To recover from the rural depopulation, reduction of arable, and loss of incomes suffered during the mid-1400s, Wrocław duchy lords and peasants turned again to time-tested methods, namely grants of land with years free from obligations and *locatio* of tenants under customary norms of German law. The appeal to past practice was explicit. In a charter of 1500 Master Andreas Heune of St. Mathias told how, after the wars had stopped, he had publicly proclaimed in Wrocław his offer of customary freedoms to those who would take up deserted land. The diploma attests to his success. It gives to Martin Cubitz two mansi at Siechnice with full rights of inheritance and alienation in return for the same dues recorded there since the mid-1300s. Almost twenty years later a successor to Heune, Master Erhard Schulz, was still articulating the same notion of restoring that which once had been. To refute Wrocław's allegation that his new mill at Siechnice illegally diverted the Oława, he explained that two had stood there until war destroyed village and mills alike, leaving only a place still called "die gebrante mole" and another where remains of a sluiceway were visible. The village had been "rebuilt" ("widergebawt"), and now he would likewise replace the two old with one new mill.[29]

Conscious intent to reconstruct the countryside by traditional means and to traditional norms went beyond one hospital foundation. The agreement of 1504 between the Church of Wrocław and Silesian territorial authorities gives long passages to the handling of ecclesiastical dues from resettled properties. A leitmotif is behavior "nach alter Gewonnhait" as "in den verganngen Jaren gegeben," be it for the form of tithe or other payment, the rate of assessment, or the procedures for actual receipt. Empty lands in Silesia, the parties assumed, would be restored through traditional grants of years without obligations and the church, too, was to observe such "until the properties are brought into cultivation and their freedom has expired."[30] Already two years before, King Władysław had issued to the Wrocław citizen Hans Haunold a familiar-sounding permission to put out his demesne farm at Złotniki to hereditary peasant tenancies and erect a privileged tavern there.[31] It is the last known *locatio* from the Wrocław duchy and the only one after the 1390s.

Effective and extended use of customary incentives to cultivate abandoned lands is especially well documented from the lordship of the cathedral mansionarii at Małuszów. The early sixteenth-century rent book records repeated successful grants of such land with initial years free from obligations.[32] Bartusch Keyser took up a deserted half mansus in 1503 and received four years of freedom, which he can be seen enjoying in the following years' accounts. Bartusch joined Paul Szala, whose exemption had a year to run in 1504/05, and was himself then joined by three more men who took up 2.25 mansi among them and would begin to pay rents only in 1509 or 1510. Later Bartusch and at least two of the others are visible with their lands productive and paying rents. Then Andreas Lissag accepted in 1515 a mansus with liberty for two years and carried through the agreement to become a long-time resident of the village.

In 1520 the lords of Małuszów for the first time departed from their traditional way of promoting restoration of uncultivated land. They gave 1.5 mansi which "seint etzliche Jar wuste gelegen" to the taverner not as a customary tenancy with free years but on a two-year lease for a money rent set at half the traditional rate. The taverner so held and paid in the next two accounts. After a gap in the record, this was in 1528 the new norm. During each of the next four years three or four peasants were paying small sums for tenure of "agri deserti;" on the one such holding measured in mansi Wenzel Brosky worked ¾ mansus for only a half mark rent, one third the customary rate.

A listing of agreements made at the village court session of 10 October 1531 encapsulates the stepwise shift from tradition to innovation in the handling of abandoned arable at Małuszów. Andreas Wurff was treated in time-honored fashion, getting four years free to take up an empty half mansus, rebuild the ruined house, and then pay the "censum antiquum." Lorenz Ossig, Gregor Schoda, Hans Brosky, and Wenzel Brosky entered individually into holdings of "agri deserti" totaling 3.75 mansi from which they were to pay annual dues a half or a third the customary rate. A sixth peasant, Stephen Rigan, tenant since at least 1528 of the very farm Andreas Lissag had once restored, also came before that village court—to be fined 1.25 marks for seeding deserted fields without the lord's permission.

Available farmland and customary incentives to bring it into use gave opportunities for peasant survivors of the mid-century storm and their children. More abundant resources per capita thus sustained an Indian summer of prosperity for the traditional German law peasantry of the Duchy of Wrocław.[33] In the years around 1500 landed wealth and equality among peasant household farms were notably high, tenant communities achieved social stability, and their members dealt on local and regional markets for land and its products.

Extant surveys and rental accounts document larger holdings and greater equality among landed tenants between the 1490s and early 1530s than in former times. One body of data so demonstrating came from the six villages near Środa where the town's parish priest recorded the farms which owed him payments for tithe in 1494. As already tabulated in Table 10.4b above, those fifty-eight tenants averaged just over two mansi each and in several places the most common holding was that large or larger. No other assemblage of peasants in the duchy is ever recorded with farms of such size (no other collection of data included villages from this area, either). But large peasant farms were not at this time peculiar to the vicinity

Table 11.2. Distributions of tenant holdings (*mansi censuales*) in eight Wrocław district villages, 1504–1532

Place, date, and area covered	Number of tenants	Holdings at size (mansi) of:												Mean	Std. dev.	Index of inequality
		0.5	1.0	1.25	1.5	1.75	2.0	2.25	2.5	2.75	3.0	3.25	3.5			
Matuszów 1504 20 of 20 rental mansi	13	1	3	1	3	1	2	1		1				1.54	.44	.230
Biestrzyków 1514 10 of 10 rental mansi	4						2				2			2.50	.50	.085
Mędłów 1518/24 8.5 of 8.5 rental mansi	4				1		1		2					2.125	.41	.104
Mędłów 1531 8.5 of 8.5 rental mansi	4				1		2				1			2.125	.54	.137
Matuszów 1532 20.5 of 20.5 rental mansi	9			1	1	1	2	1			1	1	1	2.29	.72	.178
Czernica 1532 18 of 18 rental mansi	12		6	2			2			2				1.50	.67	.249
Muchobór Wlk. 1532 32 of 32 rental mansi	19	1	3		4		10		1					1.63	.50	.154
Tarnogaj 1532 11.5 of 11.5 rental mansi	12	3	7		2									0.96	.29	.179
TOTAL: on 129 m	77	5	19	4	12	2	21	2	3	3	4	1	1	1.68	.70	.226
% of tenants	100	6.5	25	5	16	2.5	27	2.5	4	4	5	1.5	1.5			
cumulative %		6.5	31	36	52	54.5	82	84	88	92	97	99	100			
Land in holdings (m)		2.5	19	5	18	3.5	42	4.5	7.5	8.25	12	3.25	3.5			
% of land		2	15	4	14	3	32.5	3.5	6	6.5	9.5	2.5	3			
cumulative %		2	17	21	35	37	70	73	79	85	95	97	100			

Note. Sources: WAA I, III d 34, *sub annis* 1504 and 1532; Dittrich, "Eckersdorf," p. 252; WAA I, III d 13–16, *sub annis* 1518 and 1531; WAP Rep 15, 228, pp. 44–51; and WAA I, IV a 43, *sub anno* 1532. Free holdings of schulzen and priests are omitted.

of Środa. An early sixteenth-century sample of villages and tenants from the district of Wrocław is given in Table 11.2.[34] The most common farms were as big as those around Środa. An average of 1.68 mansi neared the 1.70 known from two mid-century Wrocław district villages and exceeded the 1.5 mansi found there before the 1430s.[35] Fifteenth-century gains were thus sustained into the sixteenth.

The rise in landed endowments affected most tenants in the Wrocław district; wealth did not there polarize. Average farm sizes differed from village to village, but the index of population inequality (.226) and the average village by village index (.164) are as low as or lower than in the late 1430s and 1440s there. Tenants had more even access to landed resources than before the crisis.[36] As Figure 11.1 shows, however, peasants near Środa in the mid-1490s were less equally endowed—though still more than in other parts of that district a century before.

How much were large and more equal peasant farms intermediate results of improved physical security after the wartime decimations and how much factors independently promoting reduced defaults and greater stability of peasant populations? Sparse data cannot test such causal hypotheses. The Małuszów rent book does, however, reveal among tenants in the first third of the sixteenth century sharply lower rates of turnover than in the earlier hard years. In the Holy Spirit accounts from the 1430s, one tenant in ten disappeared from one year to the next; with many not replaced, the population fell. At Radomierzyce in the 1450s numbers held but five of seven initial householders were gone after nine years. During 1502–32 at Małuszów almost every vacancy was filled. But with an average annual change of only one in twenty, turnover of half the tenants took almost ten years. Six of the nine sitting tenants in 1532 bore surnames continuously recorded there since 1502.[37] Still greater stability occurred at Mędłów, where three of four individuals present in 1518 were still there nineteen years later.[38] Stable peasant communities were formed by durable peasant families.

The same tenant families actively engaged in lively local markets for land and supplied agricultural commodities to the towns. Incidental references to land transactions among peasants are almost numerous. Records from lordships of the Holy Trinity Hospital seen by the eighteenth-century antiquarian Klose once even gave prices—ranging from eight to twenty-four marks the mansus at Klecina in the late 1480s, for instance.[39] At Mędłów in the late 1520s a sale moved a half mansus from the farm of Wyczek to that of Woytek.[40]

Of peasants dealing in land the Małuszów rent records again give the

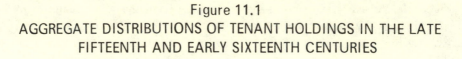

Figure 11.1
AGGREGATE DISTRIBUTIONS OF TENANT HOLDINGS IN THE LATE
FIFTEENTH AND EARLY SIXTEENTH CENTURIES

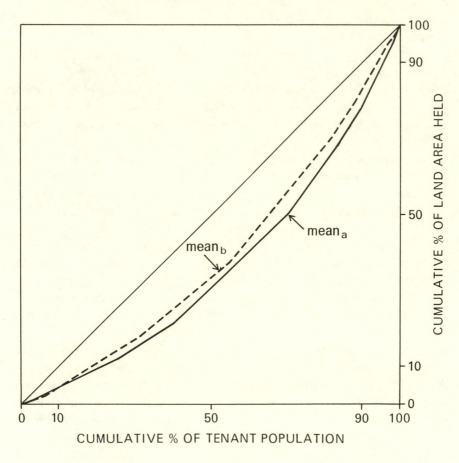

a ——— 58 tenants on 123 mansi in six villages near Środa, 1494. (from Figure 10.3)
b – – – 77 tenants on 129 mansi in eight villages in the Wrocław district, 1504–1532. (data from Table 11.2)

most orderly demonstration, showing fifteen cultivated parcels changing hands in their thirty-one year span. Land moved between persons of the same surname (which may be construed as involving kinship links), and with no known prior connection. In eleven cases an existing tenement passed whole to a new cultivator, but four plainly transferred land from one farming unit to another. The complex liveliness of early sixteenth-century peasant society is best conveyed through an individual case assembled from this rich account.

The known career of Bartusch Kosel manifests several relevant processes.[41] He entered the roll of tenants at Małuszów in 1506 by paying rents for 1.375 mansi, half the amount cultivated since at least 1502 by Simon Kosel who, moreover, also had 1.375 mansi in 1506. Some years of account are missing here, but by the next, in 1511, Simon had passed from the scene and Bartusch paid for the full 2.75 mansi. Is it safe to infer that Simon had been an elder kinsman (father?) of Bartusch who endowed the latter with half the family holding in advance of his full inheritance? In the next year (1512), however, Bartusch reduced his farm to two mansi by transfering .75 mansus to the previously unknown and landless Jacob Keiser. This man had trouble meeting his rent payments, kept that land for four years, returned it to Bartusch, and vanished. In the late 1510s Bartusch was again the largest tenant in Małuszów.

Bartusch had more opportunities. A fellow tenant, George Polsky, died in 1520 after three years' unsuccessful struggle to work the 2.25 mansi he had taken over from Peter Lessky. Bartusch bought from the heirs 1.25 mansi of this farm (which had not been broken since 1511),[42] and thus in 1521–22 had four mansi, the largest farm known in the Małuszów accounts. This much he did not keep. When a lacuna in the record ends in 1528, Bartusch had two mansi and (his son?) Martin Kosel, one. The two mansi Bartusch retained at least through 1532 made him no longer a large but a middling tenant; he sat, however, on the village court in both 1529 and 1531, the only years in which the rent book gives its membership. A long-time and respected village resident dealt actively in village land.

Evidence of peasant marketing comes from sources generated away from the villages. Some report actual occurrences. A contemporary added to two Wrocław chronicles notice of August floods in 1501, and explained the city's subsequent shortage of bread and beer by mention that high water had prevented villagers from bringing foodstuffs there.[43] Municipal ordinances and court cases from the previous decade fined peasants and townspeople who tried to arrange sales before grain reached the marketplace; laws of the 1520s added similar rules for wool.[44]

Other references make general assumptions, as when Pancratius Vulturinus lauded the cheap victuals "you will find from an ample circle" around Wrocław or when Franz Bottner or the cathedral chapter connected grain prices to peasant behavior.[45] Perhaps an item of city propaganda put normal expectations most clearly. In a 1509 petition that the king restore its staple right over the transit trade, Wrocław argued that bringing in more merchants and shippers would benefit peasants because the ensuing demand for grain, food, and fodder would drive prices up. This in turn would be good for nobles, said the town, because then peasants could better pay their rents.[46] Available markets contributed to the well-being of peasants near Wrocław, but even their prosperity always remained within the web of lordly claims.

Landowners behaved after 1480 as if waked from a fifty-year nightmare. Clerics and citizens of Wrocław especially took up where they had left off. Managers of church estates hurt during mid-century aggressively restored their previous strength. Landowners from the towns expanded their rural interests at rates reminiscent of their late fourteenth-century predecessors.

The best examples of a rejuvenated clerical enthusiasm for careful hus-bandry of landed wealth are the substantial monastic estates, all of which were around 1500 the responsibility of active, effective, and, coincidentally, long-serving corporate leaders. As the particular situation of a house al-lowed or required, such abbots or masters resettled empty lands, monitored traditional incomes, reclaimed rights and properties once sold, pledged, or usurped, and rationalized their interests through selective purchases or sales. Of course such thrusting could raise conflict with competitors, but into the 1520s most monastic estates had again become successful economic enter-prises, though some risked ambitions outstripping their capital resources.

In most respects St. Vincent provides sufficient illustration. John Löb-schütz became abbot of that deteriorated house in 1480 and until 1505 la-bored for its restoration.[47] He began at the center, the abbey's home lordship in *Olbino*, where mills and fishponds were rebuilt, more of the latter, a tavern, and other buildings constructed, and the adjoining property called *Rzepina* regained through a testamentary donation. Abbey estates sold or pledged by his mid-century predecessors he redeemed: Opatowice for 312 marks in 1484; Grabiszyn for a thousand in 1490. In 1492 the abbot ended a decade-long dispute with neighbors to the abbey lordship of Krobielowice. For a thousand florins he bought them out, obtaining the village of Wojtkowice and its subordinate demesne *Gąska*. Rights over lands at Pracze Widawskie and/or Widawa came from another testamentary gift in 1500. During his last decade John devoted more effort to abbey lands out-side the Wrocław duchy—and to paying for all of this with credits totalling more than 1500 marks at a cost of annual *census* worth more than 123.[48]

John's successor, Jacob Paulewski, capped restoration of St. Vincent's estate with a royal charter in 1507 that expressly forbade secular jurisdiction over it,[49] but some financial strain was likely being felt. In 1508 Jacob sold to the merchant Nicholas Uthman rights over Pracze, which may have been thought a wise use of property not easily integrated with other abbey interests. But already two years before Jacob had borrowed 1500 florins from Hieronymous Uthman to buy Wierzbno and thereafter sold further rents to raise more than another 500 florins.[50] When Jacob died in January, 1515, the need for cash was acute. Within months his elected successor, John Fabri, had raised at least 335 florins by selling more *census* but that well was going dry. When St. Vincent asked the cathedral chapter in June if it would lend up to 1400 florins against incomes from Grabiszyn, the canons learned the village already "ultra modum esse gravatam" with rental charges and declined. John went to Rome for confirmation in office and died on the return journey. After he left the abbey's administrators pawned all remaining rights at Pracze and Widawa to the Uthman, who would retain them past mid-century.[51] Still, St. Vincent remained under its next two abbots a well-situated and important corporate member of Wrocław's ecclesiastical elite.

In circumstances opportune for administrative success other clerical leaders had their own.[52] Even long-fragile St. Mathias regained properties and financial health under Master Andreas Heune (1483–1506).[53] So confident had peace made even the locally impotent that the ranks of monastic lords swelled at the turn of the century. A house of Celestines at far-away Oybin in Lusatia obtained Kulin from the old noble family Pak for religious considerations, credits, and more than five hundred florins.[54]

On other church-owned properties tightening of managerial oversight took forms less to corporate advantage. Integrated administration of the estates of the Church of Wrocław remained a sacrifice to that institution's internal complexity, political involvement, and scattered possessions. Bishop and chapter could still hope to sway the crown or persuade Silesian authorities against intrusive secular jurisdiction, taxes on church land, and, in the mid-1520s, Lutheran threats to property and tithes.[55] To bishops John IV Roth (1482–1506), John V Thurzo (1506–20), and Jacob von Salza (1520–39), what they had around their titular see mattered less than their own principality and residence at Nysa. On what remained near Wrocław to the bishop's *mensa*, now administered as the "Bresslisch Hald," more lordships were by 1530 pledged, leased, or enfeoffed to hereditary lay sublords than in the bishop's hands.[56] To him land still better served other than purely economic ends.

Authority over the cathedral island and many lordships near Wrocław had devolved upon the cathedral chapter, but responsibility for these lands

and incomes was diffused among many prebends and subsidiary corporations. Since 1471, for instance, jurisdiction over Kryniczno had belonged to
the "hospital" (really residence) of scholars at the cathedral school.[57] Even
earlier, war-related fluctuations in the yield of individual lordships caused
the chapter to divide its common estate among several administrators and
to devise means to rotate prebends among those canons in residence. Each
watched closely over his own properties and collectively on one another,
if only for their own future prospects, but managerial unity scarcely
survived.[58]

A quasi-private lordship was more obviously formed from the Wrocław duchy properties of another preoccupied and even more distant clerical administrator, the bishop of Lebus. By 1499 his five holdings neatly
grouped around an administrative center at Borek Strzeliński had gone
from direct episcopal control to management by lease to a noble *Amtmann*.
After 1525 this was Nicholas Tschesche, from a family near Grotków, and
his heirs, who occasionally observed the terms of their contract.[59]

Some distinctively urban foundations regained less well their economic
strength and public respect, thus leaving openings for a reformed Wrocław
to impose municipal control. When the prior of the Holy Spirit hospital
declared himself Lutheran in 1525, the city council immediately took into
its own hands all the foundation claimed (notably Zębice).[60] The Hospitallers of Corpus Christi were accused of mismanagement for their declining
membership and sales of properties. By 1540 Wrocław was able to take over
the commandery and all its lands through a 4000 florin loan to the king.[61]
But these events pertain more to the aggressive acquisition policy of the
sixteenth century municipal corporation than to the internal history of ecclesiastical estates.

By 1530 some ideological preconditions for ecclesiastical lordship around
Wrocław were changing. Though military needs in 1529 provided a legitimate opportunity, only then could the citizens have consummated as they
did their long irritation with the privileges of St. Vincent. To remove possible cover for feared Turkish invaders they razed the ancient abbey at *Olbino* and compelled the canons to take up residence at the old Franciscan
church of St. Jacob in town.[62] Thus a later generation undid much of the
work of John Löbschütz. Yet this future cannot change the importance or
the success of late fifteenth- and early sixteenth-century church estates and
their managers. Financial distress had been overcome, alienated rights and
properties reclaimed, and, where possible, the advantages of continuous
and consistent needs and policies again exploited. In 1530 these distinctive
landowners claimed lordship in 119 places, more than in 1480 and just
slightly fewer than in 1425. A solid third of the duchy's rural settlements
contained church property.[63]

A 1522 petition to King Louis by the nobility of the Wrocław duchy drew attention to one more way in which relations among landowners then bridged back across the mid-fifteenth century. When the "armen Ritterschaft" complained that citizens of Wrocław had bought out the greater part of the nobility,[64] they exaggerated little. After two generations of stagnation in the townsmen's share of rural estates a new wave of acquisitions had swelled. Their 22 percent of the duchy's settlements and 29 percent of those with known lordship in 1480 climbed by 1530 to 31 and 38 percent. Of individual holdings their share rose from 27 percent to 35.[65] What had begun in the fourteenth century now in the early sixteenth brought the townsmen, not to the mere parity with knights of a century before, but to collective quantitative superiority among all landowning groups. And yet this impressive parallel to fourteenth-century behavior conceals critical differences. To elucidate these is to begin to identify why and how an apparent and largely intended restoration of pre-crisis conditions became instead a transformation of the very bases of rural life. The role of lordship was central.

Braking the lordship cycle

The townspeople who assumed preeminence among sixteenth-century landowners differed in orientation from their predecessors a century and more before. Once those could rightly be labeled *citizen* lords; now these were more *lords* of urban origin. Their economic sense of self and their social recognition of place were changing. Shifts in property relationships among the largest landowning group were paralleled among others. As a result the structural motility of landed wealth so prevalent earlier in the duchy's history now decelerated.

Behind alterations in ways citizens handled landed property lay adjustments in the commercial position of their city. For much of the 1400s Wrocław had been an active player in a multi-lateral trading network.[66] Its merchants pushed east into Lithuania, Russia, and the rim of the Pontic steppes. At Lwów in the 1450s they gained direct access to goods flowing from the Orient via the Black Sea. At home members of textile and metalworking crafts with strong export orientations competed in numbers with those from local provisioning and retail trades.[67] Broad western contacts sustained the city's function as middleman. Wrocław merchants dealt with the Low Countries, with Venice, and with the towns of upper Germany, whose own traders soon began to follow higher profit margins eastward.[68]

These familiar and favorable commercial conditions underwent subtle transformations during the later fifteenth and early sixteenth centuries. The easternmost tendrils shriveled with rupture of Lwów's Black Sea connection after 1475, closure of Novgorod in the 1490s, and growing competition from indigenous Polish, especially Cracow, merchants. Augsburgers and Nürnbergers now contested the place of Wrocław. The Fuggers, for instance, appeared in Silesia in 1488, used Wrocław merchants as agents during 1503–17, and then sent their own employees. Westward through the city passed their shipments of Hungarian copper, but not the output from their Silesian mines.[69] More immediately disconcerting was the strength of Cracow. Conflicting claims to staple rights erupted into a trade war from 1499 to 1515 with notably harmful effects. A Wrocław chronicler still recalled a decade later how a 1511 Polish embargo impoverished the city's craftsmen, bakers, and innkeepers; the cathedral chapter recognized in 1513 how it had cost the tavern at Widawa on the Polish road its custom and thus the operator his ability to pay rent.[70]

The dispute over the Wrocław staple, itself a response to perceived commercial problems, was more symptom than cause of a narrowing and shortening of the town's mercantile focus. In the early sixteenth century Wrocław was becoming a place of more regional than European significance, serving as a transit point for east- and west-bound goods and as the chief node for Silesian exchanges. The export trades, first metals and then textiles, slipped from its leading crafts.[71] Even some regional exports of growing value remained outside its commercial control: Silesian mines used the city's capital but not its trade routes; Silesian linen grew up elsewhere (and mainly after the 1550s). Wrocław was always the most important single trading center in Silesia, that should not be doubted, and later in the century its merchants did create profitable new components in their Polish trades. But around 1500 wealthy mercantile and craft families had reason to question whether expanded or continued investment in trade was preferable to safer and remunerative alternatives.

Distinctive tones of elite urban culture were fading. Since the reign of Sigismund successful town families eagerly bought coats of arms and patents of nobility. Each of the fifteen councillors and assessors in office in 1474 so improved the formal status of his line. City fathers raised their sons to perform credibly in tournaments they sponsored on the market square.[72] Young men from Wrocław served their own or other princes as knights and grew into careers as princely advisors. One case in point is Nicholas Popplau. Born about 1440 to a merchant just then moved to Wrocław from Legnica, and still after university in 1467/68 factor in Cracow for the family firm, he then joined Emperor Frederick III as a knight and courtier. Nicholas toured Europe in 1483–86, went twice as an emissary to Muscovy, and died in Egypt in 1490 while a pilgrim to Palestine. Yet as late as 1473 he still participated in a hereditary division of the family's Wrocław properties.[73] In a later generation George Sauermann (1492–1527), son of a Wrocław town councillor, took a humanist education at Wittenberg, Leipzig, and Bologna, consorted with Ulrich von Hutten, and put his literary and diplomatic talents to the service of Charles V. But then George's father, Conrad Sauermann, was in 1515 one of six *Ratsherren* expelled from the council "because, having many properties under other rulers, they brought much evil to the city."[74] Perhaps with wiser ambitions were the half dozen town families who then placed sons among the cathedral canons.[75]

The capital such men were prepared to spend on country properties might come less from that temporarily surplus to the needs of business and more from a liquidation of trading interests. Hans Popplau, nephew to the well-traveled Nicholas, indubitably made just that decision. As principal heir in 1499 to his father, Caspar, and hence chief of the lineage, Hans continued for fifteen years the family cloth trade. After 1512, however, he progressively withdrew his capital from the family firm, winding it up in 1515 and the next year buying three whole lordships and a part of a fourth. In 1522 he closed his last mercantile accounts and bought four more rural properties.[76] What Hans Popplau did wholesale and in the full light of good documentation, others were doing piecemeal and, to historians lacking the Popplau account books, covertly. Knightly rural residents from town families are one indicator. So is the gradual loss of town councillors with inherited wealth in land.[77] For such people governance of a commercial center was losing importance. Families for whom land had once safely supplemented mercantile incomes now saw it substituting for them.

In these circumstances fundamental relationships between citizens and their rural properties began to shift. Individual estates grew larger. Their possessors showed concern to transmit these as coherent economic units. Town families retained and increased the same lordships through successive generations.

Aggregate quantitative data on land ownership in the late fifteenth and early sixteenth centuries establish the trend towards larger citizen estates.[78] In 1480, when the available sample is at a low ebb, 58 citizens are recorded with 87 holdings in 77 places; the slightly larger data for 1530 find 64 citizens with 124 holdings in 107 places. An average of about 1.5 holdings per lord rose to almost two. At the end of the period of crisis owners from the city with but one or two holdings (51) had outnumbered those with more (7) by a ratio of more than seven to one. Fifty years later the records identify 53 small citizen lords and 11 large ones; the ratio had dropped below five to one. Considered against the whole set of landowners in the duchy and against the 30 percent increase in total citizen possessions, small city-based lords increased by a quarter from 31 to 38 percent and large ones doubled from 4 to 8 percent. Finally, whereas in 1480 citizens with small estates together had 61 properties, 70 percent of those known to be in citizen hands, by raising its total to 72 in 1530 this group had fallen back to a less than 60 percent share of townspeople's holdings.

The broad statistical trend to larger citizen estates also reprised late fourteenth-century movements. In fact, looking only at the split between large and small citizen lords, the level of concentration had by 1530 still not regained that of 1425, when each group had about the same amount. But methods designed for long-term comparison may not convey the immediate impact of the change around 1500. In no earlier sample year can any private lay landowner be documented with as many as ten properties. Hans Popplau had eleven in 1530, in at least seven of which he was the only lord on record.[79] No non-institutional landowner in 1480 had more than five properties. Three townsmen did in 1530.[80] In sharp contrast to a century before, such larger estates were now also longer-lasting.

Chapter 7 established how neither fourteenth-century elites nor their estates long survived. What a successful individual gathered was then treated not as an endowment for a future lineage but as a congeries of assets to be divided among members of the next generation. Equality among all male and female heirs assured rapid dispersal of property into the hands of other kin groups, whether by marriage or by sale. This effect was compounded by the regularity with which adult males married and produced children, thus further reducing the size of the portions falling to each heir. Hence the descendants of the well-to-do slipped from the stations their fathers or grandfathers had achieved.

By around 1500 landed urban families were approaching intergenerational transfer differently than had their predecessors. Apparent constraint of male marriage and reproduction, concentration of *landed* wealth on males, even especially favored individual males, and transmission of land in coherent management units point to a growing consciousness of multi-generational patrilines as significant foci of personal commitment among leading townsmen. A family called "de Jenkowicz" or "Jenkwitz" after their home village near Brzeg illustrates the slow shift from one behavioral pattern to the other.[81]

Little distinguished the main fourteenth-century line of Jenkwitz (Table 11.3) from their contemporaries in Wrocław. Henry [2] established their place among the leading citizens and Henry [3] that among landowners. He held at five places when he died in 1427. But he fractionated that estate among his heirs such that Henry [4] received only urban land and Polakowice and the sisters split the rest. With the wealth went the standing of this branch, who held no office after 1438 and no land or other mark of elite status by 1499.[82]

Control over female inheritance and male marriage helped heirs of the early-deceased third son of Henry [2], Mathias, maintain the ascent of the Jenkwitz in mid-fifteenth century Wrocław. In 1425 the three siblings established a consortium which lasted to the death of George fifteen years later. George and Mathias [2] operated as partners, endowing their sister with annuities but not rights of ownership in land. To the half of Sadków which was their paternal legacy they added the rest in 1435 and then a half of Bogunów.[83] Each brother acted officially for the collectivity, but only Mathias married, and he did so twice. Thus when George died Mathias gained sole possession of all they had accumulated, which he in turn passed to his one surviving son, Mathias [3]. The girls were married well, to be sure, but from the late 1440s until his death without issue in 1484, this Mathias Jenkwitz, heir of two lordships and purchaser of another four, was among the wealthiest in the duchy.[84] In him alone culminated his own, his father's, and his uncle's patient efforts.

That the name of Jenkwitz still continued among the Wrocław elite after the death of Mathias [3] was thanks to another scion from the ancestral stock still rooted near Brzeg. Lawrence Jenkwitz, a Wrocław citizen and merchant of the second rank in the 1450s and 60s, bore the additional name of "Posadowsky auf Postelwitz" from an ancestral marriage connection, but the identity of heraldic devices used by the earlier Wrocław Jenkwitzes and by Lawrence and his descendants establishes the latters' consciousness of kinship and continuity.

The line of Lawrence certainly constrained male marriage and female inheritance of land to concentrate wealth and advance its position. Their first lordship, Sulimów, canon Ambrose acquired in 1474 and passed to his merchant brother and nephews.[85] In the next generation Peter [2] followed his uncle in the cathedral chapter while Agnes received instead of land two successive husbands from the top business and political strata of her other brothers. Ambrose [2] owned rural land only briefly in the 1520s but sat for 44 consecutive years on the Rat. Nicholas [2] joined him there for 17 years while through two decades building an estate of nine lordships (6 in the duchy, 3 outside) and keeping seven.[86] Together the brothers in 1533 paid impressive sums to Charles V for imperial sanction of the family's noble rank. Among their children again no land went to daughters. Most males were celibate or pursued promising opportunities elsewhere. In each group only one remained with the resources to reproduce an elite lineage at Wrocław: Abraham (born some months after his father's death) inherited five lordships and standing to serve 39 years on the Rat; the lawyer Kilian twice married very well before dying without issue. With those two men, family consciousness and discipline had carried the Jenkwitzes to a sixth generation in the leading circles of Wrocław and the duchy.

Table 11.3. The Jenkwitz

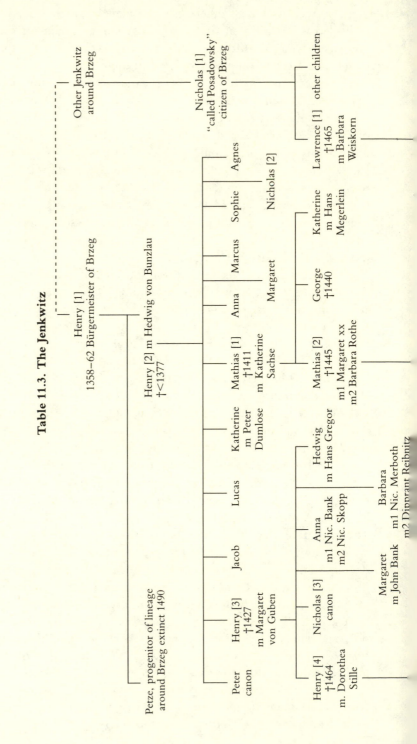

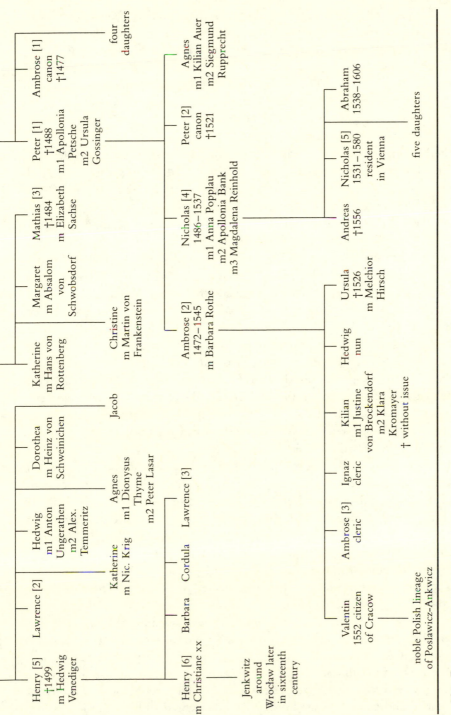

Henry [5]
†1499
m Hedwig
Venediger

Lawrence [2]

Hedwig
m1 Anton
Ungerathen
m2 Alex.
Temmeritz

Dorothea
m Heinz von
Schweinichen

Jacob

Katherine
m Hans von
Rottenberg

Margaret
m Absalom
von
Schwobsdorf

Mathias [3]
†1484
m Elizabeth
Sachse

Peter [1]
†1488
m1 Apollonia
Petsche
m2 Ursula
Gossinger

Ambrose [1]
canon
†1477

four
daughters

Katherine
m Nic. Krig

Agnes
m1 Dionysus
Thyme
m2 Peter Lasar

Christine
m Martin von
Frankenstein

Agnes
m1 Kilian Auer
m2 Siegmund
Rupprecht

Peter [2]
canon
†1521

Henry [6]
m Christiane xx

Barbara

Cordula

Lawrence [3]

Ambrose [2]
1472–1545
m Barbara Rothe

Nicholas [4]
1486–1537
m1 Anna Popplau
m2 Apollonia Bank
m3 Magdalena Reinhold

Jenkwitz
around
Wrocław later
in sixteenth
century

Valentin
1552 citizen
of Cracow

Ambrose [3]
cleric

Ignaz
cleric

Kilian
m1 Justine
von Brockendorf
m2 Klara
Kromayer
† without issue

Hedwig
nun

Ursula
†1526
m Melchior
Hirsch

Andreas
†1556

Nicholas [5]
1531–1580
resident
in Vienna

Abraham
1538–1606

five daughters

noble Polish lineage
of Poslawicz–Ankwicz

Note. For sources, see notes to text.

A sense of family identity and the discipline to curb female inheritance and male reproduction in its interest visibly emerged among the Jenkwitzes during the fifteenth century. But whether from lack of opportunity or inclination they had no evident concern for the coherence or integrity of any particular properties. The assembly and special transmission of certain lordships as a cohesive lineage estate is better seen among a younger kin group called Krig or von Krikow (Table 11.4).

For three generations the objects of the Krigs' special attention were in the bottomlands of the northern Środa district. In the late 1430s Peter [1] Krig bought Wojnowice and some rights at Białków to go with his lands elsewhere.[87] The year of his death his heirs jointly acquired all of Białków and planned with their neighbors to build artificial fishponds.[88] When they divided the inheritance the sons of the second marriage, Melchior and Nicholas, took Wojnowice and Białków and let the rest pass to their half-brothers, to their sister, and then out of the family. Melchior and Nicholas together obtained other properties, but at their separation in 1464 the original legacy stayed with Nicholas. He had already purchased Wilkostów on the east of what he owned, and now acquired more rights at Wojnowice, Prężyce, and Gosławice. At his death about 1476 Nicholas Krig left an estate of six lordships, four contiguous there northwest from Wrocław and two separate in the opposite direction.[89] Two sons died early. The daughters got the scattered properties and Peter [3] sole possession of the spatially consolidated portion. There in the next 27 years he added other rights and two more lordships, Księginice and *Skaszyce*. Around the nucleus of his grandfather's long-retained acquisition Peter had what was by 1507 the most unified and nearly the largest private estate in the duchy.[90]

Now Peter used what his lineage had built to raise it one more step. In 1512 he exchanged his entire estate for the hereditary captaincy and lordship of the town and castle of Kąty, a royal fief at the edge of the duchy.[91] To fit his new position he had King Lewis formally declare his hereditary nobility—but, with his sons, also kept his citizenship at Wrocław. Peter [4] had learned the family recipe, for after succeeding his father in possession of Kąty he bought in 1526 three more villages within six kilometers of it.[92] Then his premature and childless death halted his efforts and the disciplined upward trajectory of the Krigs.

The Jenkwitz and Krig families offer well-documented and relatively simple examples of behavior increasingly common among leading kin groups at Wrocław. Real property they channeled by preference to males. A pattern of patrilineal stem structures emerged such that a single favored son received all, larger, or especially well-placed parts of the patrimony; he married and continued the lineage. His disfavored siblings did not. When

Table 11.4. The Krig

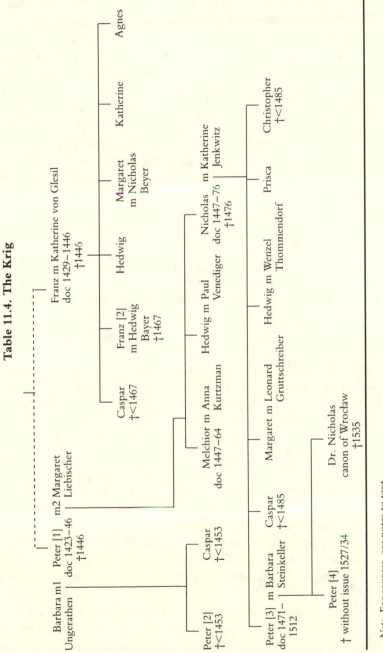

Note. For sources, see notes to text.

Caspar Popplau set out the disposition of his estate in 1499 he designated to his son Hans four entire lordships (three contiguous, the other not far away) and to his five daughters shared lands and rent charges at three others. An incapacitated male he treated as female: Thomas Popplau, a mute, got only annuities charged against the properties of Hans.[93] But each such arrangement was ad hoc and thus the evidence to hand is entirely behavioral. Recorded actions of leading townspeople give rise to the inference that they had come to see the male patriline as important to them and to their social place.

Confirmatory hints of shifting consciousness include citizens' acquisitions of hereditary noble rank and subsequent flaunting of armorial devices on houses, moveables, and tombs. As such symbols passed to new generations in the male line, they reminded later men of their own membership in an institution they shared with their ancestors. Formal expression of solidarity with future members of a patriline came only after the 1520s as lords of urban origin gradually adopted legal mechanisms to inhibit current possessors from alienating a landed patrimony.[94] In many ways, then, elite citizen families, estates, and the link between them all gained longevity.

Qualitative changes in familial relations and the treatment of property visible among the late fifteenth- and early sixteenth-century urban elite had objective and correlate effects in the countryside. Impermanence no longer accurately characterized citizen lords or their estates. At least a third of the propertied lineages of 1530 could trace possession of specific lordships to and before the days of their grandsires. The tenacious Krigs were no longer unusual. Wojkowice, for instance, belonged for three generations after 1441 to the Haunolds. Their successors in 1507, the Hornigs, were in at least their third generation when a new set of heirs took possession in 1558.[95] All these paled, however, beside the Rothes at Wilczków. Hans Rothe acquired his first land there in 1375 and his son, Peter, proprietary rights in 1420. Their descendants remained through the entire fifteenth century and by the 1530s the last to sit on the Wrocław city council, another Hans, was calling himself "Rothe zu Wiltschaw." He died, still possessed of the village, in 1542, but his descendants, who had by then withdrawn from urban life and joined the nobility, lasted, as did their lordship over Wilczków, until 1617.[96] Individual Rothes died, but in 1530 the Rothe lordship at Wilczków had lived for 150 years.

Paralleling the new social context and durability of land ownership among sixteenth-century citizens were the growing estates of other urban lords, the municipalities of Wrocław and Środa. Wrocław had long claimed some suburban lands and back in the fourteenth century bought more, but as late as 1468 they were incidental to town affairs. Rumblings of greater interest in land were heard in the 1490s, but major expansion, driven by fiscal and political motives, got under way in the 1520s. The properties of the hospitals were acquired as part of the city's Reformation and its office of captain let it turn viceregal authority over Krępice into private lordship. Michalowice the town bought in 1526 and Jenkowice in 1528. Wrocław had property in ten places in 1530 and would acquire by purchase, pledge, and political pressure more in coming years.[97] At its own smaller scale Środa did the same.[98] Together the two corporations controlled in 1530 about half the thirty-one holdings Table A.1 records for "other" landowners. They added scale and longevity to lordship.

Whence came the lands which so raised the importance of urban-based owners during the late fifteenth and early sixteenth centuries? Mostly from the knightly nobility, whose possessions in the duchy shrank proportionately. Among surviving representatives of that group, however, larger and more durable estates also became more common.[99] Table A.1 has the statistical summary: 74 places with noble lords in 1480 had become 60 in the more complete records of 1530; 88 noble holdings became 74; 64 known lords became 41; 33 families became 24. These are raw data. Controlling for shifting sample sizes shows measures of the land held by squires dropping by about a fifth and of their numbers among all landowners by about a fourth. For the first time in the years sampled, in 1530 this group controlled surely less than a quarter of the land in the duchy and perhaps less than a fifth. Losses were everywhere in proportion to the knights' earlier holdings. As a result, their remnants in the Wrocław district were all but erased and their strongholds in those of Środa and even Uraz again threatened.

Nearly all the net decline occurred among small noble holders, whose numbers and properties were halved between 1480 and 1530 (Table A.2). Knights with one or two holdings accounted for a fifth of the duchy's identifiable property at the end of the mid-century crisis, but fifty years later just a tenth. Larger estates showed a relative strength even greater than among citizens. The five knights with three or more holdings in 1480 became eleven in 1530; their eighteen properties (5 percent of known lordships) became thirty-nine (11 percent). For the first time recorded, large noble landowners controlled in 1530 most of the property of their status group.

The growing scale of noble estates probably related to ways surviving knightly lineages had improved the durability of their position. Though knights seem less forthcoming about details of family arrangements, like contemporary citizens more of them now looked to pass land to males and to favor a single son with properties forming a spatially coherent core patrimony. Peter Sack, for instance, castellan at Środa, by 1515 had lands in

Szczepanów, Jaśkowice, and Cesarzowice which he then persuaded the king to shift from fief to proprietary status. In 1538 he obtained confirmation that all three properties could pass from one son to another, with female inheritance only in default of male heirs.[100] Such ability for brothers to deal together looks critical. The noble Garwolski family obtained Bagno through a female connection and then lost it in 1505 for lack of a male heir. Regranted in 1511 to Hans Keltsch, another knight, it passed among his sons in the 1530s and thus remained in that family beyond the 1560s, when it went into the third generation.[101]

Then greatest among the duchy's noble lords were the Debitsches, who plainly worked to create a territorial property unit and keep it under individual control. Hans Debitsch acquired from an in-law in 1472 Golędzinów, Zajączków, Wojciechów, and parts of Lubnów and Bukowiec, all but the last lying north and east of Uraz. To this core in the next thirty years Hans added more of Lubnów and Bukowiec plus, precisely in the middle of what he already had, part of Pęgów. From 1510 all belonged to one successor, Ernst Debitsch, who had at least two brothers, but who handled for his kin all extra-familial property affairs. Ernst, too, built the patrimony with more acquisitions at Lubnów and Pęgów. Rights inherited from cognates elsewhere, however, he and his co-heirs resigned. When Ernst died in 1541 the family lands had been expanding from a fixed core for some seventy years.[102]

Whatever the means, in the sixteenth century knights, too, could often look back at lengthening family possession of certain lordships. The roster in 1530 included some old fourteenth-century names: Lawrence Seidlicz at Damianowice held land then eighty years in his family; Hans and Christopher Sommerfeld were at Jastrzębce where their name had owned since 1436.[103] Newer lineages were also well represented: a Kreiselwitz held at least part of Cesarzowice since before 1437 and of Ogrodnica since 1468; a Schindel is recorded at Sadowice from 1441.[104] Each of these family lordships lasted beyond the 1550s.

By 1530, processes at work among nobles, citizens, and corporations had caused lords with three or more properties to possess most of those where an owner is known. The quantitative dominance of small landowners was passing. Even more significantly, different behavior among landowners changed the framework for agrarian life by halting the lordship cycle.

With the late fifteenth and early sixteenth centuries unified control of rural property by a single owner became normal. In place after place the singular title *Erbherr* gained literal truth as cycles of lordship rolled once more through a consolidation phase and then stopped. The evidence is not the mere acts of consolidation, for those, of course, had been part of the old structure. It is rather the failure of fragmentation—and then the passage of a whole lordship, whether by sale or inheritance, from one owner to another. Hence across the duchy the ending of the cycle was necessarily slow, incremental, cumulative, and never complete. To Sadków it came early: what George and Mathias [2] Jenkwitz brought together in 1435 was not again separated, though the village passed from the Jenkwitzes to the Dompnigs in 1484 and thence to the Prockendorfs in 1490.[105] At Jarząbkowice the final consolidation came later: brought together by the Holy Trinity Hospital in 1497, the lordship passed by sale through Skopp, Hornig, Schewitz, and Popplau hands in the next twenty years but then and thereafter remained intact.[106]

The process can be quantified in the case of Świniary. Here between 1375 and 1449 lords from seven families had averaged a tenure of barely eleven years, none lasted twenty-five, and for only sixteen years did one lord have all. Then between 1453 and 1549 only two families in succession owned Świniary. Peter Frankenstein established a unitary lordship in the former year, and this was but briefly broken while his daughter Ursula had half. Her cession to unseparated fellow heirs in 1501 was the final consolidation of Świniary, but it had then already been one for most of a half century.[107] Neither status nor market mechanisms had ceased to affect the disposition of landed property but the typical unit had become an entire village. Across the whole duchy in 1530 only one settlement in four knew more than one lord. The earlier cycles had become a one-way flow.

The tendency of consolidation permanently to supplant subdivision did heighten conflict among competing lords. Who would achieve unchallenged authority in a place? Whose autonomous rights would be curbed? All sorts of landowners pressed all sorts of issues. In the fall of 1485 Melchior Ungerathen and John Keuschberg disputed over the village court at Wierzbice while the nuns of Trzebnica fended off a claim Hans Debitsch of Lubnów had advanced on Kotowice.[108] George Kreiselwitz of Buczki tried in 1511 to get his argument with the cathedral penitentiary decided by a secular court; the bishop's official fought back.[109] The next February the hereditary holder of the chapter's fief at Księże Małe reported that he had caught men from the St. Mathias lordship of Księże Wielkie fishing through the ice on the Oława where it flowed through his lands. Gear was seized, men were arrested, the Master of St. Mathias arrived in high dudgeon, inspections and witnesses were demanded. The dispute rumbles for two years through the chapter's minute book, punctuated with representations from Wrocław city councillors, assertions that ecclesiatical liberty was at stake, rumor that weapons had been seized, appointment of episcopal mediators, and offers from both the chapter and the hospital to buy the other's property. A new lessee of Księże Małe pulled out, allegedly due to threats from St. Mathias.[110] That landlords' squabble between two churches had not yet calmed when the chapter was also considering how canon Prockendorf's refusal to bury a man from Bogdaszowice who died excommunicate for non-payment of church dues was causing "all the nobles of the district" to grumble threats against the clergy.[111]

No doubt the scribal proclivities of churchmen and the differential survival of certain records around Wrocław make a disproportionate share of known disputes over lordship pit layman against cleric, but the traditional claims of spiritual authority to some rights in all lordships meant, in this environment of consolidation, a general sense of cleavage and tension. Much of the 1504 treaty the royal governors and chancellor mediated between the Silesian Estates and the cathedral chapter aimed to establish a framework for settling local arguments. It specified procedures for collection of tithes, regulated new taverns, equalized fiscal burdens, curbed use of ecclesiastical punishment to enforce secular dues, required churchmen to cooperate in resettling deserted lands, and reserved the wealth of intestate rectors for parish use under the lord's supervision.[112] From the lay landowner's point of view, or even that of a churchman who happened to lack ecclesiastical jurisdiction over his land, this went far towards limiting interference in his lordship. On the other hand, major ecclesiastical landowners in the Wrocław duchy sought and gained clear privileges against secular authority over their lands and subjects. Each would rule his own.[113]

The consequent clearer delimitation of jurisdiction was matched with a lively concern for establishing limits on the land itself. Wrocław and St. Vincent had the rector of the Corpus Christi Commandery arbitrate in 1487 the boundary between them at Siedlec, which involved placement of fourteen stone markers and specification that the town controlled the lake and the abbey the river for fishing; a new agreement about the parties' woodlands forty years later referred to and used that description. In 1509 and 1521 the same two lords tried to sort out what belonged to *Rzepina* and what to *Olbino*, appealing to a royal charter from Mathias and a ducal one from the 1260s, taking sworn testimony from local inhabitants, and looking for traces of a woodland that had been cut down.[114] Every ditch and hillock mattered. When peculations by the prior of Holy Spirit caused three and a half mansi at Wysoka to be seized and sold in 1527, the buyer, Hieronymous Hornig, made sure they were formally separated from that lordship and joined to his own at Radomierzyce.[115]

At the extreme this thrust to more sharply defined and more consolidated lordships transcended traditional units of settlement to create multi-village territories under a single lord. These had as yet no formal standing, so the existence of each must be ferreted from records showing a single person owning and transferring together several contiguous places. Among such genuine property complexes was that assembled in the 1460s by Hieronymous Ungerathen, who added Żar to what he and his brother Mathias already had at Lutynia; the two lordships went together from the Ungerathen heirs to Hans Haunold in 1498 and remained with that lineage into the 1540s.[116] In 1492 St. Vincent joined to its old Krobielowice its newly purchased Wojtkowice and *Gąska*.[117] Among nobles there were the five adjacent properties of the Debitsches northeast of Uraz and those of Nickel Tschesche around Borek Strzeliński.[118] Bledzów and Ślęza had a common owner from the 1480s as did Wilków and Sobkowice; Wierzbica and Owsianka went as one from 1514.[119] Such were the logical extension of mechanisms now at work among all landowning groups.

It is time to reiterate the findings of this protracted and at times necessarily minute examination of landowners and their properties in the late fifteenth- and early sixteenth-century duchy. After the crisis church corporations took up attentive management and townsmen extensive acquisitions much as they had left off, but for the latter several relevant contexts had changed. Economic, cultural, and social assumptions of wealthy citizens encouraged greater investment in land and attention to its passage intact from one generation to the next. This raised the average size and longevity of citizen estates. Municipal estates and those of the surviving noble landowners moved in the same directions. Within each landowning group, then, dominant patterns in the handling of property had changed. As seen from the countryside, a structural feature of lordship, its erratic but continual cycling between phases of dispersion and reassembly, its inconstancy and disunity, was replaced with a new unity, durability, and, hence, authority. Dispersion of rights among many ephemeral owners locked for their own purposes in a lordship cycle had formerly been synergistic with lords' distance from rural life, with village autonomy, and with peasant freedom. Around 1500 that condition was no more.

§§ 12 §§

STRAWS IN A CHILLING WIND

Die Leute nicht freie sein.

The Wrocław town council decides an appeal by peasants from
Krępice against their lord, 1525; *UD*, pp. 225–226.

Winds of change blew cold through late fifteenth- and early sixteenth-century villages of east central Europe and peasants shivered. In Poland one generation's sequence of statutes imposed servitude and patrimonial jurisdiction on cultivators whom lords then squeezed for an exportable surplus. In Hungary the single blast of the Diet's revenge for the 1514 peasant revolt affirmed earlier rumblings that non-nobles had no rights. In Bohemia whole districts bowed to the whim of great private lords.

Silesia, and especially its center, lacked overpowering magnates, innovative and effective lawmakers, great staple exports and dramatic events but still the new wind blew, sweeping the regime of German law before it. By the late 1500s, elite dominance over a rapidly impoverished servile population would distinguish a different rural order.[1] But the discontinuity took shape a century before. Around Wrocław acts of individuals in particular villages, circumstantial words of court proceedings, and articulated intentions in specific laws form a pattern of changing minds and expectations. Incremental, idiosyncratic, and incomplete though the movement was, a decisive balance had by 1530 tipped against peasant freedom and towards lords' power. On the one side peasant rights were eroded, village leadership crippled, and peasant resistance suppressed. Legal and institutional defenses of peasant autonomy lay open. On the other side landowners directly asserted in the countryside their authority and interests. In sum, during the deceptively warm calm of reconstructed rural prosperity, one set of relationships, even one mental framework, yielded before another. Dried leaves and chaff on a village street swirl in a new direction before trees begin to sway.

Portents of servitude

The rising regional flow against traditional peasant rights was manifest around Wrocław in new constraints on the mobility of tenants, alienability of tenures, and allocation of productive labor. Nowhere were these novelties general, instantaneous, nor yet absolute. They were, however, present and multiplying.

By the late fifteenth century the judicial climate of the duchy was turning against the right of peasants to move freely. Arguments in Paul Merot's 1485 case against Franz Bottner spoke of labor supply and grain prices, but the issue was Merot's wish to leave his hereditary tenancy at Żerniki Wrocławskie. There the duchy court was firm: he could go only after he put the farm in full and proper cultivation.[2] A like harbinger in 1511 was the new schulz of Oporów, whose lord elsewhere would not let him sell his former farm.[3]

"Merot vs. Bottner" was no isolated incident. The report of it survives in a collection of legal precedents and principles compiled at that very time by a veteran of Wrocław's courts, Caspar Popplau, brother to the knight Nicholas and father to the future merchant become landed gentleman Hans. Caspar's unsystematic and unofficial manual, "Der Rechte Weg," enunciates the legal thinking he assimilated in twenty years' service on town and duchy tribunals.[4] On peasant rights his tone is unmistakable. A free man taking a tenancy becomes a "Pawer" [*Bauer*, "peasant"]. As such he is liable to provide guarantors for three years rent and all his property is at risk if he defaults.[5] Only six months advance notice and default from legitimate poverty ("rechtem armut") permit free departure (this entry follows "Merot vs. Bottner").[6] Roman law citations confirm the necessity of the lord's consent and glosses on *Sachsenspiegel* forbid other lords to receive runaways. Thirty or forty years' tenure creates presumptive rights against expulsion but countervailing hazards. No peasant born on a lordship may leave without permission and, though such an heir may not be driven out, his appeal is to the lord's court and his is the burden of proof.[7] Caspar Popplau sat to hear Paul Merot's case. It was his second year on that court. Had he already formulated such understandings of the law?

The repressive tone of Popplau's private scholarship is echoed in public agreements among the next generation of Silesia's rulers. A 1505 assembly first bound peasants in the province to their land, but representatives of Wrocław did not attend.[8] Another in 1512, at which they were present, repeated those provisions and the more comprehensive agreement of 1529 developed them further, barring unapproved movement to tenants, gertner, or their children and encouraging lords to retrieve those who disobeyed.[9] How much were the laws wishful elite thinking? People at Małuszów were still moving some years later with no word of permission. They moved much less than had their peers a century before. Was that only because times were now safer for farmers?

Incrementally curbed, too, were peasants' rights freely to convey land in tenancy, which the men of Małuszów still then in practice enjoyed. Again Popplau's collection sets the tone with exemplary cases and theoretical dicta. The Wrocław courts found in the matter of a disputed inheritance at an unnamed village that peasant holdings could be conveyed only before the lord's village court. Sales of rental tenure required, as a matter of principle, the landowner's consent; if violated, the buyer lost the land and what it held. Among precedents from Legnica Popplau found the same rules controlling division or merger of tenant farms, and from Roman law he learned that even squatters on deserted land owed the rents once due from it.[10]

Such thinking let lords intrude on peasant land markets by demanding payment for entry to tenures, something not formerly known to Silesian peasants. The *Markgroschen*, so-called from a standard rate of one groschen in the mark (2.8 percent), was first demanded from rent-free holdings of schulzen or taverners, but spread before 1550 to rental tenancies, especially on church estates. As well or instead some owners demanded from villagers the very laudamium they themselves had escaped a generation earlier. At 10 percent of the sale price it imposed greater costs on peasant land transactions. St. Vincent was claiming laudamium from the schulz at Kostomłoty as early as 1472. Lay lords at Siemidrożyce took such payments against peasant opposition by the 1540s.[11] Within a generation some meaningful entry fine would be normal in Wrocław duchy villages. Constraints, controls, and higher costs help explain why the kinds of human movements once typical in villages under German law subsequently stopped.

Traditional freedom from forced labor was also infringed upon. Around 1500 services, if not yet onerous ones, were imposed upon even some German law tenants. Something called *Hofarbeit* was being demanded from gertner in villages near Środa during the mid-1400s,[12] but comparable claims against regular landed peasants are recorded only a generation or two later. Ordinary rental mansi owed five days a year at Wierzbica in 1496, three in the fields and two in the meadows.[13] Obligations of similar magnitude and with limiting provisions or monetary compositions are thereafter not rare. A property at Rędzin in 1521 contained three peasants and four gertner owing in collective total thirty-eight days a year or one white groschen per day.[14] Labor rents around Wrocław before 1530 were thus as nothing beside those assessed in days per week in contemporary Poland. Even they, however, intruded and irritated people who remembered or knew of other arrangements. The community of Krępice in 1527 acquiesced to a yearly forty heller, two hens, and fifteen eggs per mansus in lieu of "the very heavy *Hofarbeit* to which they are bound."[15]

An effective preliminary to successful gnawing at customary peasant freedoms was local and incremental subversion of traditionally autonomous village leaders, the free and hereditary schulzen. Their claims to special status evaporated. A sequence of texts for *Oldrzewie Małe* tells part of the tale. Back in 1417 the local demesne farm had been owned by the schulz from Ołtaszyn. That situation had long passed, however, when in 1511 a royal charter confirmed Caspar Ungerathen's proprietary rights over part of the village and, explicitly, two "free schulzen and fiefholders" ("freyen Scholtzen und Lehenleutten"). A 1529 sale by Ungerathen's nephews referred to two "free peasants" ("freyen Pauern"), as did one five years later. Debasement of social nomenclature would continue, too, for in two texts from the early 1560s they were become mere "inhabitants" ("Inwohner") and "peasants" ("rusticos").[16] Even the freedom had departed.

Participation by village headmen in regional governance had ended long before. Schulzen gave way to citizens on the Wrocław district court by 1400, while keeping three seats on the Środa court into the late 1450s. But twenty years later only knightly lords and townsmen gave judgement on panels above the village.[17]

More immediate harm came to village leadership when lords bought out hereditary schulzen and assigned their functions to appointees with less secure tenure. The offices had on earlier occasions been sold to landowners—as under economic stress in the 1420s and 30s—but then commonly regranted to new hereditary successors. Later sales less often had that result. Already in 1480 the schulz at Klecina held only for life. Sebald Sauerman paid off the hereditary occupant at Wierzbica and the brothers Dompnig that at Komorniki, both in 1505; Hans Hornig did the same at Mokra four years later.[18] So too did less thrusting landowners like the cathedral chapter, which in 1514–15 replaced schulzen at Kębłowice and Nowa Wieś Wrocławska. Among church lordships surveyed somewhat after 1530 about one village in ten held no schulz but a mere "court administrator" (*Gerichtsverwalter*).[19] How were such lord's men to sustain leadership and external representation for their fellow villagers?

Nor did the few schulzen who still at this late date built on their position augur well for the interests of their neighbors. At Biestrzyków in 1511 Plusske Rossel, son of a solid local peasant, held the post of demesne manager (*Hofmeister*). Four years later he was also exercising the lord's jurisdiction over local peasant disputes and in 1518 he died as schulz in Kamieniec Wrocławskie. Within ten years a known descendant claimed Wrocław citizenship and in ten more the family itself owned half of Żerniki.[20] At the same time Woitke Gomolka, schulz of Jagodno, was expanding his lands through purchases at Turów and schulz Stephan of Brodno doing the same around Jaśkowice and Jastrzębce.[21] All three were exploiting loosely managed church lordships, while Rossel's climb began and may have continued as a lord's official. How effectively would he have defended village rights against the lord who employed him?

Peasants unwillingly witnessed their own exploitation and piecemeal debasement. They responded with traditional community forms of resistance. Usually led by hereditary schulzen and other village notables they opposed intrusions on what they saw as their customary rights. This often meant waging what were by now equally customary battles. Low level opposition to tithes and to novel dues thus remained almost endemic. Local schulzen and communities at Popowice on one side of Środa and Bielany on the other rejected claims from the town rector for certain payments.[22] Doubtless the cathedral chapter took no pleasure from the many incidents recorded in its minute books. In 1502 a canon excommunicated people of Smolec for refusing grain tithes. The rector of *Szczepin* complained in 1511 that inhabitants of the chapter's own Oporów beat up the servants he sent to collect his tenth sheaves from the fields. Such actions could gain desired results. Demands in 1513 from holders at suburban *Siebenhuben* to pay in kind rather than the then much disordered currency were met "ut in terrorem ipsorum rusticorum."[23]

In this setting villagers around Wrocław soon recognized the one sixteenth-century innovation wholly in accord with their traditional stance. Reformation ideologies and anti-clericalism offered satisfying grounds for peasant action. At Domaniów, where the rector had during the 1300s complained of collective tithe refusals, these and other obligations to the Trzebnica nuns again went unpaid as early as 1519.[24] Resistance to ecclesiastical authority spread. The cathedral custos recorded in 1524–25 no tithe incomes from Iwiny and Radomierzyce "because of the Lutherans." By 1532 the monks of Oybin had received nothing from Kulin for more than a decade, and the next year villagers in chapter lordships at Bogusławice and Rzeplin rejected the cathedral clergy sent as their rectors, claiming the right to elect their own. Of course lay authorities quickly saw that evangelical enthusiasm threatened all lordship and in Silesia, too, if not the Wrocław duchy, moved against socially radical reform. In limited circumstances a form of elite support might be available, that will be clear below, but normally not so. The nuns had their rents again by 1523 and the custos his tithes in 1526; King Ferdinand ordered collection of the Kulin dues in 1533.[25]

Authorities who heard disputes over basic peasant obligations to pay and to work would not often defend "subjects" (*subditi, Untertanen*) against their *Erbherrn*. That lesson was sharply taught to the men of Krępice, whose traditionally anomalous free peasant fiefs a harsher age would no longer understand or tolerate. When the Wrocław town council firmly grasped viceregal power during the 1400s it began to assimilate rule over Krępice to more familiar patterns. The councillor it set over the village acted like any other aggressive lord. By early 1525 the villagers had taken too much. The community ("gemaind") managed to gain a hearing before the Rat and accused the administrator, Hans Berlin, of "forcibly imposing many new services" ("gewaldiglich zu vilen newen Diestparkeiten benotget") against their rights. They offered in evidence their written charters. No other villagers in the duchy could have put so strong a case before so public a panel. The council saw in their action mere error, disobedience, and uprising ("empoerunge") and in their charters, no discernible rights. The land belonged to the council and "die Leute nicht freie sein." Forced to beg pardon and to swear obedience, the peasants had with their fully traditional appeal achieved only official declaration that they were obliged to serve.

Twice, about a year later, for further disobedience men of Krępice were jailed, made to find pledges for good behavior, and ordered to sell their holdings. A contemporary noted in the margin of the city court book entry, "Hansz Berlin vulgo der Paver feindt" ("the peasants' enemy"). Another eighteen months passed and the community again stood before the council. This time, however, they asked permission, so long as it pleased the council and the king in whose name it governed and in full submission to "Hansen Berlin als Ihrem erbherrn," to lighten the burden of their obligatory duties by taking annual payments instead. With resistance so crushed, the council agreed.[26]

Villages less peculiarly advantaged than Krępice could rely no better on their own traditional means of defense. In January, 1532, Bartusch Kosel and two fellow assessors from the Małuszów court stood in the bishop's palace at Wrocław, repudiated by their schulz and threatened with prison for refusing rents.[27] Five years later Domasław's schulz and jurors discussed *Hofarbeit* with their hereditary lord and the man to whom he had pledged their village. Once the peasants accepted three annual plow services per mansus the lords agreed to a fixed cash rate for works not needed and limits on the distance the workers should travel, but only so long as nothing prejudiced hereditary lordly rights.[28] So, too, at Siemidrożyce about this time did Melchior Keltsch introduce the laudamium over peasant objections.[29]

But more often than not the services, the new payments, the curbs on peasant rights came in quietly and without apparent overt opposition. With their historic leadership departed or cowed, peasant communities in the Wrocław duchy had lost their old capacity for successful self-defense before it was tested and found wanting.[30] The failure of country people to withstand repressive innovation stemmed equally from the new strength and drive of their lords. Serfdom and subsequent pauperization came in central Silesia through individual acts of local authority.

The Erbherr takes control

All trends intersected in a primary shift of agrarian structure: contraction of distance between lord and peasant. Landowners became around 1500 more closely involved in the affairs of their properties and their tenants. This redounded, on balance, to the disadvantage of the latter. *Erbherren* absorbed or faced down competitors within and without the village to seize command of the juncture between peasants and the larger society. Lords ruled their subjects. Aggressive managers attended to the profitability of their lands and their demesne farms. They created in their lordships a new regime.

To argue that late fifteenth- and early sixteenth-century lords around Wrocław coopted and replaced autonomous influences in their properties sets further contexts around events already narrated. It is the process of consolidation carried to and beyond the gathering of property rights into a single bundle. Owners, pledge-holders, hereditary lessees, and those with preemptive rights jostled for advantage. By one means or another one claimant or another now usually emerged with the prize, the unimpeded authority of a sole owner, lord, and possessor. Others posed separate challenges, be they a schulz standing with hereditary tenure and customary law between lord and fixed-rent tenants, a cleric backed by episcopal sanctions demanding tithe or parish dues, or a creditor siphoning off peasant payments and hailing village debtors into an external court. There lay the long-term significance of that replacement of other lenders traceable to the 1470s or so, of those curbs on ecclesiastical claims by violence, coerced agreements, or new religious sentiment, and of those weakened, impoverished, or subverted schulzen. Lords aimed thus to squeeze out or hedge about what opposition they could not buy up.

To the same interpretive context belong lords' interventions in two other hitherto separate social subsystems, the market and the law. Urban indignation at violations of town marketing rights swelled under Mathias, but repeated law-making had little effect. Illegal taverns remained a steady irritant, not merely between towns and clerical lords, as some petitions suggest, but as Środa well knew in the 1530s–40s, with lay owners as well.[31] Lords who bought up hereditary free taverns, like Sebald Sauerman at Wierzbica, or who established their own, as Środa accused Adam Wolff at Samborz, Henry Kreiselwitz at Ogrodnica, and others elsewhere,[32] gained more than revenues. They inserted their own authority into yet another formerly independent avenue of contact between their peasants and the world beyond the village.

Capital jurisdiction over most villagers in the Wrocław duchy had entered private possession by the early fifteenth century, but fragmented lordship then made exercise of *iura ducalia* more remunerative than authoritative. The contribution of private jurisdiction to the shaping of a new rural regime was thus delayed until final consolidations gave it value for that purpose. As a single *Erbherr* now drew this right, too, into his sole purview, its potential was realized and more. Early sixteenth-century compilations, notably the *Constitutio Criminalis Carolina* of 1532 which applied around Wrocław, imported authoritarian norms from learned Roman theory and, by freeing holders of patrimonial jurisdiction to declare for their subjects their own law, weakened the protective force of ancient custom.[33]

Around 1500 *Erbherren* were thus emerging as the chief and often sole mediating link between peasant communities and the larger surrounding society. As the new rural regime took shape they seized the strategic place held by the schulz in the old. To the *Erbherr* turned the expectations of outsiders who had claims in a village. When fellows from Kostomłoty and Zabłoto wrecked the toll gate at Środa, the town magistrates, who had had them in custody, wrote to the abbot of St. Vincent asking that they be punished.[34] A cleric whose tithes or *census* went unpaid was to turn first to the lord and, if the lord failed him, prosecute the lord in the church courts.[35] As captain of the duchy the Wrocław council called on landowners to clear debris from flood-prone watercourses, to maintain roads and bridges, and, when Silesia feared the coming of the Turk, to muster their militarily capable subjects.[36]

Expectations reflected practice. Around 1500 lords handled many different connections between peasants and the rest of society. They took responsibility for enforcing what others demanded of their subjects. These might be financial: what a schulz once did was a task of "Lord Albrecht Sauerman" at Radomierzyce in 1529, who collected from the people ten florins owed for the lease of land at Wysoka and paid it to the Holy Spirit Hospital.[37] Other claims had a more public character, as when St. Vincent, the cathedral chapter, and the city of Wrocław joined to have local peasants pay for construction of new bridges over the Ślęza between Grabiszyn,

Oporów, and Muchobór Wielki.[38] Nicholas Krig, lord of Pasterzyce in 1531, punished one of his own tenants for acts in contempt of the Małuszów lord's court.[39]

Perhaps as often as lords pressed external claims against their subjects, they projected village concerns outward and upward. To protect villagers served peasant interests (and the lord's own). Some cases followed horizontal lines. The chapter acted for men of Biestrzyków and of Bliż caught up in feuds with outsiders, and for Peter Woywoda of Wilkowice, to whom a peasant from a village near Oława owed money.[40] Lords of Małuszów and of Żerniki Wrocławskie together mediated an inheritance dispute between people from the two villages.[41]

Lord and peasant interests best coincided when it came to repelling ostensibly superior claims of almost any kind. The district of Środa in 1473 assessed a tax on Święte, so Bishop Rudolf wrote sharply to remind Wrocław that those people belonged only to his jurisdiction.[42] The chapter defended its tenants against former lords or neighboring lords, laymen, nuns, or fellow canons.[43] At Domasław between 1526 and 1529 the lord, Hans "the Peasants' Enemy" Berlin, bare months from crushing resistance at Krępice, and the village leaders, among them men who would submit to labor services under Berlin's successor, together struggled against the absentee curate, Balthasar Logaw, cantor of Holy Cross. In one reported confrontation Logaw accused Berlin of bringing "Lutheran hooligans (*Buben*)" into his church. Berlin, whose forebearance amazed the villagers, retorted "because you will not keep watch over my people with God's law like a [proper] pastor, I must see to it they are cared for with that and do not live like beasts."[44]

Lutheran ideas were not required for lords to speak for their villages against the intrusions of clerics. Hans Berlin himself had demonstrated that with characteristic verve more than a decade earlier. In October, 1512, Bogunów was plundered and burned during the feuds over Christopher von Reisewitz. Berlin was (in right of his wife) *Erbherr*, and by early in the new year had approached the cathedral chapter for freedom from tithes while villagers rebuilt. The canons offered six years full exemption and six more at a reduced rate. Berlin demanded eight and eight. He then stuck to his demand through two meetings with appointed negotiators, a threat that if he seeded his own fields he would be tithed at the full rate, and yet another appearance before the entire chapter.[45]

Others than brash sixteenth-century lay lords like Hans Berlin also stubbornly contested tithes. Back in the 1460s the abbot of St. Mary and his peasants of Brochów defied three definitive sentences from church courts to make the rector of St. Maurice take only what they asserted were the customary rates.[46] But the church records do give some of the best examples of how lords were taking on the tasks once done by schulzen. In three days at the turn of 1513–14, Albert Scheuerlein, *Erbherr* at Jagodno, first won absolution from the cathedral chapter for a woman whose family had been banned for tithe refusal and then gained a mediated agreement on what the villagers would be expected to pay—which he, Scheuerlein, would collect and give in their name.[47]

The *Erbherr*, then, is around 1500 caught in the act of replacing the schulz as "broker" between peasant society and the non-peasant elite.[48] The change of actor changed the role itself. A schulz is recognizably what sociologists call a "village notable," defined by his marginality and successful in his mediative function from his simultaneously serving the values of both local community and exterior society. The schulz as broker embodied the balance between lord and peasant fundamental to the regime of German law. The new broker was not a notable, not marginal, not between lord and peasant, but the lord himself. He derived his authority from sources wholly external to the village community and peasant society. The lord as broker embodied pervasive and immediate elite control over peasants. When that control penetrated the very core of village affairs, the old distance separating lord and peasant had collapsed. In the emerging regime confrontation of lord and peasant was direct and unequal. Lords linked and lords ruled.

During the late fifteenth and early sixteenth centuries lords were imposing and exercising their superior authority over and within village communities around Wrocław.[49] They made their position clear. The first substantive entry in the village court book begun at *Olbino* in 1528 is the oath each villager swore:

> I, [gives name], pledge and swear to be loyal, true, and subject to the most worthy Lord John, Bishop and Abbot, His Grace, as my legitimate natural hereditary lord, and to the praiseworthy foundation of St. Vincent at Wrocław, to watch out for the property and best of His Grace and of the abbey, and to protect [it] from evil, with my entire ability, so help me God.[50]

Wrocław's first act upon taking possession of the Holy Spirit Hospital in 1525 was to extract a like oath from those on its lordships, as did Hans Colmann, the citizen who took Domasław in pledge in 1537. Colmann's contract further specified that he would run the village court, a display of authority the lords of Popowice had been sure to make since the 1470s.[51]

These men wielded power to enforce their authority. As lord of Popowice the rector of Środa, John Ruster, exiled from the village a peasant who would not obey.[52] The canon in charge of Jelenin reported in early 1516 that he had led soldiers to capture disobedient peasants and thrown the rebels in prison. Only sufficient personal pledges would get them out.[53] Jail was in early 1532 threatened against those who refused rents at Małuszów. The taverner there, a man with a troublesome reputation (the year before it had been false beer measures and a brawl with the herdsman), was also at community request held for five days, fined, and required to give six personal guarantors for future peace with the "herschafte unnd gemeyn."[54] The last phrase is a telling one; not schulz and community but lordship and community form the village now.

Not only the criminal and disobedient felt the strength of the *Erbherr*. His power sliced deep into the economic rights and resources of all villagers. The lord intervened in the disposition of land and wealth among subject households (not yet, it seems, gratuitously, but no less tellingly). The cathedral chapter took over and settled a dispute over a land survey at Kończyce and intervened when two men at Rzeplin exchanged a *census*. At Popowice by mid-century the lord was determining how many sheep each subject was to keep.[55]

Lords manipulated what they took from their tenants, too. In this they might show consideration, as at Polanowice where the chapter forgave some rents for poverty and then reduced all because of flood damages.[56] Economic intervention was, however, arbitrary, not customary, and very much in the lord's own interest. At Kryniczno in 1510 the decision to take cash for grain dues, with a rate set by the market price, would be enforced even if the peasants objected; the same rule applied to payments in lieu of *Hofarbeit* at Domasław.[57] The power of the lord made even fixed obligations, that fundamental principle of tenant rights under German law, a potential victim of the desire for revenues. The student hospice of St. John received the dues from Kryniczno but five marks a year therefrom went to the mansionarii of Holy Cross. This repurchaseable *census* the schulz and community had themselves established for fifty marks back in 1406, but in 1511 the cathedral chapter decided the scholars needed more funds. They imposed a "contribution" on the peasants of Kryniczno so the hospice could buy the rent.[58] That was one way aggressive lordship could solve its problem of debased customary rents.

What peasants paid the *Erbherr* received. Ruling lords were economic managers who used their authority to generate incomes from their properties and rights. Control of his lordship let the *Erbherr* direct the use of its resources. Was this lesson of survival learned in the mid–fifteenth century, when lords' distance from the agrarian economy proved so costly to them? Manipulating the height and form of tenant obligations helped insure the lord's incomes from rental land against debasement and default. Authority, available resources, and demand to be filled also encouraged lords to re-assess the potential of producing on their own accounts in traditional and innovative ways.

Growth of demesne production accompanied the spread of serfdom in sixteenth-century Silesia, beginning slowly before and attaining peak rates after 1550. Landlord farms made from former woodland or by dispossessing schulzen and tenants marketed surpluses of cereals, livestock, and other commodities. Some relied exclusively on compulsory peasant labor, but in northern and central Silesia self-contained enterprises commonly employed paid servants and gertner, and across the province as a whole lords using a mix of free and forced workers were probably most numerous.[59] Estate farming in sixteenth-century Silesia thus more closely resembled that in contemporary Bohemia and Hungary than in the Polish kingdom, where export grain production and heavy use of forced peasant labor were central by 1500.[60] Nonetheless the province had reversed three centuries of shrinking landlord involvement in the productive activities of the countryside.

Around Wrocław in the late fifteenth and early sixteenth centuries landowners were establishing foundations for their later preeminence in various rural economic sectors. They invested time, energy, and capital in traditional pastoral and arable farming and in promising new pursuits. As significant as any particulars, however, is the growing concern for close economic management these collectively reveal.

Local circumstances meant not all such activities were new. Most fully documented at this time are landlord farms reminiscent of the fourteenth century, small livestock or mixed farming enterprises on bottomland or black earth sites. Those in corporate estates were managed in time-honored ways. Krzyki, for instance, belonged to the Holy Trinity Hospital, whose administrator in the late 1480s let out highly detailed lease/labor contracts for operation of its eight or nine mansi, three hundred sheep, and seventy-odd other animals.[61] The "Hofemann" signed on for three years and the shepherd for one, each receiving maintenance, shares in the product, and a cash salary. Their responsibilities were minutely inventoried. Another managerial mode required closer supervision and use as needed of a wage labor force. Canon Stanisław Borg had the chapter's Kozanów for life and continued residence. He spent more than seventy marks on capital improvements and hired workers from Gądów Małe. When plans to leave Wrocław in 1516 caused him to surrender the farm, the chapter quickly approved provisional assignment to canon Henry Esewein, "lest for lack of a governor this demesne be desolated in its fields or suffer any other waste."[62] Landowners knew that successful demesne farming demanded continual attention.

Vague and isolated records hint that some upland farms with more emphasis on grain production were similarly managed,[63] but simply too little is known about these—and about arrangements on all lay lordships. This is a serious gap, for such properties later had considerable quantitative importance[64] and their gradual expansion is fully visible in the period of interest here. In the mid-1490s Nicholas Luckow had already added to his four mansi of demesne at Jugowiec another four that had been rental land, while at Ogrodnica nearby the heirs of Peter Kreiselwitz had taken over the fields of the scholtisei and some deserted land. Sebald Sauerman augmented his demesne farm at Wierzbica in 1496 when he bought the four mansi of the schulz and two of the taverner.[65] Thus Wrocław duchy lords early drew upon all easily accessible sources of arable to expand their demesnes.

Wholly new landlord farms wait another generation. About 1525 Nicholas Tschesche at Borek Strzeliński bought out claimants to four empty mansi, added two more from an unknown source, built barns, stables, and a house for a farm manager, and had this run in parallel to the nine-mansi demesne he already worked there.[66] By the early 1540s the squire (from a one-time city family), Hans Rothe of Jakubowice, and the senior Wrocław councillor, Stephen Heugel, were both buying out peasants to make large new *Vorwerke* at Domasław and at Krępice respectively.[67]

Managerial concerns of lords with relatively labor-intensive grain farms are reflected in local and regional efforts to manipulate the supply and cost of labor. Compulsory work by tenants was one response: specifications of *Hofarbeit* normally included plow and harvest services. That wage labor long had equal or greater importance is shown by its repeated regulation through ordinances of princely Diets and the Wrocław council. In 1513, for instance, the former set maximum rates for many rural workers, from plowmen, dairy maids, cooks, and wagoners paid by the year a mark and more to mowers, diggers, or carpenters making a groschen or two a day. Wrocław attended directly to the grain harvest. Proclamations issued early each July set the current coin to be given daily for rye, wheat, and grass cutters, rakers, and binders. Around the city these workers could get up to half again what the provincial legislation allowed (2.5 or 3 as opposed to 2 groschen for mowers of rye) and those working on wheat always rated a further premium. Maximum wage rates responded to employers' perceptions of supply shortages and so did negative incentives built into the city legislation. Able-bodied vagrants were to be reported by inn-keepers and given three days to take work at the wages set, leave, or be beaten.[68]

A third response to labor needs of the grain harvest was continued hiring of migrants from Poland. They entered the written record by the hungry hundreds whenever the early summer weather failed to get the central

Silesian crop ready by their arrival in the first week of July.[69] All such means answered in lords' interests the needs of their farms for workers.

Landlord farms around early sixteenth-century Wrocław drew labor from the market and sent product there. The city's regulations and tolls were special complaints of the nobility in 1522. Knights argued against violations of their privileges when "we drive with our grain into the city . . . and with our fish on the fish market and other of our country produce."[70] So noble operators of demesne enterprises produced for sale grain and other commodities, notably fish.

Non-agricultural rural production especially attracted innovation and investment from fifteenth- and early sixteenth-century landowners around Wrocław. Forestry, fisheries, artificial fish culture, and manufacturing promised returns to careful managers. Natural woodlands near the city and its markets were worth attention. Leonard Steyrer called Gressel, a town councillor until he was expelled in 1515, used controlled burning to improve the timber growing on his land beside Kozanów; his example caused the cathedral chapter to consider the same technique. If only from the canons' own experience with the Polanowice woods, they knew that timber was valued for road repairs, housing construction, and fuel. They disputed with their peasant subjects boundaries between demesne and common woodland. Wrocław's corporation also made special efforts to hold the woods at Rędzin.[71]

Ownership of wild fisheries brought gains to those who were alert to defend their rights and to update each year the leases to fishermen who, as before, worked the Odra and its branches. Early sixteenth-century lords were much concerned for the fisheries they controlled, witness the long dispute over that in the Oława between Księże Małe and Wielkie and another precipitated when fishers from Wrocław followed their quarry on to waters then flooding cathedral chapter land at Kozanów.[72] Such attention was rewarded. The fishery gave 2.5 marks of the 18.5 the city received in 1468 from lordship over Kowale. The annual lease of that at Kotowice brought Trzebnica 7 marks in 1523, when rents and fiscal rights over the whole village yielded only 35.[73]

Barthel Stein, master of the Corpus Christi Commandery and humanist encomiast of Silesia, remarked in 1513 on the many artificial fish ponds around Wrocław.[74] Rich evidence affirms his testimony. Fish culture constituted a creative response of late medieval landowners to labor shortages, surplus land, and market opportunities.[75] Because the relative chronology of east-central European pisciculture is unsure, it cannot be determined whether this innovation first arrived at Wrocław from Bohemia—where advanced methods had a good foothold before the Hussite revolution—or from elsewhere in Silesia or Poland.[76] By the late fifteenth and early sixteenth century the artificial rearing of fish was a noteworthy development throughout the region.

Lords in the Duchy of Wrocław actively developed their ponds from the mid-fifteenth to the early sixteenth century. Consortia of citizens and nobles first built several in the wet terrain of the north-central Środa district.[77] Elsewhere in the duchy no comparable projects are verifiable before the 1470s, although the chronicler at St. Mary later recalled that heavy floods of 1464 damaged "innumerable fish ponds in Silesia."[78] By 1500 all sorts of landowners were constructing, operating, and dealing in ponds everywhere that subsequent maps show such standing waters in the duchy.[79] A law of 1513 set a groschen a day as the diggers' pay.[80] Still, the multipond complexes which by then sprawled across the northern third of the Środa district remained the most important concentration among the two dozen or more groupings known in the duchy by the second quarter of the century.

Artificial fish culture required large-scale engineering, technical sophistication, entrepreneurial talent, and social authority. Earthen dams in watercourses drowned former fields and meadows, while operational needs to drain ponds regularly called for sluices and outlet channels. Hence most pond builders had to gain agreement from several landowners and to consider how they would deal with peasants whom their work injured or displaced. Negotiations over the "Stockichten Teich" between Białków, Mrozów, and Wojnowice busied the Schellendorf brothers, Peter Krig, and Krig's heirs for almost a decade; both parties agreed to compensate flooded peasants in accord with knowledgeable estimates of damage.[81] Effective running of the enterprise also demanded holding tanks and regular stocking. Ponds at Zabór in 1494 received 9000 three-year-old carp raised by Hans Dompnig. By this time Wrocław had a lively market in cultivated fish, supplied in bulk by, among others, Peter [3] Krig.[82]

The commercial rearing of fish demanded capital beyond the capacity of peasants. Only lords could mobilize the reputed thousand florins John Löbschütz spent about 1490 to repair and enlarge the pond complex at St. Vincent. Then he put eight hundred marks more into a big new pond just across the Widawa from the duchy—and that did not include the value of tolls he first exchanged for complete authority over the village.[83] Returns were commensurate if all went well. Ursula Bank was able as early as 1472 to borrow a hundred marks against security of only half her incomes from what could not have been a large pond at Magnice.[84] No wonder the nobility expressly defended their rights freely to market fish in Wrocław. And no wonder the first European compendium on artificial fish culture, though written by the Moravian prelate Jan Skalý z Dubravka (Jan Dubravius) for Anton Fugger in 1525, first came into print in 1547 at the press of Andreas Vingler in Wrocław.[85] Careful and profit-oriented landowners there had long known the value of such expertise.

The pond sites and water needed for fish production were common if not ubiquitous in the duchy. But its few landless peasants made successful promotion of rural industry depend on the rare combination of good access to raw materials and markets. Any lord was pleased to have revenues from traditional rural crafts,[86] but before 1530 more capital-intensive activities are found only quite near the city. At Złotniki, for instance, Hans Haunold received in his 1502 privilege express permission to erect a "Hammer."[87] The new idea worked. A quarter-century later Hedwig Kupferschmiedin ceded to Benedict Kinast Kupferschmied her "Kupferhammer" in that place.[88] A hammer-mill there had water power from the Bystrzyca and in the city a day's journey away its customers and its (imported) supplies of raw copper.

Landowners closer to the city had more lucrative opportunities as dangerous and noxious processing operations moved out to suburban sites, not among the southerly market gardens but north and west along the river channels. A rendering plant was built in 1493 on streamside meadows in *Szczepin*. Across the Odra an older industrial zone grew. The tar works formerly at the city's Odra gate moved in 1521 to a new site in *Olbino*. Slaughter houses had multiplied there and spread downstream into *Rzepina* since the mid-fifteenth century. Wax and gunpowder manufacturing followed. In the 1530s were added a wire mill and a copper hammer like that at Złotniki. This one paid yearly to Wrocław, lord of the land and community, eight marks in rent.[89] Over the next couple of centuries lords of settlements along the river from Szczytniki to Osobowice would erect and own distilleries, lime and plaster works, paper mills, starch factories, and other heavy quasi-industrial operations.[90]

In the years around 1500, then, lords began rapidly to close the distance that had separated them from rural economic activity. In ruling peasant subjects, linking village communities to a larger social whole, managing their own demesne enterprises, and seeking the labor and markets to make the last remunerative, early sixteenth-century landowners had ceased to treat their properties as mere territorially-defined rights to regular incomes. They were themselves now possessors of productive resources and lords over men.

Shifts in the format and vocabulary of the records lords kept may be taken to symbolize a changing of minds. This investigation began with texts from a patrimonial age. Charters of Henry the Bearded regularly named peasants whose personal servitude and social category established their specific social relations and obligations. During the age of German law, however, characteristic rural records differed; lords held and transferred villages described in terse summary statements: so many *mansi censuales* at such and such a rate per mansus and the schulz has a certain amount of free land and duties. Lists of named tenants were rare then, for lords did not rule men so much as own identifiable territory with particular charges against it.

The situation altered some during the fifteenth century. Genuine rent and income registers became more common as the elite learned from experience that abstract claims to income were not, in fact, revenue received. It made good sense to list tenant, holding, obligation, and actual payment and, in effect, to think of land along with the men who gave it value. Until sometime in the sixteenth century, however, land and people still usually went together. A tenant mattered—and thus had his name listed by some lord's officer—because he held land. Those without land—and here both gertner and the wholly landless come quickly to mind—were not, as a matter of course, worthy of record.

The last, too, began to change in the sixteenth century. By its end lords were keeping track of men not, in the first instance, by their holdings, but by their social category.[91] Peasants, gertner, cottagers, servants, craftsmen, or whatever status, they belonged to the lord as his subjects, paid to him their obligations, and hence, whatever the resources he might allow them to use, had importance to him in their persons.

The personal and patriarchal outlook of the elite surfaced earlier in passing phrases than in whole genre of records. As early as 1469/70 Bernhard Wende ceded "the schulz, peasants, and patronage right" at Proszków where previous texts spoke only of the village and its court.[92] Constantine Meissner installed a new free schulz at Domasław in 1514 but specified that he was to "hold" only to Constantine himself as his *Erbherr*.[93] Then during and after the 1520s come charters wherein lords transfer "a peasant," "two peasants," or the like.[94] The lord's peasants had become "his people" and that meant he had responsibility for them. The Kolovrat agreement of 1504 speaks often of "die Lewt" and of the need to ensure they "nit zu Schaden kemen" and "nicht zu Grunde verderpt werden."[95] The assumptions required only clarification from Lutheran ideology to become Hans Berlin's "*I* must see to it that . . . *my* people [mein Leute] are cared for and do not live like beasts."[96] But Hans was simultaneously "the Peasant's Enemy," and his apparant paradox of care and enmity encapsulates the two faces of the new *Erbherr*: the peasants were "his" and his was the responsibility for their care; they were not animals but they were not free people.

Thus even around Wrocław, even with what were by east-central European standards rich agricultural resources, nearby urban markets, and a dense population of prosperous farmers, the chill of neoserfdom slowly seeped across the land. For the pluralism of the age of German law, unequal though it always was and already lamed in the fifteenth-century crisis, it substituted a closing of options, a hierarchical rigidity, a sense of authority, monopoly, and constraint. The positive-sum game, which had in the thirteenth and fourteenth centuries enriched most groups in the rural duchy, lords and peasants alike, now, for all the efforts of some to restore it, ended. The new was a zero- or negative-sum game; its rules placed a premium on power. Those who had it and knew to wield it won in early modern central Silesia as elsewhere in the larger region. Those who lacked it, the peasant population or, in contemporary parlance, *arme lewte*, bowed before it as they had not for three hundred years past.

§§ 13 §§

RETROSPECT: RURAL LIVES AROUND LATE MEDIEVAL WROCŁAW

. . . réalité est faite, sans fin, d'individus et de combats; l'évolution humain est le produit d'innombrables causes partielles et de conséquences multiples, directes et indirectes. . . .

Robert S. Lopez, *Naissance de l'Europe*, p. 12.

A circuitous journey of exploration through a small but complex historical terrain reaches an end (with regret for byways untraced on harsh practicality's curtailed itinerary). The announced intent was to identify major elements of human experiences in the medieval countryside around Wrocław and to understand how these came about. In prospect, three contextual questions were offered for provisional ordering of observations. What was the trajectory of economic change? How did relationships of lords and peasants form an agrarian society? What agents shaped the successive east-central European transitions to the developmental dynamic of freedom in the High Middle Ages and the repressive sterility of neoserfdom at their close?

The analytical issues deserve final summation. Economic growth in the central Silesian countryside did lag behind and then converge toward patterns earlier begun further west. By 1200 increases in human numbers and elite wants were prompting experiments for greater production. A native Polish elite took the initiative in reorganizing relationships between themselves, peasant cultivators, and land resources. To gain willing collaborators they adjusted the risks and benefits from farming, removing themselves from close connection with agriculture and the lives of those who practiced it. They imported institutions and encouraged immigrants that would help achieve their purposes. The proven arrangements of the German law rewarded *locatores* who led peasants to build a larger and more productive rural economy based on peasant family farms with links to urban markets.

Except when high cereal prices tipped the balance, tenant farming held for over two hundred years a slight but effective edge over larger landlord farms.

Economic troubles at the close of the Middle Ages had connections to problems elsewhere—early fourteenth-century harvest failures, bullion shortages, a "spillover" from crisis in Bohemia—and distinct domestic aspects. Plague was here first delayed and then survived with little damage to economic activity. Then in the 1400s symptoms of rural crisis followed exogenous stresses. They were chiefly political and meteorological, but resembled in their effects, notably depopulation and lower landed incomes, those seen in other parts of Europe. The Duchy of Wrocław surely generated less agricultural product in 1480 than it had in 1350 and marketed less, too, but per capita wealth among peasant survivors had probably grown. The trigger for "recession" is not easily found in antecedent conditions of this regional economy.

The operation and eventual transformation of rural society around late medieval Wrocław depended on synergy between agrarian institutions and the social environments of lords and peasants. Especially critical for the autonomy of village communities under the German law was the economic and social "distance" of lords from their properties. Between the twelfth-century and the fifteenth landowners around Wrocław found most property better met their socially defined needs when treated as a source of regular revenues than as a bundle of potentially productive resources. Cyclic social processes and historical processes were connected. When lords collectively changed the social function of property a change of agrarian relations followed.

On the long-obscure social terrain within the village, leadership by schulzen balanced the distance of lords. But while headmen brokered community dealings with non-peasant society, peasants moved in a complex web of individual relations. Initiatives freely exercised under the German law deny stereotypes of repressed and quiescent east-central European peasants.

The regional setting well sustains the departure of contemporary east-central European historiography from inappropriate dependence on ethnocultural variables. Certainly the area around Wrocław became and remained during the later Middle Ages a zone of complex ethnic mingling. Encounters there among persons of native Polish and migrant German or other origin encouraged a distinct Silesian identity. But ethnic difference was no determinant of socio-economic behavior in the countryside, for lords and peasants of whatever cultural distinction shared common experiences—of clearing new land in the 1270s, of failed harvests during the 1310s, of plagues escaped in 1348–51 but not 1361 or 1372, and of wealth destroyed in 1428, 1459, or 1474.

Shared among protagonists of whatever ethnic origin were also the peasant liberty of the High Middle Ages and servitude of their end. Both tranformations were driven by lords demanding net revenues, but necessary preconditions, operational motives, and peasant responses differed. Growing populations and markets and available resources and technology gave thirteenth century possessors of rights over land the confidence to release productive factors to immigrant and native peasants in return for risk-free fixed money dues. Freedom and the gains from greater productivity gave cultivators incentive to accept the offer.

Servitude came along a path of multiple contingencies and consequences. After lords gained private possession of lucrative public jurisdictions, they learned in the fifteenth century the dangers of fixed cash incomes and distance from productive resources. When only those who controlled resources could assuredly receive revenues, at least some lords lost confidence that the regime of German law could still satisfy their wants. The same economic troubles and their effects—impoverishment of schulzen and others, rapid turnover of tenant households, weakening of pluralism in the village—corroded the defenses of peasant communities. Then each completed consolidation of all owners' rights reduced local competition among the elite. In the circumstances of about 1500 not incentives but coercion achieved the control by the lord that then seemed to assure the revenues of a more unitary landowning group.

The past was not lived by historian's issues but by whole human beings. This exploration found complex regional and individual experiences at the simultaneous intersection of all the themes. At the level of data and criticism, empirically supportable generalizations take statistical and stochastic rather than law-like and deterministic form. At the level of understanding and explanation are found contingency and pragmatic human responses to situations. In retrospect, four sequentially overlapping interpretive ideas—development, stable pluralism, survival, exploitation—helped carry this treatment forward from the twelfth century to the sixteenth. Each in succession framed settings for individuals of all social stations. Occasionally even the shaping of particular lives can be made out.

The developmental transformation of agrarian relationships dominated the twelfth through the fourteenth centuries. Pressures of peasant numbers and elite wants could drive a developmental dynamic only through creative entrepreneurial responses by people of both high and ordinary standing. What a Duke Henry or an Abbess Gertrude instigated gave to others indispensable roles. Visible participants were the *locatores* like Lambert of Tyniec at Zabłoto in the 1240s, Hanco Dremelik at Siechnice in the 1350s, and then Menzelinus, whose plans for Stabłowice the plague shattered. Obscured by the very structures which promoted innovation are the peasant cultivators who adopted new institutions and methods.

Developmental success was a multi-cultural enterprise. Around Wrocław early changes were autochthonous, what became key village institutions were imported, German peasant immigrants demonstrated the worth of new institutions and of new arable, and indigenous people rapidly multiplied the success. To make development work in high medieval central Silesia it had to benefit all participants, lord and peasant, migrant and native. From the late twelfth century through at least the 1350s, perhaps the 1410s, the agricultural sector of the duchy was, taken globally, a situation in which all gained.

A socio-economic system, the regime of German law, resulted from high medieval development and gave structural shape to times here called "the long fourteenth century." Almost everywhere some options or alternatives were available—resources in bottomlands, black earth, and loam; strategies for the social use of property; choices of economic opportunities. Fundamental relationships between lords and peasants were, however, firm, and manifest in stable institutional settings and notionally traditional total transfers from agriculturalists to the elite. Members of the latter like Nicholas Sittin, Conrad of Borsnicz, and their heirs competed with their peers in a constrained environment shaped by socio-biological cycles of lives and families. In autonomous communities farmers retained the yield of greater productivity or self-exploitation. Only late and locally did their larger numbers press against limited resources and an ossifying agricultural technology. Personal mobility, occupational and marketing opportunities, credit and kinship networks reinforced the ability of villagers—glimpses were caught of a Nicholas of Stary Dwór and a Nicholas Unverworn—to negotiate safely with the several changing elite individuals who claimed ownership rights in land. Differences in ethnicity and culture also remained plural elements in the countryside.

In the fifteenth century a new situation supplanted development and pluralism because external forces damaged the agricultural system. For some people it became a question of physical and for others of social survival. All suffered when production fell and then peasants shifted their own losses to their lords—who had to choose their own response. The same conditions that let Bartek Rusticus refuse to pay tithe led Czasław Sommerfeld and Henry Dompnig to sustain elite position by means not earlier acceptable. Some survivors acheived success but the regime of German law was crippled.

An exploitative regime of neoserfdom in the duchy grew from the four-teenth-century assimilation of sovereign authority and the fifteenth-century loss of revenues experienced by all landowners. It advanced after changes in key social situations of both lords and peasants. The successive careers of Nicholas, Caspar, and Hans Popplau—town-born courtier, repressive ju-rist, merchant retired to lordship—caught one configuration. The coerced leading villager Bartusch Kosel and Plusske Rossel the lord's agent exem-plified peasant counterparts. *Erbherrn* around 1500 had the strength to move against peasants and the motivation to secure greater real incomes from agriculture. Hans Berlin showed that none could deny their will. If the global positive-sum conditions of earlier centuries were long-gone, then each rural lordship was potentially a zero-sum game in which the lord was well-placed not to lose. Social, physical, economic, and mental structures damaged during the fifteenth century became mere wreckage for removal or materials for reuse in new forms shaping a starker regime. When freedom failed peasant prosperity was an ephemeral substitute.

The medieval Duchy of Wrocław was an unusual place. Its small terri-tory held good agricultural resources and a large market. Its history estab-lished greater local cultural variety than may have been the norm elsewhere even in east-central Europe, for it included urban and rural, German and Slavic, and centers of secular and ecclesiastical cultures. An enduring politi-cal fracture zone reduced large-scale "state" influence and made "big" events also local ones with direct effect in the countryside. In consequence the Duchy of Wrocław is "representative" not of Silesia—where other re-gions had much lower urbanization and poorer soils, for instance—, not of Poland—with which it shared not half of the story here told—, and not of east-central Europe as a whole—where development generally came a little later and serfdom a little earlier and state politics mattered more, by and large. But can any real region or area stand for others over a long time?

The Duchy of Wrocław is no representative of east-central Europe. Its inhabitants were collectively well-documented participants in particular versions of human experiences also shared by others in that region. As else-where, people responded to situations as they perceived them. This book has set those situations and people around Wrocław into the shared western pasts we call the Middle Ages.

§§§§§§§

Appendices

Appendix A

MATERIALS AND METHODS FOR MEASURING LONG-TERM CHANGE IN LORDSHIP AND FARM MANAGEMENT

The Duchy of Wrocław is rich in two kinds of records unusual in medieval rural history, surveys which describe many settlements at a single time and conveyances of property among lords. Neither can be used simply. Techniques to extract quantitative data from these documents must recognize and control for their original purposes and character. This appendix presents the main sources and methods used to estimate changes in landownership and in the relative importance of demesne and tenant farming.

Sources: surveys and conveyancing

1. The "Liber fundationis episcopatus Wratislaviensis" (*LFE*) of about 1300 catalogs rights and properties belonging to the Church of Wrocław. Besides lordships and tithe villages in the *mensa episcopalis*, it includes grants from the *mensa* of life tenures to individual prelates and fiefs to episcopal vassals. Missing are the chapter's corporate holdings and those of cathedral prebends. A second manuscript also contains a fragmentary version listing only *mensa* properties around Wrocław.[1]

The medieval diocese of Wrocław and *LFE* contained four regional archdeaconries, two of which divided the duchy. Included with other areas in the Wrocław archdeaconry were the Wrocław and Uraz districts. Under several administrative and territorial headings this register covers 41 identifiable settlements in the Wrocław district, indicating ownership arrangements and the presence of peasant tenants or demesne. But only 8 such entries are complete descriptions of land in the village. Nor are any such among the 6 more places listed from the Uraz district.[2] The Środa district in the archdeaconry of Legnica, was surveyed in *LFE* by type of income—field tithes, fixed grain tithes, fixed money tithes, etc.—more than territorial unit. This causes several places to be mentioned more than once. Cathedral clerks often knew little of secular boundaries. Hence entries can correctly be assigned to only 12 Środa district settlements and only the 3 which belonged to the bishop have reasonably complete inventories of the land there.[3]

Scholars agree that *LFE* was compiled at the turn of the century but not as a single document.[4] The Wrocław register was begun during 1295–99 and completed before the death of Bishop John III Romka in 1301, while relevant parts of the Legnica register date, as there indicated, to 1305.[5] Because the whole was a working text, some individual entries even contain, especially in the names of subordinate possessors, accretions as late as the 1350s. The ultimate published edition is a tenurial palimpsest and its details best verified against other available records.

LFE was a tool for the financial administration of the bishops. Because their rights included both ownership and tithes, their own and secular lordships occur among the 59 Wrocław duchy settlements there listed, 11 of which are full numerical descriptions of the place. For the purposes of this discussion, the *LFE* is treated as representing conditions around 1300 in a sample of 25 percent of the 234 settlements then documented in the duchy.

2. A mid-fourteenth-century "Registrum villarum, allodiorum et jurium ducatus Wratislaviensis et districtus Nampslaviensis," now no longer extant, was published in 1843 as "Das Landbuch des Fürstenthums Breslau" (*LB*).[6] Neither the editor, Gustav A.H. Stenzel, nor the sole later commentator, Carl Brinkmann,[7] then made entirely clear whether they dealt with one codex containing two versions, a draft (*Konzept*) and a fine copy (*Original*), or two separate manuscripts, K and O. Brinkmann also mentioned another with the date 1361 but did not specify if this was where Stenzel obtained the *exactio* (*Geschoss*) payments which he appended to the *LB* proper.[8] It is clear, however, that the *LB* as published by Stenzel contains items from more than one original.

Disparate contents and organizing procedures mark *LB* as an early effort to account for sovereign lands and rights and not the product of an experienced bureaucracy. But in a society where some owners had special rights over their properties it made good sense to mix organization according to geographical criteria with separate headings for ecclesiastical landlords and for demesne holdings. Each rubric groups numerical descriptions of rural settlements, examples of which head chapters 5 and 6 above. No landowners are systematically omitted, but lay lords are not always named and independent demesne farms in the Środa district are nowhere listed.

The whole of *LB* contains 385 separate entries for Wrocław duchy settlements in the main survey sections and another 165 in separate listings of mills, service obligations, *exactio* receipts, and so on. Many places appear more than once, for demesnes entered as part of the whole village often recur in catalogs of demesnes and places with divided lordship may appear twice. After these are combined and the handful of unidentifiable names (without further information attached) eliminated, *LB* produces for the Duchy of Wrocław itself a list of 284 identifiable places, 207 of which have all their land described.[9]

The enquiry which produced *LB* began in 1352 with a letter from Emperor Charles telling the Wrocław council to help the chancellor, Dietmar Meckenbach, investigate and improve the administration of sovereign rights and incomes.[10] What Stenzel published, however, comprised sections from both the draft (K) and the fine copy (O) that resulted. Brinkmann suggested that K served chancery officials as a working office copy while O became the permanent file record. Ordinarily the editor used O as his basic text and noted the dozen or so cases in which the K counterparts differed, usually by giving more details. But Stenzel also printed from K materials not in O, notably lists of mills and of taxes received. In O only the general statement of ducal rights bears a date, 1353,[11] but parts of K are dated 1358 and 1361[12] and the codex described by Brinkmann had a partly legible cover date, either 1363 or 1373.[13] The extreme dates within the text as published by Stenzel, then, are Wrocław's municipal incomes of 1348/49 and the *exactio* receipts of 1361. Brinkmann would not date the entire collection more precisely than that, but suggested that the basic Wrocław duchy survey (#1–220) was done in 1353 while demesnes (#221–386) may have been listed as late as 1358.[14]

LB was an official survey of rural properties in the duchy made for fiscal purposes by royal clerks with the aid of the city council. The differing incidence of various fiscal rights called for care in distinguishing among demesne, free, and tenant holdings, while *exactio* returns offer a useful check as to its accuracy. Although the two most important sections may have been compiled as much as five years apart, it still seems appropriate to treat them as a single set of complementary information. The survey of 1353 covers 80 percent of the 354 settlements then in the duchy and gives full numerical information about land distribution in 58 percent of them.

3. Surviving as WAP, AMW, C 20 is the helpfully titled and dated "Registrum omnium bonorum sive villarum et allodiorum in districtibus Wratislaviensi, Noviforensi et Awrassensi super pecunia Burnegelt anno etc. XXV" (RB).[15] It records payment in 1425 of a tax called "burnegelt" assessed at one groschen per mansus in the Wrocław and Uraz districts and a half groschen per mansus in the Środa district (although a few places in the latter paid the full rate). Systematic use of this manuscript is complicated by peculiar features of the tax and its collection.

RB is organized very like *LB*, mostly by district but with separate sections for ecclesiastical estates. Sample entries appear as head notes to chapters 6 and 9 above. Because partial payments of tax from some places were recorded separately and because the clerks at times confused two names for the same place, the register's 212 entries actually refer to 199 separate and identifiable settlements, for 61 of which all land seems accounted.[16]

The tax receipts themselves help check the accuracy of village sizes recorded in RB, and more aid in understanding it comes from a previously unnoticed manuscript. An untitled fragment of a similar text was done by a contemporary hand resembling that of RB itself.[17] The badly battered six leaves which survive record "mansi censuales" in 67 places of which 60 are legible. These replicate the sequence of settlements in RB from "Seschiz" to "Brecenaw,"[18] but leave out a total of 12 entries there. All such omissions are, however, of places either out of the usual alphabetical sequence or repeated elsewhere in RB under a different and older name. Of the 60 pairs of entries legible in both manuscripts, 41 have the same form of name and number of rental mansi. Another 11 such pairs find the RB entry originally the same but visibly corrected to a different number. The fragment, then, seems to have served as a model or draft for assessing the tax eventually compiled as RB.

LB was created as a permanent fiscal register, but RB records the receipt of a particular and unusual tax, the "burnegelt." Thus entries in the two documents are not entirely synonomous. The 1425 assessment seems unique in Silesia, for the term is no customary local one but a Germanization of the Czech *berna* or "aid." In Bohemia, where it had been used since the early Luxemburgs, the *berna* was incident on all subjects of landlords but not on direct exploitation properties.[19] Perhaps in consequence, demesne lands in the Duchy of Wrocław were not taxed and rarely listed in the RB account.[20]

A second important difference between village entries in RB and those in *LB* also derives from the peculiar incidence of the "burnegelt." Unlike most other texts, that of 1425 does not use the term "mansi censuales" to refer exclusively to tenant-held rental mansi. In contrast to normal Silesian practice, efforts were seemingly made also to assess the "burnegelt" against free holdings of schulzen, village priests, and the like. Consequently RB commonly grouped these lands among the "mansi censuales," the "taxable [rather than "rental"] mansi."[21] At Jerzmanowo, for instance, RB records 60 "mansi censuales" and describes 60 mansi, including 3 of the priest, 2 of the schulz, and another that was also somehow peculiar, all of which precisely replicates the situation of the whole village in both 1353 and 1443, when 54 mansi were in the hands of tenants.[22] If read literally, however, the RB entry falsely suggests an 11 percent increase in the number of rental mansi at Jerzmanowo. Plainly and of critical importance, therefore, individual entries in RB can be correctly understood and compared only when they are read in the context of other references to that settlement.

RB also contains notably fewer settlements than either *LB* or the 1443 tax account, 199 as opposed to 284 and 235 in the others respectively. Some omissions are systematic: independent demesne settlements; lordships of the bishops of Wrocław and Lebus; lordships of the Wrocław cathedral chapter. Two nearly contemporary texts help fill the lacunae. The Lebus property register from 1405 includes four of the same Wrocław duchy holdings as appear in the 1443 tax roll. Full information about eight properties of the Wrocław bishop is available in a fragmentary income account dating from 1421/25.[23] For the sake of more complete and representative data from the period immediately before the Hussite wars, the settlements recorded in these texts were added to those from RB itself to give a total sample of 211, 58 percent of the 362 places then in the duchy, and a sub-set of 73 (20%) with full numerical descriptions of their lands.

4. Among the papers of the late eighteenth-century Wrocław antiquarian Samuel B. Klose now in WAP is his holograph copy of a manuscript entitled "Districtus Wratislaviensis liber de mansis comparatus sub anno 1443 per religiosum validum et strennuum ac honestos viros dominos, magistrum s. Mathiae, Mulich Haugwitz militem Wenceslaum Reichil consulem et Henricum Jenkwitz collectores pecuniae ejusdem" (KLM). The original was reported missing in the generation after Klose's death. Klose published a summary, but there translated place-names, gave for each only the total size and amount of deserted land, and left out entries without such information and other remarks in the manuscript.[24]

KLM covers the entire duchy (not just the Wrocław district of its title) and includes lordships of normally-exempt churches. Like earlier survey texts its 19 titles mix geographical and ownership criteria of organization. Duplications among the 273 individual entries reduce the count of identifiable settlements to 235. Only 44 have full numerical information on all land in the settlement, but 165 give enough to calculate the proportion of land then deserted. In addition to information about land types, most entries give the amount and date of the tax payment and the amount, if any, still owed or dismissed for cause. As in RB, some lay landlords are also named.

Mentioned nowhere is the purpose or occasion for the 1443 assessment, although both explicit statement and comparison of payments to village resources gives a rate of 12gr per occupied tenant mansus, tavern, or mill wheel in the Wrocław and Uraz districts. In the Środa district, however, the normal rate was 6gr. This half rate recalls King John's special privilege cutting the *exactio* (*Geschoss*) there in 1341.[25] The tax, then, is most likely the *exactio*, levied and collected by a committee with representatives from all three important landowning groups. Their efforts resulted in a 67 percent sample of the 344 places then inhabited in the duchy, but only 12 percent with full numerical details. Again the exempt demesnes are most often missing.

5. The four survey documents offer much numerical information about land and economic organization in large but not complete samples of Wrocław duchy settlements at times significant to its economic history. Most ecclesiastical lordships are there well accounted for, but identification of lay lords is less complete and even the best survey, *LB*, omits some 20 percent of the 345 places then known from the duchy's documents. And the latest survey dates to 1443. Different materials, not a single large text but the mass of charters preserved individually, in ecclesiastical cartularies like LN, and in official registers like RF, complement the surveys and provide valuable further information for use in conjunction with them.

Conveyancing arrangements in the duchy and the registers of texts arising from them were adequately introduced in Chapter 1. Except for scattered fortuitous examples of the full texts which survived as the landowners' copies or happened to be published before 1945, most conveyancing charters now survive only as summaries in RF. But comparison of randomly-surviving full originals with their entries in that register demonstrate the care with which it was assembled.[26] It reproduced the language of the originals, Latin until the 1360s, German thereafter. Especially for texts up to the mid-fifteenth century, the secretary transcribed the exact date, listed the captain before whom the transaction was consummated, and summarized the content of the charter, paying especial attention to the persons involved and the exact nature of the rights and properties being transferred. He omitted only the lengthy formulae and repetitions so beloved of lawyerly bureaucrats, important for possible legal disputes, but relatively irrelevant for knowing what passed from whom to whom. All test possibilities affirm the substantive accuracy of texts preserved in RF, and hence confidence in their use.

The distribution of lordships

Conveyancing charters are only one, if a most important, source to identify lords over the duchy's rural settlements. They are supplemented by the surveys and all other documents from the medieval duchy, nearly all composed in landowning circles and for their purposes. Conveyances offer a skeleton for the sequence of owners, but other surviving texts help to flesh it out. Controlled and systematic exploitation of information on landlordship began by assembling for each of the 384 rural settlements all of the documents pertaining to it as, for example, was done for Kobierzyce to start Chapter 7. From each such collation a lordship series was then constructed. As Chapters 7–8 and 11 amply demonstrate, these need not be unbroken to account for who owned what in a settlement during most of the fourteenth, fifteenth and early sixteenth centuries.[27]

Certainly 384 such capsule histories, each with its peculiarities, gaps, and differently dated changes of lordship, are at best a marginal improvement on the unstructured mass of individual texts. As such they have but antiquarian interest. Only after development of more general propositions can the particulars of lordship changes in a Kobierzyce or any other one place gain a context and serve as illustrative examples. Only by the fullest possible view of the evidence, too, can the many holdings of Wrocław citizens apparent to the most cursory glance at conveyances from the fourteenth or the early sixteenth century be rightly judged in relation to other landowning groups.

The technique here adopted was comparative statics, the construction from the ownership histories of profiles of the landowning elite at five dates. Those chosen, 1300, 1353, 1425, 1480, and 1530, took the greatest advantage of concentrations of survey, conveyancing, and other documentation while also approximating points inherently critical to the rural history of the duchy. All evidence is exploited. From the history of each rural settlement the lord or lords at each date were, if known, listed and identified. After classification according to both social order and number of properties held, the summary profiles appear in Tables A.1 and A.2.

Because landowners and their properties receive extensive substantive treatment in Chapters 7, 8, and 11, the tables here need only explanatory comment. All lords of all property are, of course, never known, so the first prerequisite is to assess the coverage of the samples created by those that are recorded. Section a of Table A.1 offers the only possible test statistic, a comparison of all the settlements known (both up to 1540 and in each sample year) with those for which landlords are known in each sample year. Comparison of settlement numbers works with a relatively fixed base population (in the statistical sense); knowing how many settlements have identifiable lords also tells how many do not. Holdings and individual landlords, however, are only known if they are documented; no estimate is independently possible of the number of landlords not known or the number of holdings of unknown lordship. Of settlements, then, all samples after 1300 are quite full; lords in at least three-fourths of the duchy's settlements are identified for each profile.

The sample for 1300, however, is slim, comprising less than half of the

Table A.1. The possession of lordships: comparative statics, 1300–1530

	1300	1353	1425	1480	1530
a. The samples					
1. Settlements in the duchy[a]	234	354	362	345	340
2. Settlements with known lordship	163	317	291	266	278
Known lordship samples as percent[b] of:					
3. Settlements documented to 1540 (row 2/384 × 100)	41%	83%	76%	69%	72%
4. Settlements in the sample year (row 2/row 1 × 100)	70%	89%	80%	77%	82%
b. Settlements with lordships of[c]					
5. Ecclesiastical corporations	101	123	124	111	119
6. Settlements with ecclesiastical lordships as percent of those with known lordship (row 5/row 2 × 100)	62%	39%	43%	42%	43%
7. Settlements with ecclesiastical lordships as percent of settlements then in the duchy (row 5/row 1 × 100)	42%	35%	34%	32%	35%
8. Nobles	39	131	80	74	60
9. Settlements with noble lordships as percent of those with known lordship (row 8/row 2 × 100)	24%	41%	27%	28%	22%
10. Settlements with noble lordships as percent of settlements then in the duchy (row 8/row1 × 100)	17%	37%	22%	21%	18%
11. Citizens of Wrocław	27	88	101	77	107
12. Settlements with citizen lordships as percent of those with known lordship (row 11/row 2 × 100)	16%	28%	35%	29%	38%
13. Settlements with citizen lordships as percent of settlements then in the duchy (row 11/row 1 × 100)	12%	25%	28%	22%	31%
14. Others[d]	25	54	38	30	28
15. Settlements with other lordships as percent of those with known lordship (row 14/row 2 × 100)	15%	17%	13%	11%	10%
16. Settlements with other lordships as percent of settlements then in the duchy (row 14/row 1 × 100)	11%	15%	11%	9%	8%
c. Individual holdings[e]					
17. Holdings of known lordship	207	579	415	328	348
Holdings of:					
18. Ecclesiastical corporations	104	125	124	114	119
19. Ecclesiastical holdings as percent of those with known lordship (row 18/ row 17 × 100)	51%	21%	30%	35%	34%
20. Nobles	48	226	118	88	74

	1300	1353	1425	1480	1530
c. Individual holdings[e] (cont.)					
21. Noble holdings as percent of those with known lordship (row 20/row 17 × 100)	23%	39%	28%	27%	21%
22. Citizens of Wrocław	28	147	118	87	124
23. Citizen holdings as percent of those with known lordship (row 22/row 17 × 100)	14%	25%	28%	27%	35%
24. Others	27	81	55	39	31
25. Other holdings as percent of those with known lordship (row 24/row 17 × 100)	13%	14%	13%	12%	9%
d. Lords					
26. Landlords identified	85	351	213	172	140
27. Ecclesiastical corporations	16	17	18	18	19
28. Ecclesiastical landlords as percent of those identified (row 27/row 26 × 100)	19%	5%	8%	10%	14%
29. Nobles	35	167	84	64	41
30. Noble landlords as percent of those identified (row 29/row 26 × 100)	41%	47%	39%	37%	29%
31. Noble landlord families[f]	(23)	(79)	(39)	(33)	(24)
32. Citizens of Wrocław	25	97	65	58	64
33. Citizen landlords as percent of those identified (row 32/row 26 × 100)	29%	28%	·30%	34%	45%
34. Citizen landlord families[f]	(21)	(60)	(39)	(34)	(39)
35. Others	9	70	46	32	16
36. Other landlords as percent of those identified (row 36/row 26 × 100)	10%	20%	22%	18%	11%

Notes.

[a] For 1300 only, settlements then documented. Each total includes places for which the latest known record comes after the previous sample year.

[b] All percentages are given to the nearest whole number.

[c] In section b, rows 5–16, each settlement counts only once for each *kind* of landlord. Thus a place with properties of two different nobles still contributes but one to the entry in row 8, but if a noble and citizen each have properties in the same place it counts separately for both groups. Hence raw counts need not total the same as in row 2 and percentages need not add to 100.

[d] "Others" here include sovereign dukes, municipal corporations, citizens of Środa, schulzen and other free but non-noble countrymen, and persons not identifiable as to social order. For shifts among them, see text.

[e] In section c, rows 17–25, the property of each individual landlord in each settlement where he or she held counts once for that group. Thus in contrast to section b, rows 5–16, two noble landlords in one place contribute two holdings to the noble count. The raw counts add up to the totals in row 17 and, except for rounding errors, the percentages to 100.

[f] As identified by common surnames.

Table A.2. The scale of lordships: comparative statics, 1300–1530

		All lordships	Small lordships (1–2 holdings)								
		Total[a]	Total	%[b]	Eccles.	%	Nobles	%	Citizens[c]	%	Others	%
1300	Landlords	85	69	81%	7	8%	32	38%	23	27%	7	8%
	Holdings	207	77	36%	8	4%	39	19%	21	10%	9	4%
1353	Landlords	351	315	90%	6	2%	155	44%	87	25%	67	19%
	Holdings	579	316	62%	8	1%	184	32%	100	17%	69	12%
1425	Landlords	213	182	85%	5	2%	79	37%	54	25%	44	21%
	Holdings	415	207	50%	6	1%	94	23%	62	15%	45	11%
1480	Landlords	172	147	85%	6	3%	59	34%	51	30%	31	8%
	Holdings	328	171	52%	7	2%	70	21%	61	19%	33	10%
1530	Landlords	140	103	73%	7	5%	30	38%	53	38%	13	9%
	Holdings	348	128	37%	8	2%	35	10%	72	21%	13	4%

Table A.2. (*continued*)

		All lordships	Large lordships (3–15 holdings)										Church of Wroclaw	
		Total[a]	Total	%[b]	Eccles.	%	Nobles	%	Citizens[c]	%	Others	%	(Eccles.)	%
1300	Landlords	85	15	18%	8	9%	3	4%	2	2%	2	2%	1	1%
	Holdings	207	83	40%	49	24%	9	4%	7	3%	18	9%	47	23%
1353	Landlords	351	35	10%	10	3%	12	3%	10	3%	3	1%	1	0.3%
	Holdings	579	170	29%	69	12%	42	7%	47	8%	12	2%	48	8%
1425	Landlords	213	30	14%	12	6%	5	2%	11	5%	2	1%	1	0.5%
	Holdings	415	166	40%	76	18%	24	6%	56	13%	10	2%	42	10%
1480	Landlords	172	24	14%	11	6%	5	3%	7	4%	1	0.6%	1	0.6%
	Holdings	328	118	36%	68	21%	18	5%	26	8%	6	2%	39	12%
1530	Landlords	140	36	26%	11	8%	11	8%	11	8%	3	2%	1	1%
	Holdings	348	182	52%	73	21%	39	11%	52	15%	18	5%	38	11%

Notes.
  [a] Landlord and holding totals from Table A.1, rows 25 and 17.
  [b] Percentages are all of the total in the column marked Total[a], which is identical in both parts of the table. All percentages greater than 1 are rounded to the nearest whole number.
  [c] "Citizens" are citizens of Wrocław. "Others" include dukes, municipal corporations, citizens of Środa, schulzen and other free but non-noble countrymen, and persons not identifiable as to social status.

total set of villages ever known and only 70 percent of the certainly incomplete set actually documented up to that year. This sample predates the officially sanctioned conveyancing system, hence its inadequacy. It has, however, certain useful features and should not be ignored. Notice the raw totals for the two groups, clerics and townspeople, who voluntarily used written charters rather extensively in the late thirteenth century. Ecclesiastical totals are good-sized, for churchmen already held land in 101 places, 27 percent of those ever documented in the duchy. Their estates were, as discussed in Chapter 3, primarily well-recorded creations of the twelfth and thirteenth centuries. Later accretions were relatively few and mostly evident new acquisitions, not properties which had long escaped documentation. For townsmen the reverse is true. Despite their rather anxious use of written evidence for lordship rights, only 25 individuals held 28 properties in 27 places.

"Others" are summarized together to simplify the tables. In 1300 the two dukes of Wrocław and Głogów held 18 of these properties and in 1353 the king still retained 3. More such holders were the municipalities of Wrocław (1353–1530) and Środa (1480–1530), a handful of Środa citizens, and numbers of schulzen and other villagers with lands directly subject to the sovereign. Only two citizens of Środa, Anna Vogt in 1425 and Thomas Zimmerman in 1530, possessed 3 or more holdings and the sole unclassifiable individual so fortunate was one Martin Bobko in 1353. Only because the holdings of the Church of Wrocław were always so much more numerous than those of its nearest rival, St. Vincent with 13 in 1353, is it shown apart from the other large owners.

No doubt reality was much messier than the quantifiable evidence may imply. Much of that messiness or nuancing is central to non-quantitative discussions throughout this·book. The sources will not, however, sustain any systematic measurement or numerical comparison of variables like the acreage, sale value, or incomes from land in lords' estates.

Some might propose "correcting" for probable correlations.[28] Ecclesiastical corporations sought and often gained sole ownership over whole villages—which might mean their share of rural land was greater than the proportion of sites where they owned. Citizens and knights more often had only fractions of villages—which would make them still smaller proprietors than numbers of holdings or settlements indicate. Conversely, however, churchmen always and citizens until the late fourteenth century mostly owned in the Wrocław district where average settlement size was well below that in the Środa and Uraz districts where more knights had authority. To factor such considerations into the counts displayed in Tables A.1 and A.2 would, however, achieve a spurious pretense of accuracy through two additional methodological errors. The tabulations would necessarily thus be removed yet another step from the textual evidence. All general "corrections" commit the ecological fallacy of imputing to individual members of a group stochastic attributes of the whole.

It is better to accept the profiles for what they are, the best possible crude summaries of the available evidence, and to infer from them only rough conclusions of the sort for which only broadly-based statistical information can make a prima facie case. The numbers appearing in Tables A.1 and A.2 are large enough and the places covered representative enough after 1300 to permit inference in Chapters 7, 8, 10, and 11 of aggregate structures and trends. Microscopic detail and comparison among individuals is from this evidence neither valid nor attempted.

The relative importance of demesne and tenant farming

Surveys, conveyances, and other historical records commonly identify the form or forms of managerial institutions in each settlement at certain times. These particulars are the raw data for long-term assessment of the relative importance of the direct exploitation demesne and the tenant village across the entire duchy. Two estimates are here made: of the frequency of institutional arrangements, i.e., the presence of demesne or rental lands in Wrocław duchy settlements; and of the quantity and proportion of arable so operated.

1. Institutional arrangements in rural settlements and on landowners' holdings

Different fiscal and other requirements on demesne and rental land meant late medieval writers and clerks were normally careful to distinguish between them. *LB* lists "villae" separately from "allodia," and specifies the "mansi ad allodium" in places otherwise out to tenants.[29] Peculiarities of RB have been mentioned, but it and KLM still repeatedly make the same distinctions as the earlier text.[30] The same vocabulary contrasting *mansi censuales, Zinshufen, villa, Dorf,* on the one hand, with *allodium* or *Vorwerk* on the other, permeates the conveyances.[31]

Contemporaries applied their vocabulary with evident and patterned discrimination. Thus in 20 references between 1337 and 1566 Kazimierzów was never called a *villa,* only a demesne, while Brodno, in 20 other texts dating 1235–1523, is *villa* or *Dorf* with *mansi censuales, gebawr erbe,* or *tzinsshafftige huben,* but not once *allodium* or *Vorwerk.*[32] More commonly, however, the particular nomenclature and description of a place evolved over time with a consistency confirming that verbal changes reflected real shifts in the institutions present. Bieńkowice, for instance, was an "allodium" in all 5 of its charters between 1340 and 1354 as well as the 1353 *LB*.[33] But in 1360 the same owners as in 1353 and 1354 called it a "villa." Three years later "czinse" here were noted in a charter and in later years these references continued. Rental mansi at Bieńkowice appear in both the 1425 RB and the 1443 KLM, while into the 1530s no further documents ever mention a demesne at this place.[34] So Bieńkowice was until 1354 never called anything but a demesne and after 1360 gives no sign of being anything but a village of rent-paying tenants.

In a last and more complicated example, the earliest references to Wierzbice from 1324, 1336, and 1338 mention both demesne and tenant lands. The demesne, moreover, is said to be 10 mansi, well less than the 60 mansi always documented for this place, and thus suggesting the coexistence here of both managerial modes.[35] But in *LB* no demesne appears; of the 60 mansi, tenants held 54, a schulz and a priest 2 each, and the last 2 were "leftovers."[36] Nor did demesne lands leave any trace in the 14 extant sale charters from 1354–1414 or the 1425 tax roll.[37] In 1443, however, the tax clerk recorded "2 1/2 Hufen allodiium" to mark a reappearance of demesne subsequently confirmed in conveyances during the later fifteenth and early sixteenth centuries.[38] All of this information suggests that while parts of Wierzbice were rented out to peasant tenants throughout its documented medieval history, the demesne lands of the 1330s had been divided up by 1353 and direct exploitation by the landlord was restored only in 1425/43 to remain into the sixteenth century.

For purposes of tabulation the convention was here adopted to date changes in the institutional vocabulary for a place by the first record of the new terminology. Thus Wierzbice is said to have both tenancies and demesne from its first documentation in 1324 until 1353, tenancies only from 1353 to 1443, and both again from the latter date up to 1540 and the end of this study. Bieńkowice is a demesne before 1360 and then tenancies.

These diagnostic procedures were carried out for every settlement known to have existed in the Wrocław duchy up to the 1530s. With contemporary documents verifying for each place the presence or absence of each of the two kinds of arrangements, tenancies (rental land) and demesne, but with both sometimes simultaneously present, every rural settlement can be designated at any given time as one of three possible "settlement types:" a *tenant village*, a *demesne*, or a *village with demesne*.[39] For places like Brodno or Kazimierzów, the settlement type never changed, but for those like Wierzbice or Bieńkowice the result is a successively dated sequence of settlement types. Wierzbice is a village with demesne from 1324 to 1353, a tenant village from 1353 to 1443, and a village with demesne after 1443; Bieńkowice is a demesne from 1282 to 1360 and a tenant village thereafter. For no

Table A.3. Current settlement types: comparative statics, 1300–1530

	Settlements[a]	Tenant villages		Villages with demesne		Demesnes	
1300	234	51		80		103	
			22%		34%		44%
1353	354	80		113		161	
			23%		32%		45%
1425	362	116		125		121	
			32%		35%		33%
1480	345	112		131		102	
			32%		38%		30%
1530	340	109		133		98	
			32%		39%		29%

Note.
[a] For 1300 only, settlements documented.

place did more than three such successive settlement types emerge from the late medieval evidence. With each settlement so classified over time, the final step was to count up the settlement types current among all places existing in the duchy at dates of special interest and rich documentation (1300, 1353, 1425, 1480, and 1530). This generated the summary profiles of "current settlement types" shown in Table A.3.

Again, little explication belongs here. Notice that although the number of settlements on record grows as documentary coverage becomes complete between 1300 and 1353, the relative proportions change little. Examining each settlement type over time, the villages rose both absolutely and relatively from 1353 to 1425, but then, slowly losing in actual count at about the same rate as the total set of settlements declined, kept the 32 percent share. Demesnes exhibited a different pattern after the mid-fourteenth century, falling in numbers even more rapidly throughout. The mixed settlement type, however, increased regularly and hence more quickly than did the number of settlements present in the duchy. After 1425 only this perhaps more symbiotic arrangement with lord and peasant lands at the same site continued to grow in numbers and relative frequency.

Data in Table A.3 can be transformed to other statistics of interest. Since the village with demesne contains both of the "simple" forms, that number or percentage added to both of the others measures the frequency of demesnes compared to tenancies overall: for example, in 1353 193 or 55 percent of settlements had tenancies and 274 or 77 percent had demesnes. Equally relevant is to know that, also in 1353, of those 274 demesnes, 161 (59%) did not share the site with peasant tenants but 113 (41%) did.

Procedures used for whole settlements can also tabulate arrangements

Table A.4. Major landlord groups and managerial arrangements: comparative statics, 1300–1530

	1300	1353	1425	1480	1530
Holdings of known lordships[a]	207	579	415	328	348
Ecclesiastical corporations:					
Holdings	104	125	124	114	119
Tenancies only[b]	28%	36%	48%	50%	50%
Tenancies with demesne	19%	17%	25%	28%	30%
Demesne only	53%	47%	27%	22%	20%
Nobles					
Holdings	48	226	118	88	74
Tenancies only	18%	18%	20%	12%	12%
Tenancies with demesne	41%	44%	39%	54%	55%
Demesne only	41%	38%	41%	34%	33%
Citizens of Wrocław					
Holdings	28	147	118	87	124
Tenancies only	11%	30%	43%	25%	33%
Tenancies with demesne	11%	19%	36%	53%	45%
Demesnes only	78%	51%	21%	22%	25%

Notes.

[a] Only a count of holdings (each lord's in each place) is here feasible. Compare Table A.1, part c, rows 17, 18, 20, and 22.

[b] "Tenancies" here replaces the "tenant villages" of Table A.3 because a holding might well include some tenancies but not the entire village or peasant community. The concept of land rented out to tenants is, however, the same.

on the properties of identified landowning groups. Where there was one lord his managerial setup was the settlement type of the place. But when several owners divided lordship, the conveyances in particular must be examined most carefully to ascertain who held demesne and who tenancies in places then with both. Hence the distributions in Table A.4 of managerial institutions among the three major landowning groups, ecclesiastics, nobles, and townsmen, cannot be as complete as even the known lordship samples (Table A.1), but are the fullest such estimates from all extant documentation. No group here profiled replicated on its properties the duchy-wide distributions of Table A.3, although most changes are comparable.

2. Measuring land in demesne and in tenancies

Tabulating settlements and landholdings by their changing institutional type indicates the direction and extent of agrarian trends. This is helpful by itself and will soon also aid in evaluating other more detailed but less widespread kinds of information. But treating each settlement or holding as a unit and assessing change by counting these does not measure the actual distribution of land between lord and peasant farms. Neither settlements nor holdings were uniform in size or in the ratio of demesne land to peasant land. Quantities of land are regularly reported only in the four survey texts, *LFE, LB*, RB, and KLM. Only by closer examination of their data can more precise estimates be attained. In fact, however, the first of these, the *LFE* of 1300, proves too limited in coverage and detail to be other than an incidental comparison. *LB* and RB have received considerable scholarly attention and must be the principal objects here.

Curiously, prewar German historians never tried to exploit effectively either the 1353 or the 1425 text, being satisfied to note that almost every modern settlement appeared therein and to extract quantitative descriptions of individual villages. No one added up the lands of various types even for one list, much less compared them.[40] When in 1953 Wacław Korta edited and published the 1425 text, he was the first to total and compare the amounts of tenant and demesne land in the two surveys.[41]

Korta apparently worked with 213 places he considered to be in both lists with sufficient information to be helpful, simply taking each entry as written and adding up the total sizes, rental mansi, and mansi in demesne.[42] His rather confusing totals and proportions are:

	1353	1425
Total land	3443¼ mansi	2839¼ mansi
Tenant land	2323¼ mansi (67%)	2703 mansi (95%)
Demesne land	1204¾ mansi (35%)	46 mansi (0.16%)

Although the total area of the places in his sample declined markedly (by 18%) during times when very few new places may be found, Korta did not comment thereupon. He emphasized instead the 60 settlements where tenant lands increased between 1353 and 1425 and the reduction of demesnes in his sample from 116 to a mere 14. Although the total tenant and demesne lands in 1353 exceed the total sizes (!), and schulz and other free lands are simply ignored, the numbers Korta presented do support his assertion of significant shifts from demesne to the rental economy between the mid-fourteenth and early fifteenth century.[43]

Shortly after the appearance of Korta's work Roman Heck focused on exactly the matters Korta had ignored to cast doubt on the validity of his statistics. By pointing out that the *burnegelt* tax favored recording tenant holdings and omitting demesnes, Heck drew attention in general terms to the possibly-skewed distribution of settlements listed in 1425.[44] Heck reworked the totals for the 1353 *LB*, now using all settlements (323 including the Kąty district) and concluded that in that year 61.9 percent of the land was out to tenants and 28.5 percent in demesne. Noting further that more demesnes than villages in *LB* lacked enough numerical information to contribute to the totals, he estimated that about 30 percent of the duchy's land was then in landlord farms.[45] Heck did not, however, redo Korta's calculations for 1425 or attempt to revise his interpretation; he later even used Korta's evidence and conclusions elsewhere.[46]

Heck's criticisms impelled reexamination of the RB manuscript earlier described in this appendix. This revealed mistakes in Korta's edition, systematic omissions in the text, and the consequent need to read each entry in RB in the context of other contemporary information about that settlement. The scope of the early fifteenth-century survey can be improved by adding places with similar information from other contemporary sources. Then the 1425 document and others like it can be used to study the average size of settlements or of various types of land within them (schulz or church holdings, for example) or to learn how specific places changed.

The question of shifts in the aggregate distribution of tenant and demesne lands demands a criterion beyond accuracy in individual entries, viz. the representative quality of the samples of settlements given in the surveys. In other words, do the sets of localities in these documents and especially the sets with enough numerical information for construction of totals and proportions, present a measurably valid profile of all the settlements then in the Wrocław duchy? The rest of this discussion moves progressively from statistics acquired directly from the corrected survey texts to others which use this same information in a way more accurately representative of the entire duchy.

Consider first what each text offers as a "full information sample," i.e. those sets of settlements in each for which correctly read survey entries describe numerically all of the land.[47] Although the number and identity of settlements in these samples vary from survey to survey, each is the fullest possible set of verifiably complete information for each year. Table A.5 summarizes this data for the variables now of concern. The full information samples correspond with Korta's conclusion that tenant lands increased at the expense of demesne, both on the long term and especially between 1353 and 1425 (but the amount of change is well below his assertion). The proportions for 1353 also concur with those Heck obtained from all entries, complete or not. Note, too, that after 1353 land outside the tenancy-demesne dichotomy (schulz, priest, and other free holdings) changed little.

What then is wrong with the distributions in Table A.5? Answer: the raw data from the survey and tax rolls are inherently biased against de-

Table A.5. Rental and demesne land in all settlements
with full information, 1300–1353–1425–1443

	1300	1353	1425	1443
Settlements in duchy[a]	234	354	362	344[c]
Settlements in survey text	59	284	211	235
Settlements with full information	11	207	73	44
Total land described[b]	251m	4968m	1239m	721m
Rental land	126m	3001m	956m	587m
percent of total	50%	60%	74%	71%
Demesne land	77m	1429m	219m	177m
percent of total	31%	28%	17%	22%

Notes.
[a] 1300 only, settlements documented.
[b] All land quantities are in mansi (m).
[c] The 1443 total drops because standard procedures retain in the count of settlements for 1425 several places last documented in the late fourteenth and early fifteenth centuries. Those no longer appear for 1443.

mesnes and demesne lands and, as such, do not provide a representative sample or summary of aggregate land distribution and its changes. Heck noticed this characteristic of both the 1353 and 1425 documents, but beyond guessing that demesnes probably covered a bit more land than his figures indicated, he neither evaluated the degree of distortion nor tried to compensate for it. Both can be done.

A way to assess the bias of the surveys and their full information samples is to compare the proportions of places with each type of land in the entire duchy to those in the surveys and samples. In statistical terms, Table A.6 compares the *sample* proportions with the *population* proportions already established in the settlement type distributions of Table A.3.[48] With near total consistency the proportion of villages (places with rental lands) in both the texts and the samples is well above that which existed in reality while conversely the proportion of demesnes is well below their actual frequency. The disparity is, moreover, greatest in the critical year of 1425, when a sample containing 3 villages for every 2 demesnes severely distorts a real world with a ratio of 1 to 1. Especially because measurable bias differs among the samples, these unrepresentative sets of data cannot accurately or consistently depict real changes in the relative shares of demesne and tenant land.[49]

If simply taking all settlements with full information in one corrected survey and comparing the relative frequency of tenant and demesne lands

Table A.6. Settlements with rental and with demesne lands in the duchy, the survey documents, and the full information samples

	1300	1353	1425	1443
a. Settlements with rental lands [a]				
in the Wrocław duchy	131 of 234	193 of 354	243 of 344	243 of 344
percent of total in duchy	56%	55%	67%	71%
in the survey text	35 of 59	177 of 284	185 of 211	209 of 235
percent of total in text	59%	62%	88%	89%
in the full information sample	4 of 11	144 of 207	55 of 73	37 of 44
percent of total in sample	36%	69%	75%	84%
b. Settlements with demesne land [b]				
in the Wrocław duchy [c]	183 of 234	274 of 354	247 of 362	231 of 344
percent of total in duchy	78%	77%	68%	67%
in the survey text	41 of 59	210 of 284	116 of 211	128 of 235
percent of total in text	70%	72%	55%	55%
in the full information sample	8 of 11	144 of 207	33 of 73	32 of 44
percent of total in sample	73%	69%	55%	75%

Notes.

[a] In terms of the "current settlement types" of Table A.3, tenant villages plus villages with demesne.

[b] In terms of the "current settlement types" of Table A.3, demesnes plus villages with demesne.

[c] Percentages will add up to more than 100% because villages with demesne are counted in both sections.

therein with like information from a similarly defined set from another survey can yield no meaningful result,[50] more indirect methods are needed to obtain representative samples and hence measurably accurate estimates of aggregate land type distributions. Simple random sampling founders on the inherent bias of those places with full information, but combining the known current settlement type distributions and the numerical details available in the full information samples improves the estimates. Two procedures served as a mutual check.

The first method uses what statisticians call a "proportionate stratified random sample"[51] for the two years of chief concern, 1353 and 1425. From each year's full information sample 25 settlements were selected at random. Each set so selected, however, had to reproduce in both its current settlement type distribution and its distribution of settlements among the 3 districts the same characteristics as then prevailed among all known settlements. Thus in 1353 the current settlement type distribution of 23 percent tenant villages, 32 percent villages with demesne, and 45 percent plain demesnes (see Table A.3) set for the sample a parameter of 6 places with tenancies but no demesne, 8 places with tenancies and demesne, and 11 places with demesne land only, while in the 1425 stratified sample, the current settlement type distribution of 32–35–33 percent demanded a sample of 8, 9, and 8 places respectively. In addition, because the duchy's settlements were in both years 65 percent in the Wrocław, 29 percent in the Środa, and 6 percent in the Uraz district, each sample needed 16, 7, and 2 places from them respectively.[52] Thus each sample replicated on two critical variables the composition of the population it was intended to represent. The results obtained by this sampling technique were as follows:

1353 sample proportions:	54% tenant land	34% demesne land
1425 sample proportions:	63% tenant land	29% demesne land.

The samples, in effect, created distributions for 557 and 440 mansi respectively, or about 7 percent of the land in the duchy. By using the binomial theorem to determine the limits of the sample proportions to a confidence of 90 percent,[53] the following population proportions emerged:

1353:	$54 \pm 3\%$ tenant land	$34 \pm 3\%$ demesne land
1425:	$63 \pm 4\%$ tenant land	$29 \pm 4\%$ demesne land.

Further application of the binomial theorem to changes in land distribution indicated that, also within confidence intervals of 90 percent, tenant lands grew by 9 ± 5 percent while demesne lands fell by 5 ± 5 percent. The former change is statistically significant, the latter barely so. The proportionate stratified random sampling procedure yielded measurably accurate estimates, but like any sampling technique, abandoned some of the data.

All available data contributed to the estimate acquired through the second technique employed; it might be called weighted and pooled means.[54] For each of the two survey years 1353 and 1425[55] the full information sample was divided into subsets of each settlement type in each district (Wrocław district villages, Środa district villages, Uraz district villages, Wrocław district villages with demesne, etc.). For each of the 9 subsets thus created (3 districts × 3 settlement types) were calculated the mean size (all settlement types), land out to tenants (villages and villages with demesne), and land in demesne (demesnes and villages with demesne). For instance, in 1353 the full information sample contains 45 Wrocław district villages with an average size of 27.5 mansi and 23.5 mansi out to tenants. Each of these sub-totals must, however, then be weighted to accord with the actual frequency of that settlement type in that district. Hence since the Wrocław district in 1353 actually contained not 45 but 54 villages, the means were multiplied by 54 to allow for their contribution of 1485 mansi to the duchy's total arable area and 1270 mansi to the total of land out to tenants. In the

same year 8 Uraz district villages with demesne appeared in the full information sample to average 37.6 mansi, 23.5 mansi out to tenants, and 9.3
mansi in demesne, but because in fact 10 such places then existed, their
contribution was estimated at 376, 235, and 93 mansi respectively. This procedure of determining the average size of each component and then weight-
ing for its known frequency created a total duchy-wide distribution of 7597
mansi, 4034 mansi out to tenants, and 2851 mansi in demesne for 1353 and
respectively 7047, 4649, and 1883 mansi for 1425. These estimates convert
to the following proportions:

1353:	53% tenant land	38% demesne land
1425:	66% tenant land	27% demesne land.

With the sole and bare exception of the demesne land estimate for 1353, the
proportions acquired by the second method fall within the 90 percent confidence interval estimated by the first.

Because KLM contains full information for no Uraz district settlements
and comparatively few other places as well, no proportionate stratified random sample could be made for 1443. The fully subdivided weighted mean
tactic was ruled out too. It is possible, however, to subdivide and weight
only according to the duchy-wide current settlement type distribution for
that year.[56] This procedure gives a distribution of 68 percent tenant land and
21 percent demesne land for 1443, a relatively small shift from the 66 and
27 percent of 1425 and one well in accord with the considerable slowdown
in changes of settlement type.

The more representative and hence reliable estimates, which are mutually corroborative and exploit all extant data, depict long-term aggregate
trends in the relative shares of tenant and demesne lands between 1300 and
1443. In 1300, when the settlements in *LFE*, though too few for statistical
manipulation, seem fairly representative of known settlements, about half
of the land in the duchy was probably out to tenants. This may be a minimum limit because many demesnes are simply absent from the documentation until 1353. But when the distribution for 1353 is examined and
estimated, it confirms with considerable likelihood that the amount of tenant land had risen very little during the preceding half century. Peasants
themselves probably operated farms on only a little more than half of the
duchy's lands, while a good third was still in demesne. Reasons for little
shift from demesne to rental land during the first half of the fourteenth
century are developed in Chapter 6 and corroborated by the German law
evidence discussed in Chapter 4.

According to the best possible approximations from available data for

Figure A.1
THE RELATIVE IMPORTANCE OF DEMESNE AND TENANT FARMING.

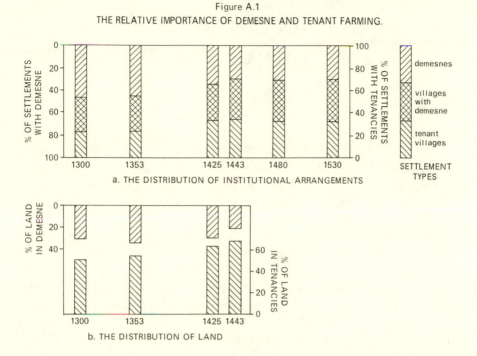

a. THE DISTRIBUTION OF INSTITUTIONAL ARRANGEMENTS

SETTLEMENT TYPES

demesnes

villages with demesne

tenant villages

b. THE DISTRIBUTION OF LAND

1425, tenant lands then covered some two-thirds of the arable in the duchy and demesnes only about one fourth. Korta's conclusion of a significant shift since the mid-fourteenth century was not wrong. Plainly inaccurate, however, was his assertion that at the eve of the Hussite wars nearly all of the duchy's farmland was in peasant hands and that direct exploitations had virtually ceased to exist. During the two-generation interval between *LB* and *RB*, lands out to tenants most likely grew by about 10 percent of the total or about 20 percent of their former proportion. Most of this increase came at the expense of the demesnes which concurrently declined by that same 10 percent of all lands or over 25 percent of their own area in 1353. The evidence from 1443, less extensive and less conducive to the creation of valid estimates as it may be, does corroborate the change since 1353, but otherwise proves little further change after 1425. These findings, then, appear in Figure A.1.

Appendix B

NOTES ON MONEY
IN MEDIEVAL SILESIA

Monetary transactions for rents, tithes, taxes, and sales of produce or land made the circulating medium an important external parameter of rural economic relationships around Wrocław. Like much else in Silesia, the coinage system developed from a Polish prototype through close identification with Bohemian arrangements into a confusion of competing local authorities which the Habsburgs only later brought to heel. This appendix notes conditions with effects remarked throughout the study.

Through the thirteenth century Silesian moneys, supported by the growing silver and gold production of the Sudetes, were struck from the Polish mark of 183.5 grams, which was also the main unit of account. The mark (mk) was no coin. *Locatio* charters may refer to rents of a quarter mark silver and conveyances to prices of many marks, but people paid these in *denarii*, nominally 240 to the mark, and later in *quartenses* (one-fourth of a *skot*) at 96 to the mark.[1] Moneyers used a 75 percent alloy called "usual silver," which made the mark of coins contain only about 137.4 grams of pure silver.[2] This amount serves in this study to convert to silver all nominal values predating 1310.

Close contacts between some Silesian and Bohemian mints and spread of Bohemian coins eastwards in the thirteenth century presaged the early fourteenth-century creation in Silesia of a Bohemian monetary as well as political hegemony. For two hundred years the Prague groschen (gr) would dominate Silesian exchanges. This manifestation of the European return to large silver coins was first struck in 1300. Its original high weight (3.85 grams) and near purity soon succumbed to debasement's allure, but the groschen still became the premier circulating medium throughout central Europe, and inspired emulation in Poland and the German states. In Silesia it prevailed by the second or third decade of the century.[3] By 1325–30 Silesians stopped minting *quartenses* and would until the 1460s make only small coins. Although the groschen was first struck at 64 to the Prague mark of 253 grams and remained tied to that Bohemian standard, in Silesia the smaller Polish mark meant that a "mark groschen" or "marce grossorum numeri consueti polonici" counted only 48 coins. Other units of account also acquired groschen equivalents, the *firdung* (*fertonis*) at 12, the *lot* at 3, the *skot* at 2, and the *quartensis* at ½. Even as the groschen haltingly lost weight and fineness, these terms remained pegged to it and lost their one-time reference to weights of silver.

Figure B.1 depicts the debasement of the groschen during the two and a half centuries of its minting. Between 1300 and the Hussite wars it lost some two-thirds of its original silver content and over half that it had held when it first gained preeminence in Silesia. The coin fell quickly under the last Przemyslids and John. Charles IV, however, managed for three decades to keep the groschen stable and even tried to revalue it upwards just before his death. This reform failed, but the value to which Wenceslas lowered the coin in 1380 held for another twenty-five years. Considerable monetary stability thus characterized the second half of the fourteenth century. Two debasements in 1406 and 1408 resulted from Wenceslas's political troubles. Then the king's death and ensuing Hussite revolution marked a major break. Bohemian coinage ceased from 1418 to about 1428 and again from the early 1430s until 1459.

Need for a piece smaller than the groschen was met by the heller (hl), a little coin of poor alloy which spread from Schwäbisch-Hall across the Germanic lands and into Silesia by the 1320s. Sometimes also called *obolus, nummus, pfennig,* or even *denarius,* this initially one-sided coin was in the fourteenth century normally figured at twelve to the groschen, even though it rarely held that much silver.[4] Wrocław received the right to issue its own heller in 1362 and long kept them stable. A steep fall began in the 1420s (Figure B.1)—and inspired sharp popular libels against councillors Beda and Nicholas Rempel for so defrauding the poor. Heller debasement did hurt the poor more than the well-to-do when wages adjusted more slowly than prices and groschen were more stable. On a longer scale the more continuous drop of the groschen certainly eroded the fixed rental incomes of the elite to the advantage of peasants who paid them. In any case, contemporaries were well aware of the immediate impact monetary changes had on rural and urban economies. Undeterred, Wrocław put out in 1429 heavier new heller almost devoid of silver, which quickly shoved even those of 1422 off the changers' benches.[5] Forced to such tokens to finance its anti-Hussite efforts, Wrocław in 1438 abandoned the issue and with it seemingly all minting, not to resume until 1460.

Monetary shortages disturbed the Silesian economy of the fifteenth century as those elsewhere. Production at the great Czech mines of Kutna Hora declined and, with the political collapse of the Luxemburg state system, helped precipitate the break in groschen issues. Responsibility for the Silesian money supply thus devolved on local mints, but their long periods of idleness seem to reflect a downturn in the province's specie production as

Figure B.1
SILVER IN THE PRAGUE GROSCHEN AND THE WROCŁAW HELLER, 1300-1550

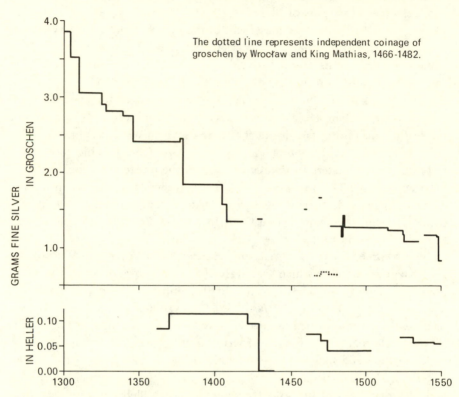

Note. The groschen portion of the graph is from tables in Castelin, pp. 28–29, and Szwa-grzyk, "Szerokie grosze," pp. 48–70. Heller are from Friedensburg in *Münzgeschichte,* II, *passim,* "Breslauer Pönfall," pp. 89–100, and "Münzen König Ferdinands," pp. 213–230 and 282–284.

well.[6] As early as 1410 the Duke of Legnica complained that drainage prob-lems had eliminated all of his once large revenues from mines. Other rec-ords hint at reduced gold and silver yields elsewhere. Ewa Maleczyńska refused to court the possibility of a "mining crisis," but could provide no evidence from the early and mid-fifteenth century to demonstrate continued high yields, prosperity, and expansion. Instead the instances offered of ad-vancing technique and production skip quietly from the late fourteenth century to the last few decades of the fifteenth. Prospectors' guides of the mid-1400s, whose obscure geographical references and almost occult rec-ommendations mark an interest allegedly aroused by mining success, more likely found a ready audience because specie shortages could be met only through new discoveries or improved methods of drainage. Debasements and monetary anarchy in the fifteenth century argue as well for a serious dearth of monetary metals—unless the Silesian experience was unique in western and central Europe.

To say that money was scarce and mintings rare in the mid-fifteenth century is not to assert the lack of a monetary history then. On the contrary, the 1450s and 60s generated more records related to coinage than did the whole fourteenth century. Foreign coins of poor and unknown alloy flooded the province, counterfeiters plied their trade, and local authorities sought repeatedly to regain control. Confusion perhaps peaked soon after 1450. Rosicz noted that in 1456 coins from Bohemia, Moravia, Meissen, Austria, Bavaria, Kłodzko, Görlitz, Poland, "et qualiter queris moneta" had common course in Wrocław. Local and collaborative regional efforts to suppress some of these coins or to regulate exchange values reveal by their very frequency their utter lack of lasting success.[7] Not even Mathias Corvinus could impose his will on the anarchic state of Silesian money. Two major efforts to stabilize the coinage shattered on opposition of the towns and incompatibility between the king's monetary and his fiscal needs.[8] Corvinus did, however, sponsor in Wrocław the first Silesian minting of groschen— the one issue to differ greatly in silver content from simultaneous Bohemian ones.

Escape from monetary disarray was long delayed. By the later years of Mathias's reign comprehensive reform had been abandoned. Silesian mints issued little but poor heller and the people made do with whatever coins could be had. When some princes tried in 1503 to strike still lighter heller, Wrocław's angry reaction did result in a new coinage agreement of April 1505. Towns and dukes were all to mint so-called *Weissgroschen* valued at the same 36 to the Hungarian florin as current Bohemian groschen but containing barely two-thirds the silver. Some were struck and some circulated, but available documents are inadequate to determine their relative importance as a circulating medium. Later agreements suggest they too, quickly lost value. At the same time Bohemian, Polish, and old Wroclaw groschen coined under Mathias continued to circulate freely.

Monetary confusion and the many badly debased heller drove the groschen from its ancient position as the premier medium of exchange. While gold, chiefly the Hungarian florin (ducat, *gulden*, fl) took over the largest transactions, the heller ruled everyday trade. Even the term "groschen" may around 1500 have meant more often a number of heller, usually twelve but sometimes fourteen, the so-called *Zalgroschen*, than an actual coin.[9]

The end came only in the 1540s. King Ferdinand issued a new and larger silver piece, the taler, in 1540 and then, fearing its incipient absorption into the prevailing chaos, first made it the basic unit of his monetary system (30 *Weissgroschen* to the taler) and in 1547 stopped production of groschen altogether.[10] After some years for the new medium to replace the old, the age of the groschen had ended.

To obtain long-term trends by conversion of nominal values to silver after 1310, the procedure here followed has assumed marks groschen where not otherwise specified and used the most recent (and hence least valuable) issue. Gresham's law normally meant poorer coins quickly replaced older, more valuable ones. When other media of payment (marks silver, marks heller, florins, etc.) were specified, like methods were used.

Appendix C

ON THE NAMES OF PLACES
AND PEOPLE

The materials and methods of this study and the need clearly to communicate its results make critical the comprehension of names given in the three medieval languages of the primary texts and the three modern of the scholarship and the standardizing of those used in the book itself. Only consciously consistent handling of personal and place names can rightly link references in separate sources (or even one and the same text), avoid deceptive anachronisms, and maintain narrative clarity. Perfect achievement of the latter two incompatible ends is unlikely, but seemingly reasonable compromises are followed wherever practicable.

1. Toponyms

Primary texts contain place names of Polish and German origin variously transposed or translated into the inconsistent orthography of medieval Latin and/or German. Relevant secondary works in modern German, Polish, and Czech use various modern forms as well. All place names were fluid until the advent of official printed maps and lists and some remained fluid thereafter. Many in the Wrocław duchy were first recorded as (sometimes ignorantly) Latinized versions of Polish sounds. Some first appear in Latin itself, and others are German at the start.

During the Middle Ages several changes affected the place names of the duchy. Polish sounds were often incrementally Germanized, at least in the orthography of the increasingly numerous vernacular German texts or of those written in Latin by German speakers. Other Polish roots were either translated directly into German equivalents or mistranslated into a similar-sounding but meaningful German word. And people simply took up new and different names for a few places.

Similar processes continued in modern times. Some traditional village names were more formally Germanized in the nineteenth century and many with Polish roots were expunged for "genuine German" names during the 1930s. Then in the late 1940s Polish authorities wholly re-Polonized the Silesian map. Most places around Wrocław for which an ancient Polish root could be ascertained (sometimes incorrectly), were given the modern Polish form of that same root and suffix. Those without such a heritage received Polish translations of the traditional pre-1930s German name or some more arbitrary label. Some new Polish names were modified a second time shortly thereafter. The effect is that nineteenth- and twentieth-century German works refer to villages with formally Germanized and modernized versions of their late medieval names, the last decade of German scholarship may use names with no historic character, and postwar Polish writers employ an eventually standardized nomenclature mostly modernized from high and late medieval forms of Slavic origin.

For most places in the medieval duchy the modern Polish forms best resemble the sounds late medieval writers seem to have been trying to reproduce. For that reason and because those are the names of the places now in the late twentieth century, modern Polish names are used for all Silesian and Polish sites now existing. To call the city Wrocław rather than Breslau is the least anachronistic approach. It does, admittedly, give an incorrect impression for those less numerous places which until 1945 always had clearly German names. Anachronism there is the price of consistency. German equivalents are shown in the Gazetteer.

Some inhabited sites in the medieval duchy no longer exist or have lost their one-time distinct identity, so no modern Polish names are available. Most such places were in the Wrocław district and for those Józef Domański has diligently reconstructed the original form of the name.[1] Disappeared medieval settlements in the districts of Środa and Uraz are handled in the same fashion, using, where informative and verifiable, citations given in Adolf Moepert's book on the former district.[2] All reconstructed toponyms are given within asterisks (as *Czepankowicz* or *Burkhardsmul**) to conform with standard linguistic practice.

The precise form of name given in a particular primary text is employed (in italics or quotation marks as appropriate) only when the form itself is an object of discussion or cannot be equated with a known place. After 1300 the latter are rare.

Places outside of Silesia are treated with common English names or, failing these, forms from the language now there spoken. Hence it is Prague, not Praha, but Kutna Hora, not Kuttenberg and Leipzig, not Lipsk.

2. Anthroponyms

People belonging to the community of the medieval duchy receive in primary texts and secondary studies the same bewildering and then anachronistic variety of names as do places. This book tries to use standardized forms. Occasional exceptions include individuals known in English by their non-English name (like Jan Długosz) and names taken from a primary text to recapture a special historic flavor. Barring these (or accidental lapses) the following practices are followed.

a. GIVEN (CHRISTIAN) NAMES

1. Forms with close English equivalents are given as English: Johannes, Hans, Jan, Janek are all John; Henricus, Heinrich, Henryk, Heynko are all Henry
2. Forms with clear modern equivalents are standardized to that equivalent in the "home" language: Stanislaus, Stanek, Stanko are Stanisław; Theodoricus, Ditko are Dietrich
3. Names without a common or appropriate modern equivalent are standardized to a single orthographically-tidy representation of the medieval form: Mikora; Dzierzykraj; Hieronymous (not Jerome); Pansław; Bartholomeus (not Bartholomew).

b. COGNOMENS AND SURNAMES

Besides posing the normal linguistic and orthographic problems, second names were during the later Middle Ages around Wrocław gradually shifting from individual cognomens or patronymics to relatively fixed family surnames. In any given instance the stage of development may be wholly obscure. Furthermore, names derived from place names (de/von/-ski) then only gradually and partially came to denote noble rank. Some nineteenth and twentieth century writers are too quick to read mere geographical surnames as if they were aristocratic titles. Hence this source of error and false impression here also must be considered. With trepidation the following practices have been attempted.

1. Detectable family names are standardized to a single, preferably medieval and text-based, form. Hence to the mid-fourteenth century these tend to be Latinate and thereafter relatively Germanic. Where the Germanic form in particular gives a false-sounding impression, a more Slavicized version from the written evidence is preferred.
2. Names of geographic origin are standardized to the form used in most of the texts referring to the individual or family in question. On rare occasions for durable families the form used for the fourteenth century is modified in the fifteenth simply because the great weight of the documentation so compels (Hugowicz fairly replicates early texts, but Haugwicz the later ones; the cognate village name, Jugowiec, is not used for the family.)

3. Names in the type of de/von + toponym are translated as "of + toponym" except in the cases of certain families who after the mid-fourteenth
   century came unambiguously to treat the entire phrase (or just the toponym) as a hereditary surname. Names with the Polish form toponym
   + -ski are handled similarily. Hence, for example: thirteenth-century *de
   Cracovia* = of Cracow; fourteenth-century *von Burne* = of Żródła; but
   fifteenth-century *von der Heide* = von der Heide (not of Błonie); and
   sixteenth-century *Zindalsky* = Zindalski (not of Wojnowice).

4. Social status is never inferred from a form of name alone.

NOTES

Chapter 1

Notes conserve space with short or abbreviated citations. Full references are in the Bibliography.

1. Some may know Wrocław better by its German name, Breslau. See p. 10 and the Gazetteer.

2. Pounds, *Economic History*, pp. 90–122. Explanatory paradigms are encapsulated in the titles of Lopez, *Commercial Revolution* and Duby, *Early Growth: Warriors and Peasants*.

3. Pounds, *Economic History*, pp. 440–487; Miskimin, *Economy of Early Ren.*; Abel, *Strukturen*, and works there cited.

4. Zientara, "Depresja," pp. 262–274, called for more closely focussed research on east-central Europe and its special experience in the late Middle Ages. Małowist proposed relative lags in medieval development to explain both the region's later distinctiveness and its internal differentiation: "Inequality," pp. 15–28, and "Growth," pp. 319–357. Hopes for an economic history familiar with both late medieval trends and east-central European particulars have not been fulfilled.

5. Modern anthropologists and comparative sociologists have written more about peasant society than a wise historian should try to read. Important studies are listed and central issues summarized in "The nature of a peasant society" in Macfarlane, *English Individualism*, pp. 9–33. (Macfarlane's work rests on a fundamentally anachronistic comparison of late medieval and early modern English peasants with nineteenth-century Polish peasants barely a generation removed from a servitude sharper than England ever knew; to tell scholars like him of another earlier east-central European countryside is one hope here.)

6. For example: Goody, *Family and marriage*; the section on "Demand" in Cipolla, pp. 3–63; Duby and LeGoff, Goody et al., *Family and Inheritance*; Duby, *Early Growth*, pp. 48–72, 157–180, and 232–256.

7. A revisionist précis is Barraclough, "Introduction: Towards a new concept of European history," in his *Eastern and Western Europe*, pp. 7–14. For ways later national and racist ideas were imposed on this region's medieval history see Graus, "Slavs and Germans," pp. 15–42 in the same collection.

8. Zernack, pp. 786–789. Thus the revision (1961) of Aubin et al., *Geschichte Schlesiens*, I, retained from prewar editions the conceptualization of institutional and economic history into "Die slawische Zeit" and "Die deutsche Kolonisation." Reciprocally, "national relations" and "national antagonisms" appear almost as often as "class conflict" as subheadings in the collective Maleczyński, ed., *Historia Śląska*, I. This framework also shaped the agrarian history of the province. The only genuine early synthesis, Dessmann, pp. 1–93, began with the "German colonization" of the thirteenth century and explained the shift from medieval free tenant farming to early modern serfdom on grounds that German settlers were no longer available and Slavs had to be used instead. Analysis of any kind is curiously thin in Roman Heck's chapters on the tenth through sixteenth centuries in Inglot et al., pp. 38–105, a work for a general audience. For German readers the same applies to Haase, pp. 62–144. These are not works of investigative or interpretive scholarship. Also tied to traditional paradigms is the factually informative dissertation of Matzen-Stöckert.

9. Halecki, *Borderlands*. East-central European topics are treated in one comparative context in Hoffmann, "Outsiders."

10. Schlesinger, "geschichtliche Stellung." The influence of this approach is visible in Schlesinger, ed., *Ostsiedlung als Problem*, especially essays by Schlesinger, "Problematik," pp. 11–30; Graus, "Problematik," pp. 31–75; and Trawkowski, "Rolle," pp. 349–368.

11. Graus, "Germans and Slavs," pp. 29 and 42. Łowmiański wrote in the 1985 valedictory volume of his *Początki Polski*, 6, p. 833, on the cultural role of immigrant German knights

in thirteenth-century Silesia, "Był to materiał do utworzenia partykularnego narodu śląskiego, ale ten zależenia od okoliczności historycznych mógł pozostać w ramach nadrzędnego narodu polskiego." That without modern nationhood Silesia may earlier have had its own autonomous identity is a useful idea.

12. A *European* perspective on medieval settlement in east-central Europe was called for by Zernack, pp. 801–804. From the Middle Ages the problem of transition is well-posed by Małowist in "Growth" and "Inequality;" from an early modern retrospect it is the concern of Mączak et al., *East-Central Europe*.

13. Hence interpretive debates and comparative issues are where possible here relegated to the notes.

14. This makes valuable now that prewar and even much older scholarship which preserved information from sources since destroyed. It remains true despite recovery in 1980 from the German Democratic Republic of some formerly unknown remains of the Wrocław archive. See Wörster, pp. 262–265, and Irgang, "Urkundenforschungen," pp. 366–367. Recovered materials have not been accessible for this study.

15. Pfeiffer, *Patriziat*, pp. 197–200 describes the conveyancing and registration system and reports its official and private use. The best review of the records themselves is still Bobertag, "Gerichtsbücher," pp. 102–175. See further discussion in Appendix A.

16. Statistical methods used with the survey texts and the charters of conveyance are treated in Appendix A.

Chapter 2

1. On the traditional importance of the bottomland-plain distinction, see especially Szulc, pp. 16–25. More general information is from Schlenger, pp. 31–52, and Geisler, *Atlas*, sheets 2–3, 19, and 21.

2. After the Duchy of Wrocław acquired jurisdiction over the intervening bit of Oleśnica territory in 1567 [RF, III, 312 and IV, 2777], the long-unruly Uraz district was absorbed into the Wrocław district.

3. Generally for what follows see Halecki, *Borderlands*, pp. 1–172; Dvornik, *Slavs*, pp. 1–88, 120–212, 232–246, and 283–361; Manteuffel; Gieysztor, "Medieval Poland," pp. 31–165; Aubin, et al., *Geschichte Schlesiens*, I; Maleczyński, *Historia Śląska*, I:parts 1–2; Jasiński, *Rodowód Piastów*, I, 39–186; Schwarzer, pp. 54–90.

4. Lands of a third brother, Conrad, a minor in 1163 and dead by 1173, went to Bolesław. Zientara, "Bolesław," pp. 367–394.

5. Zientara, *Brodaty*. Baszkiewicz, *Powstanie zjednoczonego*, explained the political strength of many thirteenth-century Silesian rulers by the economic precocity of that province, but see also Labuda, "Uwagi o zjednoczeniu," pp. 125–149.

6. Appelt, "Vincenzstift," pp. 219–227 rejected the authenticity of a charter dated to 1214 (*KdS* #248 and *SUB*, I, #351) and thus pushed back to 1223 the first acceptable evidence of Środa's German law (*KdS* #282 and *SUB*, I, #225).

7. Mularczyk, "Walk o władzę" and "Podziały Śląska."

8. *SR* #1536.

9. For the role of Henry IV in Polish history see Knoll, pp. 15–17.

10. *LBU*, II, 3–8,

11. Łokietek's resurrection of the kingdom is a great event of Polish history but less significant to the Wrocław duchy, simply because the later Piasts did not achieve their goal of reuniting Silesia with the other Polish provinces. On the successes of Łokietek, see Knoll, pp. 14–41; Baszkiewicz, *Powstanie zjednoczonego* and *Polska czasów Łokietka*; Dąbrowski, *Korona królestwa*.

12. *SR* #3401 and *HPR*, 3F. After 1314 the borders of the medieval duchy were changed in two ways, one of which affects this study. During the fourteenth and fifteenth centuries a handful of villages along the eastern border of the Wrocław district passed for varying lengths of time from the Oława district of the Brzeg duchy to the Wrocław duchy, apparently at the wish of local landlords who bought these transfers from impecunious dukes of Brzeg. Map 1.1 indicates the sites; they are objects of this study only when they were in the Duchy of Wrocław.

Two other districts with temporary or tenuous constitutional connections with Wrocław will receive no further attention here. The district of Kąty, a triangular sliver of land bordering the Środa district on the south, was part of the Świdnica duchy and various of its successor states from 1291 to 1419 and thereafter an episcopal property. Often it was held as a pledge by others, including Charles IV briefly in the 1350s, when it was surveyed for *LB* (Reiter, pp. 4–10). To the east the Namysłów district, strategically located in the wooded swamps of the upper Widawa River near the Polish border but separated from Wrocław by the entire width of often hostile Oleśnica, knew a longer legal connection with the Wrocław duchy. Charles IV acquired this strongpoint from the Duke of Brzeg in 1359 and immediately declared it incorporated into his Duchy of Wrocław. Rulers of Wrocław often had concern for the defence of Namysłów, but the two areas were never really united. Like Kąty, Namysłów is treated as a part of the duchy only in sources from Charles' reign. Even the term used to refer together to these royal possessions, "ducatus Wratislaviensis et districtus Nampslavienses," confirms their distinction. See Bobertag, "Gerichtsbücher," pp. 102–108 (though in error on the Uraz district).

13. Koebner, "Zaudengerichte," pp. 31–82; Helbig, pp. 102–106.

14. *BUB* #152.

15. Menzel, *Jura ducalia* is chiefly based on the Cistercian house at Kamieniec Ząbkówski, but his interpretation also applies to the Wrocław duchy. The issue is treated fully in Chapter 8 below.

16. For scholarly synthesis of the city's medieval history see Maleczyński, "Dzieje Wrocławia," pp. 11–336 with discussion of population size pp. 84–85.

17. Knoll, pp. 59–61; Pustejovsky; Menzel, "Trennung," pp. 262–274.

18. *BUB*, pp. 124–125; *LBU*, I, 66–69.

19. Knoll, pp. 96–97, 179–194, 204–207, 218, 226–227 and 232. To the end of his reign Casimir sought in vain for a way to dislodge the Luxemburgs from Silesia.

20. *LBU*, I, 8–12. See also Sanmann.

21. John himself had appointed a captain for Bohemia during his absence in 1313. Kopietz neglects earlier Přemyslid and contemporary Polish use of this office.

22. Brinkmann, pp. 395–405.

23. The land registers began while Conrad of Borsnicz was captain in 1336 (*SR* #5538 and Bobertag, "Gerichtsbücher," p. 145). Fees for registering land transactions were regulated in 1339 and 1341 (*BUB*, #160 and #170).

24. The incumbents and their terms of office in Bobertag, "Gerichtsbücher," pp. 161–163.

25. Goerlitz, *Verfassung*, pp. 101–104.

26. *NRB*, pp. 30–32 and 243–244.

27. *BUB* #174.

28. *BUB* #184.

29. Rachfall, *Gesamtstaatsverwaltung*, pp. 43–45 and Menzel, *Jura ducalia*, pp. 52–54. John reserved only service obligations and payments in lieu thereof in his 1327 confirmation that landowners were exempt from tax (*BUB*, pp. 117–120; *LBU*, I, 67–69).

30. Tz-S, pp. 550–552. To judge from an explicit statement in *LB* #89 and the rates in RB and KLM, the reduction became permanent. The 1353 records also suggest mint money rates were halved in the Środa district to 3 groschen per mansus.

31. Budgetary data from *HPR*, pp. 101–113, here given roughly because the original contains several arithmetical errors. The *Geschoss* and mint money totals for the Środa and Wrocław districts accord with semi-annual assessments for Walpurgis 1361 and three other undated but contemporary terms printed as *LB*, #116–450 with notes. No fiscal records cover the Uraz district.

32. For comparative synthesis see Russocki, pp. 171–188.

33. Rachfall, *Gesamtstaatsverwaltung*, pp. 45–64 (with regard for centralizing and statist prejudices) and compare Croon, pp. 2–18.

34. The 1327 privilege is *BUB*, pp. 117–120; *LBU*, I, 67–69. In 1346 the "communitas vasallorum nostrorum Wratislaviensis districtus" helped appoint members to a royal commission (*RBM.*, IV, 1661) and in 1400 "wir ritter und knechte lantleute des furstintumis czu Bresslaw und czu dem Neumarkte" sent a long list of grievances to the king (*NRB*, p. 254). The history of the Estates of the duchy has not been written nor, in the absence of materials once in the archives, is it likely to be. They certainly were active, however, long before the reign of Mathias.

35. Kopietz, pp. 68–71.

36. WAP, AMW, G 3, fol. 11r.

37. Those for 1361–79 were reconstructed from court records by Kopietz, pp. 72–78, and for 1380–1611 (excepting a few years in the late fifteenth century) appear in WAP, AMW, C 15.

38. Maleczyński, "Dzieje Wrocławia," pp. 85–162, summarizes economic and social evolution during the fourteenth century, but now compare the interpretation by Małowist, "Trade," pp. 547–549.

39. On Wrocław's power over the duchy see Hoffmann, "City-State," pp. 173–199.

40. *BUB*, pp. 179–180 and 212; *HPR*, pp. 101–133.

41. Henry of Lasan bought land after his term of office (RF, II, 578, and IV, 2820–2837) and Bishop Conrad was no stranger.

42. Klassen, *Nobility*, pp. 55–58, but for detailed identification of Škopek and other Czech captains of the duchy I am indebted to John Klassen for permission to use unpublished results of his research. On John of Milheim see Odložilík, "Chapel of Bethlehem," pp. 125–141.

43. Most details are in Markgraf, "Unruhigen Zeiten," and Grünhagen, "Aufstand," but more sympathy for the guildsmen appears in Maleczyński, "Dzieje Wrocławia," pp. 159–163.

44. Estimates from a city tax register of 1403 differ according to the numbers assigned to non-taxable groups, especially the clergy; see Maleczyński, "Dzieje Wrocławia," pp. 85–87. On the maintenance of public order see Heinisch, pp. 68–91.

45. Silesian reaction or reactions to the Hussites is fiercely disputed among German and Polish historians. The most detailed narrative account, Grünhagen, *Hussitenkämpfe*, is marred by a crudely anti-Slavic and German nationalist stance, while post-war Polish scholarship highlights all possible cases of lower-class and ethnicly Polish sympathy for Slavic revolutionaries. See, for example, Maleczyńska, "Udział Śląska;" Heck, "Hussitenaufstandes;" Heck and Maleczyńska, eds., *Ruch Husycki*. More balanced and subtle is Dziewulski, "Społeczeństwo," who noted different reactions in Silesian groups and regions and evaporation of peasant support after experience of Hussite raids.

46. Kronthal, "Asenheimer."

47. Two different but equally valuable books in English make Poděbrady one of the most accessible figures in the entire story: Heymann, *George of Bohemia*, and Odložilík, *Hussite King*. A more Silesian and ecclesiastical perspective is available in Jan Drabina's "1453–71," "Tempelfeld," "Stosunek zakonów," and *Kontakty z Rzymem*.

48. Heck, "Elekcja kutnohorska," pp. 193–235.

49. The only full, if dated, biography outside of Magyar is Fraknói, *Mathias Corvinus*.

50. *PCC*, I, 271.

51. Wendt, "Stände," pp. 157–176. Polish feudal law, still operative in Silesia as well as the kingdom, imposed on fief holders restricted inheritance rights, increased military services, and wardship by the suzerain rather than family members; see Skwarczyński," pp. 292–310 and Chapter 7 below.

52. Markgraf, "Heinz Dompnig."

53. Lhotsky, pp. 185–202.

54. Sigismund's activity during 1504–06 also arose from his own interests as duke of Głogów and of Opawa. See Nowogrodzki.

55. Drabina, *Kontakty z Rzymem*; Laug, "Kolowratsche Vertrag," pp. 37–56, "Domkapitel," pp. 88–104, and "Auseinandersetzung," pp. 51–62.

56. Thus the Habsburg, Albert, installed his ally, Margrave Albert of Brandenburg, in 1439, Poděbrady paid off his rivals Henry and John of Rožmberk in 1455–1458, and Corvinus appointed his important supporter, Zdeněk of Šternberk in 1469.

57. Charters for post-1424 conveyances of the chancellorship are compiled in WAP, AMW, C 3. A city family acquired the office under Sigismund and it remained in private hands until 1504, when the town council bought possession from the holder and perpetual confirmation from the king.

58. Stobbe 1867, p. 161; *NRB*, pp. 281–283. The Wrocław cathedral chapter knew in the early 1500s that what it called the "convocatione nobilitarium in territorio et sub dominio civitatis Wratislaviensis" was often a tool of the *Rat* (e.g. ACW, I, 439, 680–686, 783, and 878).

59. Treated in Hoffmann, "City-State" from the complete petition published in Klose, *Inneren Verhältnisse*, pp. 31–32. For other examples of Wrocław manipulating duchy adminis-

tration in the interests of the corporation and its citizens, see Klein, ed., pp. 362–363; Wendt, "Landbesitz," pp. 215–228; *UD*, pp. 227–229. Compare from the perspective of urban cultural awareness Petry, "Breslau," pp. 162–169.

60. Dillon, *King and Estates*.

Chapter 3

1. For themes of this chapter see Dembińska and Podwińska, eds., *Historia kultury materialnej*, and Trawkowski, "Przemiany społeczne," pp. 62–118. On ways late medieval monastic myth about twelfth-century founders' heroic deprivation and deeds in a desolate wilderness long warped modern scholarly minds, see Epperlein, pp. 303–335.

2. Gieysztorowa, "Badania," pp. 530–556, and "Research," pp. 5–17.

3. Ładogórski, *Zaludnieniem*, pp. 172–175; Maleczyński, "Wsi przed kolonizacja," pp. 131–132. See also Maleczyński, ed., *Historia Śląska*, I:1, 242–247.

4. Trawkowski, "Roli kolonizacji," p. 188.

5. ". . . in diebus illis, cum dominus dux antiquus Boleslaus . . . diversis in locis suis rusticis terram distribuerit, dedit hanc silvam cuidam rustico suo proprio, Glambo nomine. Hic idem rusticus Glambo primo exstirpabat illum locum, qui nunc dicitur Magnum Pratum" (Grodecki, ed., *Księga Henrykowska*, p. 276).

6. Tyszkiewicz, pp. 17–32 and 36–40. Minor differences between Tyszkiewicz's identification of documented place names and that of later onomastic research, notably Domański, *Nazwy miejscowe*, do not alter his findings. Further.examination of the documentary evidence for settlement during 1150–1250 indicates that the relative preponderance of church properties introduces no spatial bias; the pattern of densely- and sparsely-settled landscapes is unchanged when the fewer lay properties are treated independently. For direct reference to clearance of woodlands in this area, see *SUB*, II, #364–365.

7. On the pattern in the Wrocław district see Tyszkiewicz, pp. 6–13 and 36–40. Compare Kaźmierczyk and Podwińska, "Badania," pp. 451–462, and "Wyniki badań," pp. 463–477. Sparse habitation of the loams and moraines is confirmed by frequent thirteenth-century mention of forests and wildlife there, as, for example, *KdS* #198; *SUB*, I, #171, and II, #275; *SLU* #29, 48, and 110; *SR* #1081 and 2630; *LFE*, B150.

8. Podwińska, "Habitat agraire," pp. 733–735.

9. For what follows see Trawkowski, "Rozwój osadnictwa," pp. 113–115; Podwińska, *Zmiany form*, pp. 21–223; Lalik, "Radło i źreb," "*Sors et aratrum*;" Podwińska, "Habitat agraire," pp. 730 and 741–747; Gieysztor, "Villages désertés," p. 610.

10. *KdS* #296; *SUB*, I, #247 (compare Domański, *Nazwy miejscowe*, #240); *KdS* #129, 198, and 349; *SUB*, I, #114, 171 and 279.

11. *SLU* #9.

12. *KdS* #55; *SUB*, I, #45. See also *KdS* #107 and 235; *SUB*, I, #95 and 198; *SR* #1163, 1706, 3391, and 3400; *LFE* B32.

13. *KdS* #103, 107, and 130; *SUB*, I, #83, 95, and 115. See also *KdS* #128 or *SUB*, I, #114.

14. *KdS* #103 is *SUB*, I, #83, but editorial identifications of "Yaxonouo" must be revised in light of *Księga Henrykowska*, p. 286,, as suggested by Domański, *Nazwy miejscowe*, #139. For *viciniae* see *KdS* #91; *SUB*, I, #77, and II, #341; *SR* #876; *BUB*, p. 11.

15. *SUB*, II, #287; Podwińska, *Zmiany form*, pp. 250–255.

16. Onomastic evidence for Krajków, Rzeplin, Wilkowice, Milejowice, and Żurawina is handled in Domański, *Nazwy miejscowe*, #212 and 265–268, but Szukalice also occurs in charters from the early 1250s (*SLU*, #1, 13, and 19). That *Jaszkotle* was also until around 1300 not a place but an area is shown in Hoffmann, "Nazwy," pp. 12–13 and 17–24.

17. *SR* #2922 and 2950. Moepert, *Ortsnamen*, p. 34.

18. *SR* #2492, 2497, and 2630; Stenzel in *Übersicht* 1841, pp. 179–180.

19. Maleczyński, "Wsi przed kolonizacja," pp. 132–133; Ładogórski, *Zaludnieniem*, pp. 169–170. When Grüger, "Besiedlung," pp. 22–25, denied Maleczyński's claims of good-sized Polish villages around 1200, he forgot the differences between the thickly settled Trzebnica region and the foothills of a Ziębice district only then being opened up.

20. Podwińska, "Habitat agraire," pp. 735–736 and 743.

21. Podwińska, *Zmiany form*, pp. 104–223; Gieysztor, "Villages désertés," p. 610. Com-

pare western analogues in Hoffmann, "Origins," pp. 33–45; Cheyette, pp. 182–206; Chapelot and Fossier, pp. 70–72, 127–128, and 135–150.

22. *ChronBMV*, p. 172: "Et licet prius et pro tunc Prokaw et Buchta due villule fuerunt, ex tunc tamen et usque nunc simul sunt una villa in terminis suis, que simpliciter Prokaw nominatur." See also *KdS* #71 and 105; *SUB*, I, #61 and 97, and II, #258 and 259; *UFO*, #51; Domański, *Nazwy miejscowe*, #4, 5 and 38.

23. *KdS* #296; *SUB*, I, #247 and compare #313 (not in *KdS*).

24. *UD*, pp. 248–251. In 1234 Abbess Gertrud called it "Domaycerke," using the old Polish word for church, *cyrki* (*SUB*, II, #86). This form gave way before 1300 to its German equivalent, "Thomaskirch" (Domański, *Nazwy miejscowe*, #129).

25. In order of their last documentation: *Nabitin*—known from an authentic text only in 1175 (*KdS* #55; *SUB*, I, #45); *Odrzyca*—known only in 1193 (*KdS* #70; *SUB*, I, #60); *Strzemlino*—known only in 1204 (*KdS* #107; *SUB*, I, #95); *Świętniki* belonging to St. Vincent—known from 1193 (*KdS* #70; *SUB*, I, #60) to 1204 (*KdS* #107; *SUB*, I, #95); *Uścimowo*—known only in identical passages from 1208 and 1218 (*KdS* #130 and 193; *SUB*, I, #115 and 181); *Żórawin*—known from 1175 (*KdS* #55; *SUB*, I, #45) to the 1240's (Seidel, *Beginn*, p. 153, or, if the grant to Dean Benicus is this place, *SUB*, II, #287); *Buchta*—known 1204 to 1243 (see note 22 above); *Guzowicy*—known in 1155 and 1245 (*KdS* #35; *SUB*, I, #28 and II, #287); *Jasbromie*—known only in 1245 (*SUB*, II, #287); *Coci Episcopi*—known only in 1249 (*SUB*, II, #364–365); *Bronikowo*—known 1193 to 1250 (see note 22 above); *Sokolnicy*—known 1149 to 1253 (*KdS* #25, 70, 87, 103, 107, and 130; *SUB*, I, #19, 60, 75, 83, 95, and 115; *UFO*, #60); *Kochlowo*—described in 1267 (*SR* #1271) and further documented in 1269 and 1274 (*SR* #1324 and 1452; Haeusler, "Bemerkungen," pp. 275–276).

26. *KdS* #130 and 193; *SUB*, I, #115 and 181.

27. Lalik, "*Sors et aratrum*," pp. 3–9, contrasts the many recent noble donors of properties confirmed to the bishopric of Wrocław in 1155 (*KdS* #35; *SUB*, I, #28) with the exclusively ducal source of those held by the archbishop of Gniezno in 1136. Generally on lordship see Łowmiański, *Początki Polski*, 6:377–398.

28. The administrative (rather than simply military) character of the castles is well defended in Modzelewski, *Organizacja*, pp. 92–135 (partly accessible in an earlier form as "La division," pp. 1125–1138) against the assaults of Buczek in "Organizacja gospodarki," "Organizacja grodowa," and "Organizacja służebna."

29. Readers who recognize similarities with Strayer, "Two Levels of Feudalism," should also note the absence in Poland of both the western hierarchy of vassal ties and the characteristically German group of servile knights (ministerials). Immigrant German ministerials were received in Silesia as knights. Bogucki, "*Miles*," pp. 227–231; Cetwiński, "Pochodzenie," pp. 49–53; Cetwiński, *Rycerstwo* 1980, pp. 11–58; and Cetwiński, *Rycerstwo* 1982.

To sample the flavor of modern Polish scholarship on the complex early history of the country's nobility, see Wojciechowski, *Ritterrecht*, pp. 29–53; Wojciechowski, "La condition;" Gąsiorowski, "Rycerstwo," pp. 620–624; Gąsiorowski, ed., *Nobility*—especially the introduction (pp. 7–16) and selections from works of Łowmiański, Buczek, and Bieniak—; Łowmiański, *Początki Polski*, 6:594–634.

30. Korta, *Wielkiej własności*, pp. 21–57, and "Rozwój terytorialny," pp. 528–566.

31. Korta, *Wielki własności*, pp. 21–26; Richtsteig, pp. 21–24; Cetwiński, *Rycerstwo* 1982, pp. 15–17, and works there cited. Compare Radler, pp. 301–305.

32. Cetwiński, *Rycerstwo* 1982, pp. 126–127; Korta, *Wielki własności*, p. 38; *SR* #957; *SLU* #41. Compare Eistert, "Pogarell," pp. 226–290.

33. Korta, *Wielki własności*, pp. 41–42, summarizes from Wutke, "Gallici," pp. 279–311; Cetwiński, *Rycerstwo* 1982, pp. 95–96 and 188–190. See also Zientara, "Walonowie," pp. 349–368.

34. Cetwiński, "Pochodzenie," pp. 56–61; Korta, "Rozwoj terytorialny," pp. 18–38. Contrast the hyperbole of Schilling, pp. 100–103 or Engelbert, "Frauen." Doroszewska, pp. 51–55, shows more Germans at early thirteenth-century courts than on the land.

35. *KdS* #25; *SUB*, I, #19; Cetwiński, *Rycerstwo* 1982, p. 13; *SR* #802.

36. *KdS* #198; *SUB*, I, #171; *SR* #956; Cetwiński, *Rycerstwo* 1982, p. 112.

37. *SR* #802 and 957. Compare *SUB*, II, #413.

38. Midunsky, ed., pp. 22–62; Engelbert, "Walter."

39. Both had checkered early histories. St. Mary began as a foundation of Peter Włast at Górka among his rich donations near Mt. Ślęza and was moved to Wrocław in the early 1190's,

while St. Vincent, also traceable to Włast, was Benedictine until dilapidation caused its transfer to the Premonstratensians before 1193.

40. Because charters for these are among the richest sources from Poland around 1200 and because both houses later modeled forgeries on authentic ones, the texts were long objects of fierce historical debate. Contemporary scholarly agreement is manifest in equivalent assessments in *KdS* and *SUB*. Compare Matzen-Stöckert, pp. 146–158.

41. *KdS* #55; *SUB*, I, #45; "Si qui autem Poloni non pertinentes ad alicuius dominium fuerint abbatis coloni, non cogantur alii cuiquam aliquod solvere vel servitium aliquod exhibere." In here seeing an authentic immunity I follow Menzel, *Jura ducalia*, pp. 32–33, as opposed to Korta's assertion (*Wielki własności*, pp. 143–144) that exemptions were only for immigrants. See also Grodecki, *Początki immunitetu* and Łowmiański, *Początki Polski*, 6:532–576.

42. Korta, *Wielki własności*, pp. 143–159.

43. *SUB*, II, #342. More examples are *KdS* #91, 105, 107 and 163; *SUB*, I, #77, 94, 95 and 142.

44. Matuszewski, ed., *Najstarszy zwód*, p. 167: *Ius polonorum*, art. 6, requires a peasant to reply to accusations only before his own lord. Vetulani argued that this compilation especially reflected Silesian conditions but Matuszewski's reluctance to attempt so specific a location remains more convincing. See Vetulani, "Niemiecki spis," and "Nowe wydanie;" Matuszewski, "Śląskie pochodzenia."

45. *KdS* #91; *SUB*, I, #77; Seidel, "Leubus."

46. Appelt, "Vinzenzstift," pp. 225–226; *UFO*, #66.

47. *KdS* #333; *SUB*, I, #364; *SR* #973.

48. Korta, *Wielki własności*, p. 90, and "Rozwój klasztornej."

49. Korta, *Wielki własności*, pp. 51–55 (e.g. *SR* #956).

50. *KdS* #130; *SUB*, I, #115.

51. Korta, *Wielki własności*, pp. 90–91, finds purchased only 26 (4.7 percent) of the 549 church villages in Silesia by 1266.

52. *KdS* #68 and 91; *SUB*, I, #58 and 77; *SR* #712, 725a, 802, 876, 957; *SLU* #41.

53. *KdS* #55, 59, 81, 86, 91, 251, 294 and 295; *SUB*, I, #45, 49, 70, 74, 77, 311, 312, 248, and 314; II, #5 and 17. See also a case from the 1290s in *UD* #2–3. On kin right in Polish law see Kolańczyk; Gieysztor, "Lignage;" Bieniak, "Rody."

54. *KdS* #68, 41, 103, 105, 130, 152, 153, and 235; *SUB*, I, #58, 61, 83, 94, 115, 129, 130 and 230. Purchase of Adelaide's portion of Budziszów in 1252 also exemplifies St. Mary's consolidation practices, for the abbey had earlier bought the other half from her late husband (*SR* #802). Compare also Brochów and Domaniów as described above.

55. For St. Vincent, Trzebnica, and the Holy Spirit Hospital see *KdS* #70 and 174; *SUB*, I, #60 and 147; *BUB*, #10. Compare Constable, pp. 99–197.

56. Findings here support positions of Grodecki, "gospodarki folwarcznej," pp. 58–60; Cetwiński, *Rycerstwo* 1982, pp. 108–130; and Łowmiański, *Początki Polski*, 6:245–247, against Korta, *Wielki własności*, pp. 94–124, and Haeusler, *Geschichte*, p. 81, who concede no quantitative significance to demesnes in the twelfth and thirteenth century economy. The latter count uncritically the few references in rare, inconsistent, and unrepresentative early documents and leave a mystery the many plainly long-standing demesne farms of the late 1200s.

57. Celestine III gave the two older houses the same clause in 1193—"Sane laborum vestrorum, que propriis manibus aut sumptibus colitis, sive de nutrimentis animalium vestrorum, nullus a vobis decimas exigere vel extorquere presumat" (*KdS* #70 and 71; *SUB*, I, #58 and 61)—and in 1216 Innocent III much the same to the Cistercians (*KdS* #174 and 175; *SUB*, I, #147 and 148). The *sane laborum* formula was established under Innocent II for this purpose; see Constable, pp. 234–245. All four privileges also forbade violence "infra clausuras locorum seu grangiarum vestrarum," for which see Bader, *Dorf*, pp. 148–168.

58. *KdS* #103; *SUB*, I, #83, and II, #86; *UFO* #77; Korta, *Wielki własności*, pp. 97–103.

59. *KdS* #55 and 175; *SUB*, I, #45 and 148; II, #350; *SR* #1966; Korta, *Wielki własności*, pp. 105–106; Siedel, *Beginn*, pp. 105–109.

60. *KdS* #105 and 107; *SUB*, I, #94 and 95. See also *SUB*, II, #181, 193, and 301; *SR* #1742, 3415, and 3905.

61. *KdS* #129; *SUB*, I, #114; Korn, *BUB* #10 and 17.

62. *KdS* #55; *SUB*, I, #45. Seidel, *Beginn*, pp. 96–97, on the later history of the *Olbino* demesne is interesting conjecture.

63. *SUB*, I, #295, and Stenzel in *Übersicht* 1841, p. 78 for "milit[es] quos propriis exco-

lunt aratris." Hugo is in *SR* #1271, 1324, and 1452. See also *KdS* #251; *SUB*, I, #311; *UFO* #70; *SR* #1050 and 2240; and the discussion of *aratrum* below.

64. (Relatively) well-described early demesnes in the future Wrocław duchy include: *Żórawin* and *Olbino* in 1175 (*KdS* #55; *SUB*, I, #45); Szczytniki in 1204 (*KdS* #107 and 109; *SUB*, I, #95 and 96); an unlocated holding given by Duke Henry to St. Mary in 1204 (*KdS* #105; *SUB*, I, #94); Polanowice in 1267 (*SR* #1275).

65. Grodecki, "Książęca," p. 27, and Missalek, p. 251. The Trzebnica charter (*KdS* #104; *SUB*, I, #93) equates one plow horse and two oxen in setting peasants' rents, but the description of stock on the Szczytniki demesne (also in 1204), makes it dubious that horses then plowed on direct exploitation properties (as Korta, *Wielki własności*, pp. 108–109). What Duke Henry called "duos equos," Abbot Gerard transformed into "duos herpicarios" (*herpex* = harrow) (*Kds* #107 and 109; *SUB*, I, #94 and 95). On the use of horses for harrowing and carting but their lagging diffusion into *demesne* plow teams, see Podwińska, *Technika*, pp. 287–290, and, for late twelfth-century England, Langdon, pp. 48–62, especially 58–59.

66. Polanowice had 12 oxen and 2 *iumenta* of twice the value per head. Were they also plow beasts? A demesne at Rzeplin in 1253 had 3 mansi (*SLU* #13).

67. *SLU*, #13; *SR* #1331; Hoffmann, "Nazwy," pp. 2–9.

68. Seidel, *Beginn*, p. 153. See also *SLU*, #13 and *SR* #1275.

69. Other than the Trzebnica information (of which more below although most places lay outside the later Wrocław duchy), what Korta (*Wielki własności*, pp. 124–142) offers as records of rent levels comes almost entirely from German law villages and thus tells little about an earlier Polish economy.

70. Trawkowski, *Gospodarka*; Korta, "W sprawie gospodarki;" Seidel, *Beginn*, pp. 103–105.

71. Trawkowski, *Gospodarka*; Epperlein, pp. 327–335.

72. Lalik, "Radło i źreb," and "*Sors et aratrum*," pp. 10–12; Trawkowski, "Rozwój osadnictwa," pp. 107–115; Tymieniecki, "Przemiany," pp. 21–35. The *aratrum* thus functioned precisely like the *mansus* (*Hufe, łan*) in the German law system or the eight-ox team of Domesday England. The interacting concepts of physical, familial, successional, and assessment units encompassed in *źreb* (*sors*) and *aratrum* (*radło*) resemble those outlined by Herlihy, "Carolingian Mansus," pp. 79–89.

73. *KdS* #103 and 130; *SUB*, I, #83 and 115.

74. *SUB*, II, #301; *SR* #1742 and 1078, but for location see *SLU*, #19, and *SR* #2092.

75. On peasant status groups in Silesia and Poland see Maleczyński, "Wsi przed kolonizacja," pp. 133–138, and "Ludnościa chłopska;" Korta, *Wielki własności*, pp. 175–201; Tymieniecki, "Społeczeństwo" and *Historia*, I:97–216 and 320–336; Buczek, "W sprawie 1204;" and Łowmiański, *Początki Polski*, 6:508–532.

76. Buczek, *Książęca ludność* and Modzelewski, *Organizacja*, pp. 92–135, are major treatments. See also note 28 above.

77. Domański, "Nazwy służebne," and *Nazwy miejscowe*, p. 134 and *passim*; Rospond, pp. 19–24; Matzen-Stöckert, pp. 101–102. A full display of service sites is on Map 3.1.

78. *KdS* #103, 104, 129 and 130; *SUB*, I, #83, 93, 114, and 115. See Bogucki, "Komorniki."

79. *Sanctuarii* lived near Wrocław at Świątniki, at a *Świętniki* that belonged to St. Mary and disappeared in the 1400s, and at another *Świętniki* near *Olbino*, the property of St. Vincent. The last, known only around 1200 (*KdS* #70, 87, and 107; *SUB*, I, #60, 75 and 95), had in 1193 seven households (see Domański, *Nazwy miejscowe*, pp. 40–41 and 103–104). Bishop Thomas gave to the Teutonic Order in 1249 a property where his cooks lived near Wojszyce (*SUB*, II, #364–365).

80. *KdS* #337; *SUB*, I, #281. This derivation was first suggested by Tyc, pp. 42–43.

81. As *aratores* in the 1227 tithe agreement (*KdS* #337; *SUB*, I, #281) and as *rataj* with freedoms worth granting to the Clares' holdings in 1257 (*SR* #973). Ratyń gained recorded mention only in 1324 (Domański, *Nazwy miejscowe*, #41).

82. *KdS* #104, 129, 130; *SUB*, I, #93, 114, 115.

83. Vanishing free peasants are a theme of tenth- through thirteenth-century Polish history. Some likely became knights with land and freedom but more probably lost both. See studies by Małecki, pp. 391–423; Matuszewski, "Causae;" Buczek, "prawie chłopów," pp. 88–95; Tymieniecki, *Smardowie*; Wasilewski, pp. 1–23. Łowmiański, *Początki Polski*, 6:429–507 reviews the complex disputes. For a wholly contradictory position see Kossmann, "Bauernfreiheit" or "Bauern und Freie."

84. *KdS* #68; *SUB*, I, #58. On the longer-lasting unfree *decimi* (*dessitli*) see Poppe.
85. Discussion of *hospites* and *ascripticii* draws heavily on Lalik, "*Sors et aratrum*," pp. 19–22, who mediated a dispute over inheritance rights between Matuszewski, "Causae," and Buczek, "prawie chłopów." See also Wolfarth.
86. *KdS* #104; *SUB*, I, #93.
87. Matuszewski, *Najstarszy zwód*, pp. 233–234.
88. *KdS* #68; *SUB*, I, #58.
89. Note the terms used in *KdS* #71 (*SUB*, I, #61) and for all inhabitants of Kotowice collectively in *KdS* #130, pp. 39–40. Compare the 1288 foundation of Holy Cross (*UFO*, pp. 124–128), where most villages still had Polish customs. On Czech analogs see Fritze, pp. 503–520.
90. Matuszewski, *Najstarszy zwód*, pp. 169–173; Podwińska, *Zmiany form*, pp. 275–341. See western parallels in Bader, *Dorfgenossenschaft*, pp. 266–383.
91. *BUB*, p. 11; *KdS* #91; *SUB*, I, #77; *SR* #876.
92. Matuszewski, *Najstarszy zwód*, p. 155. Haeusler, *Geschichte*, p. 77, finds thirteenth-century *włodarze* in rent-collecting and judicial roles, but those around Wrocław are later (*LB* #51; Kurnik, p. 20).
93. Matuszewski, *Najstarszy zwód*, pp. 227–231.
94. Kurze, pp. 460–465; Santifaller, "Beziehungen," p. 402; Schulte, "Parochial-Verfassung," pp. 390–397; Knötel, pp. 179–204.
95. In general see Maleczyński, "Wsi przed kolonizacja," pp. 138–143 and Korta, *Wielki własności*, pp. 124–142, although the latter's indiscriminate handling of German law innovations and their antecedents obscures the earlier situation.
96. *KdS* #104; *SUB*, I, #93.
97. The most comprehensive Silesian listings remain those in Tz-S, pp. 10–32, and Haeusler, *Geschichte*, pp. 54–56.
98. All cited occur with Polish and/or Latin names in Wrocław duchy charters from 1202–52. See *KdS* #103, 104, 105, 107, 109, 163, and 248; *SUB*, I, #83, 93, 94, 95, 96, and 142; II, #339 and 342; *SLU*, #9.
99. *KdS* #248; *SUB*, I, #351.
100. Matuszewski, *Najstarszy zwód*, p. 197; *KdS* #323 and 337; *SUB*, I, #261 and 281. Górka, *Leubus*, pp. 53–64, showed that special tithes on new land were also indigenous to Poland.
101. *LFE*, B and D *passim*; *SUB*, I, #295.
102. Tymieniecki, "Przemiany," pp. 28–32; Korta, *Wielki własności*, pp. 140–143.
103. Maleczyński, "Wsi przed kolonizacja," pp. 142–143.
104. *SUB*, II, #343.
105. "Chinino" may be Radakowice (*KdS* #103, 130 and 193; *SUB*, I, #83, 115 and 181); Zonowid in *KdS* #68 and *SUB*, I, #58. *Ius polonorum* mentions run-aways (Matuszewski, *Najstarszy zwód*, pp. 233–235).
106. Maleczyński, "Wsi przed kolonizacja," pp. 144–145, says Silesia thus developed money rents before the rest of Poland.
107. Tymieniecki, "Przemiany," pp. 28–32, has rising demands from lords force productivity increases, as does Korta (*Wielki własności*, p. 143), who conflates German law rents.
108. Dąbrowski, *Rozwój*; Podwinska, *Technika*.
109. *KdS* #129 and 337; *SUB*, I, #114 and 281; *SR* #1104; Stenzel in *Übersicht* 1841, p. 110. On slash-and-burn in early thirteenth-century Silesia and in forested parts of twelfth-century France and Germany, see Tyc, pp. 42–43. Remains of domestic animals from tenth-through thirteenth-century levels near Wrocław's cathedral indicate regular consumption of pork and beef (Myczkowski, pp. 150–171).
110. *SR* #973, 1257, 1301, 2042; *HPR*, p. 16; *UFO*, p. 112. On much eating of local wild fish by residents near the cathedral, see Kozikowska, pp. 3–14.
111. *BUB* #17; *SR* #1301.
112. *SR* #904. Hops and fruit culture gain special mention in *Ius polonorum*, too (Matuszewski, *Najstarszy zwód*, pp. 231–233).
113. Klichowska, "Materiały," and "Znaleziska;" Dembińska, *Konsumpcja*, pp. 58–65; Dąbrówski, *Rozwój*, pp. 88–89.
114. Podwinska, *Technika*, pp. 179–254.
115. Matuszewski, "Nowożytnego zaprzęgu," pp. 637–663; Zak, pp. 625–635; Podwińska, *Technika*, pp. 287–291; *KdS* #107 and 109; *SUB*, I, #95 and 96.

116. Examples near Wrocław are *KdS* #105; *SUB*, I, #94 and *SR* #1275 See also Chmielewski, "Uwagi;" Gieysztor, "Trójpolówki;" Trawkowski, "Roli kolonizacji," pp. 188–190; Tymieniecki, "Technika;" Podwińska, *Technika*, pp. 173–179. Count Unimir had "tres agros" at Popowice in 1260 (*UFO*, pp. 103–104).

117. Dembińska, *Przetwórstwo*, pp. 63–72 and 78–81 diminishes the enthusiasm of Trawkowski, "Młyny." For a thirteenth-century hand mill see Semkowicz, ed., *Vita Hedwigis*, pp. 556–557.

118. A mill in *SUB*, I, #19 (*KdS* #25) has caused the passage to be thought an interpolation.

119. *KdS* #129 and 296; *SUB*, I, #114 and 247.

120. *KdS* #129; *SUB*, I, #114.

121. *KdS* #296; *SUB*, I, #247.

122. *KdS* #59; *SUB*, I, #49. The first recorded in Silesia was a "Wgyasd" of 1149/50 (*KdS* #26; *SUB*, I, #23). Podwińska, *Zmiany form*, pp. 202–224.

123. Schulte, "Ujazd," pp. 211–220. The nine Silesian places named Ujazd are not in the duchy.

124. *KdS* #130 and *SUB*, I, #115. Compare Ozorowice in the same text and in *KdS* #103 or *SUB*, I, #83, and, in the latter, Tyniec Mały, too. See also *SR* #876 and 907; *KdS* #91, 175, 198, and 349; *SUB*, I, #17, 148, 171, and 279.

125. At Czernica in 1265 new boundaries merged lands already the bishop's with those now bought from Henry III (*SLU*, #56).

126. *KdS* #91 and 198; *SUB*, I, #77 and 171; *SR* #876.

127. *SLU*, #111. Schulte's original view ("Ujazd," pp. 200–235) that *lgota* freedoms were developed before and independently of the German law movement was rejected by Schilling, pp. 307–309, in part because he dated German law in Silesia back to the twelfth century. The earlier thesis is reaffirmed by Eistert, "Klarenkloster," pp. 75–77, and by Grodecki, "Wole i lgoty," p. 56, works which Matzen-Stöckert, pp. 100–101, ignores.

128. *KdS* #55; *SUB*, I, #45; *Księga Henrykowska*. For discussion see Korta, *Wielki własności*, pp. 159–173; Zientara, "Bolesław," pp. 389–390.

129. *SLU*, #56 and 65.

130. *UD*, pp 197–198 (compare introductory pp. 55–56)

131. Planned development took place in the late 1200s without German law at Żerniki, Gaj, Sępolno, and Zagródki (*SR* #1109, 1431, 2054 and 2335), while nine places, some explicitly described as tenant villages with fixed money dues, had "iure polonico" in the episcopal register of 1300: Małuszów, Rynakowice, Księże Małe, *Zielona*, Prawocin, Bogusławice, Milejowice, Wilkowice, and Bliż (*LFE* B25, 27, 40–43, 47, 53–55). For later evidence see Haeusler, *Geschichte*, p. 286; *LB* #50–51; *UD*, introductory pp. 56–59; and Maleczyński in *Historia Śląska*, I:1, 281–283.

132. For a broad sample see Piekarczyk; Francastel; *L'artisanat et la vie urbaine en Pologne médiévale*, Ergon (supplement to *KHKM*), vol. 3; Gieysztor, "Villes et campagnes" and "Wieś i miasto." The urban quality of these places is fully acknowledged in Sporn, pp. 170–172. Compare Łowmiański, *Początki Polski*, 6:649–731. For Wrocław Maleczyński, "Dzieje Wrocławia," pp. 24–72, the sketch by Morelowski, and the synthesis of Młynarska-Kaletynowa, *Wrocław*, wholly supersede the claims for German initiation of all genuinely urban life made in Markgraf, "Deutsche Stadt," and retained in Aubin *et al.*, *Geschichte Schlesiens*, I, 438–446.

133. Nowakowa; *KdS* #170; *SUB*, I, #60 and II, #26.

134. Dembińska, "Town Consumption." Gieysztor, "Forum to Civitas," p. 16, called attention to the importance of wealthy urban consumers. Hołubowicz, pp. 56–69, estimated the much smaller Opole ate 10–15 percent of grain production from 600 peasant farms. Ostrowska, pp. 164–179.

135. Kaźmierczyk, *Wrocław lewobrzeżny*.

136. *KdS* #55, 103, 130 and 296; *SUB*, I, #45, 83, 115 and 247.

137. Trawkowski, "Ołbin," pp. 78–89, used evidence from *KdS* #25, 55 and 70 (*SUB*, I, #19, 45 and 60), which continues in later texts, *KdS* #86, 91, 107, 248; *SUB*, I, #74, 77, 351 and II, 26; Bobertag, "Gerichtsbücher," p. 164.

138. Młynarska-Kaletynowa, "Rozwój sieci," pp. 349–361.

139. Besides items already mentioned, see Maleczyński, *Najstarsze targi*, and the revision by Karol Buczek, *Targi*, pp. 37–58 and 92–112. Compare Schlesinger on German markets in east Elbia, "Marktgründungsurkunden," pp. 408–440.

140. Acceptance of Środa as a Polish market depends (first) on its old name, "Szroda" in the first text of 1223 (*KdS* #282; *SUB*, I, #225), referring to a Wednesday (*środa*) market day and not to the site of the place midway (*środek* = center) between castles at Wrocław and Legnica, and (second) on its new name, "Novum Forum" (Neumarkt) indicating no more than economically minor changes of site and institutions in an older market settlement.

Other possible markets in the future duchy are tenuous. If the "forum in Kenese" given by Duke Mieszko in Pope Celestine's 1193 charter for St. Vincent is Księże Wielkie and not some other place, it is the only such reference in the five records of this village up to 1253 (*KdS* #25, 70, and 87; *SUB*, I, #19, 60 and 75; II, 62; *SR* #839). Markets at Domasław and Legnica are first mentioned only in a text composed in the 1240s or early 1250s (*KdS* #248; *SUB*, I, #351; Appelt, "Vinzenstift," pp. 219–227).

141. *KdS* #25, 70, 103, 107, 130; *SUB*, I, #19, 60, 83, 95, 115; *SR* #878; Schulte, "Kostenblut," pp. 246–248; Kuhn, "Städtegründungspolitik," p. 57.

142. Cieśla, pp. 159–225 is also summarized as Rabęcka, pp. 372–375; Buczek, *Targi*, pp. 69–79.

143. *Żórawin* (*KdS* #55; *SUB*, I, #45), Wilkszyn (*KdS* #86; *SUB*, I, #74), Uraz (*KdS* #130; *SUB*, I, #115), Kozanów (*KdS* #129; *SUB*, I, #114), Oporów (*KdS* #130; *SUB*, I, #115), and Ślęza (*SR* #675 and the text in *BUB*, p. 11). The Domaniów tavern occurs only in the 1234 German law *locatio* as do four others in the 1250s.

144. *KdS* #103 and 130; *SUB*, I, #83 and 115; *BUB*, 33. The town thus fired the first shot of a long war over urban commercial monopolies (*Meilenrecht*) and brewing rights.

145. *SUB*, II, #131; *SR* #1275; Matuszewski, *Najstarszy zwód*, pp. 191–193. See also *SR* #1044.

Chapter 4

1. *SUB*, II, #86; text and German translation are also in Helbig and Weinrich, eds., II, #16. *SR* #1968 and *LFE* B6 show it worked.

2. *SR* #6669; *BUB* #210.

3. Gieysztor, "Forum to Civitas," pp. 7–30, sketched the debate between evolutionary and revolutionary interpretations of German law in Polish towns. Then see Kuhn, "deutschrechtlichen Städte;" Wędzki; Buczek, "Z problematyki osiedli;" Sporn; and Łowmiański, *Początki Polski*, 6:705–707.

4. Kuhn, "Städtegründungspolitik" 1971, pp. 32–34 and 48–49. Helbig, pp. 98–99; Appelt, "Vinzenzstift," pp. 227–228.

5. Helbig and Weinrich, II, #34. Maleczyński, "Dzieje Wrocławia," pp. 24–72; Morelewski, pp. 191–215; and Rutkowska-Płachcinska, "Stadtgemeinde," pp. 354–359, deny that Wrocław had before 1241 the autonomous German commune advanced by Grünhagen, "Beamten," pp. 428–437; Markgraf, "deutsche Stadt," pp. 524–544; Schilling, pp. 218–225; and Goerlitz, *Verfassung*, pp. 3–5 (with great caution). After 1241, however, *ibid.*, pp. 6–20, is the best guide to the city's constitution.

6. Zientara, "Z zagadnień prawa," p. 335; Thieme, pp. 147–149; Matuszewski, "Landrecht," pp. 113–118.

7. Around 1300 land- and leaseholders who wanted to answer for their properties according to German rather than Polish legal norms obtained privileges to appear *in foro theutonico*. These concern a landowner's rights vis à vis the duke or other claimants and not the lord-peasant relationship created by a German law *locatio*. Compare at *Łukaszewice* the owner's privilege of 1306 with the permission for *locatio* in 1350 (*UD*, #4 and 20) and see also *SLU*, #105, 117, 128, and 130; *SR* #4421 and 4500. On such titles to land see Chapter 7 below.

8. *SLU*, pp. 47–99, and Zientara, "Żródła i geneza;" and "Z zagadnień prawa," pp. 334–336, also cover older studies.

9. Generally concerning the rights and obligations of German law peasants there is little dispute but much literature. For a sampling, see Rachfahl, "Grundherrschaft;" Helbig, pp. 110–112; *SLU*, pp. 221–253; Tymieniecki, *Historia*, I, 396–411 and 436–467; Trawkowski, "Rozwój osadnictwa," pp. 120–128.

10. *SLU*, pp. 269–281; Schlesinger, "Bäuerliche Gemeindebildung," pp. 234–274; Helbig, pp. 112–114; Tymieniecki, *Historia*, I, 416–432; Podwińska, *Technika*, pp. 173–179.

11. No doubt the size of the mansus varied slightly among Wrocław duchy villages

while this system was used, but the general standard seems to have been maintained even in the seventeenth century. Compare Sreniowski, pp. 301–337, and Walter Kuhn, "Hufe," pp. 152–157.

12. Maleczyński, *Historia Śląska*, I:1, 393–394 and 398–426. The rural schulzen under Polish law found in late thirteenth-century Little Poland by Gąsiorowski, "Szerzenie," pp. 76–77, are not present in central Silesia.

13. Current knowledge of the Polish economy reduces the long list of supposedly distinctive signs of German law offered by e.g., Aubin in *Geschichte Schlesiens*, I, 59–60, who trusted mansi and fixed tithes more than did his own authority, Schlenger, pp. 203–238 and 128–133. But Menzel does not sharply distinguish between common and diagnostic criteria in either *SLU*, pp. 136–149, or his preliminary "Urkundenwissenschaft," p. 155, with the result that Matzen-Stöckert, pp. 210–217, though aware of possible ambiguities, appears to use Aubin's criteria.

14. The historiography is listed in Helbig and Weinrich, I, 28–36, and II, 45–60, and surveyed by Kaczmarczyk, "Kolonizacja," pp. 218–326. More thoughtful treatments are Schlesinger, "Problematik," pp. 11–30 and Trawkowski, "Rolle," pp. 349–368. Traditional interpretations for Silesia are Aubin, *Geschichte Schlesiens*, I, 417–453, and Maleczyński, *Historia Śląska*, I:1, 280–287, 291–293, and 393–428, with the former updated and recapitulated with great clarity in Appelt, "Siedlung," pp. 1–19.

15. Appelt, "Frage," pp. 193–206, shows the consensus. *KdS* #55, 91, 122; *SUB*, I, #45, 77, 101; Helbig and Weinrich, II, #1–3.

16. *KdS* #252 and 254; *SUB*, I, #211 and 210. Appelt, "Vinzenzstift," pp. 227–230, and "Frage," pp. 199–206; *SLU*, pp. 293–299.

17. Compare Aubin in *Geschichte Schlesiens*, I, 427–431, Maleczyński in *Historia Śląska*, I:1, 285–287 and 395–426, and Menzel's thirteenth-century texts in *SLU*, pp. 299–341.

18. Maleczyński in *Historia Śląska*, I:1, 397; Aubin in *Geschichte Schlesiens*, I, 431–432. Gąsiorowski, "Szerzenie," p. 83, disputed Maleczyński because a third of the items on his list of places with evidence of German law to 1341 (*Historia Śląska*, I:1, 398–426) dated to the fourteenth century. Gąsiorowski forgot that only a dated contract or permission can provide a *terminus post quem* for a *locatio*; mere evidence of a schulz, the criterion in 176 of Maleczyński's 211 entries after 1300, can be no more than a *terminus ante quo* and hence no proof that villages were still being given German law. Sadly, *SLU* stops with 1300.

19. Difficulties arise because the generation after about 1210 replaced charters produced by recipients with the products of newly-organized ducal chancelleries. See Bielinska, pp. 409–422 and compare Irgang, "Urkundenwesen," pp. 1–47.

20. *SUB*, I, #225, 351, 354, and 364, and II, #156, 193, and 357; *KdS*, #248, 253, 282, and 333. Understand the texts in terms articulated by Menzel in *SLU*, pp. 99–127 and 298–310; Zientara, "organizacja rynku," pp. 689–691; Appelt, "Frage," and "Vinzenzstift," pp. 219–228; Schilling, pp. 214–218 and 234–235.

21. *SUB*, II, #107, 181, and 193; Helbig and Weinrich, II, #18–19; 1253 contract for Wierzbno, *SLU*, #14.

22. *SUB*, II, #274. This does not generally disagree with Matzen-Stöckert, pp. 196–199, but some particulars differ because Matzen-Stöckert used modern rather than medieval districts and because I remain (with Menzel in *SLU*, pp. 300 and 306) unconvinced that *SUB*, I, #364 is an authentic *locatio* for Trestno (which was never other than a demesne farm) or that *SUB*, II, #159, identifies Jastrzębce as a German law village in 1239.

23. See the theoretical models simply expressed in Gould, *Diffusion*, pp. 19–21.

24. *LFE*; *LB*; RB. Coverage of the duchy's villages in *LFE* is insufficient to warrant that the absence of German law evidence for a place by 1300–09 means it did not have it. But *LB* is full enough that, in general, very few places with German law by 1353 should have been missed. *LB* and RB should give nearly complete summaries of the German law villages then present.

25. In *SLU*, pp. 136–148, Menzel advances a formal typology.

26. *SLU*, #114. Kuras, pp. 92–112, treats failed or pseudo-grants.

27. LN, fols. 26v–27r and 30r; *RS*, II, #917 and 924.

28. Maleczynski's claim that *locatio* stopped about 1300 probably came from examining no evidence after the 1341 end of the published *SR*; while Aubin's more correct long-term chronology missed the medium-term rhythm of a two-wave movement. Do not, however, infer from extant grants that interest in German law was *greater* in the mid-fourteenth century

than in the late thirteenth. Places in the Wrocław district, focus of the second wave of activity, are overrepresented in the grants. Of the 232 places which ever received German law, two-thirds (154) were in the Wrocław district and one-third (78) in those of Środa and Uraz, but of the 73 grants, four-fifths (60) were to Wrocław district places and only one-fifth (13) to others.

29. Tyc, pp. 109–115, for the period up to 1333 and Stefański, pp. 6–13, together list and date 285 grants and evidence from 514 sites out of about 2500 potential recipient villages (Ładogórski, *Zaludnieniem*, p. 163). Stefański's study stops at the death of King Casimir. Tymieniecki, "Prawo czy gospodarstwo?" p. 285, noted German law by the first third of the fifteenth century in 34 percent of the 658 places in the Poznań judicial district.

30. Schilling, p. 328, and Meitzen in *UD*, p. 103, suggested 1000 to 1500 immigrants entered only Silesia in each year of the thirteenth and early fourteenth centuries.

31. Kuhn, "Siedlerzahlen," pp. 131–154. Zientara, "Nationality Conflicts," p. 212, pointed out that the modern populations whose very rapid growth Kuhn said sustained his hypothesis were unusually compact ethnocultural communities in areas essentially virgin to their form of exploitation.

32. Maleczyński, *Historia Śląska*, I:1, 291–294, but compare Zientara, *Brodaty*, pp. 163–181.

33. *KdS* #253; *SUB*, I, #354. A report written in the 1280s about Germans, "tam agricolis quam militibus" joining in a fight among the young sons of Henry I is probably a confused fabrication. See Zientara, "Konrad," for the earlier debate and the judicious comment of Łowmiański, *Początki Polski*, 6:828–830.

34. *SUB*, II, #86, 181, and 193; *SLU*, #8 and 48; *NRB*, p. 383; *SR* #1081.

35. *SUB*, II, #346; Irgang, "Statuten," pp. 21–30.

36. *SLU*, #93 and 123.

37. In Schlesinger, ed., *Ostsiedlung als Problem*, there is apparent agreement on how migrants entered Silesia between Zientara, "Einwanderer," pp. 338–345, and Kuhn, "Landesherren," pp. 256–261. But the figure of 20 percent ethnic Germans is from Trawkowski, "Roli kolonizacji," p. 187, who compared proportions of the province settled before and after the early 1200s. Cetwiński, "Pochodzenie," pp. 50–57, and *Rycerstwo* 1980, pp. 11–58, affirms the native origins of the Silesian elite up to 1300: of 947 nobles and knights named in Lower Silesian texts, only 93 identifiably came from Germany, and of the 55 immigrant families so detected, 45 arrived after 1270.

38. "Theuthonicos vel alterius cuiuslibet ydiomatis homines" (*SLU* #8).

39. Zientara, "Walonowie," pp. 351–357.

40. *LFE* B39; "QBBB," pp. 197–198.

41. *SUB*, II, #107; *SR* #3763 and 3765. A late fourteenth-century redaction of the *Chronica principum Poloniae* (Stenzel, ed., pp. 126–127), described the drubbing peasant "Gallici" from Janików and Wierzbno gave plundering soldiers of Duke Władysław of Legnica-Brzeg in 1312. Compare Dąbrowski, *Dziejopisarstwo*, pp. 165–168, and Zientara, "Walonowie," pp. 359–362. Lambert of Tyniec, *locator* at Zabłoto in 1240 (*SUB*, II, #181 and 193) has as distinctively "western" a name as the other Walloons from his home village. Other immigrants were memorialized in the historic name of Bielany, the suburb of Środa, first recorded in 1289 (*SR* #2107 and 2107b) as "villa Flemingi" and later "Flämischdorf."

42. Domański, *Nazwy miejscowe*, pp. 127–159; Moepert, *Ortsnamen*, p. 9. On the durability of Polish culture in and around Wrocław see, *inter alia*: Rombowski, pp. 355–408; Kłoczkowski, pp. 541–557; Maleczyńska, "Niektóre zagadnienia," pp. 219–233; Pyrek, pp. 104–107; Urban, "Materiały," pp. 149–195. The zeal of post-war Polish scholars unearthing the "Polishness" of Silesia and Wrocław should not obscure the strength of what they found.

43. *SUB*, II, #339; *SR* #1081; *SLU*, #48; *NRB*, p. 383. See also *KdS* #333; *SUB*, I, #364; *UFO* #103. For earlier native participation further northwest, see Schulze, "Slawen," pp. 321–336.

44. Earlier at Rzeplin Radzław and Smilo undertook the *locatio* and across the Ślęza at Szukalice it was Sventos (*SLU*, #13, 19, and 46). The latter had as late as 1329 successors named Stasz and Swantosław (*SR* #4819). Of 43 named *locatores* in the Wrocław duchy grants of Figure 4.2, 12 have clearly German names like Dithmar, Albert, Gerhard, or Tilo, while 11 have very Polish sounding ones, Bogusław, Nagod, Witosław, etc. Polish *locatores* are also found by Grüger, "Besiedlung," pp. 19–20, and from the 1260s in Great Poland (Tyc, pp. 30–38), while for Czech *locatores* see Graus, "Problematik," p. 53.

45. *SUB*, I, #353; *KdS* #333; *SR* #1571.

46. Wohlbrück, I, 456 note **.

47. Cetwiński, "Pochodzenia," pp. 42–46.

48. Bellmann, *Slavoteutonica*.

49. Cetwiński, "Pochodzenia," pp. 45–48.

50. Weinrich, "Übersetzung," treats with insight the complex interaction between one reality of thought and spoken German and another of written Latin, but not the further complication of vernacular bilingualism.

51. Zientara, "Nationality Conflicts," and "Struktury narodowe."

52. Zientara, "Einwanderer," pp. 345–348; Symmons-Symonolewicz, "National Consciousness."

53. Distinctive complexities of Silesia well emerge from Heck, "O Piastowskich tradycjach." See also Kuhn, "Landesherren," p. 261; Grüger, "Volkstum;" Łowmiański, *Początki Polski*, 6:832–833.

54. "ad locandum ibidem Theutonicos in jure et libertate Theuthonicali" (*SUB*, II, #193).

55. "potestam plenariam exponendi, hereditandi, locandi et venendi dictos mansos agrorum rusticis, incolis et agricolis iure hereditario" (*UD*, #14). See also *SLU*, #29 and 48 or LN, fols. 38v–39r.

56. In *SLU*, pp. 214–217 and 253–269, Menzel also covers earlier studies; Matzen-Stóckert, pp. 280–282, lists many particulars—both only for the thirteenth century.

57. Among the duchy's grants only that for Gaj in 1273 suggests a landlord himself handling *locatio* (*SLU* #76). See George, pp. 13–15 and 23–26; Kötzschke, *Unternehmertum*.

58. *UFO*, #103: "Judicium omnium causarum judicio scultutus judicabit predictus."

59. *NRB*, pp. 216–217; Schulte, "Kostenblut," p. 253. The *fogtding*, so named from the abbey's Vogt, is the *Dreiding* of general custom; compare Matuszkiewicz, pp. 60–61.

60. *SLU*, #112; Matuszkiewicz, pp. 59–60.

61. The schulz's intermediate position in the tenurial arrangement is well summarized in Opitz, pp. 16–17. The schulz's control over peasant land conveyancing in *Platea Romanorum* is specified in the 1260 *locatio* (*LFE* B39; "QBBB," p. 198) and at Jenkowice in a 1297 text (*SLU*, #136).

62. Compare *SUB*, II, #193 or *SLU*, #112 to *BUB* #285 or LN, fols. 143r–144r. See also *UD* #14 and LN, fols. 34v–35v.

63. *SR* #2114, 2596, and 3407; *SLU*, #101 and 136; *UD*, #14; *BUB*, #285. For parallels in Great Poland see Tyc, pp. 62–71, or Stefański, p. 18.

64. *KdS* #253; *SUB*, I, #354, and II, #181 and 193. Of the 43 named *locatores* in the duchy, 19, all in the thirteenth century, lack further identifying characteristics.

65. *SR* #1081 and 1331; *SLU*, #1, 14, 77, and 101; *NRB*, p. 383; *UFO*, #94.

66. *SLU*, #112, 115, 122, and 123. On these men see Pfeiffer, *Patriziat*, pp. 63, 67, 110, and 166.

67. LN, fols. 370r–371r, 38v–39r, 34v–35v. That Nicholas Sittin, Nicholas Brunonis, and John Nossen had little in common with other contemporary *locatores* like "Hanco alias Johannes dictus Dremelik, rusticus in Kochern" (*UD*, #14), is plain in Pfeiffer, *Patriziat*, pp. 179–181, 88–89, and 174. Compare *RS*, II, #917.

68. LN, fols. 375v–376r, 143r–144r; *UD* #14; *BUB* #285; *RS*, II, #615.

69. *SLU*, p. 253.

70. Compare *SUB*, II, #86 with *SLU* #109, *UFO* #94, or *UD* #14.

71. See note to Figure 4.2. The mean share of the thirteenth century *scholtiseien* was 10.9 percent of contracted arable, and of the fourteenth century ones, 10.7 percent.

72. *SUB*, II, #193; *SLU*, #110 and 112; *UD* #14; *BUB* #285; LN, fols. 143r–144r.

73. *SLU*, pp. 260–262. Silesian schulzen had better rights than those in Brandenburg (Opitz, pp. 8–16).

74. *UD* #14.

75. *SR* #1354; *SLU* #14. See also *SLU* #89 or *SUB*, II, #357. Unlike in Great Poland, grants of the 1300s from near Wrocław do not erode the rights of schulzen (Stefański, pp. 24–25).

76. Neither *SLU*, #51 nor 109 mentions a rate, but p. 201 suggests a range of 10 to 20 mk in the late thirteenth century.

77. For 40 m in Muchobór Tilo and Arnold paid 360 mk (9 mk/m), while the *locatores* of Piłczyce, Jaszkotle, and Kotowice owed rates of 10, 12, and 6 marks respectively (*SLU*, #112, 114, 122, and *UFO*, #94).

78. LN, fol. 143r–144r. See also LN, fol. 375v–376r; *UD* #14; *RS*, II, #615.

79. *SLU*, pp. 269–281; Matzen-Stöckert, p. 278; Tymieniecki, *Historia*, I, 416–492.

80. For cases see *KdS* #253; *SUB*, I, #354, and II, #86; *SR* #973 and 1301). On "low justice" as innovation see Tyc, pp. 62–68.

81. Besides the above, see *SLU*, #14, 101, and 136; *LFE* B 376; *KdS* #311. At *Dreidingen* lords intervened in matters of particular importance within the low justice rubric, i.e., disputes between lord or schulz and the peasants, appointment or confirmation of a new schulz, and appeals from the schulz's decisions.

82. Explicit early reference around Wrocław to a peasant oath of obedience to the schulz comes only from Sedzice near Trzebnica in 1312 (*SR* #3307).

83. A local assessor, Przybysław, witnessed his lord's revision of the schulz's rights at Jenkowice in 1297 (*SLU* #136), perhaps in part because the villagers' obligations were involved. See also Helbig, pp. 107–110.

84. *Kirchenväter* are known from rural Silesia in the mid-1200s (Loesch, "Forschungen," p. 163).

85. See for examples from German law texts *KdS*, #253; *SUB*, I, #354. and II, #274; *SLU*, #65, 115–116; *UFO*, p. 136; LN, fols. 38v–39r; *UD*, #14 and 15; RF, IV, 2617–2629. See also Tymieniecki, "Prawo czy gospodarstwo?" pp. 282–284; *SLU*, pp. 221–234.

86. Only texts of the 1300s do more than describe the schulz's free mansi and then refer to "the others;" those above are *RBM*, IV, #1575, and RF, I, fol. 24v. More general application of these same terms is demonstrated in Opitz, p. 16. The classicizing chancellery of Charles IV in the 1350s used "emphyteutic" tenure (see *UD* #15, *RBM*, VII:1, #130, and RF, III, 2300–2317), which had since 1287 also appeared in Great Poland (Tyc, p. 70).

87. *SLU*, #136. Opitz, pp. 17–19 and 50–58, demonstrated that lords did not then control peasant land sales.

88. *LFE* D13.

89. *SLU*, #112, and #136, with its annual payment of one ham from each two mansi at Jenkowice in 1297, also suggests multiple-mansus holdings. Muchobór is an old-settled Polish village and Jenkowice in the loess of the southern Środa district where traces of a territorial community lasted past 1300. As *SLU*, pp. 202–203, notes, this contradicts the hypothesis of Kuhn, "Bauernhofgrössen," pp. 210–267 that at *locatio* Germans received two mansi and Slavs one.

90. *KdS* #282; *SUB*, I, #225: "in divisione mansorum per sortem more Theutonico." Trawkowski, "Roli kononizacji," p. 190, sees here the first sign of a regulated three-course rotation in Silesia. For Święte in 1256, "cum primo convenerint aestivalia cum hyemalibus" see *SLU* #29.

91. *SR* #1872. Other notably resistant areas included the area along the Odra below the mouth of the Widawa, the Strzegomka-Bystrzyca bottoms below Katy, and the wet woodlands between the Odra and Oława around Kotowice, pow. Wrocław.

92. By 1300: 73 German law sites; 54 (74%) plain; 19 (26%) bottomland. By 1530: 232 German law sites; 143 (62%) plain; 89 (38%) bottomland. The difference between the 1530 distribution of German law sites and that of all settlements is statistically significant at the 95% level.

93. Dąbrowski, *Rozwój*, p. 125; Chmielewski, *Gospodarka rolna*, pp. 100–105. Dembińska, "Próba obliczenia," pp. 7–16, argues for a maximum normal yield of wheat, rye, barley, and oats at only three to one. The problem is to reason from the well-equipped demesne with good soils but uninspired workers to the poorer peasant farm worked by a family living from their yields. See also the production budget calculation below.

94. Of the 42 surviving grants to 1312, 18 fail to mention free years, but most ducal permissions specify no obligations (like *SLU* #8). See note to Figure 4.2; Matzen-Stöckert, p. 282.

95. For like customs elsewhere see *SLU*, pp. 249–251; Kaczmarczyk, "Ciężary," pp. 15–19; Stefański, p. 27.

96. *SLU*, p. 248; compare Tyc, pp. 63–67.

97. Tz-S, pp. 550–552; Kaczmarczyk, "Cziężary," pp. 299–308.

98. *KdS* #253; *SUB*, I, #354, and II, #274; RF, IV, 2617–2629; *SLU* #115, and see also #109.

99. For Szukalice compare *SLU*, #13 and 19, and for Przesławice and Mnichowice, *SLU* #109 and *SR* #1331. See also *SUB*, II, #107 and 193; *UD*, #14; *SLU*, #14, 29, 101, 112, and pp. 245–246.

100. Compare Tyc, pp. 77–82, and Stefański, pp. 30–32.

101. *SLU*, #48 and 112; LN, fol. 370–371r; Matzen-Stöckert, pp. 284–285. Payments of Kotowice fishers in 1294 (*UFO* #103) were the same as in 1203 (*KdS* #104; *SUB*, I, #93).

102. Honors are recorded at Szczepankowice in 1289 (*SLU*, #101) but the payments were specified only in contracts of the late 1300s (*BUB* #285 and LN, fols. 143r–144r).

103. *SUB*, II, #193.

104. Kaczmarczyk and Sczaniecki, pp. 65–73; Tyc, pp. 74–83; Stefański, pp. 27–29; Korta, *Wielkie własności*, p. 139; *SLU*, pp. 235–240; Matzen-Stöckert, pp. 282–283.

105. See, for example, the episcopal income register of about 1300 for church-owned villages like Radoszkowice, Siedlakowice, or Miłoszyce (*LFE* B10, B33, and B64). Of course peasants knew perfectly well the titles by which outsiders took portions of their product and were especially willing to refuse tithes.

106. A 1273 gift of incomes from Piersno (*SR* #1442) explicitly equates the *maldratum* with 12 measures, but the size of the measure is less sure. Dembińska, *Konsumpcja*, p. 186, offered 128 liters as a Poland-wide estimate from eighteenth century local units, but Dąbrowski, *Rozwój*, p. 124, preferred 107 liters, a value 16 percent smaller. An approximation of 3 or 3 1/2 bushels to the measure is close enough for general appreciation of the payment required, but the difference affects any precise calculation of the disposition of a peasant's harvest (see below).

107. *SLU*, #13 and 19.

108. All seven instances are on loams and four in the Środa district (*SR*, #1081 and 2233; *SLU*, #48, 84, 89, 110, and 111).

109. Szukalice, where revision after one year of the 1253 contract replaced fixed tithes with real tenths, was even said to offer little difficulties to the *locator* (*LN*, fol. 430r), clearly identifying it as an older settlement where the change meant reversion to previous practice. The real tenths of the Domaniów contract, however, were by 1300 a fixed amount of grain (*LFE* B6).

110. Concern here with rents established by new German law grants is only in the context of the movement itself. Rent levels in general are treated in chapters 6 and 11.

111. For monetary conversions see Appendix B. Both the early norm and the upward drift of rents set in *locationes* around Wrocław parallel general Silesian conditions described for the period up to 1266 in Korta, *Wielki własności*, pp. 135–143, and the long-term development in Great Poland available in Tyc, pp. 74–82, and Stefański, pp. 27–30. See also Münchberg, and Kaczmarczyk, "Ciężary," pp. 19–30.

112. *SUB*, II, #181 and 193. Thirteenth-century grain prices are too few to work with specific cereals (see Chapter 6).

113. Dąbrowski, *Rozwój*, pp. 124–126, calculates production but not the distribution of the harvest.

114. In *SLU*, pp. 236–237, Menzel suggests net annual obligations in the range of 20–25 percent by reasoning that, if tithes paid at .25 mk or 12 measures the mansus were a privilege, the total should be less than 20 percent of annual grain production. He carries the exercise no further.

115. Abel, *Agrarkrisen*, p. 274, offers pre-industrial data to convert cereal weights to volumes, thereby translating to a caloric minimum of 350 liters/adult/year and a minimum normal cereal component of 250 liters/adult/year the constants presented in Slicher van Bath, "Oogstopbrengsten," pp. 34–35, and in Clark and Haswell, pp. 61–62. Were Dąbrowski's 228 liter/hectare seeding rate replaced by the 200 liter/hectare figure considered normal in Slicher van Bath, "Oogstopbrengsten," p. 32, and his measure of 107 liters by the 128 liter measure advanced by Dembińska, *Konsumpcja*, p. 186, both of which depress the calculation of total yields, the Zabłoto peasant with a 4 to 1 yield ratio still retained 33.5 measures from a 70 measure harvest and could feed 12.3 to 17.2 adults at the minima mentioned above.

116. Compare Chmielewski, *Gospodarka rolna*, pp. 68 and 101–102; Dembińska, "Próba obliczenia," p. 15; Żytkowicz, "Plony zbóż," pp. 242–250.

117. At the higher constants mentioned in note 115 above, the 3 to 1 yield ratio permits the peasant only 16.0 of a 52.5 measure harvest (31%), still feeding 5.9 to 8.2 persons.

118. See Chapter 3, Maleczyński, "Wsi przed kolonizacja," pp. 142–143, and the production of only 32 measures from a like-sized twelfth-century holding estimated by Chmielewski and Dąbrowski in Baranowski et al., p. 41.

119. Attempts were made to simulate the diffusion of German law in the duchy according to a conditional probability model which employed neighborhood effects to spread the innovation from initial to potential adopters (villages). A Kolmogorov-Smirnov test of significance indicated no similarity between the simulated and actual distributions. Within the confines of the duchy contiguity is no predictor for the spread of German law.

120. When Menzel finds for all Silesia in *SLU*, p. 202, more thirteenth-century charters from secular lords than clerics, he counts many from dukes for the frontier forests. Compare Korta, *Wielkie własności*, pp. 159–173, and for Great Poland, Tyc, pp. 97–103 and 109–115, and Stefański, pp. 14–15.

121. *KdS* #122; *SUB*, I, #101 and #293. Schilling, pp. 25–29, rightly denied earlier activity by St. Vincent, but his focus on new settlement lowered his assessment of what this house achieved during the 1230s and 1240s. For provisions of their charters, see Matzen-Stöckert, pp. 243–248.

122. *SUB*, II, #107.

123. *SUB*, II, #181 and 193. The ducal charter called for "eo jure, quod ville Theutonicale beate Marie de Wratislavia sunt locate," while Tyniec Mały, a St. Mary village, provided not only the *locator*, but also (compare *SUB*, II, #357) the precedent for a rent in barley otherwise unknown.

124. *KdS* #248 or *SUB*, I, #351, understood after Appelt, "Vinzenzstift," pp. 225–226.

125. On Kostomłoty, *SR* #878; Schulte, "Kostenblut," pp. 246–248; Appelt, "Vinzenzstift," p. 226; Kuhn, "Stätegrundungspolitik," p. 57. The two permissions, one even calling for "Środa law like the villages around Kostomłoty," are *SLU*, #12 and 38.

126. Tz-S, #39, 47, 49; *SLU*, #14 and 37.

127. *SLU*, #72 and 73.

128. *NRB*, pp. 216–217; Schulte, "Kostenblut," pp. 253–266; Appelt, "Vinzenzstift," p. 226.

129. *SLU*, #75 and 99; *SR* #3463 and 5454.

130. Korta, *Wielki własności*, pp. 164 and 173. In *SLU*, p. 210, Menzel counts surviving charters rather than sites.

131. Nothing suggests German law at Księże, Grabiszyn, or *Olbino* up to 1353 (*LB* #37, 123, 227, 295–298, 363, and following 450), but they had schulzen on the abbot's *Landding* in the 1420s (Schulte, "Kostenblut," pp. 254–255 notes). Without German law were *Sokolnicy*, *Swarocin*, Świątniki, Widawa, and Wrocław-Opatowice, and Popowice. The Opatowice near Strzelin, no longer by 1353 a possession of St. Vincent (*LB* #36 and 246), first had a schulz only in 1405 (Ludat, ed., *Stiftsregister*, p. 37).

132. Seidel, *Beginn*, pp. 140–152, outlines the progress of Lubiąż from large scale settlement on compact outlying holdings (which he would date to the 1210s) through reform of isolated villages and granges to fourteenth-century conversion of granges and former demesnes. The Church of Wrocław, its management always complicated by division of control between bishop and chapter, looks similar from the Wrocław duchy perspective. For a study organized differently see Matzen-Stöckert, pp. 233–242.

133. *SLU*, p. 184; Tyc, pp. 72–74.

134. Schilling; Zientara, *Brodaty*, pp. 163–181, and "Bolesław," pp. 389–392. Compare *SLU*, pp. 206–209, and Matzen-Stöckert, pp. 256–261.

135. *SR* #1081; *NRB*, p. 383; *SLU*, #48. The last failed.

136. *SLU*, #84 and 110.

137. *SLU*, #115 and 118.

138. *LFE* B148–B156. No charters or contractors are known.

139. Korta, *Wielki własności*, p. 170, finds large lay lords in only 3.2% of the Silesian villages with German law by 1266, but their later increase is seen in their having issued a third of the extant lay-issued texts from the 1200s (*SLU*, p. 210). See Matzen-Stöckert, pp. 261–270 for those.

140. *SLU*, #51. He also may have been the first lord to charge his *locator* a fee. Cetwiń-

ski's identification (*Rycerstwo* 1982, p. 94) of this man (and place) with one near Ząbkowice agrees with neither the witnesses nor other students (e.g. Domański, *Nazwy miescowe*, p. 95).

141. *SLU*, p. 210, finds only one charter from a townsman before 1300. Matzen-Stöckert, pp. 270–274, lists ten sites where they installed German law between 1264 and 1342, but several are surely only demesnes with a title in German rather than Polish law (see note 6 above).

142. Pfeiffer, *Patriziat*, pp. 179–181, has the family come from Zittau in Lusatia before 1300. But *RS* (e.g. I, #211) identifies it with Żytna near Trzebnica.

143. *SR* #5707, 5820, and 6669; RF, I, fol. 19r.

144. LN, fols. 370r–371v. *Cruce* soon vanishes from the record. Domański, *Nazwy miescowe*, #302; *RS*, I, #211 and 836.

145. *LB* #17; RF, I, fols. 20v–22v.

146. *SR* #6665. Compare Grünhagen, "Reste," p. 39.

147. A synthesis from *KdS* #296; *SUB*, I, #247 and 313 and II, #86; *SR* #1968, with grain yields estimated in the range of 3 or 4 to 1 and rents at the 8 scot of 1234 and the 9 of 1286.

148. Compare for Tyniec Mały *KdS* #68, 130, 135, 152, 153, and 235; *SUB*, I, #58, 115, 342, 129, 130, and 198 with *KdS* #253; *SUB*, I, #354 and II, #357; and for Kotowice *KdS* #102, 103, 104, 130, 174, and 242; *SUB*, I, #84, 83, 93, 115, 147, and 340 with *UFO*, #103 and *LB* #127 and 173. For Rzeplin and Szukalice see *SUB*, II, #287 and *SLU*, #1, 13, 19, and 46.

149. At the periphery of this, the site of Pisarzowice was in 1218 an uninhabited part of the Wilkszyn circuit, and the two episcopal holdings, Kryniczno and Święte, are unknown until 1245. See *KdS* #198; *SUB*, I, #171, and II, 287; *SR* #6326 and 6717; Seidel, *Beginn*, pp. 92–93. Święte and Komorniki, only the name (chamberlains' village, *Kemmererdorf*) of which implies an old Polish settlement (it is first recorded in 1294; *LBU*, II, 7), lie not on the loam but on a small intrusion of morainic sand.

150. *BUB* #14; *SLU*, #8 and 29.

151. *SR* #1081; *SLU*, #48, 84, and 110.

152. *LFE* D275: "Item Mocre est nova plantacio, solvit iij marcas, sed plus tenetur solvere." By 1353 Mokra had 50 mansi, 34 for tenants (although 8 were deserted), 5 of the schulz, 3 for the parish priest, and 8 in demesne (*sic* in *LB* #161).

153. Źródła: "Fons" in 1278 (*SR* #1567); German law evidence ca. 1305 (*LFE* D282). Juszczyn: "Lambertivilla" in 1286 (*SR* #1945); German law evidence ca. 1305 (*LFE* D13 and D283). Błonie: documented 1294 (*LBU*, II, 7) with one of the rare original German names, *Heide* (compare *SR* #3384); German law evidence 1336 (*SR* #5714). Jugowiec: "Hugoldivilla" in 1305 with German law evidence (*LFE* D12 and D284). Chwalimierz is like Błonie, recorded with the clearly German name, *Vrankontal*, in 1294 (*LBU*, II, 7), but with sure signs of German law only in 1338 (*SR* #6041).

154. *SLU*, #111. See also *LFE* D263, D6, and D25.

155. *UD*, introductory pp. 53–59, text p. 197.

156. *KdS* #103 and 130; *SUB*, I, #83 and 115; Kuhn, "Auras."

157. *NRB*, p. 383.

158. *SR* #1156 identifies the *locatio* with Wojciechów and *SLU*, #48 with a place near Brzeg, but others prefer Gosławice (Stenzel in *Jahresberichte* 1844, p. 102; Maleczyński, *Historia Śląska* I:1, 403; Domański, "Z problematyki," p. 321).

159. *LFE* B148-B156, where the villages have a wondrous medley of German, Polish, and hybrid toponyms: "Cunradswalde sive Gorowo, Patendorf sive Buccowetz, Woyczsdorf, Grunbach sive Borow, Rynbergk, Jakil sive Jaycowitz, Siffridivilla, Rychinwald."

160. *SR* #2630 and 3357.

161. *UFO*, pp. 124–128 and 136; *SLU*, #104; *SR* #3605.

162. *UFO*, pp. 148–152, "Vraz cum suo districtu."

163. 63 settlements with datable German law grants have a size in mansi available in 1353 or (4 of them) in 1425 (*LB* and RB). Of these, the 28 which received German law between 1339 and 1395 average only 14 mansi while the 35 with grants from 1221 to 1312 average almost twice that, 27 mansi. Stefański, pp. 5–12 finds grants in contemporary Great Poland concentrated on the old-settled areas near major towns.

164. *SR* #6302. *ChronBMV*, p. 196 refers simply to "locandi et exponendi allodium Prokaw in villam jure Theutonico."

165. *BUB* #210: "ut bona vestra allodialia in districtibus Wratislauiensi et Nouiforensi personis quibuslibet in emphiteosim locare et ut super dictis vestris bonis allodialibus ville de nouo construi et plantario pro terre augmento et communis boni utilitate."

166. Hoffmann, "Nazwy," pp. 9–17.

167. LN, fols. 38v–39r: "agricolis et ruricolariis pro annua census allodium suum Gandaw dictum." See also *RS*, I, #335 and 343.

168. *LB* #75. Equally cogent examples are the activities of Nicholas Sittin around Bielany described above and the planned *locatio* of *Łukaszewice* in 1350 (*UD* #20).

169. *BUB* #28 and 37; Tz-S, #57; Markgraf, "Verkaufsstätten," pp. 173–180.

170. *HPR*, pp. 39–40.

171. *BUB* #107, a general marketing code published in 1321, mentions those bringing "frumenta ad forum cum curribus suis."

172. By 1300 the Silesian "mile" was probably about 6.5 km. (Stolle, *"miliare,"* pp. 11–19). Definitive on the *Meilenrecht* in Moravia and Silesia is Küchler, but see also Wrocław's privileges of 1266, 1272 and 1290 in *BUB*, #28, 29, 39, and 56.

Chapter 5

1. *SLU*, #13, 19, and 51; see also #55.

2. In east central Europe the meaning of *allodium* as direct exploitation demesne (*Vorwerk, folwark*) developed in the twelfth century and was consistent and standard during the fourteenth through sixteenth centuries. See Pfeiffer, *Patriziat*, pp. 207–210; Heck, "Gospodarce folwarcznej," pp. 170–175; Rutkowska-Płachcinska, "Rezerwy," pp. 411–435; Korta, *Wielki własności*, pp. 94–115; Pach, p. 1223. *Allodium* does not here mean "alod." As shown in Chapter 7 below, around Wrocław the terms *proprietas* and *beneficium* or *feudum* expressed the conceptual dichotomy between property and fief.

3. *KdS* #129–130; *SUB*, I, #114–115, Wattenbach, ed., *Protzan*, pp. 170–172; *LB* #307.

4. Except for the Poland-wide analysis of Rutkowska-Płachcinska, "Rezerwy," most scholars have considered the late medieval demesne farm only as a contrast and precursor to the forced-labor latifundium that produced cereals for export sale in early modern east central Europe. This approach has largely obscured the place of the earlier enterprises in their own time. See Dessmann, pp. 16–18; Grodecki, "Gospodarki folwarcznej." pp. 60–66; Heck, "Gospodarce folwarcznej," pp. 175–179; Inglot, "Zagadnienie wpływu," pp. 353–354, and the conceptually-labored comparative treatments of Harnisch, "Gutsherrschaft," pp. 214–220, and "Probleme," pp. 252–255 and 269–274. The ill-documented general essay of Mühlen, p. 86, pointed out that demesne and tenant farming were in the later Middle Ages two competing agricultural systems, but the implications of this structural fact are rarely drawn. See, however, the well-considered studies of the Altmark and the Uckermark in Engel and Zientara, especially on this issue, pp. 53–72 and 274–324.

5. Statistical estimates summarized in this paragraph are developed in Appendix A (and there encapsulated in Figure A.1) where, too, are supplied the justifications for their mild divergence from those given for 1353 in Matzen-Stöckert, pp. 401–408, and their marked disagreement with those offered for 1425 in Korta, "Księga."

6. *UFO*, pp. 124–128.

7. *SLU*, #51; HGZ, fol. 2v. Compare also *LFE* B26; RF, III, 2367–2378; Heyne, *Bisthum*, II, 715.

8. *LFE* B46 and B31; *ChronBMV*, p. 183. Compare RF, II, 936 and LN, fol. 34v–35v. Ludat, *Bistum Lebus*, pp. 101–102, found the bishop's Silesian demesnes larger than those he had in the Kingdom.

9. Matzen-Stöckert, pp. 378–385, calculates 7.4 mansi for farms in the Wrocław [and Uraz] district and 7.0 for Środa, but the sample constituted by this data is uncontrolled. Matzen-Stöckert stresses the 4–11 mansi range of normal farm size, but half those in the distributions she gives are between 4 and 8.

10. Piersno: *LB* #177; RF, II, 992-1005; Matzen-Stöckert, p. 328. Grabiszyn: *LB* #295–298; Matzen-Stöckert, p. 307, omits as unlocatable *LB* #296, which puts the Reichel farm "ibidem."

11. Chi-square testing of the distribution of places with tenants only, tenants and de-

mesne, and demesne only against their sites in bottomlands or elsewhere produces test statistics of 12.81 and 23.36 for 1353 and 1425 respectively. With 2 degrees of freedom the independence of the two distributions may be rejected with a confidence of 99% at values above 4.61 and with 99.5% at values above 10.60. Places operated as demesnes alone consistently supply the extreme departures from the frequencies predicted by a null hypothesis of independence. In 1425, for example, 79 of 121 such localities lay in the bottomlands, while the null hypothesis would predict only 58.5.

12. *UD*, p. 263. They got 7 more marks for the lake at Chomiąża (*Ibid.*, p. 262). See also *SLU*, #105; *SR* #5717; *KdS* #117; *SUB*, I, #332; *RS*, II, #690; *LN*, fols. 251v and 368r; *UD*, pp. 136–137; Kurnik, pp. 17–20; *RF*, IV, 2061–2068; Wendt, *Landgüter*, pp. 214–217.

13. *SLU*, #105; Heyne, *Bisthum*, II, 710; *RF*, I, 127–132.

14. Wendt, "Verpfandung," pp. 158–159 note 4.

15. For examples see *SR* #1268, 2234, 2236, 2613, and 6444; *LFE* D25; *LB* #283; *HPR*, pp. 74 and 105–109; Dyhernfurth, pp. 25–26; Ligęza, pp. 449–450. Treatment of such facilities is in Chapter 9.

16. Of the 80 sites, 36 (45%) were independent demesnes and 44 (55%) demesnes sharing a settlement with tenants at the time their production was recorded. Like the general pattern already shown, the black earth properties were mostly of the former type (15 of 22 = 68%) and those on the loam and moraines of the latter (22 of 29 = 76%) Sites on the bottomland (18), loess (6), and black earth but with significant bottomland resources (5) have no pronounced association with a particular management type.

17. The texts do not specify but the 8 horses at Jarząbkowice in 1352 (*RF*, I, 214–220) are far from the 62 mixed head at Kozanów in 1321, the 54 at Gądów Mały in 1336, or the 116 at Sołtysowice in 1360 (*LN*, fol. 368r; *SR* #5680; WAP, AME, G3, fol. 13v). These totals include no sheep.

18. Szulc, pp. 16–32, 70–77, and 84. For parallel moves toward pastoralism in lowland and sandy areas of late medieval Brandenburg see Krenzlin, pp. 59–72.

19. *UD*, p. 5: "in una pecia ubi locata est curia."

20. *SR* #1663, 1706, 2832, 3391, 3400; *LFE* B32; "QBBB," p. 196.

21. *DT*, p. 160. Compare *LB* #236; *RS*, II, #779; *RF*, IV, 2598.

22. See, for example, *SR* #5684 and *RF*, I, 195, or IV, 3040.

23. *HPR*, pp. 105–106.

24. HGZ, fols. 37v–38r, 59v–60r, 77v–78r, 98v–99r, and 114v–115r.

25. Compare Dembińska, "Próba obliczenia," pp. 7–16, and Chmielewski, *Gospodarka rolna*, pp. 84–97.

26. *DT*, p. 160.

27. Grünhagen, "Protokolle," pp. 136–137. Compare Dittrich, "Eckersdorf," pp. 245–246, and WAP, AMW, G3, fol. 10r–v.

28. HGZ, fol. 59v.

29. *HPR*, pp. 107–109

30. *HPR*, pp. 105–106.

31. *HPR*, pp. 129–130. The same account from 1427 has similar numbers: cattle 7mk 4gr; pigs 2mk; goats 47gr (Klose, *Von Breslau*, II:2, 382–383).

32. Production is best described for harvest years 1433/34 and 1434/35 (HGZ, fols. 25v–26v and 60v–61r).

33. *SR* #5680. Compare *SR* 1275, 2372, and 5747; *LN*, fol. 368r; WAP, AMW, G3, fols. 10r–v and 13v; *RF*, III, 2155–264 [sic].

34. *SR* #1275; *DT*, pp. 65–66.

35. *SR* #2042; *KdS* #355; *SUB*, I, #361; *UD*, p. 263.

36. *UD*, pp. 148–151. For further examples see *ibid.*, pp. 154 and 262–263; *SLU*, #13 and 19; *SR* #1268, 6201, 6555; *DT*, pp. 65–66.

37. *RF*, I, 198–199; see also *SR* #1817.

38. HGZ, fol. 59v.

39. *SR* #1104 with the text published by Stenzel, *Übersicht*, 1841, p. 110; Stobbe, p. 344; *HPR*, pp. 107–109; HGZ, fol. 26v.

40. On the general advance of stock raising in late medieval Poland see Rutkowska-Płachcińska, "Gospodarce hodowlanej," pp. 584–597, but compare also Dembińska, "Gospodarka hodowlana," and Chmielewski, *Gospodarka rolna*, pp. 120–146.

41. Tithe disputes arose over the demesne at Kębłowice in 1366 (Görlich, *Vincenz*, p. 138)

and at Bielany in the early fifteenth century (Kindler, pp. 193–194). For annuities and other liabilities in grain from demesnes on the loam see *SR* #2236, 2237, 3284, 3830, 4505, 5880, 6262; Heyne, *Bisthum*, II, 715; RF, II, 626–634 and IV, 2717–2724; HGZ, entries for Lisowice and Jarząbkowice, passim. Demesne farms on the loess practiced the same open field short fallow grain farming (*SR* #4240, 4260, 4803a, 4858d, 4870h; Dyhernfurth, pp. 17 and 27–28).

42. Compare the numbered stints at Jastrzębce, Wróblowice, Jarząbkowice, and Żerniki (*SR* #3367, 4268, 6183; RF I, 214–220; Heyne, *Bisthum*, II, 715) with the generalities for Stablowice or Radakowice (*SR* #6005; RF, III, 2012–2021).

43. *SR* #6005 and RF, IV, 2740–2769. The Stablowice arrangement was again recorded in 1362 (RF, IV, 2661–2692). See also the same situation at Jarząbkowice (RF, I, 214–220)

44. *SR* #2336 and 2337; *NRB*, (1906), pp. 218–119.

45. Grodecki, "Gospodarki folwarcznej," pp. 64–66, provides evidence for grain exports from demesnes in Kujavia and Sądecz by the late thirteenth century and Zientara finds the same in the Uckermark (Engel and Zientara, pp. 274–324).

46. *HPR*, pp. 105–106.

47. HGZ, fols. 77v–78r. *Ibid.*, fols. 25v–26v or 60v–61r, tells the same about Trestno. On St. Mathias' operation of Bierdzany as a "kitchen estate" see Dittrich, "Fürstentum," pp. 247–248.

48. Dyhernfurth, pp. 25–26.

49. *SR* #4817 and 5686. To argue (as Eistert, "Pogarell," p. 233) that the 9 gardens belonging to the Jarosławice *scholtisei* in the latter text are evidence of *Dreschgartner* and *Robot* services not only needlessly injects modern concepts into a fourteenth century situation, it ignores the clear separation in the text between the gardens and the *peasants*' labor services and the explicit limitation of these to plowing (not a *gertner* service at all). See also the discussion of *gertner* late in this chapter.

50. Ludat, *Bistum Lebus*, pp. 127–128. The other two did only three or four days a year.

51. *SR* #5762; *LB* #37 and 123; LN, fol. 126v.

52. HGZ, fol. 37v.

53. *HPR*, pp. 107–109; HGZ, fols. 26v and 59v.

54. Mentioned *Ibid.*, fols. 78v, 99r, and 115v, but not extant.

55. RF, III, 2412. Compare the servants of Peter Kosak at Probostwo in 1406 (Heyne, *Neumarkt*, pp. 338–340).

56. Korta, "Księga," #46, 61, 85, 88, 144, 145, 150, 156, 157, 182, 186, 191, and 199.

57. *HPR*, pp. 107–109; HGZ, fols. 25v–26v and 98v–99v.

58. HGZ, fols. 59r–61r and 78v.

59. *LB* #123 with note.

60. HGZ, fol. 78v. Compare also fols. 38r and 99v. Another laborer seeks "verdintes lonis" from the Środa priory in Heyne, *Neumarkt*, pp. 339–340. On wage labor on contemporary Polish demesnes see Rutkowska-Płachcińska, "Rezerwy," pp. 425–435.

61. HGZ, fol. 99v. The rate is well below a reaper's wage.

62. A Polish assembly in 1398/99 legislated jurisdiction over people going to Silesia "ad laborandum" (Hube, *Prawo*, p. *62*).

63. Korta, "Księga," p. 231 (and after him, Heck in Maleczyński, *Historia Śląska*, I:2, 62–63) counted only 34 places with gertner, but he omitted the first entry, Brzoza, with two (RB, fol. 1v; Korta, "Księga," #5) and read the 12 at the gallows just outside Wrocław as part of the entry for Jaszkotle (fol. 6r; #99, last part). In addition, RB entries for at least 11 places fail to mention gertner reported in other texts, viz.: *SR* #4870a, 4870b, 4870h, 5975, and 6801; Dyhernfurth, pp. 25–26; RF, I, 473; RF, II, 817–826; RF, III, 265–269, 2000–2008, 2085–2096, 2097–2113, 2367–2378; RF, IV, 3039; Jesuiter, VII:III #11 (6). Finally, note the gertner recorded at places not in RB in Ludat, *Stiftsregister*, pp. 36 and 38; Grünhagen, "Protokolle," pp. 136–137; "QBBB," pp. 212, 215, and 225; HGZ, fol. 99v.

64. The assertion by Korta, "Księga," p. 231, and Heck in Maleczyński, *Historia Śląska*, I:2, 62–63. For the examples mentioned see *KdS* #129 and 130; *SUB*, I, #114 and 115; *SR* #4870b, 4870e, and 6081, and others in *SR* #5975, 6005, 6772; RF, I, 473, II, 817–826, III, 265–269, 2085–2096 and 2097–2113; IV, 3039; Tz-S, p. 172. *LB* surveys *royal* incomes and rights, and thus includes the *Olbino* gertner and their haying obligations (*LB* #123), but not aspects of the rural economy which remained outside the fiscal net. Compare also the frequency of gertner in villages in Great Poland (Stefański, pp. 32–33) and on the widespread Silesian and Polish properties of Lebus (Ludat, *Bistum Lebus*, pp. 96–97 and 128–132).

65. Klotz, pp. 115–129, is the fullest treatment, modifying points raised by Knapp and Kern, pp. 76–83, and Opitz, pp. 20–25, and used by later writers like Ludat, *Bistum Lebus*, pp. 96–97, and Juhnke, pp. 102–104. Symptomatic of his anachronistic treatment of the fourteenth century evidence is the assertion (pp. 121–122) that the gertner established in Gajowice by Abbot Conrad of St. Mary in 1345 (Tz-S, p. 172), owed services (they did not) and the inference that a schulz who owed service ("as customary") was peculiarly diagnostic of a gertner settlement. Dyhernfurth, pp. 16–20, noted gertner with German names by the 1320s, but otherwise too eagerly equated *orti* with *ortulani*.

66. A point made and then dropped by Klotz, pp. 117–121.

67. References in *HPR*, pp. 1–88, were amplified by Walter, "Gertrudskapelle," p. 77, and further illustrated in *SR* #3079. For Środa see *SR* #2855 and 4910; Heyne, *Bisthum*, I, 505.

68. *UD*, p. 222.

69. Tz-S, p. 172; *ChronBMV*, p. 201; Wendt, *Landgüter*, pp. 180–184; *HPR.*, pp. 84 note 1, 99–100, and 128–129; RB, fol. 6r; Szulc, pp. 36–42 and 83; and see Chapter 9 below.

70. The absence of demesne farms is verified by all other references, notably RF, as described in Appendix A, for the following places with gertner in 1425 (an asterisk [*] indicates those without demesne as early as 1375):

Brzoza*	Jerzmanowo	*Leimgruben**
Bogunów	Jaksonów*	Krzeptów
Bielany Wr.*	Mnichowice	Księginice, pow. Wrocław
Bratowice*	Piotrków Borowski	Łowęcice
Domasław	Wojtkowice*	Wszemiłowice*
Damianowice	Wierzbice*	

Gertner also lived without local demesnes at Kręczków and Świnobród in 1405 and elsewhere on the Lebus properties (Ludat, *Bistum Lebus*, pp. 128–132, and *Stiftsregister*, p. 38).

71. *SR*, #4870b, 4870e, and 4870h.

72. RF, II, 265–269 and 2097–2113; IV, 3039.

73. HGZ, fol. 99v. See also Borek Strzeliński in Ludat, *Stiftsregister*, p. 36, and Biestrzyków in Grünhagen, "Protokolle," pp. 136–137.

74. *SLU*, #13, 19, and 46; Wattenbach, *Protzan*, pp. 170–172; Grünhagen, "Protokolle," pp. 136–137.

75. *SR* #4870b; Markgraf, "Unrühigen Zeiten," p. 74. The John Flamming whose grain fields, farmstead, and barns at Sulimow were described in such detail in 1361 (*DT*, p. 160) was also a townsman, if of lesser position (Pfeiffer, *Patriziat*, p. 142).

76. *SR* #4870b. For *coloni* and *advocati* on corporate farms see *UD*, pp. 4 and 141; *SR* #4057; *RS*, II, #40 and #690; *ChronBMV*, p. 215.

77. HGZ, fols. 39r, 99v, and 115v. An unnamed *colonus* paid in the Wysoka rye in 1436 (fol. 78r) and John "Hoffeman" paid the tax from John of Błonie's demesne at Jaszkotle (RB, fol. 6r).

78. *HPR*, pp. 105–109.

79. *SR* #5747; WAP, AMW, G 3, fols. 10r–v. See also Görlich, *Vincenz*, pp. 79–80, and Heyne, *Neumarkt*, pp. 338–340.

80. The Clares leased out 7 mansi at Jeszkowice in 1332 for 2 years at 6 marks a year (*SR* #5159). The well-stocked 3 mansi at Lubnów brought John Cnuso 5⅔ marks per year in 1336 (*SR* #5747). St. Mary charged for the 2 mansi at Gajowice 1.5mk plus 6 capons annually. A lease at the owner's pleasure is *SR* #5684.

81. Wattenbach, *Protzan*, pp. 170–172; LN, fol. 368r. For like provisions at Polanowice in 1267 and Biestrzyków in 1410 see *SR* #1275 and Grünhagen, "Protokolle," pp. 136–137.

82. *SLU*, #105; "QBBB," pp. 195, 211, and 225. See also *LFE* B25.

83. *SLU*, #114.

84. *SR* #3050, 3260, 3422, and 4334; *LFE* B35; LN, fols. 26v–30r; *LB* #305; *RS*, I, #9 and 386, II, #656, 917, and 924; *UBB*, pp. 315–317; *RBM*, VII: 2, 372–373. Later records include "QBBB," pp. 212 and 223–225; WAA II: XI Piłczyce; Grünhagen, "Protokolle," p. 157; Klose, *Inneren Verhältnisse*, p. 190; WAA I, II e 11, p. 50.

85. LN, fols. 40r–44v, 376r–376v, and 471r–472v; Grünhagen, "Protokolle," p. 126. For full discussion of both properties during the fourteenth century see Hoffmann, "Nazwy," pp. 13–16 and 21–22. See more hereditary leases at Księże Wielkie (*SR* #1459, 1461, 6187), Mokry Dwór (Pfotenhauer, *Kamenz*, pp. 228–229), Zagródki (*SLU*, #130; *SR* #2386, 2608,

2609; Heyne, *Bisthum*, I, 601; *LFE* B36; "QBBB," p. 196; *ChronBMV*, p. 205) and Nowy Dwór (*Ibid.*, p. 209).

86. *SR* #1459 and 1461; Pfotenhauer, *Kamenz*, p. 228 note; *ChronBMV*, p. 183. While the other two transactions give both size and price, that for Mokry Dwór lists only the price. The per mansus rate is based on *LB* #258 and the 1386 renewal (Pfotenhauer, *Kamenz*, pp. 228–229). Compare also the 10mk per mansus price specified for Piłczyce above (LN, 26v–27r) and the 20mk per mansus obtained by the bishop for Zagródki (*SLU*, #130; *SR* #2386; and Heyne, *Bisthum*, I, 601) and by the cathedral chapter for Kończyce in 1332 (*SR* #5143).

87. *SLU*, #130; *SR* #1459, 1461, 2386; Heyne, *Bisthum*, I, 601; *LFE* B36; *ChronBMV*, p. 183.

88. Pfotenhauer, *Kamenz*, pp. 228–229. Compare LN, fols. 26v–27r and 34v–35v and *SR* #5143.

89. *ChronBMV*, p. 200.

90. *SR* #1459; *ChronBMV*, p. 183.

91. LN, fols. 370v–371r (abbreviated in *RS*, I, #211 and 836). Heyne, *Bisthum*, I, 874, and II, 715, describes economic leases by St. Clare of *Weinberg* in 1352 and a demesne at Zerniki in 1411.

92. *ChronBMV*, p. 205. St. Mary acquired the hereditary leasehold under the bishop by gift of a lay holder in 1300 (*SR* #2608–2609). The Bishop of Lebus may, judging by his receipt of fixed incomes from 9 mansi "pro allodio" in Borek Strzelinski in 1405, have had them out on lease. He received the same as from rental land, one mark, one modius wheat, and one modius oats per mansus per year (Ludat, *Stiftsregister*, p. 36). See also HGZ, fol. 2v, for the comparable rates paid by the hereditary holder of 12 mansi in demesne at Lisowice in 1430. For comparison with rents on tenant-held mansi see Chapter 6.

93. Rutkowska-Płachcińska, "Rezerwy," pp. 426–433, argues from cases like Borek Strzelinski (mostly in the kingdom, not Silesia) that revenue per mansus is the critical variable and that thirteenth- through fifteenth-century owners received as much or more from a demesne mansus as from one in tenant hands. She neglects, however, the relative costs of returns under the two systems.

94. *HPR*, pp. 105–106. The text gives a *summa* of 56mk 38gr, but the entries specified add up to only 54mk 38gr. The 1378 total also differs from the sum of entries by about 0.5mk.

95. *HPR*, pp. 107–109, does not total all expenditures listed and also gives a "summa omnium . . . super edificiis" of 33mk 34gr much larger than the 26mk 38gr 2hl specified as spent on these projects. Difficulties arise from the account's mixing payments made to the administrator, John Nossen, and those made by him from these monies for specific items. On the normal 10% interest rate see Chapter 8 and for peasant rents see Chapter 6 below.

96. HGZ.

97. Study of land prices requires that conveyances state both the size of the property sold and the amount of money paid for it. The latter is more often critical because, even in the original charters, issuers came increasingly in the mid- and late 1300s to report only the formulaic "um eyn genant gelt." See, for example, the sale of Pasterzyce in 1344 published in full in *DT*, pp. 67–68, or that of Borek from 1373 in *BUB*, pp. 232–233. All cases here discussed have the necessary information.

Land prices have hitherto been little and uncritically examined. Meitzen, *Boden*, III, 411–412, merely generalized from his previously published collection of documents from Domasław (and, unbeknownst to him, *Łukaszewice*) to assert that Silesian land prices (of any and all kinds) remained fixed in nominal terms until the 1490s and thus slowly declined in silver value with the debasement of the coinage. Pfeiffer, *Patriziat*, pp. 203–205, considered land prices (again of all kinds) only to argue that the Wrocław magnates whom he studied took advantage of increases to speculate in rural properties. His evidence is ten examples of places where two or more price citations (not necessarily on a per mansus basis) indicate an increase. So convinced was he, however, of a uniform upward movement, that he declared one sale record (*SR* #4280) fraudulent just because it had a price higher than two later ones. Like Meitzen, Pfeiffer treated only nominal prices, recognizing that these were not his modern mark but doing nothing about it. Several of his exemplary price increases were really drops in silver value.

98. *SR* #3355.

99. *SR* #2844, 4979, 6081, 6132, 6143, 6270.

Chapter 6

1. The early history of Tyniec Mały and the *locatio* of 1219/28 (probably 1221) were discussed in chapters 3 and 4 above. Thereafter see *SUB*, II, #193, 357, and 397; *SR* #935, 1633 [a possible forgery and the only reference to a demesne here during this period], and 3666; *RS*, II, #169. For *Milino* see also *SR* #4856.

2. *ChronBMV*, p. 199, is undated, but a later copy (WAA II, V B 2p) gives 1330; *SR* #5601, 5671, and 5827–5828. This may have been the occasion for fabrication of *SR* #1633. All post-1337 references to *Milino* are retrospective (see those of 1372 and 1462 in Domański, *Nazwy miejscowe*, #179). *LB* #50 and 354.

3. *ChronBMV*, pp. 199 and 215.

4. *Ibid.*, 218: "Hic eciam dominus Mathias abbas allodium in minori Tincz exposuit pro quibusdam rusticis Polonis in agros rusticales ad certos census annuos in peccuniis et frumentis, qui quasi quandam villulam ibidem construxerant quam fratres yronice Matczkendorf vocaverunt et nec peccuniam hereditatem nec census annuos solvunt, sed et concordiam quandam desuper factam postea minime servaverunt." Judging from RB, fol. 9r, this happened between 1425 and 1429.

5. Compare the analysis of Engel and Zientara, and, for the West, syntheses of Genicot, pp. 660–742, and Pounds, *Economic History*, pp. 440–487. In finding temporal and spatial *variations* in rural conditions and trends between the mid-1200s and the early 1400s, the present study dissents from previous uniform, stable, or unilinear treatments. In "Gospodarce folwarcznej," pp. 175–179, in Maleczyński, *Historia Śląska*, I:2, 37–99, and in Inglot et al., pp. 68–105, Heck had the "market-money" economy expand steadily from the late 1100s through late 1400s, which he illustrated with scattered and general examples and accompanied with a perfunctory bow towards possible difficulties in the mid-fifteenth century. Aubin, *Geschichte Schlesiens*, I, 417–483, confused Germanization and economic history; he could see only smooth growth to a "Golden Age" under Charles IV that a subsequent "Slavic reaction" destroyed. Dessmann, pp. 14–18, thought the thirteenth and fourteenth centuries an age of *Grundherrschaft*, but Haase, pp. 80–130, lost the latter between periods of settlement and of serfdom. Interpretations thus conflict without engaging their differences and conform only in neither treating the evidence systematically nor refining conclusions to fit particular generations or regions.

6. In 1353: 354 places, 274 with demesne (77%), 193 with tenancies (55%). In 1425: 362 places, 246 with demesne (68%), 241 with tenancies (67%). For methods and evidence, see Appendix A.

7. Some demesnes had been abandoned by 1353, but the 274 places with demesne land then is probably a fair minimum estimate of those which ever had it in the fourteenth century. The 122 places where withdrawal is recorded are 44% of the 274.

8. LN, 38r–40r, and Hoffmann, "Nazwy," pp. 9–17. See for other cases, LN, 30r–35v; *RS*, I, #211 and 836; II, #917 and 924; "QBBB," pp. 212 and 223–225; *LFE* B22 with *LB* #12).

9. See Appendix A, table A.4. Of 28 citizen holdings known in 1300, 6 had tenants and 25 demesne, but the 118 in 1425 included 92 with tenancies and 67 with demesne. By comparison the churchmen shifted rather less, going from 47% with tenancies, 72% with demesnes on their 104 holdings in 1300 to 83% with tenancies, 52% with demesnes on 124 holdings in 1425.

10. Seidel, *Beginn*, pp. 105–109.

11. Fibiger, pp. 302–305; *LB* #20–22 and 240–241; *UD*, pp. 144–147; RF, I, 37r. Compare activities of the Dominican nuns of St. Katherine (*LB* #46, 48–49, and 86; RF, II, 742–743; RB, fol. 3v), St. Clare (*LB* #29–30 and 309–310; RB, fol. 8r), and the Hospitallers (*LB* #34; RF, I, 263–286; RB, fol. 3v; Sommerfeldt, pp. 81–83; Wendt, *Landgüter*, pp. 180–184).

12. Pfeiffer, *Patriziat*, pp. 144–148, 177, and 276–277, or Stein, pp. 86–89, 108–109, and 146–147.

13. For citizens still with farms on the black earth in the 1420s, see RF, III, 279–295, IV 2987–3002; RB, 4v and 12r; *UD*, pp. 40–42 and 48, and for cereal monoculture on independent demesnes there, RF, I, 195; *LB* #354; "QBBB," pp. 196 and 218; *SR* #2054; WAA II, IV a 1; Heyne, *Bisthum*, I, 601; HGZ, *passim*.

14. Like the *locatio* charters, other records from the late 1200s to early 1400s rarely distin-

guished what was owed for tithe and what for rent, saying, especially on the ecclesiastical properties where most originate, "quam pro decima tam pro censu." Kaczmarczyk and Sczaniecki, pp. 71–72, refer to texts from all over the kingdom, from Silesia, and from the Wrocław duchy.

15. "Die Reallasten an Geld-und Getreidezinsen erlitten in allen behandelten Ortschaften im Laufe der Jahrhunderte überraschend geringe Veränderungen." (in UD, introductory p. 114).

16. Müncheberg, pp. 21–35, was accepted and used by Heck in Maleczyński, Historia Śląska, I:2, 46–47 and 76–78.

17. Medians and modes in Table 6.3 help control for variations in the means caused by a few extreme cases. They confirm and moderate the upward trend.

18. Most villages owed a mixture of wheat, rye, and barley or oats, but from the evidence listed in the note to Figure 6.3 the proportions did not vary in any meaningful way.

19. LFE B376 and "QBBB," pp. 215 and 224. Lesser dues (not the object of this discussion) were nominally the same.

20. The problem noted at Table 6.3 of two sites with high money dues and unknown grain obligations in 1326–75 affects assessment of changes during the late fourteenth century in total obligations. If the higher sum of the components better estimates average dues around 1350, then the mid-century grain equivalent of 21.1 measures also exceeded that of 1386–1430. In either case, however, the largest grain equivalent remains 1280–1300/05.

21. Landowning groups were unequally active in granting German law and dividing demesnes, but no significant associations were found between the class of owner and the level of rents.

22. The issue of the Peter's Pence has mainly been its use, with elaborate factors to correct for different rates and incidence of assessment, by Tadeusz Ładogórski in Zaludnieniem, pp. 67–142. For criticism see Buczek, "Rachunki świętopietrza," and "O wiarygodności;" Kuhn, "Bevölkerungsdichte," pp. 31–45, and Gieysztorowa, "Badania," pp. 527–529. Ładogórski's replies, "Spór" and "Nowy pogląd," are not altogether reassuring restatements of his technical claims.

23. Specific figures from Gieysztorowa, "Badania," pp. 522–526, barely modified earlier estimates there cited. See also the brief English treatment in Gieysztorowa, "Research," pp. 5–17.

24. Gieysztorowa, "Badania," pp. 542–553; Kuhn, "Bevölkerungsdichte," pp. 60–68.

25. Dziewulski, "Nowa praca," pp. 49–51; Maydorn, pp. 44–62. The Wrocław and Legnica archdeaconries split the Wrocław duchy.

26. Ładogórski, Zaludnieniem, pp. 103–131 and 139. Kuhn, "Bevölkerungsdichte," pp. 42 and 66, accepted all but the last of Ładogórski's corrective factors for the Silesian evidence and thus found the Peter's Pence a reasonably accurate measure for population in this province, partly because it supported his contention of much lower densities further east. Maleczyński, Historia Śląska, I:248–251) used an estimator of 2719 known villages plus 10% for those unknown and a (arbitrary) mean of 122 persons per village to get 475,130 persons without and 493,130 with the region of Oświęcim-Zator; this reappears in Inglot et al., pp. 112–113. The consequent density is 10–11 per square kilometer. The lowest (and unsubstantiated) estimate of "about 360,000" was by Rogmann, pp. 419–422.

27. The 1,252,000 figure used for 1578 by Ładogórski, Zaludnieniem, p. 140, was taken from Dziewulski, "Zaludnienie," p. 432. The resultant growth of 272% would rank well-developed Silesia second only to late-developing Mazovia.

28. Dziewulski, "Nowa praca," pp. 44–46 and Chapter 10 below.

29. Dziewulski, "Nowa praca," pp. 46–51, also showed that Peter's Pence records much understate the size of towns in the Opole region (where locally detailed accounts do survive from around 1400). His work, incidentally, invalidates a purported 42% population decline during the late 1300s deduced therefrom by Russell, "Recent Advances," p. 98 note 79. Russell's article is not reliable on Polish materials. Its discussion (p.96) of Ładogórski, Zaludnieniem, and of Vielrose (used in German translation), reverses the positions of the authors.

Kuhn, "Bevölkerungsdichte," pp. 64–66, neared the Ładogórski estimates because he derived a still lower average density of 3 persons per mansus from assuming a household of 6 but claiming average holdings of 2 mansi. The latter thesis (see Kuhn, "Bauernhofgrössen," pp. 265–266), is denied by Dziewulski's Nysa studies and by evidence from the Wrocław duchy treated in chapters 9 and 11 below.

30. Ładogórski, "Spór," pp. 33–34 and 44–51.

31. Ładogórski, *Zaludnieniem*, pp. 156–157; Kuhn, "Bevölkerungsdichte" p. 42.

32. All estimates rely on the 1353 *LB* because it covers the whole duchy like no other text. Ładogórski (*Zaludnieniem*, pp. 156–157) calculated at 100/village and 25/demesne which, after the improperly associated and incompletely recorded Kąty district is deleted, gives about 10,000 for the Środa district and 28,000 for the duchy as a whole. Since *LB* omits 36 of the 39 independent demesne farms then known in the Środa district (its only significant omission), another 900 or so persons should be added.

Most authors who used the total of mansi in the duchy did not allow for documented places missing from *LB*. Their estimates (Ładogórski's is 6690 without the Kąty district) are thus about 6% too low; the duchy held approximately 7000 mansi in the mid-fourteenth century. Dziewulski ("Nowa praca," pp. 46–48) suggested from his study of the Nysa district an average holding of 1.1 mansi with 6 persons on it, to get 5.5 persons per mansus. When applied to the Wrocław duchy materials his constants yield some 31,000 from settlement evidence and 38,500 from the total mansi.

Kuhn's assertion of a 2 mansi mean holding ("Bauernhofgrössen," pp. 265–266; "Bevölkerungsdichte," pp. 64–66) pulls the density down to only 3 persons per mansus and 21,000 on the 7000 mansi in the duchy. In "Seelenzahlen," pp. 11–15, Kuhn applied his constants to data compiled from *LB* by Matzen-Stöckert. After some prestidigitation with un-sized demesne farms (but not places missing in *LB*) Kuhn got 14,754 people in the Wrocław district outside the parishes of the city, 10,938 in the Środa district (with Kąty), 1,941 in the Uraz district, and thus a total of 27,633 in the duchy outside of town parishes

33. The size of peasant tenures is examined in Chapter 9. Ludat, *Bistum Lebus*, pp. 106–110 found 86% of people in the bishop's Silesian and Polish lordships living on peasant farms.

34. The lower figure, actually given as 14,000–15,000, is that of Mendl, pp. 162–163, and the higher from Ładogórski, *Zaludnieniem*, p. 160. Other and earlier guesses in Rogmann, pp. 428–429, or Maleczyński, "Dzieje Wrocławia," p. 206, have little basis in evidence, while the decline from 12,000 in 1300 to 10,000 in 1403 asserted in Russell, *Regions*, pp. 100–101, makes untenable assumption about population trends and uses less than the best estimate for the latter year.

35. "Tanta enim fames in Almania extitit, ut multi relictis agris suis fugerunt in Poloniam. . . ." (Bielowski, ed., "Rocznik dawny," p. 682. A famine of 1282 is said to have affected Silesia only in a compilation of 1410 (Bielowski, ed., "Rocznik Henrykowskich," p. 702). Two annals compiled around 1310 at Krzeszów and Lubiąż mention a famine of 1282 but locate it in Bohemia, not Silesia (Bielowski, ed., "Rocznik Grysowski," p. 696, and "Rocznik lubiaski," p. 708). On the dating and reliability of these texts see Korta, *Annalistyka*, pp. 198–229 and 231–247.

36. *LFE* D12.

37. *SR* #5879. More examples are *SR* # 5994, 5995, and 6023.

38. "desertarentur vsque ad vnicum mansum" (*BUB*, pp. 124–125).

39. *LB* #3 (a short total), 6 note, 55, 97, 100, 104, 109, 122 note, 125, 129, 132, 134, 161, 180, 206, 208, 210, 213, 218, and 219. In the 17 where it was measured, 166 mansi (9.8 per settlement) lay empty. They were 3.1% of the mansi inventoried. Compare Matzen-Stöckert, pp. 372–373 and 420. Where specified, most deserted mansi of 1353 were rental. These plainly concentrated on the poorer soils; of the 20 sites 8 were on the loam of the Bystrzyca valley and the central Środa district, 4 on the Uraz moraines, 7 in the bottomlands, and but 1 on the black earth. Recent hostilities along the duchy's northern frontiers (see p. 144 below) and the possibility that wooded mansi in the bottomlands had never been farmed make those in the Uraz district and east of Wrocław less likely symptoms of economic distress, but the contrast between frequent desertion in the Środa district and its rarity on the black earth seems to signify a temporary retreat from the very marginal lands which had been opened up a generation or so before.

40. Bielowski, ed., "Rocznik Henrykowskich," p. 703, claims many deaths from famine in Wrocław in 1317, as do the brief early fourteenth-century notes, Kętrzyński, ed., "Varia," p. 590. Compare also Lucas and, more locally, Kershaw.

41. Evidence from the autobiography of Charles IV and from an addition to the *Chronicon principum Poloniae* is summarized in *SR* #6021. See also Roepell, p. 410.

42. See Watts, pp. 543–547; Pounds, *Historical Geography*, pp. 325–339; and works there cited.

43. The only sources to assert plague in Silesia in 1348–49 were later compilations which implicitly generalized from the experience of the rest of Europe; contemporary local records fail to mention or suggest either an epidemic or unusually heavy mortalities. The evidence was examined in Grünhagen, "Karl," pp. 34–42, but see also the description of the disease's spread in Carpentier, pp. 1062–1092.

44. *LB* #342 note. Compare notes at *LB* #16, 263, and 358.

45. Bielowski, ed., "Rocznik większy," p. 690; Semkowicz, ed., "Osobliwości," pp. 740–745; Rosicz, *Gesta*, p. 40 (misdated to 1371). Grünhagen, "Karl," pp. 39–42, assessed the evidence.

46. In 1425 14 places (of 211 in the survey and like texts) had empty lands. The 11 with numerical information contained 57 deserted mansi (5.2 per settlement). This 2.1% of the 2752 mansi there accounted had no spatial peculiarities. See Appendix A.

47. *RBM* , VII:4, #1154; RF, I, 133–139, and II, 621–623; LN, 471r–471v.

48. *BUB*, #107

49. Only two records of livestock prices survive from before the 1430s. Stock on the Polanowice demesne in 1267 was valued per head at 0.5mk for cattle, 0.375mk for sheep, and 0.167mk for hogs (*SR* #1275). Sales from the royal demesne at Borów in 1377 brought much lower nominal prices: 16.25gr per cow, 4.4gr per calf, 36.7gr per horse (*HPR*, pp. 105–108). In the only comparable case, the silver price of 69 grams for a cow in 1267 was almost twice the 39 grams in 1377. This fall seems to match that in grain prices established below.

50. Friedensburg, "Getreidepreise." Heck used Friedensburg's fifty-year estimates in "Gospodarce folwarcznej," p. 179.

51. Friedensburg, "Getreidepreise," pp. 42–45, converted into gold Reichsmarks, a meaningful standard in 1906, but too dependent on the gold-silver ratio for permanent use, especially since the prices were paid in silver coins.

52. See Appendix B note 1.

53. Friedensburg, "Getreidepreise," pp. 19–24.

54. *Ibid.*, pp. 13–19; Friedensburg, *Münzgeschichte*, II, 30–31 and 69–70; Beyer, pp. 121–122.

55. See note 40 above.

56. *HPR*, pp. 104–107; WAP Klose, Kl 49 (Kl 48), 2v–3r.

57. *SR* #2362 and 3160

58. *SR* #3538, 3640, 3740, and 3947. See also *SR* #4611, 4659, and 4951 for John of Lübeck's piecemeal restoration in 1327–30 of a demesne at *Januszowice* and *Siedlec*. Owners of one at Przesławice, who had in 1324 permission to put it out to tenants, did so only after 1347 (*SR* #4370 and RF, III, 2000–2008).

59. English lords also responded to high early fourteenth century grain prices by retaining demesnes they had been phasing out (Mate, pp. 15–16), and, a century or more before, had handled inflation's threat to fixed money incomes by taking back leased demesnes (Harvey, pp. 3–30).

60. *SR* #6023

61. "Attendentes sterilitatem et vilitatem agrorum districtus nostri Noviforensis," Tz-S, pp. 550–552. Like cuts had been granted in 1337 by rulers of the neighboring Legnica, Złotoryja, and Chojnów districts (Rachfahl, *Gesamtstaatsverwaltung*, p. 43). As late as 1443 taxes in the Środa district were still half those elsewhere (KLM).

62. *SR* #5714; Klapper, ed., pp. 163–164. Rents were refused at Pietrzykowice in 1329 (*SR* #4817) and tithe at Cesarzowice near Środa in the 1340s (*RS*, I, #718). Compare tithe refusals around 1340 near Świdnica in Unterlauf, ed., pp. 353–354. See the geography of contemporary desertions in note 39 above.

63. Compare for England, Kershaw, pp. 47–50, and for France, Fourquin, p. 191. Recall, too, the slowdown during 1300–30 of German law grants in Great Poland.

64. See Appendix B.

65. In *SR* #6121 and 6172 creditors worry about future repayment in poorer coins.

66. "in Wratislaviensi districtu sepe plurima fierent dampna." Stenzel, ed., *Chronica*, p. 129.

67. Rosicz, *Gesta*, p. 52.

68. RF, IV, 2925; *DT*, pp. 163–164.

69. The working copy of *LB* #23. 263, and 358.

70. RF, II, 675–699 (for 1351).

71. *BUB*, pp. 185–186.

72. Engel and Zientara, pp. 366–367.

73. Grünhagen, ed., "Correspondenz," pp. 356–357.

74. *BUB*, p. 171.

75. RF, IV, 2661–2692; RB, fol. 5r. The Eichelborn property at *Zielona*, a prosperous and valuable holding in the 1350s, was abruptly in 1362 "vacua penitus et deserta" (RF, III, 2510–2520).

76. Engel and Zientara, pp. 64–67 and 325–384; Kuhn, *Siedlungsgeschichte Oberschlesiens*, p. 143.

77. All texts are in *UD*, pp. 197–229, where (introductory pp. 53–59) the tenurial peculiarities are also laid out. No claim is here made that absolute values of holdings in Krępice equalled those of more normal peasant land, only that changes in their price should parallel those for customary tenancies.

78. The fourteenth- and early fifteenth-century history of the duchy thus controverts the rising exploitation, higher labor rents, and exacerbated class conflict then found in Poland by Heck, "Walki klasowe," pp. 441–444.

Chapter 7

1. *SR* #5178; *LB* #82. "Koberwitz" is derived from the Slavic personal name *Kobier* (Domański, *Nazwy miejscowe*, #156). Other of Otto's lands appear in *SR* #5707.

2. *SR* #5800.

3. Except as otherwise indicated, further information on the lords of Kobierzyce is from RF, I, 462–466.

4. On the Molheim family see Pfeiffer, *Patriziat*, pp. 63–66.

5. Details in Pfeiffer, *Patriziat*, p. 183, suggest that he had access to texts now vanished. See also *DT*, pp. 14–15.

6. RB, fol. 3r; Korta, "Księga," #35.

7. Pfeiffer, *Patriziat*, pp. 233–234 and 263.

8. *UD*, pp. 21–23 #27. "Allod," "allodial," and related terms do not occur in this context.

9. RF, III, 2367–2378. For earlier and later examples see *SR*, #3006, 3007, 3568, 4570, and 4974; RF, I, 358–367 and II, 774–782; Eistert, "Pogarell," p. 268; *UD*, p. 201; *LB*, #499.

10. *SR* #4366; *SR* #4614 and 4630 are two more early cases.

11. *SR* #5807.

12. RF, IV, 2966–2978. Other conveyances by sale and inheritance of lordships identified as fiefs are RF, I, 399–406; II, 478; III, 2367–2378; and IV, 2700–2716.

13. *RBM*, 7:5, #1421. See also *RI*, 8:2, #6674; RF, I, 62v; III, 2465–2476.

14. RF, II, 925–933, and IV, 2966–2978. For a broader look at female rights to land, see below, pp. 181–185.

15. RF, II, 578. The Stroppen family had bought the village in 1357 and passed it by inheritance at least twice. For later escheats elsewhere see RF, III, 2367–2378; IV, 2700–2716.

16. Markgraf, "Unruhigen Zeiten," p. 76.

17. RF, I, 399–406, and III, 2409–2425; see also RF, II, 1024–1028 and 1045–1048. Pfeiffer, *Patriziat*, pp. 195–196, does not clearly distinguish between hereditary fiefs and true proprietary rights. Conveniently forgetful or undocumented conversions also occurred, like the mansus at Małkowice described in 1369 as "once a fief and . . . now *erbe*," or that at Świniary which changed between 1404 and 1439 (RF, II, 702–730 and III, 2465–2476).

18. In general see Wojciechowski, *Ritterrecht*, pp. 29–53 and 103–105. Among later scholars Kolańczyk has stressed and Bardach, "Uwagi," has minimized the importance of lineage solidarity in early Polish land law, but Wojciechowski's position is that followed, especially for the middling and lesser landowners important in the Wrocław duchy, in Rymaszewski; Koczerska, pp. 42–63; Sczaniecki, pp. 102–104; and Gawęda, pp. 53–55. Fourteenth-century developments in the duchy increasingly diverged from those in the kingdom.

19. The Holy Spirit Hospital bought Lisowice in 1276–77 by dealing with two knights, Dietrich, son of Boruta, and Reinold of Themeriz; their wives, both named Elizabeth; and several other women, all kin to the late Count Unarc (*SR*, #1276, 1529 and 1550; *BUB*, pp. 45–47).

20. *BUB*, pp. 110–111.

21. Texts and commentary (oblivious of Polish antecedents) by Gaupp in *SLR*, pp. 84–115, 144–146, and 195–196.

22. *UD*, 35.

23. RF, II, 817–826. Compare RF, I, 1r–3v and *SR* #5317.

24. *SR* #3050; LN, fol. 29v; WAA II, IX Piłczyce. Compare Gądów Mały in Hoffmann, "Nazwy," pp. 14–17, and a lay rear fief at Sośnica in RF, III, 2409–2425.

25. WAA II, V B 2c. See also *SR* #4066, 4290, 4345, 4346, 4405, 4421, 4500, and 5163; *RBM*, IV, #1345–1346; RF, II, 817.

26. That no social stratification was concealed in this nomenclature is clear from terminological studies and personal examples in Bogucki, "*Miles*," pp. 222–253, and Zgorzelska, pp. 279–303. See also Witzendorff-Rehdiger, "Adel."

27. As institution and human gene pool the Silesian nobility originated in and only slowly separated from the distinctive medieval Polish elite, not the German one described in Freed, "Origins" and "Reflections," or Arnold, *German Knighthood*.

28. As mentioned in Chapter 3, the social origin and initial status of Polish knights are disputed, but more scholars agree on how they achieved recognition as nobles during the fourteenth and fifteenth centuries. See Wojciechowski, "Condition" (1936), pp. 664–671, and (1937), 27–36; Wojciechowski, *Ritterrecht*, pp. 29–53 and 103–105; Górski, "Structures," and "Rycerstwo;" Sczaniecki; Gąsiorowski, *Nobility*; Łowmiański, *Początki Polski*, 6: 634–649.

29. Goerlitz, *Verfassung*, pp. 16–17; Pfeiffer, *Patriziat*, pp. 40–43.

30. Pfeiffer, "Entwicklung," pp. 99–117.

31. *SR* #6231. See also the Molheim in note 4 above. Pfeiffer, "Entwicklung," pp. 110–112 organizes data from Pfeiffer, *Patriziat*, pp. 6–90 to determine that fourteen of the fifteen identifiable members of Wrocław's combined council and court in 1287 (first in the unbroken record, but otherwise supposedly representative) were kin to what he calls the *Uradel*.

32. Witzendorff-Rehdiger, "Adel," pp. 193–212. The mid-century shift of one branch of the Reste family (later von der Wede) from citizen to knightly rank is seen in RF, IV, 2923–2930.

33. *SR* #3367 and 4268. See also *SR* #3712 or 5989, including lordships in other principalities belonging to Wrocław citizens.

34. Goerlitz, *Verfassung*, pp. 79 and 101; *BUB*, pp. 110–111, 120, 136, and 142–145; *NRB*, p. 253.

35. See discussion of *LFE* in Appendix A.

36. The issue of citizen and knightly landholding around fourteenth-century Wrocław was engaged in Hoffmann, "Citizens," which summarized the innumerate and contradictory views on the landed wealth of Wrocław citizens strongly asserted by Wendt, "Landbesitz," pp. 215–216, Pfeiffer, *Patriziat*, p. 206, and their followers (Kraemer, p. 34; Heck in Maleczyński, *Historia Śląska*, I:2, 56; and Menzel, *Jura ducalia*, p. 155) and offered earlier versions of data now in Tables 7.1 and A.1 and elsewhere in chapters 7–8 and Appendix A.

37. The figure of 16% citizens at places where lords can be identified in 1300 and 12% at places then in any way documented must be deflated. Most of the other places documented by about 1350 probably also existed in 1300 but few of them would have had citizens as lords.

38. *SR* #1664, 2145, and 3904. The Stillevogt family land at Romnów (*SR* #2249), between the Bystrzyca and Strzegomka, was not in the Middle Ages consistently assigned to the Środa rather than the Wrocław district. Comparing Map 7.1 with Map 3.1 further suggests that most early-fourteenth-century citizen lords fit into interstices among the church estates of the Wrocław district.

39. A net increase from no citizen properties before the 1241 municipal charter to 27 in 1300 is a mean rate of about one every two years, while 61 added between 1300 and 1353 is more than one a year. The total of places with citizen lands then rose by only 13 between 1353 and 1425.

40. In Table 7.1 citizens of Środa are counted with "other" landlords because their small place among the duchy's landed elite contrasts with that of Wrocław people. A few men from Środa regularly held parcels in their suburb of Bielany (RF, I, 1103–1126), but otherwise only the Vogt family of hereditary town judges owned rural land in any of the years profiled: Agnes Vogtin had Buczki, Michałowice, and Chwalimierz in 1425 (RF, I, 67r–71r and 127–132; II, 763–767).

41. Even if all 37 documented places in 1353 for which no lord may then be identified

were assigned only to the knights, that group would still hold in only 47.5% of the duchy's settlements.

42. *SR* #3232, 4589, and 5178 are just examples.

43. This applies to the Borgk at Mokronos Dolny (RF, II, 770), the Borsnicz at Jarosław (RF, I, 382), Lutko of Waldow and some knightly Restes at Brzoza (*SR* #5317; RF, I, 55r–56v), the land at Raszków held successively by a Falkenhain, the heirs of Conrad of Windmoel, and a Clonicz (RF, III, 2061–2068), the Seidlicz at Chmielów (*SR* #3760), and the Schellendorf at Ratyń and Lutynia (*SR* #4366), among others.

44. Among the early fourteenth-century knights who were themselves either the first documented holder or the direct descendant thereof and subsequently bought out by citizens of Wrocław were the Pogorzel at Jaroslawice in 1314 (Eistert, "Pogarell," p. 268) and the heirs of Dobko at Dobkowice in 1337 (*SR*, #3537, 5589, and 5996). For more examples see *SR* #2930, 4683, 5845, and 6060 or RF, I, fol. 76v.

45. About 1300 noble owners are recorded across the duchy in approximate proportion to the varying density of nucleations, but by 1353 61 percent and by 1425 82 percent of known noble properties were outside the Wrocław district. Precise counts of lordships are as follows:

	1300	1353	1425
Wrocław district	22	51	14
Środa district	15	63	52
Uraz district	2	17	12
Totals	*39*	*131*	*80*

These statistics actually exaggerate the survival by 1425 of noble lords in the Wrocław district, for of the 14 places then counted, 5 were within 5km of the boundary with the Środa district and 3 in a tight cluster along the Widawa beside the Oleśnica duchy. Another site is classed as noble only because the citizen's daughter who owned it by inheritance from her father had married a knight.

46. Poor early evidence for ducal possession of specific places underrepresents the rate of decline before 1353, but loss of the last remnants is visible. Charles IV redeemed Borów from the Rideburg brothers in 1353 (RF, I, 37c–37d) and in 1377–78 the demesne was still run on the royal account (*HPR*, pp. 105–106), but before 1387 it had passed by the king's gift to Stefan Poduske (*DT*, p. 60). Growers of hops at Małkowice and gertner at *Olbino*, who were directly subject to the king in 1353 (*LB* #2 and 123), also had other lords before 1400.

47. Wendt, "Landbesitz," pp. 216–217; *Landgüter*, p. 3; Kraemer, pp. 19–36. All Wrocław's lands then lay close to the city and served primarily the needs of the citizens' draft and meat stock, although some parcels were rented to peasants. Incidental brief holdings of lesser municipalities (though not Środa at this time) also appear in RF, I, 76v–79r, and IV, 2860–2861.

48. Unidentifiable except as to name were in 1353 45 individuals with 49 holdings in 33 places and in 1425 21 with 22 in 19. The 4 such in 1300 each owned one property and together held in 3 places. The patterns and character of all available evidence on land ownership argue strongly that successful identification of these individuals would little change the relative share of the duchy's rural lordships possessed by the church, citizens, and knights.

49. Neither the duchy's three principal landowning groups nor the importance of citizen control of rural lands made it unique in fourteenth century east-central Europe. The Altmark of Brandenburg contained no center of ecclesiastical administration comparable to Wrocław and its easy access by water to Hamburg encouraged small-scale grain export activity by townsmen, but its profile of lordships in the late fourteenth century still much resembled that here asserted for the Wrocław duchy. From the Brandenburg *Landbuch* done for Charles IV in 1375, Evamaria Engel found that the margrave owned only two villages and, even with his taxes and justice rights, received only 3% of the incomes from the agricultural sector, while the three other landowning groups whose incomes derived from arable acreage, the church, the lay nobility, and the townsmen, possessed about 20%, 22%, and 41% respectively (Engel and Zientara, pp. 105–188).

50. Except for the Church of Wrocław, no lords of estates here classified as large were all that huge on any absolute scale. Silesia (and Brandenburg, too) lacked in the thirteenth and fourteenth centuries the vast consolidated private estates which then covered whole districts and dozens of villages in Bohemia and Lusatia (Lehmann, pp. 119–121; Klassen, *Nobility*, p. 6).

51. The discussion here is informed by that famous dispute, although plainly I have more confidence in the careful use of such techniques to develop a limited body of valid assertions than did some of those whose debates were finally summarized by Lawrence Stone (*Crisis*, pp. 144–156).

52. The halt in donations of land might be attributed to King John's 1338 requirement of sovereign approval for any gifts to churches in the "city and territory of Wrocław" (*BUB*, #157), but the royal action was more symptom than cause of a turn of piety to objects other than traditional monastic or collegiate houses. As amply shown below, gifts to older foundations stopped more than a generation before the decree but the continued growth of newer houses with a different clientele was little impeded.

53. No text is a full and accurate list, what with continual buying, selling, leasing, exchanging, and amalgamating, but the composite evidence is compiled in Table A.2 (and partly reproduced in Table 7.2). Lordships of the cathedral chapter are treated in Dola, *Kapituła*, pp. 69–82.

54. Most of this rich endowment was in the future Brzeg and Oleśnica duchies, but it included lordship in Domasław, Żerniki Małe, Rybnica, and Sępolno. After a farm at Tarnogaj replaced the latter, these remained the only Holy Cross lands around Wrocław. See *UFO*, pp. 124–124, and *SR* #2054. Compare *LB* #335; KLM, fol. 35; RF, I, 166; and WAA II, IV a 1.

55. *BUB*, #95; *SR*, #3794–3799, 4780, 4783; *UBB*, #267.

56. Heyne, *Bisthum*, II, 32; *UBB*, #296; Urban, *Wykaz AAW*, #183–184 and 203. See also Schindler, *Domkapitel*.

57. Urban, *Studia*, pp. 29–31.

58. *SR* #1602; LN, fols. 370r–371r; *UBB* #297; *RS*, I, #211, 836, and 840.

59. "QBBB," pp. 205–225.

60. Dola, *Kapituła*, pp. 84–106, notes inadequate evidence on specific endowments before the seventeenth century, but their presence and separate management since the thirteenth.

61. Compare *SUB*, II, #287, and *UBB*, pp. 339–343. Also from the bull of 1245, Bogusławice, Małuszów, Zacharzyce, and Żurowice still belonged to the Church in 1382, though administrative peculiarities kept them from the charter. (See *LFE*, B27-B30; "QBBB," pp. 195 and 218; KLM, fol. 34.)

62. *UFO* #60, is a papal confirmation of the abbey's properties in 1253. Thereafter *Sokolnicy* and the St. Vincent claims in *Opatowo* simply vanish. For sales of properties see *SR* #1047 and *NLChron*, p. 61 and for the appearance of lay lords on St. Vincent lands, *SR*, #1013 and 3078, and RF, I, 481.

63. *NLChron*, p. 90.

64. *Ibid.*, pp. 92–98; *RS*, I, #106, 122, 131, 161, and 462; RF, II, 2456–2461; *LB* #247. Of course Nicholas rode the rising economic outlook of the 1340s.

65. *NLChron*, pp. 101–122; RF, I, 511, and III, 2456–2461; *RI*, 8:1, #5771.

66. RB, fol. 9r.

67. *ChronBMV*, pp. 183–200; *SR*, #2207, 3191, 3326, 3585, 4585, 5008, 5065, 5212; *LB* #55. WAA II, V B 2b and RB, fol. 9r, list Wrocław duchy properties of St. Mary.

68. *ChronBMV*, pp. 200–219.

69. Probably because Cistercian monks at Lubiąż, nuns at Trzebnica, and their main groups of properties were outside the shrunken Wrocław duchy, neither gave much special attention to what they did own there. Lubiąż tried briefly in the 1320s and 30s to consolidate an estate from its own and Trzebnica lands in the northwest corner of the Środa district. After this foundered on jurisdictional disputes with local lay lords and Duke Henry, and Lubiąż continued to liquidate its grange economy, occasional sales of scattered or outlying lordships by both houses left each with only a few holdings in the duchy. For materials towards a narrative see *UD*, pp. 248–269; Hoffmann, "Nazwy," pp. 9–17; Seidel, *Beginn*, pp. 43 and 153; *SR*, #2100, 3875, 4070, 4130, 4223, 4224, 4908, 5553, 5908, and 6619; an interestingly forged version of the Lubiąż foundation charter (*KdS* #113 = *SUB*, I, #326); Wendt, "Verpfandung," p. 159; RF, III, 2408; Jesuiter, III:I, 4–5 ; and compare on the generally moribund grange economy of eastern Cistercian foundations by the fourteenth century Roehl,

pp. 110–115. The same maintenance of an existing position was true of houses with more recent origins but primary landed interests elsewhere: Holy Cross; the Bishop of Lebus; the Teutonic Order; a house of Poor Clares from Strzelin; and a Cistercian abbey from Kamieniec Ząbkówski. For treatment of one such, see Ludat, *Bistum Lebus*, pp. 73–96, 176–181, and 205–206.

70. *SR*, #1301, 2652, 2893 3550, and 4631. Boundary disputes at Chrząstowa with St. Mary's culminated in clear division of the property in 1336 (*SR*, # 5717, 5745, and 5765).

71. *SR* #3679 and 4320.

72. See, for instance, the complex arrangements for 23mk 30gr in annual rents from several villages, some already owned by the convent, which Dytwin bought in 1340 for a legacy to his daughters Anna and Margaret, both nuns therein (*SR* #6423).

73. *SR* #5203; Heyne, *Bistum*, I, 870; *RBM*, IV, #1533; *RS*, I, #220 and 229.

74. *LB* #25–32, 103, and 539; Heyne, *Bistum*, I, 870 and 874.

75. Lay lords took over Iwiny, Jeszkowice, and *Weinberg* (RF, I, 395–398, and II, 866–875; Heyne, *Bistum*, I, 874). See the "Bona monasterii Sancte Clare" in the tax returns of 1425 and 1443 (RB, fol. 8r, and KLM, fol. 17) and add forests and meadows at Redzin, exempt from fiscal obligations (RF, III, 2049–2060).

Comparable but even longer abilities to attract landed donations and purchase other properties were shown by Wrocław's Dominican convent, St. Katherine. Its accumulation between the late 1290s and 1405 of lordships clustered on the black earth above the Oława River and along the southern edge of the duchy is seen in *SR*, #2714, 3391, and 3400; *LB*, #46, 47, 49, 86, and 87; RF, I, fol. 37r, and II, 742–743; RB, fol. 9v; and KLM, fol. 22.

76. *SR* #2857. Henry VI let go all ducal claims in 1326 (*SR* #4572).

77. *SR*, #5047, 5163 , 5617, and 6559.

78. Fibiger, pp. 302–306; confirmed in Heyne, *Bisthum*, II, 703, and RF, I, 167–171, and II, 771.

79. Fibiger, pp. 306–314; *RI*, 11:1, #5817; Heyne, *Bisthum*, III, 944; RB, fol. 8v. Two other charitable corporations, the Commandery of the Knights of St. John at the Corpus Christi church and, at the same site, the Holy Trinity Hospital, also expanded their estates towards the end of the fourteenth century. Both relied primarily on purchase, though for Holy Trinity payment actually came from a city council responding to the experiences of plague. Wendt, "Verpfandung," pp. 156–159 clarified the complex relationship between these two corporate entities, although his findings are not in the poorly documented Szczesniak, pp. 20–22. For their estates see also Hoffmann, "Nazwy," pp. 2–9, Wendt, *Landgüter*, pp. 180–194; and RF, I, fols. 37c-37d, and pp. 255 and 275–278, and III, 2408. The Holy Spirit Hospital, on the other hand, after acquiring Lisowice in 1277, never changed the four properties it held (see *SR* #6320 and *BUB* #165).

80. The grant to father and son jointly in 1282 is only in RF, I, 481; passage from father to son two years later is *SR* #1856.

81. *SR* #2226, identified as Domański, *Nazwy miescowe*, #51.

82. *SR* #3128 and 4589; for the latter's German immigrant ancestors see Cetwiński, *Rycerstwo* 1982, pp. 130 and 195.

83. *SR* #1856, 3160, and RF, II, 1057–1060.

84. *SR* #2514 and 2643.

85. *SR* #4066, 4290, 4345, 4346, 4405, 4421.

86. *SR* #3232.

87. Examples which follow belong to statistically important types of landowners, but are not purported to constitute a random sample (from what population?) or even one representing all significant covariations among subgroups of lay lords (e.g. noble and citizen; large and small; early, mid-century, and late). This methodological disclaimer is not to be misconstrued. Fully documented cases of all sorts of fourteenth-century lay estates can be and have been reconstructed from the extant evidence. But since no subset shows its own distinctive features, only an illustrative few deserve recapitulation.

88. In 1336 John's ignorance of his own local vassals almost cost John and Conrad Schellendorf the rights of their families to Ratyń and Lutynia (see p. 185 below).

89. *SR* #5178 and 5800.

90. *SR* #5707; compare RF, I, 206–212.

91. Another small noble lord who actively used the land market, the squire Luthold Sommerfeld, constructed entirely by purchase during the 1330s and 1340s a tidy estate in the

Środa district: village lordship and a fortified dwelling at Mokra, a demesne farm at *Opalin*, and fiscal payments from Krępice. See *UD*, p. 201; *DT*, pp. 65–66; *SR* #5974; RF, II, 774 and 883.

92. RF, IV, 2733–2737, reveals the error of Pfeiffer, *Patriziat*, pp. 128, 155 and 174, who assigned this transaction to John Winter and located the land in Stoszyce.

93. Pfeiffer, *Patriziat*, pp. 103, 107–108, 181, 224 and 308; Witzendorff-Rehdiger, "Herkunft," pp. 124–125; Stein, pp. 83–84 (not always a reliable source on land transactions).

94. *LB* #11, 14, and 66; RF, I, 330–346.

95. RF, I, 175–183, 322–328, 330–346 and 511–512, II, 901–909, and IV, 2617–2619, and 2938–2940; WAP Rep. 135, E 96, pp. 4–5.

96. Relevant property records not in note 95 above are RF, I, 143–147, 399–406, and 459; Pfeiffer, *Patriziat*, p. 181.

97. Schwarz ought to have known another four vendors, too. His first purchases at Krobielowice, Świniary and Kobierzyce were from men with city backgrounds like his own and the land at Jaksin came from the captain of the duchy, Conrad Falkenhain, with whom a town councillor like Schwarz should have had some contact (RF, I, 399–406, 462–466, and 511–512, and III, 2465–2476).

98. *RBM*, 7:1, pp. 87–88 #122.

99. *DT*, p. 165.

100. RF, I, 175–182, 322–328 and 399–406 and IV, 2938–2940; WAP, Rep. 135, E 96, 4–5. Schwarz sold sublordship at Ozorzyce after getting a royal grant of *locatio* rights to improve its value (RF, II, 912–916 and Pfeiffer, *Patriziat*, p. 181). See also RF, I, 143–147, 459, 462–466, 511–512 and III, 2465–2476.

101. Cetwiński, *Rycerstwo* 1982, pp. 68, 101, 136, 156, 175, and 177; Schieckel, p. 109; *SR* #3007, 4726, 5845 and 5988. Haugwitz, I, 90–103, missed at least the critical record of Poppo's death in 1367, and eagerly linked into families all members of this large and widespread lineage.

102. Wały had also earlier belonged to the family (RF, I, 239–246, III, 2085–2096, and IV, 2882–2891). Compare *SR* #6031.

103. RF, I, 239–246, 421–423, and 510; III, 2085–2096; IV, 2613–2616. See also the purchases of the nobles Nicholas Grzebkowicz at Smolec Mały in 1382, Lutko Radak at Siemidrożyce in 1403, and Franz Schellendorf at Solna before 1425 (RF, II, 901–909, and III, 2237–2257 and 2358–2366).

104. Sales under what might be thought extreme conditions include *SR* #2514 and RF, III, 2358–2366 (land held in right of a spouse); *SR* #5807 and RF, IV, 2820–2837, and II, 1024–1028 and 1045–1048 (fiefs); *SR* #5715 and RF, II, 848; II, 854–859; III, 2358–2366 (inherited family lands).

105. *SR* #6618. For earlier examples of consent among city families properly subject to the Madgeburg custom of Wrocław courts and Polish landowners under *ius hereditarium*, see *SR* #1276, 1529, 1550, 2930, 3679, and 4478; *BUB*, #46 and 49.

106. *UD*, pp. 147–148; RF, III, 2499–2507. Because the Roraw were likely of twelfth-century Walloon immigrant stock and much intermarried with local knights and the owners of Żybiszów indigenous non-knightly free landowners (see Chapter 9 below), they might just have retained archaic Polish customs of extensive kin-right. But when one from a city family of German origin, Peter Steinkeller, officially in 1415 consented to a sale three years earlier by his brothers of land at Sośnica to another city man of similar background, John Sachse (RF, III, 2409–2425), it looks as if all elements of the lay elite were familiar with a view of kin right broader than that declared in law.

107. This is not to imply that purchases from kinsmen or from strangers of land previously sold by a kinsman were rare (see, for example, Franz Dompnig's acquisitions of lands once his brother's at Boreczek and Jaksonów in RF, I, fols. 39r–42v and pp. 330–346). What cannot be shown, however, is one exercising a *right* to preferential treatment, rather than merely buying land known to be available.

Not all rights of repurchase or comparable legal curbs on alienation arose from a general kin right. Sales with rights of re-purchase reserved to the seller were common, as in Peter Schwarz's 1362 dispute with Henry Sittin over possession of Żerniki Wielkie (*DT*, p. 165, #238:17–18). These contracts can not be studied because they were registered not in the *libri perpetuorum* like full conveyances but in the *libri reemendorum*, neither now extant nor normally copied into RF.

108. Koczerska, pp. 42–63, surveys female inheritance and property rights in marriage in late medieval Poland. The daughter's dowry or marriage portion is described similarly in the duchy's code of 1356, both in passages taken wholly from *SSp* (articles 10 and 26) and in one which modified that on a related point (article 359); see *SLR*, pp. 144–145 and 195–196.

109. Landed rights and property could go to a daughter's husband without being called a *dos*. The widow of John Schertilzan, Katherine, gave in 1348 to her son-in-law, Reinczko of Swenkenfeld, eight marks annual rent on her property in Bogdaszowice, and promised, if he had children by his wife, the land itself. By 1364 Reinczko possessed it "by gift of Katherine" (RF, I, fols. 29r–34r). For a later example see RF, II, 952–960 and IV, 2923–2930 and Pfeiffer, *Patriziat*, tables 7 and 35.

110. Articles 36 and 45 of the duchy's code (*SLR*, pp. 147–149) replicate *SSp Landrecht*, I: 20, 1–5 and 24, 1–4. The Royal Six then interpolated into their model an article (37) distinguishing between an "umbegobet" (unendowed) widow, who rightly received both *Gerade* and *Morgengabe*, and "begobet" (endowed) one, who received only the former. Legal texts from Wrocław and its duchy (i.e., the 1356 code and the roughly contemporary systematic compilation of Magdeburg law used by the city's courts) never clarify whether "endowment" here refers broadly to any contractual provision or narrowly to one explicitly in lieu of *Morgengabe*. Gaupp argued for the more limited interpretation by analogy with a Magdeburg case (not one certainly known in Wrocław) where an explicit cash value replaced the objects normally specified as a *Morgengabe* (*SLR*, pp. 118–124 and 147). If this were true, all the landed dowers discussed below ought to have been a mutually exclusive alternatives to *Morgengabe*; if not, a wife could receive both land and movables. The land records of the duchy contain by their very nature little mention of movables, but it may be significant that they nowhere document a woman with both dower and *Morgengabe*. Especially telling are two carefully detailed agreements from 1336 and 1340 about the widow's rights of Lusha Stille, which mention *Gerade* and *lypgedinge* but not *Morgengabe* (*SR* #5596 and 6507). But in an agreement made in Wrocław in 1434 the heirs of Hans Teschner and his widow, Barbara Hern, exchanged some lands, outstanding debts, and stocks of grain and firewood for a contractual right to 150 marks on Teschner's property "als irer morgengabe" (*UD*, p. 52). The best proof of Gaupp's contention would, however, still be to find a woman who clearly did receive both *Morgengabe* and *dotalicium*. For the city law, see Laband, ed., pp. 140–154.

Even the *Gerade* might affect landed property rights. In 1336 John Molnsdorf owed his stepmother 80 marks from Mokronos Dolny for the movables "que vulgo gerad dicitur." His brothers-in-law, Albert and Conrad Falkenhain stood surety for his payment and received in turn possession of Mokronos as their security against loss (*SR* #5617 and a version misdated to 1356 but with more details in RF, II, 770).

111. "Leyp getzeug kan den frauen nymant gebrechen." *SLR*, article 39 replicates *SSp Landrecht*, I:21, 2 and in general pp. 147–149. Compare Koczerska, pp. 42–63. Land records from around Wrocław neither confirm nor deny shifts in the relative value of dower and dowry asserted as a European phenomenon in Herlihy, *Households*, pp. 98–100.

112. *SR* #5617 or 5705; RF, IV, 2700.

113. *SR* #5584; RF, I, 175–182 and II, 642–659. For further representative examples see *SR* #5154, 6189 note, and 6514; RF, I, 310; III, 2123; or III, 2510–2520.

114. RF, II, 626–634 and *BUB*, pp. 246–247. For two other explicit examples, see *SR*, #6517 and RF, III, 2510–2520. See also RF, I, 418–419 and III, 2300–2319 and 2337–2357.

115. Articles 39 and 54 of the duchy's code replicate *SSp Landrecht*, I: 20: 2 and 32. Cases according therewith appear in *SR* #6911; RF, II, 912–916; *DT*, pp. 64–65.

116. RF, I, 167–171 and III, 2300–2317. In both cases the property was plainly the husband's acquisition and possession, not something the wife herself brought to the marriage. Later cases are in RF, I, 29r–34r, 52v–54v, and 310–319; II, 1009–1017.

117. *SR* #5596 and 6507.

118. RF, II, 590–592; John Dompnig gave Wierzbica to his wife, Katherine, in 1408 (as his widow she sold it thirteen years later) and a kinswoman of his, Anne, similarly got Pełczyce from her spouse, Patrick Sebinwirt, a decade later (RF, III, 321–324 and II, 1029–1044). Compare also RF, II, 770 and 1009–1017.

119. *SR* #3326 and 5658; RF, II, 854–859.

120. In 1314 one citizen father, Mathias Scriptor, arranged that incomes from half his demesne at Smardzów should go for life to his daughters, Margaret and Agnes, nuns of St.

Katherine in Wrocław. They would personally inherit the property and with the consent of the prioress could alienate it, but the convent itself had no authority before the deaths of the girls. *SR* #3400. For other examples see *SR* #5740 or *UD*, pp. 30–31.

121. RF, II, 961–977. For other transfers during the father's lifetime see *RS*, I, #602 and 621, and II, #1013; RF, II, 595, and III, 2097–2113 and 2337–2357).

122. The general statement in article 26 came from *SSp Landrecht*, I: 13, 1 and received further specification in discussions of daughters' succession to their mother's *gerade* (article 10 = *SSp Landrecht* I: 5, 2) and their right to incomes from land under the law of fiefs (article 359, not in *SSp*; see *SLR*, pp. 144–145 and 195–196. The issue is familiar to western social historians through the studies of Yver, especially as disseminated by Le Roy Ladurie, "Family Structures."

123. *UD*, p. 30; RF, III, 2097–2113. See also RF, II, 615–619 and 961–977 and the dispute recorded in *RS*, I, #621 and II, #515.

124. On a daughter's equal right to land under Polish and Silesian custom of the thirteenth century see Wojciechowski, *Ritterrecht*, pp. 43–44; Gawęda, pp. 53–59; and especially Lesiński, *Stanowisko kobiety*, pp. 49–56. Later laws of King Casimir and his successors encouraged a girl's brothers or even male cousins to take the land and give her a cash settlement or charge on it (*Ibid.*, pp. 55–56; Koczerska, pp. 42–63). Parity for female heirs affected German law in the Wrocław duchy as early as 1339, when King John altered the city's Magdeburg precedents to reflect it in cases of representation by grandchildren of a deceased parent's claim on a grandparent's estate (*SLR*, pp. 94–95).

125. *SLR*, pp. 84–98, 144, 146, and 195–196. Article 9 modified *SSp Landrecht* I:5,1, and article 30, *SSp Landrecht* I:17,1.

126. For example, see *SR* #6700–6701.

127. RF, IV, 2661–2691, with details especially in the charter whereby the new recipient alienated it again in 1428. Compare the escheat of Jenkowice in 1408 (RF, I, 358–367).

128. See note 13 above and, for more, *RI*, 8:2, #6674 and 6680; RF, I, fol. 62v, and IV, 2870–2879; *RBM*, 7:5, #1421.

129. *SR* #6063 and RF, III, 2337–2357 (other female heirs here, too). See also *SR* #3415 and 3905 and RF, I, 7v.

130. *UD*, p. 43, #70. Compare RF, III, 2337–2357

131. RF, III, 2337–2357. Other cases include *SR* #6044, 6055, and 6063; RF, III, 2337–2357 and II, 961–977.

132. *SR* #3415; *UD*, pp. 43–45; RF, IV, 2870–2879.

133. RF, III, 2337–2357. For more instances, see *SR*, #3905 and 6556; *UD*, p. 45; RF, IV, 2870–2879.

134. Bardach, "L'indivision;" Koczerska, pp. 90–109. Article 77 of the duchy's code (*SLR*, p. 152) distinguished between heirs who had or had not "gesundirt vnde geteilet" from siblings.

135. RF. I, 370–381, and III, 2337–2357.

136. Arrangements among two generations of the Pak family are in *SR* #4589, 4967 and 6583 and RF, II, 1057–1060. At Raszków in the 1340s kin of Conrad of Windmoel wanted land to go from uncle to nephew but had to settle for three nieces (RF, III, 2061–2068).

137. *SR* #3823.

138. *SR* #5636. To prevent further exploitation of his ignorance John eventually had to annul all grants of expectations (*BUB*, pp. 160–161). Wrocław duchy customs diverged from those in the Kingdom of Poland, where male collaterals soon could preempt land from direct female heirs (see note 124 above).

139. For examples see *SR* #6911; *UD*, p. 35; RF, III, 2428–2444.

140. One son named John also ceded his expectation in 1390, but this seems not to have been observed. *DT*, p. 160, #128:5; RF, IV, 3077–3083. See also *SR* #6044.

141. *SR* #4290, 4346, 4405 and 4421.

142. Stephan was hereditary lord before the last record of either his brother or his sister. *SR* #5845 and 6060; *RS*, I, #260, 473, 474, 683, 684, 796, 798, and 799; RF, I, 76v–79v and 175–182; III, 2409–2425; and the family background in Cetwiński *Rycerstwo* 1982, pp. 70, 120, and 139–140. A similar case at Smolec Mały during the 1350s is in RF, III, 2337–2357.

143. *UD*, p. 31, #42. See also *RS*, II, #1013.

144. *SR* #4201; Wutke, "Kreuzstiftkanoniker," p. 268 (a text not in *SR*); *RS*, I, #342,

and II, #1031; RF, II, 936–945, and III, 2142–2150. Pfeiffer, *Patriziat*, p. 75, was more wary of linking various persons called "de Ratibor" than were Witzendorff-Rehdiger, "Herkunft," p. 119, and Stein, p. 69.

145. RF, I, 147–154, and 399–406, III, 2499–2507; *LB*, #323, 329 and 469; *RB*, fol. 4v. This trading family did not attain the Wrocław *Rat* and may later have shifted their interests out of the duchy (see Pfeiffer, *Patriziat*, p. 95).

146. RF, I, 206–212 and 462–466. Otto's family was not close kin to some Gluboses who between the 1340s and 1380s had two small lordships north of Uraz (RF, I, 347–354, and II, 642–659).

147. For the Sittin family, see Pfeiffer, *Patriziat*, pp. 113, 143–144, 176, 179–181, and 243. Witzendorff-Rehdiger, "Herkunft," p. 112, speculates on earlier origins and Stein, pp. 65–66, contains minor errors of fact.

148. *SR* #5058, 5707, 5846, 5887 and RF, I, 206–212, and IV, 2617–2619 mention hereditary properties at Żerniki Wielki and Bledzów. With Cesarzowice Nicholas endowed the entry of kinswomen to the convent at Strzelin in 1336, while rights at Gniechowice and Leśnica were soon held by his nephews and his wife's family, the Blanke (*SR* #5740, 5845, 5997 and 6060; RF, I, 175).

149. *SR* #5569, 5761, 5800, 5820, 6255, 6321 and 6669; *RS*, I, #211, 678, 685, 836, and 840; LN, fols. 370r–371r; RF, I, 19v–22v, II, 917–924, and IV, 2987–3002.

150. *UD*, p. 17; *RS*, II, #462 and 566; RF, I, 20v and II, 917–924. See also RF, I, 19v–22v and II, 917–924.

151. *UD*, pp. 21–23. A daughter endowed as a nun is not mentioned here. On the passing Sittin possession of small holdings at Pełczyce see RF, II, 1029–1044.

152. WAP, AMW, G3, fols. 12v–13r; *UD*, p. 25.

153. Only Pfeiffer, *Patriziat*, p. 180 has the gist of the text.

154. *UD*, pp. 28–29.

155. *Ibid.*, p. 29, #37 looks like an incomplete text of the agreement, but none better has been found. The later history of the lordships does not depart from what would be expected if only what is there recorded had modified the provisions of 1362–63.

156. *UD*, pp. 31–39; RF, I, 20v–22v, II, 917–924, and IV, 2987–3002.

157. Family members arrived late in the thirteenth century from the Meissen area (Cetwiński, "Pochodzenie," pp. 49 and 57 and *Rycerstwo* 1982, pp. 129, 140, and 149–150). During and after Conrad's time many of that surname occur in Wrocław duchy records. Some were the brothers of the captain and their descendants, others had less clear ancestry. But the men and women discussed here are all plainly of Conrad's paternity and make with their properties a complete and consistent story. They were the richest and longest of the Borsnicz lines in the duchy.

For the lands of Conrad and his wife, including those alienated before his death, see Kopietz, pp. 23–24 and texts in *SR* #5591, 5634, 5638, 5708, 5831, 5845, 5900, 6031, 6040, 6209 and 6316; *UD*, p. 6 #5; LN, fols. 374r–374v; RF, I, 322–329 and IV, 2653–2660 and 2938–2940.

158. LN, fol. 374r–374v.

159. Grünhagen, ed., "Correspondenz," p. 357; *LBU*, I, 74; *RBM*, 7:5, #1509; RF, I, 247–254, 322–328, 479; II, 731–735 and 844–848; IV, 2653–2660, 2931–2934, 2938–2940; WAP, AMW, G 3, fol. 7r.

160. Friedman vanished after 1348. For dealings of his brothers see RF, I, 322–328, and IV, 2653–2660, 2931–2934, and 2938–2940; Rössler, #672; Schulte, "Kostenblut," p. 215; Wutke, "Wilxen," pp. 157–159. Only three times, all in the early 1350's, did Conrad's brothers act without him (see additionally WAP, AMW, G 3, fol. 6r). Conrad dealt almost exclusively with kin (also RF, I, 247–254, 382, and 479 and II, 731–735). His career should recall that of his peer and contemporary, Krig Hugowicz.

161. The last rights over another's land, those at Kostomłoty, Conrad sold in 1388 (Schulte, "Kostenblut," p. 215). See also *DT*, p. 54, #43:4.

162. RF, II, 731–735. After a long gap in surviving records for Marszowice a Borsnicz was again there in the early 1490s.

163. Przesław appears only in the agreement to divide the inheritance (RF, II, 731–735) and serving beside Czenko and Henry among the Silesian mercenaries of the Teutonic Order in 1410 (Pfotenhauer, "Schlesier," p. 205). John's lands in Bagno and Wały came from his stepdaughter, Hedwig Hugowicz (RF, III, 2085–2096). For Nicholas's ecclesiastical career and

incomes see Heyne, *Bistum*, III, 888–889; Härtel, p. 286; Jungnitz, "Statistik," pp. 387–388. The family properties are RF, I, 247–254 and 479 and IV, 2653–2660.

164. Turnover rates in typical families certainly exceeded those found among English barons by McFarlane, pp. 72–79, 123, 143, and 173, but cannot be explained as there from the genetic hazards of primogeniture and impartibility. More plausible explanations come from the considerations of kin group strategies by J. P. Cooper, E. P. Thompson, and V. G. Kiernan in Goody et al., pp. 192–398, and Giesey, "Rules and Strategies," although it is the rarity of successful dynastic strategies that must be emphasized around fourteenth century Wrocław. The behavior of lords in the duchy at that time thus more resembles the "multicellular" strategy of dispersed family wealth proposed as an alternative to dynasticism in Raftis and Hogan, pp. 23–28.

Chapter 8

1. For examples see *SR* #4870b and 4870e; *DT*, pp. 65–66; *UD*, p. 202; Stobbe, "Signaturbüchern" 1865, p. 344; LN, fol. 385r.

2. One citizen "living in the village" was John Sommerfeld, scion of a noble line, at Brzezina in 1338 (*SR* #6032).

3. *LB* #455: "De Petirkow servitur cum dextrario per annum sed ibidem servit Paulus de Harta et Heinco de Cracouia 10½ septimanas, post hoc isti de Dirschdorff residuum anni." Details in *LB* #451–506 are reminiscent of fifteenth-century Polish discrimination among nobles serving as heavy cavalry, light cavalry, and infantry (Górski, "Rycerstwo," pp. 823–834). But the section is organized inconsistently and includes so many collective obligations like that of the Dirsdorfs that elaborate statistical analysis is vain. Matzen-Stöckert, pp. 439–454, tabulates all data and variants but draws no conclusions.

4. Pfotenhauer, "Schlesier," pp. 204–214.

5. Despite the nobles' military heritage and profession, social violence among lords seems rare at this time. One from Siemidróżyce allegedly forced the priest of Kostomłoty to take cash for his real grain tithe (*SR* #4870b) and a dispute over rents from Jenkowice caused Dietrich Doring and Henry Roraw to kidnap the auxiliary bishop of Wrocław (Pfotenhauer, "Weihbischöfe," pp. 252–254). Nicholas Rempel purportedly used his position on the Wrocław council to extort gifts from a landowner who needed rights confirmed (Markgraf, "Unruhigen Zeiten," p. 76). Vaguely reported or politically inspired difficulties of certain ecclesiastical landowners were mentioned earlier. But these isolated cases compare to the general disorder which so distressed the fifteenth-century countryside and its chroniclers (see Chapter 10). The silence might be from lack of the right sorts of documentation from the earlier period, but the instances mentioned sound different in kind, more particular responses to existing disputes within the landed elite than generalized and effectively unprovoked assaults upon the wealth and persons of landowners and their tenants.

At least some lords fortified private rural dwellings at this time (RF, II, 774–782 and IV, 2942–2958; RUL #9; Grünhagen, "Protokolle," pp. 136–137). But the comfort and safety of defensible manor houses then also caused lesser Polish nobles to leave peasant-style housing (Górski, "Rycerstwa," p. 835).

6. Markgraf, "Unruhigen Zeiten," pp. 73–76.

7. Notably Pfeiffer, *Patriziat*, pp. 206–222 and 317–318 (but also Menzel, *Jura ducalia*, p. 155) imputed a special managerial mentality to citizen landowners. The behavioral anecdotes he offered as evidence have equivalents among "traditional" owners (Hoffmann, "Citizens," pp. 295–298).

8. *SR* #3619, 4817, 6224; LN, fols. 46r–47r; Heyne, *Bisthum*, II, 541–542; Schulte, "Kostenblut," pp. 251–255; RF, II, 621–622; Grünhagen, "Protokolle," pp. 136–137; RB, fols. 8r and 9r.

9. One short-lived abbot of St. Mary, Jacob Steyner (1416), had previous managerial experience, though the abbey's later chronicler thought it inappropriate that he had been "simplicianus . . . eo quod semper allodia rexit" (*ChronBMV*, pp. 215–216). St. Mary's *advocati* were laymen (RB, fol. 9r), but the bishop of Lebus had a cleric as "provisor" at Borek in 1394 (Wohlbrück, II, 21–22). For lay and clerical agents of St. Clare see *SR* #4817 and 6224.

10. *SR* #4870b and RB, fols. 10r–10v are the transcript of a church court's inquiry and a tax return, not the normal run of texts concerning lay lordships.

11. *LFE*; WAP, AMW, K 113; *UD*, pp. 252–269; Ludat, *Stiftsregister*; "QBBB," pp. 210–225.

12. *LFE* B28; "QBBB," p. 196. Compare treatments of *Szczytniki* in WAP, AMW, K113, fols. 7v–8r; Opatowice in Ludat, *Stiftsregister*, p. 37; and Rynakowice in "QBBB," p. 211. Presentation of lordship as statements of what existed and what it should yield is parallelled in the public sphere by the format of *LB* and of a fragmentary manuscript preliminary to RB (WAP, AMW, C 27).

13. LN, fol. 368r; WAP. AMW, G 3, fol. 13v; Grünhagen, "Protokolle," pp. 136–137.

14. *DT*, pp. 65–66. Compare *DT*, pp. 71–72, and LN, fol. 385r.

15. A key text from the 1430s, the rental book of the Holy Spirit Hospital (HGZ), contains its first yearly account in 1431. It earlier has the form of a chartulary or a survey.

16. *HPR*, pp. 43, 46–49, 58, 64, 72–75, 77–83, 85, and 87.

17. *HPR*, pp. 116–117, and compare pp. 105–109.

18. *HPR*, pp. 129–130.

19. In government records the earliest extant income accounts are the *exactio* returns from the 1360s so confusingly reproduced in *LB* #416–450 (and tabulated in Matzen-Stöckert, pp. 434–438) and RB. Both derive from the city's administration of the duchy.

20. For what follows see especially in Figure 6.3b and Table 6.3.

21. Nothing around Wrocław suggests a use of cereal rents for commercial purposes as by townsmen with land then in Brandenburg (Engel and Zientara, pp. 147–187). The trend to cash payments argues that lords here wanted more liquid receipts.

22. *LFE* B35; *LB* #305; "QBBB," pp. 212 and 223–225. Totals here given correct one arithmetical error in the text.

23. *LFE* B376. The other entry for Radoszkowice in *LFE*, B10, seems to reflect a later situation when most episcopal rights had been let out to a lay sublord.

24. "QBBB," pp. 215 and 224.

25. *LFE* B33; "QBBB," pp. 196 and 211. The rent-free lands of the parish priest were not listed in either survey and those of the schulz only for his service and meal payments in 1421/25. Compare *LB* #13.

26. *UD*, p. 263, #4.

27. The lands and tithe rights of the bishop in the Wrocław duchy were about 1420 to yield him before expenses at least 978 marks and 363 malder a year ("QBBB," pp. 210–225).

28. *SR* #2382 and 6150. At lower consumption levels 13 rental mansi and a half share of lordship over the schulz in Klecina were to support eight disabled poor in the Corpus Christi hospital (*SR* #5945).

29. *SR* #3391 and 3400; *UD*, pp. 30–31.

30. *SR* #6976. Compare *SR* #5617, 6471 and 6785; RF, II, 626.

31. A Polish ordinance of 1474 made five marks annual income the threshold for cavalry rather than infantry service and twenty marks the boundary between light and heavy horse (Górski, "Rycerstwo," pp. 832–834). Around Wrocław this would have been unrealistic even a century earlier.

32. Even in the fourteenth century inheritance did not have to split individual properties. Between 1359 and 1408 Solna passed whole through three generations of Schwarzes (RF, II, 901–909).

33. *CdM*, VII, 616–617, #847–850; *RS*, II #798; RF, I, 175–182. See also *SR*, #6040, 6618, and 6911; *UD*, pp. 21–23; RF, III, 2337–2357.

34. RF, III, 306–311. For comparable behavior elsewhere, see RF, I, 399–406; II, 702–730; III, 321–324.

35. RF, II, 925–933; III, 2069–2081 and 2428–2444.

36. RF, II, 702–730.

37. RF, I, 255–262. Perhaps because citizens could endow with other than land, knights and owner-occupiers predominate among known cases where a dower fragmented a lordship. More such are *SR*, #5935, 5936, 6032, 6440, and 6979 and RF, I, 175–182; II, 763–767 and 774–782; IV, 2717–2724.

38. See Chapter 5 above. In 1347 the canons leased out the village of Święte for the same financial reasons (*RS*, I, #564).

39. *SR* #2316; *LFE* D6 and D25. More and later fiefs from the bishop are in *LFE* B10, B26, B28, B32, and B35; *UBB*, #283; *RBM*, 8:1, #61; 7:2, 372–373, #602; "QBBB," p. 211. Such intermediate personal authority over other members of the elite, common in the medieval

West, was rare in Silesia and Poland, where even simple knights normally depended directly on the prince (Wojciechowski, "Condition," pp. 695–98). For other clerics with elite tenants see WAA II, IV a 1 or *SR* #6073.

40. RF, I, 469. Compare *SR* #4964.

41. RF, III, 2409–2425. For comparable exercise of lordship by sublords on church properties see *SR* #2355 and 2386; WAA II, IX Piłczyce; Urban, *Wykaz AAW*, #726; *RS*, I, #575.

42. *SR* #4104 and 5352; RF, I, 23v, and III, 2118; LN, fol. 377r. Other subordinate lords operate more or less freely in *SR* #1397, 2608, 2609, 3050, 3415, 3904, 3905, 6073, and 6903; *RBM*, 7:2, 372–373, #602; *RS*, I, #621, and II, #515; LN, fols. 469v–471v; WAA II, IV a 1; WAA II, IX Piłczyce.

43. *SR* #3619.

44. *ChronBMV*, pp. 199–200. See also LN, fol. 470v.

45. Discussion here is purposely limited to pledges and sales of rents in the context of lords handling land. Roles of credit and debt in the countryside are treated in Chapter 9. For comparative legal perspectives see Planitz; Noonan, pp. 154–164; Lesiński, *Kupno renty*.

46. In the 1390s Peter of Milino used both to pay off an old debt to Franz Schreiber, and Bishop Wenceslas, "forced by need," sold a large *census* on Wilkowice to St. Mary (*DT*, pp. 12–13; LN, fol. 384r–385r). Earlier see *SR* #5832 and 5901 and RF, II, 925.

47. For examples, *SR* #6179, 6471 and 6976; RF, I, 155, 175–182; II, 702–730, 817–826; IV, 2914–2933, 2942–2958; Jesuiter VI:I, #57.

48. In December 1336 Albert Haze gave Jaśkowice to secure John and Heinemann Gallicus against possible losses from their guaranteeing his payment of 30 marks to Nicholas de Glogovia by the next Michaelmas (*SR* #6517). See also *SR* #5614, 5617, and 5983.

49. *SR* #5614 and 5679. Compare RF, I, 214.

50. Jesuiter, VI:I, #8 and #58; VII:III, #11 (20) and (24); V:IX, #12; RF, III, 2155 [258]-264.

51. *DT*, pp. 158–159. For additional examples of the terms of rents, see *SR* #5936; *UD*, pp. 23–26 and 32–33; *DT*, pp. 19–20; RF, I, 287 and 399–402; II, 626–634; III, 2409–2425; IV, 2914–2930.

52. On mills (RF, IV, 2805 and III, 2409–2425) and on arable (RF, I, 133–139; II, 626–631; IV, 2717–2724 and 2841–2852).

53. RF, I, 52v–54v; II, 702–730; III, 2428–2444; *LB*, #83. For more good-sized and/or frequent sales around the same time, see *SR*, #6175, 6204, and 6768; RF, II, 774–782; IV, 2717–2724, 2914–2922, 2923–2930, 2938–2940, and 3039–3059; *UD*, pp. 25–26.

54. *LBU*, I, 71; Korn, *Gewerberecht*, pp. 96–97. The city sold annuities at interest slightly below that paid by rural property owners, but the rate also fell slowly (Beyer, pp. 121–122). Friedensburg, *Münzgeschichte*, II, 69–70, confused rates in different forms of credit and loans to princes (inherently risky) with and ones against the incomes of more ordinary landowners.

55. For examples see *SR* #5191, 5742, 5743, 5903, and 6004; *BUB* #144, and *RBM*, IV, #1345–1346.

56. *SR* #6584. See also *SR* #5730 and 5874; Beyer, p. 116; *UD*, p. 154.

57. *SR* #3810.

58. *SR* #5742 and RF, II, 901–909. See also Dyhernfurth, pp. 25–29 and RF, IV, 2740–2769.

59. Debts in the 1350s and sales in the 1360s at Sadków are in RF, III, 2428–2444. For more examples see RF, II, 774–782, and IV, 2841–2852; *SR* #4066, 4290, 4345, 4346, 4405, 4421, and 4500.

60. *SR* #5926 and *DT*, pp. 158–159. For more cases see *SR* #5924, 6048, 6175, 6395, and 6396; *UD*, pp. 155–158; WAA II, V B 2c; Urban, *Wykaz AAW*, #519, 544, and 612.

61. RF, I, 399–406. Also WAA I, III d 2, 36–37.

62. Dyhernfurth, p. 27; RF, III, 2000.

63. *DT*, p. 54; WAA II, V B 2b; Kindler, pp. 196–197.

64. RF, IV, 2596–2612.

65. RF, IV, 2925.

66. *SR* #6371; WAA II. IX Piłczyce. I omit conditional sales or delayed payments as in *SR* #5994 and 5995; RF, II, 642–659;

67. *SR* #5845 and 3232. The Gluboses also liquidated their holding at Kobierzyce in a setting of debts (p. 152 above).

68. Pfeiffer, *Patriziat*, pp. 203–205 and 317, blamed rising land prices and rapid turnover

of properties on the distinctively speculative behavior of Wrocław citizens, driven by a capitalist mercantile mentality. His hypothesis is echoed in Eistert, "Wüstungen," p. 138, and by Heck in Maleczyński, *Historia Śląska*, I:2, 56. The error in this view of price movements has been established above, as were parallels in various kinds of behavior between citizens and other lords (whom Pfeiffer never studied).

69. RF, II, 675–699, 975, 1061–1069, and 2300–2317. Pfeiffer used no specific cases to diagnose fast deals as speculative.

70. The label by Pfeiffer, *Patriziat*, p. 204, who reports only the nominal prices. Other information from RF, I, 187–194.

71. All from the chartulary, WAA I, IV a 8, fols. 95v–96r. In *Patriziat*, p. 204, Pfeiffer mentions only some of these sales, wrongly assigns those between the two farms, and gives no source for his information. See also *DT*, pp. 7–8.

The histories of *Bartuszowice* and *Zdanów*, two small places later merged to Stary Śleszów and offered by Karl Eistert ("Wüstungen," pp. 138–142) as examples of citizens "flipping" land for speculative gains, also fail on closer examination to sustain that interpretation. Lordship over *Bartuszowice* was fragmented by the family of a minor knight, Arnold of Turów, and another knight with urban connections, Henry of Molnsdorf, reconsolidated it. *Zdanów*, was gathered up after 1345 by a consortium linked by kinship with the Dompnig family, and then passed to one member, Peter Beyer, who probably carried out the actual merger. (Eistert did not know of Beyer's membership in the original consortium.) See RF, I, 15r–15v, 80v, and III, 2300–2317, 2497. In both cases, then, the citizen owners showed long-term interest in improving their lordships.

72. RF, I, 76v–79r.

73. As noted (before Pfeiffer's book appeared) by the posthumously published antiquarian Rüffler, p. 124.

74. RF, I, 487–495. See a like case in RF, III, 270–272.

75. RF, III, 297–300 and I, 45r–47r. Compare RF, I, 214–220.

76. RF, I, 473–478. For more partitioning sales by nobles see *SR* #5609, and RF, III, 2409–2425; IV, 2662–2692.

77. WAP, AMW, Q 154, 1, fol. 7r. Compare RF, I, 20v–22v.

78. LN, fols. 471r–472r.

79. WAA I, IV a 8, fol. 95v: "videtur quod ex duis allodiis quodlibet de vj mansis predictus franciscus a duis personis emptis et comprentis villa fabricavit. . . ."—as written in 1441.

80. I rejoiced to find parallel articulation of the concept in Berman, pp.43–46. As elsewhere in this chapter, consolidation is a matter of individual lordships and distinct from the accumulation of properties by the estate builders of chapter 7.

81. *SR* #3331. See parallel cases in *SR* #4932 and 5669; *SR* #4066, 4345, 4346, 4405, and 4421; RF, I, 1r; RF, I, 370–381; RF, II, 675–699; RF, III, 2428–2444; RF, II, 774–782, and I, 76v–79r.

82. RF, II, 961–977 (transactions in 1417 and 1418 were not at Piotrowice but at Pietrzykowice and *Piotrowice Małe*). More knightly consolidators appear in RF, II, 2131–2139; RF, III, 270–277; RF, I, 454–455; *SR* #5653.

83. *SR*, #5819, 5988, and 6031 (the last is corrected *Ibid.*, p. 297), and RF, I, 239.

84. LN, fols. 377r and 472v. See also Heyne, *Bisthum*, I, 603 note; *RS*, II, #466, 559, 664, and 750; RF, III, 2118; *ChronBMV*, 183 and 214, and Fibiger, p. 305. But the Hospital of Corpus Christi did buy Borek in pieces from three previous owners (RF, I, 44v; *DT*, pp. 2–4; *BUB* #279).

85. *LB*, #349 and 350; RF, II, 675–699, and IV, 2894–2895; RB, fol. 2r; KLM, fol. 3.

86. Between 1300 and 1425 twenty-one place names in the duchy either vanish or cease to refer to a separate place; seventeen are last recorded between 1360 and 1425. Fifteen of the twenty-one (71 percent) were Wrocław district demesne farms, most of which became part of a neighboring village.

87. Peter Bayer consolidated Stary Śleszów in the 1350s–60s and then joined to it *Zdanów* and *Bartuszowice* LB #12, 277, and 278; RF, I, 15r–15v and 80v, and III, 2300–2317 and 2497; RB, fol. 4r; KLM, fol. 11). Eistert, "Wüstungen," pp. 137–142, confuses events of the 1360s and misses later ownership and taxation evidence to argue wrongly that these were abandoned because of either citizen "capitalism" or damage during the Hussite wars. Other citizen lords are seen expanding their properties by merging nearby and smaller ones in: RF, I, 206–212, and III, 2151–2154; LN, fols. 370v–371r and 359v, with RF, I, 19r; *LB*, #315 and

543, RF, I, 187–194, and IV, 2083–2085, and RB, fol. 2v; *LB*, #92, 158, 231, and 232, with RF, III, 2510–2520, *DT*, pp. 165–168, *RBM*, VIII: 4, #1154, RB, fol. 5r, KLM, fol. 13, and Domański, *Nazwy miejscowe*, #263 and 308).

88. *LB*, #113–114 and 368–370; RF, I, 430–431, II, 783, and III, 2456–2461; *SR*, #3329; *LFE* B51; *NLChron*, pp. 98 note 49, 107, 119–120 note 83, and 124 note 92.

89. RF, I, 20v–22v; *LB*, #326. No member of the family is ever called citizen, knight, or by any other designation of status, although some daughters later married into knightly families.

90. RF, IV, 3077–3083, with more evidence in RF, I, 147–154, II, 635–639, and IV, 3038; *UD*, p. 12; LN, fols. 128r–129r. To follow the evolution of place names here, see Domański, *Nazwy miejscowe*, #106, 122, 172, and 296. Hoffmann, "Nazwy," pp. 17–24, details how a contemporary of the Zweibrodts, Martin of Gądów, made from two other demesnes another village named for its founder, Gądów "at Jaszkotle."

91. Find noble creators of new lordships in *SR* #4967; RF, I, 187 194, II, 901–909, and IV, 2083–2085.

92. WAP, Rep. 15, 228, p. 54, describes it in the early 1530s.

93. RF, I, 322–328 and IV, 2938–2940 and 2796–2800. Compare RF, IV, 2632–2640.

94. Menzel, *Jura ducalia*, well covers the institutional phenomenon in late medieval Silesia; most of his conclusions are followed here. But because Menzel's main systematic study was of church estates, he may postdate the practical completion of it. Noted below are departures of developments around Wrocław from Menzel's province-wide findings. On the general growth of landlord jurisdiction over east-central European peasants see Blum's classic, pp. 823–826, and compare the more economic Makkai, pp. 225–238, and Kamiński, pp. 253–268.

95. *SR* #4589 and 4968. More are *SR* #4554, 5635, 5879, 5970, 6326, and 6842; Wutke, "Zwei Urkunden," p. 231; RF, I, 279.

96. *SR* #6209 and RF, IV, 2942–2958. Compare also *SR* #4137, 4744, 5125 (still pledged 20 years later in *LB* #517), 6209, and 6316; RF, I, 34v–36v; III, 279–295; II, 626–634.

97. RF, I, 58v–61r. See also *SR*, #3268, 3704, 3943, and 6586; RF, I, 473–478; II, 1024–1028; IV, 2841–2852.

98. The extant record for some settlements is not always consistent. At Jarząbkowice, for instance, Paschco bought the mint money from King John in 1345 but five and six years later sold the lordship with full high justice and exemption from all taxes, a description then repeated in subsequent coveyances (RF, I, 214–220; *RBM*, IV, #1596). Compare also labile terminology in RF, I, 1r–3r and 76v–79r; III, 279–295; IV, 2596–2612.

99. Bobertag, "Gerichtsbücher," pp. 168–169; RF,, I, 382–390. Other records of private ownership of taxes before capital jurisdiction include: *SR* #6586 and RF, II, 702–730; RF, IV, 2661–2692; *SR* #5127 and RF, I, 399–406; *SR* #3873, 5384, and 5723, with *LB*, #183 and 516, and RF, I, 442–450; *SR* #6669 and RF, I, 20v–22v; RF, II, 590–592; RF, III, 279–295).

100. *SR* #4748, 3760, 5127, 5164, and 5317; *RBM*, 7:1, #122. Evidence from the duchy does not support Menzel's assertion that especially townspeople then preferred fiscal to judicial privileges (*Jura ducalia*, pp. 155–157).

101. RF, IV, 2632–2640. Compare like terms in RF, I, 34v–36v.

102. Unlike other Silesian areas mentioned in Menzel, *Jura ducalia*, pp. 77–79.

103. *SR* #3568 and 4570. Compare *SR* #5892.

104. *SR* #6175; RF, II, 615–619 and 1024–1028.

105. RF, IV, 2796–2800. For other private dealings see *DT*, pp. 12–13; *SR* #4526 (compare *SR* #3853).

106. *SR* #4137.

107. *SR* #4160 and 5143; *NLChron*, p. 105 note 61. For more tension between land- and justice-lords see *SR* #6111 or 6767.

108. Henry IV gave the bishop in 1290 the first unlimited transfer of ducal jurisdiction to a landowner, but it covered only the church's territory around Nysa and Otmuchów (*LBU*, II, 198–200). For what follows see Menzel, *Jura ducalia*, pp. 81–83.

109. *UBB*, #269–270 and 275.

110. *UBB*, #276, #278, and #283. The charters of conveyance, all dated 3 Kalends January 1349, appear in LN, fols. 352r–354v and 373r–375v (*RS*, II, #189–197). In the 1430s Abbot Jodocus of St. Mary followed a similar policy and bought the ducal rights over its Tyniec Mały and Jarosławice (*SR* #6111; Rössler, #310–311; RF, IV, 2796–2800, and *ChronBMV*, pp. 226–228 and 232). For complicated struggles and buy-outs on the lands of

Lubiąż see Wutke, "Wilxen," pp. 151–160, which better accords with extant texts than does Seidel, *Beginn*, pp. 89–94. The authentic records are *SR* #5807, 6326, and 6717; *LB*, #500; RF, III, 2445–2453; IV, 2931–2934; Wutke, "Zwei Urkunden," p. 231; Wattenbach, "Dittmans Chronik," p. 281.

111. RF, II, 952–960 and 1024–1028. See also RF, III, 2428–2444, and IV, 2841–2852. Even the owner-operators at Krępice bought from the Radaks their dues in lieu of service which King John had alienated (*UD*, pp. 200–203, #6–7 and 13).

112. Menzel, *Jura ducalia*, p. 152 seems to qualify his general belief in a process incomplete before the sixteenth century with a passing remark about the union of landlord and ducal authority in the Wrocław duchy during the fourteenth. This chronology was as well the impression of one of the first and most careful students of the Wrocław duchy land records, Bobertag, in "Gerichtsbücher," p. 114. Reiter, pp. 56–59 found the same in the district of Kąty.

Still the proposition that the surviving evidence displayed in Figure 8.2 approximates the rate and timing of a real process is not self evident. The sample covering only 139 places looks too small and haphazard, especially with its sharp reduction in new sites with evidence after about 1440.

Defence of the proposition begins from the fact that in the mid-sixteenth century, when scholars agree that Silesian landowners had full jurisdiction over their peasants (Menzel, *Jura ducalia*, p. 144; Heck in *Historia Śląska*, I:2, 85–87), landlords with ducal rights can be *proven* only in those 139 sites in the duchy. But 110 of those 139 had those rights by 1425 and in that year only 12 places were surely under a jurisdiction not that of the landowner. We note further in support that (1) the positive documentation is itself so inconsistent from one text to another that ducal jurisdiction could easily have belonged to owners elsewhere without ever being recorded; (2) even where early charters explicitly reserved ducal justice while granting fiscal incomes, lords with jurisdiction can later be found without any new grant; and (3) those places for which good written records of ducal rights are extant were mainly large settlements (86% villages) where the rights were most valuable and hence should have been longest retained by the dukes. All this argues for the undocumented cases coming with or before the documented 139.

Alternatively, it is unlikely that many lords acquired ducal rights later than the documented cases, viz. in illicit silence during the mid-1400s. (1) Those putative lords never tried to legitimate those usurpations as even illegal claimants earlier had done. This would have made sense only if by the fifteenth century most lords could have been assumed to hold those rights. (2) King Mathias and his officials, who worked intensely to revive royal authority during the 1480s, never once raised the (thoroughly inviting) issue of recent private appropriation of indisputably sovereign prerogatives to tax and judge.

Hence the extant evidence, even when treated conservatively by requiring explicit mention that the landowner had judicial rights, probably does more or less accurately represent the rate at which ducal rights came into owners' hands. In well more than a simple majority of the duchy's rural settlements this had happened by the time of the Hussite wars.

113. *SR* #4554, 4570, 4574, 4585, 4589, and 4631.

114. *SR* #5800 and 5875; RF, I, 214–220; III, 2379–2388; IV, 2740–2769; *RBM*, IV, #1582.

115. RF, I, 58v–61r, and III, 279–295. That five places first appear in 1351 is, however, mere coincidence, for all are passing mentions that the lordship included ducal jurisdiction.

116. *LB* #406a–415a and #507–522; Matzen-Stöckert, pp. 455–457.

117. Compare *LB* #514 with *SR* #5442 and *LB* #416. See also reservations of justice in *RBM*, VII:1, #122.

118. For those not earlier mentioned see *SR* #3684, 4554, 5800, 6060, and 6834; RF, I, 174–175; III, 2379–2388; IV, 2740–2769.

119. As elsewhere, compare Menzel, *Jura ducalia*, pp. 145–152.

120. Bobertag, "Gerichtsbücher," pp. 166–167; RF, IV, 2632–2640. Nicholas Sittin got justice at Bielany in 1341 but not at Solna, which he held 1344–56 (RF, I, 20v–22v, and II, 901–909).

121. *SR* #4968 was confirmed in RF, I, 330–346; RF, I, 58v–61r. See also RF, III, 279–295 and RUL, #5–6.

122. RF, III, 2069–2081. Compare RF, II, 626–634.

123. RF, III, 2012–2021 and 2428–2444.

124. *KdS* #115; *SUB*, I, #328. Compare also *KdS* #112–114 and 118; *SUB*, I, #325–327 and 333. The Lubiąż forgeries are fully discussed in Menzel, *Jura ducalia*, pp. 124–129.

125. *SR* #3138, 4223, 4224, 4570, and 5892.

126. *KdS* #242 and 355; *SUB*, I, #340 and 361. Menzel, *Jura ducalia*, pp. 120–124, treats the literature.

127. Heyne, *Bisthum*, II, 771 and 774–775; Haeusler, *Geschichte*, pp. 375–376; Sommersberg, I:2, 1015–1017.

128. *SR* #1604, 2893, 4571, 4574 and 4631. Note, too, Charles's grants to a favored cleric, Bishop Thomas of Sarepta, in 1364 (*RI* VIII:1, #4051; Pfotenhauer, "Weihbischöfe," p. 249; Heyne, *Bisthum*, II, 204–205.

129. *SR* #4828 and 6176; *RS*, I, #339; *NLChron*, pp. 98 and 107. Schulte, "Kostenblut," pp. 215–216, is definitive.

130. Schulte, "Kostenblut," pp. 255–258; Menzel, *Jura ducalia*, pp. 129–134. Elsewhere in the Wrocław duchy the Premonstratensians bought these rights between 1350 and the 1420s (Schulte, "Kostenblut," pp. 214–215; *NLChron*, p. 105 note 61; RF, IV, 3015). But at Wierzbno, where dealings among Duke Louis of Brzeg and various Wrocław duchy knights and citizens with the *iura ducalia* had for a time in the mid-fourteenth century caused the village to be transferred to the Wrocław duchy, the abbey gained them only in 1502. For St. Mary and Lubiąż see note 110 above.

131. Menzel, *Jura ducalia*, pp. 22 and 79, acknowledging that this meaning was articulated long ago by Gustav A. H. Stenzel himself. But to agree that "der spätmittelalterliche Übergang der *iura ducalia* von den Landesherrn an die Grundherrn die Dominialverfassung in Schlesien wesentlich grundgelegt hat" (p. 22) is not to take the anachronistic position that fourteenth century lords got these rights with that long-term purpose in mind. Their actions must be perceived in terms of their own age, which neither designed nor built "Gutsherrschaft."

132. Synodal statutes certainly used in the diocese of Wrocław are available as edited by Stenzel in *Übersicht*, 1841, pp. 180–182. For the 1290s–1330s dispute at Siemidrożyce see *SR* #2492, 2497, 4803a, 4858c–d, 4861a–f, 4870b–h, and 4946a.

133. Mentioned in *UBB*, introduction, p. xvi.

134. Wohlbrück, I, 456 note, corrected in *SR* #6237.

135. In this the duchy was like the rest of the region. See Mularczyk, "Patronatu;" Kurze, pp. 246–250 and 460–465; Michael, *Patronat*, pp. 248–251; Loesch, "Forschungen," pp. 160–163; Schmid, "Grundung" and "Pfarrorganisation;" Klassen, *Nobility*, pp. 27–46.

136. *SR* #3904. See also RF, I, 20v, 416; III, 2367; *BUB* #300.

137. *SR* #2580–2589.

138. Text in Heyne, *Bisthum*, I, 454–455 note. Dispute over tithes around Siemidrożyce spurred creation of the new church there(*SR* #2631 and Stenzel's edition in *Übersicht*, 1841, pp. 179–180). Trzebnica's forgers made sure patronage was included in their version of the abbey's rights to Chomiąża (*KdS* #355 = *SUB*, I, #361).

139. *SR* #4594, notarized in *SR* #4757 and confirmed by Charles IV (*RI*, 8:1, #1474 and 6069; *RS*, II, #612 and 654). Compare the parish of Borek Strzeliński in Ludat, *Stiftsregister*, p. 36.

140. *UD*, pp. 139–140; Fibiger, pp. 302–303; *SR* #3330; RF, III, 279–295.

141. *SR* #5593; RF, III, 306–311. A 1428 conveyance of Mokra traces lordship and *Kirchlehn* through five successive owners (RUL #10). Pfeiffer, *Patriziat*, p. 422, notes the careful formulae used to avoid simony when patronage was part of a sale.

142. RF, II, 961–977. See also *SR* #5604; RF, I, 330–346, III, 2012–2021, and IV, 2942–2958.

143. RF, IV, 2632–2640.

144. Heyne, *Bisthum*, II, 700 and 704; Fibiger, pp. 305–306.

145. For three cycles of Chrzanów, ca1250–1417, see *SUB*, II, #413; *SR* #6466a, 6624, 6625, and 6775; RF, II, 675–699, and IV, 2894–2895; *LB*, #349–350; RB, fol. 2r; *UD*, p. 12, #15. The two and a half at Raszków are in *SR*, #5143 and RF, III, 2061–2068.

146. RF, IV, 2870–2879, and I, 358–367. For a wide variety of lordship cycles as well documented as those outlined above, see *SR* #3051, 3854, 5164, 5427, 5701, 5937, 5964, and 6037 (Gaj); RF, I, 1r–3v (Olbrachtowice), 58v–61r (Brzezica), 76v–79r (Damianowice), 195–196 (Gurse), 214–220 (Jarząbkowice), 330–346 (Jaksonów), 473–478 (Karczyce); II, 731–735 (Marszowice), 830–839 (Mrozów), 917–924 (Pasterzyce), 961–977 (Piotrowice),

980–981, 956, and 961–977 (*Piotrowice Małe*); III, 270–277 (Zakrzyce); 279–295 (Święta Katarzyna), 306–311 (Skałka), 2044–2048 (Ramułtowice), 2069–2081 (Ratyń), 2300–2317 (Stary Śleszów), 2428–2444 (Sadków); IV, 2653–2660 (Ozorowice), 2740–2769 (Strachowice).

147. *BUB* #17; *SR*, #1257, 1545, 2623, 2710, 3409, 3410a, 5047, 5370, 5617, and 6226; RF, II, 770–771, 827, and 850; Fibiger, pp. 303–305, 311, and 313; *UD*, pp. 145–147 and 248–251; *LB*, #22, 70, and 322; RB, fol. 8v; Dittrich, "Kreuzherren," pp. 124–127.

Chapter 9

1. As rediscovered by Raftis in *Tenure*.

2. *UD*, introductory pp. 53–59 and text pp. 197–229; compare RF, I, 498–507. For the other sites mentioned, see RF, I, 487–495; II, 675–699, 1029–1044; III, 854–859. Further instances at Smolec Mały (RF, III, 2337–2357) and Zakrzyce (RF, III, 270–277) are not to be construed as completing an exhaustive list, for elsewhere they may have gone before adequate records begin.

3. *UD*, p. 211. As late as 1443 the biggest holding in the half of Krępice which then paid tax contained only 4 mansi and eight more averaged 1½ (KLM, fol. 32). Its largest earlier farm had no more than 6 mansi (*UD*, pp. 204–205).

4. RF, II, 1029–1044 and I, 487–495. Compare RF, III, 854–859.

5. See for explicit midcentury mention of holdings "with feudal law," RF, II, 675–699 or *UD*, p. 209.

6. Compare RF, I, 487–499, with the terms of the charters of 1282 (*Ibid.*, not in *SR*) and 1284 (*SR* #1856). Other escheats and regrants may be found in *UD*, pp. 214 and 218.

7. *UD*, pp. 201, 203, and 208; RF, II, 676; *LB* #452, 463–464. Service building bridges was, however, unique to Krępice.

8. RF, I, 487–495 and II, 675–699. At Chrzanów, Krępice, and Okrzeszyce landholders under feudal law were subject to regulated three course rotations (RF, II, 675–699, and 854–859; *UD*, 205 and 216). Compare *RS*, I, #972, and RF, III, 2049–2060.

9. *SR* #4227; RF, II, 1029–1044. Nothing suggests any blood relationship among the three lines. For the same at Krajków see *SR* #1856 and 5705; *RS*, I, #764; RF, I, 481 and 487–495. Other names recall nearby villages, as RF, III, 854–859 and 2337–2357.

10. Compare in Chapters 3 and 7 above.

11. *SR* #4290.

12. RF, II, 854–859. In RB, fol. 4r, John Krischwicz with 3 mansi sounds like the last owner-operator at Okrzeszyce. Two other such cases are in RF, II, 675–699 and 1029–1044.

13. RF, III, 270–277.

14. For examples of service and of payments in lieu of it, see *LFE* B 376; *SR* #2596 and 5686; RF, IV, 2820–2837; *UD*, pp. 144–145 and 263; Schulte, "Kostenblut," p. 215; *BUB*, pp. 236–237; WAA I, II e 11, 81–83 and 129. Lords invest schulzen in LN, fol. 25v; *RS*, II, #169; WAP, Rep. 55, #40; Wohlbrück, II, 403.

15. WAP Rep. 135, E113f, 3–4; Kindler, pp. 48 and 50.

16. *SR* #3098, 3996 and 4459; WAP Rep. 135, E113f, 3; Kindler, p. 48; RF, II, 702–730; *NLChron*, pp. 118–119 note 81.

17. LN, fols. 143r–144r; Wohlbrück, *Bisthum Lebus*, II, 21–22.

18. *UD*, p. 46. Comparable interactions in other places are RF, I, 99 and 103–126, and *RS*, II, #169. Involvement of wives in several such cases may hint at endogamous marriages. Firm evidence for this is not available from the Wrocław duchy, but it would replicate behavior among the village officials and wealthy peasants further west. See Bader, *Dorfgenossenschaft*, pp. 284–291, and "Dorfpatriziate." Certainly women at times were schulzen in their own right. "Kunigunda, scultetissa in Schonvelt," sold a rent on it in her own name and that of her sons sometime in the 1350s (RF, III, 2405–2408) and others like "Agneta Schultissin zu Krolkowitz" or "Katherina Schultissynne von Michilwicz" also acted in the absence of a male with the title (RF, IV, 2733–2737, and Stobbe, 1866, pp. 179–180).

19. *UD*, pp. 144–145.

20. *LB*. Compare Matzen-Stöckert, pp. 354–359.

21. RB lists 211 places of which 139 had schulzen, but gives the size of land for only 47;

the mean is 2.3 mansi. KLM mentions schulzen in 148 of its 235 places, but again the mean size of 2.7 mansi is based only on the 16 with quantified entries.

22. Tz-S, pp. 583–585.

23. Stints for schulzen at 15 more places appear in *SR* #1968, 2596, and 6826; *RS*, II, #169 amd 917; LN, fols. 143r–144; Wohlbrück, II, 21–22, and 403; *BUB*, pp. 236–237; RF, I, 287–301, and II, 1024–1028; *DT*, p. 233; HGZ, fol. 3v; *UD*, pp. 69–70; *UFO*, p. 136. General privileges at three more are in RF, I, 103–126; RUL, #18; Kindler, pp. 48–50; and WAP Rep. 135, E113f, 4. This surely underrepresentative sample supports no regional or chronological patterns in rearing of sheep by schulzen. Another agricultural privilege, rent-free possession of extensive acreage for cultivation of hops, enriched fourteenth century schulzen at Małkowice (*SR* #3098; RF, II, 702–730).

24. For taverns and mills in the hands of schulzen see *SR* #3098 and 3138; Ts-S, #15; *UD*, p. 16; RF, II, 702–730, III, 2097–2113, and IV, 2820–2837; Ludat, *Bistum Lebus*, pp. 98–99. Crafts are listed in WAP, Rep. 55, #40; Tz-S, pp. 583–585; *UFO*, p. 136; *SR* #1968 and 3138; *UD*, p. 16; *DT*, p. 233; RF, IV, 2820–2837.

25. For examples see *HPR*, p. 129; *UD*, p. 263; *DT*, p. 233; RF, I, 16v, 76v–79f [sic], and 418–419; RF, III, 2097–2113.

26. *SR* #5982 and RF, I, 266–267; *SR* #6514. For other cases, see RF, II, 590–592, and IV, 2740–2769.

27. *SR* #3098 and RF, II, 702–730.

28. RF, II, 925–933, and see also I, 99–102.

29. RF, II, 917–924.

30. RF, II, 810–814. Also see RF, I, 52v–54v and III, 2481–2496.

31. *HPR*, p. 106.

32. RF, I, 26v–29r, and III, 2300–2317.

33. *SR*, #6428 and 5615. For another case see RF, II, 866–875.

34. *SR*, #4481–4482; LN, fol. 300r–301r; and p. 000 below.

35. RF, I, 103–106.

36. *SR* #6259; Stobbe, 1866, pp. 179–180. See also WAP, Rep. 55, #40; RF, I, 267 and 287–301. A synod of the Gniezno province in 1357 forbade hereditary division of the scholtisei in church villages and required cash payments to younger heirs by the eldest (Opitz, p. 18).

37. *SR* #3996. For similar temporary or partial acquisitions of schulz holdings by local lords see Haeusler, *Geschichte*, p. 376; *SR* #6826; RF, III, 279–295; WAP, Rep. 135, E113f, 3–4. Pfeiffer, *Patriziat*, pp. 220–221, asserts a decline in schulz status and wealth beginning in the late fourteenth century, but almost all his evidence comes after the 1430s.

38. See Mendras, pp. 133–137.

39. Schulte, "Kostenblut," p. 255; *SR* #6589; RF, IV, 2966–2978; *DT*, pp. 158–159; *UD*, p. 46.

40. Schulte, "Kostenblut," pp. 254–255.

41. Frauenstadt, pp. 242–244. For examples in the Wrocław duchy see Tz-S, pp. 583–585; *SR* #5686; *UD*, pp. 69–70.

42. "Spreche abir eyn schultheis das her synem herren synen czins gegebin hette. . . ." Compare *SLR*, art. 84, with *SSp Landrecht*, I, 54 (the issue is proof of payment). See village collections in WAP Rep. 55, 40; *BUB*, pp. 236–237; Wohlbrück, II, 21–22.

43. RSC records in seven of the eleven years with adequate information between 1406 and 1421 the schulz of Radomierzyce handling tithes due from his village. Later the warden had collections made by a subordinate and did not say who actually paid.

44. RB—e.g. for Stabłowice at the head of this chapter.

45. In general, Goerlitz, *Verfassung*, pp. 101–104 and *NRB*, pp. 30–32 and 243–244. For a case see *RS*, I, #764.

46. *NRB*, p. 263; Schulte, "Kostenblut," p. 255. Schulzen held four of the five seats on the cathedral chapter's similar court in 1374 (LN, fol. 46r).

47. *UD*, pp. 159–160. Compare Schulte, "Kostenblut," p. 250, or *RS*, II, #318.

48. *SR* #5962; *NRB*, pp. 344–345; *DT*, pp. 54 and 158–159.

49. *DT*, p. 54. More cases in Grünhagen, "Preticz," p. 471; *UD*, p. 160; Pfotenhauer, *Kamenz*, pp. 35–36; LN, fols. 253r–253v.

50. *SR* #5714. Just outside the duchy the heirs of the schulz in Wawrzęcice refused tithes owned to the Domaniów church (*SR* #3496) and others led refusals near Świdnica (Unterlauff, pp. 353–354).

51. Concern here is with the socio-economic status and role of rural priests, not their spiritual capacities.

52. See pp. 228–230 above. Papal provisions to village churches near Wrocław occur in *SR* #3842 and Wagner, pp. 293–294.

53. RF, I, 450, and II, 615–619; Rössler, #293 and 298. Other country priests of noble origin are in *SR* #2613, 4653, 5230, 5444, and 6041; *LFE* D6 and D25; RF, I, 347; II, 817–826 and 925–933; III, 2061; 2097–2113; IV, 2700–2716.

54. *SR* #3330; RF, III, 279–295 and IV, 2595–2612; Pfeiffer, *Patriziat*, pp. 110, 177, and table 11. Compare Reinboth Watzinrode in RF, I, 29r–34r, and Pfeiffer, *Patriziat*, pp. 103–104.

55. Wagner, p. 293; Compare Peter Rhedern from Brzeg, appointed to Uraz by Holy Cross in the 1350s (Rössler, #240 and 258).

56. Kindler, pp. 192–193. For more exemplary ecclesiastical careers see *SR* #4861a–b, 4564, 5047, 5138, and 5370; Ptaśnik, ed., I, 356–368; *UD*, pp. 139–140; Engelbert, *Quellen*, p. 39.

57. Ludat, *Stiftsregister*, p. 36.

58. Heyne, *Bisthum*, I, 454–455. A papal provision to Piotrowice in 1371 (Wagner, p. 294) assessed it at 15 florins (ca 4.75 marks) per year. See also Kindler, pp. 192–193.

59. *LB* lists the lands of 68 churches in the duchy; they averaged 2.2 mansi and more than 70 percent were between 1.5 and 2.5 m. Compare Matzen-Stöckert, pp. 364–370. In RB and associated texts 31 glebes of known size average 2.1 m, and 28 in KLM, 2.0.

60. The standard is argued by Loesch, "Forschungen," pp. 160–162, and around Wrocław implied in Tz-S, pp. 426–427; *SR* #3763 and 5046; Heyne, *Bisthum*, II, 534–535; *LB* #176 and 179; HGZ, fols. 2v, 21v, etc.

61. *SR* #4861b and 5230; RF, IV, 2942–2958. The priest's general tax exemption was why his lands were noted in *LB*. Several RB entries (i.e. fols. 2v and 12v) specify that he did not pay.

62. HGZ, fol. 2v, 13r, where the local landowners were laymen.

63. *UFO*, p. 136; *LFE* B30 and B32; "QBBB," p. 196.

64. *SR* #3574, 3691, 4861a, 4861f, and 4870d, for examples.

65. *SR*, #5047; *RS*, II, #318; Klapper, pp. 163–164; Fibiger, pp. 302–303; *UD*, pp. 139–140; Heyne, *Bisthum*, I, 454–455; Görlich, *Vincenz*, p. 108 note 1; RF, III, 1097–2113; Ludat, *Stiftsregister*, p. 36.

66. Heyne, *Neumarkt*, p. 336. See also Dittrich, "Kreuzherren," pp. 153–154.

67. *SR* #6041; RF, III, 2061. For similar instances see *SR* #5653; RF, I, 347–354; 615–619, 817–826, and 925–933; III, 279–295 and 2097–2612 and 2700–2716; Heyne, *Bisthum*, I, 925–926; Rössler, #240, 293, and 298.

68. Heyne, *Bisthum*, II, 534–535; *SR* # 3763 and 3785; Heyne, *Neumarkt*, p. 336.

69. *SR* #5370 and 5047.

70. WAP Rep. 67, #679, 805, 806, and 816. See also Engelbert, *Quellen*, #131.

71. Heyne, *Bisthum*, II, 769–770.

72. *UD*, pp. 50–51. After an apparent agreement in January, 1433, the court in September held the case subject to ecclesiastical jurisdiction. See also Heyne, *Bisthum*, I, 454–455; Klapper, pp. 163–164.

73. *SR* #3574, 3691, 4403, 4728, 4861a, 4861f, 4870d, and 4920.

74. Heyne, *Bisthum*, II, 110–112. Papal tithes on clerical incomes were paid grudgingly about 1340 (Ptaśnik, I, 356–368) and in 1400 loudly protested by 41 priests of the Środa archpresbyterate (Jungnitz, "Statistik," pp. 387–402).

75. Examples include *SR* #2437, 2437, 2897, 4844a, 4858a–b, 4868a–b, 4870a–c and f, 4916a, 4907a, 4919a, 4924a, 4929a, 4930a, 4932a, 4936a, 5507, and 6096.

76. Stenzel, ed., *Catalogus*, pp. 251–252. Heck, "Hussitenaufstand," pp. 219–220, argues that Stephen was not then unusual in Silesia as a whole, but compare Urban, *Studia*, pp. 82–83.

77. Names are here as HGZ, fol. 12r. Compare 17r and 21r.

78. The earliest data from around Wrocław thus contradict the thesis of Kuhn, "Bauernhofgrössen," pp. 265–267, that since the time of *locatio* German tenants had significantly larger (2 mansi to 1) farms than did Poles. Kuhn assumed that modal farm sizes (and even most individual tenures) did not change between the 1200s and the 1700s. This goes against the evidence of Reiter, pp. 41–46, and of this and later chapters. But because records of peasant land before the Hussite wars come only as "snapshots" of a place at one date, they cannot be

tested for connections between farm size and changes in family composition, which the relatively free alienation and inheritance rights of the duchy should have fostered. Compare Berkner, pp. 398–418, and Goody, ed., *Developmental Cycle.*

79. Sommerfeldt, pp. 82–83.

80. LN, 46r–47r.

81. *DT*, p. 53; RW, S 96–97; HGZ, fol. 108v.

82. RW, S 52. *Peinliche sache* were excepted.

83. *UD*, pp. 148–151. The court found for the hospital.

84. LN, 375v–376r.

85. The case (*DT*, p. 54) was appealed to the *iudicium provinciale*, but all participants seem otherwise ordinary tenants.

86. RF, II, 1009–1017. In 1381 a peasant from Sulimów, Niczko Markard, bought six mansi at Wierzbno as a fief of the duke of Brzeg (Rössler, #924; RF, IV, 2596–2612).

87. In the words of the presumably fourteenth-century Środa code, the tenant must work with those "di her bekost mit siner spize unde mit lone; tut her is andirweide luetin czu czinze adir czu pflege, so ist her selbir eyn unrecht czins man deme gute." *NRB*, p. 188, differs only in dialect from *SSp Lehnrecht*, 60, 2.

88. *SLR*, art. 337 and 84 (pp. 190 and 152–153)—"Is en sal keyn czins man vor synen herren dulden obir synen czins den her iclichs tages jerlich gebin sal"—replicate *SSp Landrecht*, III, 79:1 and I, 54:1.

89. Compare *SLR*, art. 84 (pp. 152–153) to *SSp Landrecht*, I, 54:2–3.

90. *SLR*, art. 225 (p. 172) replicates *SSp Landrecht*, II, 59:1.

91. RW, L 56, summarizes an appeal (apparently of the mid-1400s) in which the Magdeburg court upheld claims by an unnamed Wrocław duchy village that their lord's imposition of larger fines was against established custom and therefore illegal.

92. *SLR*, art. 353 (p. 194) introduced common marriage property to Silesian law:
Nymt eyn schulteise adir eyn gebouwer der do gut vnd erbe hat. eyn weip. vnd stirbet das weip ane geburt des mannes. so sal alles das gut das si czu im bracht hat, halb bleiben bey dem manne. vnd halb bey iren neestin. vnd sullen en en vorbas me night habin enczusprechin. Stirbet aber das weip vnd lesit eliche kinder di si mit im gehabit hat. so sullen di kinder alle di gut di do uatir vnd mutir sint. halb nemen, vnd sullen halb bleibin bey dem vatir. Das selbe gleich her wedir ab der uatir stirbet ane geburt.
For a discussion see Gaupp, "Gütergemeinschaft."

93. Text and commentary on the bishop's code are in Gaupp, "Gütergemeinschaft," pp. 71–76, and in Tz-S, pp. 632–634. Compare Haeusler, *Geschichte*, pp. 306–307. For its use to determine descent of a tenure at Polanowice in 1418 see Goerlitz, "Recht," p. 151.

94. References abound to plural "heirs" and "children" and verify specific discussions of the form and process of division. See *SLR*, art. 353 (p. 194); Laband, ed., book 4, II:23 (p. 154); Gaupp, "Gütergemeinschaft," pp. 71–72. For nineteenth- and early twentieth-century peasant impartibility in Silesia see Huppertz, pp. 25–63 and map 1, or Hartke and Westermann.

95. Opitz, pp. 16–17, emphasized the limitation of the landowner's right to proper receipt of his rents as transmitted by the schulz and (pp. 44–79) showed that entry fines payable to the lord for his consent to transfer of tenant land were introduced in the late fifteenth and early sixteenth centuries. The earliest reference to landlord consent in RW, D 4–5, comes from 1454.

96. *SLR*, art. 225 (compare *SSp Landrecht*, II, 59:1).

97. Compare Tyc, p. 70, and RW, T 85–95 and U 22.

98. Müncheberg, pp. 21–35, and see also Carsten, p. 81.

99. *SR* #4861f; compare *SR* # 4861a. He went about 5 km.

100. This discussion surely minimizes both the frequency of migration (because only those described as migrants are countable) and the distances people moved (because the search for place names behind personal names has mostly been limited to Wrocław duchy sites). But the intent here is only to show that peasants in the duchy did exercise their rights of mobility.

101. *UD*, p. 214. Others came from Brzezina, Wojnowice, Mrozów, and Leśnica (*UD*, pp. 212–213 and 221–222).

102. Sommerfeldt, pp. 82–83.

103. As Table 9.1 above, from HGZ, fols. 12r–12v, 14v–16v, and 19v–22r. Because the first full annual entries, some from 1431 and others from 1433, show little deserted land or

default on obligations, they may be presumed more to reflect the previous peaceful conditions than those of mid-century rural crisis.

About 1360 *Leimgruben* had 13 migrants among the 23 gertner tenants; 5 came from Wrocław duchy sites (*HPR*, pp. 99–100 and notes). At Partynice in 1350 five of ten leading villagers came from other places, four within the duchy (*RS*, II, #318).

104. *SR* #4932 and *DT*, p. 103 (with other instances from Jerzmanowo and Węgry on pp. 146 and 150). See also *RS*, II, #982.

105. RF, IV, 2820–2837.

106. WAP, AMW, K 8. Mendl, pp. 154–185, determined that the list contains 2272 correct original entries, but did not study it as evidence for migration. Reichert, *Familiennamen*, was much interested in those derived from places of origin, but neither calculated the frequency of appearance for each name nor compared the various types. Thus while his findings (pp. 73–85) support the argument here made for considerable rural-urban migration, notably from areas close to Wrocław, his data was not gathered or presented in a form suitable for systematic study of the issue.

107. A count of 205 persons assumes that each individual entry refers to a different person, even if the names were the same. If identical names, like the "Jacob Hugesdorff" which appears in three widely separated points of the list (fols. 11v, 20r, and 23r; the list is organized by quarters and streets), in fact refer to the same individual, there were 188 persons (8% of the total). The count of 95 places however, allots to only the closest of ambiguous place names all individuals which bore such a family name. Thus John "Bresener" (9v), Peter "Bresener" (59v), and Hans "Bresym" (62r) with surnames from *Brese*, could have come from Brzezina, Brzoza, or Brzezica (all then *Brese*).

108. *Ibid.*, fols. 53r, and 66r. Migration in and from the countryside around Wrocław thus resembles (given differences in available sources) the late medieval English movements discussed globally by McClure, pp. 167–182, and treated at the microscopic level of inter-village marriages by Bennett, pp. 219–221.

109. *UD*, p. 222.

110. WAP, Rep. 67, #466 (original lost).

111. *SR* #5274; full text in *NRB*, p. 231. Compare the murder in Wrocław of a man from Grabiszyn (Stobbe, 1866, p. 362).

112. *UD*, p. 39; *DT*, p. 53.

113. Görlich, *Vincenz*, p. 107 and notes. The abbot refused the gifts and postponed his decision.

114. LN, 11v–12r. See also Heyne, *Bisthum*, II, 32; Kopietz, p. 44.

115. *DT*, p. 56. For more cases see *RS*, II, #169; *UD*, p. 39.

116. *SR* #4870c and 4870d.

117. *UD*, pp. 161–162. See also inquests in *SR* #5717 and Heyne, *Bisthum*, I, 869.

118. On the ultimate (early 1800s) spread of gardening villages south of Wrocław, see Szulc, pp. 36–42, 83–84, and map B. Wendt, *Landgüter*, pp. 165–167, attests from the late 1400s to the peculiar local name and folk culture associated with them.

119. *HPR*, pp. 34 and 39; *SR* #4587; Wendt, *Landgüter*, pp. 157–167.

120. Tz-S, p. 172, *RS*, I, #275; *ChronBMV*, p. 195. Compare obligations on normal rental mansi in Figure 6.3b(1) above.

121. *HPR*, p. 84 note 1 (identified as Wendt, *Landgüter*, pp. 180–184); *ChronBMV*, pp. 199–201; Wendt, "Verpfandung," p. 159 ; *BUB*, pp. 236–237.

122. RB, fols. 6r and 8r. Other sites are not in the return (Gajowice, *Platea Romanorum*) or appear without information on lands, tenants, and payments (Borek, fol. 1r).

123. Trace unchanging rent rates on city lands here from the late 1350s to 1468 through *HPR*, pp. 84 note 1, 87 note 1, 99–100, and 128; WAP, AMW, K 113, 6v–7r; Beyer, p. 116 note; Klose, *Inneren Verhältnisse*, pp. 271–272. By comparison, two gardens, one of 2 *jugera*, the other of unknown size, at *Platea Romanorum* rented for 1 and 1.25 marks respectively in the 1430s (HGZ, fols. 38v, 59r, 98r, and 113r).

124. WAP, AMW, K 113, 6v. Grünhagen in *HPR*, pp. 99–100 and notes, called this the "German rental," but there conflated it with a now-vanished slightly earlier fragmentary Latin one.

125. KLM, 5r (in attributing this village to St. Vincent instead of St. Mary either the original or Klose's transcript erred). For later description of the farms, see Wendt, *Landgüter*, pp. 180–184, and Szulc, map b.

126. This practice in mid-fourteenth century *Leimgruben* and *Neudorf* is documented in Wendt, *Landgüter*, pp. 160–165, and "Verpfandung," pp. 158–159 note 4.

127. WAP, AMW, K 113, 7v–8r; *HPR*, pp. 128–129; *SR* #6144; *LB* #123.

128. For the cases mentioned: RF, III, 2521–2525; *BUB*, pp. 99–100; WAP, AMW, K 113, 7v; *LFE* B18. More are in *LB* #250 and *SR* #3000.

129. Tz-S, pp. 426–427. Compare *SR* #6364; *LB* #123 note; LN, fol. 378v–379r.

130. *LFE* B18; Tz-S, pp. 426–427.

131. WAP, AMW, K 113, 7v; *HPR*, p. 129.

132. *UD*, p. 152. Wrocław consumers then ate from the Odra chiefly bream, pike, and perch (Kozikowska, pp. 6–7).

133. *UD*, p. 16; RF, II, 722–723. The abbot of Lubiąż hoped for much the same in his 1310 *locatio* of Bartoszowa (*SR* #3138).

134. *SR* #3763, 3785, 4317, 4324 and 6144; RF, I, 511; II, 786; *LB* #123); *HPR*, pp. 107–109. A rural linen industry is all many associate with pre-modern Silesia, but it developed during the 1500s in the hills around Swidnica and Jawór, not the plains of the Wrocław duchy (Aubin, "Leineweberei," pp. 115–121 and 145–150).

135. A miller and a malter had fully free commercial properties in *Platea Romanorum* (*SR* #4317 and 4324). Wenceslas Pechman's sale of an annuity on his *Olbino* *Pechhaus* in 1425 was also unencumbered (WAP, AMW, Q 154, 2, fol. 24r).

136. For examples, see *SR* #3098, 5899, 6170, and 6695; Bobertag, "Gerichtsbücher," pp. 169–170.

137. *SR* #3086 and 3113.

138. Wutke, "Gallici," p. 304.

139. *SR* #2495; RF, I, 413–415; HGZ, fols. 21v and 84v. See also *SR* #3098, 4750, 4948, 6170, and 6181; RF, IV, 2661–2692; WAP, AMW, G 3, fol. 4v; Ludat, *Bisthum Lebus*, p. 98.

140. See, for examples, HGZ, fols. 16r, 24r, 48v, and 89v; RF, I, 511, and II, 786; *SR* #4750, 4948, 6170, and 6181; Bobertag, "Gerichtsbücher," pp. 169–170; Wutke, "Gallici," p. 304.

141. Upkeep: *SR* #2495 and 3086; *RS*, I, #161; RF, I, 29r–34r.

142. Tavern rents: *SR* #1322, 3086, 4117, 5604, 6170, and 6446; WAP, AMW, G 3, fol. 4v; *HPR*, pp. 105–106; RF, II, 961–977; Wutke, "Gallici," p. 304.

143. Dembińska, *Przetwórstwo*, pp. 197–224; Stenzel, "Müllern, p. 338; *RS*, II, #573; RF, I, 413–415. Besides a heavy obligation of 12 *maldrata* of ground meal, the tenant of a mill on the Widawa had to mast two pigs for his lord (*SR* #2495).

144. *SR* # 6144; *LB* #123; Görlich, *Vincenz*, pp. 80–81; HGZ, fols. 21v and 84v; RF, II, 598.

145. Kopietz, p. 43 note 2.

146. *SR* #4861f.

147. *SR* #4750; WAP, AMW, G 3, fol. 4v; HGZ, fols. 84v and 120r (with other cases on 21v and 24r). On combinations of craft work and farming typical in the later Prussian state see Skalweit.

148. Stenzel, "Müllern," pp. 331–340, mentioned a *ius molendini* of ⅟₁₈ (5.5%) at Świdnica in 1362, but not the 1336 ordinance, which appears in *BUB*, pp. 134–135. Note that incomes in kind parallel the miller's usual obligations in kind.

149. *HPR*, pp. 107–109.

150. Signs of poverty among this group are rare and ambiguous. Taverners who did not pay rents at Wierzbno in the 1330s and Stabłowice in the 1350s seem to have denied the lord's right to them (*SR* #4948, 6170, 6181; WAP, AMW, G 3, fol. 4v). A pitch boiler in *Olbino* did in 1425 sell for 20 marks a two mark *census* (WAP, AMW, Q 154, 2, fols. 24r–v).

151. *UD*, p. 39; WAP, AMW, Q 154, 1, fol. 6r.

152. RF, II, 599–602. For other investments see Stenzel, "Müllern," p. 338, and HGZ, fols. 88r, 89v, and 105v.

153. HGZ, fols. 16r–v, 24r, 48v, 67v, 89v, 106v, 107r, and 122v. Another mansus in 1438 left Andres behind only the schulz.

154. For legislation see Korn, ed., *Gewerberecht*, pp. 96–99 and 109–110, and for its contentious application to ecclesiastical retail of beer, Dix, pp. 16–18.

155. Kindler, p. 43. Compare Tz-S, pp. 547–548, and Grotefend, "Streitigkeiten."

156. Korn, *Gewerberecht*, pp. 14–15, 68, 83, 96–99, and 109–110; Stobbe, 1866, pp. 176–177; WAP Rep. 135 E 99 e, #2–3; Mahlendorff, pp. 7–10, 14–17, 40–42, and 45–56.

157. Heyne, *Bisthum*, II, 697–699, and III, 936–939. Even puny Leśnica tried to constrain crafts in nearby villages (RUL, #3).

158. Małowist, "Trade," pp. 544–547; Samsonowicz, "Przemiany," pp. 697–703; Kehn, pp. 59–115; Nowakowa.

159. *SR* #1102 and 2116; *HPR*, p. 1; *BUB*, pp. 79–80; Kuhn, Städtegründungspolitik," 1972, pp. 50–51.

160. *LB* #430b-c and 450; RUL, #5. Compare also *SR* #3983, 5700, 5935, 5936, and 5997; Kopietz, p. 43; RUL, #3, 6, and 8; RB, fol. 13r

161. *UFO*, pp. 148–152; *LB* #124; RF, II, 844–848. Kuhn, "Städtegründungspolitik," 1972, pp. 33–35, and "Auras," pp. 212–215, speculated that tithe arrangements in 1288 are an earlier sign of a town.

162. *SR* #878 is treated in Schulte, "Kostenblut," pp. 246–248, and Kuhn, "Städtegründungspolitik," 1971, p. 57. For later disputes see Heyne, *Bisthum*, II, 697–699, and *BUB*, pp. 213–214.

163. *SR* #2334, 2457, 2944, 3138, 3726, 4570, and 5892; Kuhn, "Städtegründungspolitik," 1972, pp. 37–39; *LB* #283, 410, 412; WAP, AMW, G 3, fols. 9v–10r; *HPR*, pp. 105–109.

164. Wohlbrück, II, 69–70.

165. Review Map 3.1. An ill-attested market at Domasław may briefly have filled the gap (*KdS* #248; *SUB*, I, #351; Chapter 4 note 20 above).

166. *SR* #2116, 4961f, 5935, 5936, 5700; Kopietz, p. 43; RUL, #3; WAP Rep. 135 E96, #5; RF, II, 844–848. Trades documented for both markets and ordinary villages in the duchy are those found in the Kingdom of Poland by Lalik, "Petites villes," pp. 20–24, and Samsonowicz, "Kleinstädte," pp. 191–205. For comparable low-level nodes in the English market net see Hilton, "Market towns."

167. *DT*, p. 233. See also Tz-S, #15; *SR* #1968 and 3138; RF, I, 454, II, 722–723, and IV, 2820–2837 and 2870–2879, *UD*, pp. 16 and 144–145, WAP Rep. 55, #40, and Wutke, "Gallici," p. 304.

168. See for examples *UD*, p. 16; RF, I, fols. 1r–3v, and II, 722–723; *SR* #3785.

169. Görlich, *Vincenz*, pp. 80–81; *SR* #1268, 1403, and 5582; WAP, AME, Q 154, 2, fol. 24r; *DT*, p. 150; Ligęza, pp. 449–450. In contrast, the Oleśnica duchy then contained several rural forges (Haeusler, *Geschichte*, p. 290).

170. Ciesla, "Taberna," pp. 159–225; Ludat, *Bistum Lebus*, p. 98; Tz-S, pp. 583–585.

171. *SR* #3086 and 3113. At Wierzbno in 1361 the village court met in the "stuba tabernae" (Heyne, *Bisthum*, II, 708).

172. See, for example, *SR* #1397 and 2334; RF, I, 20v–22v, III, 2123–2130, and IV, 2641–2644; *DT*. p. 51; LN, fol. 385r; *UD*, p. 263. Only two isolated references to windmills survive, near Kryniczno (*LFE* D25) and somewhere in the Uraz district (*LB* #556).

173. By comparison, Pistoia (urban and rural) then had a mill for every 140 persons or 7.5 km² (Muendel, "Pistoia"), while in Little Poland the density averaged just one per 75 km² and even around Cracow reached only one in 21 km² (Podwinska, "Młynów"). Addition of the duchy's second and urban mills as well as city dwellers would bring its totals up to about 100 mills for around 45,000 persons in the early fifteenth century (1 per 15.5 km² or 450 persons).

174. For the "Four-wheeled Mill" near Krobielowice see *NLChron*, pp. 97–98; *RS*, I, #106, 122, 131, 161, and 462; RF, I, 511–512, and II, 786. Of the 26 mills the 1353 fiscal survey put on the Bystrzyca system and the Ślęza, 19 had two or more wheels and the others no size given (*LB* #526–546). Written descriptions of these structures (Dembińska, *Przetwórstwo*, pp. 90–135) are illuminated by the unique excavation of a rural mill near Brzeg (Bagniewski and Kubów).

175. For problems of water supply at a mill on the Oława see *UD*, pp. 151–152. The duchy's largest, the "Seven-wheeled Mill" was on the Odra at Wrocław, but most mills on these streams had only one wheel (*LB*, #523–525, 547–561). Muendel, "Florentine," pp. 99–100, also found more mills on upland streams.

176. RF, III, 2097–2113. For more examples see *SR* #2495, 3619, 4374, and 5368; *BUB*, p. 107; RF, II, 917–924.

177. Like the discussion of village priests, this of parishes is limited to certain social aspects. For religious life in late medieval Silesia, see Urban, *Studia*, pp. 75–86 and 156–184.

178. The foundation charter notes problems in times of flood (Heyne, *Bisthum*, II, 454–455 note). See also Görlich, *Vincenz*, pp. 85–86 and 108; Jungnitz, "Pfarrspregel," pp. 30–32.

179. Ludat, *Stiftsregister*, p. 36. Compare St. Maurice at *Platea Romanorum* in Heyne, *Bisthum*, III, 600, and Święta Katarzyna in *LFE*, B30 and B32; "QBBB," p. 196, *UD*, pp. 139–140, and Fibiger, pp. 302–303. Few private or filial churches were built: *SR* #2623, 2710, 5047, and 5370; Heyne, *Bisthum*, II, 534–535.

180. The early Uraz parish is described in the 1288 foundation charter of the Holy Cross chapter (*UFO*, pp. 124–128) and discussed speculatively in Kuhn, "Auras," pp. 212–215. Churches at Brzezina and Wilkszyn are recorded by the late 1330s and at Pęgów, Golędzinów, and perhaps Lubnów in 1353 (Ptaśnik, I, 356–358, with place names corrected as in *SR* #5409; *LB* #126, 128, 129; Heyne, *Bisthum*, II, 115). Differences between parish structures of Polish and German tradition are noted in Schulte, "Parochial-Verfassung," pp. 390–399, and Loesch, "Forschungen," pp. 158–163.

181. Heyne, *Bisthum*, II, 454–455; *UD*, pp. 50–51; Klapper, pp. 163–164.

182. *UD*, p. 222; Heyne, *Neumarkt*, p. 336; *NRB* p. 263. *Kirchenvater*, the lay heads of parishes otherwise well-known from mid-Silesian records are not clearly recorded in the duchy at this time, but compare Loesch, "Forschungen," p. 163, and Schmid, "Gründung" and "Pfarrorganisation."

183. *SR* #4870b and 4870e.

184. *SR* #3763, 3785, and 5046. For donations by small holders see Jungnitz, "Pfarrspregel," p. 31, or *NRB*, p. 256. Michael, "Dorfschule," pp. 227–230, listed none in the pre-Reformation duchy but a "schuler" was at Bukowiec in 1414 (Heyne, *Neumarkt*, p. 336).

185. In the 1353 and 1425 fiscal texts the central villages average about 36 mansi against a mean for the duchy of 25–30.

186. Compare the pattern of cities, market towns, and taverns on Map 9.1 with the theoretical model of central sites developed and manipulated in Lösch, pp. 101–135. The foregoing analysis may, as well, be seen as replicating at a local level that in Russell, *Regions*, pp. 15–38.

187. *SR* #6707 and RF, I, fol. 1r; WAA II, IV a 1. See further *SR* #5926, 6175, and 6395–6396; RF, I, 462; Rössler, #492 and 1178; *HPR*, pp. 128–133; WAP, AMW, Q 154, 2, fols. 17v–18r; Heyne, *Bisthum*, III, 572; *UD*, pp. 155–158.

188. LN, fols. 377v–378r; *NLChron*, p. 121 note 6. See also Sommerfeldt, pp. 82–83; LN, fols. 294v–295r; WAA I, IVa 8, fol. 98r; *ChronBMV*, p. 209; Urban, *Wykaz AAW*, #652.

189. WAP Rep. 67, #104. Nine villagers at Kębłowice in 1374 borrowed from their schulz (LN, fols. 46r–47r).

190. *UD*, pp. 199 (compare *SR* #5959) and 213; HGZ, fol. 108v.

191. *SR* #5009; *NRB*, pp. 222–224; WAA I, IV a 4a, fols. 30r–30v; WAP Rep. 55, #94. See also *SR* #4248, 4481–4482, and 5419; Heyne, *Bisthum*, III, 576.

192. *SR* #5714; WAA I, IV a 8, fols. 60v–61r.

193. *SR* #6112; *UD*, pp. 204–213, and, for another case, p. 4. Peasants borrow from Jews in *SR* #5603 and WAP, AMW, G 3, fol. 8v.

194. Nicholas later managed to redeem part of it. His neighbor Matzke also then had to sell part of his lands for rents overdue to a city lender. *UD*, pp. 207–211.

195. *UD*, pp. 33–35, 37, and 40–41; WAP Rep. 55, #94; WAA I, IV a 4, fols. 30r–30v; WAP Rep. 67, #104.

196. LN, fols. 375v–376r.

197. *HPR*, p. 106.

198. *SR* #6444; *UD*, p. 213. For further instances see Stobbe, 1864/65, p. 351, and *NRB*, p. 263.

199. *SR* #6707; compare *SR* #5714 and RF, I, 462.

200. *UD*, p. 208.

201. HGZ, fol. 82v.

202. Sommerfeldt, pp. 82–83.

203. WAP Rep. 55, #91. See also *UD*, pp. 152–153.

204. For these and others see *SR* #6428; RF, II, 854, and III, 2405–2406; *UD*, pp. 39, 152–153, and 218; HGZ, fols. 15r and 108v.

205. RF, I, 26v–29r, and III, 2300–2317. Compare *SR* #6428.

206. *SR*, #5615.

207. Rössler, #489, 491, and 492.

208. *SR*, #6231 and 6395.

209. Pfeiffer, *Patriziat*, p. 151.

210. Heyne, *Bisthum*, III, 576; *UD*, p. 47. Different sources from the Wrocław duchy do

make its extra-village debt networks more visible than its counterparts to the intra-village ones analyzed in Clark, "Debt," pp. 268–271, but the quality and effects of the relationships are comparable.

Chapter 10

1. An early attempt at much that follows was Hoffmann, "Warfare."
2. Gerlich, *Habsburg, Luxemburg, Wittelsbach.*
3. Mosbach, pp. 83–84; RF, III, 279–295.
4. Mosbach, p. 94. All documented sites of destruction in this and subsequent conflicts are shown on Map 10.1.
5. Görlich, *Vincenz*, p. 99; *ChronBMV*, p. 215.
6. Grünhagen, ed., *Geschichtsquellen*, pp. 64–66; Rosicz, *Gesta*, p. 47. Heck, "Hussiten-aufstand," pp. 226–228, made much of popular support in 1428, but Dziewulski, "Społeczeń-stwo," pp. 27–28, established the special circumstances.
7. Rosicz, *Gesta*, pp. 47–48; Markgraf, "Rosicz," pp. 246–248.
8. From evidence in Grünhagen, *Geschichtsquellen*, p. 172; RB, fol. 5r compared to RF, IV, 2681; *ChronBMV*, p. 220; LN, fol. 19v.
9. Bolkenhain, p. 10; Wendt, "Verpfandung," p. 159.
10. Only a royal warning to the Środa district court (*NRB*, p. 264) suggests a danger in 1431. For 1432 see a contemporary note from Strzelin (Grünhagen, *Geschichtsquellen*, pp. 157–158).
11. As reported by an anonymous eye-witness in Wachter, *Geschichtsschreiber*, pp. 25–26. See also *ChronBMV*, p. 233; Ermisch, "Verhältniss;" Maleczyński, *Historia Śląska*, I:2, 246–249.
12. Rosicz, *Gesta*, pp. 55–56. Compare Ermisch, "Königloser Zeit," pp. 19–20, 50–55, and 64, and Kronthal, "Asenheimer."
13. Rosicz, *Gesta*, p. 59, and *Chronica*, p. 581.
14. Kindler, pp. 196–197. Seyfrid Seidlicz forcibly refused a *census* on Gałów (Bauch, *Schulwesen*, pp. 122–123).
15. Jungandreas, p. 176.
16. Stobbe, 1867, p. 446 (Dominic's "youth" got him off with a fine). Men of the Skopp family were in the 1450s accused of robbing fellow citizens (Pfeiffer, *Patriziat*, pp. 266–267) and then outlawed for a gang murder (*UD*, pp. 64–65).
17. Klose, *Inneren Verhältnisse*, p. 74.
18. *NRB*, pp. 344–345.
19. Stobbe, 1870, pp. 194–195. For further cases see *UD*, #19:12; Stobbe, 1867, p. 161; *NRB*, pp. 350, 352, and 255; Klose, *Inneren Verhältnisse*, p. 105.
20. Stobbe, 1868, p. 173; *NRB*, p. 355.
21. *UD*, p. 55; Steinhausen, ed., I, 369.
22. *PCC*, I, 202–203 and 213–214.
23. Ermisch, "Königloser Zeit," p. 279; Klose, *Inneren Verhältnisse*, pp. 66–67 and 101.
24. Nell, p. 316, stresses how banditry fractures existing socio-economic relations.
25. *PCP*, I, 17–18.
26. Rosicz, *Gesta*, pp. 75–76; Eschenloer, *Historia*, pp. 55–62. Compare Menzel, "Eschenloer."
27. Eschenloer, *Historia*, pp. 140–141 and 232.
28. *PCC*, I, 33.
29. Eschenloer, *Geschichten*, II, 303–304 and 309–311.
30. *Ibid.*, pp. 312–326; Johnsdorf, pp. 112–114. Other reports are in Schultz and Grünhagen, pp. 383–384, and Semkowicz, ed., "Rocznik," pp. 735–736. Compare Korta, *Annalistyka*, pp. 322–325.
31. Eschenloer, *Geschichten*, II, 327–328. With the vicinity of Wrocław "wuste," Mathias and his army went in March to the lands of St. Mary around Sobótka for a week's rape and plunder (Johnsdorf, p. 115).
32. Grünhagen, *Geschichtsquellen*, p. 172.

33. LN, fol. 19v; KLM, fol. 28.

34. Johnsdorf, p. 115. Compare effects of endemic violence on other local rural economies in, for example, Flanders (Nicholas, pp. 333–340) or Northwest England (Elliott, p. 61).

35. The direct meteorological and indirect economic evidence is treated in terms of climatological theory in Lamb, *Climatic History*, pp. 449–461, who rated the periods 1310–19 and around the 1430s and −50s the worst for most of Europe. Compare his earlier *Changing Climate*, pp. 58–108; Alexandre; LeRoy Ladurie, *Times of Feast*, pp. 264–268. In east-central Europe 1360–1430 was relatively warm and dry and 1430–1500 cool and wet. Summer subtropical anticyclones and a maritime flow of air in winter gave way to maritime cyclones ruling the warmer months and continental air masses the cooler. (Flohn, pp. 347–357; reworked by Richter, pp. 249–254)

Note that the argument here advanced does not infer economic conditions or changes from general climatic change as censured in, for example, Anderson, "Climatic Change," but follows his recommendation to examine shifts of weather patterns and changing frequencies of meteorological "shocks" to economic activity. Wrocław's "shocks," however, precisely fit what are arguably the broad patterns of late medieval climate.

36. Santifaller, *Kopialbücher*, p. 276; *HPR*, pp. 137–138 and 179; Kętrzyński, ed., "Varia," p. 590.

37. Rosicz, *Gesta*, pp. 62–85, is then the most complete account, but often confirmed by Eschenloer, *Historia*, pp. 56, 103–104, and 188–189; Bielowski, ed., "Rocznik magistratu," p. 686; *ChronBMV*, p. 249; Schultz and Grünhagen, pp. 376–377.

38. Weikinn, vols. I and II, under years as indicated. The Odra later flooded during the summer four times between 1537 and 1550, in 1570, and three years during the 1590s.

39. After several such floods before 1854, none occurred until 1888 and then 13 in the next 20 years (Hellmann and Elsner).

40. Eschenloer, *Geschichten*, II, 338. See also Eschenloer, *Historia*, pp. 220 and 223, and Rosicz, *Gesta*, p. 85. The failure of cold winters seriously to affect agriculture around Wrocław corresponds with findings for Holland by de Vries.

41. Rosicz, *Gesta*, pp. 75 and 85; Eschenloer, *Historia*, pp. 213, 242, and 264–266, and *Geschichten*, II, 266, 270, and 299–300; Henel, p. 320.

42. Eschenloer, *Historia*, pp. 229–233 and 103–104; Rosicz, *Gesta*, pp. 80–81; *ChronBMV*, pp. 249–250; Schultz and Grünhagen, pp. 376–377. See further Rosicz, *Gesta*, p. 67; Eschenloer, *Historia*, pp. 188–189; Johnsdorf, pp. 115–116; *UD*, pp. 159–162.

43. Brandon found runs of wet years in late medieval Sussex often cut yields by up to 15 percent. In Brandenburg and Upper Saxony during the cool wet period after 1430 peasants simply abandoned farms on impermeable soils (Richter, pp. 249–254). See also Dunin-Wasowicz; LeRoy Ladurie, *Times of Feast*, pp. 289–292.

44. Eschenloer, *Historia*, p. 229. Background for what follows is Day, "Bullion Famine."

45. See Appendix B, especially Figure B.1.

46. WAA I, IV a 8, fols. 30v–31r. Compare the 1430s–50s history of a *census* on a tenure at *Polska Nowa Wieś* in *NLChron*, p. 129 note 104 (where "fl." must be an error for "ft."). For more cases see *UD*, p. 223; WAA I, IV a 4a, fols. 23v–24r and 19r–19v; Klose, *Inneren Verhältnisse*, p. 190.

47. WAA I, IV a 4a, fols. 27v–28v, with fols. 21r–21v a similar case from 1474. See also WAP Rep 135, D273, fol. 10r–10v, and Jesuiter, VI:III, #11:58.

48. Szwagrzyk, "Szerokie grosze," pp. 65–66.

49. Normal increases during the months of shrinking reserves before a new harvest went unremarked by chroniclers. The scale of extreme fluctuation is best compared with some careful short-term price series. Braudel and Spooner, pp. 465–466, graph seasonal variations at Paris, 1591–99, and Udine, 1636–45. No maximum for a given year there exceeds by more than 2.3 times that year's minimum and the multiple surpasses 2 only in three years at Paris. Likewise during the great famine of 1315–16 in England the wheat price index rose only from 1 to 2.4 (Farmer, p. 218).

50. Rosicz, *Gesta*, p. 49.

51. Grünhagen, "Annalistische Nachlese," p. 189: "et sic pauperes congregati in Wratislavia ex multis opidis et villis in maxima multitudine in plateis et in cimiteriis hospicia habuerunt et jacuerunt, fame et frigore perierunt;" Rosicz, *Gesta*, p. 51; *ChronBMV*, p. 225. In 1434 the Holy Spirit Hospital received from its demesne at Trestno less than half the grain of the previous year (HGZ, fols. 25v–25v and 60v–61r). Did peasant cultivators lose the same?

52. Henel, p. 320; Rosicz, *Gesta*, p. 53.

53. Rosicz, *Gesta*, p. 53; Heyne, *Wohlau*, pp. 195–196; Eschenloer, *Geschichten*, II, 264–266; Eschenloer, *Historia*, pp. 229 and 242; Schultz and Grünhagen, p. 382; Bielowski, "Rocznik magistratu," p. 686. A general account of the 1437 famine is Abel, *Strukturen*, pp. 85–95. Schmitz found poor harvests after bad weather the chief and war damage the second precipitant of famine in medieval Europe.

54. "Da sahe man die armen Leuten schaaricht aus Slesien und allen umliegenden Landen kommen; ein Scheffel Kleien kauften die Gebaur gar gerne umb zehen Groschen." Eschenloer, *Geschichten*, II, 264–266 and *Historia*, p. 242.

55. *Peasants* seeking food distinguish these shortages from the normal pattern of subsistence crises as narrowly urban phenomena caused by rural producers covering their own short supplies out of what they usually sold. For widely scattered examples see Braudel, *Mediterranean*, I, 328; Nicholas, pp. 122–123; Gould, "Price Revolution," p. 86. Nor were most central Silesian peasants market-oriented specialists who, because they always bought their food, were vulnerable to an urban inflation (compare Ringrose, p. 769). Thus the peasant food shortages around fifteenth-century Wrocław must mean that the producers themselves could not control enough production to cover their own needs.

56. Rosicz, *Gesta*, pp. 44 and 53; Grünhagen, "Annalistische Nachlese," p. 186; Henel, pp. 308 and 320; Bielowski, "Rocznik magistratu," pp. 685–686; *ChronBMV*, p. 214.

57. Rosicz, *Gesta*, pp. 62–63; Bielowski, "Rocznik magistratu," p. 686; Klose, *Inneren Verhältnisse*, p. 110; Schultz and Grünhagen, p. 377.

58. ". . . nisi quantum interdum ex contagione villanorum accidit." Eschenloer, *Historia*, p. 146.

59. Thus only tenants at Zębice owed rent to the hospital. Villagers at Wróblowice paid 1.5 measures of rye per mansus for a ducal right and the rest cash in lieu of tithe. HGZ, *passim*.

60. RSC 1449–57 was done by none other than the chronicler Sigismund Rosicz (see Schulte, "Rosicz," pp. 334–336). It is the only part of the successive registers the wardens kept from 1406 to the 1700s to record more than total receipts and defaults.

61. RB, fols. 11r–13r (Zębice is not in the document).

62. KLM is discussed further in Appendix A. Abandoned land signifies rural consumption crises of more than short-term nature in the interesting analytical framework of Stewart, pp. 61–80.

63. The published register from 1443 (Klose, *Von Breslau*, II:2, 443–447) exaggerates the desertions because it omitted everything except settlement size and abandoned land and interpolated "unbewohnt" after 7 places which are blank in Klose's own holograph transcript (KLM) of the lost original. Both *LB* and RB contain blank entries for places which other texts confirm were then inhabited, so this occurance in KLM is not acceptable evidence of desertion. Because Grünhagen used the printed data in *Hussitenkämpfe*, pp. 276–278, his statistics are invalid.

64. In 1419 during a brief pause in the Teutonic Order's war with Poland, 20.8% of the 31,525 mansi in Prussia were empty (Abel, *Wustungen*, p. 43). Jäger, pp. 222–237, warns to discriminate between desertions caused by war or other external influences and those from a Malthusian "agrarian crisis," but the Wrocław and the Prussian situations seem wholly comparable.

65. KLM, fols. 10, 19, 26–29, and 31 have less deserted land at Łowęcice, Ilnica, and Jarząbkowice, but of the 225 mansi there listed for the nine villages, 41 (18.2%) were abandoned.

66. PCP, I, 18. In the less-affected zone near the city Radomierzyce had no spaces in 1443 (KLM, fol. 5) or in RSC, 1449–57.

67. Eschenloer, *Geschichten*, p. 328; RSC, 1471–88.

68. The end to growth and subsequent decline of rural population was likely not the same in the city. Maleczyński, "Dzieje Wrocławia," p. 206, suggested a 1% fall from 19197 in 1403 to 18945 in 1470, and listed other careful estimates ranging up to a 30% increase. Wrocław's walls were not then extended but there are signs of greater internal density. Unchanged urban demand against shrunken production would cause higher prices and intermittent crises of subsistence.

69. RSC [all four mss.].

70. *ChronBMV*, pp. 218 and 226.

71. WAA I, III d 2, pp. 29–30; Heyne, *Bisthum*, III, 989.

72. Arnold et al., p. 356. For more defaults see *UD*, p. 158; WAP Rep. 55, 124; HGZ, fol. 113v; WAA I, IV a 8, fols. 31v–32r and 98v; Schulte, "Vermischte," p. 242; Perlbach, "Zur Geschichte," pp. 259–260; Eistert, "Klarenkloster," pp. 81–82.

73. KLM, fol. 28; WAP Rep 135, E99e, II, #7–8; more or less accurately summarized in Kindler, pp. 89 and 91.

74. RSC, 1471–88.

75. Dyhernfurth, pp. 20–21.

76. HGZ, fols. 19v, 42v–43r, 64r, 103v, and 119v.

77. HGZ, fols. 18v–19r, 41v–42r, 63v–64r, 82v–83r, 95v–96r, 102v–103r, and 118v–119r. As shown in Table 10.3, 51% of the payments required from Zębice tenants were defaulted. Conditions were similar at Jarząbkowice (HGZ, fols. 23v–24r, 48v–49r, 67v–68v, 89v–90v, 106v–107v, and 122v–123v) and Radakowice (HGZ, fols. 21v, 46v–47r, 66v, 87v–88r, 105v, and 121v).

78. HGZ, fols. 20v, 44v, 65v, 85v–86r, 104v, and 120v.

79. RSC, 1449–57. Ilnica's high and general non-payment of the early 1430s fell sharply after 1436. Prominent persistent defaulters were the schulz, Michael Radak, and the parish priest, John Wyzczeky (HGZ, fols. 20r, 43v, 65r, 84r, 104r, and 120r). Compare Radakowice in HGZ, fols. 87v–88r, 105v, and 121v.

80. Meyer, *Studien*, pp. 63–68 describes a manuscript (now lost) recording hundreds of excommunications obtained by St. Vincent against mid-century defaulters on tithe.

81. *UD*, pp. 158–159.

82. *ChronBMV*, pp. 218 ("exemit") and 226 ("redemit"). In 1442 the same abbot dismissed arrears owed and gave two more years of exemption to the schulz of Jugowiec (WAP, Rep. 55, 24).

83. HGZ, fols. 48v, 67v, 86v, 87v, 89v, and 106v. That lords were wise to query peasant non-payment is well illustrated in Lorcin, "Ruse paysanne." Surely Silesian peasants and lords were as astute as their French counterparts.

84. HGZ, fols. 18v, 41v, 95v, 81v–82v, 102v, and 118v.

85. HGZ, fols. 43v and 106r.

86. HGZ, fols. 21r, 44v, 46r, 69r, 108r–109r, and 84v.

87. At Radomierzyce most of a generation later the succustos visibly coerced no one, but only two delinquents had small residual sums forgiven (RSC, 1449–57).

88. HGZ, fols. 22r, 24v, 43r, 45v, 46r, 47v, 48r, 65r, 66r, 86v, 106r–v, and 122r.

89. RF, II, 810–814. Compare two like cessions of lordship during the 1440s in RF, I, 52v–54v and II, 914–924.

90. RF, I, 76v–79v (see also 22v); III, 2465–2476; IV, 2661–2692; WAP Rep. 55, 110; *UD*, p. 158.

91. *NLChron*, pp. 127–129. See further WAP Rep. 55, 111, and six more cases at Domasław in 1438–40 (*UD*, pp. 56–58).

92. *UD*, p. 48; WAA I, III d 2, pp. 24–25 and 28–29. See also HGZ, fols. 58v, 77v, and 97r.

93. HGZ, fol. 98r; WAA I, III d 2, p. 36; WAA I, IV a 4a, fols. 23v–24r; WAP Rep 135 E113f, pp. 5–6.

94. RW, G 65.

95. "die einwoner in den dorfern, nemlich das gebaür volk in den Breslischen, Neunmargtischen und Namslowischen weichbilden gessessen" (*NRB*, pp. 281–283; summarized in RW, N 83).

96. *UD*, pp. 56–58. See also *NLChron*, pp. 128–129 note 102.

97. *NLChron*, pp. 127 and 129 with note 104.

98. WAA I, III d 2, p. 36. See also *NLChronik*, pp. 128–129; WAA I, IV a 4a, fols. 23v–24r.

99. *UD*, p. 223, #23:13; HGZ, fol. 64r. For additional examples see HGZ, fol. 108v, and *UD*, pp. 215–217, #19:5–8.

100. *UD*, pp. 50–51. Further confirming village credits are cryptically opaque references in 1450s litigation from Domasław (*UD*, pp. 58–63, #101–109, 111–115, 118–122, and 124–126).

101. *UD*, pp. 215–216, #19–20.

102. *UD*, p. 223, #23:10. The fifth citation mentions no coin.

103. Wenczko's shortage of funds in 1435 is further corroborated by his later need to pay

a penalty and obtain a guarantor for overdue rents (HGZ, fol. 96r).

104. HGZ, fol. 82v. His payment of full rents on time in 1436 and 1437 is also recorded on fols. 81v and 102v.

105. HGZ, fols. 67v–68v, 89v, and 106v–107r, also records other farms enlarged with deserted land. On Zębice see fol. 82r.

106. HGZ, fols. 84v, 104r, and 120r. For similar cases elsewhere see fols. 92r and 106v–107r.

107. The many farms of two mansi there in 1494 were asserted by Kuhn, "Bauernhof-grössen," pp. 238–240, to come from remarkably large original thirteenth-century holdings, but the flaw in his reasoning has already been noted (Chapter 9, note 78). The issue receives further treatment in the next chapter (p. 329), but clearly the contextual isolation of the 1494 land distributions lets them reveal only a fragment of late fifteenth century reality, not its antecedents.

108. HGZ, *passim*; Klose, *Inneren Verhältnisse*, pp. 271–272, and compare *HPR*, p. 129, and WAP, AMW, K 113, fol. 1r–1v).

109. "Wenn yn guten geczeyten, do das getreyde mehe geguldin hat, hat er der huben genossin. Nu itzunder das getreyde wenig gilt, wil der . . . die huben lassin legin." Klein, ed., pp. 361–363.

110. Merot's claim of difficulty finding labor points at an obscure but possibly significant influence on villagers' responses to mid-century conditions. Population decline and the ability of small holders to enlarge their farms to the point of self-sufficiency in basic foodstuffs should have cut the supply of rural wage labor and, even with stable demand, raised its price. The rising cost of labor is a commonplace in the post-plague European economy. But around Wrocław rural wage rates are poorly documented. Lacking earlier comparisons, we note only that rye reapers at Wysoka and Trestno in the late 1430s made 4 groschen a day and meals, which exceeded in nominal and, especially, silver value that imposed by statute in the duchy during the 1510s, 36 old heller (3 groschen at the overvalued official rate). See HGZ, fols. 38r, 59v, 60v, 63r, 78v, and 99r–99v, and compare Klose, *Inneren Verhältnisse*, pp. 185–186. If this indicates a short- or medium-term upswing in the 1430s, it too profited surviving small holders. Conversely, tenants with well more than two mansi, like some at Wróblowice in 1438 and several at Komorniki or Jugowiec in 1494, would have found the cost of hired labor—if available—constraining their ability to produce or dispose freely of large quantities of grain beyond the needs, obligations, and productive capacity of their own families.

111. Heck, "Hussitenaufstand," pp. 225–233, well represents this interpretation, as do contributions by him and by Maleczyńska in Maleczyński, *Historia Śląska*, I:2, pp. 89–94 and 229–250.

112. Stobbe, 1867, p. 154. See also *UD*, p. 225.

113. RW, R 3; *NRB*, p. 356; Stobbe, 1867, p. 181, and, for another refusal of obedience, p. 156.

114. *ChronBMV*, pp. 247–248, reports another case, too.

115. Arnold et al., #2204; Schulte, "Vermischte," p. 242; WAA II, IV a 1; *ChronBMV*, pp. 169–170.

116. Kindler, pp. 89–91; WAP Rep 135, E99e, II, #7–8.

117. Dyhernfurth, pp. 20–21.

118. Kindler, p. 75; Klose, *Inneren Verhältnisse*, p. 66.

119. Heck, "Hussitenaufstand," p. 225, listed only the 1420 inquiry from Stobbe, 1866, pp. 360–362. Since Wrocław's elite so feared heretics, Heck's assertion that documentary silence means there really were many thereabouts fails to convince.

120. Heck, "Hussitenaufstand," pp. 226–228; Grünhagen, *Geschichtsquellen*, pp. 64–66; Dziewulski, "Społeczeństwo," pp. 27–28. See note 7 above.

121. Grünhagen, *Geschichtsquellen*, p. 103; Stobbe, 1867, pp. 151–159; Heck, "Hussitenaufstand," pp. 228–233.

122. *ChronBMV*, pp. 220 and 233; RF, IV, 2632–2640; *DT*, p. 315; *PCC*, I, pp. 202–203.

123. Grünhagen, *Geschichtsquellen*, p. 172.

124. Bauch, *Schulwesen*, pp. 122–123; WAA I, IV a 36, fols. 1v–3v; Heyne, *Bisthum*, II, 192–197. See also Arnold et al., p. 356, and Heyne, *Bisthum*, III, 888–889.

125. *ChronBMV*, pp. 169–170.

126. RSC 1475. He excused his failure to transmit tithes by the "magnis dampnis quis plures consumpssisset et expendet. . . ."

27. A thorough discussion is Urban, *Studia*, pp. 127–149 and 221–233. See also Marshall, pp. 41–51; Rosicz, *Chronica*, pp. 580–582.

128. LN, fols. 61r–62r; Bauch, *Schulwesen*, pp. 126–127; see generally Dola, *Kapituła*, pp. 57–110.

129. Fibiger, pp. 309–319; Heyne, *Bisthum*, III, 944–947; Dittrich, "Kreuzherren," pp. 124–127; RF, II, 827; KLM, fols. 9 and 18.

130. Wendt, "Verpfandung," pp. 159–160; RF, I, fol. 29v; KLM, fol. 2.

131. *ChronBMV*, pp. 218–226: "propter penuriam monasterii, provenientem ex destructione bonorum ipsius per nephandos hereticos et alios, ad debita solvenda hinc inde contracta et specialiter ad solvendum supremum jus in Jeraslawicz tunc emptum."

132. *ChronBMV*, pp. 237–256, 169–170, and 172–173. Recovery was costly. To rebuild the abbey's burned mill took two years, 920mk, and unaccounted food and drink for the workers.

133. *NLChron*, pp. 125–132; Klose, *Inneren Verhältnisse*, p. 161; Görlich, *Vincenz*, p. 130 note 2.

134. *NLChron*, p. 132: "Et demum intrans monasterium, tam in spiritualibus quam secularibus quasi desolatum et viduatum sine honore invenit, quia vix decem fratres in toto reperit, item omnia allodia deserta, sine sepibus et inculta jacuerunt vel alia a monasterio alienata."

135. Jesuiter, V:9, #18; VI:1, #16, #24, and #55; VII:3, #11 (38), (29), and (39). The repurchaseable debt instruments among these transcripts give insights unavailable elsewhere.

136. RF, III, 2155 [258]-264; Jesuiter, *passim*. Compare the "economic battering" sustained by noble landowners in disorderly contemporary Brandenburg (Hagen, pp. 90–93).

137. Szwagrzyk, "Szerokie grosze," pp. 65–66.

138. *ChronBMV*, p. 226; *SR* #5827 note; WAP, Rep. 55, #110.

139. HGZ, fols. 18v, 42r, 64r, 82r–83r, 102v, and 118v–119r. For another case see *UD*, pp. 158–159.

140. RB, fol. 11r, and KLM, fol. 26.

141. See Appendix A, Figure A.1b.

142. For methods and tabular presentation of these statistics see Appendix A, Table A.3 and Figure A.1a.

143. Mid-fifteenth-century demesne farms did not differ from those of the fourteenth. Wysoka and Trestno, so well documented during the 1430s, were already seen in Chapter 5 to resemble like enterprises a hundred and more years older. Holy Spirit then also leased demesne land at Lisowice to two laymen who, when they were able to cultivate this in peace, seemingly employed wage laborers in grain production (see HGZ, fols. 12r, 17r, 22v–23r, 40v–41r, 62v–63r, 80v–81r, 101v–102r, and 117v–118r). Compare elsewhere LN, fol. 19v, and Klose, *Inneren Verhältnisse*, p. 190.

144. See above Chapter 4, especially Figures 4.1 and 4.2.

145. Table A.4 and discussion in Appendix A, pp. 389–390.

146. See Table 6.2 and pp. 120–121.

147. See pp. 380–387.

148. The point was argued from preliminary study of the quantifiable data in Hoffmann, "Citizens," pp. 298–303, with references to earlier scholarship.

149. The average estate also remained unchanged: 1.95 holdings per lord in 1425; 1.91 in 1480.

150. RF, III, 2028–2041.

151. RF, I, 127–132.

152. WAA II: XI Piłczyce; Grünhagen, "Protokolle," p. 157; Klose, *Inneren Verhältnisse*, p. 190.

153. Dittrich, "Kreuzherren," pp. 247–248; Heyne, *Bisthum*, III, 945; Fibiger, p. 313; RF, II, 988–989. Compare Mokronos Górny in Dittrich, "Kreuzherren," pp. 124–126, and RF, II, 850.

154. RF, II, 980–981, and I, 418–419. Conrad Runge and Conrad Luckow took over Jakubowice and Siemidrożyce from the heirs of Peter Roster Muhlschreiber in 1441 . For more examples see RF, I, 25a-26b, 76b–79a, 133–139, 310–319; III, 265–269, 315–317, 2012–2021, 2069–2081, 2358–2366 and 2379–2388; and IV, 2801–2805; Dyhernfurth, pp. 30–31. As in the above examples, the new noble owners came from families previously well-documented among the duchy's knights; they were not recently enobled members of the urban elite.

155. RF, III, 2409–2425. For more knights who replaced other owners after 1425 but left before capture by the 1480 tabulation see RF, I, 433–438 and 462–466; II, 558–566; and IV, 2661–2692.

156. RF, I, fol. 37d [sic].

157. Heyne, *Bisthum*, III, 1070–1071; Sommersberg, I:2, 797–798.

158. See a decision of the *iudicium curiae*, WAP Rep. 16, IV 6 a, pp. 4–5, and Kindler, pp. 80 and 196–198. At times Sommerfeld and Hans Runge each had a noble seat on the court (WAP, AMW, C 15).

159. RF, I, 127–132; Markgraf, "Heinz Dompnig," p. 187.

160. It is not likely a result of incomplete data. Less full coverage in 1480 does mean fewer holdings to add up to large estates, but if significant this should also affect the count of noble properties. Those figures suggest no shift of scale.

161. Eschenloer, *Historia*, p. 261. But compare pp. 337–339 below on mid-century profits from trading eastwards.

162. Beyer, pp. 100–113.

163. Petry, *Popplau*, pp. 146–147.

Chapter 11

1. Johnsdorf, p.121, tells how troops Mathias quartered in central Silesia during 1489–90 "devastarunt terram et villas non minus quam foret inimici."

2. Provisions of a *Landfriede* made at a princely Diet in Wrocław, 1482 Oct 27 (*PCC*, II, 66–67) echo for another fifty years in the 400 folios of WAA I, VI a 1. Those set out in 1512 "contra grassatores, spoliatores et incendarios" were applied by the cathedral chapter to calm a village feud at Kończyce (*Ibid.*, pp. 44–45; *ACW*, I, 465, 480–487, 723, 729, 739, and 781).

3. Klose, *Inneren Verhältnisse*, pp. 12–50; *ACW*, I, 516 and 519.

4. "Sunder ym Dorffe, wehr das dorffe bewacht, bewacht auch die mole." *UD*, p. 165.

5. Lamb, *Changing Climate*, p. 101.

6. Stenzel, ed., *Chronica*, pp. 167–168; Fibiger, p. 318; Semkowicz, "Rocznik," p. 739; *ACW*, I, 885–888; Pfotenhauer, "Pförtner," pp. 266–267.

7. Friedensburg, "Getreidepreise," p. 9.

8. The city suffered in 1482–83, 1496, 1507, 1516, 1525, and 1542, but sometimes for less than a month: *NLChron*, p. 135; Henel, pp. 363 and 371; Klose, *Inneren Verhältnisse*, p. 111; Semkowicz, "Rocznik," p. 740; Pfotenhauer, "Pförtner," p. 268.

9. Petry, *Popplau*, pp. 92–94.

10. WAA I, IV a 4a, fol. 34r–35r. A comparable incident from 1530 is reported in Kindler, p. 202.

11. Semkowicz, "Rocznik," pp. 737–738; *ACW*, I, 740. Like cases are *ACW*, I, 503, 554, 619, 701, 772, and 839.

12. Dziewulski, "Zaludnienie," pp. 419–492.

13. As calculated by Heck in Maleczyński, *Historia Śląska*, I:2, 63, from "QBBB," pp. 210–225 and WAA I, II e 11, pp. 85–99 (this manuscript contains material from 1530 to 1593).

14. Klose, *Inneren Verhältnisse*, pp. 185–185 and 208–210; WAA I, VI a 1, pp. 101–104 and *passim*; Schulte, "Erntearbeiter," pp. 190–192.

15. Heyne, *Neumarkt*, pp. 386–393. All land uncultivated in 1494 was at Proszków, but recent resettlement was noted at Ogrodnica and Komorniki. For references to empty rental land at several places on into the 1530s see *ACW*, I, 560; *UD*, p.165; WAA I, III d 34, *sub anno* 1531; WAA I, VI a 1, pp. 126–127.

16. *NLChron*, p. 132; Moepert, *Ortsnamen*, p. 116; WAA I, VI a 1, p. 125; RF, III, 2560; WAP Rep 15, 228, pp. 54–59.

17. *UBB*, pp. 368–369.

18. To most literary tastes the Silesian youths who trudged off to Cracow or Padua in the 1480s or 90s, sat at the feet of Conrad Celtis, and proved their poetic skills with praise of their home province, churned out turgid stuff indeed. Still their rich fields, fat flocks, and exiguous supplies of flour, bread, and beer suggest one undeniable vision of Silesian agriculture then. For examples, see the "Epistola descriptiua" of Wrocław-born Bernhardinus Feyge (Caricinus), published in Cracow in 1499 (Bauch, "Humanismus," pp. 125–126) or lines 71–82 and

161–165 of the more polished *Panegyricus Silesiacus* written before 1506 by Jelenia Góra's Pancratius Vulturinus (ed. Drechsler). A sympathetic reader is Fleischer, "Silesiographia."

19. Klein, ed., pp. 362–363.

20. By about 1550 Silesian rye prices at 20gr the measure doubled those of 1500; the rise went on to the Thirty Years War (Friedensburg, "Getreidepreise," p. 42). On increase from the 1530s of copper prices at Wrocław see Fink, p. 340.

21. Other dues were also the same for long periods (see WAP, AMW, Q 29, I, 2v and 6v; II, 3r and 5v; III, 9r–9v; and compare HGZ). And perhaps more often than the texts can show, from year to year lords accepted cash for obligations in kind. This happened at Czernica in 1532 as it had in 1511, when the cathedral chapter also, "following the observed custom," took money for tithes from Mnichowice (*ACW*, I, 342 and 345–346.

22. WAA I, IV a 41–43, *passim*.

23. WAA I, III d 34, *passim*.

24. WAA I, III d 13–16, *passim*. Domański and Sille, pp. 209–210, finds Trzebnica receiving full rents and taxes from Kotowice in 1523/24.

25. WAP, AMW, Q 29, I, fols. 2v–6v, and II, fols. 3r–5v, and WAA I, III d 98, *sub annis notis*.

26. RSC, *passim*. The cathedral chapter would, however, hear and accommodate with remissions unusual circumstances—a destructive raid, a bad harvest—in a village. See for cases *ACW*, I: 340, 516, 519, 523–524, 528, 534, and 701.

27. For like structural continuity across a late medieval crisis, see Rotelli, *Piemonte*.

28. Manifest interest in the recent past blossomed at Wrocław during the 1450s–90s in LN (Turoń, "*Liber Niger*"); the histories of Rosicz and Eschenloer; *ChronBMV* and St. Mary's chartulary (Wattenbach, "*Repertorium Heliae*"); the chronicles and chartularies for St. Vincent by Nicholas Liebental; and the legal researches of Caspar Popplau (Goerlitz, "Verfasser"). The descriptive and retrospective Silesian literary tradition represented in the next generation by humanist-trained authors had antecedents more extensive than Fleischer, "Silesiographia," attests.

29. *UD*, pp. 164–167. See also Fibiger, pp. 318–323.

30. *UBB*., pp. 366–370, notably articles 4 and 8.

31. RUL, #39.

32. WAA I, III d 34 is not paginated or foliated but the years of account are numbered. Compare at Kryniczno *ACW*, I, 560.

33. The relative well-being of *central* Silesian peasants is noted in Heck, *Studia*, pp. 30–51 and 288.

34. All places on Table 11.2 are in old-settled areas, mostly on the black earth. Małuszów and Mędłów, with their large farms and equality, were full of tenants with Slavic-sounding names: e.g. Simon Piotrak, Stenzel Woytke, Wenczil Brosky, Matschek Arula, Woytek David, Wyczek. The smallest average farm on the table is at Tarnogaj in 1532, where the dozen tenants included Borsche, Berger, Cranse, Rost, Wanger, Nickel Essig, and Paul Pusch. If the particulars in the extant written record accurately represent the past, that from the Wrocław duchy fails to sustain ethnic determinism of the peasant situation.

35. See Figure 9.1.

36. Compare Table 10.4a and Table 9.1.

37. WAA I, III d 34, *passim*.

38. WAA I, III d 13–16, *passim*; WAA I, III d 32, *sub anno* 1536.

39. Klose, *Inneren Verhältnisse*, p.308. Long-term comparison is vitiated not only by great differences among these few price citations but also by earlier ones coming only from tenurially eccentric Krępice, where early fifteenth century levels of almost 20mk the mansus had been halved by the 1460s.

40. WAA I, III d 13–16. Land markets among the next generation of peasants should be examined from sources seemingly not available for the Middle Ages. Village court registers from central Silesia are mentioned in Laband, "Gerichtsbücher," pp. 20–22; WAP Rep 135, E113f, p. 5; Bruchmann, "Quellen" and "Schöffenbücher." Examples still found at Wrocław begin only in the late 1510s and -20s, so can offer little germane to this study. Their chaotic early years give evidence of dealings in land, but larger conclusions must range well beyond the 1520s. See WAP, AMW, Q 347, 1 and WAP, AMW., Q 348, 1a.

41. WAA I, III d 34, *sub annis notis*.

42. By 1522 the schulz had the rest of the Polsky tenure. Three or four times, then,

Bartusch Kosel is recorded in transactions which moved land among existing farms. Real tenurial and operational units were not fixed in medieval German law villages.

43. Stenzel, ed., *Chronica*, pp. I, 167–168.

44. Klose, *Inneren Verhältnisse*, pp. 81–85, 211, and 214. Kindler, p. 75, has villagers marketing at Środa.

45. "Exiguo defert alimenta clientulus aere / Empta foro; reperis spatiosis omnia circis," Vulturinus, *Panegyricus*, lines 161–162; Klein, ed., p. 362; *ACW*, I, 506.

46. As cited in Rauprich, "Streit," pp. 83–84. Compare the close correlation between English peasants' wealth and access to markets in Biddick, pp. 823–831. Wrocław peasants thus contradict the scenario of Graus, "Problematik," p. 69, who blames the revival of demesne farming on rent rates frozen by lack of market opportunities.

47. John's reputation gains from the full account by his own chronicler, Liebental, but good charter evidence confirms the reports. Both are in *NLChron*, pp. 132–140. See also Görlich, *Vincenz*, pp. 133–136; Heyne, *Bisthum*, III, 933; RF, IV, 2911.

48. Some new borrowing refinanced debts incurred for Grabiszyn (Görlich, *Vincenz*, p. 133).

49. WAP Rep. 67, #377.

50. *NLChron*, pp. 32 and 35–37; Görlich, *Vincenz*, p. 137; Heyne, *Bisthum*, III, 933.

51. *NLChron*, pp. 37–38 and 141; *ACW*, I, 785–786; Görlich, *Vincenz*, p. 139.

52. For achievements of St Mary's Benedict Johnsdorf (1470–1503) and Thomas von Falkenhain (1503–29) see *ChronBMV*, pp. 260–261, and Wattenbach, "*Repertorium Heliae*," pp. 202–205. On the "rechter Restaurator" of Lubiąż, Andreas Hoffman, see Wattenbach, "Dittmans Chronik," pp. 282–284; Grotefend, "Signaturbuche," pp. 202–207 and 281; RF, III, 2408 and 2453. What little may be learned about the estates of Wrocław-area convents also points to recovery of lost rights and properties. For Trzebnica see Heyne, *Bisthum*, III, 1083; Bach, pp. 110–131; RF, II, 575; Domański and Sille. Meager traces about the Dominican nuns of St. Katherine and about St. Clare are in Dittrich, "Eckersdorf," pp. 258–259, and Heyne, *Bisthum*, III, 1004.

53. Fibiger, pp. 318–323; Dittrich, "Kreuzherren," pp. 247–248; Heyne, *Bisthum*, III, 945 and 947; RF, II, 989.

54. Wutke, "Oybin," pp. 37–41; Kindler, p. 159; RF, I, 442.

55. *UBB*, pp. xcviii–ci and 365–371; Sommersberg, I:2, 798–800; Heyne, *Bisthum*, III, 326–330; Bauch, "Roth;" Marshall, pp. 51–59.

56. WAA I, II e 11, pp. 76–98 and 125–130.

57. Bauch, *Schulwesen*, p. 127; Heyne, *Bisthum*, I, 425.

58. Dola, *Kapituła*, pp. 84–106; Laug, "Domkapital;" *ACW*, I, 696–698.

59. Ludat, *Bistum Lebus*, pp. 205–206; Wohlbrück, II, 399–404.

60. Wendt, *Landgüter*, p. 5; Heyne, *Bisthum*, III, 134; WAP, AMW, Q 29, 1, fols. 8v–9v.

61. The above follows Wendt, "Verpfandung," pp. 160–166, and Luchs, pp. 363–365, and not the unsupported Szczesniak, pp. 21–22.

62. Wattenbach, "Abbruch;" Wendt, "Kirchenpolitik." A continuator of Liebental (*NLChron*, p. 141) tells how this and royal taxes caused financial distress under abbot John Tyle (1529–45).

63. See Appendix A, Table A.1, rows 5–7. A useful appreciation of the cultural climate remains Dersch, "Vorabend."

64. The text is in Klose, *Inneren Verhältnisse*, p. 31.

65. See Appendix A, Table A.1, lines 11–13 and 22–23.

66. In general for what follows see Małowist, "Trade," pp. 549–550; Henning; Wolański; Wendt, *Orient*, pp. 6–84; Rauprich, "Handelslage." Henning's reading of trends at Wrocław convincingly shadows the more rosy picture given for the entire province by Wolański.

67. Henning, p. 121; Mendl, pp. 164–176; Eulenberg, pp. 267–272.

68. Scholz-Babisch; Ahlborn; Stromer; Petry, *Popplau*, pp. 62–74.

69. Fink, pp. 294–340.

70. Rauprich, "Streit," pp. 54–116; Samsonowicz, "Przemiany," pp. 703–706; Semkowicz, ed., "Rocznik," pp. 737–738; *ACW*, I, 503–504.

71. Henning, p. 121, argued that key craftsmen were too few in sixteenth century Wrocław for any serious export production.

72. Tync. See also Maleczyński, "Dzieje Wrocławia," p. 265; Pfeiffer, "Entwicklung," pp. 112 and 116–118; Witzendorf-Rehdiger, "Adel," pp. 207–208.

73. Petry, *Popplau*, pp. 142–145; Pfotenhauer, "Popplau." Nicholas's contemporaries, Christopher and Leonard Skopp, did keep their Wrocław citizenship, but lived as rambunctious rural squires (RF, I, 477; Pfeiffer, *Patriziat*, pp. 266–267).

74. Bauch, "Sauermann." Conrad held the castle at Jelczyce from the bishop. For more knights from city backgrounds see RUL, #60; Foerster, "Ribisch."

75. *ACW*, I, 696–698. Unlike some German chapters, that at Wrocław never barred canons of non-noble birth (Pfeiffer, "Entwicklung," p. 118; Dola, *Kapituła*, pp. 128–130).

76. Petry, *Popplau*, pp. 28 and 146–152, also noted (p.3) the frequency of "dieses Aufgehen alter Kaufmannsfamilie im Landadel." Tync, pp. 99–100, shows a general mid-sixteenth-century move by leading old Wrocław families from trade to the land.

77. Pfeiffer, "Entwicklung," p.113.

78. See Appendix A, notably Table A.1 and Table A.2.

79. RF, I, 14v, 196, 220, 406, 455, 473–498; II, 602, 735, 900; III, 277; Jesuiter, VI:III, #11.

80. Paul Monaw: RF, I, 147, 182; II, 795, 875; III, 2123–2130; IV, 2957–2958. Nicholas Uthman: RF, I, 824; II, 619, 810–814; III, 2131–2139; IV, 2628–2629; *NLChron*, p.141; WAP Rep 15, 228, p. 58.

81. For data see Stein, pp. 115–121, and Pfeiffer, *Patriziat*, pp. 255–258 and table 18. The former's reconstruction better fits extant record sources.

82. RF, I, 17r, 34r–36v, 48r–49r, 183–186, 358–367; II, 586, 988–989, 1024–1028, 1045–1048; IV, 2733–2737, and 3074–3075; RB, fols. 1v, 4r, 4v, and 11v; *DT*, p. 315; Fibiger, pp. 312–314; Dittrich, "Kreuzherren," pp. 247–248; WAA I, III d 2, pp. 36–37. See also Wutke, "Jenkwitz."

83. RB, fol. 4v; RF, I, 34v–36v, and III, 2428–2444.

84. RF, II, 558–566 and III, 2409–2425 and 2428–2444.

85. RF, IV, 2596–2612.

86. RF, I, 1r–3v, 11v; II, 592; IV, 3083.

87. Most facts are in Stein, pp. 159–161, and Pfeiffer, *Patriziat*, pp. 263–265 and table 23. Peter and his business partner and likely brother Franz took up residence, wives, and municipal office in Wrocław in the 1420s. See also RF, III, 2028–2041; IV, 2979–2986; RUL, #12, 13, and 16.

88. RF, I, 18v–20r; RUL #19.

89. RF, I, 42r; II, 883–900; III, 2028–2041; IV, 3003–3010, 3074–3075; RUL, #19.

90. RF, I, 18v–20r, 455; II, 850, 883–900; IV, 3009; Jesuiter, V:III, #7. See also Dittrich, "Kreuzherren," pp.124–126.

91. RF, I, 18v–20r, 455; IV, 2979–2986, 3010; RUL, #43–44.

92. RF, I, 29r–34r; III, 311, 2123–2130.

93. Klose, *Inneren Verhältnisse*, pp. 162–163; Petry, *Popplau*, pp. 148–149. See also a lesser urban kin group, the Krapfs, in *UD*, pp. 70–73.

94. Pfeiffer, *Patriziat*, p. 203, typically ignored the purpose and chronology of citizen use of the Roman law *fideicommissum*. He only lamented that those who used it were abandoning the "capitalist" mentality of the town.

95. RF, II, 866–875, and IV, 2898–2911; Pfeiffer, *Patriziat*, p. 296. The Hornigs gained noble status in 1549 (Witzendorf-Rhediger, "Adel," p. 208).

96. RF, IV, 2928–2930; *UD*, pp. 83–85; Pfeiffer, *Patriziat*, pp. 184–185; Witzendorf-Rhediger, "Adel," p. 208.

97. The city had at least fifteen lordships in the duchy by 1550 and closer to twenty by the start of the Thirty Years War; almost ten were still municipal property in 1900. See Wendt, "Landbesitz," pp. 216–218, and *Landgüter*, pp. 3–5 and 202–208; Kraemer, pp. 19–61.

98. Kindler, pp. 81–84 and 153–160. Compare also RF, III, 2294, and Pfotenhauer, "Pförtner," p. 293.

99. Those who in 1522 wrote to King Lewis as the "Ritterschaft" or "Adel" of the duchy (Klose, *Inneren Verhältnisse*, pp. 31–32; reprinted in Hoffmann, "City-state," pp. 198–199) are best approximated with the families whose members then shared the four annual noble (as opposed to citizen) seats on the *iudicium curiae* (WAP, AMW, C15). During 1480–1530 families of recent urban origin were not there represented—with the single exception of Hans Popplau in 1514–15. What follows, and specifically the profile of noble landownership in 1530, includes no estates built by a citizen who then became one of the "Ritterschaft." The process of socio-cultural change was not so abrupt.

100. Kindler, p. 115, used texts no longer extant.

101. RF, I, 239–246. Compare similar behavior among the Luckows and the Haugwitzes at Radecz (RF, III, 2528–2533).

102. The Debitsch estate may be tracked through RF, I, 231–235 and 247–254; II, 578, 657, and 925–933; III, 2489 and 2528–2533; and IV, 2860–2861. Supplemental records are Jesuiter, VI:III, #11:102; *UD*, pp. 83–84; and Haeusler, *Geschichte*, p. 316. Ernst died an outlaw and his fiefs forfeit for attacks on Uraz, but his heirs fought the charge strongly enough to retain four of the six properties (see Wendt, *Landgüter*, pp. 207–208).

103. RF, I, 76v–79r and 99–102; Kindler, pp. 80–81 and 196–198.

104. RF, III, 265–269; IV, 3039–3059; WAA I, III d 2, pp. 210–211. Records from the duchy do not, however, prove these long tenures were sustained by the formal entails then adopted in the Polish kingdom by first magnates, then *szlachta*. Cooper, pp. 198–199, reviewed earlier scholarship but Gawęda, pp. 53–59, has found magnate entails a century earlier, in the 1470s.

105. RF, III, 2428–2444. Compare Piotrowice, Damianowice, and Karczyce in RF, I, 76v–79r and 473–478; II, 961–977.

106. RF, I, 214–220. For late fifteenth- and early sixteenth-century consolidations at Węgry, Mrozów, Źródła, Mokra, Olbrachtowice, and Kulin see RF, I, 1r–3v, 45r–47r, 439–442; II, 830–839; IV, 2870–2879; RUL, #34–42; Wutke, "Oybin," pp. 37–41.

107. RF, III, 2465–2476.

108. *PCC*, II, 97; Haeusler, *Geschichte*, p. 376. Since Debitsch was gobbling up lands on two sides of Kotowice (see p. 348 above), his reaching for the convent's vill is no surprise.

109. *ACW*, I, 295–296.

110. *ACW*, I, 364–367, 370–371, 375, 378, 448, 517, 521, 526, 528, 536, 539, 540–542, 557, 569, 572, 574–575, 577, 591, 594, 599, 603, 614–616, and 650. Clearly both chapter and hospital hoped continued pressure would bring the other to sell and thus let it consolidate the two lordships of Księże.

111. *ACW*, I, 637.

112. *UBB*, pp. 365–370; Laug, "Kolowratische Vertrag," pp. 37–56.

113. Landlords gained freedom from external authority in two other ways. Entry fines to royal fiefs, valued at 10% of the purchase price, had been abolished for nobles of the Środa district in 1387, but citizens of Wrocław and knights of that district had to wait until 1469 and 1497 respectively (Opitz, pp. 44–50 and 95–100). Also in this context belong both the efforts in 1475 and 1484–90 of Corvinus and his supporters to enforce royal authority over fiefs and the collapse of that policy upon the king's death (Wendt, "Stände," pp. 165–176; *PCC*, II, 78, 92–93, 104–107, 116–118, and 207–214.) Not for almost a half century before and as long after those events had Wrocław duchy lords seriously to fear state interference with the ways they and the courts on which they sat handled their estates.

114. Klose, *Inneren Verhältnisse*, pp. 297–302, includes more cases, as do Wernicke, "Bemerkungen," pp. 298–299, and *ACW*, I, 243 and 537.

115. RF, I, 378 and 381; Dittrich, "Eckersdorf," p.249.

116. RF, II, 615–619; III, 297–300. Compare RF, III, 2337–2357.

117. This was the last record of the latter place; common ownership was a first step towards common identity. See *NLChron*, pp. 132–135 and 137, and the confirmatory secular records in RF, I, 155–158 and IV, 2898–2911 (where the compiler confused *Gąska* and Wojtkowice with Gąsiorów and Wojkowice). Compare dealings by Lubiąż in RF, III, 2445–2453; Wattenbach, "Dittmans Chronik," 281; Seidel, *Beginn*, p.94.

118. See notes 102 and 59 above.

119. RF, I, 206–212; Wutke and Türk; RF, III, 321–324.

Chapter 12

1. That order is depicted in Heck, *Studia*, who credited (pp. 288–302) relatively greater peasant prosperity and access to markets for its belated arrival in Silesia *et fortiori* around Wrocław. The operational assumptions of the new regime are those Witold Kula wrestled to reimagine in *An Economic Theory*. Kula's theory of how the system came to work does not, however, explain how it came to be. One classic explanation was well stated by Jerome Blum, who stressed noble legislative power and export markets. Laszlo Makkai elegantly reformu-

lated the competing hypothesis, which emphasizes the pressures of rising landlord demand for purchasing power against a sparse and unproductive agricultural population. As will become plain, these interpretations neither separately nor together account for developments around Wrocław. The weakness and temporal disjunction there of the economic and political preconditions elsewhere thought critical suggests mechanical causality had less importance than cultural preconceptions and individual contingencies. But one principality with visible internal differences can only display, not be the prototype for, a general regional shift towards authoritarian lord-peasant relations.

2. Klein, ed., p. 363.

3. *ACW*, I, 340.

4. Goerlitz, "Verfasser." RW is arranged by provenance of cases and principles cited. Popplau indexed it by subject in "Remissorium über den Sachsenspiegel, Weichbildrecht, Lehenrecht, Landrecht, und Breslischen Stadtrecht" (WAP, AMW, J8), where the key word "Pawern" (pp. 681–691) lists all entries mentioned below. For an early study see Böhlau.

5. RW, T85, T90, and S96–97 are extracts from a late collection of glosses on *Sachsenspiegel*.

6. RW, K11–12. Had Merot tried to make a case for his *rechtem armut*? The decision speaks not thereto.

7. RW, T87–89, T91–92, and U22.

8. Heck, *Studia*, p. 41, citing WAA I, VI a 1, pp. 7–8.

9. WAA I, VI a 1, pp. 44–45 and 164–170. See Frauenstadt, p. 247.

10. RW, D4–5, K85, R31, and U4.

11. Opitz, pp. 50–79, 109, and 356–361.

12. Heyne, *Bisthum*, III, 1017; Kindler, pp. 198–199.

13. Pfeiffer, *Patriziat*, p. 218 note.

14. Wendt, *Landgüter*, pp. 20–21; RF, III, 2049–2060. See also *UD*, pp. 74, 81–85 and 164–168.

15. *UD*, p. 226: "vil beschwerliche hoffarbayt, dazu sy verpflicht."

16. RF, II, 874–875.

17. Goerlitz, *Verfassung*, pp. 101–104; *NRB*, pp. 30–32 and 243–244.

18. RF, I, 437; II, 782; III, 323. Pfeiffer, *Patriziat*, pp. 220–221, gives more cases, asserting the decline in status and autonomy was continuous from the late fourteenth century, but offering only sales to landowners, with six of nine instances dating after 1480 and two from the 1430s. A classic study is Rutkowski.

19. *ACW*, I, 687–688 and 857; WAA I, II e 11, pp. 85–91, 96–98, and 125–130.

20. Dittrich, "Eckersdorf," p. 252.

21. RF, II, 587 and 815; Kindler, pp. 201–202.

22. Kindler, pp. 92–93 and 98. See also Dyhernfurth, pp. 20–21.

23. *ACW*, I, 130, 306, 554, 612 and 897–898, includes other cases.

24. For treatment broader than here attempted see Heck, "Reformacja."

25. RSC, *sub annis dictis*; Wutke, "Oybin," pp. 43–44; Domański and Sille, p. 210.

26. *UD*, pp. 225–226.

27. WAA I, III d 34, 1532.

28. *UD*, pp. 84–85. The two lords had earlier agreed that the choice between labor and money was theirs alone (*UD*, pp. 81–83).

29. Opitz, pp. 356–358. Such actions violated one of Popplau's Magdeburg precedents, where fifty years previous custom stopped a lord from raising fines for missing a court (RW, L56).

30. Better-known peasant struggles in the Duchy of Świdnica differed little from those near Wrocław. At Piotrowice near Jawór in 1527 armed villagers, their schulz in the van, assaulted the royal governor who had come to put down their opposition to new rents. Arrests, shameful public penances, and a few expulsions quelled the disturbance. Conspiracies and confrontations the next summer at Janice near Lwówek Śląskie focussed on a lord who preempted peasant produce. A court of nobles confirmed his rights but told him to give fair price, avoid novelties, and not pressure schulzen once the rents had been paid. Kern, "Bauernunruhen," pp. 25–29, gives most details, but see also Meyer, *Gemeinde*, pp. 52–53. (This unrevised 1944 dissertation has no cases from the Duchy of Wrocław.) For suppression of more plainly religious unrest around Głogów see Grünhagen, "König Ferdinand," pp. 70–72; Maleczyńska, "Niektóre zagadnienia;" Heck, "Reformacja," pp. 40–46.

31. Küchler, pp. 60–63 and 69–75. Exemplary texts from the duchy are *NRB*, pp. 280–285; *PCC*, II, 95–96; and *UBB*, p. 367.

32. RF, III, 324; Kindler, pp. 139–140. See also *UD*, pp. 163–164 and 168.

33. Orzechowski, pp. 229–245; Lindgren, pp. 57–88.

34. Kindler, p. 75.

35. Items 5 and 7 of the Kolovrat treaty, *UBB*, pp. 366–368.

36. Klose, *Inneren Verhältnisse*, p. 219; Pfotenhauer, "Pförtner," pp. 272–273. WAA I, II e 11 was a response.

37. WAP, AMW, Q 29, 1, fol. 5. Contrast earlier activities of a well-endowed hereditary schulz there (RF, I, 370–381; RSL, 1406–57). For lords involved in other private financial dealings of tenants see *ACW*, I, 748–749, 753, 763, and 786).

38. *ACW*, I, 844 (and a like case on p. 306).

39. WAA I, III d 34, 1531. For lords elaborately concerned with local criminal justice, see *ACW*, I, 578, 588–590, 597–598, 611, 616, 625, 632–633, 642–643, 652–656, 658–659, 671, 674–676, 678, 694, 702, 704, 744, 823, 835, and 837–839.

40. *ACW*, I, 254, 257, 260, 493, 527, 529, 637 and 894, includes further examples.

41. WAA I, III d 34, 1531.

42. *PCC*, I, 133–134. Likewise did the cathedral chapter in 1516 plot ways for peasants from Ołtaszyn and Polanowice to evade summons to the Wrocław district court (*ACW*, I, 855 and 898–899).

43. *ACW*, I, 340, 773, and in the Księże fishery dispute with St. Mathias as discussed p. 349 above.

44. "Weil ihr aber als ein Pfarrer meine Leuthe mit Gottes Rechte nicht vorsehen wollt, muss ich demnach sehen, das sie damit versorgt werden und nicht wie ein Viehe leben." *UD*, pp. 74–79.

45. *ACW*, I, 516, 519, 523–524, 528, and 534. For the situation see RF, I, 36v, and Klose, *Inneren Verhältnisse*, pp. 33–50.

46. *ChronBMV*, p. 255. Lords of all sorts arranged tithes for their peasants in *ACW*, I, 342, 607, and 717).

47. *ACW*, I, 617 and 619, with verification from RF, II, 586–587. Allegedly unjust bans for refusal of uncustomary tithes were protested with at least partial success by other citizen lords (*Ibid.*, pp. 130, 726, and 897–898).

48. Vocabulary and concept were introduced by Wolf, "Aspects," pp. 1072–1076, and elaborated by Mendras, pp. 133–137. Interpretation of the schulz in these terms was on pp. 241–242 above.

49. For legal aspects of lordly control see Meyer, *Gemeinde*, pp. 85–87, 100, 119, and 145–148.

50. "Ich N.N. holde und schwere dem hochwirdigen Herrn Joanni Bischoffe und Abbt, seiner Gnaden als meinem rechten natürlichen erbherren und dem löblichen Stiffte-Sanct Vincenz alhie tzu Bresslaw getreu, gewehr und underthenig tzu sein, seiner Gn. und des convents gutt und bestes tzu ertrachten und arges zu verhütten, noch meinem gantzen Vermogen, dartzu mir Got helffe." Laband, "Gerichtsbücher," p. 22.

51. Heyne, *Bisthum*, III, 134; *UD*, pp. 81–83; WAP Rep 135 E113f, p. 5. Compare the abbot of St. Vincent at Kostomłoty in 1506 in *NLChron*, pp. 31–32.

52. Kindler, p. 98 and note.

53. *ACW*, I, 846, gives no cause for the dispute. The chapter about the same time called for "severe imprisonment" for the "impertinence and malevolence of the peasant Paul Golisch in Szukalice" and jailed some peasants from Polanowice "qui renuunt ducere frondes [?garlands] pro ecclesia Wratislaviensi" (*Ibid.*, 847 and 658). Recall how Wrocław broke resistance at Krępice.

54. WAA I, III d 34, 1532.

55. *ACW*, I, 723, 729, 739, and 781; WAA I, III d 2, pp. 33–35; *NRB*, p. 286. At Polanowice the lord often came into interminable disputes among buyers, sellers, alleged heirs, and other claimants to rights of the scholtisei (*ACW*, I, 301, 402, 406, 418, 421, 552, 586, 616–617, 621, 623, 627, 633, 641, 670–671, 745, 870, 895, 906, and 937).

56. *ACW*, I, 785, 818, 844, and 927 (with more such acts).

57. *Ibid.*, p. 266; *UD*, pp. 81–85. For equally arbitrary responses to problems the unstable coinage posed for rent payments see *ACW*, I, 503, 701, 740, and 772.

58. WAA I, IV a 8, fols. 60v–61r; *ACW*, I, 318.

59. Heck, "Gospodarce folwarcznej," pp. 195–210.

60. Historiographic context and comparative perspectives on landlord farming elsewhere in contemporary east central Europe are accessible through Makkai; Harnisch, "Gutsherrschaft," pp. 220–240, and "Probleme," pp. 251–274; and Żytkowicz, "Trends." Hagen, p. 93, makes revival of demesne farming in the Prignitz a direct response to losses of income.

61. Klose, *Inneren Verhältnisse*, pp. 306–307. For like arrangements elsewhere see *Ibid.*, pp. 190–191 and 307–308; Dittrich, "Eckersdorf," pp. 253–254; WAP Rep 15, 228, p. 52; Pfotenhauer, "Pförtner," p. 294; WAP, AMW, Q 29, 1, fols. 3–6.

62. *ACW*, pp. 252–253, 451–454, 477, 478, 634, 856, and 871 (". . . ne allodium ipsum propter carentium gubernatoris in suis agris desoletur aut dispendium aliquod patiatur").

63. Kindler, pp. 202–204; *ACW*, I, 524 and 730.

64. Heck, "Gospodarce folwarcznej," pp. 187–191, and compare Matějek, who examined an area near Opole in 1588.

65. Heyne, *Neumarkt*, pp. 390–391; Pfeiffer, *Patriziat*, p. 240.

66. Wohlbrück, II, 404.

67. *UD*, pp. 86 and 227–229. The laggard new creations explain why settlement types changed little before 1530 (p. 326 above).

68. Klose, *Inneren Verhältnisse*, pp. 185–186 and 208–210.

69. Schulte, "Erntearbeiter," pp. 190–192. The much earlier evidence was mentioned p. 105 above.

70. "So wir mit unserm Getreyde in yre Stadt faren, so müssen wir das vorzollen, und werden wegen des Zollis von ynn gepfandt, unser Kleyder von Halsse geryssen, unser Pferde aus den Wagen gespannen, und mit unsern Fyschen vff dem Fyschmargkt und andir unser Landtnahrung dy wyr hynein furen dorch yre neue Offsecze bedrangkt. . . ." (Klose, *Inneren Verhältnisse*, p. 32).

71. *ACW*, I, 273, 438, 615, 575, 702, 785, 865–866, and 923; Wernicke, "Bemerkungen," pp. 298–299. See also Kindler, pp. 155–157.

72. On the Księże dispute see above p. 349 and for Kozanów, *ACW*, I, 526 and 573. All kinds of landowners evidenced in charters and agreements their interest in fisheries located from one end of the bottomlands to the other: Jesuiter, VI:III, #11:65; *ACW*, I, 670–671, 701, and 722; *UD*, pp. 165–167; RF, III, 313; Kindler, pp. 158–160; Pfotenhauer, "Pförtner," p. 295.

73. Klose, *Inneren Verhältnisse*, pp.271–272; Domański and Sille, pp. 209–210. For returns from other fisheries see *Ibid.*, pp. 212–213, and Klose, *Inneren Verhältnisse*, p. 306. Fresh wild fish consumed by Wrocław's Dominicans in the 1490s had to be purchased from local catches (Blasel, pp. 29–34).

74. Stenus, pp. 6–8.

75. Pfeiffer, *Patriziat*, pp. 212–213, seems right to say that a single 1363 reference is the only pre-war hint at fish culture around Wrocław, but his treatment otherwise exaggerates the role of "rücksichtslos kaufmännisch" urban magnates.

76. Neither Nyrek nor Szczygielski gave much attention to the problem of origins.

77. The earliest known undertaking was in 1434, when Hans Bank loaned George Schellendorf 85mk to build a pond at Wojnowice from which Bank could also take fish. Several other new constructions followed thereabouts during the 1440s. See Pfeiffer, *Patriziat*, p. 213 (with some texts now lost); RF, II, 774–782; III, 2445–2453; IV, 2979–2986; RUL, #16 and 19; Jesuiter, IV:VI, #3; VII:I, #2; VII:III, #11.

78. *ChronBMV*, p. 249.

79. Sites recorded above and others in RF, III, 2069–2081 and 2367–2378; IV, 3066–307 [sic]; Görlich, *Vincenz*, p. 137; Wattenbach, "Dittmans Chronik," p. 281; Kindler, pp. 198–199; WAP Rep 135 E113f, pp. 6–7; Heyne, *Neumarkt*, p. 84; RUL #53; *ACW*, I, 408, 504, and 772–773; and Jesuiter, VI:III, #11:119 may be compared with the especially clear map by Wieland.

80. Klose, *Inneren Verhältnisse*, p. 186.

81. RUL, #16 and 18; RF, IV, 2979–2986; Pfeiffer, *Patriziat*, p. 213. Also compare Kindler, pp. 198–199; WAP, Rep 135 E113f, pp. 6–7; Görlich, *Vincenz*, p. 137; Heyne, *Neumarkt*, p. 84; RUL #60.

82. Pfeiffer, *Patriziat*, pp. 212–213 note. Henry [5] Jenkwitz blamed losses on fish ponds for part of his financial trouble. See also Blasel, pp. 29–34; RF, III, 2069–2081.

83. *NLChron*, pp.132–135.

84. Pfeiffer, *Patriziat*, p. 213 note.
85. Dubravius.
86. E. g. RF, III, 2069–2081; IV, 2692; *UD*, pp. 165–168.
87. RUL #39.
88. RF, I, 187–194.
89. Wendt, *Landgüter*, pp. 167 and 130–133.
90. Szulc, map C.
91. WAA I, II e 11 is a good early example, but many later are in Heck, *Studia*, pp. 56–78.
92. RF, III, 2367–2378.
93. *UD*, p. 70.
94. For examples: RF, II, 583, 875, 1005; III, 2130.
95. *UBB*, pp. 366–367.
96. *UD*, p. 78.

Appendix A

1 "QBBB," pp. 195–203.
2. *LFE*, B1–58, B64, B148–156, and B370–388. See the introduction, pp. lxx–lxxii, and Eistert, "Berichtigungen," pp. 347–351.
3. *LFE*, D1–70 and D261–284.
4. Stolle, "*Registrum*," pp. 133–156; Maetschke, pp. 22–33.
5. "Compilatum est presens registrum per Albertum anno domini millesimo trecentesimo quinto" between *LFE*, D282 and D283.
6. No *LB* manuscripts seem to have survived 1945.
7. Brinkmann, pp. 395–412, treated *LB* in detail as a precursor to Charles's later survey of Brandenburg, but Matzen-Stöckert, pp. 30–33, refers only to Stenzel's discussion.
8. *LB* #416–450, gives four sets of payments, only one of which is explicitly dated to 1361. Brinkmann, p. 401 claimed (and nothing suggests otherwise) that all were of about the same age.
9. *LB* is the only survey to include the districts of Kąty and of Namysłów, which the need for consistency omits from this long-term study. That is the chief (and non-recognition of the sites of demesne farms identified by the names of owners another) reason why the 284 places here found in *LB* are less than the 327 counted by Matzen-Stöckert, pp. 305–331, or the 323 by Heck in "Gospodarce folwarcznej," p. 175, and in Inglot et al., p. 73.
10. *BUB* #205; Brinkmann, p. 395.
11. *LB* #406a–406e and 406p–415. Intervening (406f–406o) are the city's accounts for 1348–49 which Stenzel took from K.
12. *LB* #1 and #419 notes.
13. Brinkmann, pp. 396–397.
14. *Ibid.*, pp. 402–408.
15. RB was published as Korta, "Księga," pp. 235–256. Comparison of that edition with the manuscript revealed many dubious readings, including several of numbers (necessary corrections are listed in Hoffmann, "Studies," pp. 273–275).
16. Korta, "Księga," worked with 213 places said to be in both *LB* and RB. Since Korta's edition numbered 214 entries but he noted several duplications and places not adequately recorded in *LB*, it is obscure how he reached the 213 figure.
17. WAP, AMW, C 27.
18. RB, fols. 5r–11r (Korta, "Księga," #86–163).
19. Bosl, pp. 407–408, summarizes from the definitive study by Krofta, pp. 1–26, 237–257, and 437–490. On the same exemption for the "aid" (*pobór*) in Angevin and Jagiellonian Poland see Gieysztor, "L'impot," p. 327.
20. Compare, for instance, the explicit mentions in *LB* #191 and in texts of 1404, 1405, 1425, 1439, and 1443 (RF, I, 127–132; KLM, fol. 27) of a demesne farm at Chwalimierz wholly ignored in RB, fol. 11v (Korta, "Księga," #169). Rüffler, pp. 126–127, who wrote in the 1920s, attributed general recognition of this fact to unpublished writings of the nineteenth-century archivist, Colmar Grünhagen, but Korta, "Księga," seems unaware of it.
21. Although *census* normally meant "rent" (*Zins*) and *censualis* "rent-paying" or "tenant-held" when applied to land, an alternative denotation of any monetary obligation, specifically

to pay public taxes, is not unknown. In Matthew 22:17 the Pharisee asks, "Licet censum dare Caesari aut non?" (Mark 12:14 and Luke 20:22 substitute *tributum*). Compare entries for both terms in the medieval Latin glossaries of DuCange, II, 274–276; Dieffenbach, p. 112 (*census* as *Gelt* as well as *Zins*); Niermeyer, pp. 166–168 (where the basic meaning of *census* is "tax"); and the Bayerische Akademie, II:3, pp. 452–453 and 458.

22. RB, fol. 2v: "Hermansdorff 60 mansi censuales et taberna. Plebanus hebet 3 mansos, non dat. Petrus scultetus presentavit 1 marcam, 3 scotos de 54 [sic. Korta, "Księga," #28, erroneously gives 44] mansis. Item 9 ortulani non dant. Stephanus Smed habet 1 mansum. Non dat. Scultetus etiam non dat de duabus [*sic*] mansis." Compare *LB* #3 and KLM, fol. 5.

Like effects arise where RB gives only the tenant-held "mansi censuales" and the unwary assume these made up the whole village. At Chwalimierz RB, fol. 11v, accounts for only 22 of the 30 mansi well-recorded before and after 1425 (*LB* #191; KLM, fol. 27). Compare Bartoszowa in RB, fol. 5v; *LB* #84; KLM, fol. 12.

23. Ludat, *Stiftsregister*, pp. 36–38; "QBBB," pp. 210–225.

24. Klose, *Von Breslau*, II, 443–449.

25. Tz-S, pp. 550–552.

26. Compare, for instance, the transfer on 30 March 1412 by Lucas von der Nysa to his sons Otto and Stephan of his expectations at Bogdaszowice and a nearby mill as given in full in Curtze, ed., p. 86, and in summary in RF, I, fol. 31r. Further examples are summaries in RF, I, 86–93, I, 498–507, and II, 615 and 663–672 of transactions concerning Domasław, Krepice, and *Łukaszewice* for which full texts appear in *UD*, pp. 1–88 and 197–229. Meitzen's erroneous identification there of *Łukaszewice* as a demesne farm in Domasław has been corrected in Domański, *Nazwy miejscowe*, #175, and (earlier but unbeknownst to Domański) by Heinrich von Loesch in *SR*, VII, 195–196.

27. Three more cases of the collation techniques used to establish lordship series occur in Hoffmann, "Nazwy," pp. 2–25, where sequences of buyers and sellers help distinguish among settlements with virtually identical names. No claims to originality are here made for this tactic of compiling village *Besitzgeschichten*. Its old and honorable, if antiquarian, place in Germanic scholarship is shown in Dittrich, "Eckersdorf," pp. 243–265; Dyhernfurth; Eistert, "Wüstungen," pp. 137–142; Granier, pp. 346–352; Heyne, "Krintsch," pp. 630–638; *UD, passim*; Schulte, "Kostenblut," pp. 209–266; Rüffler, pp. 114–162.

28. As Ładogórski, *Zaludnieniem*, did to convert Peter's pence returns into population estimates (see Chapter 6 note 30).

29. See for example *LB* #3, 76, or 196.

30. For example, RB, fols. 3r, 11v, and 12v (Korta, "Księga," #35, 168, and 193) and KLM, fols 2, 27, and 28.

31. For the terms see Chapter 5 note 2 and works there cited.

32. Kazimierzów: *SR* #5922; *LB* #280; RF, II, 810–814; *PCC*, I, 202–203. Brodno: *UFO* #41; *UD*, pp. 248–251 and 263; *SR* #3875, 4070, 4223, 4224, 5908, and 6619; KdS #355; *SUB*, I, #361; Heyne, *Bisthum*, I, 933 and II, 774–775; RB, fol. 11r; Domański and Sille, eds., p. 213.

33. *SR* #6466 (and, in the original Latin, RF, I, fol. 8v); RF, fols. 8v–9v; *LB*, #230. *SR* #1706 from 1282 says nothing of this.

34. RF, I, fols. 9v–10v; *DT*, pp. 167–168; RB, fol. 1v (Korta, "Księga," #11); KLM, fol. 2.

35. *SR* #4312, 5657, and 6174.

36. *LB* #5.

37. RF, IV, 2942–2957; RB, fol. 5v (Korta, "Księga," #95 as corrected) records the same 54 *mansi censuales*.

38. KLM, fol. 15 (this text often mixes German and Latin); RF, IV, 2957–2958.

39. The ensuing typology of settlement types is exhaustive and the three terms mutually exclusive, thus permitting statistical treatment as a multinomial.

40. Most German authors simply ignored the then unpublished RB. Pfeiffer, *Patriziat*, p. 198, discussed the development and administration of taxes on land by going directly from *LB* to KLM.

41. Korta, "Księga." Surprisingly, Matzen-Stöckert's 1976 study still went straight from *LB* to KLM and did not refer to Korta's work.

42. Korta, "Księga," pp. 226–227. Compare the problems with this approach discussed p. 378 above.

43. *Ibid.*, p. 231, "W świetle uzyskanych danych na podstawie porównania omawianych źródeł da się stwierdzić, że od drugiej połowy wieku XIV i w początkach XV w księstwie wrocławskim dokonywały sie zmiany w kierunku dość silnego powrotu do gospodarki czynszowej kosztem ziemi allodialnej." Korta's point that this also proves that the spread of tenancies had not stopped by 1400 is less well taken; comparison of conditions at two dates can tell nothing of variations in the rate of change during the interval between them.

44. Heck, "Gospodarce folwarcznej," pp. 175–176 note.

45. *Ibid.*, pp. 170–173.

46. Maleczyński, *Historia Śląska*, I:2, 46; Inglot et al., p. 73. Subsequently (and without mention of Heck) Matzen-Stöckert, pp. 405–407, calculated from *LB* (with the Kąty district) 52.1% rental and 23.4% demesne land. Matzen-Stöckert and Heck handle differently land described as woods, waste, or not cultivated.

47. All land must be accounted for. Thus if a settlement has a demesne but the available information does not allow determination of its size, that settlement cannot be included in the full information sample for that survey year.

48. In the rest of this appendix the term *population* will be used only in its statistical sense to mean the entire set of settlements or lands existing in the Wrocław duchy at a particular time. It does not refer to numbers of people.

49. Representation of districts also departed inconsistently from actuality. In 1353, when 65% of the duchy's settlements were in the Wrocław district and 29% in the Środa district, the full information sample has 70% and 25% from them respectively, but in 1425 the same real relationship compared with 82% in the Wrocław district and 14% in the Środa district. Since both the German law data covered in chapter 4 and that of changes in settlement types show more conversion of demesnes to tenancies in the Wrocław district than elsewhere at that time, the greater share of Wrocław district places in the sample from 1425 further exaggerates the increase in rental land. The 1443 full information sample, while well replicating the ratio of the two larger districts, contains no places from the Uraz district.

50. The even more narrowly defined samples which can be made by taking only those places with full information in both of two or more surveys (e.g. 1353 and 1425) all turn out still more heavily biased toward villages and against demesnes.

51. The method was first devised to ensure adequate representation of each distinct group within a subdivided population (a feature not guaranteed by ordinary random sampling). See Parten, pp. 226–236, or Kish, pp. 189–198.

52. Too few demesnes with full information from the Uraz district precluded a sample larger than 25 or better stratification by the population proportions of Wrocław district villages, Środa district villages, Uraz district villages, Wrocław district villages with demesne, and so on. The lack of full information for Uraz district places in 1443 also prevented use of the stratified technique then.

53. The 90% confidence interval is that pair of values between which the parameter being estimated (here the proportions of demesne and of tenant land) will fall in 90% of the random samples of given size taken from that population. For the techniques here employed see, besides works cited in note 51 above, Mendenhall, pp. 147–152 and 162–165. Note that use of the method here does assume that, within each stratum, the full information samples are themselves random with respect to amounts of each land type in their selection of which places appear.

54. In fact, this closely resembles the "disproportionately stratified sample" described in Parten, pp. 483–484, and Kish, pp. 195–196. It does not qualify because here no samples other than the full information sets are created. But like the first technique described, this too relies on the full information sets of each settlement type being representative of all places of that type (i.e., that the Wrocław district villages with full information in 1425 do represent in size and amount of tenant land all Wrocław district villages in that year, and so on).

55. The method cannot be followed for 1300 because no villages with demesne appear in that full information sample. A slightly variant technique necessary for 1443 is discussed below.

56. The duchy-wide current settlement type distribution for 1443 was 33% tenant villages, 38% villages with demesne, and 29% demesnes (see Table A.6). To check the accuracy of this less satisfactory procedure it was also carried out for 1353 and 1425 and the results compared with those acquired by the preferred methods discussed above. For 1353 the duchy-wide stratification profile gave total estimated proportions of 51% tenant land and 37% de-

mesne land compared with 53% and 38% by the fully subdivided procedure, and for 1425 the estimates were even closer, 65% and 27% compared with 66% and 27%. When the duchy-wide version was limited to the Wrocław and Środa districts as the 1443 data requires, the 1353 set gave a breakdown of 51% and 39% while that for 1425 yielded 66% and 27%. Since none of these less satisfactory procedures departed greatly from the estimates developed by the best means available, use of the duchy-wide profile on the 1443 information should create little additional risk of error.

Appendix B

1. Suggestions in Friedensburg, *Münzgeschichte*, II, 315, of a smaller Polish mark are refuted by Pošvář, "Pieniądz," pp. 13–16. Proximity of the 183.5 gram Polish mark to the mark of Cologne does hint at early German influence on Polish mints, but Meinhardt, pp. 44–48, depends too exclusively on Friedensburg and German authorities to make convincing his assertion of entirely German models for thirteenth-century Silesian coins. Maleczyński, "Z dziejów gornictwa," pp. 236–283, provides background on Silesian mining (*not* an activity of the Wrocław duchy).

2. Friedensburg, *Münzgeschichte*, II, 25–26. See also his "Münzstätte," pp. 91–101, and *Schlesischen Münzen*.

3. General discussion of central Europe in Kiersnowski, *Wielka reforma*, I, 166–224, is specified for Bohemia and Silesia in Castelin; Szwagrzyk, "Szerokie grosze," pp. 87–89; Pošvář, "Pieniądz," pp. 31–32. See also Spufford, pp. 273 and 284.

4. Meinhardt, pp. 49–51, summarized and updated Friedensburg, *Münzgeschichte*, II, 53.

5. Rosicz, *Gesta*, p. 45, repeated a crude ditty nailed one night to the *Rathaus* door. More generally see Friedensburg, *Münzgeschichte*, I, #79, and II, pp. 72–79. Treatment of money in Maleczyński. *Historia Śląska*, I:2, 159–162, is chiefly about counterfeiting.

6. Day, "Monetary Contraction," and "Bullion Famine," provide systemic meaning for Silesian facts treated in isolation by Maleczyńska in *Historia Śląska*, I:2, 100–101, and Maleczyński, "Z dziejów gornictwa," p. 248.

7. Rosicz, *Gesta*, p. 72. Failure of a 1455 agreement among Silesian princes is no surprise, since it decreed 480hl to the fl and 17hl to the gr, while the fl was also to equal 28gr (or 476hl). See Friedensburg, *Münzgeschichte*, I, #4, and II, p. 54.

8. *Ibid.*, II, 84–92 and 176–178.

9. *Ibid.*, II, 92–101; *Historia Śląska*, I:2, 157–163; Friedensburg, "Breslauer Pönfall," pp. 89–100, and "Münzen König Ferdinands," pp. 213–230 and 282–284; Meinhardt, pp. 51–53. Silesian gold coinage was always quite small. Wrocław received the right to coin gold in 1360 but did so only after 1517.

10. Pošvář, "Talary," pp. 318–325; Friedensburg, "Breslauer Pönfall," pp. 100–126.

Appendix C

1. Domański, *Nazwy miejscowe*, is an indispensible tool for correct historical study of the region.

2. Moepert, *Ortsnamen*.

NOTES TO MAPS AND FIGURES

Figure 4.2. Places with datable grants of German law, 1220–1549

The following datable German law texts underlie the graphs, with tabulations using the earlier date if several charters exist:

1221	Tyniec Mały *KdS* #253; *SUB*, I, #354.
1234	Domaniów *SUB*. II, #86
1235	Wierzbno *SUB*, II, #107 (permission; contract in 1253, *SR* #808, *SLU* #14)
1240	Zabłoto *SUB*, II, #181 and 193.
1244	Janików *SUB*, II, #274.
1240s	Kostomłoty *KdS* #248; *SUB*, I, #351.
1250	Karczyce *SUB*, II, #410.
1251	Rzeplin *SLU* #1. Contracts in 1253, 1254, and 1262 are *SLU*, #13, 19, and 46.
1251	Szukalice Same texts as Rzeplin except for 1262.
1251	Polanowice *SLU* #7. Repeated 1268 (*SLU* #65).
1251	Pisarzowice *SLU* #8.
1252	Wilkowice *SLU* #9.
1252	*Zielona* *SLU* #11 and *SR* #1641.
1256	Święte *SLU* #29.
1260	*Platea Romanorum* *LFE* B39 and "QBBB," pp. 197–198.
1261	Łowęcice *SR* #1081.
1261	Warzyn *NRB*, p. 383 and *SR* #1102.
1263	Gosławice *SLU* #48, but identified as Stenzel in *Jahresberichte*, 1844, p. 102 (*SR* #1156) and Matzen-Stöckert, pp. 224–225.
1264	Pietrzykowice *SLU* #51.
1265	Turów *SLU* #55.
1265	Czernica *SLU* #56. Contract in 1273; *SLU* #77.
1269	Mnichowice *SR* #1331 and Matzen-Stöckert, p. 223, but identified as Hoffmann, "Nazwy," pp. 2–9.
1272	Czeczy *SLU* #73.
1273	Wrocław-Gaj *SLU* #76.
1277	Mrozów *SLU* #84.
1280	Wrocław-Żerniki *SLU* #89.
1286	Szczepankowice *SLU* #101.
1289	Przesławice *SLU* #109.
1289	Mokra *SLU* #110.
1289	Ligotka *SLU* #111, but identified as this place by comparison with *LFE* D271, *LB* #187. and RF, I, 93–94.
1291	Muchobór Wielkie *SLU* #112.
1291	Piłczyce *SLU* #114.
1291	Nadolice Wielkie *SLU* #115.
1292	Kamieniec Wr. *SLU* #116.
1292	Swojczyce *SLU* #116.
1292	Maślice *SR* #2233.
1292	Kozanów *SLU* #118.
1293	Jaszkotle *SLU* #122.
1293	Kojęcin *SLU* #123.
1294	Kotowice, pow. Trzeb. *UFO* #103; *SR* #2339.
1310	Bartoszowa *SR* #3138.
1312	Chrząstowa Mała *SR* #3286 and 3296.

1339	Smolec Wielkie *SR* #6302.
1341	Blizanowice *SR* #6665.
1341	Bielany Wrocławskie *SR* #6669.
1342	Partynice *SR* #6954.
1342	Królikowice *SR* #6842.
1344	*Cruce* LN, fols. 370r–371r; *RS*, I, #211 and 836 (repeated 1348).
1345	Iwiny RF, II, 866.
1345	Święta Katarzyna RF, III, 282 (for 7½ mansi of demesne in a village with other evidence of German law before 1260, as reported in *SLU* #41). *RS*, I, #303 omits *locatio* rights.
1345	Boguszyce *LB* #20 note; RF, I, 37v.
1345	Gądów Mały LN, fols. 38v–39r; *RS*, I, #343.
1345	Strachowice *RS*, I, #337.
1345	*Oporzyce* *RS*, I, #305.
1346	*Leimgruben* *HPR*, p. 84 note 1.
1348	Owsianka *RS*, I, #794 (probably never exercised).
1350	*Lukaszewice* *UD* #20.
1350	Boreczek RF, I, fols. 39r–42r.
1351	Brochów *RI*, 8:2, #6672; *ChronBMV*, p. 196; *RS*, II, #541.
1351	Cesarzowice, pow. Wr. RF, I, fol. 24v.
1352	Pustków Żurowski LN, fols. 375v–376r; *RS*, II, #615.
1354	Siechnice *UD*, #14–15 (permission followed in 1357).
1357	Mokronos Górny *UD*, #15; Fibiger, pp. 303–305.
1359	Żerniki Małe RF, IV, 2617–2629.
1359	Marcinkowice *RBM.*, 7:1, #130.
1359	Stary Śleszów RF, III, 2300–2317.
1362	Kębłowice *LB* #320 note.
1364	Budziszów, pow. Wr. *RI.*, 8:2, #7121; *ChronBMV*, p. 200.
1373	Wrocław-Borek *BUB*, #285.
1375	Kończyce LN, fols. 34v–35v.
1386	Mokry Dwór Pfotenhauer, ed., *Kamenz*, #278.
1393	Bliż LN, fols. 143r–144r.
1395	Biestrzyków LN, fols. 24v–25r, and Dittrich, "Eckersdorf," p. 245.
1502	Złotniki *RUL*, #39.

Not accepted as actual grants of German law *locatio* are 7 thirteenth-century charters used in *SLU* and Matzen-Stöckert, pp. 223–227, for sites in the later Wrocław duchy. Especially by comparison with Moepert, *Ortsnamen*, p. 115, nothing connects with Wszemiłowice the "Semyanouo" of a 1257 contract (*SLU* #32). Six other cases (*SLU* #53, 69, 105, 117, 128, and 130) refer not to German law villages but to individuals with leasehold, sublordship, or even lordship under substantive German rather than Polish law (see chapter 4 page 62 and note 6).

Matzen-Stöckert, pp. 225–226, gives 9 sites with 11 charters for *locatio* between 1300 and 1342. Six of the sites are those above, but Blizanowice in 1341 is omitted. Matzen-Stöckert adds *UD* #4 for *Łukaszewice* in 1306 and *SR* #4421 and 4500 for Strachocin in 1325–26; these texts describe landowners with proprietory rights under German rather than Polish law and not the (intended) creation of a German law village.

Map 5.4. Demesne farm production, ca.1250–ca.1425

Production on demesne farms at the sites shown is recorded in: *SR* #1275, 1377, 2037, 2054, 2236, 2237, 2362, 3284, 3367, 3402, 3409, 3904, 3930; 4163, 4240, 4260, 4268, 4334, 4505, 4579, 4803a, 4817, 4858d, 4870h, 5143, 5352, 5680, 5684, 5747, 5800, 5994, 6005, 6262, 6073, 6183, 6712, 6713; RF, I, fol. 46r, pp. 195, 214–220, 271–274, 310–319, 473; RF, II, 567–575, 626–634, 642–659, 835, 936–945, 952–960; RF, III, 2012–2021, 2024, 2097–2113, 2155–264 [sic], 279–295 [sic], 2367–2378, 2389–2404, 2409–2425, 2481–2496; RF, IV, 2661–2692, 2717–2724, 2740–2769, 3040; Kindler, pp. 193–194; Grünhagen, ed., "Protokolle," pp. 136–137; WAP, AMW, G 3, fols. 10r–v and 13v; *LB* #283; *KdS* #355; *HPR*, pp. 25, 105–109, and 129–130; *SUB*, I, #361; *LFE* B14 and D25; Dyhernfurth, pp. 17, 27, and 28; HGZ, *passim*; *DT*, pp. 65–66 and 160; Stenzel in *Übersicht* 1841, pp. 110 and 178; Görlich, *Vincenz*, pp. 86 and 136; LN, fol. 368r; Jesuiter, VII: III, #11 (3); *ChronBMV*, p. 183; Heyne, *Bisthum*, I, 601, 820, and II, 715; Heyne, *Neumarkt*, pp. 338–340; *SLU*, #13, 19, 46, 105; Kurnik, p. 18; Stobbe, p. 349; *BUB* #52.

Figure 5.1. Demesne land prices, 1260–1431.

Nominal prices per mansus were calculated from the sources here listed and converted to silver prices by methods given in Appendix B: *SLU*, #76 and 128; *UD*, p. 5 #4, p. 11 #13, pp. 13–14 #17, and pp. 141–142 #10–11; *SR*, #1050, 1696, 1871, 1965, 2249, 2844, 3218, 3355, 3331, 3543, 3585, 3701, 3791, 4300a, 4417, 4683, 4900, 4939, 4951, 4979, 4986, 5011, 5014, 5022, 5212, 5368, 5390, 5391, 5602, 5665, 5890, 5966, 5994, 6005, 6017, 6037, 6080, 6081, 6132, 6143, 6220, 6262, 6270, 6290, 6371, 6428, 6448, 6466, 6467, 6553, 6622, 6702, 6786, 6874; Stelmach, pp. 95–97; *NLChron*, p. 98 note 49, p. 107; *DT*, pp. 7–8 and 54; LN, fols. 26r–26v, 466v–468v; *RS*, II, #156. Pfeiffer, *Patriziat*, pp. 203–204; *RI.*, 8: 2, #6676; *BUB* #283; WAA I, IV a 8, fols. 95r–97v; Dyhernfurth, pp. 25–27.

Map 6.1. The retreat from demesne cultivation, 1300–1425.

Map 6.1 identifies points of *change* between the situations earlier shown on maps 5.1, 5.2, and 5.3. Sites where tenants were introduced on demesnes, or demesnes were abandoned or reduced are to be found through collation of information in: *BUB*, #285; *ChronBMV*, pp. 200–214; WAP, AMW, K113, 1r–1v; Domański, *Nazwy miejscowe*, #244; *DT*, pp. 54, 72–73, and 114–115; Dyhernfurth, p. 27; Sommerfeldt, pp. 81–83; Heyne, *Bisthum*, III, 540–542; HGZ; Hoffmann, "Nazwy," pp. 9–17; *HPR*, p. 84 note 1; KLM, pp. 26 and 32; Kronthal, p. 2; *LB* #2, 6, 9, 15, 16, 20, 22, 29, 34, 46, 48, 49, 52, 62, 63, 64 note, 65, 67, 68, 70, 75, 81, 85, 92, 93, 95, 98, 115, 122, 162, 164, 177, 180, 181, 184, 185, 187, 190, 198, 205, 208, 210, 217, 218, 238, 240–241, 245, 246, 256, 258, 259, 274, 277, 285, 287, 288, 302, 309–310, 319, 328, 332, 358, 359, 366, 367, and 371; *LFE* B22, D25, and D271; LN, fols. 33v–35v, 38r–40v, 46r–47r, 128r–129r, 143r–144r, 300r–301r, and 376v–377r; Ludat, *Bistum Lebus*, pp. 176–181; Ludat, *Stiftsregister*, p. 37; "QBBB," pp. 211–213 and 223–225; RB, *passim*; WAA I, IV a 8, fols. 96v–97v; RF, I, 8v–10v, 13r–14v, 19v–20r, 34v–36v, 37r, 39r–42r, 52v–54v, 58v, 67r–69r, 76v–79v, 93–94, 127–132, 161–171, 147–154, 159–166, 198–203, 206–212, 247–254, 263–286, 310–319, 370–381, 393–394, 399–406, 406–408, 439–442, 449–450, 467, 473–478, and 510; RF, II, 519–523, 535–546, 558–566, 579–583, 586–587, 590–592, 615–619, 626–634, 675–699, 702–730, 742–743, 763–767, 770, 830–839, 866–875, 901–909, 912–916, 917–927, 936–945, 960, 961–977, 992–1005, 1024–1028, 1029–1044, 1049–1056, and 1057; RF, III, 265–269, 306–311, 2000–2008, 2012–2021, 2028–2041, 2044–2048, 2300–2317, 2337–2357, 2358–2366, 2409–2425, 2465–2476, 2499–2507, and 2510–2520; RF, IV, 2596–2612, 2661–2692, 2740–2769, 2870–2879, 2914, 2942–2958, 3003–3010, 3018–3030, 3039–3059, 3074, and 3077–3083; *RS*, I, #335 and 343; Schulte, "Kostenblut," p. 255 note 1; Seidel, *Beginn*, pp. 92–94; *SR* #2117, 2630, 3138, 4589, 4630, 4748, 4950, 4962, 4748, 5740, 5970, 5879, 6237, 6410, 6011; Stobbe, 1866, pp. 179–180; *UBB*, pp. 339–343; *UD*, pp. 18–21, 27–28, 31–32, 40–41, 48–49, and 144–147; Wendt, *Landgüter*, pp. 123–133, 180–184, and 202; Wohlbrück, I, 456 note **.

Figure 6.2. Landlord prices for rental land, 1257–1430.

Nominal prices per mansus were calculated from the sources here listed and converted to silver prices by methods given in Appendix B: *SLU*, #56, 115, and 122; *SR* #957, 1045, 1768, 2353, 2545, 2944, 3129, 3236, 3330, 3342, 3407, 3450, 3695, 3810, 4286, 4690, 4912, 4950, 5150, 5153, 5194, 5317, 5554, 5570, 5583, 5604, 5642, 6040, 6480, 6617, 6873, 6942; *RS*, II, #98; Pfeiffer, *Patriziat*, p. 204; *DT*, pp. 6–7, 9–10, 165; LN, fols. 468v–468Ar; Rössler, #461, 523, 556; Dyhernfurth, pp. 25–26; RF, II, 850.

Figure 6.3. Major tenant obligations, 1234–1430.

Figure 6.3, which is presented in four parts or versions, indicates rental values by a letter for places which offer such information at more than one date and by a dot for those from other places. When only one payment is known (the other being unknown, not known to be zero), the entry appears on the one graph only, but not on the graphs for the totals. Conversions from nominal to silver values follow the current silver content of the coinage as detailed in Appendix B. Grain values are from Table 6.4 below.

Places with more than one record of tenant obligations during the period 1234–1430 are as follows:

A	Domaniów	E	Święte	I	Biskupice Podgórne
B	Zabłoto	F	Pietrzykowice	J	Radoszkowice
C	Rzeplin	G	Chomiąża	K	Rynakowice
D	Szukalice	H	Jenkowice	L	Piłczyce
				M	Kowale

Lines connecting letters indicate only the net direction of change between two records, and not continuous change over time.

Major obligations of tenants are recorded as follows. (An x after the date indicates a *locatio* charter.):

Domaniów	1234x	*SUB*, II, #86
Zabłoto	1240x	*SUB*, II, #181 and 193
Tyniec Mały	1248	*SUB*, II, #357
Rzeplin	1253x	*SLU*, #13
Szukalice	1253x	*SLU*, #13
Wierzbno	1253x	*SLU*, #14
Rzeplin	1254x	*SLU*, #19
Szukalice	1254x	*SLU*, #19
Małkowice	1255	*SR* #904
Święte	1256x	*SLU*, #29
Platea Romanorum	1260x	*LFE* B39; "QBBB," pp. 197–198
Łowęcice	1261x	*SR* #1081
Warzyn	1261x	*NRB*, p. 383
Rzeplin	1262x	*SLU*, #46
Gosławice	1263x	*SLU*, #48
Pietrzykowice	1264x	*SLU*, #51
Turów	1265x	*SLU*, #55
Czernica	1273x	*SLU*, #77
Mrozów	1277x	*SLU*, #84
Kostomłoty	1278	*SR* #1573
Żerniki	1280x	*SLU*, #89
Chomiąża	1285	*SR* #1872
Szczepankowice	1286x	*SLU*, #101
Domaniów	1286	*SR* #1968
Przesławice	1289x	*SLU*, #109
Mokra	1289x	*SLU*, #110
Ligotka	1289x	*SLU*, #111
Muchobór Wielkie	1291x	*SLU*, #112
Maślice	1292x	*SR* #2233
Jaszkotle	1293x	*SLU*, #122
Kotowice	1294x	Tz-S #94; *UFO* #103
Zagródki	1297	*SLU*, #130
Jenkowice	1297	*SLU*, #139
Widawa	1298	*SR* #2495

Biskupice Podgórne	ca1300	*LFE* B26
Radoszkowice	ca1300	*LFE* B10 and B376
Rynakowice	ca1300	*LFE* B25
Święta Katarzyna	1300	*SR* #2596
Święte	ca1305	*LFE* D5
Kryniczno	ca1305	*LFE* D6
Żurawina	1326	*SR* #4507 (The 3mk 16gr and 6 malder 8 measures of grains must be the total from the 6⅔ mansi, not a rate per mansus.)
Pietrzykowice	1329	*SR* #4817
Jarosławice	1336	*SR* #5686
Strzeganowice	1346	Heyne, *Bisthum*, I, 603 note
Wilczków	1352	RF, IV, 2923–2930
Pustków Żurowski	1352x	LN, 375v–376r; *RS*, II, #615 omits relevant details
Osobowice	1352	Heyne, *Bisthum*, I, 874; *RS*, II, #691 omits relevant details
Piłczyce	1353	*RS*, II, #917; LN, fol. 30r–v
Siechnice	1354x	*UD*, pp. 144–145 #14
Kowale	ca1360	WAP, AMW, K 113, fols. 1r–1v
Szczytniki	ca1360	*Ibid.*, fol. 8r
Zabłoto	1363	Tz-S #178
Poświętne	1369	LN, fols. 378v–379r
Strachowice	1369	RF, IV, 2740–2769
Prawocin	1369	Tz-S, #161 note 7
Wrocław-Borek	1373x	*BUB*, pp. 236–237
Kończyce	1375x	LN, fols. 34v–35v
Jenkowice	1386	Wutke, "Jenkwitz," p. 161
Wróblowice	1386	*DT*, p. 60
Kowale	1387	*HPR*, p. 129
Bliż	1393x	LN, fols. 143r–144r
Borek Strzeliński	ca1405	Ludat, *Stiftsregister*, p. 36
Kręczków	ca1405	*Ibid.*, pp. 37–38
Opatowice	ca1405	*Ibid.*, p. 37
Świnobród	ca1405	*Ibid.*, p. 38
Brodno	1410	*UD*, p. 263
Chomiąża	1410	*Ibid.*, 262–263
Lipnica	1410	*Ibid.*, 263
Biskupice Podgórne	1421/25	"QBBB," pp. 211 and 225
Radoszkowice	1421/25	*Ibid.*, pp. 215 and 224
Rynakowice	1421/25	*Ibid.*, p. 211
Jelenin	1421/25	*Ibid.*
Miłoszyce	1421/25	*Ibid.*, pp. 213 and 224
Piłczyce	1421/25	*Ibid.*, p. 212
Siedlakowice	1421/25	*Ibid.*, p. 211
Zębice	1430	HGZ, *passim* (the rent is older).

Figure 6.4. Cereal prices (rye and "grain"), 1250–1430.

Price citations, all from the Wrocław duchy, were assembled from the following sources, many of which were unknown to Friedensburg: *SR* #847, 1044, 1482, 2054, 2480, 3662, 3869, and 4117; Friedensburg, "Getreidepreise," pp. 13–24; Dyhernfurth, p. 28; *BUB*, p. 204; Bielowski, ed., "Rocznik większy," p. 690; *HPR*, pp. 104–107; *UD*, p. 148; RF, I, 279; Kindler, p. 194; *ChronBMV*, p. 219. Calculations of a per measure price from citations given in a different form are by the present author. Conversions to silver use methods described in Appendix B.

Figure 8.1. Prices for annual census on landlord's property

The graph displays the prices of sales recorded in *SR* #3794, 4918, 4932, 5288, 5749, 5668, 6011, 6035, 6112, 6121, 6144, 6175, 6204, 6286a, 6363, 6370, 6485a, 6507, 6557, 6768, 6977, and 6985; *RS*, II, #799, 937, and 1089; Wutke, "Kreuzstiftkanoniker," p. 268; RF, I, 29r; LN, fol. 384r–385r; *UD*, pp. 14–15, #18; 20–21, #26; 23–24, #28; 25–26, #32–33; 27–28, #35; 30–31, #40–41; 36, #54; 42, #68; 54, #96; 55, #98; and 56, #100; Fibiger, p. 313; *LB*, #522; Rössler, #318, 441, 471, 492, 717, 791, and 1088; *HPR*, pp. 131–133; *DT*, pp. 4–5, #5; 12–14, #11–12; 19–20, #17; Wutke, "Landbüchern," pp. 256–263; Dyhern-furth, pp. 28–29; Bauch, *Schulwesen*, pp. 119 and 125; Heyne, *Bisthum*, II, 709–710 and 721–722; III, 888–889; Kindler, p. 108; Stobbe 1867, pp. 438–439; Jesuiter, V:IX, #12, 13, and 21; VI:I, #8, 16, 21, 22, 24, 37, and 55; VII:III, #11 (6, 8, 9, 11, 14, 19, 28, 26, and 38); WAP, AMW, Q 154, 1, fol. 5r–5v; WAP, Rep 55, #94; WAA II, IV a 1; Urban, *Wykaz AAW*, #304, 404, 508, 510, 590, 658, 681, and 717.

Figure 9.1. Aggregate distribution of tenant holdings in 14 villages, 1351–1433

Data is from the cumulative % entries in Table 9.1 and thus derived from the sources there cited. The Lorenz curve must fall between the diagonal (curve of absolute equality) and the right angle formed by the lower and the right hand margins of the graph (curve of absolute inequality). The index of inequality (Gini coefficient) measures the departure of the actual distribution from absolute equality as the proportion of the limiting triangle which lies above and to the left of the actual distribution. The greater the inequality, the more this statistic approaches 1; the greater the equality, the more it approaches 0. For uses and limitations of these measures see Alker and Russett, pp. 359–363, and Paglin, pp. 598–609.

Figure 9.2. Prices of annual census on villagers' holdings

Prices of *census* on villagers' holdings are recorded in *SR* #4481–4482, 5009, 5120, 5419–5420, and 5720; LN, fols. 46r–46v, 253r–253v, 293v–295r, 300r–301v, 375v–376r, and 377v–378r; Heyne, *Bisthum*, II, 708, and III, 576; *UD* pp. 47, 57–58, 33–34, 152–153, 204, 207, 209, 211, 212–213, 213, and 218; Sommerfeldt, pp. 82–83; *NRB*, p. 256: Kindler, p. 107; WAP, AMW, Q 154, 2, fols. 17r–18v and 24r–24v; WAA I, IV a 8, fols. 30v–31v and 60v–61r; WAP Rep 55, #91 and 94; *NLChron*, p. 121 note 86; Stobbe, 1866, pp. 179–180; Urban, *Wykaz AAW*, #532 and 653; WAA I, IV a 4a, fols. 30r–30v; WAP, AMW, Q 154. 1. fol. 6r; WAP Rep 67, #104; HGZ, fol. 19r.

Figure 10.1. Cereal prices (rye and "grain"), 1400–1530.

Prices after 1425 are from the following: *ChronBMV*, p. 225; HGZ, fols. 25r–26v, 75v–78v, 95v, 99v, 103r; Grünhagen, "Annalistische Nachlese," pp. 188–189; Heyne, *Bisthum*, I, 641; Rosicz, *Gesta*, pp. 65, 68, and 73; Stobbe, 1868, p. 174; Heyne, *Wohlau*, pp. 139 and 195–196; Klose, *Inneren Verhältnisse*, pp. 182–183; Eschenloer, *Geschichten*, II, 264–266 and 336–337. Conversions to prices per measure and in silver were by the present author using methods described in Appendix B.

Figure 10.4. Landlord prices for demesne and rental lands, 1409–1509

Price citations from Pfeiffer, *Patriziat*, pp. 203–204; Dyhernfurth, pp. 26–27; RF, II, 850; *UD*, pp. 54 and 65–67; Klose, *Inneren Verhältnisse*, p. 190; Jesuiter, VI:III, #11:58; *NLChron*, pp. 132–135; Wutke, "Oybin," p. 41. Conversions to prices per mansus and silver equivalents by the present author use methods described in Appendix B.

GLOSSARY

Specialized or specially defined terms of repeated occurrence are briefly defined in alphabetical order with original languages [G = German, L = Latin, P = Polish] and abbreviations where relevant. In running English text these words are normally italicized only at their first appearance and the German nouns are not capitalized.

advocatus L [G:*Vogt*; P:*wojt*]—generally "deputy;" ranging from ducal judges or lay judges for ecclesiastical lords to various property managers or supervisors.

allodium L—see demesne.

aratrum L [P:*radło*]—literally "plow"; in 11th–13th c. Poland a measure of land area used to assess obligations.

Bede G [L:*petitio specialis*]—special ducal subsidy taken from the 14th c. in times of need. See also *Geschoss*.

Bürger G—see citizen.

ćwiertna P—see "measure."

campus L—local economic grouping of *źreby*, 11th–13th c.

captain [L:*capitaneus*; G:*Hauptmann* or *Landeshauptmann*; P:*starosta*]—royal governor.

Church of Wrocław—the corporate entity of the bishop, his cathedral, and his cathedral clergy, the latter including the cathedral chapter of canons, their vicars, and other subordinate but ordinarily autonomous units.

circuitio L [P:*ujazd*]—12th c. Polish custom of the duke delineating a privileged area by ceremonially riding its bounds.

citizen [L:*civis*; G:*Bürger*]—term of free status derived from recognized membership in a collectively privileged municipal community.

civis L—see citizen.

custos L—warden (ecclesiastical or managerial office).

czuda P [G:*Zaude*]—Polish law district court, established ca.1300 and abolished in the Wrocław Duchy in 1337.

demesne [L:*allodium*; G:*Vorwerk*; P:*folwark*]—land in hands of the lord/owner and, especially, not part of (hereditary) peasant tenant farms subject to the administrative authority of the schulz.

district [L:*districtus*; G:*Weichbild*]—territorial unit of government centered on a town.

Eigen G—see property.

Erb—[prefix] G [L:*hereditarie*]—denotes hereditary and permanent conditions or status, as *Erbherr* or *dominus hereditarius* for a lord and *Erbzins* or *census hereditarie* for a rent.

exactio L—see *Geschoss*.

famulus L [G:*Gesinde, Knecht*, etc.]—(permanent) servant or hired hand.

ferto L [G:*Virdung*]—generally the fraction "one fourth," but commonly .25 mk = 12gr; hence *fertones* or *Virdungen* as obligations of .25mk.

florin—see *gulden*.

folwark P—see demesne.

German law [L:*ius Theutonicum*; G:*deutsches Recht*; P:*prawo niemiecki*]—distinctively recognized legal and institutional customs imported from German-speaking lands further west into Silesia and Poland during the 12th–13th c. and there employed into the 16th c. When here used without qualifier, refers in particular to village community organization using these customs.

Gertner G [L:*ortulanus*; P:*zagrodnik*]—literally "gardener"; status designation for a village small-holder and day laborer as distinct from a peasant with land in the village fields.

Geschoss G [L:*petitio*, also *exactio generalis* or *collecta*]—ducal land tax, initially irregular at times of need, but by the early 14th c. a fixed annual payment assessed on peasant, gertner, and urban landholdings. Demesne and schulz lands and many ecclesiastical holdings were exempt.

Gesinde G—see *famulus*.

groschen (gr) G [L:*grossus*; P:*grosz*]—large silver coin struck in Bohemia, 1300–1547, and at times in Silesia, the principal circulating coinage in Silesia during the later Middle Ages. Normally valued at 48 to the mk.

gulden (fl) G—florin; large gold coin of reasonably good and stable alloy during the 14th–16th c., principally in Silesia those coined in Hungary.

heller (hl) G also *pfennig* [L:*hallensis*, also *obolus, nummus*, etc.]—small coin of poor silver alloy struck from the 14th c. by many central European mints. Normally 12 to the gr in the 14th c. and higher thereafter.

Hofgericht G—see *iudicium curiae*.

Hofrichter G—see *Landrichter*.

Hufe G—see *mansus*.

iudicium curiae L [G:*Hofgericht*, also *Mannrecht*]—ducal/royal court for the Wrocław Duchy; a public court presided over by the captain or the *Hofrichter* from the Wrocław district and with a panel of assessors drawn in equal numbers from citizens of Wrocław and knights to hear cases involving property and lordship in the duchy as well as appeals from the *iudicia provincialia*.

iudicium provinciale L [G:*Landgericht*]—district court; a public court presided over by the *advocatus provincialis* (G:*Landvogt*) and later by the *Landrichter* (also *Hofrichter*) which applied the German law custom of the district in civil and criminal cases.

iura ducalia L—rights to tax and exercise high and appellate justice over a territory or village, originally ducal prerogatives.

ius militium L [also *ius militare*]—fiscal and judicial privileges claimed by knights under Polish customary law, including to pay tithes from their own lands to any church they chose.

jugerum (j) L [G:*Morgen*]—unit of area, 30 to the *mansus*, which see. In Silesia generally about .56 hectares.

Kirchenvater G—vestryman, member of lay group responsible for fabric of a church.

Knecht G—see *famulus*

knight [L:*miles*; G:*Ritter*]—term of elevated free status originally claimed for performance of military service to Polish dukes and magnates and subsequently in Poland and Silesia treated as the normal label of privileged ("noble") rank.

Landrichter G [L:*iudex provincialis*]—chief judge of the district court; see *iudicium curiae.*

laudamium L & G—fine payable to the lord upon entry to a landholding.

leftovers [L:*excrescentia, remanencia*; G:*Überschar*]—land in a German law village not included in the original survey and distribution to tenants.

lgota P—literally "lightening"; 12th c. Polish concession of reduced obligations as an incentive for agricultural settlement.

locatio L [G:*Lokation*]—act of establishing a German law village.

locator L [G:*Lokator*]—contractor handling the establishment of a German law village.

łan P—see *mansus.*

maldrata L—see *Malter.*

Malter G [L:*maldrata*]—unit of dry volume containing 12 "measures," which see. Hence *Malterzehnt* or *decimas maldratas* for tithes paid as a *Malter* of grain.

mansus (m) L [G:*Hufe*; P:*łan*]—unit of area, especially arable, and thus commonly an assessment unit for obligations resting upon land under German law, 13th c. +. Defined as 30 iugera [morgen] each of 300 square rods or 9000 square rods. In Silesia generally (and the Wrocław Duchy exclusively) the "Flemish" m of about 16.8 hectares or 42 statute acres.

mark (mk) G [L:*marca*; P:*grzywna*]—unit of weight and of money. Not a coin. The Polish mk used in Silesia into the early 14th c. weighed 183.5 grams, but the "usual silver" alloy of 75% then used in coins contained about 137.4 grams of silver. After the early 14th c. mk ordinarily referred to "marcae grossorum numeri consueti polonici," the unit of 48 Bohemian groschen that originally weighed the same as a Polish mk but, with debasement, became a unit of account.

measure [L:*mensura*; G:*Scheffel*, also *Mass*; P:*ćwiertne*]—unit of dry volume, 12 to the *malter*; in central Silesia during the later Middle Ages approximately 128 liters.

Meilenrecht G [L:*ius miliare*]—legal monopoly by a town corporation over market exchanges in the surrounding area.

miles L—see knight.

mint money [L:*pecunia monetalis*; G:*Münzgelt*]—ducal tax taken from the 1290s in lieu of profits from arbitrary recall and reminting of coins; converted by the 1330s to an annual payment from cultivated land assessed together with the *Geschoss*, which see.

Morgen G—see *jugerum.*

official [L:*officialis*; G:*Offizial*]—principal canon law judge for the bishop.

opole P [L:*vicinia*]—territorial community under traditional Polish customs, 11th–13th c.

ortulanus L—see *Gertner*.

petitio L—see *Geschoss* and *Bede*.

poradlne P—tax assessed on a "plow"; see *aratrum*.

property [L:*proprietas*; G:*Eigen*]—(especially) land held by hereditary and familial right as opposed to the conditional tenure of a fief or a tenancy.

proprietas L—see property.

Rat G—the ruling council of a city or town.

Ratmann G—see town councillor.

Ritter G—see knight.

Ritterschaft G also *Mannschaft*—the self-alleged collectivity of knightly landowners from a district or the duchy acting as a political group, a concept probably earlier expressed in Latin by the term *terrigenae*, which see.

Royal Six [G:*Königliche Sechse*]—royal appellate court for the Wrocław Duchy on matters of law, 1346 + .

scabinus L—see *Schöffe*.

Scheffel H—see measure.

Schilling G—12 of anything, especially 12hl = 1gr or 12gr = .25mk = 1 *ferto*; not a coin.

Schock G [L:*sexagena*]—60 of anything, especially 60gr = 1.25mk; not a coin.

Schöffe G [L:*scabinus*]—juror, assessor, member of judicial panel.

Scholtisei G—the village landholding permanently attached to the office of *schulz*, which see.

Schulz G [L:*scultetus*; P:*sołtys*]—hereditary village head man in a village under German law.

scot [L:*scotus*; G:*skot*]—¹⁄₂₄mk; not a coin.

scultetus L—see *Schulz*.

Setzschulz G—village head man appointed by the lord and serving at the lord's pleasure; see *Schulz*.

sors L—see *źreb*.

terrigenae L—the politically significant in a territory; see also *Ritterschaft*.

ujazd P—see *circuitio*.

vicinia L—see *opole*.

Vogt G—see *advocatus*.

Vorwerk G—see demesne.

zagrodnik P—see *Gertner*.

Zaude G—see *czuda*.

źreb P [L:*sors*]—(isolated) farm, farmstead; 11th–13th c.

PRONUNCIATION GUIDE

A Simplified Guide to Polish
for Anglophone Readers

Polish spelling	pronounced like English
a	*a* in *father* but shorter
ą	nasalized *ow* in *known*
b	b
c	ts
ch	*h* in *hue* but stronger, almost like German *ch* in *ach*
ci	soft *ch* in *ouch* (same as Polish *ć*)
cz	*tch* in *switch*
ć	soft *ch* in *ouch* (same as Polish *ci*)
d	d
dź	hard *dg* or *j* in *fudge* or *jam*
e	*e* in *let*
ę	nasalized *e* in French *fin*
f	f
g	*g* in *gay*
h	*h* in *hue* but stronger, almost like German *ch* in *ach* (same as Polish *ch*)
i	long *e* in *feet* without any glide
j	consonantal *y* in *yet*
k	k
l	l
ł	consonantal *w* in *wet*
m	m
n	*n* in *linen* or *nn* in *cannon*
ń	soft *n* in *lenient* or *ny* in *canyon*
o	*o* in *open*
ó	long *oo* in *fool* or *u* in *tune* without the final glide
p	p
r	trilled or rolled *r*
rz	palatalized *z* in *azure* (same as Polish *ż*)
s	s
si	softened *sh*, a further forward version of German *ch* in *ich*
sz	*sh* in *show*
ś	softened *sh*, a further forward version of German *ch* in *ich* (same as Polish *si*)
t	t

u   long *oo* in *fool* or *u* in *tune* without the final glide (same as Polish ó)

w   *v* in *vest*

y   midway between short *i* in *sit* and short *e* in *set*

z   z

zi   voiced Polish *ś*, further forward than English *z* in *azure* (same as Polish *ź*)

ź   voiced Polish *ś*, further forward than English *z* in *azure* (same as Polish *zi*)

ż   palatalized *z* in *azure* (same as Polish *rz*)

As a general rule Polish stresses the prefinal syllable (penult).

Hence some places in the Wrocław duchy might be represented in phonetic English (the stressed vowel is underlined) as follows:

Wrocław	Vr_o_ – tswav
Wojciechów	Voy – ch_e_ – huv
Księże	Kshee – _e_n – zhe
Cieszyce	Chee – ye – sh_i_ – tse
Zajączków	Zay – _o_nch – kuv

BIBLIOGRAPHY

1. Unpublished Archival Sources in Wrocław Collections

Archiwum Archidiecezjalne. [WAA]

[Cited after Wincenty Urban, *Katalog Archiwum Archidiecezjalnego we Wrocławiu, Rękopisy*, Archiwa, biblioteki i muzea kościelne, vols. 10–16 (Lublin, 1965–68).]

Katalog, part I (original manuscripts)
II e 11. Mvster Register des Bischtvmbs Breslaw, 1593.
III a 1. Statuta, Consuetudines, Ordinaciones et Conclusiones. Item onera prelaturarum et offica prelatorum. Item Chronica episcoporum Ecclesie Watislaviensis.
III a 31. Liber Niger [chartulary of cathedral chapter].
III d 2. Donatio D. Vicariis S. Johannis Wrat. Copiae litterarum censualium . . . vicariorum.
III d 13–16. Registrum proventuum vicariorum perpetuorum ecclesiae maioris Wratislaviensis, 1518–1524; 1518; 1520–1521; 1531–1538. 4 vols.
III d 28. Regestum succustodiae dextri chori ecclesiae Wratislaviensis 1406–1459.
III d 32. Reg. prov.: villae Mandlaw, 1536–1631.
III d 34. Malsen. Zinsregister 1502–1532.
III d 49. Regestum Subcustodis 1507–1787.
III d 59. Regestrum altaris SS Erasmui, Wenceslai, Barbarae et Hedwigis [1511–1904].
III d 98. Regest. altar. SS Trium Regum in eccl. S. Elizab. [1512–1898].
IV a 4a. Copiae litterarum censualium vicariorum perpetuorum ecclesie collegiate Sancte Crucis Vrat. in et extra civitatem Vratislaviensi et Districtu diversorum 1521.
IV a 8. Registrum literarum censuum et redditum precentoris et mansionariorum Cripte ecclesie sancte Crucis Wrat. . . . MCCCCXLI.
IV a 36. Registrum censuum scolarium S. Crucis. 1478–1479.
IV a 41–43. Regestum perceptorum et expositorum [viz. distributionum] mansionariorum collegiae ecclesiae sancti Crucis, 1464–1485, 1487–1512, 1531–1541. 3 vols.
VI a 1. Fürstentagsbuch, 1504–1531.

Katalog, part II (modern transcriptions)
IV a 1. betr. Breslauer Kreuzstift. Abschriften aus dem Breslauer Staatsarchiv 1305–1476.
V B 2a. Augustiner Chorherren Breslau Sand Akten 1112, 1148–1384, 1391.
V B 2b. Augustiner Chorherren Breslau Sand Akten 1406–74.
V B 2c. Augustiner Chorherren Breslau Sand Akten 1504–1655.

V B 2p. Augustiner-Chorherren. Breslau, Sandstift Rechnungssachen. 1250–1683.
IX Acta Parafii: Piłczyce. Incorporationsb. v. 1435 ff.

Archiwum Państwowe. [*WAP*]

Rep 15, 228. Registrum proventuum Decanatis Ecclesiae Sancti Johannis.
Rep 15, 230. Registrum Redditum Succustodie dextri chori ecclesiae Wratislaviensis.
Rep 15, 293. Registrum Succustodiae dextri chori de anno 1471 usque 1488.
Rep 16, IV 6 a. Verschiedene Land- und Hofgerichtsverhandlungen aus den Jahren 1449–1617.
Rep 55. Archiv der regulirten Chorherren auf dem Sande zu Breslau, bei Unser Lieben Frauen. Register, 1212–1796.
Rep 67, Registra 1–2. Archiv der regulirten Chorherren zu S. Vincenz in Breslau.
Rep 135, B72. Inhaltsverzeichniss der ausserurkundlichen Papiere des Jesuiter-Collegium zu Breslau, 1352–1788.
Rep 135, C150e, Zg134/37. Regesten der Urkunden des Schlossarchivs Deutsch-Lissa 1404–1790.
Rep 135, D273. Diplomaten des Minoritenklosters zu Neumarkt (1331–1753).
Rep 135, E96. Stenzel, Gustav, A. H., "Beiträge zur Geschichte von Lissa im Fürstenthum Breslau aus Urkunden des Königl. Schlesischen Provinzial Archivs und gedruckten Werken."
Rep 135, E99e. Privilegia der Stadt Neumarckt.
Rep 135, E113f. "Das Auenrecht in Pfaffendorf, Kreis Neumarkt."
Rękopisy Klose, Kl 49 (Kl 48). Preise, Einnahmen, Ausgaben.
Rękopisy Klose, Kl 132 (Kl 128). Districtus Wratislaviensis liber de mansis comparatus sub anno 1443 per religiosum validum et strennuum ac honestos viros dominos, magistrum s. Mathiae, Mulich Haugwitz militem, Wenceslaum Reichil consulem et Henricum Jenkwitz collectores pecuniae ejusdem.

Archiwum Państwowe, Archiwum miasta Wrocławia. [*WAP, AMW*]

C 3. Erstlich ist die Cantzlei dess Furstenthumbs Breslaw, Newmargt unde Nambslaw.
C 15. Verzeichniss der Mitgleider des Hof- oder Mannengerichts auf der Kaiserlichen Burg zu Breslau 1380–1611.
C 20. Registrum omnium bonorum sive villarum et allodiorum in districtibus Wratislaviensi, Noviforensi et Awrassensi super pecunia Burnegelt anno etc. XXV.
C 24, 1–5. Repertorium Investiturarum in Praediis Ducatus Wratislaviensis, quae in Libris ejusdem Cancellarie continentur. [Repertorium Frobenianum]. 5 vols.
C 27. [untitled fragment of a 14th century *Liber de Mansis* from the Wrocław Duchy].
G 3. Auszüge aus dem verlorenen Breslauer Stadtbuche Hirsuta Hilla, 1328–1360; nach einer Abschrift aus dem Ende des 17. oder Anfang des 18. Jahrhunderts in den Handschrift Fol. 220 der Fürstensteiner Majoratsbibliothek abgeschrieben von O. Frenzel, Custos der Stadtbibliothek, Breslau 1878.
J 7. Der rechte Weg.
J 8. Remissorium über den Sachsenspiegel, Weichbildrecht, Lehenrecht, Landrecht, und Breslischen Stadtrecht.

K 8. Registrum exaccionis in anno nativitatis dni MCCCCIII. Item anno nativitatis MCCCCIIII.

K 113. Das seint die czinse die stat angehorende [1354].

Q 28. Heilige Geist: Zinsbuch 1430–37.

Q 29, 1–3. Percepta censum hospitalis Sancti spiritus. 3 vols.

Q 154, 1. Matricula omnia privilegiorum . . . hospitalis S. Trinitatis. Anno domini millesimo quinquegentismo tercio.

Q 154, 2. Verzeichnis der Zinsbriefe des Hospitals [S. Trinitatis].

Q 347, 1. Item dys buch gehoret dem eynwonerm vnnd gebawern czum Dompslaw, dem gerichte signaturen czu czeichnen.

Q 348, 1a. Register des gerichts in dem guth vnd dorff Procz an der Oder im 1513 jar.

Bibliotek Zakładu im. Ossolinskich, PAN.

12007/II. Percepta claustri Trebnicen. ad anu domi, 1523.

2. Published Primary Sources, Collections, and Registers

Altmann, Wilhelm, ed. *Die Urkunden Kaiser Sigmunds, 1410–1437,* 2 vols. *RI,* ed. Johann Böhmer *et al.,* vol. 11. Innsbruck, 1896–1900.

Appelt, Henrich, and Winfried Irgang, eds. *Schlesisches Urkundenbuch.* 2 vols. Vienna, 1963–75.

Arndt, W., ed. "Chronicon Polono-Silesiacum," pp. 553–570 in *MGH, SS,* vol. 19. Hannover, 1866.

Arnold, Robert, et al., eds. *Repertorium Germanicum. Regesten aus den päpstlichen Archiven zur Geschichte des deutschen Reichs und seiner Territorien im XIV. und XV. Jahrhundert.* Berlin, 1897.

Bielowski, August, ed. "Rocznik Cystersów Henrykowskich, 970–1412," pp. 699–704 in MPH, vol. 3. Lwów, 1878.

———, ed. "Rocznik Grysowski Większy, 1230–1306," pp. 696–697 in MPH, vol. 3. Lwów, 1878.

———, ed. "Rocznik lubiąski, 1241–1281, oraz wiersz o pierwotnych zakonniach Lubiąża," pp. 707–710 in MPH, vol. 3, Lwów, 1878.

———, ed. "Rocznik magistratu Wrocławskiego, 1149–1491," pp. 680–688 in MPH, vol. 3. Lwów, 1878.

———, ed. "Rocznik wrocławski większy," pp. 688–690 in MPH, vol. 3. Lwów, 1878.

———, ed. "Rocznik wrocławski dawny, 1238–1308," pp. 680–685 in MPH, vol. 3. Lwów, 1878.

Bierbach, Arthur, ed. *Urkundenbuch der Stadt Halle, ihrer Stifter und Klöster.* 2 vols. Geschichtsquellen der Provinz Sachsen und des Freistaats Anhalt, 2d series, vols. 10 and 20. Magdeburg, 1930–39.

Bindewald, Helene, ed. *Deutsche Texte aus schlesischen Kanzleien des 14. und 15. Jahrhunderts.* Vom Mittelalter zur Reformation, vol. 9. Berlin, 1935–36.

Boček, Antonin, et al., eds. *Codex diplomaticus et epistolaris Moraviae.* 15 vols. Olomouc, 1836–1903.

Bolkenhain, Martin von. "Chronik des Martin von Bolkenhain," pp. 1–18 in *Ges-*

chichtschreiber Schlesiens des XV. Jahrhunderts, ed. Franz Wachter. SrS, vol. 12. Breslau, 1883.

Curtze, Maximilian, ed. "Schenkungurkunde d. d. Breslau, Mittwoch vor Ostern 1412," *Schlesische Provinzial-Blätter*, 2d series, 13 (1874), 85–86.

Domański, Józef, and Karl Sille, eds. "Trzebnicka księga rachunkowa z lat 1523– 1524," *KHKM*, 29 (1981), 187–217.

Dubravius, Jan. *Iani Dubravii De Piscinis ad Antonium Fuggerum*, ed. Anežka Schmitova. Sbornik filologický, vol. I, no. 1. Prague, 1953.

Eike von Repgow. *Sachsenspiegel*, ed. Karl A. Eckhardt, 2d ed. rev. 2 vols. Monumenta Germaniae Historica, Fontes Iuris Germanici Antiqui, 2d series vol. 1:1–2. Berlin, 1955–56.

Engelbert, Kurt, ed. *Quellen zur Geschichte des Neisser Bistumlandes auf Grund der drei ältesten Neisser Lagerbücher*. QD, vol. 10. Würzburg, 1964.

Erben, Carolus [Karel] J. et al., eds. *Regesta diplomatica nec non epistolaria Bohemiae et Moraviae*. 7 vols. Prague, 1855–92, 1928–63.

Eschenloer, Peter. *Geschichten der Stadt Breslau, oder Denkwürdigkeiten seiner Zeit, vom Jahre 1440 bis 1479*, ed. J. Kunisch. 2 vols. Breslau, 1827–28.

———. *Historia Wratislaviensis et que post mortem regis Ladislai sub electo Georgio de Podiebrat Bohemorum rege illi acciderant prospera et adversa*, ed. Hermann Markgraf. SrS, vol. 7. Breslau, 1872.

Fibiger, Michael J. "Series et acta magistrorum Wratislaviensium sacri ordinis crucigerorum cum rubea stella hospitalis s. Mathie," ed. Gustav A. H. Stenzel, pp. 287–381 in SrS, vol. 2. Breslau, 1839.

Gaupp, Ernst T., ed. *Das schlesische Landrecht oder eigentlich Landrecht des Fürstenthums Breslau vom J. 1356 an sich und in seiner Verhältnisse zum Sachsenspiegel dargestellt*. Leipzig, 1828; reprint Aalen, 1966.

Gierowski, Józef A., and Józef Leszczynski, eds. *Teksty zródłowe do dziejów chłopa śląskiego. Cz. 1: Do 1945 roku*. Wrocław, 1956.

Górka, Olgierd, ed. *Anonymi descriptio Europae orientalis "Imperium Constantinopolitanum, Albania, Serbia, Bulgaria, Ruthenia, Ungaria, Polonia, Bohemiae" anno MCCCVIII exarata*. Cracow, 1916.

Grodecki, Roman, ed. *Księga Henrykowska*. Biblioteka tekstów historycznych, vol. 2. Poznań, 1949.

Gross, Lothar, ed. "Ein Fragment eines Registers Karls IV. aus dem Jahre 1348," *Neues Archiv der Gesellschaft für ältere deutsche Geschichtskunde*, 42 (1922), 579– 601.

Grotefend, Heinrich, ed. "Aus dem ältesten Signaturbuche des Klosters Leubus," *ZVGS*, 12 (1874/75), 202–207 and 281.

Grünhagen, Colmar, ed. *Henricus Pauper. Rechnungen der Stadt Breslau von 1299– 1358, nebst zwei Rationarien von 1386 und 1387, dem Liber Imperatoris vom Jahre 1377 und den ältesten Breslauer Statuten*. CdS, vol. 3. Breslau, 1860.

———, ed. "Protokolle des Breslauer Domkapitels. Fragmente aus der Zeit, 1393– 1460," *ZVGS*, 5 (1863), 118–159.

———, ed. "Die Correspondenz der Stadt Breslau mit Karl IV. in den Jahren 1347–1355," *Archiv für österreichische Geschichte*, 24 (1865), 345–370.

———, ed. "Annalistische Nachlese, 1227–1450," *ZVGS*, 9 (1868), 182–190.

———, ed. *Geschichtsquellen der Hussitenkriege*. SrS, vol. 6. Breslau, 1871.

———, et al. *Regesten zur schlesischen Geschichte*. CdS, vols.7:1–3, 16, 18, 22, 29, 30. Breslau, 1875–1925.

Grünhagen, Colmar, and Hermann Markgraf, eds. *Lehns- und Besitzurkunden Schlesiens und seiner einzelnen Fürstenthümer im Mittelalter.* 2 vols. Publicationen aus den Königlichen preussischen Staatsarchiven, vols. 7 and 16. Leipzig, 1881–83.

Haeusler, Wilhelm, ed. *Urkundensammlung zur Geschichte des Fürstenthums Oels, bis zum Aussterben der Piastischen Herzogslinie.* Breslau, 1883.

Heck, Roman, and Ewa Maleczynska, eds. and trans. *Ruch Husycki w Polsce; wybór tekstów źródłowych (do r. 1454).* Wrocław, 1953.

Helbig, Herbert, and Lorenz Weinrich, eds. *Urkunden und erzählenden Quellen zur deutschen Ostsiedlung im Mittelalter.* 2 vols. Darmstadt, 1970–75.

Henel, Nikolaus. "Annales Silesiae ab origine gentis ad obitum usque D. Imper. Rudolphi II," pp. 197–484 in Sommersberg, vol. 2. Leipzig, 1730.

Hube, Romuald, ed. *Antiquissimae constitutiones synodales provinciae Gnezniensis maxima ex parte nunc primum e codicibus manu scriptis typis mandatae.* St. Petersburg, 1856.

Huber, Alfons, ed. *Regesten des Kaiserreichs unter Kaiser Karl IV., 1346–1378.* 2 vols. *RI,* ed. Johann Böhmer et al., vol. 8:1–2. Innsbruck, 1877–89.

Johnsdorf, Benedikt. "Böhmische Chronik," pp. 109–123 in *Geschichtschreiber Schlesiens des XV. Jahrhunderts,* ed. Franz Wachter. SrS, vol. 12. Breslau, 1883.

Jungandreas, Wolfgang. "Altschlesisches aus dem Breslauer Stadtarchiv," *MSGV,* 33 (1933), 172–177.

Kętrzyński, Wojciech. "Varia e codicibus Vratislaviensis," pp. 586–591 in MPH, vol. 6. Cracow, 1893.

Klapper, Joseph, ed. "Ein schlesische Formelbuch des 14. J.," *ZVGS,* 60 (1926), 157–177.

Klein, Franz, ed. "Eine bauernrechtliche Quelle des 15. Jahrhunderts aus Schlesien," *ZRG,* 78, Germanistische Abteilung, 65 (1947), 361–363.

Korn, Georg, ed. *Breslauer Urkundenbuch.* Breslau, 1870.

———, ed. *Schlesische Urkunden zur Geschichte des Gewerberechts insbesondere das Innungswesen aus der Zeit vor 1400.* CdS, vol. 8. Breslau, 1867.

Korta, Wacław. "Nieznana księga podatkowa księstwa wrocławskiego z 1425 r.," *Sobótka,* 8 (1953), 223–256.

———, et al., eds. *Regesty Śląskie.* 2 vols. Prace Komisji Nauk Humanistycznych PAN, Oddział we Wrocławiu, vols. 2 and 11. Wrocław, 1975–83.

Kötzschke, Rudolf, ed. *Quellen zur Geschichte der Ostdeutschen Kolonisation im 12. bis 14. Jahrhundert.* Leipzig, 1912.

Kronthal, Berthold, and Heinrich Wendt, eds. *Politische Correspondenz Breslaus im Zeitalter des Königs Matthias Corvinus.* 2 vols. SrS, vols. 13–14. Breslau, 1893–1894.

Laband, Paul, ed. *Das Magdeburg-Breslauer systematische Schöffenrecht aus der Mitte des XIV. Jahrhunderts.* Berlin, 1863.

Ligęza, Elżbieta. "Dokument księcia wrocławskiego Władysława z 27 VII 1269 roku," *Sobótka,* 27 (1972), 445–450.

Ludat, Herbert, ed. *Das Lebuser Stiftsregister von 1405. Studien zu den Sozial- und Wirtschaftsverhältnissen im mittleren Oderraum zu Beginn des 15. Jahrhunderts.* Giessener Abhandlungen zu Agrar- und Wirtschaftsforschung des europaischen Ostens, vol. 9. Wiesbaden, 1965.

Maleczyński, Karol, ed. *Kodeks dyplomatyczny Śląska.* 3 vols. Wrocław, 1956–1964.

———, et. al., eds. *Liber mortuorum abbatiae S. Vincentii Vratislaviensis.* MPH, series nova, vol. 9, fasc. 1. Warsaw, 1971.

Markgraf, Hermann, ed. *Politische Correspondenz Breslaus im Zeitalter Georgs von Podiebrad. Zugleich als urkundliche Belege zu Eschenloers Historia Wratislaviensis.* 2 vols. SrS, vols. 8–9. Breslau, 1873–1874.

Markgraf, Hermann, and J. W. Schulte, eds. *Liber fundationis episcopatus Wratislaviensis.* CdS, vol. 14. Breslau, 1889.

Matuszewski, Józef, ed. *Najstarszy zwód prawa polskiego.* Warsaw, 1959.

Meinardus, Otto, ed. *Das Neumarkter Rechtsbuch und andere Neumarkter Rechtsquellen.* DQ, vol. 2. Breslau, 1906.

Meitzen, August, ed. *Urkunden schlesischer Dörfer. Zur Geschichte der ländlichen Verhältnisse und der Flureinteilung ins besondere.* CdS, vol. 9. Breslau, 1863.

Midunsky, Max-Joseph, ed. "Die Urkunde Papst Hadrians IV. für das Bistum Breslau vom Jahre 1155," *ZVGS,* 70 (1936), 22–62.

Perlbach, Max, ed. *Pomerellisches Urkundenbuch.* Danzig, 1882.

Pfotenhauer, Paul, ed. *Urkunden des Klosters Kamenz.* CdS, Vol. 10. Breslau, 1881.

Ptaśnik, Jan, ed. *Acta Camerae Apostolicae.* Monumenta Poloniae Vaticana, vols. 1–2. Wydawnictwa Komisji Historycznej Akademii Umiejętności w Krakowie, vols. 71–72. Cracow, 1913.

Rosicz, Sigismund. "Chronica et numerus episcoporum Wratislaviensium," pp. 576–584 in *Katalogi Biskupów Wrocławskich,* ed. Wojciech Kętrzyński. MPH, vol. 6. Cracow, 1893.

———. "Sigismundi Rosiczii Gesta diversa transactis temporibus facta in Silesia et alibi," pp. 37–86 in *Geschichtschreiber Schlesiens des XV. Jahrhunderts,* ed. Franz Wachter. SrS, vol. 12. Breslau, 1883.

Rössler, R. "Urkunden Herzogs Ludwig I. von Brieg," *ZVGS,* 6 (1864), 1–96 and 11 (1872), 429–462.

Sabisch, Alfred, ed. *Acta capituli Wratislaviensis 1500–1562. Die Sitzungsprotokolle des Breslauer Domkapitels in der ersten Hälfte des 16. Jahrhunderts.* 2 vols. Forschungen und Quellen zur Kirchen- und Kulturgeschichte Ostdeutschlands, vols. 10:1–2 and 14:1–2. Cologne, 1972–76.

Santifaller, Leo, ed. *Nikolaus Liebental und seine Chronik der Äbte des Breslauer St. Vincenzstifts.* Analecta Praemonstratensia, vol. 25. Tongerloo, 1949.

Schulte, Wilhelm [Lambert], ed. "Quellen zur Geschichte der Besitzverhältnisse des Bistums Breslau," pp. 171–279 in his *Studien zur schlesischen Kirchengeschichte.* DQ, vol. 3. Breslau, 1907.

Schultz, Alwin, and Colmar Grünhagen. "Annalistische Nachlese. Fortsetzung, 1449–1500," *ZVGS,* 9 (1868), 373–388.

Semkowicz, Aleksander, ed. "Rocznik Wrocławski (Annalia seu contigentia in civitate Wratislavia) 1415–1517," pp. 737–740 in MPH, vol. 3, Lwów, 1878.

———, ed. "Niektóre osobliwości (Quaedam memorabilia) do r. 1378," pp. 740–745 in MPH, vol. 3. Lwów, 1878.

———, ed. "Vita Hedwigis maior," pp. 510–633 in MPH, vol. 4. Lwów, 1884.

Skowrońska, Anna, ed. "Kilka nie drukowanych dokumentów biskupa Tomasza I z lat 1239–1259," *Sobótka,* 13 (1958), 305–317.

Sommerfeldt, Gustav. "Ländliches Zinswesen in Schlesien, 1381," *Archiv für Kulturgeschichte,* 4 (1906), 81–83.

Sommersberg, Friedrich Wilhelm von, ed. *Silesiacarum rerum scriptores aliquot adhuc inediti . . . confecit opus non Silesiae modo sed et vicinarum gentium res adornans Fridr. Wilh. de Sommersberg.* 3 vols. in 4. Leipzig, 1729–32.

Steinhausen, George, ed. *Deutsche Privatbriefe des Mittelalters*. 2 vols. Denkmäler der Deutschen Kulturgeschichte, Abt. 1: Briefe, Bd. I. Berlin, 1899–1907.

Stelmach, Roman. "Nieznany dokument Henryka VI z 26 V 1323 roku," *Sobótka*, 34 (1979), 95–97.

Stenus, Bartholomeus [Barthel Stein]. *Descripcio totius Silesie et civitatis regie Vratislaviensis*, ed. Hermann Markgraf. SrS, vol. 18. Breslau, 1902.

Stenzel, Gustav A. H. "Älteste Nachricht von Hopfenbaue in Schlesien," *Schlesische Provinzial-Blätter*, 98 (1833), 485–487.

————. "Catalogus abbatum Saganensium," pp. 178–528 in SrS, vol. 1. Breslau, 1835.

————, ed. "Chronica principum Poloniae," pp. 38–178 in SrS, vol. 1. Breslau, 1835.

————, ed. "Chronica abbatum Beatae Mariae virginis in Arenae," pp. 156–286 in SrS, vol. 2. Breslau, 1839.

————, ed. "Das Landbuch des Fürstenthums Breslau," pp. 48–141 in *Übersicht 1842*. Breslau, 1843.

————, ed. *Urkunden zur Geschichte des Bisthums Breslau im Mittelalter*. Breslau, 1845.

Stobbe, O. "Mittheilungen aus Breslauer Signaturbüchern," *ZVGS*, 6 (1865), 335–356; 7 (1866), 176–191 and 344–362; 8 (1867), 151–166 and 438–453; 9 (1868), 165–181; 10 (1870/71), 192–196.

Tzschoppe, Gustav A., and Gustav A. H. Stenzel, eds. *Urkundensammlung zur Geschichte des Ursprungs der Städte und der Einführung und Verbreitung Deutscher Kolonisten und Rechte in Schlesien und der Ober-Lausitz*. Hamburg, 1832.

Unterlauff, Max, ed. "Ein schlesische Formelbuch des 14. Jahrhunderts," *ZVGS*, 28 (1893), 310–355.

Urban, Wincenty. *Katalog dokumentów Archiwum Archidiecezjalnego we Wrocławiu*. Część I. Rome, 1970.

————. "Repertorium dokumentów Archiwum Archidiecezjalnego we Wrocławiu," *Studia theologiczno-historyczne Śląska opolskiego*, 2 (1970), 285–421.

————. *Wykaz regestów dokumentów Archiwum Archidiecezjalnego we Wrocławiu*. Warsaw, 1970.

Vulturinus [Geier], Pancratius. "*Pancratii Vulturini Panegyricus Slesiacus*, die älteste Landeskunde Schlesiens," ed. Paul Drechsler, *ZVGS*, 35 (1901), 35–67.

Wachter, Franz, ed. "Coronatio Adalberti regis Romanorum Ungarie et Boemie," pp. 21–28 in his *Geschichtschreiber Schlesiens des XV. Jahrhunderts*. SrS, vol. 12. Breslau, 1883.

Wagner, August. "Schlesisches aus dem vatikanischen Archive in Rom aus den Jahren 1316–1371," *ZVGS*, 25 (1891), 287–305.

Wattenbach, Wilhelm. "Martin Sebastian Dittmans Chronik der Aebte von Leubus," *ZVGS*, 1 (1856), 271–297.

————, ed. *Das Formelbuch des Domherrn Arnold von Protzan*. CdS, vol. 5. Breslau, 1862.

Wieland, I. W. *Principatus Silesiae Wratislaviensis . . . a I. W. Wieland . . . delineata . . . rectificata per . . . Matthaeum Schubarth*. Nürnberg [ab Haeridibus Homannianis], 1736.

Wutke, Konrad. "Studien zur älteren schlesischen Geschichte, 3. Über die Datierung einer Urkunde betr. Kattern z.J. 1260 bzw. 1264," *ZVGS*, 44 (1910), 236–242.

———. "Zwei Urkunden K. Johanns v. Böhmen zum Jahre 1339. (Betr. Schreiberdorf und Deutsch-Lissa i. Kr. Neumarkt)," ZVGS, 51 (1917), 231–248.

———. "Aus verloren gegangenen Brieger Landbüchern," ZVGS, 51 (1917), 248–266.

———. "Über die Datierung und die Echtheit der Leubuser Urkunde vom Jahre 1320 bzw. 1324 betr. Wilxen," ZVGS, 52 (1918), 151–160.

———. "Eine verschollene Urkunde über Nippern, Kreis Neumarkt, aus der Zeit von 1279 bis Mitte 1281," ZVGS, 66 (1932), 283–287.

———. "Eine Jahresgedächtnisstiftung für den Breslauer Kreuzstiftkanoniker Eckard dd. Breslau 1330 (?) Mai 4," ZVGS, 67 (1933), 265–269.

Zakrzewski, Ignacy, and Franciszek Piekosiński, eds. Codex diplomaticus Majoris Poloniae. 5 vols. Poznań, 1877–1908.

3. Secondary Sources

Abel, Wilhelm. Die Wüstungen des ausgehenden Mittelalters. 3d ed. rev. Stuttgart, 1976.

———. Agrarkrisen und Agrarkonjunktur. Eine Geschichte der Land- und Ernährungswirtschaft Mitteleuropas seit dem hohen Mittelalter. 3d ed. rev. Hamburg, 1978. [original Berlin, 1935].

———. Strukturen und Krisen der spatmittelalterlichen Wirtschaft. Quellen und Forschungen zur Agrargeschichte, vol. 32. Stuttgart, 1980.

Ahlborn, Joachim. "Die Nürnberger Fernkaufleute Marcus und Matthäus Landauer und deren Handelsbeziehungen zum Osten (15. Jahrhundert)," ZO, 19 (1970), 303–321.

Alexandre, Pierre. "Les variations climatiques au Moyen Age (Belgique, Rhénanie, Nord de la France)," AESC, 32 (1977), 183–197.

Alker, Hayward R. Jr., and Bruce M. Russett. "Indices for Comparing Inequality," pp. 349–372 in R. L. Merritt and S. Rokkan, eds., Comparing Nations. The Use of Quantitative Data in Cross-National Research. New Haven, 1966.

Anderson, John L. "Climatic Change in European Economic History," Research in Economic History, 6 (1981), 1–34.

Appelt, Heinrich. "Die Echtheit der Trebnitzer Gründungsurkunden (1203/18)," ZVGS, 71 (1937), 1–56.

———. "Klosterpatronat und landesherrlichen Kirchenhoheit der schlesischen Herzöge im 13. Jahrhundert," pp. 303–322 in Mitteilungen des österreichische Instituts für Geschichtsforschung, Ergänzungsband 14. Innsbruck, 1939.

———. "Das Breslauer Vinzenzstift und das Neumarkter Recht," ZO, 9 (1960), 216–230.

———. "Die mittelalterliche deutsche Siedlung in Schlesien," pp. 1–19 in Deutsche Ostsiedlung im Mittelalter und Neuzeit. Cologne, 1971.

———. "Zur Frage der Anfänge des deutschen Rechtes in Schlesien," ZO, 27 (1978), 193–206.

Arnold, Benjamin. German Knighthood, 1050–1300. Oxford, 1985.

Aubin, Hermann. "Die Anfänge der grossen schlesischen Leineweberei und -handlung," VSWG, 35 (1942), 105–178.

————, et al., eds. *Geschichte Schlesiens*. Vol. 1: *Von der Urzeit bis zum Jahre 1526*. 3d ed. Stuttgart, 1961.

Bach, Aloysius. *Geschichte und Beschreibung des fürstlichen jungfräulichen Klosterstiftes Cistercienser Ordens in Trebnitz*, ed. August Kastner. Archiv für die Geschichte des Bistums Breslau, vol. 2. Neisse, 1859.

Bader, Karl S. "Dorfpatriziate," *Zeitschrift für die Geschichte des Oberrheins*, 101 (1953), 269–274.

————. *Das mittelalterliche Dorf als Friedens- und Rechtsbereich*, Studien zur Rechtsgeschichte des mittelalterlichen Dorfes, vol. 1. Graz, 1959.

————. *Dorfgenossenschaft und Dorfgemeinde*. Studien zur Rechtsgeschichte des mittelalterlichen Dorfes, vol. 2. Weimar, 1962.

Bagniewski, Zbigniew, and Piotr Kubów. "Średniowieczny młyn wody z Ptakowic na Dolnym Śląsku," *KHKM*, 25 (1977), 3–30.

Baranowski, Bohdan, et al. *Histoire de l'économie rurale en Pologne jusqu'à 1864*. Wrocław, 1966.

Bardach, Juliusz. "Uwagi o rodowym ustroju społeczeństwa i prawie bliższości w Polsce średniowiecznej," *CPH*, 4 (1952), 407–458.

————. "L'indivision familiale dans les pays du Centre-Est européen," pp. 335–353 in Duby and LeGoff, eds., *Famille et parenté*. Rome, 1977.

Barraclough, Geoffrey, ed. *Eastern and Western Europe in the Middle Ages*. London, 1970.

Baszkiewicz, Jan. *Powstanie zjednoczonego państwa polskiego na przełomie XIII i XIV wieku*. PAN Komitet Nauk Prawnych. Studia nad Historią Panstwa i Prawa, Series 2, vol. 1. Warsaw, 1954.

————. *Polska czasów Łokietka*. Warsaw, 1968.

Bauch, Gustav. "Ritter Georg Sauermann, der erste adelige Vorfahr der Grafen Saurma-Jeltsch," *ZVGS*, 19 (1885), 145–181.

————. "Beiträge zur Litteraturgeschichte des schlesischen Humanismus," *ZVGS*, 26 (1892), 213–248; 30 (1896), 128–164; 31 (1897), 123–164; 32 (1898), 49–104 and 392–393; 34 (1900), 370–378; 37 (1903), 120–168; 38 (1904), 292–342; 39 (1905), 156–198; 40 (1906), 140–184.

————. "Analekten zur Biographie des Bischofs Johann IV Roth," pp. 19–102 in his *Studien zur schlesischen Kirchengeschichte*. DQ, vol. 3. Breslau, 1907.

————. *Geschichte des Breslauer Schulwesens vor der Reformation*. CDS, vol. 25. Breslau, 1909.

Bayerische Akademie der Wissenschaften and Deutsche Akademie der Wissenschaften zu Berlin, eds. *Mittellateinisches Wörterbuch bis zum ausgehenden 13. Jahrhundert*. Munich, 1970 + .

Bellmann, G. *Slavoteutonica. Lexicalische Untersuchungen zum slawisch-deutschen Sprachkontakt im Ostmitteldeutschland*. Studia linguistica germanica, vol. 4. Berlin, 1971.

Bennett, Judith M. "Medieval Peasant Marriage: An Examination of the Marriage Licence Fines in the *Liber Gersumarum*," pp. 193–246 in Raftis, ed., *Pathways to Medieval Peasants*. Toronto, 1981.

Berkner, Lutz K. "The Stem Family and the Developmental Cycle of the Peasant Household: An Eighteenth-Century Austrian Example," *AHR*, 77 (1972), 398–418.

Berman, Constance H. *Medieval Agriculture, the Southern French Countryside, and the*

Early Cistercians. A Study of Forty-three Monasteries. Transactions of the American Philosophical Society, vol. 76, part 5. Philadelphia, 1986.

Beyer, Otto. "Schuldenwesen der Stadt Breslau in 14. und 15. Jahrhundert, mit besonderer Berücksichtigung der Verschulderung durch Rentenverkauf," *ZVGS*, 35 (1901), 68–143.

Biddick, Kathleen. "Medieval English Peasants and Market Involvement," *JEcH*, 45 (1985), 823–831.

Bielinska, Maria. "Kanzlei- und Urkundenwesen Polens im 12. und 13. Jahrhundert," *Mitteilungen des Instituts für österreichische Geschichtsforschung*, 80 (1972), 409–422.

Bieniak, Janusz. "Rody rycerskie jako czynnik struktury społecznej w Polsce XIII–XV wieku (Uwagi problemowe)," pp. 161–200 in Henryk Łowmiański, ed., *Polska w okresie rozdrobnienia feudalnego*. Wrocław, 1973.

———. "Clans de chevalerie en Pologne du XIIIe au XVe siècle," pp. 321–333 in Duby and LeGoff, eds., *Famille et parenté*. Rome, 1977.

———. "Knight Clans in Medieval Poland," pp. 123–176 in Gąsiorowski, ed., *The Polish Nobility*. Wrocław, 1984.

Blasel, Carl. *Geschichte von Kirche und Kloster St. Adalbert zu Breslau.* DQ, vol. 16. Breslau, 1912.

Blum, Jerome. "The Rise of Serfdom in Eastern Europe," *AHR*, 62 (1957), 807–836.

Bobertag, Georg. "Die Gerichte und Gerichtsbücher des Fürstenthums Breslau," *ZVGS*, 7 (1866), 102–175.

———. "Die Rechtshandschriften der Stadt Breslau," *ZVGS*, 14 (1878/79), 156–207.

Bogucki, Ambroży. "Termin *miles* w źródłach śląskich XIII i XIV w.," pp. 222–263 in Stefan K. Kuczyński, ed., *Społeczeństwo polski średniowiecznej*, vol. 1. Warsaw, 1981.

———. "Komorniki i podkomorzy w Polsce piastowskiej," pp. 75–133 in Stefan K. Kuczyński, ed., *Społeczeństwo polski średniowiecznej*, vol. 3. Warsaw, 1983.

Böhlau, Hugo. "Die 'Summa Der rechte Weg gnant,' " *ZRG*, 8 (1869), 165–202.

Bosl, Karl, ed. *Handbuch der Geschichte der böhmischen Länder.* Stuttgart, 1966 + .

Brandon, P. F. "Late-Medieval Weather in Sussex and its Agricultural Significance," *Transactions of the Institute of British Geographers*, 54 (1971), 1–17.

Braudel, Fernand. *The Mediterranean and the Mediterranean World in the Age of Philip II*, tr. Sian Reynolds. 2 vols. New York, 1972.

Braudel, Fernand, and Frank Spooner. "Prices in Europe from 1450 to 1750," pp. 378–486 in E. E. Rich and C. H. Wilson, eds., *The Cambridge Economic History of Europe.* Vol. 4: *The Economy of Expanding Europe in the Sixteenth and Seventeenth Centuries.* Cambridge, 1967.

Brinkmann, Carl. "Die Entstehung des märkischen Landbuchs Kaiser Karls IV.," *Forschungen zur brandenburgischen und preussischen Geschichte*, 21 (1908), 373–433.

Bruchmann, Karl G. "Quellen zur bäuerliche Sippen- und Hofgeschichte Schlesiens (Vornehmlich aus den Bestände des Staatsarchives Breslaus)," *Schlesische Geschichtsblätter*, 1936 no. 1, 3–32.

———. "Die schlesischen Schöffenbücher und ihre Verzeichnung," *Schlesische Geschichtsblätter*, 1939 no. 4, 21(93)-26(98).

Buczek, Karol. "Uwagi o prawie chłopów do ziemi w Polsce piastowskiej," *KH*, 64:3 (1957), 86–99.

———. "W sprawie interpretacji dokumentu trzebnickiego z r. 1204," *PH*, 48 (1957), 38–77.

———. *Książęca ludność służbna w Polsce wczesnofeudalnej*. PAN Komisja Nauk Historycznych, Prace, vol. 1. Wrocław, 1958.

———. "Rachunki świętopietrza jako podstawa badań nad zaludnieniem Polski XIV wieku," pp. 77–102 in *Medievalia w 50-rocznicę pracy naukowej Janą Dąbrowskiego*. Warsaw, 1960.

———. "O wiarygodności rachunków świętopietrza i methodach polemiki naukowej," *KHKM*, 11 (1963), 83–100.

———. *Targi i miasta na prawie polskim*. Warsaw, 1964.

———. "Z badań nad organizacją gospodarki w Polsce wczesnofeudalnej (do początku XIV w.)," *KHKM*, 17 (1969), 193–230.

———. "Z badań nad organizacją grodowa w Polsce wszesnofeudalnej. Problem terytorialności grodów kasztelańskich," *KH*, 77 (1970), 3–30.

———. "Z problematyki osiedli wczesnomiejskich w Polsce," *Studia Historyczne*, 19 (1976), 325–334.

———. "Organizacja służebna w pierwszych wiekach państwa polskiego," *Studia Historyczne*, 20 (1977), 353–376.

———. "Prawo rycerskie i powstanie stanu rycerskiego w Polsce," *PH*, 69 (1978), 23–44. [Translated as "The Knight Law and the Emergence of the Nobility Estate in Poland," pp. 87–122 in Gąsiorowski, ed., *The Polish Nobility*. Wrocław, 1984.

Carpentier, Elisabeth. "Autour de la Peste Noire: famines et epidémies dans l'histoire du XIVe siècle," *AESC*, 17 (1962), 1062–1092.

Carsten, Francis L. *The Origins of Prussia*. Oxford, 1954.

Castelin, Karel O. *Česká drobná mince doby předhusitské a husitské (1300–1471)*. Prague, 1953.

Cetwiński, Marek. *Rycerstwo śląskie do końca XIII w. Pochodzenie—gospodarka—polityka*. Prace WTN, series A, no. 210. Wrocław, 1980.

———. "Pochodzenie etniczne i więzy krwi rycerstwa śląskiego," pp. 40–85 in Stefan K. Kuczyński, ed., *Społeczeństwo Polski średniowiecznej. Zbiór studiów*, vol. 1. Warsaw, 1981.

———. *Rycerstwo śląskie do końca XIII w. Biogramy i rodowody*. Prace WTN, series A, no. 229. Wrocław, 1982.

Chapelot, Jean, and Robert Fossier. *The Village & House in the Middle Ages*, tr. Henry Cleere. Berkeley, 1985.

Chayanov, Alexander V. *The Theory of Peasant Economy*, ed. Daniel Thorner, et al. The American Economic Association Translation Series. Homewood, Ill., 1966.

Cheyette, Frederic. "The Origins of European Villages and the First European Expansion," *JEcH*, 37 (1977), 182–206.

Chisholm, Michael. *Rural Settlement and Land Use; An Essay in Location*. New York, 1967.

Chmielewski, Stefan. "Uwagi o narzędziach rolniczych w Polsce w początkach gospodarki czynszowej," *KHKM*, 3 (1954), 166–180.

————. *Gospodarka rolna i hodowlana w Polsce w XIV i XV w. (Technika i rozmiary produkcji)*. Studia z dziejów gospodarstwa wiejskiego, vol. 5, part 1. Warsaw, 1962.

Cieśla, Irena. "Taberna wczesnośredniowieczna na ziemach polskich," *Studia Wczesnośredniowieczne*, 4 (1958), 159–225.

Cipolla, Carlo. *Before the Industrial Revolution: European Society and Economy, 1000–1700*. 2d ed. rev. New York, 1980.

Clark, Colin, and Margaret Haswell. *The Economics of Subsistence Agriculture*. 2d ed. rev. New York, 1966.

Clark, Elaine. "Debt Litigation in a Late Medieval English Vill," pp. 247–279 in Raftis, ed., *Pathways to Medieval Peasants*. Toronto, 1981.

Constable, Giles. *Monastic Tithes: from their Origins to the twelfth century*. Cambridge Studies in Medieval Life and Thought, new series, vol. 10. Cambridge, 1964.

Cooper, J. P. "Patterns of inheritance and settlement by great landowners from the fifteenth to the eighteenth centuries," pp. 192–327 in Goody et al., eds., *Family and Inheritance*. Cambridge, 1976.

Croon, Gustav. *Die landständliche Verfassung von Schweidnitz-Jauer. Zur Geschichte des Ständewesens in Schlesien*. CdS, vol. 27. Breslau, 1912.

Dąbrowski, Henryk. "Uwagi nad początkami opactwa Cystersów w Lubiążu," *Sobótka*, 13 (1958), 169–177.

————. *Rozwój gospodarki rolnej w Polsce od XII do połowy XIV wieku*. Studia z dziejów gospodarstwa wiejskiego, vol. 5, no. 1. Warsaw, 1962.

Dąbrowski, Jan. *Korona królestwa polskiego w XIV wieku. Studium z dziejów rozwoju polskiej monarchii stanowej*. Wrocław, 1956. [Also accessible as "Die Krone des polnischen Königtums im 14. Jahrhundert. Eine Studie aus der Geschichte der Entwicklung der polnischen ständischen Monarchie," trans. C. Woesler, pp. 399–547 in Manfred Hellmann, ed., *Corona Regni. Studien über die Krone als Symbol des Staates im späteren Mittelalter*. Wege der Forschung, vol. 3. Darmstadt, 1961.]

————. *Dawne dziejopisarstwa Polskie (do roku 1480)*. Wrocław, 1964.

Day, John. "The Great Bullion Famine of the Fifteenth Century," *Past & Present*, 79 (1978), 3–54.

————. "The Question of Monetary Contraction in Late Medieval Europe," pp. 55–71 in his *The Medieval Market Economy*. Oxford, 1987 [originally published 1981].

Dembińska, Maria. "W sprawie badań nad gospodarka hodowlana w Polsce w XIII i XIV w.," *Przegląd Zachodni*, 11 (1955), 622–626.

————. "Próba obliczenia wysokości plonów w królewskich dobrach allodialnych w XIV wieku," *Studia z dziejów gospodarstwa wiejskiego*, 4 (1961), 7–16.

————. "Early medieval town as a centre of foodstuff consumption." *Ergon*, 3 (1962), 378–380.

————. *Konsumpcja żywnościowa w Polsce średniowiecznej*. Wrocław, 1963.

————. *Przetwórstwo zbożowe w Polsce średniowiecznej (X–XIV wiek)*. Warsaw, 1973.

Dembińska, Maria, and Zofia Podwińska, eds. *Historia kultury materialnej Polski w zarysie*. Vol. 1: part 1 *Od VII do XII wieku*. Warsaw, 1977.

Deren, Andrzej. "Akta m. Wrocławia 1221–1945. (Zestawienie grup rzeczowych)," *Sobótka*, 34 (1979), 421–436.

Dersch, Wilhelm. "Schlesien am Vorabend der Reformation," *ZVGS*, 68 (1934), 69–94.

Dessmann, Günter. *Geschichte der schlesischen Agrarverfassung.* Abhandlungen aus dem staatswissenschaftlichen Seminar zu Strassburg, vol. 19. Strassburg, 1904.

de Vries, Jan. "Histoire du climat et de l'économie," *AESC*, 32 (1977), 198–226.

Dieffenbach, Lorenz. *Glossarium Latino-Germanicum mediae et infimiae aetatis.* Frankfurt a.M., 1857.

Diels, Paul, and Richard Koebner. *Das Zaudengericht in Böhmen, Mähren und Schlesien.* Historische Untersuchungen, vol. 17. Breslau, 1935.

Dillon, Kenneth J. *King and Estates in the Bohemian Lands, 1526–1564.* Studies presented to the International Commission for the History of Representative and Parliamentary Institutions, no. 57. Brussels, 1976.

Dittrich, Paul. "Beiträge zur Geschichte des Breslauer Fürstentums. I: Zur Geschichte von Eckersdorf," *ZVGS*, 43 (1909), 243–265.

———. "Beiträge zur Geschichte des Fürstentums Breslau. II: Die Kreuzherren im Fürstentum Breslau," *ZVGS*, 45 (1911), 201–256.

———. "Beiträge zur Geschichte des Fürstentums Breslau. III: Die Kreuzherren im Landkreise Breslau," *ZVGS*, 46 (1912), 124–158.

Dix, Hans. *Das Interdikt im ostelbischen Deutschland.* Marburg, 1913.

Długoborski, Wacław, Józef Gierowski, and Karol Maleczynski. *Dzieje Wrocławia do roku 1807.* Warsaw, 1958.

Dola, Kazimierz. "Zakon joannitów na Śląsku do połowy XIV w.," *Studia theologiczno-historyczne Śląska opolskiego*, 3 (1974), 43–86.

———. "Kanonicy wrocławskiej kapituły katedralnej w latach 1418–1500," *Studia theologiczno-historyczne Śląska opolskiego*, 5 (1976), 185–315.

———. "Prałacy wrocławskiej kapituły katedralnej w latach 1418–1500," *Studia theologiczno-historyczne Śląska opolskiego*, 6 (1978), 257–307.

———. *Wrocławska kapituła katedralna w XV wieku. Ustrój—skład osobowy—działalność.* Katolicki Uniwersytet Lubelski. Rozprawa habilitacyjna—Wydział Teologiczny. Lublin, 1983.

Domański, Józef. *Nazwy miejscowe dziesiejszego Wrocławia i dawnego okręgu Wrocławskiego.* Warsaw, 1967.

———. "Śląskie nazwy służebne," *Onomastica*, 19 (1974), 5–42; 20 (1975), 5–34.

———. "Z problematyki badań zanikłych osad na Śląsku," *KHKM*, 31 (1983), 317–334.

Doroszewska, A. *Otoczenie Henryka Brodatego i Jadwigi jako środkowisko społeczne.* Warsaw, 1978.

Drabina, Jan. "Wrocławska kapituła katedralna i jej stosunek do politycznych wydarzeń lat 1453–1471," *Śląskie Studia historyczno-teologiczne*, 2 (1969), 183–204.

———. "Mikołaj Tempelfeld z Brzegu," *Wrocławskie studia teologiczne—Colloquium Salutis*, 2 (1970), 83–102.

———. "Stosunek wrocławskich zakonów do króla Jerzego z Podiebradu," *Śląskie Studia historyczno-teologiczne*, 4 (1971), 249–266.

———. "Kontakty Wrocławia z stolicą apostolską w dobie panowania Jagiellonów na Śląsku (1490–1526)," *Sobótka*, 31 (1976), 1–25.

———. "Kontakty Wrocławia z Piusem II i kurią rzymską w latach 1458–1464," *KH*, 83 (1976), 513–530.

———. "Prokuratorzy miasta Wrocławia na papieskim dworze w drugie połowie XV wieku," *Sobótka*, 32 (1977), 289–305.

———. "Stosunek Wrocławia do krucjat antytureckich w latach 1453–1529," *Sobótka*, 35 (1980), 1–17.

———. *Kontakty Wrocławia z Rzymem w latach 1409–1517* Prace WTN, series A, no. 219. Wrocław, 1981.

Duby, Georges. *The Early Growth of the European Economy: Warriors and Peasants from the Seventh to the Twelfth Century*, tr. Howard B. Clarke. London, 1974; French original, 1973.

Duby, Georges, and Jacques LeGoff, eds. *Famille et parenté dans l'occident médiéval.* Collection de l'École Française de Rome, vol. 30. Rome, 1977.

DuCange, Charles D. *Glossarium mediae et infimiae latinitatis*, ed. G.A.L. Henschel, rev. ed, 7 vols. Paris, 1842.

Dunin-Wasowicz, Teresa. "Climate as a Factor Affecting the Human Environment in the Middle Ages," *JEEcH*, 4 (1975), 691–706.

Dvornik, Francis. *The Slavs in European History and Civilization*. New Brunswick, N.J., 1962.

Dyhernfurth, Gertrude. *Ein schlesisches Dorf und Rittergut. Geschichte und sozial Verfassung.* Staats- und Sozialwissenschaftliche Forschungen, vol. 25, No. 2. Leipzig, 1906.

Dziewulski, Władysław. "Zaludnienie Śląska w końca XVI i początku XVII wieku," *Przegląd Zachodni*, 8 (1952), 419–492.

———. "Społeczeństwo śląskie a husyci," *Odrodzenie i Reformacja w Polsce*, 5 (1960), 5–44.

———. "Nowa praca o zaludnieniu ziem polskich w XIV wieku," *Zapiski Historyczne*, 27 (1962), 39–52.

Eistert, Karl. "Berichtigungen und Ergänzungen zum *liber fundationis*," *ZVGS*, 72 (1938), 347–351.

———. "Die Bedeutung der Ritter Czambor für die frühmittelalterliche schlesische Kirchengeschichte," *AsKg*, 4 (1939), 46–69.

———. "Die Wüstungen Bartuschowitz und Sdanowitz bei Alt Schlesing (früher Alt Schliesa), Kreis Breslau," *ZVGS*, 77 (1943), 137–142.

———. "Zur Geschichte des Strehlener Klarenklosters," *AsKg*, 17 (1959), 69–83.

———. "Beiträge zur Genealogie des Breslauer Bischofs Preczlaus von Pogarell (1299–1376)," *AsKg*, 20 (1962), 226–290.

Elliott, G. "Field Systems of Northwest England," pp. 42–92 in Alan R. H. Baker and Robin A. Butlin, eds., *Studies of Field Systems in the British Isles*. Cambridge, 1973.

Engel, Evamaria, and Benedykt Zientara. *Feudalstruktur, Lehnbürgertum und Fernhandel im spätmittelalterlichen Brandenburg.* Abhandlungen zur Handels- und Sozialgeschichte, vol. 7. Weimar, 1967.

Engel, Franz. "Mittelalterliche Hufenmasse als siedlungs-geschichtliche Quellen," *Abhandlungen der Braunschweigische Wissenschaftlicher Gesellschaft*, 6 (1954), 272–287.

Engelbert, Kurt. "Zum 950jährigen Bestehen des Erzbistums Breslau. 2. Bischof Walter von Breslau (1148–1169) und seine Zeit," *AsKg*, 9 (1951), 1–24.

———. "Die deutschen Frauen der Piasten von Mieszko I. (†992) bis Heinrich I. (†1238)," *AsKg*, 12 (1954), 21–51.

Epperlein, Siegfried. "Gründungsmythos deutscher Zisterziensererklöster westlich und östlich der Elbe im hohen Mittelalter und der Bericht des Leubuser Mönches im 14. Jahrhundert," *Jahrbuch für Wirtschaftsgeschichte*, 7 (1967), 303–335.

Ermisch, Hubert. "Schlesiens Verhältniss zu Polen und zu König Albrecht II, 1435–1439," *ZVGS*, 12 (1874/75), 237–284.

———. "Mittel- und Niederschlesien während der königloser Zeit, 1440–1452," *ZVGS*, 13 (1876/77), 1–72, 291–342.

Eulenburg, F. "Drei Jahrhunderte städtischen Gewerbewesens. Zur Gewerbestatistik Alt-Breslaus 1470–1790," *VSWG*, 2 (1904), 254–285.

Farmer, D. L. "Some Grain Price Movements in Thirteenth-Century England," *EcHR*, second series, 10 (1957), 207–220.

Fink, F. "Die Bergwerksunternehmungen der Fugger in Schlesien," *ZVGS*, 28 (1894), 294–340.

Fleischer, Manfred P. "Silesiographia: The Rise of Regional Historiography," *Archiv für Reformationsgeschichte*, 69 (1978), 219–247.

———. *Späthumanismus in Schlesien. Ausgewählte Aufsätze.* Munich, 1984.

Flohn, H. "Klimaschwankungen im Mittelalter und ihre historisch-geographische Bedeutung," *Berichte zur deutschen Landeskunde*, 7 (1950), 347–357.

Foerster, Richard. "Heinrich und Seyfrid Ribisch," *ZVGS*, 41 (1907), 180–240.

Fourquin, Guy. *Les campagnes de la région Parisienne à la fin du moyen âge du milieu du XIIIe siècle au debut du XVIe siècle.* Publications de la Faculté des Lettres et Sciences Humaines de Paris, Série "Recherches," vol. 10. Paris, 1964.

Fraknói, Wilhelm [Vilmos]. *Mathias Corvinus, König von Ungarn, 1458–1490.* Freiburg i. B., 1891.

Francastel, Pierre, ed. *Les Origines des villes polonaises.* École Pratique des Hautes Études, VIe Section. Sciences economiques et sociales. Congrès et colloques, vol. 2. Paris, 1960.

Frauenstadt, P. "Das schlesische Dreiding. Ein Beitrag zur Geschichte der gutsherrlich-bäuerlichen Verhältnisse," *Jahrbücher für Nationalökonomie und Statistik*, 55 (1895), 232–254.

Freed, John B. "The Origins of the European Nobility: The Problem of the Ministerials," *Viator*, 7 (1976), 228–237.

———. "Reflections on the Medieval German Nobility," *AHR*, 91 (1986), 553–575.

———. "Nobles, Ministerials, and Knights in the Archdiocese of Salzburg," *Speculum*, 62 (1987), 575–611.

Friedensburg, Friedrich. *Schlesiens Münzgeschichte im Mittelalter.* 2 vols. CdS, vols. 12–13. Breslau, 1887–1888. *Ergänzungsband.* CdS, vol. 23. Breslau, 1904.

———. "Der Breslauer Pönfall und die Münzordnung König Ferdinands," *ZVGS*, 24 (1890), 88–126.

———. "Studien zur Münzgeschichte Schlesiens im XVI. Jahrhundert. II. Schlesische Münzen König Ferdinands, geprägt vor dem Jahre 1546," *Zeitschrift für Numismatik*, 17 (1890), 213–230, 282–284.

———. "Zur älteren Geschichte der Münzstätte Breslau," *ZVGS*, 36 (1902), 91–101.

———. "Die schlesischen Getreidepreise vor 1740," *ZVGS*, 40 (1906), 5–45.

———. *Die schlesischen Münzen des Mittelalters.* Breslau, 1931.

Fritze, Wolfgang H. "Phänomene und Probleme des westslawischen Bauerntums am Beispiel des frühpremyslidischen Böhmen," pp. 494–529 in Herbert Jahnkuhn, ed., *Das Dorf der Eisenzeit und des frühen Mittelalters. Seidlungsform—wirtschaftliche Funktion—soziale Struktur.* Göttingen, 1977.

Gąsiorowski, Antoni. "Szerzenie się tzw. prawa niemieckiego na wsi slaskiej. Uwagi dyskusyjne," *RH*, 28 (1962), 75–83.

———. "Rycerstwo," pp. 620–624 in *Słownik starożytności słowiańskich*, vol. 4. Warsaw, 1970.

———, ed. *The Polish Nobility in the Middle Ages. Anthologies.* PAN, Komitet Nauk Historycznych; Polskie Towarzystwo Historyczne: Polish Historical Library, no. 5. Wrocław, 1984.

———. "Research into Medieval Polish Nobility. Introduction," pp. 7–20 in Gąsiorowski, ed., *The Polish Nobility.* Wrocław, 1984.

Gaupp, Ernst T. "Das deutsche Recht, insbesondere die Gütergemeinschaft in Schlesien," *Zeitschrift für deutschen Recht und deutsche Rechtswissenschaft*, 3 (1840), 40–83.

Gawęda, Stanisław. "Małopolskie rodziny możnowładcze w stosunki do praw spadkowych kobiet w wiekach średnich," *Prace Historyczne*, 56 (1977), 53–59.

Geisler, Walter, ed. *Wirtschafts- und verkehrsgeografischer Atlas von Schlesien.* Breslau, 1932.

Genicot, Léopold. "Crisis: From the Middle Ages to Modern Times," pp. 660–742 in Michael M. Postan, ed., *The Cambridge Economic History of Europe.* Vol. 1: *The Agrarian Life of the Middle Ages.* 2d ed. rev. Cambridge, 1966.

George, Rosemaria. "Die Grossunternehmer in der ostdeutschen Kolonisation des Mittelalters." Unpublished Phil. Diss., University of Münster, 1948.

Gerlich, Alois. *Habsburg, Luxemburg, Wittelsbach im Kampf um die deutsche Königskrone.* Wiesbaden, 1960.

Giesey, Ralph E. "Rules of Inheritance and Strategies of Mobility in Prerevolutionary France," *AHR*, 82 (1977), 271–289.

Gieysztor, Aleksander. "W sprawie początków trójpolówki w Polsce i w krajach sąsiednich," *KHKM*, 8 (1960), 71–79.

———. "Wieś i miasto słowiańskie przed XIII wiekiem: rynki lokalne i regiony ekonomiczne," *Sprawozdanie WTN*, 17 (1962), 93–96.

———. "La ville slave du Haut Moyen-Age centre du production artisanale de rayonnement commercial," *Ergon*, 3 (1962), 287–297.

———. "From Forum to Civitas: Urban Changes in Poland in the Twelfth and Thirteenth Centuries," pp. 7–30 in *La Pologne au XIIe siècle. Congrès International des Sciences Historiques à Vienne.* Warsaw, 1965.

———. "Villes et campagnes slaves du Xe au XIIIe siècle," pp. 87–106 in *Second International Conference of Economic History, Aix-en-Provence, 1962*, vol. 2. École Pratique des Hautes Études, VIe Section. Sciences economiques et sociales. Congrès et colloques, vol. 8. Paris, 1965.

———. "Villages désertés: bilan de la recherche polonaise," pp. 607–613 in *Villages désertés et histoire économique XIe-XVIIIe siècle.* École Pratique des Hautes Études, VIe Section. Centre de recherches historiques, les Hommes et la terre, vol. 11. Paris, 1965.

———. "L'impot foncier dans le Royaume de Pologne au XIVe et XVe siècle," pp. 317–328 in *L'Impôt dans le cadre de la ville et de l'État. Colloque International, Spa, 6-9-IX-1964. Actes.* Collection Histoire, série in no. 13. Brussels, 1966.

———. "Medieval Poland," pp. 31–165 in *History of Poland.* Warsaw, 1968.

————. "La lignage et la famille nobilaire en Pologne aux XIe, XIIe et XIIIe siècles," pp. 299–308 in Duby and LeGoff, eds. *Famille et parenté*. Rome, 1977.

Gieysztorowa, Irena. "Badania nad historia zaludnienia Polski," *KHKM*, 11 (1963), 522–562.

————. "Research into the Demographic History of Poland: A Provisional Summing Up," *APH*, 18 (1968), 5–17.

Gieysztorowa, Irena, and Tadeusz Ładogórski. "W sprawie nowych badań nad zaludnieniem dawnej Polski," *KHKM*, 6 (1958), 45–60.

Goerlitz, Theodor. "Der Verfasser der Breslauer Rechtsbücher 'Rechter Weg' und 'Remissorium'," *ZVGS*, 70 (1936), 195–206.

————. "Das flämische und das fränkische Recht in Schlesien und ihr Widerstand gegen das sächsische Recht," *ZRG, Germanistische Abt.*, 57 (1937), 138–181.

————. *Verfassung, Verwaltung und Recht der Stadt Breslau*. Teil I: *Mittelalter*, ed. Ludwig Petry. QD, vol. 7. Würzburg, 1962.

Golachowski, Stefan. "Niektóre formy układu pól we wsiach średniowiecznych Śląska," *Sprawozdania WTN*, 17 (1962), 97–106.

Goody, Jack. *The development of the family and marriage in Europe*. Cambridge, 1983.

————, ed. *The Developmental Cycle in Domestic Groups*. Cambridge Papers in Social Anthropology, no. 1. Cambridge, 1971.

————, et al., eds., *Family and Inheritance: Rural Society in Western Europe, 1200–1800*. Cambridge, 1976.

Gordon, Stewart. "Recovery from Adversity in Eighteenth-Century India: Rethinking 'Villages,' 'Peasants,' and Politics in Pre-Modern Kingdoms," *Peasant Studies*, 8:4 (1979), 61–80.

Górka, Olgierd. *Über die Anfänge des Klosters Leubus*. DQ, vol. 18. Breslau, 1913.

Görlich, Franz X. *Die Prämonstratenser und ihrer Abtei zum heiligen Vincenz*. Vol. I: *Urkundliche Geschichte der Prämonstratenser und ihrer Abtei zum heiligen Vincenz vor Breslau*. Breslau, 1836.

Górski, Karol. "Les structures sociales de la noblesse polonaise au moyen age," *Le Moyen Age*, 73 (1967), 73–85.

————. "Rycerstwo i szlachta wobec możnowładstwa w XIV i XV wieku," *KH*, 77 (1970), 829–845.

Gottschalk, Josef. "Der angebliche Bruderzwist unter den Söhnen der hl. Hedwig," *AsKg*, 9 (1951), 45–59.

————. *St. Hedwig Herzogin von Schlesien*. Forschungen und Quellen zur Kirchen- und Kulturgeschichte Ostdeutschlands, vol. 2. Cologne, 1964.

Gould, J. D. "The Price Revolution Reconsidered" pp. 91–116 in Peter Ramsey, ed., *The Price Revolution in Sixteenth-Century England*. London, 1971. [originally published 1964]

Gould, Peter R. *Spatial Diffusion*. Association of American Geographers Commission on College Geography, Resource Paper no. 4. Washington, 1969.

Granier, Herman. "Dyhernfurth," *ZVGS*, 35 (1901), 346–352.

Graniky, G. *Die Kulturlandschaft des Wohlauer Altkreises, ein Beitrag zur Siedlungs- und Wirtschaftskunde einer schlesischen Landschaft*. Veröffentlichungen der schlesischen Gesellschaft für Erdkunde, vol. 27. Breslau, 1939.

Graus, Frantisek. "Slavs and Germans," pp. 15–42 in Barraclough, ed., *Eastern and Western Europe in the Middle Ages*. London, 1970.

————. "Die Problematik der deutschen Ostsiedlung aus tschechischer Sicht," pp. 31–75 in Schlesinger, ed., *Ostsiedlung als Problem*. Sigmaringen, 1975.

Grodecki, Roman. "Książęce wlość trzebnicka na tle organizacji majątków książęcych w Polsce w XII w.," *KH*, 26 (1912), 433–475; 27 (1913), 1–66.

———. *Początki immunitetu w Polsce*. Lwów, 1930.

———. "Wole i lgoty," pp. 42–58 in *Studia ku czci R. Bujaka*. Lwów, 1931.

———. "Początki gospodarki folwarcznej w Polsce," pp. 57–72 in Henryk Barycz and Jan Hulewicz, eds., *Studia z dziejów kultury polskiej. Książka zbiorowa*. Warsaw, 1949.

Grotefend, Heinrich. "Die Streitigkeiten zwischen Adel und Städten der Fürstenthumer Schweidnitz und Jauer und die Privilegienbücher des Schwiednitz-Jauerschen Adels," *ZVGS*, 10 (1871), 294–314.

Grüger, Heinrich. "Die slawische Besiedlung und der Beginn der deutschen Kolonisation in Weichbilde Münsterberg," *AsKg*, 21 (1963), 1–37.

———. "Das Volkstum der Bevölkerung in den Dörfern des Zisterzienserklosters Heinrichau im mittelschlesischen Vorgebirgslande vom 13.-15. Jahrhundert," *ZO*, 27 (1978), 241–261.

———. "Schlesisches Klosterbuch 7. Trebnitz. Zisterzienserinnenabtei," *JSFWUB*, 23 (1982), 55–83.

———. "Schlesisches Klosterbuch 9. Breslau. St. Vincenz. Benediktiner-, dann Prämonstratenserabtei," *JSFWUB*, 24 (1983), 67–97.

Grünhagen, Colmar. "Ueber die Gründung von Kloster Leubus. Ein Beitrag zur Kritik der ältesten Leubuser Urkunden," *ZVGS*, 5 (1863), 193–221.

———. "Die Herren von Reste. Ein Beitrag zur Geschichte des Breslauer Patriziats im 14. Jahrh.," *ZVGS*, 7 (1866), 35–56.

———. "Die ältesten deutschen Beamten in Breslau," *ZVGS*, 8 (1867), 428–437.

———. "Hoger von Preticz und die Prittwitze," *ZVGS*, 8 (1867), 470–471.

———. "Zur Geschichte des Breslauer Aufstands von 1418 nebst urkundlichen Beilagen," *ZVGS*, 11 (1871), 188–196.

———. *Die Hussitenkämpfe der Schlesier, 1420–1435*. Breslau, 1872.

———. "Schlesien unter Kaiser Karl IV.," *ZVGS*, 17 (1883), 1–43.

———. "Schlesien unter der Herrschaft König Ferdinands 1527–1564," *ZVGS*, 19 (1885), 63–139.

Haase, A. *Schlesiens Landwirtschaft. Ein Gang durch die Geschichte der schlesischen Landwirtschaft von den ersten Anfängen bis zum Leisteungsstand bei Beginn des Zweiten Weltkrieges. Eine agrarhistorische und agrargeographische Darstellung*. Wolfenbüttel, 1981.

Haeusler, Wilhelm. "Bemerkungen," *ZVGS*, 13 (1876–77), 275–276.

———. *Geschichte des Fürstenthums Oels bis zum Aussterben der Piastischen Herzogslinie*. Breslau, 1883.

Hagen, William W. "How Mighty the Junkers? Peasant Rents and Seigneurial Profits in Sixteenth-Century Brandenburg," *Past & Present*, 108 (1985), 80–116.

Halecki, Oscar. *Borderlands of Western Civilization; A History of East Central Europe*. New York, 1952.

Harnisch, Hartmut. "Die Gutsherrschaft: Forschungsgeschichte, Entwicklungszusammenhänge und Strukturelemente," *Jahrbuch für Geschichte des Feudalismus*, 9 (1985), 189–240.

———. "Probleme einer Periodisierung und regionalen Typisierung der Gutsherrschaft im mitteleuropäischen Raum," *Jahrbuch für Geschichte der Feudalismus*, 10 (1986), 251–274.

Härtel, Richard. "Die Prälaten des Breslauer Domstiftes bis zum Jahre 1500," *ZVGS*, 24 (1890), 279–290.

Hartke, W., and E. Westermann. "Zur Geographie der Vererbung der bäuerlichen Liegenschaften in Deutschland bis zum Erlass des Reichserbhofgesetzes," *Petermanns geographische Mitteilungen*, 86 (1940), 16–19.

Harvey, P. D. A. "The English Inflation of 1180–1220," *Past & Present*, 61 (1973), 3–30.

Haugwitz, Eberhard Graf von. *Die Geschichte der Familie von Haugwitz*. 2 vols. Leipzig, 1910.

Heck, Roman. "Położenie i walki klasowe chłopów w drugie połowie XIV i w początkach XV w.," pp. 441–444 in *Pierwsza Konferencja metodologiczna historyków polskich*, vol. I. Warsaw, 1953.

———. "Uwagi o gospodarce folwarcznej na Śląsku w okresie odrodzenia," *Sobótka*, 11 (1956), 169–211.

———. "Schlesien in der Zeit des Hussitenaufstandes," tr. Bolko Schweinitz, pp. 213–235 in Maleczyńska, ed., *Beiträge zur Geschichte Schlesiens*. Berlin, 1958.

———. *Studia nad położeniem ekonomicznym ludności wiejskiej na Slasku w XVI w.* Wrocław, 1959.

———. "Reformacja a problem walki klasowej chłopów śląskich w XVI wieku," *Odrodzenie i Reformacja w Polsce*, 5 (1961), 29–48.

———. "Elekcja kutnohorska 1471 roku. W pięćsetlecie objęcia przez Jagiellonów rządów królestwa czeskiego," *Sobótka*, 27 (1972), 193–235.

———. "Rozdrobnienie feudalne na Śląsku," pp. 35–70 in Henryk Łowmiański, ed., *Polska w okresie rozdrobnienia feudalnego*. Wrocław, 1973.

———. "'Chronica principum Poloniae' a 'Chronica Polonorum,'" *Sobótka*, 31 (1976), 185–196.

———. "O Piastowskich tradycjach średniowiecznego Śląska (Problemy świadomości historycznej i narodowej)," *KH*, 84 (1977), 3–22.

Heinisch, Klaus J. "Schlesische Landfrieden," *JSFWUB*, 22 (1981), 68–91.

Hejnosz, Wojciech. "Narok polski—służba komunikacyjna," pp. 141–148 in *Prace z dziejów Polski feudalnej ofiarowane Romanowi Grodeckiemu w 70 rocznicę urodzin*. Warsaw, 1961.

Hejnosz, Wojciech. "Jeszcze w sprawie polskiego naroku," *PH*, 52 (1961), 326–337.

Helbig, Herbert. "Die Anfänge der Landgemeinde in Schlesien," pp. 89–114 in *Die Anfänge der Landgemeinde und ihr Wesen*, vol. I. Vorträge und Forschungen, vol. 7. Konstanz, 1964.

Hellmann, Gustav, and Georg von Elsner. *Meteorologische Untersuchungen über die Sommerhochwasser der Oder*. Veröffentlichungen des Königlichen Preussischen Meteorologischen Instituts, no. 230. Berlin, 1911.

Henning, Friedrich-Wilhelm. "Die Handelsfunktionen Breslaus in der ersten Hälfte des 16. Jahrhunderts," *Scriptura Mercaturae*, 6 (1972), 105–126.

Herlihy, David. "The Carolingian *Mansus*," *EcHR*, 2d series 13 (1960), 79–89.

———. *Medieval Households*. Cambridge, Mass., 1985.

Heymann, Frederick G. *George of Bohemia: King of Heretics*. Princeton, N.J., 1965.

Heyne, Johann. *Urkundliche Geschichte der Königlichen Immediatstadt Neumarkt im ehemaligen Fürstentum Breslau, von ihrer ersten Entstehung bis auf die neueste Zeit. Ein Beitrag zur Geschichte schlesische Städte.* Glogau, 1845.

———. "Uber Krintsch, ein Besitztum des Breslauer Domstifts ad S. Joannem," *Schlesische Provinzial-Blätter*, 125 (1847), 630–638.

———. *Dokumentierte Geschichte des Bisthums und Hochstifts Breslau.* 3 vols. Breslau, 1860–1868.

———. *Urkundliche Geschichte der Stadt und des Fürstenthums Wohlau von den ältesten Zeiten bis auf die Gegenwart. (Nach authentischen Geschichtsquellen, Originalurkunden und Aktenstücken). Ein Beitrag zur kirchlichen und bürgerlichen Verfassungsgeschichte niederschlesischen Städte.* Wohlau, 1867.

Hilton, Rodney. "Medieval market towns and simple commodity production," *Past & Present*, 109 (1985), 3–23.

Hoffman, Philip T. "Taxes and Agrarian Life in Early Modern France: Land Sales, 1550–1730," *JEcH*, 46 (1986), 37–55.

Hoffmann, Richard C. "Studies in the Rural Economy of the Duchy of Wrocław 1200–1530" Yale University PhD Thesis. New Haven, 1970.

———. "Warfare, Weather, and a Rural Economy: The Duchy of Wrocław in the Mid-Fifteenth Century," *Viator*, 4 (1973), 273–305.

———. "Nazwy i miejscowości: Trzy studia z historii średniowiecznej okręgu wrocławskiego," *Sobótka*, 29 (1974), 1–25.

———. "Medieval Origins of the Common Fields," pp. 23–72 in William N. Parker and Eric L. Jones, eds. *European Peasants and Their Markets: Essays in Agrarian Economic History.* Princeton, 1975.

———. "Towards a 'City-State' in East-Central Europe: Control of Local Government in the Late Medieval Duchy of Wrocław," *Societas. A Review of Social History*, 5 (1975), 173–199.

———. "Wrocław Citizens as Rural Landholders" pp. 293–312 in H. Miskimin, D. Herlihy, and A. Udovitch, eds., *The Medieval City.* New Haven, 1977.

———. "Outsiders by Birth and Blood: Racist Ideologies and Realities around the Periphery of Medieval European Culture," *Studies in Medieval and Renaissance History*, 6 (1983), 3–34.

———. "Tenure of Land, Western European," pp. 671–686 in J. Strayer et al., eds., *Dictionary of the Middle Ages*, vol. 11. New York, 1988.

———. "Tools, Agricultural: European," pp. 72–83 in J. Strayer, et al., eds., *Dictionary of the Middle Ages*, vol. 12. New York, 1989.

———. "Villages: Community," pp. 437–441 in J. Strayer et al., eds., *Dictionary of the Middle Ages*, vol. 12. New York, 1989.

Hołubowicz, Włodzimierz. "Das frühmittelalterliche Oppeln im Lichte der archäologischen Forschungsarbeiten der Jahre 1952–1953," tr. Bolko Schweinitz, pp. 35–101 in Maleczyńska, ed., *Beiträge zur Geschichte Schlesiens.* Berlin, 1958.

Hube, Romuald. *Prawo Polskie w XIV-tym wieku. Sądy, ich pratyka i stosunki prawne spólczeństwa w Polsce ku schyłkowi 14 wieku.* Warsaw, 1886.

Huppertz, Barthel. *Räume und Schichten bäuerlicher Kulturformen in Deutschland. Ein Beitrag zur Deutschen Bauerngeschichte.* Bonn, 1939.

Inglot, Stefan. "Zagadnienie wpływu antycznej literatury rolniczej na organizację folwarku na Śląsku w okresie Renasansu," pp. 353–365 in *Prace z dziejów Polski feudalnej ofiarowane Romanowi Grodeckiemu w 70 rocznicę urodzin.* Warsaw, 1960.

————, et al., eds. *Historia chłopów śląskich.* Warsaw, 1979.

Irgang, Winfried. "Die Statuten der Breslauer Synode vom 10. Oktober 1248," *AsKg*, 34 (1976), 21–30.

————. "Zur Kirchenpolitik der schlesischen Piasten im 13. Jahrhundert," *ZO*, 27 (1978), 221–240.

————. "Das Urkundenwesen Herzog Heinrichs III. von Schlesien (1248–1266)," *ZO*, 31 (1982), 1–47.

————. "Neuere Urkundenforschungen zur Siedlungsgeschichte Schlesiens und Kleinpolens (mit einer Urkunde im Anh.)," *ZO*, 31 (1982), 361–384.

Jäger, Helmut. "Late Medieval Agrarian Crises and Deserted Settlements in Central Europe" pp. 223–237 in Niels Skyum-Nielsen and Niels Lund, eds., *Danish Medieval History: New Currents.* Copenhagen, 1981.

Jasiński, Kazimierz. *Rodowód Piastów śląskich.* 3 vols. Prace WTN, series A, nos. 154, 167, and 183. Wrocław, 1973–77.

Juhnke, Richard. *Wohlau; Geschichte des Fürstentums und des Kreises.* Ostdeutsche Beiträge aus dem Göttinger Arbeitskreis, vol. 35. Würzburg, 1965.

Jungnitz, J. "Beiträge zur mittelalterliche Statistik des Bistums Breslau," *ZVGS*, 33 (1889), 385–402.

————. "Die Feststellung der katholischen Pfarrspregel Breslaus," *ZVGS*, 30 (1896), 27–54.

Kaczmarczyk, Kazimierz. "Ciężary ludności wiejskiej i miejskiej na prawie niemieckim w Polsce XIII i XIV w.," *PH*, 11 (1910), 12–30, 144–160, and 288–311.

Kaczmarczyk, Zdzisław. "Kolonizacja niemiecka i kolonizacja na prawie niemieckim w średniowiecznej Polsce," pp. 218–326 in Jerzy Krasuski et al., eds., *Stosunki polsko-niemieckie w historiografii*, Part 1: *Studia z dziejów historiografii polski i niemieckiej.* Poznań, 1974.

Kaczmarczyk, Zdzisław and Michał Sczaniecki. "Kolonizacja na prawie niemieckim w Polsce a rozwój renty feudalnej," *CPH*, 3 (1951), 59–86.

Kamiński, Andrzej. "Neo-Serfdom in Poland-Lithuania," *Slavic Review*, 34 (1975), 253–268.

Każmierczyk, Józef. "Z badan nad kształtowaniem sie wczesnośredniowiecznego ośrodka miejskiego na lewym brzegu Odry we Wrocławiu," *Sobótka*, 20 (1965), 137–170.

————. *Wrocław lewobrzezny we wczesnym średniowieczu.* 2 vols. Wrocław, 1966–70.

Każmierczyk, Józef, and Zofia Podwińska. "Badania nad osadnictwem średniowiecznym okolic Trzebnicy. Problematyka i stan badań," *KHKM*, 12 (1964), 451–462.

————. "Wyniki badań północno-zachodniej części rejonu Trzebnicy przeprowadzonych w 1963 r.," *KHKM*, 12 (1964), 463–477.

Kehn, Wolfgang. *Der Handel im Oderraum im 13. und 14. Jahrhundert.* Historische Kommission für Pommern, Veröffentlichungen, series 5: Forschungen zur pommerschen Geschichte, no. 16. Köln, 1968.

Kern, Arthur. "Schlesische Bauernunruhen 1527/28," *Schlesische Geschichtsblätter*, 2 (1909), 25–29.

Kershaw, Ian. "The Great Famine and the Agrarian Crisis in England, 1315–1322," *Past & Present*, 59 (1973), 3–50.

Kiersnowski, Ryszard. *Wielka reforma monetarna XIII–XIV w.* Warsaw, 1969.

————. *Życie codzienne na Śląsku w wiekach średnich*. Warsaw, 1977.

Kindler, Paul. *Geschichte der Stadt Neumarkt*, vol. I: *Von den ältesten Zeiten bis zum Beginn des 30 jährige Krieges*. 2d ed. Neumarkt, 1934.

Kish, Leslie. "Selection of the Sample," pp. 189–198 in Leon Festinger and Daniel Katz, eds., *Research Methods in the Behavioral Sciences*. New York, 1953.

Kisch, Herbert. "The textile industries in Silesia and the Rhineland: A comparative study in industrialization (with a postscriptum)," pp. 178–200 in Peter Kriedte et al., *Industrialization before Industrialization. Rural Industry in the Genesis of Capitalism*, tr. Beate Schempp. Cambridge, 1981.

Klassen, John M. *The Nobility and the Making of the Hussite Revolution*. New York, 1978.

Klichowska, Melania. "Material roślinny z Opola z X–XII wieku," *Materiały Wczesno-średniowieczne*, IV (1956), 179–209.

————. "Znaleziska zbóż na terenie ziem polskich od neolitu do XII wieku n.e.," *KHKM*, 9 (1961), 675–701.

Kłoczowski, J. "Ze stosunków narodowościowych na Śląsku w XV i początkach XVI w.," *Przegląd Zachodni*, 7 (1951), 541–557.

Klose, Samuel B. von. *Von Breslau. Dokumentierte Geschichte und Beschreibung. In Briefen*. 3 vols. in 5. Breslau, 1781–83.

————. *Darstellung der inneren Verhältnisse der Stadt Breslau vom Jahre 1458 bis zum Jahre 1526*, ed. Gustav A. H. Stenzel. SrS, vol. 3. Breslau, 1847.

Klotz, Ernst E. "Die Entstehung des Frei- und Dreschgärtnerstandes in Schlesien. Ein Beitrag zur Geschichte der deutschrechtlichen Kolonisation," *ZVGS*, 66 (1932), 115–129.

Knapp, G. F., and Arthur Kern. "Die ländliche Verfassung Niederschlesiens," *Jahrbuch für Gesetzgebung, Verwaltung und Volkswirtschaft im Deutschen Reich*, 19 (1895), 69–93.

Knoblich, A. "Von einer verschollenen Bibliothek des 14. Jahrhunderts und ihrem Donator," *ZVGS*, 8 (1867), 180–191.

Knoll, Paul W. *The Rise of the Polish Monarchy: Piast Poland in East Central Europe, 1320–1370*. Chicago, 1972.

Knötel, Paul. "Die Typen der schlesischen Dorfkirchen," *MSGV*, 30 (1929), 179–204.

Koczerska, Maria. *Rodzina szlachecka w Polsce późnego średniowiecza*. Warsaw, 1975.

Koebner, Richard. "Locatio. Zur Begriffssprache und Geschichte der deutschen Kolonisation," *ZVGS*, 63 (1929), 1–32.

————. "Deutsches Recht und deutsche Kolonization," *VSWG*, 25 (1932), 313–352.

————. "Die Entstehung der Zaudengerichte und der Ausgang der Kastellanei-Verfassung in Schlesien," pp. 31–82 in Paul Diels and Richard Koebner, *Das Zaudengericht in Böhmen, Mähren und Schlesien. Historische Untersuchungen*, vol. 17. Breslau, 1935.

Kolańczyk, Kazimierz. *Studia nad reliktami wspólnej własności ziemi w najdawniejszej Polsce. Rozporządzanie własnością ziemską do końca XIV w*. Studia nad Historią Prawa Polskiego, vol. 20, no. 2. Poznań, 1950.

Kopietz, Johannes. *Die Böhmische Landeshauptmannschaft in Breslau unter dem Könige Johann und dem Kaiser Karl IV*. Breslau, 1907.

Korta, Wacław. "Rozwój wielki własności klasztornej na Śląsku do połowy XIII wieku," *Sobótka*, 13 (1958), 179–205.

———. "W sprawie gospodarki wielkiej własności cysterskiej na Dolnym Śląsku w XIII wieku," *Sobótka*, 15 (1960), 63–72.

———. "Rozwój terytorialny wielkiej świekiej własności feudalnej w Polsce do połowy XIII wieku," *Sobótka*, 16 (1961), 528–566.

———. "Rozwój średniej i drobnej świeckiej własności feudalnej na Śląsku do połowy XIII wieku," *Sobótka*, 19 (1964), 18–38.

———. *Rozwój wielkiej własności feudalnej na Śląsku do połowy XIII wieku.* Monografie śląskie Ossolineum, vol. 8. Wrocław, 1964.

———. *Średniowieczna annalistyka Śląska.* Prace WTN, Series A, no. 113. Wrocław, 1966.

Kossmann, Oskar. "Bauern und Freie im Heinrichauer Gründungsbuch und in der 'Elbinger Handschrift,'" *ZO*, 19 (1970), 263–302.

———. "Bauernfreiheit im mittelalterlichen Böhmen und Polen," *ZO*, 28 (1979), 193–237.

Kötzschke, Paul R. *Das Unternehmertum in der ostdeutschen Kolonisation des Mittelalters.* Bautzen, 1894.

Kötzschke, Rudolf. *Die Anfänge des deutschen Rechtes in der Siedlungsgeschichte des Ostens (Ius teutonicum).* Berichte über die Verhandlungen der Sächsischen Akademie der Wissenschaften zu Leipzig, vol. 93, no. 2. Leipzig, 1941.

Kozikowska, Zofia. "Ryby w pokarmie średniowiecznych (X–XIV w.) mieszkańców Wrocławia na Ostrowie Tumskim jako wzkaźnik gatunków łowionych w wodach danych okolic lub dobierających tam drogą handlu," *Acta Universitatis Wratislaviensis*, 223, *Prace Zoologiczne*, 4 (1974), 3–14.

Kraemer, August. *Die wechselnde wirtschaftliche und politische Bedeutung des Landbesitzes der Stadt Breslau.* Breslau, 1927.

Krenzlin, Anneliese. *Dorf, Feld und Wirtschaft im Gebiet der grossen Täler und Platten östlich der Elbe: eine siedlungsgeographische Untersuchung.* Forschungen zur deutschen Landeskunde, vol. 70. Remagen, 1952.

Krofta, K. "Začátky české berně," *Český Časopis Historický*, 26 (1930), 1–26, 237–257, and 437–490.

Kronthal, Berthold. "Leonard Asenheimer, ein schlesischer Feldhauptmann, 1442–1446," *ZVGS*, 28 (1894), 226–258.

Krupicka, Hanns. "Die sogenannte Leubuser Stiftungsurkunde von 1175," *ZVGS*, 70 (1936), 63–110.

Küchler, Winfried. *Das Bannmeilenrecht. Ein Beitrag der mittelalterlichen Ostsiedlung zur wirtschaftlichen und rechtlichen Verschränkung von Stadt und Land.* Marburger Ostforschungen, vol. 24. Würzburg, 1964.

Kuhn, Walter. *Siedlungsgeschichte Oberschlesiens.* Würzburg, 1954.

———. "Ostsiedlung und Bevölkerungsdichte," *Ostdeutsche Wissenschaft: Jahrbuch des Ostdeutschen Kulturrates*, 7 (1960), 31–68.

———. "Flämische und fränkische Hufe als Leitformen der mittelalterlichen Ostsiedlungen," *Hamburger mittel- und ostdeutsche Forschungen*, 2 (1960), 146–192.

———. "Kirchliche Siedlung als Grenzschütz 1200 bis 1250 (am Beispiel des mittleren Oderraumes)," *Ostdeutsche Wissenschaft*, 9 (1962), 6–55.

———. "Die Siedlerzahlen der deutschen Ostsiedlung," pp. 131–154 in Karl G.

Specht et al., eds., *Studium Sociale. Ergebnisse Sozialwissenschaftlicher Forschung der Gegenwart Karl Valentin Müller dargebracht.* Köln, 1963.

———. "Bauernhofgrössen in der mittelalterlichen Nordostsiedlung," *Hamburger mittel- und ostdeutsche Forschungen*, 4 (1963), 210–267.

———. "Die deutschrechtlichen Städte in Schlesien und Polen in der ersten Hälfte des 13. Jahrhunderts," *ZO*, 15 (1966), 278–337 and 457–510 [also separate: Marburg, 1968].

———. "Die Städtegründungspolitik der schlesischen Piasten im 13. Jahrhundert, vor allem gegenüber Kirche und Adel," *AsKg*, 29 (1971), 32–67; 30 (1972), 33–69; 31 (1973).

———. *Vergleichende Untersuchungen zur mittelalterlichen Ostsiedlung.* Ostmitteleuropa in Vergangenheit und Gegenwart, vol. 16. Köln, 1973.

———. "Westslawischer Landesherren als Organisatoren der mittelalterlichen Ostsiedlung," pp. 225–261 in Schlesinger, ed., *Ostsiedlung als Problem.* Sigmaringen, 1975.

———. "Seelenzahlen der Pfarreien in der mittelalterlichen Ostsiedlung," *AsKg*, 35 (1977), 1–28.

———. "Die Besiedlung des Auraser Waldlandes," *ZO*, 27 (1978), 207–220.

———. *Neue Beitrage zur schlesischen Siedlungsgeschichte.* QD, vol. 23. Sigmaringen, 1984.

Kula, Witold. *An Economic Theory of the Feudal System. Towards a model of the Polish Economy 1500–1800*, tr. Lawrence Garner. London, 1976; Polish original, 1962.

Kuras, Stanisław. *Przywileje prawa niemieckiego miast i wsi małopolskich XIV–XV wieku.* Wrocław, 1971.

Kurnik, Walter. "Scheitnig, das Paradies der Breslauer," *JSFWUB*, 14 (1969), 17–39.

Kurze, Dietrich. *Pfarrerwahlen im Mittelalter. Ein Beitrag zur Geschichte der Gemeinde und des Niederkirchenwesens.* Forschungen zur kirchlichen Rechtsgeschichte und zum Kirchenrecht, vol. 6. Cologne, 1966.

Laband, Paul. "Die Breslauer Stadt- und Gerichtsbücher," *ZVGS*, 4 (1862), 1–22.

Labuda, Gerard. "Uwagi o zjednoczeniu państwa polskiego na przełowie XIII i XIV wieku," *KH*, 62 (1955), 125–149.

Ladenberger [Ładogórski], Tadeusz. *Zaludnienie polski na początku panowania Kazimierza Wielkiego.* Badania z dziejów społecznych i gospodarczych, no. 9. Lwów, 1930.

Lalik, Tadeusz. "Märkte des 12. Jahrhunderts in Polen," *Ergon*, 3 (1962), 364–367.

———. "Radło i źreb," pp. 25–43 in *Z polskich studiów slawistycznych*, Seria 3: *Historia*. Warsaw, 1968.

———. "*Sors et aratrum*. Contribution à l'histoire sociale de la grande propriété domainale en Pologne et en Boheme au Moyen Age," *KHKM*, 17 (1969), 3–22.

———. "Les fonctions des petites villes en Pologne au bas moyen age," *APH*, 37 (1978), 5–28.

Lamb, H. H. *The Changing Climate: Selected Papers.* London, 1966.

———. *Climate: Present, Past and Future.* Vol. 2: *Climatic History and the Future.* London, 1977.

Langdon, John. *Horses, Oxen and Technological Innovation. The Use of Draught Animals in English Farming from 1066 to 1500.* Cambridge, 1986.

Latzke, W. "Die schlesische Erbscholtisei," *Schlesien*, 3 (1958), 196–205.

Laug, Werner. "Das Breslauer Domkapitel am Vorabend der Reformation nach der 'Acta Capituli Wratislaviensis,'" *JsKg*, 54 (1975), 88–104.

———. "Der Kolowratische Vertrag von 1504, sein Wortlaut und seine Auswirkungen," *JsKg*, 56 (1977), 37–56.

———. "Die Auseinandersetzung mit der Reformation in Breslau in den 'Acta Capituli Wratislaviensis' von 1517 bis 1540," *JsKg*, 57 (1978), 51–62.

Lehmann, Rudolf. *Die Herrschaften in der Niederlausitz. Untersuchungen zur Entstehung und Geschichte.* Mitteldeutsche Forschungen, vol. 40. Köln, 1966.

Lenczowski, Franciszek. "Z rozważań nad lokacją miast śląskich," pp. 103–126 in *Mediaevalia. W 50 rocznicę pracy naukowej Jana Dąbrowskiego.* Warsaw, 1960.

———. "Stosunki narodowościowe w miastach śląskich do końca XIV w.," *Studia Historyczne*, 19 (1976), 487–504.

LeRoy Ladurie, Emmanuel. "Pour une histoire de l'environnement: la part du climat," *AESC*, 25 (1970), 1459–1470.

———. *Times of Feast, Times of Famine: A History of Climate since the Year 1000*, tr. Barbara Bray. New York, 1971 [French original 1967].

———. "Family Structures and Inheritance Customs in Sixteenth-Century France," pp. 37–70 in Goody et al., eds., *Family and Inheritance*. Cambridge, 1976.

Lesiński, Bogdan. *Stanowisko kobiety w polskim prawie ziemskim do połowy XV w.* Wrocław, 1956.

———. *Kupno renty w średniowiecznej Polsce na tle ówczesne doktryny i praktyki zachodnioeuropejskiej.* Poznań, 1966.

Lhotsky, Alphons. *Das Zeitalter des Hauses Österreich: Die ersten Jahre der Regierung Ferdinands I. in Österreich (1520–1527).* Österreichische Akademie der Wissenschaften, Veröffentlichungen der Kommission für Geschichte Österreichs, no. 4. Vienna, 1971.

Lindgren, Erich. "Der Einfluss der Carolina und der Gemeinen Strafrechtslehre auf die Breslauer Strafrechtspflege," *JFSWUB*, 12 (1967), 57–88.

Loesch, Heinrich von. "Neue kirchenrechtliche Forschungen zur Kolonisations-Geschichte Ostdeutschlands," *ZVGS*, 59 (1925), 158–163.

———. "Die Fränkische Hufe," *ZVGS*, 61 (1927), 81–108 and LXIII (1929), 33–72.

Lopez, Robert S. *Naissance de l'Europe.* Paris, 1962.

———. *The Commercial Revolution of the Middle Ages 950-1350.* Englewood Cliffs, 1971.

Lorcin, Marie-Thérèse. "Un musée imaginaire de la ruse paysanne: la fraude des décimables du XIVe au XVIIIe siècle dans la région lyonnaise," *Études rurales* [Paris], 51 (1973), 112–124.

Lösch, August. *The Economics of Location*, trans. from the 2d rev. ed. by William H. Woglom. New York, 1967.

Lucas, Henry S. "The Great European Famine of 1315, 1316, and 1317," *Speculum*, 5 (1930), 341–377.

Luchs, H. "Der Johanniter-Convent und das heil. Leichnamshospital in Breslau," *ZVGS*, 4 (1862), 356–375.

Ludat, Herbert. *Bistum Lebus. Studien zur Gründungsfrage und zur Entstehung und Wirtschaftsgeschichte seiner schlesisch-polnischen Besitzungen.* Weimar, 1942.

Ładogórski, Tadeusz. *Studia nad zaludnieniem Polski XIV wieku*. Wrocław, 1958.

———. "Spór o ocene rachunków świętopietrza i liczebność zaludnienia Polski XIV wieku," *KHKM*, 10 (1962), 33–52.

———. "Nowy pogląd na rozwój zaludnienia Polski," *KHKM*, 13 (1965), 67–70.

Łowmiański, Henryk. *Początki Polski*. Vols. 1–5: *Z dziejów Słowian w I tysiącleciu n.e.* Warsaw, 1963–73. Vol. 6:1–2: *Polityczne i społeczne procesy kształtowania się narodu do początku wieku XIV*. Warsaw, 1985.

———. "The Rank Nobility in Medieval Poland," pp. 21–54 in Gąsiorowski, ed., *The Polish Nobility*. Wrocław, 1984.

Maas, Walther. "'Loi de Beaumont' und Jus Theutonicum," *VSWG*, 32 (1939), 209–227.

Macfarlane, Alan. *The Origins of English Individualism. The Family, Property and Social Transition*. New York, 1979.

Mączak, Antoni, et al., eds., *East-Central Europe in transition: From the fourteenth to the seventeenth century*. Cambridge, 1985.

Maetschke, Ernst. "Die Entstehung des *Liber Fundationis*," *ZVGS*, 77 (1943), 22–33.

Mahlendorff, Friedrich. *Geschichtliches über die Fleischerinnungen, die Schlachthöfe und die Fleischbeschau in der Stadt Breslau*. Leipzig, 1925.

Makkai, László. "Neo-Serfdom: Its Origin and Nature in East Central Europe," *Slavic Review*, 34 (1975), 225–238.

Maleczyńska, Ewa. "Udział Śląska w zmaganiach polsko-niemieckich pierwszej połowy XV w.," *Sobótka*, 1 (1946), 24–43.

———. "Niektóre zagadnienia z dziejów Śląska na przełomie XV i XVI wieku," pp. 219–233 in Maleczyńska, ed., *Skice z dziejów Śląska*. Warsaw, 1953.

———, ed. *Skice z dziejów Śląska*. Warsaw, 1953. [Tr. Bolko Schweinitz as *Beiträge zur Geschichte Schlesiens*. Berlin, 1958].

———. *Życie codzienne Śląska w dobie odrodzenia*. Warsaw, 1973.

Maleczyński, Karol. *Najstarze targi w Polsce i stosunek ich do miast przed kolonizacya na prawie niemieckiem*. Studya nad Historya Prawa Polskiego, vol. 10, no. 1. Lwów, 1926.

———. "Życie wsi śląskiej w średniowieczu," pp. 9–20 in *Z dziejów klasy pracujący Śląska*. Sobótka supplement, series B:1. Wrocław, 1950.

———. "Z dziejów wsi śląskiej w okresie przed kolonizacja na prawie niemieckim," pp. 126–145 in *Skice z dziejów Śląska*, ed. Ewa Maleczyńska. Warsaw, 1953.

———. "Z dziejów górnictwa śląskiego w epoce feudalnej," pp. 236–283 in *Skice z dziejów Śląska*, ed. Ewa Maleczyńska. Warsaw, 1953.

———. "Dzieje Wrocławia od czasów najdawniejszych do roku 1618," pp. 11–336 in Wacław Długoborski et al., eds., *Dzieje Wrocławia do roku 1807*. Warsaw, 1958.

———, ed. *Historia Śląska*. Vol. I: *Do roku 1763*. 4 vols.; Wrocław, 1960–1964.

———. "Ze studiów nad ludnością chłopską w Polsce wcześniejszego średniowiecza," *Sobótka*, 16 (1961), 495–527.

Małecki, Antoni. "Ludność wolna w Księdze Henrykowskiej," *KH*, 8 (1894), 391–423.

Małowist, Marian. "The Problem of the Inequality of Economic Development in Europe in the Later Middle Ages," *EcHR*, 2d series, 19 (1966), 15–28.

————. "Problems of the Growth of the National Economy of Central-Eastern Europe in the Late Middle Ages," *JEEcH*, 3 (1974), 319–357.

————. "The Trade of Eastern Europe in the Later Middle Ages," pp. 525–613 in Michael M. Postan and Edward Miller, eds., *The Cambridge Economic History of Europe*, vol. 2, *Trade and Industry in the Middle Ages*, 2d ed. rev. Cambridge, 1987.

Manteuffel, Tadeusz. *The Formation of the Polish State: The Period of Ducal Rule, 963–1194*. Tr. Andrew Gorski. Detroit, 1982.

Markgraf, Hermann. "Ueber die Legation des Guido *tit. S. Laurentii in Lucina presbyter cardinalis*, von 1265–1267," *ZVGS*, 5 (1863), 81–106.

————. "Aus Breslau's unruhigen Zeiten, 1418–1426," *ZVGS*, 15 (1880/81), 63–99, addendum 564–565.

————. "Zur Biographie des Sigismund Rosicz," *ZVGS*, 15 (1880/81), 246–248.

————. "Breslau als deutsche Stadt vor dem Mongolenbrand von 1241," *ZVGS*, 15 (1880/81), 527–544.

————. "Die öffentlichen Verkaufstätten Breslaus. Kammern, Bänke, Krame, Bauden," *ZVGS*, 18 (1884), 171–208.

————. "Heinz Dompnig, der Breslauer Hauptmann †1491," *ZVGS*, 20 (1886), 157–196.

Marshall, Werner. *Geschichte des Bistums Breslau*. Stuttgart, 1979.

Mate, Mavis. "High Prices in Early Fourteenth-Century England: Causes and Consequences," *EcHR*, 2d series 28 (1975), 1–16.

Matějek, František. "Gospodarka szlachecka i chłopska na Środkowym Śląsku w XVI wieku," tr. Józef Leszczyński, *Studia i Materiały z Dziejów Śląska*, 4 (1962), 423–452.

Matuszewski, Józef. "W sprawie śląskiego pochodzenia najstarszego spisu prawa polskiego," *CPH*, 5 (1953), 198–205.

————. "Początki nowożytnego zaprzęgu konnego," *KHKM*, 1 (1953), 79–109; 2 (1954), 637–663.

————. "Causae hereditariae dokumentów immunitetowych," *CPH*, 8 (1956), 63–91.

————. "Die angebliche Aufnahme des Sachsenspiegels Landrecht I 37 in das polnische Landrecht," pp. 112–129 in *Studien zur Geschichte Osteuropas*. Part 3: *Gedenkband für Heinrich Felix Schmid*. Wiener Archiv für Geschichte des Slawentums und Osteuropas, Veröffentlichungen des Instituts für osteuropäischen Geschichte und Südostforschungen der Universität Wien, vol. 5. Graz, 1966.

Matuszkiewicz, Felix. *Die mittelalterliche Gerichtsverfassung des Fürstentums Glogau*. DQ, vol. 13. Breslau, 1911.

Matzen-Stöckert, Sigrid. *Die mittelalterliche ländliche Besiedlung der Kreise Breslau und Neumarkt*. Dissertation zur Erlangung der Würde des Doktors der Philosophie der Universität Hamburg. Hamburg, 1976.

Maydorn, B. "Der Peterspfennig in Schlesien bis in die Mitte des XIV Jahrhunderts," *ZVGS*, 17 (1883), 44–62.

McClure, Peter. "Patterns of Migration in the late Middle Ages: The Evidence of English Place-Name Surnames," *EcHR*, 2d series 32 (1979), 167–182.

McFarlane, Kenneth B. *The Nobility of Late Medieval England*. Oxford, 1973.

Meinhardt, Günther. "Schlesiens Währungssysteme," *JSFWUB*, 15 (1970), 44–57.

Meitzen, August. *Der Boden und die landwirtschaftliche Verhältnisse des preussischen Staates.* 8 vols. Berlin, 1868–1908.

Mendenhall, William. *Introduction to Probability and Statistics*, 2d ed. Belmont, California, 1967.

Mendl, Bedřich. "Breslau zu Beginn des 15. Jahrhunderts. Ein statistische Studie nach dem Steuerbuche von 1403," *ZVGS*, 63 (1929), 154–185.

Mendras, Henri. "Un schema d'analyse de la paysannerie occidentale," *Peasant Studies Newsletter*, 1 (1972), 133–137.

Menzel, Josef J. *Jura ducalia; die mittelalterlichen Grundlagen der Dominialverfassung in Schlesien.* QD, vol. 11. Würzburg, 1964.

———. "Der Beitrag der Urkundenwissenschaft zur Erforschung der deutschen Ostsiedlung am Beispiel Schlesiens," pp. 131–160 in Schlesinger, ed., *Ostsiedlung als Problem.* Sigmaringen, 1975.

———. *Die schlesischen Lokationsurkunden des 13. Jahrhunderts: Studien zum Urkundenwesen, zur Siedlungs-, Rechts- und Wirtschaftsgeschichte einer ostdeutschen Landschaft im Mittelalter.* QD, vol. 19. Würzburg, 1977.

———. "Schlesiens Trennung von Polen und Anschluss an Böhmen im Mittelalter," *ZO*, 27 (1978), 262–274.

———. "Peter Eschenloer," cols. 630–632 in *Deutsche Literatur des Mittelalters. Verfasserlexikon.*, vol. II. 2d ed. rev. Berlin and New York, 1980.

Meyer, Arnold O. *Studien zur Vorgeschichte der Reformation aus schlesischen Quellen.* Historische Bibliothek, vol. 14. Munich, 1903.

Meyer, Waldtraut. *Gemeinde, Erbherrschaft und Staat im Rechtsleben des schlesischen Dorfes vom 16. bis 19. Jahrhundert. Dargestellt auf Grund von Schöppenbücher an Beispielen aus Nieder- und Oberschlesien.* QD, vol. 12. Würzburg, 1967.

Michael, Edmund. *Die schlesische Kirche und ihr Patronat im Mittelalter unter polnischem Recht. Beiträge zur ältesten schlesischen Kirchengeschichte.* Görlitz, 1926.

———. "Die schlesische Dorfschule im 16. Jahrhundert," *ZVGS*, 63 (1929), 227–261.

Míka, A. "Nástin vývoje cen zemedelského zbozi v Čechách v letech 1424–1547," *Československý Časopis Historický*, 8 (1959), 545–571.

Miskimin, Harry A. *The Economy of Early Renaissance Europe.* Englewood Cliffs, 1969.

Missalek, E. "Der Trebnitzer Grundbesitz des schlesischen Herzogs im 12. Jahrhundert," *ZVGS*, 48 (1914), 234–259.

Młynarska-Kaletynowa, Marta. "Rozwój sieci miejskiej na Śląsku na przełomie XII/XIII w.," *KHKM*, 28 (1980), 349–361.

———. *Wrocław w XII–XIII wieku. Przemiany społeczne i osadnicze.* Wrocław, 1986.

Modzelewski, Karol. "La division autarchique du travail à l'échelle d'un État: L'organization 'ministériale' en Pologne médievale," *AESC*, 19 (1964), 1125–1138.

———. "Narok—beneficjum grodu," *KH*, 79 (1972), 623–632.

———. "Grody i dwory w gospodarce polskiej monarchii wczesnofeudalnej," *KHKM*, 21 (1973), 3–35 and 157–189.

———. *Organizacja gospodarcza państwa piastowskiego X–XIII wiek.* Wrocław, 1975.

Moepert, Adolf. *Die Ortsnamen des Kreises Neumarkt in Geschichte und Sprache. Nach den alten und neuen Kreisgrenzen dargestellt.* Einzelschriften zur schlesischen Geschichte, vol. 13. Breslau, 1935.

———. "Die ersten deutschen Dörfer um Breslau," *AsKg*, 3 (1938), 286–293.

———. "Die Echtheit der Leubuser Stiftungsurkunde in sprachwissenschaftlicher Beleuchtung," *ZVGS*, 73 (1939), 42–58.

Morelowski, Marian. "L'evolution de l'urbanisme de Wrocław," pp. 191–215 in *Les origines des villes polonaises*, ed. Pierre Francastel. École Pratique des Hautes Études, VIe Section. Sciences économiques et sociales. Congrès et colloques, vol. 2. Paris, 1960.

Mosbach, August. "Über die Gefangennehmung des Bischofs von Kujawien und Herzogs von Oppeln, Johann, Kropidło gennannt, in Breslau am 6 Dezember 1410," *ZVGS*, 7 (1866), 70–101.

Muche, Alfred. "Studien zu einem historischen Ortsregister des Bistums Breslau. Teil I: Wahren und Dyhernfurth. Zur Geschichte zweier Nachbarorte," *AsKg*, 40 (1982), 75–104.

Muendel, John. "The Grain Mills of Pistoia in 1350," *Bollettino Storico Pistoiese*, 74 (1972), 39–64.

———. "The Distribution of Mills in the Florentine Countryside During the Late Middle Ages," pp. 83–115 in Raftis, ed., *Pathways*. Toronto, 1981.

Mühlen, Heinz von zur. "Kolonisation und Gutsherrschaft in Ostdeutschland," pp. 83–95 in *Geschichtliche Landeskunde und Universalgeschichte. Festgabe für Hermann Aubin zum 23 Dezember 1950*. Hamburg, 1950.

Mularczyk, Jerzy. *Dobór i rola świadków w dokumentach śląskich do końca XIII w.* Prace WTN, series A, no. 189. Wrocław, 1977.

———. "Ze studiów nad prawem patronatu na Śląsku w wiekach średnich," *Sobótka*, 32 (1977), 133–147

———. "Dwa bunty rycerstwa śląskiego przeciw książętom wrocławskim w drugiem połowie XII wieku," *Sobótka*, 33 (1978), 1–18.

———. "Z problematyki walk o władzę na śląsku w latach czterdziestych XIII wieku," *Sobótka*, 34 (1979), 1–16.

———. "Podziały Śląska między synów Henryka II Pobożnego w połowie XIII wieku," *PH*, 76 (1985), 481–504.

Müncheberg, Gustav. *Beiträge zur Geschichte der bäuerlichen Lasten in Mittelschlesien*. Breslau, 1901.

Musztyfaga, Antoni. "Ze studiów nad osadnictwem kasztelanii Nysko-Otmuchowskiej na przełomie XIII i XIV wieku," *Sobótka*, 23 (1968), 181–197.

Myczkowski, K. "Ogólne wyniki badan szczątków kostnych i skorup zwierzęcych z wczesnego średniowiecza, wydobytych na Ostrowie Tumskim we Wrocławiu w latach 1950–1957," *Przegląd Archeologiczny*, 12 (1960), 150–171.

Nasz, Adolf. "Wpływ śląsko-łużyckiej rubieży lesnej na dynamike procesów etnograficznych," *Sobótka*, 13 (1958), 365–408.

Nell, Edward J. "Economic Relationships in the Decline of Feudalism: An Examination of Economic Interdependence and Social Change," *History and Theory*, 6 (1967), 313–350.

Nicholas, David. *Town and Countryside: Social, Economic, and Political Tensions in Fourteenth-Century Flanders*. Rijksuniversiteit te Gent, Werken uitgegeven door de Faculteit van de Letteren en Wijsbegeerte, 152e Aflevering. Bruges, 1971.

Niermeyer, Jan F., et al., ed. *Mediae latinitatis lexicon minus*. 2 vols. Leiden, 1954–1976.

Noonan, John T. *The Scholastic Analysis of Usury*. Cambridge, Mass., 1957.

Nowakowa, J. *Rozmieszczenie komór celnych i przebieg dróg handlowych na Śląsku do końcu XIV wieku*. Wrocław, 1951.

Nowogrodzki, Stanisław. *Rzady Zygmunta Jagiellończyka na Śląsku i w Łużycach, 1499–1506*. Polska Akademia Umiejętności, Wydawnictwa Śląskie. Prace Historyczne, vol. 2. Cracow, 1937.

Nyrek, Aleksander. *Gospodarka rybna na Górnym Śląsku od połowy XVI do połowy XIX wieku*. Wrocław, 1966.

Odložilik, Otakar. "The Chapel of Bethlehem in Prague," pp. 125–141 in Günther Stöckl, ed., *Studien zur älteren Geschichte Osteuropas. Festschrift für Heinrich Felix Schmid*, vol. 1. Wiener Archiv für Geschichte des Slawentums und Osteuropas. Veröffentlichungen des Instituts für osteuropäischen Geschichte und Südostforschungen der Universität Wien, vol. 2. Graz, 1956.

―――. *The Hussite King; Bohemia in European Affairs, 1440–1471*. New Brunswick, N.J., 1965.

Opitz, Emil. *Die Arten des Rustikalbesitzes und die Laudamien und Markgroschen in Schlesien*. Untersuchungen zur deutschen Staats- und Rechtsgeschichte, vol. 73. Breslau, 1904.

Orzechowski, Kazimierz. "Prawo karne i jego rola w stosunkach wsi feudalnej," *Sobótka*, 18 (1963), 229–245.

Ostrowska, E. "Wczesnośredniowieczne budownictwo drewiane na Ostrowie Tumskim we Wrocławiu," *Silesia Antiqua*, 3 (1961), 164–179.

Pach, Z. P. "En Hongrie au XVIe siècle: L'Activité commerciale des seigneurs et leur production marchande," *AESC*, 21 (1966), 1212–1231.

Paglin, M. "The Measurement and Trend of Inequality: A Basic Revision," *American Economic Review*, 65 (1975), 598–609.

Parten, Mildred. *Surveys, Polls, and Samples: Practical Procedures*. New York, 1950.

Perlbach, Max. "Zur schlesischen Geschichte aus Ermland und Danzig," *ZVGS*, 44 (1910), 256–260.

Petráň, Josef. "A propos de la formation des régions de la production spécialisée en Europe Central," pp. 217–223 in *Second International Conference of Economic History, Aix-en-Provence, 1962*. École Pratique des Hautes Études—Sorbonne, VIe Section. Sciences économiques et sociales. Congrès et colloques, vol. 8. Paris, 1965.

Petry, Ludwig. *Die Popplau. Eine schlesische Kaufmannsfamilie des 15. und 16. Jahrhunderts*. Historische Untersuchungen, vol. 15. Breslau, 1935.

―――. *Dem Osten zugewandt. Gesammelte Aufsätze zur schlesischen und ostdeutschen Geschichte*. QD, vol. 22. Sigmaringen, 1983.

―――. "Breslau in der frühen Neuzeit—Metropole des Südostens," *ZO*, 33 (1984), 161–179.

Petry, Ludwig, and Josef J. Menzel, eds. *Geschichte Schlesiens*. Vol. 2: *Die Habsburgerzeit 1526–1740*. Darmstadt, 1973.

Pfeiffer, Gerhard. *Das Breslauer Patriziat im Mittelalter*. DQ, vol. 30. Breslau, 1929.

―――. "Die Entwicklung des Breslauer Patriziats," pp. 99–124 in Hellmuth Rössler, ed., *Deutsches Patriziat 1430–1740*. Limburg/Lahn, 1968.

Pfotenhauer, Paul. "Die Kreuzherren mit den rothen Stern in Schlesien," *ZVGS*, 14 (1878/79), 51–78.

————. "Schlesier im Dienste des Deutschen Ordens im Jahre 1410," *ZVGS*, 15 (1880/81), 203–214.

————. "Die fünfzig Ritter von 1294," *ZVGS*, 16 (1882), 157–179.

————. "Nicholaus Popplau," pp. 428–431 in *Allgemeine Deutsche Biographie*, vol. 26. Berlin, 1883.

————. "Die Pförtner von Neumarkt und ihre Aufzeichnungen," *ZVGS*, 20 (1886), 260–296.

————. "Zur Geschichte der Weihbischöfe des Bisthums Breslau," *ZVGS*, 23 (1889), 241–275.

Planitz, Hans. *Das deutsche Grundpfandrecht*. Forschungen zum deutschen Recht, vol. 1, no. 4. Weimar, 1936.

Piekarczyk, Stanisław. *Studia z dziejów miast polskich w XIII–XIV wieku*. Warsaw, 1955.

Podwińska, Zofia. *Technika uprawy roli w Polsce średniowiecznej*. Wrocław, 1962.

————. "Habitat agraire en Pologne du début du Moyen Age. Soixante ans de recherches," *KHKM*, 16 (1968), 729–747.

————. "Rozmieszczenie wodnych młynów zbożowych w Małopolsce w XV wieku," *KHKM*, 18 (1970), 373–402.

————. *Zmiany form osadnictwa wiejskiego na ziemiach polskich we wcześniejszym średniowieczu: źreb, wieś, opole*. Wrocław, 1971.

Poppe, Danuta. "Ludność dziesiętnicza w Polsce wczesnoszredniowiecznej. Z dziejów kształtowania się klasy chłopskiej feudalnie zaleznej," *KH*, 64 (1957), 3–31.

Postan, Michael M. and Titow, Jan. "Heriots and Prices on Winchester Manors," *EcHR*, 2d series, 11 (1959), 392–411.

Pošvář, Jaroslav. "Talary na Śląsku," *Sobótka*, 20 (1965), 318–325.

————. "Pieniądz denarowy i groszowy na Śląsku (ze szczególnym uwzględnieniem jego związków z Czechami)," *Sobótka*, 22 (1967), 10–34.

Pounds, Norman J. G. *An Historical Geography of Europe 450BC–AD1330*. Cambridge, 1973.

————. *An Economic History of Medieval Europe*. London, 1974.

Puřs, Jaroslav, ed. *Atlas československých dějin*. Vydala Ústřední Spráwa Geodézi a Kartografie ve Spolupráci s Historickym Ustavem ČSAV. Prague, 1965.

Pustejovsky, Otfrid. *Schlesiens Ubergang an die böhmische Krone: Machtpolitik Böhmens im Zeichen von Herrschaft und Frieden*. Forschungen und Quellen zur Kirchen- und Kulturgeschichte Ostdeutschlands, vol. 13. Köln, 1975.

Pyrek, Władysław. "Z polskości mas ludowych Wrocławia w początkach XV w.," *Sobótka*, 11 (1956), 104–107.

Rabęcka, Irena. "The Early Medieval Tavern in Poland," *Ergon*, 3 (1962), 372–375.

Rachfahl, Felix. *Die Organisation der Gesamtstaatsverwaltung Schlesiens vor dem dreissigjährigen Kriege*. Staats- und socialwissenschaftliche Forschungen, vol. 13, no. 1. Leipzig, 1894.

————. "Zur Geschichte der Grundherrschaft in Schlesien," *ZRG, Germanistische Abteilung*, 16 (1895), 108–199.

Radler, Leonhard. "Hatte Graf Peter Wlost auch im Kreise Striegau Besitz?" *AsKg*, 21 (1963), 301–305.

Raftis, J. A. *Tenure and Mobility: Studies in the Social History of the Mediaeval English Village*. Pontifical Institute of Mediaeval Studies Studies and Texts, no. 8. Toronto, 1964.

————. "Social Structures in Five East Midland Villages. A Study of possibilities in the use of court roll data," *EcHR*, 2d series 18 (1965), 83–99.

————, ed. *Pathways to Medieval Peasants*. Pontifical Institute of Mediaeval Studies Papers in Mediaeval Studies, vol. 2. Toronto, 1981.

Raftis, J. A., and M. P. Hogan, eds. *Early Huntingdonshire Lay Subsidy Rolls*. Pontifical Institute of Mediaeval Studies Subsidia Mediaevalia, no. 8. Toronto, 1976.

Rauprich, Max. "Breslaus Handelslage am Ausgang des Mittelalters," *ZVGS*, 26 (1892), 1–26.

————. "Der Streit um die Breslauer Niederlage, 1490–1515," *ZVGS*, 27 (1893), 54–116.

Reichert, Hermann, E. *Die deutschen Familiennamen nach Breslauer Quellen des 13 und 14. Jahrhunderts*. Wort und Brauch, vol. 1. Breslau, 1908.

Reiter, Lothar. *Beiträge zur Besiedlungs-, Rechts- und Wirtschaftsgeschichte des Weichbilds Kanth*. Breslau, 1935.

Richter, Gertraud. "Klimaschwankungen und Wustungsvorgänge im Mittelalter," *Petermanns geographischer Mitteilungen*, 96 (1952), 249–254.

Richtsteig, Eberhard. "Peter Wlast," *AsKg*, 18 (1960), 1–27; 19 (1961), 1–24; 20 (1962), 1–28.

Ringrose, David. "The Impact of a New Capital City: Madrid, Toledo, and New Castile, 1560–1660," *JEcH*, 33 (1973), 761–791.

Roehl, Richard. "Plan and Reality in a Medieval Monastic Economy: The Cistercians," *Studies in Medieval and Renaissance History*, 9 (1972), 83–115.

Roepell, Richard. "Zur Quellenkunde der schlesischen Geschichte. I: Benedict's von Posen Chronik der Herzoge von Schlesien," *ZVGS*, 2 (1859), 402–418.

Rogmann, Heinz. "Grundlinien der Bevölkerungsentwicklung Schlesiens, Teil I. Bis zu Beginn des 19. Jahrhunderts," *Deutsches Archiv für Landes- und Volksforschung*, 3 (1939), 419–452.

Rombowski, Aleksander. "Polacy podwrocławscy (XVI–XIX w.)," *Sobótka*, 3 (1948), 355–408.

Rospond, Stanisław. "Dawny Wrocław i jego okolice w świetle nazewnictwa," *Sobótka*, 25 (1970), 9–32.

Rotelli, Claudio. *Una campagna medievale. Storia agraria del Piemonte (nordoccidentale) fra il 1250 e il 1450*. Biblioteca di cultura storica, no. 120. Turin, 1973.

Rüffler, Alfred. "Geschichte des Rittergutes und Dorfes Sillmenau, Kreis Breslau," *JFSWUB*, 21 (1980), 114–162.

Rusiński, Władysław. "Drogi rozwojowe folwarku pańszczyźnianego," *PH*, 47 (1956), 617–655.

————. "Hauptprobleme der Fronwirtschaft im 16. bis 18. Jhd. in Polen und den Nachbarländern," *Contributions, Communications: First International Conference of Economic History. Stockholm, 1960*. Paris, 1960.

Russell, Josiah C. "Recent Advances in Medieval Demography," *Speculum*, 40 (1965), 84–101.

————. *Medieval Regions and their Cities*. Bloomington, 1972.

Russocki, Stanisław. "Le role de la 'fidelitas' et du 'beneficium' dans la formation des états slaves," *APH*, 26 (1972), 171–188.

Rutkowska-Płachcińska, Anna. "Uwagi o gospodarce hodowlanej w Polsce w XIII i XIV w.," *Przegląd Zachodni*, 11 (1955), 584–597.

————. "W sprawie charakteru rezerwy pańskiej w okresie gospodarki czynsowej," *PH*, 48 (1957), 411–435.

————. "Zur Frage der Stadtgemeinde in Polen zu Beginn des 13. Jh.," *Ergon*, 3 (1962), 354–359.

Rutkowski, Jan. *Skup sołectw w Polsce w XVI wieku*. Prace Komisji Historii Poznańskiej Towarzystwa Naukowego, vol. 1, no. 1. Poznań, 1921.

Rymaszewski, Zygfryd. *Prawo bliższości krewnych w polskim prawie ziemskim do końca XV wieku*. Wrocław, 1970.

Samsonowicz, Henryk. *Rzemiosło wiejskie w Polsce XIV–XVI w*. Towarzystwo Miłośników Historii, Prace Instytutu Historycznego Uniwersytetu Warszawskiego, Badania z Dziejów Rzemiosła i Handlu w Epoce Feudalizmu, vol. 2. Warsaw, 1954.

————. "Przemiany osi drożnych w Polsce późnego średniowiecza," *PH*, 64 (1973), 697–716.

————. "La famille noble et la famille bourgeoise en Pologne aux XIIIe–XVe siècles," pp. 309–317 in Duby and LeGoff, eds., *Famille et parenté*. Rome, 1977.

————. "Soziale und wirtschaftliche Funktionen der Kleinstädte im Polen des 15. Jahrhunderts," *Jahrbuch für Geschichte des Feudalismus*, 2 (1978), 191–205.

Sanmann, H. von B. *Die Inkorporationen Karls IV.: Ein Beitrag zur Geschichte des Staatseinheitsgedankens im spateren Mittelalter*. Marburger Studien zur alteren deutschen Geschichte, Series 2, No. 8. Marburg, 1942.

Santifaller, Leo. "Die Beziehungen zwischen Ständewesen und Kirche in Schlesien bis zum Ausgang des Mittelalters," *ZRG*, 58, *Kanonistische Abteilung*, 27 (1938), 398–413.

————. *Liebentals Kopialbücher des Prämonstratenserstifts zum Hl. Vinzenz im Breslau*. Mitteilungen des Instituts für österreichische Geschichtsforschung, Ergänzungs Band, 15. Innsbruck, 1947.

Schilling, Friedrich. *Ursprung und Frühzeit des Deutschtums in Schlesien und im Land Lebus. Forschungen zu den Urkunden der Landnahmezeit*. 2 vols. Ostdeutsche Forschungen, vols. 4–5. Posen, 1938.

Schindler, G. *Das Breslauer Domkapitel von 1341–1417. Untersuchungen über seine Verfassung und persönliche Zusammensetzung*. Breslau, 1938.

Schlenger, Herbert. *Formen ländlicher Siedlungen in Schlesien: Beiträge zur Morphologie der schlesischen Kulturlandschaften*. Veröffentlichungen der schlesischen Gesellschaft für Erdkunde, vol. 10. Breslau, 1930.

Schlesinger, Walter. "Die geschichtliche Stellung der mittelalterlichen deutschen Ostbewegung," *Historische Zeitschrift*, 183 (1957), 517–542.

————. "Bäuerliche Gemeindebildung in den mittelelbischen Länden im Zeitalter der mittelalterlichen deutschen Ostbewegung," pp. 212–274 in his *Mitteldeutsche Beiträge*. Göttingen, 1961.

————. "Forum, villa fori, ius fori. Einige Bemerkungen zu Marktgrundungsurkunden des 12. Jahrhunderts aus Mitteldeutschland," pp. 275–305 in his *Mitteldeutsche Beiträge*. Göttingen, 1961 [originally published 1960].

————. *Mitteldeutsche Beiträge zur deutschen Verfassungsgeschichte des Mittelalters*. Göttingen, 1961.

————. "Zur Problematik der Erforschung der deutschen Ostsiedlung," pp. 11–30 in Schlesinger, ed., *Ostsiedlung als Problem*. Sigmaringen, 1975.

————, ed. *Die deutsche Ostsiedlung des Mittelalters als Problem der europäischen Geschichte.* Vorträge und Forschungen, vol. 18. Sigmaringen, 1975.

Schieckel, Harald. *Herrschaftenbereich und Ministerialität der Markgrafen von Meissen im 12. und 13. Jahrhundert. Untersuchungen über Stand und Stammort der Zeugen markgräflicher Urkunden.* Cologne, 1965.

Schmid, Heinrich F. "Das Recht der Gründung und Ausstattung von Kirchen im kolonialen Teile der Magdeburger Kirchenprovinz während des Mittelalters," *ZGR, Kanonistische Abteilung,* 13 (1924), 1–214.

————. "Die rechtliche Grundlagen der Pfarrorganisation auf westslavischem Boden und ihre Entwicklung während des Mittelalters," *ZRG, Kanonistische Abteilung,* 15 (1926), 1–161; 17 (1928), 264–327.

Schmilewski, Ulrich. "Die schlesischen Zehntstreitigkeiten in der ersten Hälfte des 13. Jahrhunderts," *AsKg,* 42 (1984), 159–166.

Schmitz, Hans-Jürgen. *Faktoren der Preisbildung für Getreide und Wein in der Zeit von 800 bis 1350.* Quellen und Forschungen zur Agrargeschichte, vol. 20. Stuttgart, 1968.

Scholz-Babisch, Marie. "Oberdeutscher Handel mit dem deutschen und polnischen Osten nach Geschäftsbriefen von 1444," *ZVGS,* 64 (1930), 56–74.

Schreiber, Rudolf. "Zur Auswertung von Personennamen für die Volksgeschichte," *ZVGS,* 73 (1939), 103–112.

Schulte, Wilhelm [Lambert]. "Ujazd und Lgota. Ein Beitrag zur schlesischen Ortsnamenforschung," *ZVGS,* 25 (1891), 211–235.

————. "Die Entwicklung der Parochial-Verfassung und des höheren Schulwesens Schlesiens im Mittelalter," *ZVGS,* 36 (1902), 388–404.

————. "Zur Biographie des Sigismund Rosicz," *ZVGS,* 43 (1909), 334–336.

————. "Vermischte Mitteilungen, 4: Zu Fink, Geschichte der landesherrlichen Besuche in Breslau. Breslau 1897," *ZVGS,* 46 (1912), 242.

————. "Kostenblut. Eine rechtsgeschichtliche Untersuchung," *ZVGS,* 47 (1913), 209–266.

————. "Bischof Thomas I. und die angebliche Umwandlung des Feldzehnten," *ZVGS,* LI (1917), 117–133.

————. "Polnische Erntearbeiter im 16. Jahrhundert," pp. 190–192 in his *Kleine Schriften.* DQ, vol. 23. Breslau, 1918 [originally 1908].

Schulze, Hans K. "Die deutsche Ostsiedlung des Mittelalters: Bilanz und Aufgabe," *ZO,* 26 (1977), 453–466.

————. "Der Anteil der Slawen an der mittelalterlichen Siedlung nach deutschem Recht in Ostmitteldeutschland," *ZO,* 31 (1982), 321–336.

Schwarzer, Otfrid. "Stadt und Fürstentum Breslau in ihrer politischen Umwelt im Mittelalter," *ZVGS,* 65 (1931), 54–90.

Sczaniecki, Michał. "Les origines et la formation de la noblesse polonaise au Moyen Age," *APH,* 36 (1977), 101–108.

Seidel, Viktor. *Der Beginn der deutschen Besiedlung Schlesiens.* DQ, vol. 17. Breslau, 1913.

————. "Die weltliche Stellung des Abtes von Leubus im Wandel der 13. und 14. Jahrh.," *ZVGS,* 55 (1921), 110–127.

Seppelt, Franz X. "Die Anfänge der Wahlkapitulationen der Breslauer Bischöfe," *ZVGS,* 49 (1915), 192–222.

————. "Die Epochen der Breslauer Bistumgeschichte im Mittelalter," *ZVGS*, 61 (1927), 1–11.

Skalweit, August. "Vom Werdegang des Dorfhandwerks," *Zeitschrift für Agrargeschichte und Agrarsoziologie*, 2 (1954), 1–16.

Skwarczyński, P. "The Problem of Feudalism in Poland up to the Beginning of the 16th Century," *Slavonic and East European Review*, 34 (1956), 292–310.

Slicher van Bath, Bernard H. "De Oogstopbrengsten van verschillende gewassen, voornamelijk granen, in verhouding tot het zaaizaad, ca. 810-1820," pp. 29–126 in *Afdeling Agrarische Geschiednis Bijdragen*, vol. 9. Wageningen, 1963.

————. *Yield Ratios, 810-1820*. Afdeling Agrarische Geschiednis Bijdragen, vol. 10. Wageningen, 1963.

Sporn, Th. *Die "Stadt zu polnischen Recht" und die deutschrechtliche Gründungsstadt*. Europäische Hochschulschriften, series 2, vol. 197. Frankfurt a.M., 1978.

Spufford, Peter. *Handbook of Medieval Exchange*. London, 1986.

Śreniowski, Stanisław. "Uwagi o łanach w ustroju folwarczno-pańszczyźnianym wsi polskiej," *KHKM*, 3 (1955), 301–337.

Stefański, Karol. "Wsie na 'prawie niemieckim' w Wielkopolsce w latach 1333–1370," *RH*, 37 (1971), 1–38.

Stein, Rudolf. *Der Rat und die Ratsgeschlechter des alten Breslau*. Würzburg, 1963.

Stenzel, Gustav A. H. "Beitrag zur Geschichte des Augustiner Chorherren-Stiftes der Jungfrau Maria auf dem Sande bei Breslau," *Übersicht* 1840, 113–114 and 121–128.

————. "Über die von den Müllern an die Grundherrschaften zu entrichtenden Mühlzinsen, Mehlzinsen und andere Leistungen. Ein nachgelassene Abhandlung," *ZVGS*, 2 (1859), 331–358.

Stewart, Gordon. "Recovery from Adversity in Eighteenth-Century India: Rethinking 'Villages,' 'Peasants,' and Politics in Pre-Modern Kingdoms," *Peasant Studies*, 8:4 (1979), 61–80.

Stolle, Franz. "Das *antiquum Registrum* des Breslauer Bistums, eine der ältesten schlesischen Geschichtsquellen," *ZVGS*, 40 (1926), 133–156.

————. "Das *Polonicum miliare* (schles. Meile) in der *vita s. Hedwigis* und seine Bedeutung," *Schlesische Geschichtsblätter*, (1926) nr. 1, 11–19.

Stone, Lawrence. *The Crisis of the Aristocracy 1558–1641*. Oxford, 1965.

Strayer, Joseph R. "The Two Levels of Feudalism," pp. 63–71 in his *Medieval Statecraft and the Perspectives of History*. Princeton, 1971.

Strnad, A. "Die Breslauer Bürgerschaft und des Königtum Georg Podebrads," *ZO*, 14 (1965), 401–435 and 601–640.

Stromer von Reichenbach, Wolfgang Frhr. "Nürnberg-Breslauer Wirtschaftsbeziehungen im Spätmittelalter," *Jahrbuch für fränkische Landesforschung*, 34–35 (1975), 1079–1100.

Symmons-Symonolewicz, Konstantin. "National Consciousness in Poland until the End of the Fourteenth Century: A Sociological Interpretation," *Canadian Review of Studies in Nationalism*, 8 (1981), 249–266.

Szafrański, Franciszek. *Ludwik II brzesko-legnicki feudał śląski z doby późnego średniowiecza*. Monografie śląskie Ossolineum, vol. 22. Wrocław, 1972.

Szczesniak, Bolesław B. *The Knights Hospitallers in Eastern Europe*. Studies in European History, vol. 19. The Hague, 1967.

Szczygielski, Wojciech. *Z dziejów gospodarki rybnej w Polsce w XVI–XVIII wieku.* Studia z dziejów gospodarstwa wiejskiego, vol. 9, no. 2. Warsaw, 1969.

Szulc, Halina. *Osiedla podwrocławskie na początku XIX wieku.* Monografie Śląskie Ossolineum, vol. 5. Wrocław, 1963.

Szwagrzyk, Józef. "Szerokie grosze praskie na ziemach polskich, 1302–1547," *Ze Skarbca Kultury*, 18 (1967), 41–197.

———. *Pieniądz na ziemach polskich X–XX w.* Wrocław, 1973.

Thieme, Hans. "Die Magdeburger und Kulmer Stadtrechte im deutschen Osten," pp. 144–159 in *Deutsche Ostsiedlung im Mittelalter und Neuzeit.* Studien zum Deutschtum im Osten, no. 8. Köln, 1971.

Trawkowski, Stanisław. "Ołbin Wrocławski w XII wieku," *Roczniki dziejów społecznych i gospodarczych*, 20 (1958), 69–106.

———. *Gospodarka wielkiej własności cysterskiej na Dolnym Śląsku w XIII wieku.* Warsaw, 1959.

———. "W sprawie roli kolonizacji niemieckiej w przemianach kultury materialnej na ziemiach polskich w XIII wieku," *KHKM*, 8 (1960), 183–207.

———. "Młyny wodne w Polsce w XII w.," *KHKM*, 7 (1959), 62–85.

———. "Zur Erforschung der deutschen Kolonisation auf polnischem Boden im 13. Jahrhundert," *APH*, 7 (1962), 79–95.

———. "Narok—Beneficium," *KH*, 70 (1963), 437–439.

———. "Przemiany społeczne i gospodarcze w XII i XIII w.," pp. 62–118 in Aleksander Gieysztor, ed., *Polska dzielnicowa i zjednoczona: państwo, społeczeństwo, kultura.* Warsaw, 1972.

———. "Rozwój osadnictwa wiejskiego w Polsce w XII i pierwszej połowie XIII w.," pp. 99–132 in Henryk Łowmiański, ed., *Polska w okresie rozdrobnienia feudalnego.* Wrocław, 1973.

———. "Die Rolle der deutschen Dorfkolonisation und des deutschen Rechtes in Polen im 13. Jahrhundert," pp. 349–368 in Schlesinger, ed., *Ostsiedlung als Problem.* Sigmaringen, 1975.

Turoń, Bronisław. "*Liber Niger* kopiarz biskupstwa wrocławskiego," *Acta Universitatis Wratislaviensis*, 126: *Historia*, 19 (1970), 47–96.

Tyc, Teodor. *Die Anfänge der dörflichen Siedlung zu deutschem Recht in Grosspolen (1200–1333)*, tr. Maria Tyc. Breslau, 1930 [Polish original, 1924].

Tymieniecki, Kazimierz. "Poddańcza gmina wiejska a kwestia wolnych rolników w wiekach średnich w Europie Zachodnie i w Polsce," *PH*, 23:2 (1921), 61–88.

———. "Prawo niemieckie w rozwoju społecznym wsi polskiej," *KH*, 37 (1923), 38–78.

———. "Społeczeństwo śląskie na podstawie dokumentów trzebnickich z lat 1203, 1204 i 1208," pp. 319–342 in *Studja społeczne i gospodarcze. Księga jubileuszowa ku uczczeniu 40-letniej pracy naukowej Ludwika Krzywickiego.* Warsaw, 1925.

———. "Prawo czy gospodarstwo?" *Roczniki Dziejów Społecznych i Gospodarczych*, 8 (1939/46), 275–291.

———. "Lenna chłopskie czy prawo niemieckie? (Rzecz z zakresu genezy form gospodarstwa czynszowego w Polsce średniowiecznej)," *RH*, 20 (1951/52), 59–120.

———. *Narocznicy w gospodarstwie feudalnym. Studium z dziejów gospodarczo-społecznych wczesnego średniowiecza.* Poznańskie Towarzystwo Przyjaciół Nauk. Prace Komisji Historycznej, vol. 17, part 3. Poznań, 1955.

————. "Przemiany w ustroju polskiej wsi wczesnofeudalnej i ich wpływ na wzrost sił wytwórczych," *KH*, 62 (1955), 3–35.

————. *Smardowie polscy*. Poznań, 1959.

————. "O narocznikach i . . . nie o narocznikach," *PH*, 51 (1960), 566–581.

————. "Technika rolna i organizacja społeczna w początku doby feudalnej," *RH*, 28 (1962), 57–67.

————. *Historia chłopów polskich*. 3 vols. Warsaw, 1965–69.

Tync, Stanisław. "Z życia patrycjatu wrocławskiego w dobie renesansu," *Sobótka*, 8 (1953), 69–123.

Tyszkiewicz, Lech. "Ze studiów nad osadnictwem wczesnofeudalnym na Śląsku," *Sobótka*, 12 (1957), 1–50.

Urban, Wincenty. *Studia nad dziejami Wrocławskiej diecezji w pierwszej połowie XV wieku*. Wrocław, 1959.

————. "Materiały do dziejów polskości na Śląsku w wizytacjach diecezji wrocławskiej (do początków XVIII wieku)," *Sobótka*, 14 (1959), 149–195.

Válka, Josef. "La structure économique de la seigneurie tchèque au XVIe siècle," pp. 211–216 in *Second International Conference of Economic History, Aix-en-Provence, 1962*. École Pratique des Hautes Études—Sorbonne, VIe Section. Sciences économiques et sociales. Congrès et colloques, vol. 8. Paris, 1965.

Vetulani, Adam. "Niemiecki spis polskiego prawa zwyczajowego. Uwagi źródłoznawcze," *CPH*, 5 (1953), 180–197.

————. "Nowe wydanie 'Prawa Polaków.' Na marginesie publikacji J. Matuszewskiego 'Najdawniejszy zwód prawa polskiego,'" *Sprawozdania Poznanskiego Towarzystwa Przyjaciół Nauk*, 55 (1959) [1961], 170–172.

Vielrose, Egon. "Ludność Polski od X do XVIII wieku," *KHKM*, 5 (1957), 3–49.

Walter, Ewald. "Das Patrozinium der ehemaligen St. Gertrudskapelle auf dem Schweidnitzer Anger (jetzt Tauentzienplatz in Breslau)," *AsKg*, 4 (1939), 70–83.

Walter, Ewald. "Zur älteste Geschichte des Klosters Leubus a.d.Oder," *JFSWUB*, 16 (1971), 7–40.

Wasiliewski, Tadeusz. "O służbie wojskowej ludności wiejskiej i składzie społecznym wojsk konnych i pieszych we wczesnym średniowieczu polskim," *PH*, 51 (1960), 1–23.

Wattenbach, Wilhelm. "Miscellen: 2. Ueber das *Repertorium Heliae*," *ZVGS*, 3 (1860), 202–206.

————. "Ueber die Veranlassung zum Abbruch des Vincenzklosters vor Breslau im Jahre 1529," *ZVGS*, 4 (1862), 146–159.

Watts, D. C. "A Model for the Early Fourteenth Century," *EcHR*, 2d series 20 (1967), 543–547.

Weikinn, Curt. *Quellentexte zur Witterungsgeschichte Europas von der Zeitwende bis zum Jahre 1850: Hydrographie*. 4 vols. Deutsche Akademie der Wissenschaften zu Berlin, Institut für Physikalische Hydrographie: Quellensammlung zur Hydrographie und Meteorologie, vol. 1. Berlin, 1958–63.

Wędzki, Andrzej. *Początki reformy miejskiej w środkowej Europie do połowy XIII wieku (Słowiańszczyzna zachodnia)*. Warsaw, 1974.

Weinrich, Lorenz. "Die Urkunde in der Übersetzung. Studien zu einer Sammlung von Ostsiedlungsurkunden," *Jahrbuch für die Geschichte Mittel- und Ostdeutschlands*, 19 (1970), 1–48.

Wendt, Heinrich. "Die Stände des Fürstenthums Breslau im Kampfe mit König Mathias Corvinus, 1469–1490," *ZVGS*, 32 (1898), 157–176.

———. "Breslaus Streben nach Landbesitz im 16. Jahrhundert," *ZVGS*, 32 (1898), 215–228.

———. *Die Breslauer Stadt- und Hospital-Landgüter*. Part I: *Amt Ransern*. Mitteilungen aus dem Stadtarchiv und der Stadtbibliothek zu Breslau, vol. 4. Breslau, 1899.

———. "Die Verpfandung der Johannitercommende Corpus Christi; ein Beispiel habsburgischer Kirchenpolitik," *ZVGS*, 35 (1901), 155–184.

———. "Kirchenpolitik und Stadtbefestigung in Breslau, 1529–33," *ZVGS*, 48 (1914), 74–88.

———. *Schlesien und der Orient*. DQ, vol. 21. Breslau, 1916.

Wernicke, E. "Das Wappen des Marktflecken Lissa," *ZVGS*, 19 (1885), 403–404.

———. "Bemerkungen," *ZVGS*, 16 (1882), 298–299.

Witzendorff-Rehdiger, Hans J. von. "Herkunft und Verblieb Breslauer Ratsfamilien im Mittelalter, eine genealogischer Studie," *JFSWUB*, 3 (1958), 111–135.

———. "Der ritterliche Adel und der Stadtadel in Schlesien," *JFSWUB*, 6 (1961), 193–212.

Wohlbrück, Siegmund W. *Geschichte des ehemaligen Bisthums Lebus und des Landes dieses Namens*. 3 vols. Berlin, 1829–32.

Wojciechowski, Zygmunt. *Das Ritterrecht in Polen vor den Statuten Kasimirs des Grossen*, rev. ed. tr. H. Bellée. Osteuropa Institut Bibliothek geschichtliche Werke aus den Literaturen Osteuropas, vol. 5. Breslau, 1930.

———. "La condition des nobles et le problème de la féodalité en Pologne au moyen-âge," *Revue Historique de droit français et étranger*, 4th series 15 (1936), 651–700, and 16 (1937), 20–77 [also separate, Paris, 1936].

Wolański, Marian. "Schlesiens Stellung im Osthandel vom 15. bis zum 17. Jahrhundert," pp. 120–138 in Ingomar Bog, ed., *Der Aussenhandel Ostmitteleuropas 1450–1650. Die ostmitteleuropäischen Volkswirtschaften in ihren Beziehungen zu Mitteleuropa*. Köln, 1971.

Wolf, Eric R. "Aspects of Group Relations in a Complex Society: Mexico," *American Anthropologist*, 58 (1958), 1072–1076

———. *Peasants*. Foundations of Modern Anthropology Series. Englewood Cliffs, N.J., 1966.

Wolfarth, Włodzimierz. *Ascripticii w Polsce*. PAN Komitet Nauk Prawnych. Studia nad Historia Panstwo i Prawa, Series 2, vol. 8. Wrocław, 1959.

Wörster, P. "Übergabe schlesischen Archivgutes nach Breslau," *ZO*, 30 (1981), 262–265.

Wutke, Konrad. "Die schlesischen Besitzungen des Coelestinerklosters Oybin," *ZVGS*, 48 (1914), 34–73.

———. "Zur Urkunde von 3./9. Sept. 1240 betr. die Aussetzung von Sablath, Kr. Neumarkt, zu deutschem Rechte," *ZVGS*, 49 (1915), 337–340.

———. "War Jenkwitz bei Kanth, Kr. Neumarkt, ehemals ein Pfarrdorf?" *ZVGS*, 52 (1918), 160–164.

———. "Zur Geschichte des Geschlechts der Gallici (Walch) und ihres Grundbesitzes in Schlesien im 13./16. Jahrhundert," *ZVGS*, 61 (1927), 279–311.

Wutke, Konrad, and Gustav Türk. "Die Mitglieder des Geschlechts Gruttschreiber in älterer Zeit," *ZVGS*, 75 (1941), 17–27.

Yver, Jean. *Égalité entre héritiers et exclusion des enfants dotés. Essai de géographie coutumière.* Paris, 1966.

Zak, Jan. "O genezie uprzęży końskiej na ziemach polskich," *KHKM*, 3 (1955), 625–635.

Zaniewicki, Witold H. *La noblesse "populaire" en Espagne et en Pologne.* Lyon, 1967.

Zernack, Klaus. "Zusammenfassung: Die hochmittelalterlichen Kolonisation in Ostmitteleuropa und ihre Stellung in der europäischen Geschichte," pp. 783–804 in Schlesinger, ed., *Ostsiedlung as Problem.* Sigmaringen, 1975.

Zgorzelska, Urszula. "Szlachta w terminologii źródeł górnośląskich od XIV do XVI wieku," pp. 279–303 in Stefan K. Kuczyński, ed., *Społeczeństwo polski średniowiecznej*, vol. 3. Warsaw, 1983.

Zientara, Benedykt. "Zagadnienie depresji rolnictwa w XIV–XV wieku w świetle najnowszych literatury," *PH*, 51 (1960), 262–274.

———. "Nationality Conflicts in the German-Slavic Borderland in the 13th–14th Centuries and their Social Scope," *APH*, 22 (1970), 207–225.

———. "Bolesław Wysoki—tułacz, repatriant, malkontent," *PH*, 62 (1971), 367–394.

———. "Z dziejów organizacji rynku w średniowieczu. Ekonomiczne podłoże 'weichbildów' w arcybiskupstwie magdeburskim i na Śląsku w XII–XIII wieku," *PH*, 64 (1973), 681–696. [German version "Aus der Geschichte der Marktorganisation im Mittelalter. Die ökonomische Grundlage der 'Weichbilder' im Erzbistum Magdeburg und in Schlesien im 12.–13. Jh.," pp. 345–365 in *Festschrift für Wilhelm Abel*, vol. 2. Hannover, 1974.]

———. *Henryk Brodaty i jego czasy.* Warsaw, 1975.

———. "Die deutschen Einwanderer in Polen vom 12. bis 14. Jahrhundert," pp. 333–348 in Schlesinger, ed., *Ostsiedlung als Problem.* Sigmaringen, 1975.

———. "Walonowie na Śląsku w XII i XIII w.," *PH*, 66 (1975), 353–367.

———. "Struktury narodowe średniowiecza. Próba analizy terminologii przedkapitalistycznych form świadomości narodowej," *KH*, 84 (1977), 287–311.

———. "Źródła i geneza 'prawa niemieckiego' (ius Teutonicum) na tle ruchu osadniczego w Europie zachodniej i środkowej w XI–XII w.," *PH*, 69 (1978), 47–71. [German version "Der Ursprung des 'deutschen Rechts' (ius Teutonicum) auf dem Hintergrund der Siedlungsbewegung in West- und Mitteleuropa während des 11. und 12. Jahrhunderts," *Jahrbuch für Geschichte des Feudalismus*, 2 (1978), 119–148.]

———. "Konrad Kędzierzawy i bitwa pod Studnica," *PH*, 70 (1979), 27–55.

———. "Z zagadnień prawa niemieckiego na Śląsku," *PH*, 70 (1979), 331–340. [German version "Über *ius theutonicum* in Schlesien," *APH*, 42 (1980), 231–246.]

Ziółkowska, Hanna. "The market before the Borough Charter Granting (from the 10th to the middle of the 13th century)," *Ergon*, 3 (1962), 360–363.

Żytkowicz, Leonid. "Płony zbóż w Polsce, Czechach, na Węgrzach i Słowacji w XVI–XVIII w.," *KHKM*, 18 (1970), 227–253.

———. "Trends of agrarian economy in Poland, Bohemia and Hungary from the middle of the fifteenth to the middle of the seventeenth century," pp. 59–83 in Mączak et al., eds., *East-Central Europe in transition.* Cambridge, 1985.

GAZETTEER AND
CONCORDANCE OF
TOPOGRAPHIC NAMES

The list beginning on the following page is in alphabetical order by the name form shown in **bold face**, which is that used throughout this book. Names shown within asterisks (* . . . *) are reconstructions from the earliest records of places either no longer settled or no longer separately identified. Names prefixed Wrocław- are now part of the urban municipality, but the prefix is used in this book only when needed to distinguish among two places of similar name. The same applies to places of the same name but in different districts. All medieval sites in the Wrocław duchy appear on Map 1.1. Each is here described by district and in each district by an approximate 3 by 3 grid as shown.

NW	N	NE
W	C	E
SW	S	SE

Modern Polish	Modern German	Other Forms	Identification
Bagno	Heinzendorf		settlement site in N Uraz district
Baranowice	Baara		settlement site in W Wrocław district
Bartoszowa	Schönfeld	*Bartuszowice*	settlement site in S Wrocław district
			settlement site 1313–65 in C Wrocław district
Białków	Belkau		settlement site in N Środa district
Bielany [Środa]	Flämischdorf		settlement site in W Środa district
Bielany Wrocławskie	Bettlern		settlement site in C Wrocław district
		Bieńkowice	settlement site 1353–98 in C Wrocław district
Bieńkowice	Benkwitz		settlement site in E Wrocław district
Wrocław–Bierdzany	Pirscham		settlement site in N Wrocław district
Biestrzyków	Eckersdorf		settlement site in C Wrocław district
Biskupice Podgórne	Bischwitz am Berge 1930s Linden am Berge		settlement site in W Wrocław district
Wrocław–Biskupin	Bischofswalde		settlement site in N Wrocław district
Bledzów	Grünhübel		settlement site in C Wrocław district
Blizanowice	Pleischwitz		settlement site in NE Wrocław district
Bliż	Pleische		settlement site in W Wrocław district
Błonie	Gross Heidau		settlement site in C Środa district
Bogdaszowice	Puschwitz		settlement site in SE Środa district
Bogunów	Bogenau		settlement site in SE Wrocław district
Bogusławice	Boguslawitz 1930s Schwarzaue		settlement site in E Wrocław district
Boguszyce	Bogschütz 1930s Lohbusch		settlement site in S Wrocław district
Boreczek	Wäldchen		settlement site in SE Wrocław district
Wrocław–Borek	Kleinburg		settlement site in N Wrocław district
Borek Strzeliński	Grossburg		settlement site in SE Wrocław district

Polish name	German / alternate names	Description
Borów	Markt Bohrau	settlement site in SE Wrocław district
Bratowice	Barottwitz / 1930s Schmücken	settlement site in E Wrocław district
Brochów	Brockau	settlement site in C Wrocław district
Brodno	Breitenau	settlement site in NW Środa district
Bronikowo		settlement site 1193–1250 in C Wrocław district
Brzeg	Brieg	Silesian town and duchy SE of Wrocław
Brzeg Dolny	Dyhernfurth	settlement site in SW Uraz district
Brzeście	Leibenthal	settlement site in SE Wrocław district
Brzezica	Klein Bresa	settlement site in SE Wrocław district
Brzezina and Brzezinka Średzka	Gross and Klein Breza [one in Middle Ages]	settlement site in NE Środa district
Brzoza	Gross Bresa / 1930s Erlebusch	settlement site in SE Wrocław district
Buchta		settlement site 1204–43 in C Wrocław district
Buczki	Buchwäldchen	settlement site in SW Środa district
Buczów		settlement site 1367–1436 in NE Środa district
Budziszów [Środa]	Baudis	settlement site in C Środa district
Budziszów [Wrocław]	Buchwitz / 1930s Buchen	settlement site in SW Wrocław district
Bukowiec	Pathendorf	settlement site in N Uraz district
Burkhardsmül	Schüllermuhle	settlement site in W Wrocław district
Bystrzyca [River]	Lissa	Odra tributary between Wr. and Śr. districts
Cesarzowice [Środa]	Zieserwitz	settlement site in SW Środa district
Cesarzowice [Wrocław]	Blankenau	settlement site in C Wrocław district
Cesarzów		settlement site 1295–1398 in C Wrocław district
Chmielów	Schmellwitz	settlement site in SE Środa district
Chomiąża	Kamöse	settlement site in NW Środa district

Modern Polish	Modern German	Other Forms	Identification
Chrzanów	Zaumgarten		settlement site in SW Wrocław district
Chrząstowa Mała	Marienkranst 1930s Marienwald		settlement site in NE Wrocław district
Chrząstowa Wielka	Klarenkranst 1930s Klarenwald		settlement site in NE Wrocław district
Chwalimierz	Frankenthal		settlement site in W Środa district
Cieszyce	Seschwitz 1930s Trostendorf		settlement site in SW Wrocław district
		Coci Episcopi	settlement site 1249 in C Wrocław district
Kraków	Krakau	Cracow [English]	town on Vistula R. in Little Poland; ducal and late medieval royal capital
		Cruce	settlement site 1279–1382 in C Wrocław district
Czeczy	Tschechen		settlement site in S Środa district
		Czepankowicz	settlement site 1298–1505 in C Środa district
Czerna	Tschirnau		settlement site in NE Środa district
Czernica	Tschirne 1930s Grossbrück		settlement site in NE Wrocław district
Damianowice	Damsdorf		settlement site in SW Wrocław district
Wrocław-Dąbie	Grüneiche		settlement site in N Wrocław district
Dobkowice	Duckwitz 1930s Gutendorf		settlement site in SW Wrocław district
Dobrzykowice Wrocławskie	Wüstendorf		settlement site in NE Wrocław district
Domaniów	Thomaskirch		settlement site in SE Wrocław district
Domasław	Domslau		settlement site in C Wrocław district
Wrocław-Gaj	Herdain		settlement site in N Wrocław district
Gajków	Margareth		settlement site in NE Wrocław district
Wrocław-Gajowice	Gabitz		settlement site in N Wrocław district
Galowice	Gallowitz 1930s Gallen		settlement site in C Wrocław district
Gałów	Gross Gohlau	*Garsinken*	settlement site in E Środa district
			settlement site 1318–37 in SE Środa district
	Garten		settlement site in C Środa district, abandoned in 19th century

Gądów	Alt Gandau also Polnisch-Gandau	settlement site in W Wrocław district
Wrocław-Gądów Mały	Klein Gandau	settlement site in NW Wrocław district
Gąsiorów	Ganserau	settlement site in N Środa district
Gąska		settlement site in SW Wrocław district
Gdańsk	Danzig	Port town on Baltic near mouth of Vistula R.
	Glatke	settlement site in N Środa district, now part of Głoska
Glogi	Berggloschkau also Berg-Währen and Alt-Währen 1930s Kirschberg zum Berge	settlement site in N Środa district
Głogów	Glogau	Silesian town and duchy NW of Wrocław
Głoska	Gloschkau	settlement site in N Środa district
Gniechowice	Gnichwitz 1930s Altenrode	settlement site in SW Wrocław district
Godzięcin	Thiergarten	settlement site in N Uraz district
Klein Goldschmieden		settlement site 1352–1521 in NW Wrocław district
Golędzinów	Kunzendorf	settlement site in E Uraz district
Gosławice	Gniefgau	settlement site in NE Środa district
Gozdawa	Gossendorf	settlement site in C Środa district
Górzyce	Guhrwitz 1930s Burgweiler	settlement site in SW Wrocław district
Wrocław-Grabiszyn	Gräbschen	settlement site in N Wrocław district
Wielkopolska	Gross Polen **Great Poland** [English]	Polish province N of Silesia
Gurse		settlement site in N Środa district, abandoned in nineteenth century
Guzowicy		settlement site 1155–1245 in N Wrocław district
Hohenweiden		settlement site in SW Wrocław district

Modern Polish	Modern German	Other Forms	Identification
Ilnica	Ilsnitz		settlement site in S Środa district
Iwiny	Oldern		settlement site in C Wrocław district
Jagodno	Lamsfeld		settlement site in C Wrocław district
Jajków	Jäckel		settlement site in C Uraz district
Jaksin	Jexau		settlement site in SE Wrocław district
Jaksonów	Jackschönau 1930s Schwertern		settlement site in S Wrocław district
Jakubowice	Jakobsdorf		settlement site in S Środa district
Janików	Jankau 1930s Grünaue		settlement site in E Wrocław district
Janowice	Janowitz 1930s Waldschleuse		settlement site in NE Wrocław district
Jarnołtów	Arnoldsmühle		settlement site in W Wrocław district
Jaroslaw	Jerschendorf		settlement site in SW Środa district
Jaroslawice	Jerasselwitz 1930s Gerlanden		settlement site in E Wrocław district
Jarząbkowice	Schriggwitz	*Jasbromie*	settlement site in E Środa district
			settlement site 1245 in E Wrocław district
Jastrzębce	Falkenhain		settlement site in NW Środa district
Jaszkotle	Jeschgüttel		settlement site in W Wrocław district
Jaśkowice	Jäschkendorf		settlement site in NW Środa district
Jelenin	Jelline 1930s Hirschwaldau		settlement site in SE Wrocław district
Jenkowice	Jenkwitz		settlement site in SW Środa district
Jerzmanowo	Herrmannsdorf		settlement site in W Wrocław district
Jeszkowice	Jäschkowitz 1930s Lengefeld		settlement site in NE Wrocław district
Jodlowice	Tannwald		settlement site in S Uraz district

Jugowiec	Hausdorf	settlement site in W Środa district
Jurczyce	Jürtsch 1930s Jürgen	settlement site in SE Środa district
Juszczyn	Lampersdorf	settlement site in C Środa district
Kadlup	Kadlau	settlement site in C Środa district
Kaldenhüsen		settlement site 1282–1549 in C Wrocław district
Kalinowice	Kolline	settlement site in E Środa district
Kamieniec Wrocławski	Steine	settlement site in NE Wrocław district
Karczyce	Kertschütz	settlement site in C Środa district
Karncza Góra	Kentschkau 1930s Keltingen	settlement site in E Wrocław district
Kazimierzów	Neidchen	settlement site in SE Wrocław district
Kąty	Kanth	Small town just outside SW border of Wrocław Duchy
Kegel		settlement site 1346–1411 in N Wrocław district
Kębłowice	Kammelwitz 1930s Kammfeld	settlement site in W Wrocław district
Klecina	Klettendorf	settlement site in C Wrocław district
Klodzko	Glatz	Strategic town and district between Silesia and Bohemia
Kobierzyce	Koberwitz 1930s Rösslingen	settlement site in S Wrocław district
Kobylniki	Kobelnick	settlement site in N Środa district
Kochlowo		settlement site 1267–1274 in E Wrocław district
Kojęcin	Baumgarten	settlement site in SE Wrocław district
Kokorzyce	Guckerwitz	settlement site in C Środa district
Komorniki	Kammendorf bei Neumarkt	settlement site in C Środa district
Komorowice	Wasserjentsch 1930s Schönwasser	settlement site in C Wrocław district

Modern Polish	Modern German	Other Forms	Identification
Kończyce	Kundschütz 1930s Zehnhufen		settlement site in C Wrocław district
Kostomłoty	Kostenblut		settlement site in S Środa district
Kotowice [Trzebnica]	Kottwitz [Trebnitz]		settlement site in SE Uraz district
Kotowice [Wrocław]	Kottwitz [Breslau] 1930s Jungfernsee		settlement site in E Wrocław district
Wrocław-Kowale	Cawallen, also Kawallen 1930s Friedewalde		settlement site in N Wrocław district
Wrocław-Kozanów	Kosel		settlement site in NW Wrocław district
Krajków	Kreika 1930s Rohrquell		settlement site in E Wrocław district
Kręczków	Krentsch 1930s Lindenbrunn		settlement site in SE Wrocław district
Krępice	Krampitz		settlement site in E Środa district
Kresko	Kranz		settlement site in S Uraz district
Krobielowice	Krieblowitz 1930s Blüchersruh		settlement site in SW Wrocław district
Królikowice	Siebothschütz	*Krostów*	settlement site in NE Wrocław district, merged with Jeszkowice in recent times
	Krolkwitz 1930s Weidmannsau		settlement site in S Wrocław district
Kryniczno	Krintsch		settlement site in C Środa district
Krzeptów	Kriptau		settlement site in W Wrocław district
Wrocław-Krzyki	Krietern		settlement site in C Wrocław district
Krzyków	Krichen		settlement site in NE Wrocław district
		Krzyżanowice	settlement site 1318–1417 in S Wrocław district
Krzyżowice	Kreiselwitz 1930s Kiefernberg		settlement site in SW Wrocław district

Księginice [Środa]	Kniegnitz	settlement site in N Środa district
Księginice [Wrocław]	Kniegnitz, also Polnisch-Kniegnitz 1930s Elfhofen	settlement site in C Wrocław district
Wrocław-Księże Małe	Klein Tschansch 1930s Ohlewiesen	settlement site in N Wrocław district
Wrocław-Księże Wielkie	Gross Tschansch 1930s Ohlewiesen	settlement site in N Wrocław district
Kuklice	Guckelwitz 1930s Berghuben	settlement site in S Wrocław district
Kulin	Keulendorf	settlement site in SW Środa district
Kurczów	Kurtsch	settlement site in SE Wrocław district
Wrocław-Kuźniki	Schmiedefeld	settlement site in NW Wrocław district
Lubusz	**Lebus**	Bishopric in E Brandenburg, NW of Silesia
Legnica	Liegnitz	Silesian town and duchy W of Wrocław Duchy
	Leimgruben	settlement site in N Wrocław district
Lenartowice	Leonhardwitz	settlement site in N Środa district
Wrocław-Leśnica	Lissa	settlement site in NW Wrocław district
Ligotka	Ellguth	settlement site in W Środa district
Lipnica	Schadewinkel	settlement site in NW Środa district
Lisowice	Onerkwitz	settlement site in SE Środa district
Małopolska	Klein Polen — **Little Poland** [English]	Polish province E and SE of Silesia
Lubiatów	Lubthal	settlement site in N Środa district
Lubiąż	Leubus	Silesian monastery just W of Wrocław Duchy
Lubnów	Liebenau	settlement site in E Uraz district
Ludów Śląski	Deutsch Lauden	settlement site in SE Wrocław district
Lutynia	Leuthen	settlement site in E Środa district
	Lagów	settlement site 1336–98 in C Wrocław district
Łany	Lanisch	settlement site in N Wrocław district

Modern Polish	Modern German	Other Forms	Identification
Łowęcice	Lobetinz		settlement site in C Środa district
		Lukaszewice	settlement site 1254–1511 in S Wrocław district
Lukaszowice	Grunau		settlement site in E Wrocław district
Magnice	Magnitz 1930s Magning		settlement site in C Wrocław district
Malkowice	Malkwitz 1930s Waldtal		settlement site in W Wrocław district
Maluszów	Malsen		settlement site in SW Wrocław district
Marcinkowice	Merzdorf		settlement site in S Wrocław district
Marszowice	Marschwitz		settlement site in NE Środa district
Wrocław–Maślice	Masselwitz		settlement site in NW Wrocław district
Mędłów	Mandelau		settlement site in E Wrocław district
Michałowice	Michelwitz		settlement site in SE Wrocław district
Miękinia	Nimkau		settlement site in C Środa district
Milejowice	Mellowitz 1930s Teichlinden		settlement site in E Wrocław district
		Milino	settlement site 1208–1337 in C Wrocław district
Miłoszyce	Meleschwitz 1930s Fünfteichen		settlement site in NE Wrocław district
Miłoszyn	Trautensee bei Wilxen		settlement site in NE Środa district
Mnichowice	Münchwitz		settlement site in E Wrocław district
Mokra	Muckerau		settlement site in NE Środa district
Mokronos Dolny	Niederhof		settlement site in C Wrocław district
Mokronos Górny	Oberhof		settlement site in W Wrocław district
Mokry Dwór	Althofnass		settlement site in N Wrocław district
		Molnsdorf	settlement site 1312–1411 in N Wrocław district
Mrozów	Nippern		settlement site in C Środa district

Polish name	Medieval/variant name	German name	Description
Wrocław-Muchobór Mały		Klein Mochbern	settlement site in N Wrocław district
Wrocław-Muchobór Wielki		Gross Mochbern 1930s Lohbrück	settlement site in N Wrocław district
	Nabitin		settlement site 1175 in N Wrocław district
Nadolice Małe		Klein Nädlitz 1930s Nädau	settlement site in NE Wrocław district
Nadolice Wielkie		Gross Nädlitz 1930s Nädingen	settlement site in NE Wrocław district
	Neudorf	Neudorf bei Breslau also Polnisch Neudorf	settlement site in N Wrocław district
	Niebelschütz		settlement site 1386–1533 in SW Środa district
			settlement site in W Wrocław district
Nowa Wieś Wrocławska		Maria-Höfchen	settlement site in NW Wrocław district
Wrocław-Nowy Dwór			
Nysa		Neisse	Silesian town and district S of Wrocław Duchy
Odra [river]		Oder	Principal river of Silesia, flowing NW to Baltic
	Odrzycza		settlement site 1193 in NE Wrocław district
Ogrodnica		Schönau	settlement site in W Środa district
Okrzeszyce		Unchristen from 1885 Bismarksfeld	settlement site in E Wrocław district
	Olbino	Elbing	settlement site in N Wrocław district, absorbed into the city in nineteenth century
Olbrachtowice		Albrechtsdorf	settlement site in SW Wrocław district
	Oldrzewie Małe	Klein Oldern	settlement site in C Wrocław district, subsequently absorbed into Iwiny
Oleśnica		Oels	Silesian town and duchy NE of Wrocław Duchy
Oława [river]		Ohle	Left-bank tributary of Odra R. entering at Wrocław
Oława		Ohlau	Silesian town and district SE of Wrocław Duchy

Modern Polish	Modern German	Other Forms	Identification
Ołtaszyn	Oltaschin 1930s Herzogshufen		settlement site in C Wrocław district
		Opalin	settlement site in NE Środa district, subsequently absorbed into Prężyce
Opatowice [Strzelin]	Ottwitz		settlement site in SE Wrocław district
Wrocław-Opatowice	Ottwitz		settlement site in N Wrocław district
		Opatowo	settlement site in NW Wrocław district, subsequently abandoned
Opole	Oppeln		Silesian town and duchy SE of Wrocław Duchy
Oporów	Opperau		settlement site in C Wrocław district
		Oporzyce	settlement site 1336–1425 in S Wrocław district
Wrocław-Osobowice	Oswitz		settlement site in N Wrocław district
Owsianka	Haberstroh		settlement site in SW Wrocław district
Ozorowice	Sponsberg		settlement site in E Uraz district
Ozorzyce	Oderwitz also Schildern		settlement site in E Wrocław district
		Parszowicy	settlement site in N Wrocław district, subsequently abandoned
Wrocław-Partynice	Hartlieb		settlement site in C Wrocław district
Pasterzyce	Pasterwitz 1930s Pastern		settlement site in S Wrocław district
Pełczyce	Peltschütz 1930s Buschfelde		settlement site in S Wrocław district
Pęgów	Hennigsdorf		settlement site in E Uraz district
Piersno	Pirschen		settlement site in SW Środa district
Pietrzykowice	Peterwitz also Polnisch Peterwitz 1930s Petersweiler		settlement site in W Wrocław district

Wrocław-Pilczyce	Pilsnitz	settlement site in NW Wrocław district
Piotrków Borowski	Petrigau bei Bohrau	settlement site in SE Wrocław district
Piotrowice	Gross Peterwitz	settlement site in S Środa district
	Klein Peterwitz	settlement site in W Wrocław district
Pisarzowice	Schreibersdorf	settlement site in NE Środa district
Piskorzowice	Peiskerwitz	settlement site in NE Środa district
		settlement site 1297–1491 in S Środa district
		settlement site in N Wrocław district, subsequently absorbed by the city
Polakowice	Pollogwitz	settlement site in E Wrocław district
	1930s Dreiteichen	
Polanowice	Polanowitz	settlement site in N Wrocław district
	1930s Burgweide-West	
	Polnisch Neudorf	settlement site in N Wrocław district, subsequently absorbed by the city
Popowice [Środa]	Pfaffendorf	settlement site in W Środa district
Wrocław-Popowice	Pöpelwitz	settlement site in N Wrocław district
Wrocław-Poświęte	Lilienthal	settlement site in N Wrocław district
Poznań	Posen	Chief urban center of Great Poland
Wrocław-Pracze Odrzańskie	Herrnprotsch	settlement site in NW Wrocław district
Pracze Widawskie	Protsch	settlement site in NW Wrocław district
	1930s Weide-West	
Praga	Prague	Chief town and royal seat of Bohemia
Prawocin	Probotschine	settlement site in E Wrocław district
	1930s Probstaue	
Prężyce	Brandschütz	settlement site in NE Środa district
Probostwo	Probstei	settlement site in W Środa district
Proszków	Schoneiche	settlement site in W Środa district
Przedmoście	Bruch	settlement site in C Środa district

Piotrowice Małe

Plaskota
Platea Romanorum

Polska Nowa Wieś

Praha [Czech]; **Prague** [English]

Modern Polish	Modern German	Other Forms	Identification
Przesławice	Prisselwitz 1930s Prisselbach		settlement site in S Wrocław district
Wrocław-Psie Pole	Hundsfeld		Village on Widawa R., just outside Wrocław Duchy
Pustków Żurowski	Puschkowa 1930s Hubertushof		settlement site in SW Wrocław district
Racławice Małe	Klein Rasselwitz 1930s Grenzhorst		settlement site in SE Wrocław district
Racławice Wielkie	Haidänichen		settlement site in C Wrocław district
Radakowice	Radaxdorf		settlement site in C Środa district
Radecz	Seifersdorf		settlement site in W Uraz district
Radomierzyce	Dürrjentsch 1930s Riembergshof		settlement site in C Wrocław district
Radoszkowice	Raduschkowitz 1930s Freudenfeld		settlement site in SE Wrocław district
Radwanice	Radwanitz 1930s Wasserborn		settlement site in NE Wrocław district
Rakoszyce	Rackschütz		settlement site in S Środa district
Ramułtowice	Romolkwitz 1930s Ramfeld		settlement site in SE Środa district
Raszków	Raschdorf		settlement site in NW Środa district
Wrocław-Ratyń	Rathen		settlement site in E Środa district
Rędzin	Ransern		settlement site in NW Wrocław district
Rolantowice	Lorankwitz 1930s Rolandsmühle		settlement site in S Wrocław district
Romnów	Rommenau		settlement site in SE Środa district
Rościsławice	Reimberg		settlement site in NE Uraz district
Wrocław-Różanka	Rosenthal	**Rusin***	settlement site in N Wrocław district
			settlement site 1382–86 in C Wrocław district

Rybnica	Reibnitz	settlement site in W Wrocław district
Rynakowice	Irrschnocke 1930s Königsruh	settlement site in E Wrocław district
Rzeczyca	Regnitz	settlement site in NW Środa district
Rzepina	Häselei	settlement site in N Wrocław district, subsequently absorbed by the city
Rzeplin	Reppline	settlement site in C Wrocław district
Sadków	Sattkau	settlement site in E Wrocław district
Sadków	Gross Schottgau	settlement site in W Wrocław district
Sadkówek	Klein Schottgau	settlement site in W Wrocław district
Sadowice	Sadewitz 1930s Schill	settlement site in W Wrocław district
Samborz	Tschammendorf	settlement site in SW Środa district
Samotwór	Romberg	settlement site in W Wrocław district
Samsonowicz		settlement site 1304–16 in S Środa district
Wrocław-Sępolno	Zimpel	settlement site in N Wrocław district
Siebenhuben		settlement site in N Wrocław district, subsequently absorbed by the city
Siechnice	Tschechnitz 1930s Kraftborn	settlement site in E Wrocław district
Siedlakowice	Schiedlagwitz 1930s Siedlingen	settlement site in SW Wrocław district
Wrocław-Siedlec	Zedlitz	settlement site in N Wrocław district
Siemidrożyce	Schöbekirche	settlement site in S Środa district
Śląsk **Silesia**	Schlesien	SW province of first and present Polish states
Sikorzyce	Meesendorf	settlement site in S Środa district
Skałka	Schalkau	settlement site in W Wrocław district
Skaszyce		settlement site in N Środa district, subsequently part of Księginice

Modern Polish	Modern German	Other Forms	Identification
Słup	Schlaupe		settlement site in NW Środa district
Smardzów	Schmartsch / 1930s Dörfel		settlement site in E Wrocław district
Smolec [Mały]	Klein Schmolz		settlement site in W Wrocław district
Smolec [Wielki]	Gross Schmolz		settlement site in W Wrocław district
Sobkowice	Zopkendorf		settlement site in SE Środa district
Sobótka	Zobten		Small town below Mt. Ślęza S of Wrocław Duchy
Solna	Gross Sägewitz / 1930s Segen	*Sokolnicy*	settlement site 1149–1253 in N Wrocław district
Solniki	Klein Sägewitz / 1930s Kampfwasser		settlement site in SW Wrocław district
Sołtysowice	Schottwitz / 1930s Burgweide		settlement site in E Wrocław district
Sośnica	Schosnitz / 1930s Reichbergen		settlement site in N Wrocław district
Wrocław-Stabłowice	Stabelwitz		settlement site in NW Wrocław district
Stary Śleszów	Alt Schliesa / 1930s Alt Schlesing		settlement site in SE Wrocław district
Stoszów	Stusa	*Stoszkowice*	settlement site 1341–1506 in SE Wrocław district
Stoszyce	Stöschwitz		settlement site in SW Wrocław district
Wrocław-Strachocin	Strachate		settlement site in SE Środa district
Strachowice	Strachwitz / 1930s Schöngarten		settlement site 1320–1532 in NE Wrocław district, resettled during the nineteenth century
Strzeganowice	Paschwitz / 1930s Fuchshübel		settlement site in W Wrocław district

Strzegomka [river]	Striegauer Wasser	Tributary of Bystrzyca R. in SE Środa district
Strzelin	Strehlen	Silesian town and district S of Wrocław Duchy
Strzemlino		settlement site 1204 in N Wrocław district
Sulimów	Sillmenau	settlement site in E Wrocław district
Swarocin		settlement site 1253–1378 in N Wrocław district
Wrocław-Swojczyce	Schwoitsch 1930s Günterbrücke	settlement site in N Wrocław district
Szczecin	Stettin	Port town on Odra R. near its mouth in the Baltic
Szczepankowice	Schönbankwitz 1930s Schönlehn	settlement site in S Wrocław district
Szczepanów	Stephansdorf Tschepine	settlement site in NW Środa district
Szczepin		settlement site in N Wrocław district, subsequently absorbed by the city
Wrocław-Szczytniki	Scheitnig	settlement site in N Wrocław district
Szostakowice	Schockwitz	settlement site in E Wrocław district
Szukalice	Tschauchelwitz 1930s Rübenau	settlement site in C Wrocław district
Szymanowice	Schönbach	settlement site in S Środa district
Ślęza [mountain]	Lohe Zobten	settlement site in C Wrocław district / 718 m. elevation; outlier of Sudetes range 10 km. S of Wrocław Duchy near town of Sobótka
Ślęza [river]	Lohe	Left-bank tributary traversing central Wrocław district and entering Odra R. below Wrocław
Średzka Woda	Schwarzwasser	Left-bank Odra tributary in NW Środa district
Środa Śląska	Neumarkt	market, then town and district center in W Środa district; second town of the Wrocław Duchy
Wrocław-Świątniki	Schwentnig	settlement site in N Wrocław district
Świdnica	Schweidnitz	Silesian town and duchy SW of Wrocław Duchy
Świdnica Polska	Schweinitz bei Kanth also Polnisch Schweinitz	settlement site in S Środa district

Modern Polish	Modern German	Other Forms	Identification
Święta Katarzyna	Kattern		settlement site in E Wrocław district
Święte	Bischdorf		settlement site in C Środa district
		Świętniki [BMV]	settlement site 1221–1474 in C Wrocław district, identified as property of Augustinians of St. Mary
		Świętniki [V]	settlement site 1193–1204 in N Wrocław district, identified as property of Premonstratensians of St. Vincent
Świniary	Weidenhof		settlement site in NW Wrocław district
Świnobród	Schweinbraten		settlement site in SE Wrocław district
Wrocław–Tarnogaj	Dürrgoy		settlement site in N Wrocław district
		Tiergarte	settlement site 1307–1406 in E Środa district
Trestno	Treschen		settlement site in N Wrocław district
Trzebnica	Trebnitz		Silesian town, district, and convent N of Wrocław Duchy
Turów	Thauer		settlement site in E Wrocław district
Tyniec Mały	Tinz		settlement site in C Wrocław district
		Unorowice	settlement site 1245–1443 in E Wrocław district
Uraz	Auras		settlement site, castle, and district center in S Uraz district
		Uścimowo	settlement site 1208–18 in C Wrocław district
Wieden	Wien	Vienna [English]	Principal town and ducal or royal seat in Austria
Wisła [river]	Weichsel	Vistula	Principal river of central Poland
Wały	Reichwald		settlement site in S Uraz district
		Warmutowice	settlement site 1336–72 in C Wrocław district
Warszawa	Warschau	Warsaw [English]	Principal town and ducal seat on Vistula R. in Masovia, NE Polish province
Warzyn	Wahren		settlement site in SW Uraz district

Węgry	Wangern	settlement site in E Wrocław district
	Weinberg*	settlement site in NW Wrocław district, subsequently abandoned
Widawa	Weide	settlement site in NW Wrocław district
Widawa [river]	Weide	Right-bank Odra tributary forming N boundary of Wrocław district and Duchy
Wierzbica	Schlanz	settlement site in SW Wrocław district
Wierzbice	Wirrwitz 1930s Konradserbe	settlement site in SW Wrocław district
Wierzbno	Würben	settlement site in E Wrocław district
Wilczków	Wiltschau 1930s Herdhausen	settlement site in S Wrocław district
Wilkostów	Wolfsdorf	settlement site in N Środa district
Wilkowice	Wilkowitz 1930s Weizengrund	settlement site in E Wrocław district
Wilków	Wilkau	settlement site in S Środa district
Wilkszyn	Wilxen also Oder-Wilxen	settlement site in NE Środa district
Wojciechów	Vogtswalde	settlement site in S Uraz district
Wojczyce	Polkendorf	settlement site in C Środa district
Wojkowice	Weigwitz 1930s Rossweiler	settlement site in E Wrocław district
Wojnowice [Środa]	Wohnwitz	settlement site in N Środa district
Wojnowice [Wrocław]	Zindel	settlement site in NE Wrocław district
Wojszyce	Woischwitz 1930s Hoinstein	settlement site in C Wrocław district
Wojtkowice	Woigwitz 1930s Albrechtsau	settlement site in SW Wrocław district
Wołów	Wohlau	Silesian town, district, and duchy NW of Wrocław Duc

Modern Polish	Modern German	Other Forms	Identification
Wrocław	Breslau		chief political, religious, and urban center in Silesia, located on Odra R. in N Wrocław district
Wróblowice	Frobelwitz		settlement site in W Środa district
Wszemiłowice	Schimmelwitz 1930s Zweibach		settlement site in SE Środa district
		Wynthmul	
Wysoka	Weissig 1930s Bergmühle		settlement site in C Wrocław district
Zabłoto	Sablath		settlement site in SW Środa district
Zabór Mały	Klein Saabor 1930s Klein Hirschwerder		settlement site in N Środa district
Zabór Wielki	Gross Saabor 1930s Hirschwerder		settlement site in N Środa district
Zabrodzie	Zweibrodt		settlement site in C Wrocław district
Zacharzyce	Sacherwitz 1930s Sachern		settlement site in E Wrocław district
		Zagadlowicz	settlement site 1307 in NW Środa district
Zagródki	Zweihof		settlement site in E Wrocław district
Zajączków	Haasenau		settlement site in SE Uraz district
Zakrzów	Seedorf		settlement site in NW Środa district
Zakrzyce	Sagschütz		settlement site in E Środa district
Wrocław-Zalesie	Leerbeutel		settlement site in N Wrocław district
		Zauche	settlement site 1361–1470 in SE Środa district
		Zdanów	settlement site 1250–1367 in E Wrocław district
Zębice	Sambowitz 1930s Seydlitzaue		settlement site in E Wrocław district
		Zielona	settlement site 1155–1369 in E Wrocław district
Wrocław-Złotniki	Goldschmieden		settlement site in W Wrocław district

Żar	Saara	settlement site in E Środa district
Żerkówek	Klein-Sürchen	settlement site in W Uraz district
Wrocław-Żerniki	Neukirch	settlement site in NW Wrocław district
Żerniki Małe	Klein Sürding	settlement site in C Wrocław district
Żerniki Wielkie	Gross Sürding	settlement site in E Wrocław district
Żerniki Wrocławskie	Schörborn	settlement site in C Wrocław district
Żórawin		settlement site 1175–1241 in NW Wrocław district
Źródła	Borne	settlement site in C Środa district
Żurawina	Rothsürben 1930s Rothbach	settlement site in E Wrocław district
Żurawiniec	Saarawenze	settlement site in NE Środa district
Żurawka [river]	Rothbach	tributary of Ślęza R. in E Wrocław district
Żurowice	Schauerwitz 1930s Freienfeld	settlement site in SW Wrocław district
Żybiszów	Siebischau	settlement site in W Wrocław district

INDEX

Cross References from German Place Names

Author note. These cross references link the principal German place names of the Duchy to the Polish names used in the book.

University of Pennsylvania Press
MIDDLE AGES SERIES
Edward Peters, General Editor

Edward Peters, ed. *Christian Society and the Crusades, 1198–1229*. Sources in Translation, including The Capture of Damietta by Oliver of Paderborn. 1971

Edward Peters, ed. *The First Crusade: The Chronicle of Fulcher of Chartres and Other Source Materials*. 1971

Katherine Fischer Drew, trans. *The Burgundian Code: The Book of Constitutions or Law of Gundobad and Additional Enactments*. 1972

G. G. Coulton. *From St. Francis to Dante: Translations from the Chronicle of the Franciscan Salimbene (1221–1288)*. 1972

Alan C. Kors and Edward Peters, eds. *Witchcraft in Europe, 1110–1700: A Documentary History*. 1972

Richard C. Dales. *The Scientific Achievement of the Middle Ages*. 1973

Katherine Fischer Drew, trans. *The Lombard Laws*. 1973

Edward Peters, ed. *Monks, Bishops, and Pagans: Christian Culture in Gaul and Italy, 500–700*. 1975

Jeanne Krochalis and Edward Peters, ed. and trans. *The World of Piers Plowman*. 1975

Julius Goebel, Jr. *Felony and Misdemeanor: A Study in the History of Criminal Law*. 1976

Susan Mosher Stuard, ed. *Women in Medieval Society*. 1976

Clifford Peterson. *Saint Erkenwald*. 1977

Robert Somerville and Kenneth Pennington, eds. *Law, Church, and Society: Essays in Honor of Stephen Kuttner*. 1977

Donald E. Queller. *The Fourth Crusade: The Conquest of Constantinople, 1201–1204*. 1977

Pierre Riché (Jo Ann McNamara, trans.). *Daily Life in the World of Charlemagne*. 1978

Edward Peters, ed. *Heresy and Authority in Medieval Europe*. 1980

Suzanne Fonay Wemple. *Women in Frankish Society: Marriage and the Cloister, 500–900*. 1981

Edward Peters. *The Magician, the Witch, and the Law*. 1982

Barbara H. Rosenwein. *Rhinoceros Bound: Cluny in the Tenth Century*. 1982

Steven D. Sargent, ed. and trans. *On the Threshold of Exact Science: Selected Writings of Anneliese Maier on Late Medieval Natural Philosophy*. 1982

Benedicta Ward. *Miracles and the Medieval Mind: Theory, Record, and Event, 1000–1215*. 1982

Harry Turtledove, trans. *The Chronicle of Theophanes: An English Translation of* anni mundi *6095–6305 (A.D. 602–813)*. 1982

Leonard Cantor, ed. *The English Medieval Landscape*. 1982

Charles T. Davis. *Dante's Italy and Other Essays*. 1984

George T. Dennis, trans. *Maurice's Strategikon: Handbook of Byzantine Military Strategy.* 1984

Thomas F. X. Noble. *The Republic of St. Peter: The Birth of the Papal State, 680–825.* 1984

Kenneth Pennington. *Pope and Bishops: The Papal Monarchy in the Twelfth and Thirteenth Centuries.* 1984

Patrick J. Geary. *Aristocracy in Provence: The Rhône Basin at the Dawn of the Carolingian Age.* 1985

C. Stephen Jaeger. *The Origins of Courtliness: Civilizing Trends and the Formation of Courtly Ideals, 939–1210.* 1985

J. N. Hillgarth, ed. *Christianity and Paganism, 350–750: The Conversion of Western Europe.* 1986

William Chester Jordan. *From Servitude to Freedom: Manumission in the Sénonais in the Thirteenth Century.* 1986

James William Brodman. *Ransoming Captives in Crusader Spain: The Order of Merced on the Christian-Islamic Frontier.* 1986

Frank Tobin. *Meister Eckhart: Thought and Language.* 1986

Daniel Bornstein, trans. *Dino Compagni's Chronicle of Florence.* 1986

James M. Powell. *Anatomy of a Crusade, 1213–1221.* 1986

Jonathan Riley-Smith. *The First Crusade and the Idea of Crusading.* 1986

Susan Mosher Stuard, ed. *Women in Medieval History and Historiography.* 1987

Avril Henry, ed. *The Mirour of Mans Saluacioune.* 1987

María Rosa Menocal. *The Arabic Role in Medieval Literary History.* 1987

Margaret J. Ehrhart. *The Judgment of the Trojan Prince Paris in Medieval Literature.* 1987

Betsy Bowden. *Chaucer Aloud: The Varieties of Textual Interpretation.* 1987

Michael Resler, trans. *EREC by Hartmann von Aue.* 1987

A. J. Minnis. *Medieval Theory of Authorship.* 1988

Uta-Renate Blumenthal. *The Investiture Controversy: Church and Monarchy from the Ninth to the Twelfth Century.* 1988

Robert Hollander. *Boccaccio's Last Fiction: "Il Corbaccio."* 1988

Ralph Turner. *Men Raised from the Dust: Administrative Service and Upward Mobility in Angevin England.* 1988

David Anderson. *Before the Knight's Tale: Imitation of Classical Epic in Boccaccio's Teseida.* 1988

Charlotte A. Newman. *The Anglo-Norman Nobility in the Reign of Henry I: The Second Generation.* 1988

Joseph F. O'Callaghan. *The Cortes of Castile-León, 1188–1350.* 1989

William D. Paden. *The Voice of the Trobairitz: Essays on the Women Troubadours.* 1989

William Chester Jordan. *The French Monarchy and the Jews: From Philip Augustus to the Last Capetians.* 1989

Edward B. Irving, Jr. *Rereading* Beowulf. 1989

David Burr. *Olivi and Franciscan Poverty: The Origins of the Usus Paper Controversy.* 1989

Willene B. Clark and Meradith T. McMunn, eds. *Beasts and Birds of the Middle Ages: The Bestiary and Its Legacy.* 1989

Richard C. Hoffmann. *Land, Liberties, and Lordship in a Late Medieval Countryside: Agrarian Structures and Change in the Duchy of Wrocław.* 1989

J. M. W. Bean. *From Lord to Patron: Lordship in Late Medieval England*. 1989

Mary F. Wack. *Lovesickness in the Middle Ages: The Viaticum and Its Commentaries*. 1989

Robert I. Burns, S. J., ed. *Emperor of Culture: Alfonso X the Learned of Castile and His Thirteenth-Century Renaissance*. 1990

E. Ann Matter. *The Voice of My Beloved: The Song of Songs in Western Medieval Christianity*. 1990

Patricia Terry. *Poems of the Elder Edda*. 1990

Ronald Surtz. *The Guitar of God: Gender, Power, and Authority in the Visionary World of Mother Juana de la Cruz (1481–1534)*. 1990